To All Our Children

John Hans Meyer

To All Our Children

To All Our Children

The Story Of The Postwar Dutch Immigration To Canada

Albert VanderMey

PAIDEIA PRESS
Jordan Station, Ontario, Canada

To All Our Children
The Story of the Postwar
Dutch Immigration to Canada

ISBN 0-88815-100-4

Printed and bound in Canada.
Second printing, 2004

The photographs on pages 243, 269, 271, 272, 273
and 430 are used courtesy of Malak Photographs
Limited, Ottawa.

Photographs in Chapter One, unless otherwise indicated, were provided by the author,
Helen Colijn.

Canadian Cataloguing in Publication Data

VanderMey, Albert.
   To all our children

ISBN 0-88815-100-4

1. Dutch — Canada — History — 20th century.
2. Dutch Canadians — History — 20th century.*
3. Canada — Emigration and immigration — History — 20th century.
I. Title.

FC106.D9V36 1983   971'.0043931   C83-099263-4
F1035.D8V36 1983

Contents

*This volume is dedicated
to those pioneering men and women
who left The Netherlands for Canada
in the early part of this century.
Warmly welcoming the postwar immigrants,
they encouraged them by their example,
sustained them with their presence,
and shall not be forgotten.*

Foreword

I have been asked to write the Foreword to this book on postwar Dutch immigration to Canada. I am pleased to do so, especially since I can relate some personal experiences and encounters in this regard.

For many reasons, Canada takes pride in its multi-cultural mosaic. Our culture profits from a vigorous variety of artistic and folk expressions, which is surely better than dull monolithic uniformity. Our country has benefitted greatly when people—usually young, but of whatever age—have brought with them useful skills from foreign schools and ancestral heritages. Often these were the very industrial or agricultural skills necessary for the development of this relatively new land.

The Dutch in Canada had demonstrated in the major immigration of the early 1900s that they were a welcome asset to Canada. Their imagination and diligence could be seen in the transformation of the land and its productivity in areas north of Toronto, along the banks of the Red and Assiniboine Rivers near Winnipeg, and in areas of British Columbia, just for example. It was my privilege to know three generations of some of these families.

Then in the late 1940s and 1950s many more came to what was still a raw and open country. The culture shock, even the climatic adjustment, could not have been easy. Can anyone imagine the adjustment for someone from Haarlem-mermeer or Maastricht, for example, who came to work in the bush camps of Northwestern Ontario and Manitoba, or to the wide, vacant prairie, or even to the vegetable fields of almost any province?

I know from personal experience that their vigor and optimism were sorely tried; conditions were often difficult. As a young teenager attending high school away from home for the first time, I stayed for a year with a couple just arrived from Haarlemmermeer. It was a kind of mutual reassurance period—I depended on them as a 13-year-old needing a home; they relied on me for functional vocabulary-building in English.

Of the people I remember well from those days, one is now a successful dairy farmer in the Fraser Valley; another is a contractor in water supply and municipal services installation. They have all come to know the Canadian scene very well.

I, for my part, learned to walk with *klompen;* and I learned to know their history and their ways. *Het was eerst wel moeilijk maar ook een mooie ervaring.* Most important is that I learned to appreciate their contribution to Canada.

Edward Schreyer,
Governor General of Canada

Foreword to the Second Printing

Here it is, a reprint. By popular demand! In a way, not surprising. In our multicultural world, migration history draws much interest, even fascination. The stories of this particular ethnic group are increasingly in demand as the second generation of immigrants from Holland to Canada is gradually making room for the third.

And the stories are all here, in lively narratives by the author and first-hand accounts by that brave and determined first generation: the aspirations and apprehensions upon leaving the country of one's birth, the trials and thrills of crossing the ocean, the surprises and shocks upon arrival in the land of adoption, the confusion and adjustments of the first months, the successes and failures of job hunting, the joyous arrival of the crate with belongings from home ("No hay or straw used in packing"), the pride of buying the first car, the sense of gratitude when moving into one's own house or taking possession of one's own farm, the new sense of belonging when taking out citizenship and voting for the first time. We hear of medical exams and travel arrangements, fieldmen and landing agents, chicken coops and beet shacks, abuse by employers and kindness by neighbours, language hurdles and culture shock.

These people emigrated from a country regimented by a highly centralized bureaucracy and an intricate tangle of tax laws—a densely populated and war-ravaged country where every person was numbered, every shop and trade licensed, every square inch registered, every ditch and dyke inspected. They immigrated into a huge land covering five time-zones, a land where they had to learn to get along with strange Dutchmen from other provinces and other social classes and to rub shoulders with still stranger Anglo-Saxons and Eastern and Southern Europeans. It is both entertaining and instructive to read how quickly they adopted the new language and slowly adapted to Canadian ways.

VanderMey has organized the voluminous material by topic, and his readers keep reaching for the hefty volume on the coffee table to indulge in another hour of flavouring their favourite stories—eager to note under which headings their friends and family make their appearance amid a wealth of photographs. I am proud to say that my own in-laws found a place on pages 148, 163, 171 and 397.

To All Our Children has its own place alongside studies like Ganzevoort's *Bittersweet Land* and Schryer's *The Netherlandic Presence*. Its value will grow with the years as an enduring monument to adventure and hardship, perseverance and blessing.

Professor Harry Van Dyke
Redeemer University College
October, 2004

Preface

In the spring of 1982, John Hultink, owner and publisher of Paideia Press, contacted me. "I'm looking for stories and photos for a book on the postwar Dutch immigration," he said. "Can you help me?" Before many weeks had passed, I was deeply involved in the project.

After appeals for personal histories went out, I began to sift through the boxes of material which kept coming in. I read dozens of hand-written letters, one forty-two pages long, some in Dutch, some in English, and many in-between. I contacted many people across the country, traveling here and there for interviews. During two trips to The Netherlands for other purposes, I also gathered information for *To All Our Children.*

I was eager to accept the challenge of this book, because I, too, am an immigrant. I shared Hultink's concern that the story be told now. Many of the immigrants are getting on in years. To wait any longer would mean losing their memories and insights. Indeed, while this book was in preparation, some of the contributors died. In the summer of 1982, I asked to see Rev. Martin Grootscholten, a Roman Catholic priest in London, Ontario, who did invaluable work in the immigration field. He wrote: "There is little I can do for you until August, and only if I survive this operation well. So start praying like the dickens until August and we'll see what we can do then." I was never able to see him. He died a few weeks after the operation.

This book doesn't pretend to tell every immigrant's story. The experiences included here are representative. For example, the business people we interviewed are only a few of the many successful Dutch immigrants in Canadian fields of business. Above all, we attempted, within time and space limitations, to tell as broad a range of stories as possible.

There were the last farewells, and then there were the first impressions. There were horrible boat trips and holiday voyages. Immigrants were young farmers, war brides, mothers of twelve, grandfathers, and babies. They settled across Canada, from Prince Edward Island to Vancouver Island, from the Niagara Peninsula to the far North. In myriad situations, they experienced struggle, victory, hardship, loss, homesickness, growth. They built homes, farms, churches, schools, and businesses. Some gave up and went home; some stayed to become wealthy. Many speak with nostalgia and gratitude, and a few with bitterness, as they remember how it was to immigrate.

I have tried to link their stories in a narrative which is interesting and easy to read and understand. In so doing, I have avoided burdening the reader with sociological and statistical detail. Photographs, many of them snapshots taken by immigrants, are very important. Gathering them was the most time-consuming task. We searched numerous archives and collections across The Netherlands and Canada with mixed results. Private snapshots convey first-hand immigration experience and give the book an authentic look; however, they needed the complement of quality photos taken by newspaper and magazine photographers. Many immigrants, cost-conscious, anxious, and owning only simple box cameras without flashbulbs, took only a few photos of the crossing and their first years in Canada. Shots taken *inside* the ships are almost non-existent.

All in all, though, the photos will confirm the old adage that a picture can be worth a thousand words. I hope that photos and text together will give the reader an accurate sense of how the Dutch got here, what their lives were like, and how widely they have contributed to the development and well-being of their adopted land.

The task was not easy, for much of the research and gathering of information had never been done before. The mammoth task of this book has been completed, and yet follow-up projects beg to be taken up: the broadening of a history, or the deepening of an insight. And the publisher is already considering an anthology of short stories dealing with the immigration experience. A tremendous story waits to be told by the prewar immigrants, the true pioneers, who are still living among us.

Dutch immigrants follow varied styles in writing their surnames. There are differences even within family circles. For this book, we've adopted the most common style: the first and major words of the name are capitalized (e.g. Van Zee; Van der Zee).

I'm indebted to many people, from British Columbia to Nova Scotia, for their advice and assistance. There are, first of all, the hundreds of immigrants who gave their time and hearts, who entrusted to us memories and photographs. They have made the book possible. And there are some names I would like to mention here: Albert VanderHeide of New Westminster, British Columbia, the energetic newspaper publisher who, a number of years ago, developed the idea of marketing tiles of immigrant ships, and who helped make sure that the West was adequately covered in this book; Helen Colijn of Menlo Park, California, who wrote the chapter on The Netherlands; Melle Huizinga of Edmonton, Alberta, who interviewed many people in his province; James Pot of Mount Stewart, Prince Edward Island, who did much research in The Netherlands while he was a teacher there; Anne Hutten of Kentville, Nova Scotia, George Koopmans of Telkwa, British Columbia, and G.W. Graaskamp of Hamilton, Ontario, who all submitted valuable material; Piet Madderom and Rimmer Tjalsma of *Wereld Contact* who went out of their way to look for specific photographs; Jan Heersink of Burlington, Ontario, whose counsel was appreciated; Aileen Van Ginkel of Toronto, Ontario, who did much preliminary work with the assistance of researchers at the Multicultural History Society of Ontario; the administrators and staff members of the various archives in Canada and The Netherlands; the staff at the Royal Netherlands Embassy in Ottawa, especially Gerard W.L. Seesink, the assistant immigration officer; Anthony Rypkema, vice-consul for emigration with The Netherlands Consulate General in Toronto; Pat Weaver of Toronto who edited the manuscript; Rachelle Longtin of Paideia Press and Harry DeVries who looked after the graphics; and publisher John Hultink who conceived the idea of this book and then spent countless hours developing sources and assisting with the research.

Albert VanderMey
September, 1983

Introduction

These are facts: Koosje Bol, the 100,000th Dutch immigrant to enter Canada after the end of World War II, stepped off the boat at Montreal in May of 1954. By a strange coincidence, I was born the same day, my family's first Canadian child. They disembarked on April 1, 1949, in Halifax.

Facts. My mother was seasick, more than seasick, sick to her soul. Until she saw land. My brothers and sister were curious, but stilled, wide-eyed. The train was a plunged and endless journey through nowhere, five days and nights to Alberta. They had no money. Although they didn't show it, they were afraid. The only English word they knew was "potato." My grandfather had said they were going to hell and would never come back. And he cried, with his face buried in his arm against the stable wall. Before they left, they had a photograph taken, a solemn, unblinking photograph that confronted the camera in the same way they confronted Canada.

Canada. They lived in a granary. They worked. They made $60 a month. They worked. They were homesick. They worked. They were tired. They worked. They say they were determined, but it was more than that, they were obsessed. They worked. Hand over hand, ever so slowly, they moved forward. By the time I was born, in May of 1954, they were still poor, but settled. Facts are indisputable, immutable. One lives; one dies.

But the facts are never enough. Over time and remembrance they melt and swirl, change. "The truth is—" we say, when the truth is a wide, undefinable circle around the facts. Emigrate: to leave behind a world, a life, a culture. Immigrate: to enter a new country as an alien, to settle there. To work. We say, "This is what I have done." We say, "This is why."

Why? The displacement implied by emigration/immigration is unimaginable, profound, too complex for the simple answers that are always given. "Holland was too small." "We wanted more freedom, more space." "We did it for our children, to give them a chance." Like the facts, the answers are unarguable. But there is more, so much more that is unspoken, unsaid, perhaps never even thought, nothing but an image that rests quietly in the human imagination. After all, ideas that can be captured in words are never as disillusioning—but not as glorious either—as those that can only be imagined.

Why? I have asked that question of countless immigrants: my parents, their friends, my friends' parents. The answers, the facts, cloak the images, the real reasons. Immigrate: Was it that Jericho-like shout that tore from the throats of the people when they saw the first Canadian soldier stand shining in his tank? Was it a picture of a green field stretching farther than the eye? Was it a tyrannical, domineering family? Was it a crowded, choking city? Was it another Canadian soldier who gave a child a chocolate bar; the child who took it home and said, "Look Mommy, he gave me a stick?" Was it a postcard of Canada: mountains, rivers, trees—too unbelievably beautiful to be believed? Was it Kanada/Canada, the sound of the word a breath of chinook wind that drifted enticement? Was it Canada, crisp and unsullied, no war, no occupation, no rubbled ruins? Was it the taste of tulip bulbs in the Hunger Winter? Was it a crazy conviction that money littered the streets? Who knows what trails the imagination followed? But that was it. Some ineffable image caught hold and clung to the hands of those Netherlanders, those emigrants, who let it pull them along, who thought and talked and gave logical reasons, but who followed the intangible whisper of imagination to become immigrants in Canada.

Why did you leave? Why did you come *here*? Those questions have never been answered quite completely to my satisfaction. There is still a suspended silence between the oblique moment when people first think of the idea and the irrevocable moment when they decide to immigrate. Through all ages, the strongest and hardiest, the curious and far-seeing, have moved to push beyond their own civilization. They have most often moved west, searching for the bright dream of impossibility. Against all odds, they made it possible, they took what meager means they had and made a life, their own life. We know *how* they did it; the stories are there. But we will never know what brilliant sift of wind, what far off glimmer of light prompted them. We only know they had imagination, that quality that makes human beings extraordinary, that gives them faith and desire, the eyes to see beyond the future.

I am one of those children to whom this book is addressed. Because my parents had the courage to immigrate, I was born to a wealth of possibilities that I would never have had in Holland. Like my brothers and my sister, I am happy and successful and my parents feel that they achieved what they set out to do. I am a Dutch immigrant's daughter and for the sacrifice they made I am thankful. But mostly, I am thankful for the connection between the moment they first thought, "Kanada" and the moment they decided to come here. They gave me their imagination.

Aritha Van Herk
Calgary, Alberta

Forty Days and Nights

It may as well have been for forty days
and nights that we were on the long Atlantic.
Two by two, with children most of us,
we packed our bags, walked the gangway, waved,
and leaning on a deckrail watched the sea rise
up behind us, top the dikes and take the lives
of loved ones, still waving, their raised arms
at last drowned by the flood of the horizon.
Choosing to go, you'd almost think we should
be happy,
        but added to that ocean
                        our own salt
and then, in quarters closer than the country
we'd just left, waited, walked the deck,
for ten days ate mostly variations
on a theme of onions,
            layer by layer
our former lives were peeled away, until
there was only left the small sweet core
with which to land upon our Ararat,
Québec,
        from where the train, a cattlecar
of Frisians, Groningers, and *luyden uit*
Zeeland
        took us all to destinations
pinned onto our shirts,
            male and female
we had no names, just places we were sent,
like mail from overseas.

And this may have been the land the third dove
found her branch of olive on, but it didn't
look it. We sing *I rest me in the thought
of rocks and trees*, but after fourteen days
I'd had my fill of filling the cursing farmer's
wagon with the stone and rock that dotted
all his cursed fields, and learned a lifetime's
worth of foul English, courtesy
that man, while piling up those rocks somewhere
as if they formed an altar to our God,
as if I were about to offer thanks.
If I was thankful then it was in silence,
surrounded by the ever-growing trees
which stood beside the fields, their bare trunks
the bars of my selected prison
               my chosen land
this is not, I thought
           my father's world
the *dorp* cozy, and in the middle of things,
with family, friends, with her out visiting
instead of set behind the farmer's house,
walled within a shed he'd used to park

his car, until we came (we have pictures
of this), with not a soul for her to talk to
in any tongue, on any day, except the kids.

And yet we walked one Sunday into town
and, standing on the lawn of someone's house,
took the photo we sent home, and without
saying This is where we live, told them
about indoor plumbing, how everyone had
a car.
      Was it the foolishness of pride, or
faith, that focused the Kodak Brownie on
our family? We even smiled. Who knew
if it would be a snapshot of our future?
We felt His daily care, there was protection
from the worst; we ate, had shelter, sometimes
had to laugh. Do I say it right?
                   At times
we thought it providential humor
that I, scared to death of cows and horses
was sent to work a farm;
                that once, needing
lucht in de band of a bike, and wanting
to belong, I overcame my fear of Canadese
and boldly asked the man at the pump for sky
in my band;
           that two days later I drove
the coal truck from my second job, and dumped
a one ton load down the basement chute
of the wrong house
              and the next week
wasn't paid, but shoveled those lumps of black
back through the window, until I couldn't breathe.
That week it rained. For all I cared
it may as well have rained for forty days
and nights and put the whole place under.
I've never come so close to cursing, and what
prevented it I cannot say, but looking
out the cellar saw the same sign Noah saw
and knew at once it was that band in the sky
I'd wanted all along
             to tell myself
                 to tell
the kids, so someday they'd tell theirs
that He had saved, protected us for this,
that we could show His glory, not displaced
in people who'd been moved from there to here
like shining stones of coal
           starting from below.

John Terpstra

Chapter 1

The Land They Left Behind

Amsterdam   Capital

Groningen   Provincial capital

◉   Town with more than 100,000 inhabitants

○   Town with less than 100,000 inhabitants

- - - - -   Provincial boundary

SCHIERMONNIKOOG

AMELAND

TERSCHELLING

Ems

VLIELAND

WADDEN   SEA

GRONINGEN

Leeuwarden

Groningen

TEXEL

FRIESLAND

Assen

LAKE

YSSEL

DRENTHE

NOORD-
HOLLAND

Zwolle

N O R T H

FLEVOLAND

OVERIJSSEL

North Sea Canal

Haarlem

S E A

Amsterdam

Amsterdam Rhine

Apeldoorn

Enschede

Canals

Hilversum

Twente

Leiden

Utrecht

The Hague

GELDER-

Yssel

ZUID-
HOLLAND

UTRECHT

Arnhem

LAND

New Waterway

Rotterdam

Lek

Canal

Lower   Rhine

VOORNE

Dordrecht

Waal

GOEREÉ

PUTTEN

(Meuse)

Nijmegen

HOEKSE
WAARD

Maas

Rhine

CHOUWEN

OVER
FLAKKEE

DUIVE
LAND

Den Bosch
(Bois-le-Duc)

ZEELAND

Eastern

NOORD-

WALCHEREN

THOLEN

Breda

Tilburg

Scheldt

Middelburg

BRABANT

SOUTH
BEVELAND

Western

Scheldt

Eindhoven

ZEEUWS-

VLAANDEREN

LIMBURG

Scheldt

Maas (Meuse)

W E S T   G E R M A N Y

B E L G I U M

Maastricht

| 0 | 10 | 20 | 30 | 40 | 50 | 60 | 70 | 80 km |

| 0 | 10 | 20 | 30 | 40 | 50 miles |

Prince William of Orange (1533-1584) played an important role in the Eighty Years' War, the Dutch war of independence. Beatrix, born in 1938 of the same House of Orange, is queen of The Netherlands. The royal coat of arms bears the motto je maintiendrai (I shall persevere).

The Land They Left Behind

What kind of country is The Netherlands, that country which your parents and grandparents gave up with such pluck and sense of adventure?

It's tiny. In an hour and a half, you can drive from the North Sea on the west to the German border on the east. To drive from the northern town of Groningen, near the Waddenzee, to the town of Maastricht, near Belgium in the south, takes four to five hours. In each case, you would be driving on freeways, though a few roads have traffic lights, and some congestion may slow you down.

The Netherlands is divided into eleven provinces. Starting in the north and moving clockwise, you see: Friesland, Groningen, Drenthe, Overijssel, Gelderland, Limburg, Noord-Brabant, Utrecht, Zeeland, Zuid-Holland, and Noord-Holland.

The country was for a long time staunchly Calvinist, except for Limburg and Noord-Brabant, set apart as "the Catholic provinces." There you see wayside shrines to the Virgin Mary, crucifixes under trees, and colorful saints-day processions: strong men shouldering a platform with a statue under a canopy and followed by singing choir boys and villagers devout in the faith. But many Catholics moved to other provinces and Protestants moved to Noord-Brabant and Limburg. Now, in this once predominantly Calvinist country, there are more Catholics than there are Protestants.

Since the Second World War, The Netherlands has launched a rapid industrialization program. Still, large areas in several of the provinces are tranquilly rural. According to 1979 statistics, 22.6 percent of the country is cultivated land, 3.7 percent is taken up by horticulture, 12.2 percent is covered by woods, heath, and the sand dunes along the North Sea, and 38.8 percent is pasture land for the country's four million big, fat cows. That's about one cow for every three-and-a-half inhabitants. Fourteen million people live in The Netherlands. In the most densely populated province of Zuid-Holland, there are no less than 1,075 persons per square kilometer! In the least populated province of Drenthe, however, there are only 160 people per square kilometer. Such differences bring the na-

Some Countries Just Have More Living Space

Canada (24 million inhabitants)

United States (222 million inhabitants)

China (996 million inhabitants)

Japan (116 million inhabitants

France (53 million inhabitants)

Nigeria (80 million inhabitants)

The Netherlands (14 million inhabitants)

● = 10 persons per square kilometer

tional average down to 421 persons per square kilometer. Compared to Canada this is a lot: Canada—272 times as big as The Netherlands with a total population of only twenty-four million—2.45 people per square kilometer. In fact, The Netherlands is one of the most densely populated countries in the world.

Some people say "The Netherlands;" some people say "Holland." The Netherlands (*Nederland* in Dutch) is the

Dutch of all ages ride bicycles. In the cities, bicycles are easier to park than cars.

official name, printed in every Dutch emigrant's passport: *Koninkrijk der Nederlanden,* Kingdom of The Netherlands. Holland is the country's popular name; it goes back four hundred years to when the nation was founded as the Republic of the Seven United Netherlands. The province of Holland (now divided into North and South) was then the most powerful province. As far as the

rest of Europe was concerned, Holland *was* the Republic: the part became the whole. This unofficial name for the entire country took hold, and is now cheerfully used by name, including the Royal Dutch Airlines and The Netherlands National Tourist Office: "KLM, Holland's dependable airline;" "Happy Holland Tour."

Not all the Dutch appreciate the name

Parking in Amsterdam offers a challenge.

Holland for their country. Ask a Groninger or a Frieslander which country he's from, and he will no doubt say The Netherlands. To him Holland is merely another province; if he's going to Amsterdam for business or to The Hague to discuss political matters in parliament, he will probably say that he is going *to* Holland, as if he's going to a foreign country.

Of all the provinces, Limburg has the highest hills, if that's what you want to call elevations of a few hundred feet. The highest one reaches to 1,093 feet. The Dutch grandly call this hill the Vaalser Berg (*berg* is the Dutch word for mountain).

Apart from these hills in Limburg, and even lesser bumps in other eastern provinces, The Netherlands is as flat as a pancake. One-sixth of the country is water: ponds, lakes, inland seas, rivers, and canals. Most of all this water is contained and controlled by dikes.

Dikes have been part of the country's history for at least two thousand years. When the Romans came down the Rhine to occupy the delta between that river and the Meuse and the Scheldt, they were appalled: "You can't see where water ends and land begins." Soldiers built dikes along the rivers so the nearby terrain wouldn't flood every time a winter storm

The royal family goes cycling. Prince Willem-Alexander, heir to throne, rides at the left of his father, Prince Claus. On the third Tuesday of September, parliament is opened by the queen, who arrives in a horse-drawn gilt coach.

The "boy who put his finger in the dike" was the invention of Mary Mapes Dodge, nineteenth century author of Hans Brinker; or The Silver Skates. A statue in Spaarndam celebrates the boy as a symbol of The Netherlands' struggle against the sea. At top right, another sea arm is closed off as the struggle continues. The oil tanker sails in a canal above the low-lying land.

Area reclaimed from the water in square kilometres

2500 km²

200(

1500

1000

500

0

1200–1300
1300–1400
1400–1500
1500–1600
1600–1700
1700–1800
1800–1900
1900–2000

or a melting spring snow in the Alps made the river water rise. The Romans wanted solid ground for their trading posts. The dikes also made fine highways. The Roman legions marched between fortresses, keeping, or trying to keep, the native tribes in line.

Just when the Romans were building dikes in the delta, the Frisians in the north were building mounds to live on so that flood waters could swirl around them; you can still see these *terpen* today. The Fri-

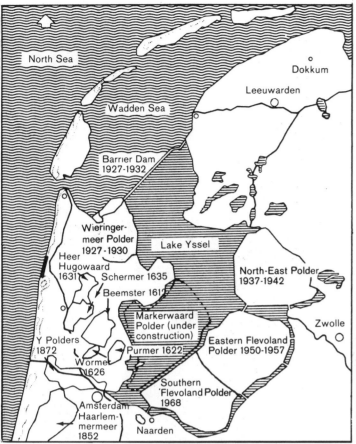

sians are the only tribe which has survived from the Roman period to modern times.

Dike building stopped when the Romans left the delta in the fourth century and was probably not resumed until the twelfth century. By that time the land near the North Sea belonged to feudal dukes or counts who made their serfs build dikes to protect the low-lying land. Men scooped up clay and sand with primitive tools and hauled it to the dikes on sleds or in sacks of hide.

When the power of the feudal lords declined and merchants became wealthy during the 17th century, the country's "Golden Age," they went into diking as a real estate investment. The merchants "made land." Dikes were built around lakes, and then windmills pumped the lakes dry. Soon hundreds of mills dotted the Dutch landscape. Windmills not only pumped water, they also sawed wood, ground flour, and pressed oil.

Diking and draining was done in a

The map shows areas reclaimed since 1612. For centuries, windmills pumped water away from Dutch soil. The Markerwaard dike has been built from Enkhuizen to Lelystad to protect a future polder.

The Land They Left Behind   21

Typical features of the Dutch landscape: a farmhouse with an attached barn, a drawbridge, dunes along the North Sea coast, Holstein cattle, and the Dutch tri-color.

haphazard manner, however. No central agency coordinated the "water housekeeping." When one landowner dammed a river to divert water from his property, the river flooded someone else's land. When a merchant drained a lake in order to go into the dairy business, local fishermen lost their livelihood.

Not until the end of the eighteenth century did the Dutch create a national *Departement van Waterstaat.* National agencies now determine when sluices let water in and out of the waterways to keep the country's water level safe; where to build bridges or dams; what water to drain and turn into land, and what to leave so that the country doesn't "dry out," leaving no water for recreation. Very little in this small country is left to the whims of individuals.

All the water pumping is now done by

mammoth machines, but because of the many windmills in the past, the notion persists that The Netherlands is a country of windmills. Some nine hundred remain —protected as national monuments, pampered and fussed over. They operate for their original purpose, or, restored, they operate for the entertainment of villagers or busloads of tourists, or else they've become museums, art galleries, or restaurants. But many a traveler has returned from The Netherlands disappointed, to say, "I didn't see any windmills," or "I saw a windmill but it didn't work." Such a pity. A windmill's long arms swooshing in the wind as the enormous oak cogwheels inside groan, gripping each other and driving a mechanism, is a wonderful thing to see.

Because The Netherlands is so small, it's a comfortable country to move about in.

You can go anywhere in a matter of hours, by car or excellent train or bus. The Netherlands is comfortable, too, because so much is small-scale and intimate. Beauty is in a clump of pines on a hillock, in marram grass waving on a sand dune, in a modern sculpture in a tiny city park, in a fine, old house serenely reflected in water. Even the famous bulb fields are small.

Changes in the landscape are subtle. A polder (diked-in land) lies beneath an enormous dome of sky, and the flat horizon is broken only by a church tower or a row of trees on the dike—if the horizon isn't "polluted" by brand new factory chimneys or concrete housing blocks. The next polder looks almost exactly the same. But the style of the farm houses is different: you are in another province. In some provinces, the barns are attached to the houses, under either a red tile roof or a straw roof pulled low over the house like a bonnet. Elsewhere, the barns are separate. In Limburg, the farms are built in a square around an atrium, just like the villas which were built there by the Romans.

In recent years, some of the old farms have had to be demolished in a process called *ruilverkaveling*, the reallotment of land. Small parcels of land are joined or exchanged to allow for bigger parcels which can be more efficiently worked. But if a new farm is built, it's usually constructed in the same local design.

Pastoral scenes in The Netherlands never last long. Soon you come to another village or town. Some of the towns, seven or eight hundred years old, have impressive walls and town gates that once were closed at night. These old towns have never grown larger than they were long ago when they were prosperous ports or trading centers. Their monumental townhalls, churches, and stately homes date back to the town's heyday.

Hundreds of stately homes line the canals in Amsterdam. These homes, now mostly used for offices, are tall and narrow because foundations were expensive (first, pilings had to be driven into the soggy soil). Their gables are often shaped like bells or steps of stairs. Jutting out from the top floor is a beam with a pulley; in this way furniture can be hoisted up

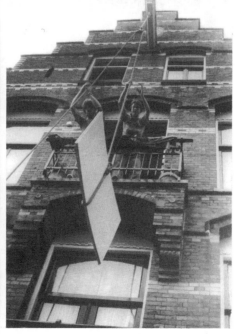

Amsterdam has more canals than Venice. Its houses have staircases so narrow that large items have to be hoisted to upper floors from the outside. Not far from the city are the famous bulb fields.

The Land They Left Behind 23

outside and in through the windows rather than be carried up the narrow stairs.

In Amsterdam, too, is one of the country's most famous museums, the *Rijksmuseum* (National Gallery) which owns one of the country's most famous paintings—known as *The Night Watch*, Rembrandt's twelve-by-fourteen-foot oil on canvas of 1642, which shows the civic guard group of Captain Frans Banning Cocq.

The Netherlands has perhaps more museums per capita than any other country in the world. A 1980 *boek van de maand* (book of the month) lists 660. Included in the list are many more art museums; not surprising in a country known not only for its Golden Age painters like Rembrandt, Hals, and Vermeer, but also for later artists like Van Gogh and Mondrian.

Various war museums record battles fought in The Netherlands during the Second World War and the five years of German occupation. Photos of resistance fighters who were shot and fugitive Jews who were found will evoke memories in those immigrants who were older children or adults when they left The Netherlands for Canada in the late 40s or early 50s.

In museum "parks" you can see old houses and windmills either moved there or rebuilt on the spot. Restored castles show what life was like in the Middle Ages. All over The Netherlands there are various collections prompted by the postwar wave of nostalgia and the feeling, "we must preserve the past." So you will see old skates set in wood, street organs turned by hand (the ones you see in the streets now are usually motor-driven), and not surprisingly in a country with some nine million bicycles, the forerunners of this useful vehicle.

In the wake of the same nostalgia, old crafts are demonstrated at summer fairs. A man is weaving a basket; a woman is plaiting a cap made of the finest lace. Woman dancers wore such caps earlier in the afternoon when they danced with their high-hatted, tail-coated men. The male and female traditional dress was either taken from the attic or faithfully copied. Nowadays few Dutch people wear what Canadians used to call the Dutch immigrants' "funny clothes." The materials are too costly, and the garments take too long to make. What's more, a woman's dress with petticoats, bonnet, apron, shawl, and *kraplap* (a collar covering shoulders and chest) just takes too

Taking in a Rembrandt; the Amsterdam home of the Concertgebouw Orchestra; a statue commemorating Anne Frank; skating on the canals; preserving the past.

A Schutterij in Limburg marches out for a competition in the koningsvogelschieten. *Milk cans, like the girl's traditional dress, will soon be things of the past. But Dutch children will probably always eat* chocolade hagelslag. *Ships crowd the inland waterways. Extensive rail lines serve all parts of the country.*

much time to put on.

Wooden shoes are still worn, but not usually with traditional dress. Wooden shoes are worn by men and women when they work in the fields or stand in the street outside their homes, washing the stoop and windows. Nowadays rubber boots often replace the *klompen*.

Another kind of craftsmanship which is receiving renewed attention is the art of building wooden, flat-bottomed boats, boats without keel but with dropboards at the side. *Platbodems*, their brown or white sails billowing, used to move cargo up and down the waterways. Bunks are now built in the holds of restored vessels, and they are used for pleasure cruising.

You can see these robust ships being sailed all over the country. Other sports are regional. Frisians vault over canals, Groningers race each other in horse-drawn tilburies, North-Brabanders wave banners, and Limburgers march with their *schutterijen* (formerly functional as civic guards). With their plumed caps and gold-braided uniforms, the guardsmen remind you of Captain Cocq's elegantly dressed company in *The Night Watch*.

After stepping smartly through town behind a brass band, the guardsmen of today shoot old-fashioned rifles at a target on top of a tall pole put up in a field.

Just as you have to travel to certain places to see particular sports, you may have to travel to eat particular foods. Thirty-six different towns make and sell their own kinds of cookies called *moppen*. Different provinces make their own kinds of spiced bread called *koek*. Fortunately, waffles from Gouda can be bought in shops or street stalls all over the country, and so, in season, can all kinds of sea produce: eel from the closed-off Zuiderzee (now called the IJsselmeer), herring from the North Sea, and mussels and oysters from the inland waters of Zeeland.

Now, what kind of people are these Dutch who all seem to insist on their own kind of cookie, their own style of farm and their own game in their own little corner of The Netherlands? It's hard to generalize about a people, but it can probably be said with a certain amount of truth that the Dutch are individualists: they like to do things in their own way. They believe in what they are doing, and

Holland's Delta Works is a massive project to control water flow.

These fishermen take time out for rest and reflection.

The seaport at Rotterdam is the world's busiest.

they will say so. Some call the Dutch stubborn.

Other "Dutch" character traits are hard to pin down. Which part of the country did these people come from? The Dutch in the south take life easier than those in the north. Which schools did they attend? What did their parents teach them? Were they raised in a small village or in a large city? The "typical" Dutch character exists no more than the "typical" Dutch look.

For centuries, people from other countries have moved to The Netherlands, and have mixed their bloodstreams with the Dutch—from Portuguese Jews and French Huguenots in the sixteenth century to, more recently, people of Malay stock and blacks from Indonesia and Surinam, former Dutch colonies. It is true that Dutch people who have been living and intermarrying in the countryside for many generations are likely to have similar physical traits. In the north, for example, many Dutch have blonde hair, blue eyes, and a sturdy physique. Elsewhere, Dutch people of equally long residence and pure Dutch ancestry tend to be dark-haired, dark-eyed, and smaller in size.

Your parents or grandparents will not hesitate to tell you which part of the country they came from. In fact, they may be prouder of their province than of the country as a whole. In that case, they will most likely call the country The Netherlands. On the other hand, your family may have no particular feeling for their province. They use the word "Holland" for the country; that's where they will say they're from.

Whether they call it Holland or The Netherlands, your relatives are bound to have opinions about what was good there when they left and what was bad; they know what heritage they treasure, and which customs and beliefs they can do without. Every immigrant, however, is likely to be proud of that one aspect of The Netherlands which is unique in the world: the inhabitants wrested their land from the water. This has given rise to the saying, "God made the world, but the Dutch made Holland." Perhaps Andries Vierlingh, William of Orange's dikemaster, said it better: "Making new land belongs to God alone. He gives to some people the intelligence and power to do it. It takes love and very much labor, and it is not everybody who can play that game."

Helen Colijn,
author of *"Of Dutch Ways"*

Chapter 2

The Vanguard

*Peter VanDyk of Gemert, Noord-Brabant, waves
from the* Waterman *in 1947. His aim was to own
his own farm. "I had a look at the
Noordoostpolder, one of the areas reclaimed from
the Zuiderzee. I don't know what turned me
off—maybe it was the emptiness—but I decided to
head for North America." Eventually he settled on
a tobacco farm near Delhi, Ontario.*

The Vanguard

Arie VanderKooij came from Maasland, in the heart of the vast vegetable-growing area west of Rotterdam. He was up early on June 17, 1947; sleep had eluded him all night. His wife had tossed and turned, too, unable to close her eyes. There was so much to think about: the evening just past and the emotional goodbyes said to so many people, the hectic day ahead of them, the uncertainty of the future. They were taking a big step. What would happen?

A few hours later, dressed in their Sunday best and toting hand-baggage and bunches of flowers, the VanderKooijs and their seven children arrived at the Holland-America Line facilities on the Wilhelmina quay in Rotterdam. In the bustling departure building, they joined another group loaded down with luggage of every description: Arie's brother and sister, their spouses and children, and a sister-in-law. Altogether twenty-five members of the family were there.

Before long, they would be on board the American-built *Waterman*, just back from the Dutch East Indies with a cargo of troops. They would join more than 1,100 others, many of them already milling about in the hall, all dressed in their best, and many clutching fresh bouquets given to them by weeping relatives. They would embark on an historic trip; they were spearheading a postwar invasion of Canada by the Dutch.

Family after family arrived, some coming in taxis, and others on foot from the railway station. But most were brought in cars and trucks driven by relatives with whom they had boarded after their own furniture had either been sold or packed in shipping crates.

There were single people too. Girls were on the way to Canada to marry the uniformed sweethearts they had cavorted with after the liberation. Boys, some of them acting as scouts for their fathers, intended to find out what Canada had to offer the farmer.

There were parents with six, eight, ten,

The VanderKooij clan gathers for a photo before boarding the Waterman *for the trip to Canada.*

ROTTERDAMSCHE BANKVEREENIGING N.V.
POTTERDAM AMSTERDAM

den Heer J.H.de Wit

VALKENBURG.

D

Leiden, 14 Juni 1947

Hierdoor deelen wij U mede dat wij het volgende in het DEBET Uwer rekening hebben geboekt:

```
getourneerd  Jan$.700.-  cheque nr. 21135 à 2,66    f.   1,862.-
                                kosten              "      10,31
             Jan$  80.-  bankpapier    2,67         "     214.--
                                kosten              "       0,50
                                                    f.   2.087,81
                                                    ============
```

Hoogachtend.
ROTTERDAMSCHE BANKVEREENIGING N.V.
kant. Leiden

49-103

The American-built Waterman *began its historic voyage on June 17, 1947. At top right, passengers gather in front of the Holland-America Line building prior to departure. The form above records the amount of money J.H. De Wit could take with him to Canada; many later immigrants were allowed to take even less. The letter, from the* Christelijke Emigratie Centrale, *announces that Canada was accepting immigrants.*

CHR. EMIGRATIE CENTRALE   's-Gravenhage,
Raamweg 26   Tel.183510
's-Gravenhage   Giro 322933

Uw schrijven van:

        In antwoord op Uw bovenvermeld schrijven berichten wij
U het volgende.
        Er bestaan momenteel mogelijkheden voor emigratie naar
Canada en wel in de eerste plaats voor boeren en tuinders die
familie in dit land hebben. Indien dit voor U het geval is, kunt
U zich aan ons bovenstaand adres daartoe opgeven, met vermelding
van naam, adres en verwantschapsgraad van Uw familie aldaar.
        Voor ongehuwden en gehuwden met hoogstens een of twee
kleine kinderen, en voor grote gezinnen met zoons en dochters
die als volwaardige arbeidskrachten mede kunnen werken, bestaat
bovendien de mogelijkheid in loondienst in Canada tewerkgesteld
te worden. Men kan slechts een klein bedrag aan dollars meenemen,
doch men behoeft dan geen familie aldaar te hebben. Het loon
dat verdiend zal worden, varieert tussen 40 en 55 dollar per
maand voor ongehuwden en ca. 75 dollar per maand voor gehuwden,
met kost en inwoning. Men zal zoveel mogelijk in of nabij een
Nederlands Protestants Christelijke kolonie geplaatst worden.
Ook hiervoor kunt U zich eventueel aan bovenstaand adres aan-
melden.
        U krijgt dan een formulier D toegezonden, dat U zo
spoedig mogelijk ingevuld en voorzien van het advies van de
landbouworganisatie, waarbij U bent aangesloten aan ons dient
te retourneren, waarna wij voor de verdere behandeling van Uw
aanvrage zorgdragen en U tijdig zullen berichten indien U een
visum zal worden verleend.

                        Hoogachtend,
                DE ALW. SECRETARIS VAN DE
                CHR. EMIGRATIE CENTRALE,

                        (I.J.M.de Bruin)

and more children, a common sight in those days. The mothers, holding the youngest in their arms, tried desperately to keep everyone together while their husbands, papers in hand, registered at the counters. A reporter for *De Rotterdammer* found "everyone full of courage." One woman told him matter-of-factly: "Well, if your husband is going, you've got no choice. But everything will turn out all right." Another pointed to her little group and said: "We'll be together over there. What could be better?"

VanderKooij felt much more relaxed now that he had come so far. There was no turning back. He could only look ahead, to the trip across the ocean, to the new home in Ontario, where three-fourths of his fellow passengers would also go, to the hard work that awaited him there, to the new life in a new country. A smile touched his face when the boarding announcement was made.

Only a few weeks earlier, J. Hugo De Wit of Valkenburg, Zuid-Holland, had received a message from the *Stichting Landverhuizing Nederland*, a foundation that had been developing candidates for emigration through the voluntary agencies in the country. The message: the time for leaving The Netherlands was at hand. The go-ahead word had been received from a representative in Canada. Arrangements had been completed to transport more than one thousand emigrants on the *Waterman*. The notice didn't mention outright that this

Emigrants applied for Canadian visas at this building in The Hague.

Passengers approached the Waterman *on a small boat.*

freighter-troopship wasn't equipped to accommodate women and children. There was only a hint: "Your attention is drawn to the fact that simple accommodation is available in the holds that have been set up for the stay of passengers. One half of the ship is for men, the other half for women and children."

De Wit didn't pay too much attention to that. He was more concerned about another detail mentioned in the notice: the *Waterman* was scheduled to leave Rotterdam on June 17. That was only a few weeks away!

The fee for the crossing was set at around 345 guilders for an adult, half that amount for a child between one and ten, and a mere twenty-six guilders for a baby.

The notice continued: "If you want to take advantage of this opportunity, please be at the Canadian immigration office at Sophialaan 1 in The Hague at 10 a.m. on

Boarding the ship meant climbing this ladder.

Passengers lined the railing to wave farewell.

A little boat came alongside and tooted a farewell song.

June 2 for a medical examination. After you have been cleared by the examiner, the immigration officer can issue a visa, provided you satisfy the other requirements. If you are married, you will have to come with your entire family . . ."

A passport was also necessary, of course, as was a declaration from the prospective emigrant that all his taxes were paid up.

The days that followed had been filled with excited activity. There were things to be sold and things to be bought. There were trips to the bank to buy dollars and put the cash which could not be taken out of The Netherlands into trust. There were letters to be written, phone calls to be made, people to be visited.

No wonder there was a broad smile of relief on VanderKooij's face when the time came for everyone to get on board. He looked forward to a relaxing trip across the ocean. The rest would be well de-

served.

However, he was soon to realize that he wasn't traveling on a luxury liner. The *Waterman*, he noticed, didn't have a gangway!

"The ship was moored some distance from the quay because repairs were being made," explains passenger John Kap of Maassluis, not far from Maasland. "About fifty passengers at a time boarded a little tugboat which took them to the side of the ship. There we stepped onto a small platform and climbed up a ladder suspended with ropes, holding onto the cables. That was quite a height, especially for those with small children. It was not the usual way to board a ship, and I can see why some people, especially those who lived inland, were somewhat hesitant or afraid."

Mrs. Peter Vriend of Houston, British Columbia, recalls: "I had a baby of just over a year in my arms while I tried to climb that ladder. Someone took the baby from me to help me get on the boat, but I wanted to keep my baby. That ladder was a scary thing."

Everyone was shown their sleeping quarters in the massive holds—the men and older boys in one part of the boat and the women and the younger children in another. Bunkbeds stood four high.

Just before departure, Kap's uncle, a functionary with the Holland-America Line, came on board to shake hands, wish good luck and pass on some information: "Don't expect too much from the trip. This boat just came in with a load of soldiers and other than hosing the decks, they haven't had time to clean it."

The ship moved slowly away from the dock. People lined the rails, trying to catch a glimpse of relatives lingering on shore. There were shouts; handkerchiefs fluttered. A group sang *Het Wilhelmus*, the national anthem.

The police boat of Schiedam, a Rotterdam suburb, had the honor of leading the *Waterman* out of the busy harbor. Most of the passengers remained at the railings, taking in sights they had never seen before

and having a farewell look at The Netherlands at the same time. Suddenly the police boat's steam whistle began to toot the well-rehearsed notes of *Vaarwel Mijn Dierbaar Vaderland* (Farewell My Beloved Fatherland). Even the hardiest on board must have swallowed lumps in their throats.

At night, John Kap crawled into his bunkbed. Exhausted, he looked forward to a long sleep, quite sure that he wouldn't be troubled by the murmurs, sneezes, arguments, and occasional guffaw.

"But I couldn't stretch my legs. The sheet was too short. I didn't want to force it, for fear of breaking something that didn't belong to me. In the morning, I discovered that the sheet was glued to the blanket by a number of fried eggs. The stench was terrible. Maybe I hadn't noticed it in the evening because I had been so exhausted."

At nine o'clock at night, feeling a bit

Small craft sailed alongside the Waterman *for a while. As the ship moved away from Rotterdam and toward the North Sea, relatives and friends kept waving from the pier.*

bored, passenger De Wit decided to stroll over to the compartment where his wife and four children were getting ready to bed down for the night. He would spend some time with them before the men were shooed away to their own sleeping quarters.

"I felt tired, so I climbed to the top bed—they stood four high—and stretched out. I fell asleep right away. When they came to inspect the place at about ten o'clock to make sure no men were around, they must have missed me. I didn't see them either, because I was dead to the world. I slept there the whole night. Don't ask me why they were so fussy. It must have been because of all those so-called war brides on board."

In the men's ward, VanderKooij didn't even have a sheet and a pillow case.

"There's no question that the conditions were crude. We felt like soldiers on the way to battle."

He didn't like sleeping by himself. During such a time of stress, it was essential for spouses to be close enough to comfort and reassure each other. Besides, the arrangement was unfair to the mothers, some of them already seasick, and having to look after all the small children and babies by themselves.

When the *Waterman* rounded the south of England and headed for the open ocean, all the passengers, young and old, had to report to the lifeboats. Vests were handed out and instructions were given. As the voyage proceeded, this exercise would be repeated a number of times, with a smaller audience each time. Why all the precautions were necessary soon became evident. Without much warning, a vicious Atlantic gale struck. As the seas began to swell, the crew hurried to close the hatches and portholes and to shove the

When the Groenewegens Left

Cornelis Groenewegen, operator of a store in The Hague which specialized in potatoes, vegetables, fruit, and fuel, displayed a sign made by a friend. "To Canada," it announced. The message thanked the faithful customers that Groenewegen and his wife, Adriana, had the pleasure of serving, even during the trying German occupation. The couple had received notice that they and their five young children— the oldest was seven and the youngest two months— could travel to Canada on the Waterman.

Groenewegen, a native of Rozenburg, west of Rotterdam, used to work on his father's farm and had peddled potatoes in The Hague before starting the

Cornelis Groenewegen thanks his customers.

The Groenewegens now, at home near Campbellville, Ontario.

dining room tables against the wall. Everything loose was tied down.

Seasickness, that age-old enemy of ocean travelers, began to take its toll. For some, the awful sickness would last until the end of the voyage. A lot of waste ended up on the decks and in the halls, and there seemed to be no one available to clean it up. Finally, someone came along with a barrel and told everyone so inclined to vomit into it. The stench surely didn't cure anybody.

VanderKooij, who had been looking forward to a luxurious trip, free of headaches, says: "Boy, was I sick. I couldn't hold anything in my stomach. Several times I did it overboard, making sure to take out my false teeth first. Some people actually lost theirs. After a while, my mouth got terribly dry and my tongue cracked. I couldn't get hold of a drink to ease my thirst. Then a boy remembered that his mother had packed a lemon in his suitcase. He got it, and I took a bite. Boy, did that hurt. I threw the thing overboard."

Kap recalls the farmer from Noord-Brabant and his four sons who shared the bunks below him: "He told me that his children were so sick they couldn't pray any more."

Kap, who didn't suffer from seasickness, felt a bit lonely. It seemed as if most of the passengers were staying in bed. The decks were almost deserted. Less than 200 people showed up for supper.

"There were couples who wouldn't see each other for five or six days," he says. "First of all, they didn't sleep together, and, secondly, they were sick in bed. And when those people finally did get together, it was wise for others to move away. What fights! I heard one woman shout: 'You and your rotten idea to

Many people came to say goodbye to the departing family.

store. He had enough qualifications to get permission to emigrate to Canada.

There wasn't much time to get everything ready for the family's imminent departure. Groenewegen's parents (that's his father on the left in front of the store at Bilthovenschelaan 86) came over for a weekend to bid farewell. None of them expected to see each other again. On a Saturday evening, Groenewegen formally transferred the business to Christian friends. The bookkeeper, an elder in his church, was also present.

"After the deal was closed," says Groenewegen, now of the Campbellville, Ontario, area, "the new owner played the small house organ and we sang many verses of the beautiful 84th Psalm. After the singing, my mother said: 'Cor, now I can let you go.' By the way, the first Bible reading at our table in Canada was from this psalm."

A farewell photo of the family in front of the store.

None of the relatives expected to see each other again.

Passengers crowd on deck to take advantage of some rare sunshine.

emigrate!' I often acted as a messenger for a husband who wanted to convey something to his wife but couldn't get out of his bed."

Kap liked to stand at the bow early in the morning, watching the boat slice through the water. His thoughts would wander —sometimes to the world somewhere ahead, beyond the horizon, but most of the time to the world he had left behind, to his wife and children, who would follow him later. Sometimes he felt so lonely that he began to wonder why he had ever decided to head for the unknown. Then he thought of the One who had created the sky and the waves and who was guiding this ship, and he didn't feel quite so lonely any more.

"I couldn't help but notice the seagulls that followed us out onto the ocean. It seemed as if they wanted to say: 'We're going to stay with you; we know what you had to leave behind.' Of course, they only wanted the bits of food that were either thrown or spewed overboard. But when

you're lonely, even a bird cocking its eye at you can make you feel a bit happier."

Mr. and Mrs. John Kottelenberg of Neede, Gelderland, just married, enjoyed the voyage tremendously, despite the misery around them. The trip was like a honeymoon. After all, they only had themselves to worry about.

"We were young, and eager to experience new things," says Mrs. Kottelenberg, now of the Shelburne, Ontario, area. "For us, the trip was rather easy. But for the bigger families, it was no picnic."

She and her husband, heading for Canada with intentions to farm, usually left their separate sleeping quarters very early in the morning in order to beat the rush to the washrooms. The facilities started to get crowded by around eight o'clock. Many of the people were ill, and sometimes the stench was unbearable.

"I was also glad to get away from the mess in the sleeping hall. In the center stood a big barrel for people whose

Arie VanderKooij, afflicted with a severe bout of seasickness, is comforted by one of his daughters. J.H. De Wit has his hands full making sure his children stay safely inside the railing. A Canadian photographer who came on board during the brief stop at Quebec City spotted the mother in traditional costume.

stomach started to turn. Often they didn't reach it in time. However, my husband and I didn't have too much trouble with seasickness. We spent most of the time on deck, watching the ocean. We found a nice, secluded spot for just the two of us. Our only problem was keeping warm: we wore winter coats and wrapped a blanket around us. It was very cold on the ocean in June."

The couple enjoyed the food, but they didn't appreciate having to stand half an hour in line for a chance to get at it.

"This was especially hard for the families with little ones. Some friends of ours from Eibergen had a six-week-old baby. The baby was bottle-fed, and the parents had such trouble getting the milk on time. It was obvious that the crew was not prepared to handle so many children. I'm sure that for many parents it was a great relief to spot the coast of Newfoundland."

Passenger De Wit has very clear memories of the food served on board. He loved it.

More scenes from the Waterman: *a family, all smiles, has weathered the crossing and is looking forward to standing on solid ground again. With the boat approaching Montreal, it's time to check the baggage.*

However, other passengers wondered why they had paid so much money to be carried by a boat that obviously didn't have enough food on board. Such complaints were inevitable. A message came over the loudspeaker to say that anyone who wanted something over and above his portion could get a ticket at the bridge and pick up the food in the coffee shop.

There were a few other things which some passengers—Mrs. VanderKooij for one—would like to forget.

"We had to keep our spoons and forks with us, clean them, and then bring them for the next meal. At coffee time, the only way to get some was to put the cup in your hand, stretch out your arm, and push through the crowd. And that standing in line for meals with a bunch of screaming youngsters . . . All those things bothered me so much that I sometimes wished I were back in Holland."

One day, well into the voyage, it was announced that icebergs were visible on the right-hand side of the ship. All those who could stand on their feet hurried to take a look. After all, one didn't see an iceberg every day. And wasn't it a sign that land wasn't too far off?

De Wit, who spent most of the daylight hours on deck—"You get to see a few things that way"—spotted the icebergs. He also saw a whale. And he saw something else . . . a mine!

"I saw it bobbing in the water some one hundred meters from the boat. Nobody ever said anything about it. I guess they didn't want the people to panic. I recognized it as a mine right away. More than one had washed ashore at Katwijk aan Zee, and I had watched as they were being detonated. As far as I'm concerned, we had a close call."

Morale plunged to a new low when the ship's sewerage became plugged. The washing hall became something like a covered swimming pool. After a while, the toilets didn't work either. People's needs were the same, and so the stinking waste spilled over and mingled with the water on the floor.

"The meat was excellent. I hadn't eaten like that for a long time. It was right after the war, you know. The butcher shops in The Netherlands weren't very well stocked yet. Yes, we got plenty to eat."

The kitchen crew even put a tub of hardened bacon fat on deck. Passengers helped themselves liberally. With a touch of salt and pepper, it made a delicious spread for sandwiches.

The Netherlands ambassador, Dr. J.H. Van Royen, waves to his fellow citizens as the Waterman *is about to dock in Montreal.*

National Film Board

Public Archive Canada

Says De Wit: "The toilet facilities were so bad that you could ask for a potty for the children. That sounded all right. But there weren't enough potties to go around."

Mrs. VanderKooij also shudders when she thinks back to the primitive washroom facilities.

"They were degrading. There were about six toilets in a row, with no doors in front of them. That stench was unbearable. But I was more concerned about the lack of privacy. One time, I arranged with a couple of women to go at the same time, and we took turns holding up a blanket."

As the *Waterman* sailed up the St. Lawrence River, passengers were told to appear in turns at the office on the bridge. There they could exchange money, receive information on where they were to be placed—most of them already knew this in The Netherlands—and receive landing instructions.

After a brief stop at Quebec City, the ship continued on to Montreal. It was June 26 when it finally edged up to its berth at dockside: The *Montreal Daily Star* reported: "Ships in port joined in the welcome with a noisy greeting from their booming whistles. Harbor craft joined in to make it the noisiest reception the harbor has seen since the days before the war." A welcoming party stood ready with speeches in hand. Among them was The Netherlands ambassador to Canada, Dr. J.H. Van Royen, who waved his hat at the mass of humanity crammed on the decks and convenient perches. Some of the passengers waved back. Others cheered. Many merely smiled, glad that the awful experience of the past ten days had finally come to an end.

The ambassador, speaking from the bridge, said some glowing words about Canada: it was a great and beautiful country. The Dutch would find a hearty reception because of the need for their labor.

"You will find that people from The Netherlands are highly thought of in Canada. That's due to the ones who came here before you and who have become known as good workers and good citizens. It's also particularly due to Her Royal Highness Princess Juliana, who stayed for a long time in this hospitable country and won many hearts for herself and her country through her charm and simplicity."

C.E. Smith, the Canadian official in charge of immigration, also spoke: "In your group are young women on the way

The arrival was front page news.

to their future husbands whom they got to know while the Canadian army served in The Netherlands. I wish them a happy and prosperous future. Others among you will go to relatives who earlier came along to this country, became successful and are now in a state to take you in and to assist you in becoming settled. Your difficulties certainly will not be as great as those of your predecessors. For those who sold their farms in order to choose their future home here and who will live for a time among strangers while they work on the land to become familiar with Canadian customs and work habits, I hope that they will find friendly surroundings and that, thanks to their drive to succeed, it won't take long before they will be settled on their own farms. Many of you will sometimes think longingly of your old home, but in time this feeling of nostalgia and loneliness will disappear—if you have the determination to make the best of the new life."

Dr. A.S. Tuinman, the energetic attaché for agricultural and emigration affairs at the Royal Netherlands Embassy in Ottawa, one of the architects of the postwar influx, offered these words:

"Your arrival on the Waterman has made a moving impression of Dutch people in Canada. A ship filled with Dutch people seeking a new future suggests to us, living far away from our land of birth, that the Dutch are still energetic and enterprising. You will undoubtedly need a fair share of this energy to make it through the difficult years ahead. I hope you will all succeed, and furthermore, I hope that you can confirm the hope placed in you by both the Canadian government and the Canadian people. It is in your own interest, as well as in Canada's, that you adjust as quickly as possible and become loyal Canadian citizens. Moreover, I hope you will not forget your country of birth. As you know, the United Nations and other organizations seek to bring nations closer together, end wars, and prepare a better future for the people of the world. To achieve that goal, people must learn to appreciate each other. Each of you can contribute much by way of example. By becoming loyal Canadian citizens and at the same time maintaining your natural ties, you can help to bring the two nations closer together, in order that the ocean you have just crossed may on all sides be

The Waterman *unloads. Each immigrant was given an identification card. This one belonged to John Kap.*

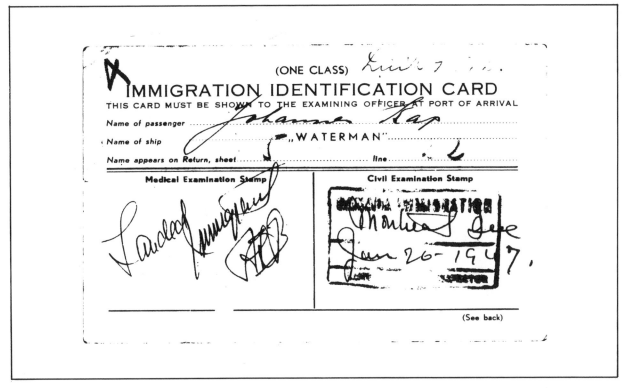

rimmed with nations living together in harmony. If this should happen, then the arrival of the *Waterman* will symbolize an event of historic importance."

There were more speeches. Then the time came for the people to leave the ship and check through immigration and customs. The scene was chaotic. Many parents had a hard time keeping their children together.

The *Montreal Gazette* reported: "As more and more passengers walked from the ship into the long customs and cargo shed, excitement increased. Surrounded by piles of baggage, the Netherlanders waited patiently for transportation to the trains. To help harassed parents, Canadian Red Cross workers proffered countless changes of baby wear while others served coffee and doughnuts to all those who became tired and thirsty during the hectic proceedings."

The crates, big and small, were hoisted out of the hold and everyone checked to make sure all their belongings were being placed together. One man asked a worker if he had seen a certain *kist*. The answer remained a mystery: it was in French.

Passenger De Wit had used straw to pack three small crates, but the customs people didn't like that at all. They feared the import of some contagious disease.

"When I went to look for my crates, I saw some tags on them. I didn't know any English, but I was level-headed enough to know that something wasn't in order."

De Wit, who traveled on to Mount Elgin, Ontario, didn't get his belongings until after they had been cleared by the health authorities.

The Immigration Committee of the Christian Reformed Church, one of the first groups who assisted the postwar immigrants, circulated a mimeographed sheet that stated in part: "Be sure to use patience and diligence as you move into the occupation we have arranged for you. And if you meet with difficulties, don't forget the Dutch proverb: 'The persistent one wins.' "

Then it was off to the trains: parents with a long row of children in tow, young farmers with new pairs of wooden shoes strapped on their suitcases, boys sweating in overcoats. But most of them were smiling. They were in Canada at last!

Chapter 3

How It All Began

Thousands of people in The Netherlands died of starvation and the cold during the last winter of the German occupation. The people in the photo lined up in a polder in Noord-Holland in 1945 for a small portion of grain and the chance to gather whatever the threshing machine left behind.

How It All Began

The Dutch didn't suddenly discover Canada after the Second World War. Far from it.

Even before the turn of the century, the Canadian West, with its millions of acres of free or cheap land, began to attract people from The Netherlands. By that time, the American agricultural frontier was filled, and so potential emigrants were forced to look elsewhere. Even former Dutch emigrants to the United States began to move to homesteads on the Canadian prairies, and some settled in such urban centers as Winnipeg.

When the Canadian West began to open up, more Dutch farmers came, attracted by glowing reports. One farmer near Carlyle, Saskatchewan, already a prosperous man by 1914, wrote: "For Hollanders and Flemings, this is the place to acquire a fortune." Could one with adventure in his blood resist such temptation?

Emigrants usually spent the first years in Canada as farmhands, railway employees, bush workers, or as urban laborers during the winter. Thus they accumulated some capital and assessed the homesteading possibilities. Before long, they were on their own, pioneers carving a living out of the wilderness.

By 1914, about 15,000 Dutch people had come to Canada. They were scattered across the West, and some had established permanent settlements. Names such as Edam and Amsterdam appeared. A group of immigrants from Nijverdal, Overijssel, settled in the Granum and Monarch areas of Alberta and called their new community Nieuw Nijverdal. Neerlandia, ninety miles north of Edmonton, was founded in an attempt to build a center where the Dutch could preserve their culture,

Public Archives Canada

Dutch Emigration to Canada 1900-1945

Year		Year		Year	
1900	25	1916	151	1932	259
1901	35	1917	94	1933	164
1902	223	1918	59	1934	148
1903	169	1919	154	1935	208
1904	281	1920	595	1936	192
1905	389	1921	183	1937	232
1906	394	1922	119	1938	376
1907	1,212	1923	1,149	1939	411
1908	495	1924	1,637	1940	238
1909	741	1925	1,721	1941	203
1910	931	1926	2,242	1942	146
1911	1,077	1927	2,465	1943	131
1912	1,524	1928	2,340	1944	159
1913	1,506	1929	2,458	1945	332
1914	605	1930	788		
1915	186	1931	269		

Source: A.S. Tuinman, *Enige aspecten van de hedendaagse migratie van Nederlanders naar Canada* (1952)

Immigrants from The Netherlands gather in an assembly hall at the railway terminal in Halifax, Nova Scotia, in the 1920s. At left, young prewar immigrants cool off in shallow water at Vancouver, British Columbia.

Above: Prewar settlers from The Netherlands clear light bush as they prepare to break up new land.
Far right: A typical frame farmhouse near Carmangay, Alberta.
Right: To get to cleared land, Stanley Mol had to build a bridge.
Below: Unemployed men on their way to Ottawa during the Depression; immigration ground to a halt during this bleak period.

religion, and sense of ethnic unity. A co-operative system encouraged agricultural development, and Neerlandia soon became one of the leading Dutch settlements in Canada.

Numerous problems faced the Dutch farmers in the West. As they struggled to overcome them, they made quite a name for themselves. In 1917, drifting soil in the Monarch area became a severe problem. Farmer Arie Koole decided to alternate strips of crop and summer fallow. Other farmers followed his example. By 1930, strip farming was practised widely as an effective defense against drifting soil. The Dutch were also leaders in irrigation projects.

Immigration came to a standstill during the First World War. But when peace was restored, the movement resumed with the encouragement of the Canadian government, the major Canadian railway companies, the emigration societies in The Netherlands, and other emigration agents. As the drawing power of the prairies and northern areas diminished—free or cheap arable land was rapidly declining—the Dutch began to spread to other areas of Canada. A number went to British Columbia, settling in the lower Fraser River valley, in the Vancouver area, and on Vancouver Island. But the majority went no farther than Ontario.

Between 1920 and 1929, more than 14,900 came to Canada, most of them settling in the mixed farming areas of southern Ontario. More and more Canadians were moving to the cities, leaving their agricultural jobs open for the newcomers. As in the West, it took the immigrants a few years to gain experience and acquire capital before they bought their own farms.

The Depression put a virtual halt to the movement. Only those with close relatives in Canada or those with lots of money could hope to make a beginning here. The

When German fire-bombs destroyed the core of Rotterdam, the Dutch armed forces capitulated to avoid further bloodshed. After five years, The Netherlands was liberated. The sketch, widely circulated after the war, shows a Dutchman thanking his Canadian liberator. At left, the liberation is commemorated in a parade through the streets of Voorburg, near The Hague.

number of immigrants fell from a high of 2,465 in 1927 to a low of 148 in 1934. People in the western world struggled to survive—including the immigrants in Canada.

Then the Second World War came along. The German occupation of The Netherlands in May of 1940 brought to an end even the limited emigration. Some refugees made their way to Canada, however. Prominent among them were Princess Juliana and her two little daughters, Beatrix and Irene, who stayed in Ottawa for the duration of the war. A third daughter, Margriet, was born at the Civic Hospital on January 19, 1943.

The dark cloud hung over The Netherlands for five years. Finally, in the spring of 1945, the sun began to shine again. The Dutch hailed their liberators—Canadian soldiers under Allied command. And they crowded into the churches to thank God for the victory and the return of freedom.

But the rejoicing was shortlived. The country's economy lay in shambles. Growth seemed impossible. Housing was in short supply, and the population continued to increase. Many people saw no future in The Netherlands for themselves and their children. They pondered the notion of getting away from the mess and starting a new life somewhere else on the globe.

The Dutch government looked toward the West. The United States was keeping its doors virtually closed. Fortunately, the Canadians were receptive. They needed more people for their vital agricultural sector. And they knew from experience that the Dutch were good farmers.

Toward the end of 1946, an immigration officer was sent to The Hague to prepare for the resumption of the immigration program, and to cope with the immediate problem of resettling the fiancées and dependents of Canadian servicemen. On January 30, 1947, Canada amended its immigration regulations to provide for the admission of sponsored agriculturalists. A few months later, Prime Minister W.L. Mackenzie King put the Canadian policy on record, affirming his country's need for more people and his intentions to develop an expansive immigration program.

The *Waterman* docked at Montreal in late June, launching a migration whose numbers within a few years would far outstrip the prewar total of more than 30,000.

Emigration fever kept on spreading in The Netherlands. The outbreak of war in the Dutch East Indies, now Indonesia, and fears that the Russians would invade western Europe added to the desire to move away. Applicants and information seekers swamped the *Stichting Landverhuizing Nederland*, an umbrella organization of government and private people that actively promoted emigration, and later developed into the *Nederlandse Emigratiedienst*.

The overcrowding problem in The Netherlands was compounded by the unfavorable outcome of the difficulties in Indonesia and the extensive repatriation of

Public Archives Canada

Dutch subjects. Unemployment and housing shortages became acute. The government was forced to take action in 1950, providing an incentive for emigration. For the first time, subsidies were available to assist those who had not had enough money to pay for the fare and the shipment of belongings.

The boat lines did a booming business, ferrying people to the far corners of the world, including Canada.

Further help was provided by the Canadian government. The immigration regulations were amended to allow non-agriculturalists into the country. By 1953, significant numbers of Dutch people with business, professional, technical, and other backgrounds had established their home in Canada.

Dr. A.S. Tuinman, the postwar agricultural and emigration attaché at the Royal Netherlands Embassy in Ottawa, had been given his instructions: try to get the Canadian authorities to reopen the doors. In September, 1946, he set to work, and detected enough interest to warrant optimism.

His job wasn't made easier by the circumstances—it was a difficult period for both countries. The Netherlands wasn't too eager to encourage the emigration of non-farm workers. Its industrial laborers were needed for reconstruction and economic recovery. Dr. Tuinman breathed a sigh of relief when he learned that the Canadians really didn't want welders or bricklayers anyway.

Officials in Ottawa feared that a postwar decline in production and the demobilization of the Canadian army would result in a period of unemployment. And so they were cautious about immigration. Certain groups had no trouble getting in—close relatives of Canadian citizens, war brides, demobilized Polish soldiers who had served in the Allied armies, and displaced persons. But there was no enthusiasm for opening the door to any John, Dick and Harry.

But then the unemployment picture did

Prospective emigrants await their turn in the waiting room of Stichting Landverhuizing Nederland.

Nederlandse Emigratiedienst

not turn out to be as dismal as feared. This was first noticeable in the agricultural sector, where a shortage of manpower continued even after most of the boys had returned from overseas.

It was in March, 1947, that the final touches were put to an understanding reached between Canadian and Dutch authorities. Agriculturalists willing to work as farm laborers would be admitted.

There was a flurry of activity in The Netherlands. People who had applied for emigration were notified. They were in-

formed that the *Waterman*, hastily pressed into service, would be leaving Rotterdam on June 17. A mad scramble to get everything ready in time was inevitable.

Dr. Tuinman, now of Arnhem, looks back upon the arrival of the boat in Montreal as a moving experience.

"We still remembered well the glorious arrival of the Canadian troops in The Netherlands toward the end of the Second World War. And now this peaceful invasion of Canada by Dutch men and women, eager to take part in the further

Right: Mr. and Mrs. Melvin Elgersma and their seven children came over with the Veendam *in May, 1947, more than a month before the* Waterman *berthed in Montreal. They must have liked the food on board—the man in the center is the cook.*

Below: The Tabinta *is about to leave. Emigrants crowd on deck to witness the departure.*

development of Canada, appeared to be a living testament of the joy and gratefulness of the Dutch people, liberated after the dark years of occupation. The arrival of the *Waterman* seemed to be the crowning of the liberation. For those responsible for the immigration initiative and organization, it was also a moment of satisfaction, hope, and confidence that this was the beginning of a large and beneficial movement of Dutch people to the new world."

But there was also worry. At first, the Dutch authorities were responsible for much of the program. The Canadians would have preferred to wait until their own immigration services were rebuilt after the curtailment caused by the war. They had given in to the urgent requests for an early start. Consequently, preparations and assistance were in the hands of inexperienced people.

However, the apprehension didn't last long. Says Dr. Tuinman: "Notwithstanding many difficulties, and thanks to the co-operation of many well-wishers and the thoroughness of the prospective settlers, this first movement made a favorable impression and was followed by many others. The first arrivals bore the brunt of our inexperience, preparing the way for those who followed."

On November 26, two months after the arrival of the second boat, the *Tabinta*, a joint press release which set out the program for 1948 was issued by Dr. Tuinman and J. Allison Glen, the minister of the Department of Mines and Resources, which included the immigration branch. The doors were being opened to admit no fewer than 10,000 agriculturalists. To facilitate the passage of the people, the Dutch government chartered the *Tabinta* and the *Kota Inten*. These were scheduled to make a total of thirteen trips, carrying some 770 passengers each time. The first two arrivals were to be at Halifax early in March, with the remainder set to dock at the St. Lawrence River ports—Quebec City and Montreal.

"Owing to present exchange restrictions," the release stated, "these Dutch families will be unable at first to establish themselves on farms in Canada. They have agreed, however, to accept agricultural employment in all parts of the Dominion with farmers whose applications for their services have been approved and who will provide living accommodation. Through these arrangements, they will acquire an excellent knowledge of Canada and of agricultural

conditions and methods in this country. The plan affords Dutch parents an opportunity to obtain for their children farmland which is unavailable at home, and will be instrumental in a greater development of Canada's agricultural resources."

By this time, the federal authorities in Ottawa were ready to assume more responsibility for the execution of the program, formally called The Netherlands-Canadian Settlement Scheme. More areas of Canada were being opened up for settlement. And the Dutch kept on coming, agreeing to work for their sponsors for at least one year. The minimum wage was $75 a month for married men and $45 for single ones. Free housing was included.

Dr. A.S. Tuinman (right) helped to develop the program which permitted Dutch agriculturalists to enter Canada. His successor was Fopke Jensma (left). The letter confirmed the placement of Arie VanderKooij, one of the early immigrants.

CANADA

IN YOUR REPLY REFER TO
No. B.30091

ADDRESS
DISTRICT SUPERINTENDENT
EASTERN DISTRICT

IMMIGRATION BRANCH

DEPARTMENT
OF
MINES AND RESOURCES

Ottawa, May 2nd, 1947.

Dear Sir:

  With reference to your application for the admission to Canada
of
  Arie Van Der Kooy, his wife, Adriana Van Der Kooy (nee de Ruiter) and their children, Arie (Jr.), Pieter, Maria Hilla, Sara, Cornelia, Adrianna and Maartje Van Der Kooy,

presently residing at

  Oostgaag C, 73 Maasland, Holland,

this is to advise that the settlement arrangements for the reception of the above-named are considered satisfactory and it will be in order for them to make application in person to the Canadian Vise Officer at the

  Canadian Legation, Sophialaan 1A, The Hague, The Netherlands.

  Provided the proposed immigrants are of good character, in possession of valid passports, can pass medical examination and otherwise comply with our requirements, vise for Canada will be granted.

  This letter should be sent to the above-named for presentation to the Canadian Vise Officer indicated for the purpose of identification.

  Yours very truly,

  District Superintendent.

Peter Verkaik, Esq.,
R. R. # 2,
Tottenham, Ontario.

The mechanics of the program were not complicated. Farmers in Canada could apply for labor from The Netherlands at the immigration offices, the National Employment Service, the provincial government offices, or the colonization departments of the Canadian Pacific and the Canadian National railways. The applications were checked out and then forwarded to the Canadian immigration officers in The Hague. The Dutch were responsible for the placements.

Then there were the medical examinations required by Canada of all immigrants, including the children. These were done by Canadian medical officers. Background inquiries also were conducted before visas were issued.

Says Harry Cunliffe of Ottawa, the chief Canadian immigration official in The Hague from May, 1976, to May, 1980: "Certainly some of the applicants were refused, but most refusals were based on the statutory health and character requirements."

In 1948, the system was reversed. Lists of prospective emigrants, who had already been medically examined at The Hague, were forwarded by the *Stichting Landverhuizing Nederland* to the agricultural attaché for transmission to Canadian immigration authorities and the other interested agencies. Placements were then worked out.

"Then, as now," says Cunliffe, "Ontario was the destination of approximately fifty per cent of the total annual immigration to Canada. There was certainly no housing standing empty in Canada in those days, and the Dutch farm families seemed to get bigger and bigger as the movement gathered momentum. I think the record was twenty-one children."

Cunliffe, who began his immigration service at Hamilton in May, 1947, speaks highly of the first newcomers, the postwar pioneers.

"Few of the Dutch immigrants spoke English then. They had come to Canada in small, crowded ships, with minimal personal effects. Families were often separated by sex to utilize all available sleeping accommodation. It must have seemed an endless journey to that first Canadian farm."

The first postwar settlers could come to Canada only if they had been placed and sponsored. Sometimes sponsors cancelled at the last minute, and then there were anxious moments and changes of destination. But most of the emigrants knew with certainty before leaving The Netherlands where they would settle.

After the successful settlement of the first wave, the Canadian government decided to take over the responsibility of placement. Sponsors were still required. However, things didn't always go according to the letter of the law.

Fopke Jensma of Ottawa, who worked in Dr. Tuinman's department beginning in 1948, explains: "It became increasingly clear that it was not easy to find sponsors in time. Processing the application took time, and the prospective immigrant needed time to prepare and arrange his affairs before departure; therefore he had to be placed no later than December or January so that he could arrive in the spring or early summer. However, in early winter, not too many Canadian farmers were thinking about hiring help, par-

Officially sponsored emigration from The Netherlands by country of future residence 1946-1982

	1946	1947	1948	1949	1950	1951	1952	1953	1954	1955	1956	1957	1958	1959	1960	1961	1962	1963
Australia	23	95	867	1,619	9,268	10,494	15,828	7,813	10,906	13,731	10,959	6,731	7,458	8,319	8,060	4,210	2,027	1,930
Brazil	40	140	135	407	281	206	281	615	578	447	288	200	234	230	249	239	143	186
Canada	9	2,361	6,899	6,856	7,033	18,604	20,653	20,095	15,859	6,654	7,651	11,724	7,284	5,323	5,457	1,799	1,553	1,701
New Zealand		8	95	101	503	3,187	4,575	2,575	768	1,266	1,355	1,065	1,733	1,338	1,158	1,375	944	594
South Africa	16	1,062	2,340	2,021	1,153	2,588	4,177	3,432	3,275	2,839	1,819	1,224	1,956	1,689	482	344	490	631
United States	369	2,911	3,128	2,605	2,883	2,262	2,634	2,843	2,708	4,012	9,220	9,074	3,745	5,332	8,700	6,045	6,176	1,572
Others	47	241	373	354	209	264	542	676	582	682	496	403	707	258	229	103	213	172
Total Dutch Emigration	504	6,818	13,837	13,963	21,330	37,605	48,690	38,049	34,676	29,631	31,788	30,421	23,117	22,489	24,335	14,115	11,546	6,786

Source: Ministry of Social Affairs and Public Health of The Netherlands, **Verslag over de werkzaamheden van de organen voor de emigratie**

ticularly people who would arrive five or six months later. On the other hand, our experience of placing immigrant farmers had demonstrated sufficient demand for Dutch settlers during the spring and summer. Therefore, placements during that time posed no great difficulties if the Canadian farmer could be assured that the immigrant was on his way or could be expected before long. As a practical solution to this problem, some prospective immigrants were approved without having a specific sponsor. One would say they were accepted on a general sponsorship, or perhaps that they were sponsored by the Immigration Branch."

That's why some people didn't learn of their destination in Canada until they were on the boat. And there were some who didn't know whether they would end up east or west or somewhere in between, even after they had landed at one of the ports of entry. In some cases, they were put up in immigration halls or hotels while they waited for further instructions.

Shortly after the war, it was no secret in the Dutch community in Canada that its ranks would soon swell. They could sense the interest being shown in emigration from the letters of relatives and friends. There was never any doubt among them that Canada would open its doors.

The Christian Reformed publications informed their readers of the possible influx of people from The Netherlands. In January, 1946, Rev. Paul De Koekkoek insisted in the *Calvin Forum* that "they must not be swallowed up by the great spaces of this great country." Things had to be done to assist newcomers and to

welcome them into the church. Heeding such advice, the church's synod formed the Immigration Committee for Canada.

Only a handful of people lay the groundwork for handling the influx into Ontario. Two men from Chatham, four from Hamilton, and five from Sarnia met together on April 30, 1946, to form a subgroup called the Christian Immigration Council for Eastern Canada. One of the decisions was to ask for an annual dona-

John and Marie Plas came to Canada in March of 1956.

1964	1965	1966	1967	1968	1969	1970	1971	1972	1973	1974	1975	1976	1977	1978	1979	1980	1981	1982	1946-1982
2,493	2,473	2,284	2,064	3,039	3,253	2,550	2,162	1,369	1,121	1,155	414	654	1,001	775	918	1,607	2,259	2,394	154,323
151	195	254	173	199	155	170	89	120	163	234	216	217	193	131	253	161	168	137	8,278
1,911	2,505	3,516	4,223	3,099	2,343	1,767	1,091	1,277	1,532	1,878	1,260	1,069	1,115	1,201	1,492	1,724	1,712	1,920	184,150
666	655	545	713	405	413	436	484	636	585	677	555	453	569	607	510	894	1,060	1,250	34,753
903	1,116	1,120	1,540	1,375	1,361	1,279	1,057	979	874	806	742	555	150						45,395
1,825	1,606	1,285	1,398	1,235	946	746	530	435	311	253	208	209	217	166	320	328	412	381	89,030
203	133	102	78	93	121	75	63	66	48	49	29	9	32	26	29	56	66	84	7,913
8,152	8,683	9,106	10,189	9,445	8,592	7,023	5,476	4,882	4,634	5,052	3,424	3,166	3,277	2,906	3,522	4,770	5,677	6,166	523,842

Rev. D.J. Scholten

|1982| nr.2|

elders

In dit nummer

Nederland
–
Amerika

200

periodiek over emigratie

This publication is issued by the various emigration societies in The Netherlands to assist people who plan to move to another country.

Help Along the Way

Organizations which existed solely to promote emigration and to assist those who wanted to get out were inundated with enquiries right after the war. People wanted to know the merits and drawbacks of each country that was opening its doors, the costs of emigrating, and information about such things as jobs, sponsors, and church life.

The task became so big and complex that the *Gereformeerde Kerk*, for example, appointed a new *Deputaatschap voor Emigratie* to look after the spiritual side of the emigration movement. The already-established *Christelijke Emigratie Centrale* would handle the other aspects—information, help with visas and other documents, placements, etc. The *deputaatschap*, which met monthly in Utrecht, consisted of six members, including A. Warnaar, the mayor of Waddinxveen, Zuid-Holland, and a frequent visitor to Canada because of his former flower business; T. Cnossen, the director of the *emigratie centrale*; and Rev. D.J. Scholten, who ministered in an agricultural area in the northeastern part of Groningen province.

Right from the start, the focus was on Canada. They promoted this land, ripe with opportunities, as the future home for Calvinists gripped by the emigration fever. One of the main reasons was the existence there of a staunch ally—the Christian Reformed Church.

This denomination, established in the United States in 1857 by a group of Dutch immigrants, spread to Canada shortly after the turn of the century. Churches were organized in key areas of settlement, such as the West Coast, southern Alberta, southern Manitoba, and southwestern Ontario. They attracted the *Gereformeerden* before the war. And they would continue to do so after the war.

Members of the newly-formed Immigration Committee for Canada of the Christian Reformed Church met with the *deputaatschap* and pledged cooperation. In fact, the committee was vitally interested in having many emigrants steered toward its churches. If thousands wanted to come to Canada, as the rumors had it, that could result in phenomenal growth for the denomination.

Rev. Scholten, who became an immigrant himself, explains some of the work of the *deputaatschap* after the movement got under way: "We were particularly interested in the spiritual welfare of the people who wanted to emigrate. We gave information to consistories and individuals. For instance, when the oldest son of a man with emigration plans went to Canada for a trial period, two things were done: he was given information about existing churches or Dutch people in his prospective neighborhood, and his name and address were forwarded to the local immigration committee or to the closest home missionary. We also arranged for ministers to act as chaplains on the immigrant boats. Later, we interviewed ministers who were interested in going to Canada or Australia to work among the immigrants."

tion of $1 per church family to cover current expenses. Another was to print a booklet of information for prospective immigrants. And they would pass on announcements of interest to the press.

The minutes also included this interesting comment: "It is generally felt that close cooperation between East and West Canada is necessary. Strong resentment is expressed against practices formerly followed by persons whose aim was to please the railroad companies more than the immigrants, with the result that settlers were placed far away from existing churches, which is detrimental to the spiritual welfare of the immigrants."

At the next meeting, on May 24, the booklet was again on the agenda. It would include information on church, school, farming, and industry in all areas of Canada. The minutes stated: "It is pointed out that in our correspondence with prospective immigrants and in our pamphlets, conditions in Canada should not be painted too bright. Simple facts should be given only . . ."

On February 18, 1947, a few months before the *Waterman* embarked on its historic voyage, an important meeting was held at the YMCA in Woodstock, Ontario. The news that everyone had been waiting for had come in a telephone call from Dr. Tuinman in Ottawa: agriculturalists would be allowed to settle in Canada soon, and The Netherlands government wanted to use the council for placing immigrants on farms.

They agreed to tackle the job. The minutes state: "If we don't accept the proposal, other organizations will take our place, with the possible result that many of our people will be misplaced. This opportunity presents a tremendous challenge to our churches for spiritual work."

However, a number of conditions were laid down: "That our own people (Christian Reformed and other orthodox groups) be placed around our churches or in new districts where it is possible to take care of their spiritual needs, and that the expense for settling of immigrants not from our churches must be carried by other sources."

It was estimated that some $4,000 would be needed to place people on farms in Ontario and another $10,000 in other territories. The church's synod would be asked to open its coffers. A delegate was dispatched to the Home Missions Board, in session in Grand Rapids, Michigan, to ask for $2,000 in the interim. Other contributions would be sought from the Dutch government, the Canadian railway companies, and the agricultural societies.

The council also:

● Suggested the appointment of two fieldmen to assist with the placement of new arrivals in southern Ontario. They would be paid $8 a day and six cents a mile for the use of their cars.

● Decided to ask the Immigration Committee for Canada to check into the possibility of having an insurance policy drawn up under which all immigrants would have $2,000 coverage for two years, covering death, sickness and accidents.

● Decided to ask the railways to supply free travel passes for the fieldmen, the *Christelijke Emigratie Centrale* to furnish a complete list of emigrants, and the Home Missions Board to place an ordained man in Montreal for missionary work and meeting new arrivals.

The wheels were in motion, and not only in Ontario. In the West, too, preparations were under way for accommodating and assisting the newcomers. Across the land, local immigration societies were formed. Meetings were held with agricultural groups and individual farmers to line up pledges of co-operation with the placements.

Rev. G.J. VanderZiel, minister of the church in Chatham, Ontario, wrote later: "What an organizing, a planning, an arranging of things before they came. As pastor in those years, I attended all those meetings, and it was all to make things easier for those who were to come in 1947 and later. Former immigrants remembered their own arrival and

A new immigrant, J. Molenkamp (center), cuts turnips on a farm in the Mackay district of Alberta. At right is Bernard Nieboer, fieldman for the Christian Reformed Church.

wanted to make it easier for the new ones. So many helped. When the train with the first immigrants, some 180 of them, arrived in Chatham in June, 1947, the old-timers were there to greet them and take them to the hall where they would meet their farmer sponsors."

Much more work awaited the army of helpers when more boats began to arrive. For example, the elders of the Christian Reformed Church in Hamilton, Ontario, were sent to Kitchener, Galt, Woodstock, and St. Catharines to find suitable meeting places for the scattered immigrants. Later, home missionaries from the United States took over, ministering to the new arrivals and organizing churches wherever the numbers were large enough. The Hamilton church prepared for its own influx by buying fifty used stacking chairs for fifty cents apiece. But when the people started coming, it took only a few large immigrant families to fill the chairs. By 1948, the congregation was so short of space that it had to meet in four different places.

As a matter of fact, the passengers on the *Waterman* weren't the first ones to set foot in Canada as a result of the understanding reached between the Dutch and the Canadian authorities. As soon as the doors were opened, some came with regularly-scheduled liners. For example, Mr. and Mrs. Melvin Elgersma and their seven children left Lichtaard, Friesland, in early May, 1947, sailing with the *Veendam*.

"We were really surprised to see so many immigrants come so soon after us," says Mrs. Elgersma, now of Cayuga, Ontario. "When we left, we had no idea that so many other people were also planning to go to Canada."

Later that month, thirteen smiling Hollanders arrived at the railway station in Chatham. They had come on the *Aquitania*, through arrangements made by the Dominion Sugar Company. They would soon be in the fields, planting and cultivating sugarbeets, which were plentiful in the area.

A reporter for the *Chatham Daily News* cornered an interpreter, and went back to his office to record the following: "At the station, the Hollanders were willing to talk about any subject but the war. The bitter days they had spent under the German heel were behind them and they were anxious to talk of the future rather than the past."

The people meeting them at the station knew that they would be back again within a few weeks to welcome a much larger contingent—passengers from the *Waterman*.

During the early years of the post-war immigration period, the Christian Reformed

Postwar Emigration from The Netherlands by Province

Province of Departure	1946	1947	1948	1949	1950	1951	1952	1953	1954	1955	1956	1957	1958	1959	1960	1961	1962	1963
Groningen											271	421	280	177	207	74	37	51
Friesland											537	771	376	231	263	81	104	78
Drenthe											232	197	170	160	165	50	24	28
Overijssel					Immigration figures for these years						428	525	514	366	336	88	82	148
Gelderland					were not available from Government records.						727	1,123	696	503	515	173	161	214
Utrecht											554	761	441	358	330	138	125	98
Noord-Holland											1,565	2,928	1,720	1,166	1,125	321	332	366
Zuid-Holland											2,005	3,005	1,893	1,531	1,391	487	409	451
Zeeland											80	134	73	68	91	54	21	21
Noord-Brabant											842	1,163	684	517	601	236	195	182
Limburg		*Source: Ministry of Social Affairs, Director for Emigration of The Netherlands:* ***De emigratie in lijnen en cijfers***									395	679	398	210	409	79	61	58
IJsselmeer Polders											15	17	39	36	24	18	2	6
Total Immigration Per Year											7,651	11,724	7,284	5,323	5,457	1,799	1,553	1,701

Church continued its all-out effort to attract newcomers to its fold. Two thousand copies of *De Gids*, a guide to the areas served by established congregations, were sent to The Netherlands.

It included general comments about Canada: "Thousands of Europeans, including the Dutch, are awaiting approval to find a new home on another continent. The war has deprived millions of what was dear to them. The effects of the war and its immense destruction continue to deepen people's anxieties and rob them of their hopes for improving their condition within the near future. As well, there is a new danger. Though men talk of peace, the threat of yet another war appears on the horizon. Should God not prevent it, the next war will be even more destructive, owing to the invention of the atomic bomb. Both politically and economically, the continent of Europe is in a deep crisis.

"Owing to the grace of God, Canada has suffered comparatively little as a result of the Second World War. None of our cities were destroyed, nor have we suffered hunger. Our young men were sent to war to help liberate the oppressed. The Dutch population is well aware of the contribution made by Canadian soldiers, particularly toward the end of the war.

"Canada is economically stronger now than it was before the war. Its industry developed rapidly during the conflict, and

Canada is now capable of diversifying. With God's blessing, Canada can now embark on a period of prosperity. Canada can now offer you better opportunities in a land that is also further removed from the disturbing rumors of yet another war. In addition, we can offer you the kind of church life that you have become ac-

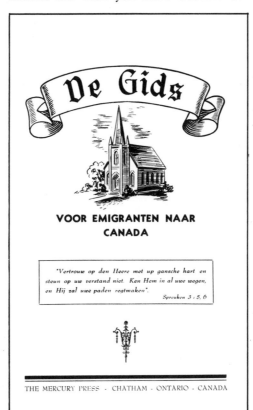

This guide, distributed in The Netherlands, was intended to steer emigrants to the Christian Reformed Church.

1964	1965	1966	1967	1968	1969	1970	1971	1972	1973	1974	1975	1976	1977	1978	1979	1980	Population of The Netherlands 1982 census
64	57	96	121	94	43	92	37	23	36	56	46	33	68	93	99	128	559,135
73	100	122	169	155	85	81	40	56	66	88	55	56	44	45	85	111	592,374
32	48	39	58	66	34	22	19	18	24	42	56	35	27	27	40	69	423,627
102	183	230	247	136	149	132	70	74	84	89	71	49	65	70	100	162	1,033,789
216	202	249	359	345	281	174	191	180	141	249	235	145	145	128	156	153	1,719,111
138	169	208	223	208	157	116	74	78	99	118	87	125	87	87	108	145	916,694
525	658	887	1,053	684	496	456	233	310	365	451	228	177	198	213	255	324	2,312,266
521	704	1,133	1,223	864	649	459	270	319	441	527	281	228	260	323	353	363	3,121,471
33	15	16	51	42	29	55	16	21	41	43	11	46	14	30	29	35	353,697
146	254	370	452	296	204	145	90	138	139	139	102	109	131	150	215	194	2,085,420
58	104	148	230	169	131	49	40	45	66	56	64	35	57	31	45	38	1,077,193
3	11	18	37	40	35	26	11	15	30	20	24	31	19	4	7	2	89,755
1,911	2,505	3,516	4,223	3,099	2,293	1,807	1,091	1,277	1,532	1,878	1,260	1,069	1,115	1,201	1,492	1,724	14,284,532

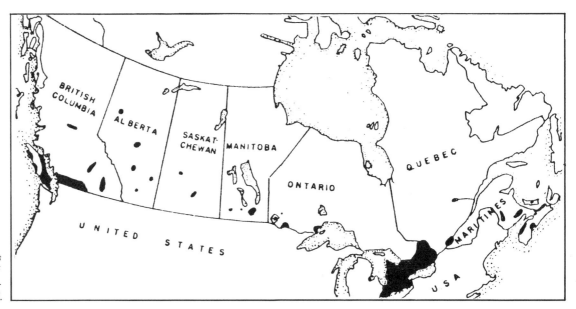

The darkened areas show where most of the Dutch immigrants settled.

customed to in The Netherlands. Many clergymen speak Dutch, and various church groups here will readily assist you in matters spiritual and social."

There were also a few words of caution: "In the event you should decide to emigrate, we would caution you against removing yourself too far from the company of fellow believers and from the church. Be mindful of the principle given to us in Matthew 16:26: 'For what shall a man be profited, if he shall gain the whole world, and forfeit his life?' As well, Matthew 6:33: 'But seek ye first his kingdom, and his righteousness; and all these things shall be added unto you.' The price of temporal prosperity and better living conditions is too high if they are obtained at the cost of one's spiritual life.

"We would also caution the emigrant against unrealistic expectations, especially during the first period. Until you have ad-

justed to Canadian society and have learned the English language, you will experience difficult moments. However, with a good measure of patience and diligence, anyone can succeed.

"Yet another danger comes from those who would try to take advantage of an immigrant's lack of knowledge about his new country. Experience shows that victims of various kinds of fraud are usually people who are averse to seeking help and advice from others."

Later, the denomination even sent a fieldman to The Netherlands to recruit emigrants.

The people in The Netherlands also learned a lot about Canada, and about the welfare of the immigrants in particular, from the many reports in the newspapers and magazines. Dutch correspondents visited Canada, and immigrants who returned to The Netherlands for a visit were sure to be approached by a local editor. People wanted to know how the immigrants were making out. After all, perhaps they had entertained plans to move abroad themselves.

Leonard Mol and his wife, who had emigrated to Canada shortly before the outbreak of the war, went back for a holiday to the province of Zeeland in 1950. Of course, many people asked about their experiences during the ten years across the ocean, the years of building a successful farm in the Chatham area. Even the *Zeeuws Landbouwblad* asked the vacationers to write a few words.

"Indeed, Canada is a land of unlimited possibilities," they wrote. "However, it is important that the emigration be careful-

Dutch in Canada by provinces

	Dutch origins	Total population	% of pop.
Newfoundland	675	563,750	0.11
Prince Edward Island	1,340	121,225	1.10
Nova Scotia	13,495	839,805	1.60
New Brunswick	4,400	689,375	.63
Quebec	8,055	6,369,065	.12
Ontario	191,125	8,534,265	2.23
Manitoba	33,875	1,013,705	3.34
Saskatchewan	17,215	965,440	1.78
Alberta	65,060	2,213,650	2.93
British Columbia	72,280	2,713,615	2.66
Yukon	400	23,075	1.73
Northwest Territories	315	45,540	.69
	408,240	24,083,500	1.69

Totals may not equal the sum of components due to rounding.
Source: Statistics Canada 1981 Census.

Emigranten kan werkloosheid wachten

Een toekomst in Canada wordt uiterst onzeker

(Van een onzer verslaggevers)

DEN HAAG, vrijdag

TERWIJL in Canada de werkloosheid catastrofale vormen begint aan te nemen, en veel emigranten in maatschappelijke nood verkeren, zijn de emigratie-autoriteiten in ons land met onverminderde ijver aan de slag om de beste vakmensen te animeren in Montreal, Vancouver of een van de andere steden van dat nieuwe vaderland een toekomst op te bouwen. Sommigen zal dat lukken. Anderen komen bedrogen uit.

Er komen alarm-
richten uit

1400 Immigranten in één keer

HALIFAX, 22 Febr. — De Volen-
n is hier vandaag aangekomen
1400 Nederlandse immigran-
Dit is de grootste groep Ne-
andse immigranten, die ooit in
eis de overtocht naar Canada
akt heeft.
immigranten werden verwel-
door de Nederlandse ambas-
, de heer Lovink.

Canadese regering wordt voorzichtig

GEEN HEE

Vader vliegt naar zieke zoon in Canada

Van een onzer verslaggevers
VLAARDINGEN, dinsdag
Met het K.L.M.-straalvliegtuig,
waarmee prinses Beatrix vanmiddag van Schiphol vertrekt om
in Ottawa het huwelijk bij te wonen van haar vriendin, Renée
Röell, reist ook de heer
Meijer uit de Lombokstraat in
Vlaardingen, die met een
triestere missie naar Toronto
snelt.
De heer Meijer gaat op weg
naar zijn zoon Piet, die levens-
gevaarlijk gewond in het ziekenhuis v... to ligt.
week ...   ...en Quebec en

GEZIN VAN NEGENTIEN NAAR CANADA

ROTTERDAM, 17 April. — Het
gezin Griffioen uit Maartensdijk
— vader, moeder en 17 kinderen
— heeft zich te Rotterdam inge-
scheept op de de "Nieuw Amsterdam" om zich te gaan vestigen in
Abbotsford (Br. Columbia), waar
het een boerderij betrekt. Voor
zover bekend, is dit het grootste
gezin, dat tot nu toe naar Canada emigreerde.
In een speciaal daarvoor ge-
urde autobus was het gezin
nsdag naar de Maasstad ge-
n. Het oudste kind is 22
e benjamin telt vier maan-
n der dochters is pas ge-
, ook haar man emi-
, evenals de verloofde
dere dochter. Ten
ok nog een vriendje
ns mee naar het
nd, zodat het ge-
uit 22 personen

Emigrantenvluchten naar Canada

's-GRAVENHAGE, 7 Febr. — In
samenwerking met de Stichting
Landverhuizing Nederland, die ten
J. behoeve van emigranten vliegtui-
ten chartert, zullen binnenkort
veer emigrantenvluchten naar
'anada worden uitgevoerd.
Het aandeel in de charterprijs
aar Canada vliegen, bedraagt
ans f 725 voor personen boven de
jaar, voor kinderen van 6 tot en
et 9 jaar f 545, van 2 tot en met
jaar f 365 en beneden de 2 jaar
75. De emigrantenvluchten naar
Canada zijn vastgesteld op 4, 11,
25 Maart en voorts voorlopig
re volgende Zondag

CANADEES FRUIT VOOR KONINGIN

SOESTDIJK, donderdag. De Canadese ambassadeur in Nederland, de heer Thomas A. Stone, heeft vanmiddag op het paleis Soestdijk aan koningin Juliana een zending kleurig blinkend fruit en de beste groentesoorten uit Ontario aangeboden.

De zending was samengesteld op verzoek van de Canadese tuin-bouwraad en de vereniging van fruit- en groentekwekers in Ontario, en bedoeld als geschenk van de vele Nederlandse emigranten, die in Ontario wonen, en als een illustratie van de belangrijke bijdrage, die deze Nederlandse Canadezen hebben gegeven aan de ontwikkeling van de tuinbouw in de streek van Toronto.

Dutch newspapers kept their readers well informed about the various happenings.

ly arranged so that the right man will land at the right place. For example, a Protestant should not be placed in the predominantly Roman Catholic province of Quebec. And a market-gardener should not be expected to work for a farmer. That happened with us once. The man was sent to us during seeding time. He was willing enough to tackle the work, but he had no experience with the machines. The resulting delays were frustrating. Another thing: it is desirable that people land in an area where they will be able to visit their own church . . ."

The Mols passed on some observations about life in Canada:

● "It is the custom not to invite anyone for funerals. The whole neighborhood comes automatically, and the neighbors are the pallbearers. When a farmer's daughter gets married, the neighbors throw a party at which each guest is expected to give a present to the bride. These are only two of the customs which newcomers are expected to adopt."

● "For women, shopping in Canada is somewhat different from what they have been used to. Other than the baker, not one retailer comes to the door. The wife has to go to town to do most of her buying. There she goes to a big store, takes a cart at the entrance, walks along aisles with all kinds of food and household articles, and picks out what she needs. There's everything: thread, tape, meat, vegetables, fruit, dustcloths, you name it. The cashier is near the exit. There, everything is neatly put into bags."

● "When, let's say, a pig is slaughtered, the meat is neatly cut into small pieces and packed in paper. The farmers keep it in refrigerators, which can be rented in a nearby milk factory or in a special building. It's rather inconvenient to go there to get a few porkchops for the evening meal."

● "A car in Canada is not a luxury. Every rural resident has one, simply because he can't do without it."

The Mols ended their message with a word directed to the wives of prospective emigrants: "Not one farmer's wife in The Netherlands can realize how hard the women across the ocean have to work. They rarely have help, because that costs too much. Most of the girls work in a factory or in the fields. The farmer's wife has to take care of the personnel. She also has to look after the vegetable garden, the lawn, and the flowers. And in the fall, it's customary for her to make all kinds of preserves . . ."

The Dutch came by the thousands to this new land, and they were welcomed with open arms. The *Halifax Chronicle-Herald* reported in December, 1951: "The immigration department in Ottawa feels that Nova Scotia and the other Maritime provinces could easily induce more Dutch immigrants because, as an official put it, 'the Dutch are maritime people and they like the smell of the sea in their nostrils' and Ottawa considers them about the finest type of immigrants Canada could hope for."

Dr. Hugh L. Keenleyside, in 1947 the deputy minister of the Department of Mines and Resources, later described the movement as "probably the most successful single scheme of its kind in Canadian history."

Canadians who gave one ethnic origin in the 1981 census

British	9,674,245
French	6,439,100
German	1,142,000
Italian	747,970
United Kingdom	529,615
Native People	413,380
Dutch	408,240

1981 Census
Statistics Canada

Deciding to Leave

Deciding to Leave

No one in Maasland could figure out why Arie VanderKooij had made up his mind to go to Canada with his family as soon as he could. He owned a fairly large vegetable-producing business, complete with greenhouse and orchard. Despite the depressed times immediately after the war when the Dutch economy was struggling to right itself, he seemed to be making a decent living. And wasn't he a true patriot who had risked his life many times as a member of the underground resistance to Hitler? He owned a citation from General Dwight Eisenhower, supreme commander of the Allies: "The name of Arie VanderKooij has been placed on record at The Supreme Headquarters Allied Expeditionary Force as being commended for brave conduct while acting under my orders in the liberation of his country 1944-45."

So why did he want to give up all he had struggled for and start anew in some strange, faraway land widely known for its severe winters, wild Indians, and vast stretches of uninhabitable bush?

"The reason is not easy to explain," he says at his home in Holland Marsh, Ontario. "I did quite a bit of underground work during the war, and I thought people would appreciate that. But it was quite the opposite. Some people in authority, with a questionable past, made things very difficult. And people who did terrible things during the war got off with light sentences, a slap on the wrist. It was all too much for me. I had to get away from that."

George Eggink of the Jarvis, Ontario, area, who left Beilen, Drenthe, in 1948, cites a similar reason.

"Yes, I was disappointed after the war. During the occupation, I was aware of a number of people who tried to stay buddy-buddy with the Germans just to keep their positions. There were others

—1947——

C.M. Hogeterp of Hamilton, Ontario, who came to Canada with his wife and seven children aboard the *Tabinta* in 1947, says: "Sure, we were deeply disappointed when the war was over. People who had worked with the Germans —policemen and others—got their positions back. We couldn't feel good about that."

But that wasn't his only reason for wanting to move away from Oudega, Friesland. The rented farm on which he milked sixteen cows was too small to provide an adequate living, and his requests for more land kept being thwarted. The information he had read about Canada in the newsletters of the *Christelijke Emigratie Centrale* persuaded him more than ever to pull up his roots and start anew in the land of The Netherlands' liberators.

When he told people of his plans, most of them thought: "It won't happen. He's just dreaming."

But when he went to The Hague to get his application papers ready and to undergo a medical examination, they found out he wasn't kidding.

"In June, 1947, I got a letter from the

emigration people, saying we could go with the *Waterman*, which would be sailing within a week. We couldn't do that, of course. So we applied right away to go on the second boat, the *Tabinta*, which was scheduled to leave on September 8. My brother and his family would go too."

Mr. and Mrs. C.M. Hogeterp at their home in Hamilton, Ontario.

who stayed in the background and never offered to help Jews or help those who went into hiding to avoid work in German factories. Then there were some who helped the Germans drag as much food as possible out of The Netherlands by assisting, for example, with the requisition of cattle and horses. And when the war was over, it wasn't long before some of these people were again in leading positions in the community."

There were many other reasons why people decided to leave behind all that was dear and familiar. There were personal reasons. There were the common reasons—the urge to get away from the congestion of The Netherlands, the desire to own a farm, fear of another war, dissatisfaction with creeping socialism, and concern for the future of the children, to name a few. Some people, particularly single young men and women, sought adventure. Others were afflicted with emigration fever, succumbing to the propaganda of the emigration societies and commercial concerns such as the Cana-

Hard times in The Netherlands: this woman wants money so that she and her family can emigrate.

Het Vrije Volk

dian railways and the boat lines. And quite a few simply followed in the footsteps of relatives.

During 1948 and 1949, after the first boatloads of emigrants had sailed for Canada, Jacob Hofstee of Berkel, near Rotterdam, felt more than ever an inner urge to get out of The Netherlands and try his luck somewhere else in the world. His family had been talking about emigration since the end of the war. There had been complications; some members of the family had died, and others had changed their minds. However, the idea of starting out somewhere else stayed with some. It seemed almost like an obsession.

"My dad renewed his efforts to emigrate," recalls his eldest son, John, of Listowel, Ontario. "At that time, only farmers could move to Canada. Dad did not qualify because he operated a parcel transport business. Australia was more open for people with other trades, so he made an application to emigrate to that country. Then, during the summer of 1950, an official of the *Christelijke Emigratie Centrale* in The Hague mentioned that Canada had eased the entrance requirements so that vegetable growers could also enter. He felt that Dad could qualify because of his previous experience in market gardening. So Dad immediately changed his application back to Canada."

Why Canada?

"There were several factors, I suppose. One was the climate, which was more like that of The Netherlands. Also, the people of the *emigratie centrale* seemed to know more about Canada, and told of the work of the Immigration Committee of the Christian Reformed Church and its fieldmen. Having that church in Canada seemed important. Canada also seemed a country with more opportunities at that time."

There were a number of reasons why the Hofstees and their relatives wanted to leave.

"Fear of another war may have been a factor, but it was not mentioned. Economically, The Netherlands was in a shambles, and Dad had a hard time making a living from his business. It also seemed that the bureaucracy was making things impossible. More and more licences and permits were required. The state-owned transportation service seemed poised to squeeze out the independents. The major reason given for emigration was that there would be much more opportunity for the children. Finally, I think we must not overlook the sense of adventure—the adventure of becoming *landverhuizers* and making it in a new country."

Mrs. Reina Feyen of Chatham, Ontario, recalls: "After the war, we started to look for a farm to rent, Kees being a farmer's son and I a farmer's daughter. At that time, the sons of farmers usually would get a farm of their own when they married. We noticed that we weren't the only ones looking for a farm. Twenty-seven applications came in when one was put up for rent."

In 1947, when his older brother took over an in-law's farm, Feyen was able to take over a small farm on the outskirts of Smilde, Drenthe. The Feyens lived there for four years, and two sons were born. More and more, they came to realize that there was no future in The Netherlands for the young, especially for the sons of farmers.

"During those years, there was a lot of advertising in the newspapers about emigration to Australia, Argentina, the United States, and Canada," says Mrs. Feyen. "Information meetings were offered, and one could write for information on how to get a sponsor, and so forth. A single man from Smilde, who had emigrated in 1948, came back home for a visit in 1950 and he told us all about Chatham and about the fieldman there, John Vellinga, who could find a farmer to sponsor us. After this, Kees felt that we

Mr. and Mrs. Kees Feyen of Chatham, Ontario.

should go. We couldn't expand where we were—there just wasn't any room."

After the liberation, Ted Smeenk opened a radio and appliance store in The Hague, not far from his home in Voorburg. It took him three years to get all but one of the necessary thirty-three permits.

"A national newspaper printed my story as an example of the unbelievable postwar bureaucracy," he says. "The officials found a reason to deny the 33rd permit after the story was published. I continued operations without a permit

—1948—

John Booy, now of Delta, British Columbia, was struck with the emigration spirit at an early age. When he was eleven, he was absorbed in stories he had read in a book on Transvaal, an area in South Africa settled by the Boers in the early 1800s. He was sure he wouldn't mind going there. This fever heightened when the headmaster told his class about plans to emigrate to Argentina. The thought of leaving The Netherlands, of starting a new life in a relatively undeveloped area of the world, never left him.

Little wonder that, two months after the war, he was quick to spot a newspaper advertisement promoting emigration. He wrote to the address, and before long he

was attending meetings at which the virtues of adopting another country were preached over and over again. At that time, he lived in Drijber, a small community near Beilen.

"My father went to the meetings too," he recalls. "In 1947, the first ones went, including a neighbor, who went to Neerlandia. My fiancée and I had already made up our minds to go to Canada. We were No. 1,200 on the list. My parents were No. 7, but they couldn't leave because my mother was expecting. In July—it was 1948—the word came that if we got married right away, we could leave in a month. Well, we were married within two weeks."

The top photo shows the farmhouse in Noord-Brabant which Mr. and Mrs. Henry Roefs left behind. They now live in this house in Berwick, Nova Scotia.

Why the Roefs Left

The exuberance that followed the long-awaited liberation abated a bit in the Donk and Beek area of Noord-Brabant. A lot of people then asked themselves: "What now?" They looked around and saw a mess.

"We had only two cows left, plus a few calves, fourteen chickens, and two pigs," says Mrs. Anna Roefs, whose husband, Henry, owned a farm there. "Before the war started, we had eight cows, ten calves, four hundred laying hens and another four hundred chicks, and a barn full of pigs. We didn't have much left. It had taken us a long time to build up the farm. Now we had to start all over again."

That, of course, wouldn't have been an insurmountable task. However, the war had left deeper scars. The couple told each other that they would never want to go through similar experiences again, even though many other people had had to endure more hardship and pain. Their children, too, seemed determined to get away from post-war Holland, from all the scary talk about the Russians and communism.

Says Mrs. Roefs, now of Berwick, Nova Scotia: "The boyfriend of one of our daughters wrote from the Dutch East Indies, where he was serving as a soldier: 'When I'm back, I don't want to stay in Holland. There's no future there in farming.' Together, the family discussed the idea of emigration. Of one thing we were sure: if one went, we would all go. The family bond would not be broken. There would be strength in togetherness."

Canada was the unanimous choice.

and got one summons after another: 'operating a business without a permit,' 'occupying business-living quarters without a permit,' 'repairing appliances without a permit,' etc."

There were other worrisome developments that made him decide to leave The Netherlands. "The Russians brought the cold war to maximum heat, and they were only an hour from our borders. The overseas Dutch colonies were demanding independence. Our trade was nil. Our manufacturing facilities had been robbed and bombed. NATO demanded an army and the tax coffers were empty. It seemed that the ship was sinking, and another war was close at hand. We did not want to go through another war . . ."

He read up on the economic and climatic conditions of Brazil, Australia, South Africa, and Canada.

"Canada topped them all: freedom of speech, freedom to work, freedom to go

Fifteen-year-old John Eisen of Apeldoorn, Gelderland, didn't mind leaving The Netherlands for some unknown country. Neither did his mother, a spry fifty-seven, and his older brother, twenty-seven. Only his two older sisters had little interest in emigration.

Before the war, the family had experienced a farm bankruptcy. The father had died in 1939. And then had come the five-year occupation by the Germans, hardly a pleasant period. Little wonder that the family wanted to get away.

"Brazil was first on the list for our new future," recalls John, now of Renfrew, Ontario. "However, emigrating to Brazil was next to impossible. So Canada became the next country to dream about. The *Christelijke Emigratie Centrale* gave us the address of a sponsor at Stratton, near Fort Francis, Ontario, and my brother, Johan, corresponded with him. The sponsor wrote back that he had a house with furniture waiting for us."

John didn't mind leaving all his friends behind, but he did regret resigning from the checker club. He was good at the game, and just that year—1949—had become second class champion of Apeldoorn.

"The farewell was a sad moment in our lives, for my sisters talked about never seeing us again."

into business, freedom of assembly, freedom of the press, freedom of religion with tolerance toward all. We read on: the highest rate of private home ownership in the world, the highest sugar consumption, one of the highest standards of living in the world, rich in natural resources, a positive export balance, consumption of meat per capita three times that of The Netherlands, cost of clothes only half, cost of living one-third, every family owned a car, lower income taxes and absence of the myriad of other taxes we struggled with in postwar Holland, a favorable climate and ten times more sunshine than we had."

S.P. Knuist, now of London, Ontario, recalls: "In December, 1948, we were officially engaged to be married as soon as a house became available. But we knew we would have to wait for a long time. Even one room was hard to get. And good jobs were scarce. I was working as a salesman in a men's clothing store in Alkmaar, Noord-Holland. So little by little, we came up with the idea to go to some other country, not necessarily Canada. Some friends were talking about going to South Africa or South America. I started to gather information. A friend who had gone to Canada wrote to us, saying that there were plenty of jobs there. By that time, more than farmers could get in. So we applied for Canada. We left on the *Groote Beer* on February 19, 1953, a few weeks after our marriage."

Dr. M.L. Van Vierssen Trip, a surgeon in Apeldoorn, had emigration on his mind ever since his own engagement to be mar-

ried. Finally, in August of 1951, at forty-six years of age and with six children, the oldest eighteen, he left for Canada.

"It wasn't that we didn't love Holland," says his wife. "But we wanted more freedom of movement. We did not wish our children to grow up with so many restrictions in the society around them."

Joe Vaessen of North York, Ontario, was itching to get married and take his bride to the New World he had heard so much about. An uncle had been living in Pennsylvania since 1921, and a brother had moved to Canada in 1954.

"In spite of our good and comfortable lifestyle in Ubach over Worms, Limburg, I and many others were infected with emigration fever. I could almost feel it. To me, it was real heroism to leave one's country so there would be more elbow room for the ones left behind."

He and his wife, Kitty, flew to Canada in 1957.

Mr. and Mrs. Joe Vaessen in 1957.

1950

Rimmer Tjalsma now lives in Mississauga, Ontario.

When Rimmer Tjalsma, twenty-four years old and single, decided in 1950 that he needed "a change" and applied for emigration to Canada, he found the authorities bending over backwards to accede to his wishes.

"It was easy in those days," he recalls at his home in Mississauga, Ontario. "Canada was mainly an agricultural country and thousands of farmers had registered for hired help. I was asked two questions: 'Can you milk a cow?' and 'Can you drive a tractor?' When I said I could, I was told a sponsor would be found for me."

Tjalsma, the son of a minister, wasn't a farmer. He worked in an office. But during the last year of the war, he had found it necessary to get out of Rotterdam just to avoid starvation. He had found work on a farm. And that was all the experience he needed to get into Canada.

He was on the boat within three months.

Teunis Schinkel of Chatham, Ontario, found it difficult to pinpoint the reason for his leaving in May of 1953. There were a number of factors that led to the decision.

"It had something to do with the fear of another war breaking out, and with the rise of communism. There was an inner compulsion to emigrate. We also noticed a certain unrest among the children. Moreover, our oldest daughter and her husband had already gone to Canada in 1948. They gave us a bit of advice, but they never urged us to go. They knew from experience that money didn't grow on trees in Canada. In the meantime, our oldest son got married and he, too, showed an interest in emigration. So, considering everything, it seemed to us better that the entire family went so as to keep it together as much as possible. One married daughter couldn't go along, however, because her retarded daughter didn't get approval."

Mr. and Mrs. Schinkel, aged fifty-three and fifty-five respectively, left Utrecht with a bit of apprehension. They realized from the start that emigration was always a tough business, and even more difficult for people their age.

"Our children, now that they are around fifty themselves, say occasionally: 'Where did you get the courage from to take such a step at such an age?' As Christians, we simply reply that God directed us in all our decisions."

Mr. Schinkel died in early 1983.

After the war, Leo Hovius and Boukje Wierenga, both from villages in southwestern Groningen, wanted to get married. It was the usual story: a housing shortage which showed no promise of getting better put an immediate ceremony out of the question. Both frowned upon the idea of living with parents.

"One day Leo asked me if I wanted to emigrate," recalls Mrs. Hovius, now of the Listowel, Ontario, area. "I had no objections to that at all. So we started making plans. Leo wanted to go to the United States, where some distant relatives lived. We got in touch with them, and they said they would help us with finding a sponsor. We visited the emigration bureau and other authorities and filled in forms. Then we got the disappointing word that it would take two years before we could emigrate. That was too long a wait. By this time—1947—a number of people from our area, including Leo's friend and his wife, were emigrating to Canada. So that's where we decided to go too. A sponsor was found in Cobden, Ontario, and permission was received to leave on the first boat in 1948."

The next order of business was to get married.

Ever since she was a child, Cornelia Annegarn of Assen, Drenthe, had a curiosity about other countries. The farther from The Netherlands, the more fascinating they seemed. In high school, she and her friend would often study the atlas after class. They agreed that one day they would surely go to America, and that the first one there would write the other a letter.

"The war came, and the liberation by Canadian soldiers strengthened my desire to emigrate," recalls Cornelia, now Mrs. J.R.T. Sheehy of Ridgetown, Ontario. "But it took years of saving the hard-earned money of a beginner's job before I had enough to pay for the trip across the ocean. Then a nurse from the hospital where I worked—*Academisch Ziekenhuis* in Groningen—went to Canada, where she stayed with acquaintances. She wrote about Canada and offered me a place in the same house until I had found work."

Nothing could hold Cornelia back now. Even an appointment as head dietician failed to sway her from her ultimate goal—a new life in a new country. But it took an agonizingly long time to get her diplomas translated, certified, photocopied, and forwarded to Canada so that she could become a member of the Canadian Diabetic Association. Letters of recommendation from professional people for whom she had worked were also necessary.

Finally, at thirty-one years of age, she was ready to go. But then an accident delayed her departure for half a year. After a bicycle mishap, her arm was in a cast, and the stern-faced officials at the Canadian immigration office in The Hague wouldn't give her permission to go until all was healed.

"Many of my acquaintances thought I was crazy to leave a good job and start all over again, but my father said: 'Follow your heart's desire.' He gave me five hundred guilders to start out with, because I had used all my savings to pay for the trip and the freight. To feel at home in the new country, I took along many of my belongings, such as a standing reading lamp, a chair, a bookcase, and a chest."

She left in March, 1955.

In 1937, when life in Europe was a daily struggle to make ends meet and when the ominous clouds of war were looming on the horizon, Jerry Rekker spotted an article in the *Friesch Dagblad*. It expounded opportunities available in Argentina for those who had ambition to start afresh.

The cover of one of the promotional booklets issued before the war by the Canadian Pacific Railway.

Tears of longing filled his eyes. He wanted so much to get away from his small rented farm in Friesland, from the endless struggle just to eke out a living, and move to a region of the world that offered a future. But he figured, sadly, that this would remain a dream forever—he just didn't have the money to move lock, stock and barrel to a faraway country.

War came. The German bombers flew over his farm on their infamous mission—reducing the core of Rotterdam to a pile of rubble and breaking the last Dutch resistance. The dark cloud that descended over The Netherlands pushed his emigration thoughts far back in his mind. Five long and difficult years would elapse before the German surrender.

When the occupation ended, Rekker was convinced more than ever that he should get away. As we have seen, he wasn't alone. His thoughts went to Canada, the land of the liberators, whose capital city had been a haven for Princess Juliana and her little girls.

"A lot of people I knew shook their head in unbelief when they learned of my plans," recalls Rekker, now of Brampton, Ontario. "Some of them were sure that there was something wrong with my head. But I knew what I was doing. The fact was that my experiences before the war had destroyed my trust in The Netherlands. And I was sure that the same game would be repeated."

He wasted no time in responding to a newspaper advertisement calling for the establishment of an emigration society. In September of 1945, his village of Giekerk had a chapter with a membership of twenty-seven, and Rekker was the chairman.

"I stressed the importance of learning English. It didn't take me long to find someone who could teach us the first principles. But not everyone could handle it. Quite a few dropped out, saying it was too difficult. Well, it wasn't easy. But some of us stuck it out."

Rekker, his wife, Julia, and their five children were on board the *Tabinta* in September, 1947, sailing for the country which promised a better future for them all.

In 1975, the National Union of Christian Schools published *To Find a Better Life*, which gives reasons that various people have given for emigrating from The

—1951

Klaas Terpstra of Hamilton, Ontario, a former part-time fieldman of the Christian Reformed Church in the Brockville area: "I worked for a family-owned business in Leeuwarden that specialized in the import and export of grain. At a certain point, I felt that I had reached the top, that I couldn't advance any further because of all the family members in the firm. It was a case of either going somewhere else or emigrating. A good friend who sold flower bulbs in Canada and knew a bit about the country talked me into the latter. He said: 'If you're thinking of moving, go to Canada.' He laid the first stone."

Terpstra, his wife, and their two small daughters sailed with the *Volendam* in 1951.

Mr. and Mrs. Klaas Terpstra at their home in Hamilton, Ontario.

Netherlands. A few recollections:

• "There were many families gripped by the excitement of emigrating to North America. Single boys who were unable to make concrete plans for a future farm or business of their own were eagerly listening to the conversations . . . In our family of five boys and five girls, there were many thoughts and much talk of the future. Expanding acreage was out of the question, and so the oldest boy began to express the desire to move to Canada, where he might someday have a farm of his own. For a girl, too, the future did not promise much more than work as a domestic. How many nights our parents must have been kept awake by the weight of the decision, debating the pros and cons of transplanting a family of ten children to an unknown environment.

"Emigration societies were hard at work, meeting with interested citizens, showing films taken by board members who had taken a trip through Canada at the expense of the CNR, the CPR, the Holland-America Line or other boat companies. Articles written by emigrants who had already settled in the land across the sea appeared in church and farm periodicals. The parents, especially the fathers, and the elder sons went to the meetings, and the younger children could feel the excitement rising. In later years I realized that mothers were not so anxious to leave friends and relatives behind; their tears dampened many a pillow.

"The map of Canada was spread out during many evening discussions. What a large country it was, and little did we realize how vast the distances were."

• "Nobody's life is the same as someone else's. Pondering our reasons for emigrating, we are conscious that these were different than anyone else's. It is even difficult to establish exactly what inspired us to leave an attractive city like Amsterdam, where we were born and raised, to abandon a lucrative position, and last, but not least, to leave behind a wide circle of relatives and good friends. Let us say it was a mixture of reasons. Already as a boy, I wanted to see more than the Lowlands, and with eagerness I read all that had to do with traveling, adventure, and foreign countries. Since I was good with figuring, it was decided that I should be a bookkeeper. And a bookkeeper I became. Later I was planning to go to the Dutch East Indies as an accountant. However, that was almost impossible because of an economic crisis then. During the Second World War, the

resistance took hold of all our actions. Relatives and friends sacrificed their lives for the sake of liberty and love for neighbors. Jail sentences, hiding, and raids were commonplace, and we all received our part of it, practising our Calvinistic principles within the reality of those days.

"After the war . . . anti-colonialism, the lust for power by Sukarno and his followers, and a weak socialistic Dutch government led to the independence of Indonesia. About that time, I started accounting and tax consultation . . . a fruitful profession. Nevertheless it did not give me so much satisfaction that the impulse for leaving the old country disappeared. On the contrary, it was growing because of my dissatisfaction with the dismantling of the Dutch kingdom, high taxes, socialistic measures, the crowded conditions in a city like Amsterdam, the heartbreaking disunity in the churches, and a self-complacency in the remaining chur-

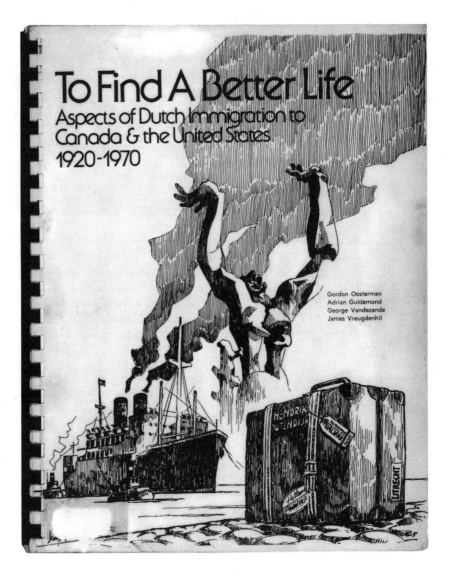

To Find a Better Life *was published in 1975.*

ches. A land of freedom, much space, new opportunities, and, above all, new possibilities for the kingdom of Jesus Christ were for us the ideal to aim at . . . Two brothers-in-law in Canada had already urged us *not* to emigrate, but to stay in the old country. A sore point for

them was the poor guidance and information particularly about the possibilities of Christian education and Christian trade unions . . . In spite of all this, we sold our business, the movers packed our household goods, we said goodbye to our parents, relatives, and friends, and left

John Reinders and his favorite pipe.

One day in the early 1950s, after a hard day's work on his rented farm at Witteveen, Drenthe, John Reinders sat down on a bale of straw, lit his pipe, and called for his eldest son, Hendrik, to join him.

"You know," he said, "you'll never guess what I've been thinking about lately."

Hendrik didn't know what to say. No, he had no inkling of what was on his father's mind. Did it have something to do with the operation of the farm?

Reinders took a deep puff, blew away the smoke, and continued: "I know this will sound strange to you. But I've pretty well made up my mind. I want to emigrate."

There was silence for a minute or two. Thoughts flashed through Hendrik's mind: "Emigrate? He's nearly sixty!" Then they started talking. Hendrik, in his mid-20s and with a young family, soon

learned that his father wanted him and the other children to come along. Not only that, he had plans to interest other farmers from the area, also of *Hervormd* faith, in going with him as a group to establish a colony in some faraway land, possibly Brazil.

Hendrik was in favor of the plan right away. He knew that he wouldn't let his father go by himself. Besides, he shared the concerns that were so prevalent in those days: rising rent and taxes, difficulty in getting your own land, a myriad of rules and regulations, encroaching socialism, the future of the children . . .

"It took me a while to accept the fact that my father wanted to go, considering his age," says Hendrik. "He had a relatively big and modern farm. By 1946, we had our first tractor. He was deeply involved in the operations of the church, school groups, the *Boerenleenbank*, and other organizations. There was really no need for him to go."

In the months that followed, they began to put plans into motion, making contact with other families from Drenthe who wanted to join the exodus. The concensus was to travel as a group to Brazil, where emigrants were welcome and where plenty of land was available for developing a Dutch colony. The families got together at a hotel in Zwolle to get to know each other and to exchange information and ideas. This became a regular outing.

Father Reinders, now in his 90s, and still puffing a pipe, remembers those days well: "We got in touch with Jan Heersink, the mayor of Steenderen, who had been in Canada, and asked him for advice. Well, one of the first things he told us was to forget about Brazil. The climate was different there. We'd be among a predominantly Catholic people. Everything he said pointed to Canada. It was obvious that he'd been impressed with this country and with the opportunities offered to those who wanted to farm. He said: 'You have to go to Canada.' Well,

the old country without any security . . . in 1952 . . . to go to a country that the Lord would show us."

● "I was a bricklayer and our house was too small for our family. We had eleven children ranging from sixteen years to nine months old. The pay was good, but the cost of living was so high that we spent all our pay for food and drink each week. The oldest son worked his second year as an apprentice bricklayer, but earned little. The second son just graduated from technical school as a mechanic. I had to earn the lion's share of

how could we argue against that advice? So all our attention was concentrated on Canada. We sought information—would there be financial advantages in going as a group, what were the rules on taking along tools and other belongings, and so on—and reported the findings at our get-togethers in Zwolle."

One man pushed an idea borrowed from a book on pioneer life: acquire a tract in the wilderness and start from scratch. But the others didn't go for that. They preferred to begin working on an established farm, get used to the climate, the soil, and the farming methods, and then acquire a farm of their own. Nevertheless, they all felt that they would end up in what they called the *rimboe*, the jungle. That's why the Reinders family decided to take along dozens of copies of *De Spiegel*, a popular Christian magazine. They figured they would need something to while away the idle hours.

Reinders, fifty-nine years old, went for the required medical checkup in Heeren-

veen. The Canadian doctor looked him over, found nothing wrong except his age, and pronounced in awkward Dutch: "Reinders, if you didn't have that family of yours standing behind you, you would never receive permission to go."

There was one last-minute setback. The husband of Reinder's daughter—she had married in 1951, after the emigration plans had been initiated—didn't want to leave The Netherlands. Of course, she had no choice but to stay. Reinders and his wife felt a bit uneasy, believing they would never see them again.

In the spring of 1952, bubbling with enthusiasm, the families from Drenthe boarded a KLM plane at Schiphol airport and began their non-subsidized trans-atlantic journey. They were headed for Drayton, a village in a rural area of Ontario. Many other immigrants were already there, working the fertile fields of their sponsors and building a new future. It was hardly a *rimboe*.

Mr. and Mrs. John Reinders lived in this farmhouse at Witteveen, Drenthe.

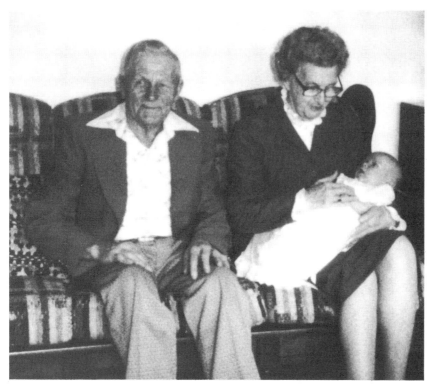

Mr. and Mrs. Kees Verburg and their first great-grandchild, Brenden Alders.

Already in 1924, Kees Verburg felt that The Netherlands was too small. He wrote to The Hague for some literature about Canada and received a number of booklets from the Canadian Pacific Railway. This firm, and others, vigorously promoted emigration in order to open up the vast Canadian West. Naturally, most of the information dealt with that part of Canada.

Verburg's parents certainly didn't like the idea of their firstborn taking off for Canada, which seemed to be on the other side of the world, and told him so. So he went to France instead. There he farmed for several years, married a Dutch girl, and had two children before returning to The Netherlands in 1932.

"Dad still wanted to go elsewhere," says his daughter, Mrs. Anne VanWijngaarden of the Wellandport, Ontario, area, "but first the Depression and later the war interfered, and it wasn't until 1950 that he started to make emigration noises again, especially since his son wanted to emigrate too. Dad investigated the possibilities in France again, but found them unsatisfactory. So Canada was hauled out of the mothballs."

The family was finally scheduled to leave Ommen, Overijssel, in the summer of 1952. Then circumstances prevented them from going at that time. The authorities, inundated with requests, rescheduled their departure for the fall of 1953.

"Father took a fit. He wasn't going to any ice-cold country in the fall and find no work. No way. He wrote long letters to all government agencies connected in any way with emigration, and finally he extracted the promise that we would be notified should a place become available. So we were on virtual standby. We sort of lived out of suitcases."

In the spring of 1953, the expected call came. Verburg could leave within a few weeks—some twenty-nine years after first toying around with the idea.

the family support. Praise the Lord that we were always healthy and had all kinds of reasons to be grateful. My wife was always optimistic and never down-in-the-dumps. We certainly were not poor in things that really count."

"I read about the wages of bricklayers in Canada. My sister emigrated in 1949 and visited Holland in 1956, giving us more news about Canada. In Holland I was a foreman with a construction company and was allowed to do bricklaying on my own as a second job. However, the tight government regulations prevented me from starting a business of my own. I had become a bricklayer at the age of seventeen without any formal training. In order to become an independent licensed bricklayer now, I had to return to school and get several diplomas, as well as have a certain amount of money. This situation caused us to decide to emigrate to Canada. In Canada, as we understood it, everyone was free, and there were opportunities for everyone who was willing to work."

Chapter 5
The Parting Is Hard

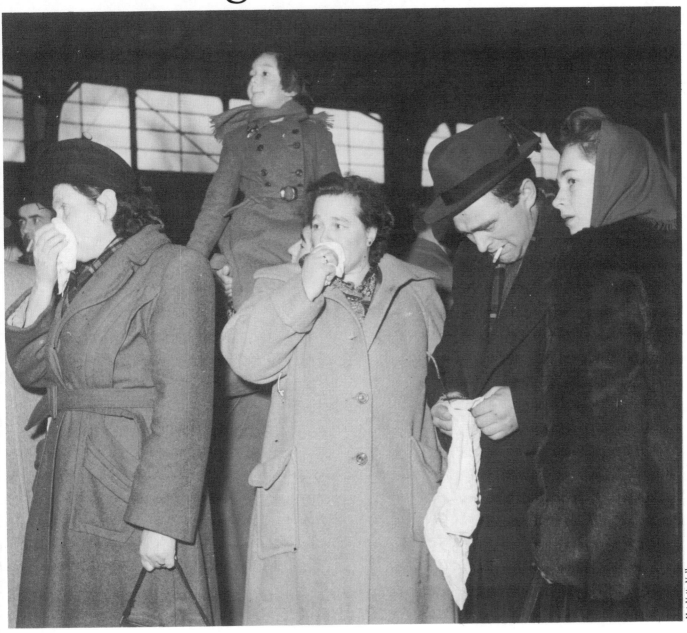

Het Vrije Volk

*Tears flowed freely as the last goodbyes were said
and the emigrants moved on, away from their
relatives.*

The Parting Is Hard

Once Henry and Anna Roefs of the Donk and Beek area in Noord-Brabant had made up their mind to go to Canada, there was no turning back.

"During the winter, we took English lessons three or four days in the week," says Mrs. Roefs, now of Berwick, Nova Scotia. "For me, it went in one ear and out the other. My mind was full of other things: what all should be taken along, the sale of the farm, taking care of the hope chests of our two oldest daughters, who were recently engaged, and so on. But my attendance did have a positive effect—I made friends with a number of couples who were planning to leave at about the same time in 1951. We talked over our plans and learned a few things from each other."

The last few weeks in The Netherlands were busy ones. There were financial matters to take care of. The farm had been sold for 45,000 guilders. Out of this, 2,000 guilders went for taxes and 4,000 cleared the mortgage. The boat trip for the family would cost 5,000 guilders. The large crate for the furniture and other belongings also took a large chunk out of the bank account. The train trip from Halifax to Pickering, Ontario, the destination, had to be paid in advance. Then there were the shopping trips.

The money that couldn't be taken into Canada because of strict exchange controls—these were eventually relaxed—was put into the trust of Henry's brother, Bert, the mayor of Deurne.

There was a farewell party for relatives on Henry's side, then one for those on Anna's side. The women of the *Boerinnenbond*, of which Anna was chairman, also came over. People from the neighborhood, friends, and relatives also stopped by for a cup of coffee, to chat about Canada, and to shake hands or give a buss on the cheek for good luck.

"The crate we ordered for our belongings was big," says Mrs. Roefs. "We packed an old washing machine, and a big kettle in which to boil the dirty clothes. There were dishes and other breakable items. These were available in Canada, too, at low prices. But what did we know? We took along many blankets, sheets, pillow cases, handkerchiefs, etc., and enough wool and sewing thread to last us

The packed belongings of Mr. and Mrs. Henry Roefs.

Time for a breather at the home of Jan A. Grootenboer of Berkel-Rodenrijs, Zuid-Holland.

Crates are loaded for shipment to the harbor at Rotterdam.

for the rest of our lives. Then there were three sewing machines and three bicycles for me and the girls—things that we made good use of. Two hams and some bacon were also put in. Only later did we learn that we weren't allowed to take meat products with us. Fortunately, we didn't have any trouble over that. The sad thing was that when we finally opened up the crate in Canada, the meat was so yellow that nobody wanted to touch it. It cost us more than 3,600 guilders to ship everything to Canada. And we had to pay another $50 to have it shipped by train from Pickering to Ajax."

March 15, the day of departure, arrived quickly. Amid great excitement, flashes of nervousness were evident. Everyone got

Right: It's May 22, 1948. The family of J.A. Grootenboer of Berkel-Rodenrijs, not far from Rotterdam, is ready to leave for the harbor to board the Tabinta.

Below: Ann, the youngest, tries out the bassinet in which she will travel to Manitoba.

dressed in his and her Sunday best and went for a big breakfast in the neighborhood. After a farewell visit to the old home, where all the eight children had been born, the family went to the cemetery to say farewell to loved ones, including little Nelly, the eleven-month-old daughter who had died suddenly of diphtheria during the war. Then they went inside the Roman Catholic church for a special mass and a farewell message from the priest.

"We entered three buses—one for us, one for relatives, and one for the *Boerinnenbond*," says Mrs. Roefs. "The people lined the street and waved. Then off we went. It wasn't until early evening that we boarded the *Volendam* in Rotterdam. My husband and I, both over fifty, were glad that all the farewells were behind us. I was so tired, I could barely stand on my feet. But my day wasn't over yet. I had to answer a number of letters from friends."

The emigrants were usually so busy with their preparations that they had little time to think about the enormity of the step they were about to take. The milkman had to be told that deliveries were no longer needed after such and such a date. Clothes had to be bought. Old clothes had to be given away or sold.

Countless questions had to be answered: why are you going, where are you going, what's Canada like, what will your husband be doing, are you happy about going, will we ever see you again . . . ?

Papers had to be put in order. There were medical exams. Says Mrs. Trudy Smit of Brossard, Quebec, who emigrated with her sister in 1956: "The worst thing was all the injections. I think that we were prepared for the tropics." There were all the ties that had to be broken. There were all those farewells, to the son's teacher, to the neighborhood butcher, to the childhood friend . . .

The sadness crept in when the truck with the crate pulled in front of the house. The furniture disappeared. Before long, the house was empty. And the family was forced to move in with relatives or friends for a few days.

Then it was off to Rotterdam. And goodbyes were said to loved ones. The tears flowed freely.

Mrs. Wilma Bergstra of Shallow Lake, Ontario, recalls: "On the day of our depar-

In Rotterdam, the family of Teunis Schinkel of Utrecht, who left in May, 1953, gathers for what many thought would be the last picture of them together. As a busload of emigrants bound for Canada leaves a village in 1950, neighbors and acquaintances wave goodbye.

Het Vrije Volk

The author (front row right) poses with his family before they board the Waterman in the spring of 1952. Above, Leo Hoens of Eindhoven, Noord-Brabant, spends a few last minutes with his brothers and sister.

Clockwise from top left: the excitement is too much for a youngster; Mrs. Scheffer writes to her brother; the Vonk family waits to leave; relatives wave and wave; a farewell kiss.

De Spiegel

Above right: Uppermost was the question: "Will I ever see them again?"
Above left: The family group picture—a common sight at the harbor area in Rotterdam.
Below: Eyes filled with tears tell the story.

De Spiegel

ture, more than thirty-three years ago now, we went with a bus from Friesland to Rotterdam. Suddenly the passengers began to sing patriotic songs. Well, that touched me, and I began to cry. And once I started, I couldn't stop. Not that I didn't want to go. The singing made me feel for the first time the big step my husband and I were about to take. We had been married for only two weeks."

In the town of Kampen, Overijssel, people talked about those who had left for other shores. Gerald Prins, a carpenter, overheard them. He felt somewhat hurt by the derogatory remarks. After all, he was actively planning to make the big move to Canada himself.

One morning, he overheard a group of men in the shop talking about a family that had left recently for Australia. One piped up: "I heard they were so disappointed when they arrived that they wanted to crawl back to The Netherlands."

Prins, who couldn't stand this sort of negative talk, walked up to the man and asked: "Where did you hear that?"

"They were saying that in town," the man said.

"But who told you that?"

"I don't know. I don't remember."

"If you hear that story being told again, you can tell the person that it's pure nonsense. The family hasn't even arrived in Australia yet. It's a long ways, you know. Please, don't spread any false stories."

The man simply shrugged his shoulders.

The sponsor of Mr. and Mrs. Nan Mulder of Hippolytushoef, Noord-Holland, wrote from Onion Lake, Saskatchewan, in 1949: "We were glad to receive your letter of introduction. As for the furniture you will need: all of your own furntiture, except for a stove which we will try and get. You will also have a house of your own. We have a mixed farm and live two miles from a school. Our village lies on the Alberta-Saskatchewan border, about thirty miles north of Lloydminster. We farm about four hundred acres, keep about fifty pigs and forty head of cattle, also horses. We farm mostly with a tractor. We do not have electricity. We would like you to come as soon as you possibly can."

Before departing on the *Tabinta* in 1947, C.M. Hogeterp of Oudega, Friesland, sold most of his furniture to relatives. Three small crates held beds, blankets, sheets, clothes, and some household items. A fourth one held just one article: a small pedal-organ, around which the family had stood on many a Sunday to sing their favorites.

"Two of our girls played the organ, so we took it along," says Hogeterp. "Besides, our living room wouldn't have been the same without it. Unfortunately, it turned out that the organ couldn't take Canada's climate. It eventually dried out and we had to get rid of it."

The last Sunday before their departure was filled with emotion. After the morning church service, friends crowded around with handshakes and words of farewell. People looked at the Hogeterps as if they would never see them again. Some of them probably were still wondering why this family would want to leave.

"In the afternoon, we visited my wife's parents and went to their church. An

At top is a scene from 1948: a last-minute check of the luggage in Rotterdam. The other photo, taken in 1950, shows relatives trying to catch a last glimpse of emigrants on the way to Canada.

Long and Loving Farewells

During the first years of the emigration movement, the Holland-America Line, the principal carrier of emigrants to Canada, discouraged relatives from going to Rotterdam on the day of departure. A mimeographed letter of instructions and tips to passengers sailing on the *Kota Inten* in March, 1948, stated: "In order to avoid needless bustle in Rotterdam, passengers are advised to say goodbye at home to their family and friends. During the embarkation process, visitors will not be allowed in the office or in the buildings of the Holland-America Line under any circumstances. Customs agents will not let anyone other than the passengers on board the ship."

This advice was largely ignored. People still went to Rotterdam in droves. Even if they lost sight of their departing relatives, they could still grieve as the ship disappeared in the distance.

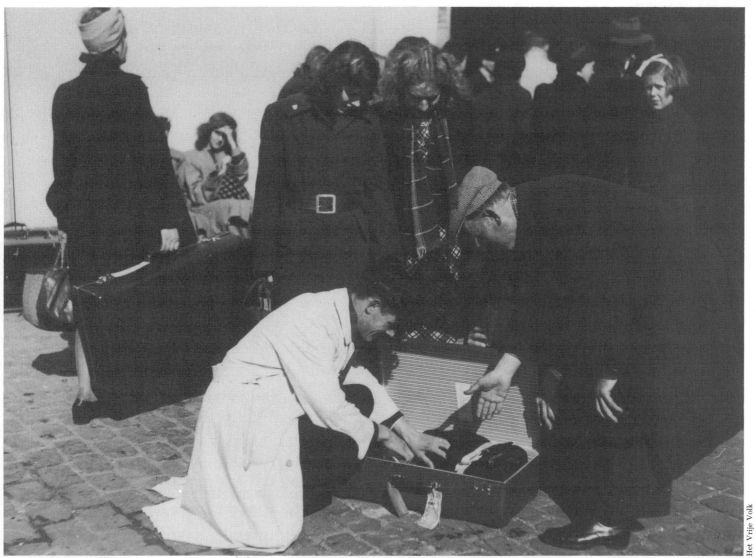

elder read the sermon and then announced that we were leaving for Canada. The congregation was asked to sing *Dat's Heren Zegen Op U Daal*. I felt a lump in my throat. After the service, more people shook hands with us. Some cried."

George Eggink still remembers the Bible verse that the minister of the *Gereformeerde Kerk* in Beilen, Drenthe, where he was a deacon, read to him on the Sunday before his departure in 1948: "Jesus Christ is the same yesterday and today and forever."

Emigration was difficult for children too. They had to leave behind the familiar places in their neighborhood, their circle of friends, their teacher, and most of their relatives, including grandma and grandpa. Many had never heard of Canada before. Some had been told it was a vast stretch of wilderness inhabited by cowboys and Indians, and that it was like Siberia in the winter. The thought of moving to the unknown didn't sit too well with those who were quite content with their surroundings. They were too young to understand why their parents had decided to take them away.

Mrs. Paulina Bootsma of Brantford, Ontario, nine years old when her family decided to leave Pijnacker, Zuid-Holland, in 1950, recalls her anguish when her father made the announcement at the dinner table.

"All my older brothers and sisters became very excited. They wanted to know so many things that everyone was talking at once. Even my little brother, sitting in his high-chair, laughed and clapped his hands with glee, although he didn't understand the reason for the commotion. But I was quiet. I didn't want to move to another country and leave all my friends behind. Moreover, I was frightened of water, and the thought of taking a boat across that big ocean didn't appeal to me."

The news of the family's plans traveled fast. Neighbors and friends came over. Some asked Paulina if she was excited about the big move. She slowly shook her head. Then they looked at her sympathetically and smiled.

"I went to all my favorite spots to say goodbye. I went far into the meadow and spotted the little daisies I used to pick. I guess I even said goodbye to the little ladybugs that crawled up my fingers and then flew away. I also went to the neighboring farmer to see him milk his cows and feed the horses. One day, while all our furniture was being packed into a huge crate, I went to my best friend's house. When it was time to go home, my friend walked me back. I hugged her, and we both cried a little. It felt funny to say goodbye. It seemed to hurt, as if something was pricking me deep inside."

Her next-door neighbor, with whom she chatted almost daily on her way home from school, came over to give her a pretty brooch as a farewell gift. Both had tears in their eyes. Then it was time for the family to leave. They got into a car and were driven to relatives in another community, where they would stay for ten days.

"Then came the time to say goodbye to them. How grandma cried. She hugged us over and over. All the aunts and uncles and cousins hugged and kissed us too. Uncle Tom said to me: 'Until we see you again.' I looked at him with surprised eyes. My parents had told me that we would probably never see any of them again. Uncle Tom, smiling, said: 'If we will not see each other on Earth again, we'll meet in Heaven.' I smiled too, and a little ray of sunshine entered my heart."

Paulina was impressed with the hugeness of the *Volendam* that lay moored at the dock. The hustle and bustle of the big throng of people was also a new sight. She was a bit bewildered by it all.

"Soon it came time for us to say goodbye to the relatives who had come to see us off. I hid my face against the shoulder of my grandpa. I had never seen tears in his eyes. I did not want to see any then. I can remember thinking: 'Why must we go so far away?'"

Mrs. Paulina Bootsma as a nine-year-old and with her first grandchild, Paulina Verdonk.

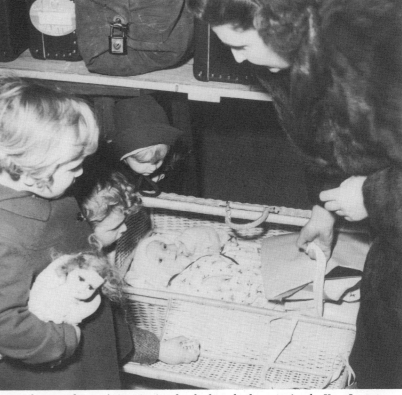

Strain shows in the man's face (top) as he checks in his baggage for the Kota Inten.
*Emigrants heading for Canada in the spring of 1950 wait in front of the customs office
in Rotterdam. At left, little Rennie Baarda seems dead to the world while her parents
(they now live near Smithville, Ontario) wait for the go-ahead to board the* Volendam *in
July, 1951. The photo above shows baby all set for the trip to Canada in a special travel crib.*

The Parting Is Hard 85

"Five years after the war," says Mrs. Nel Molenaar of the Langley, British Columbia, area, "our family of nine was going to Canada. As a child eleven years old, I found this terrible. I had never liked changes. Worse still was the fact that my oldest and dearest brother would stay behind in The Netherlands. In those days, no one talked of a trip back to the Old Country. Emigration was 'goodbye forever.' "

As the family waited in The Hague for the train that would bring them to Rotterdam, Nel was secretly hoping that it would never come, that somehow they would be able to stay in The Netherlands.

"I was getting more and more unhappy. Then, suddenly, there was a familiar face. Our minister wanted to say goodbye to us all for the last time. In his hand he carried an enormous bag filled with candies, a rare treat for us in those days. My fear and sadness disappeared."

Twenty years later, Nel, now married, had a near neighbor whom she knew well: her old minister who had also become an immigrant. When his work as adviser to the congregation was criticized now and then, Nel winced, thinking: "He knew exactly how to help a young member of his former congregation get through a difficult day."

On April 27, 1948, when the cables of the *Tabinta* were loosened and the strains of *Het Wilhelmus*, the Dutch national anthem, faded away, Mrs. Kim Veeneman had tears in her eyes and a lump in her throat. Then her thoughts went back a few years, to when the Canadian liberators were stationed in her home town of Apeldoorn, Gelderland, and she felt much better.

"During the summer of 1945, the Bach choir, of which I was a member, performed on the bandstand in the Oranje Park to honor the soldiers. Included in the program was the Canadian anthem, "O Canada." We had a great time studying and rehearsing this, because the English language was foreign to most of us. Our director was as confused as we were. However, the president of the choir thought himself an expert, for he had a bookstore and came in contact daily with

Dutch customs officers go through their routines. Passengers board the ship. A father has to show his documents before his family is allowed on board.

the Canadians. He said we should sing "O Canada" a little off key, for that was the way it was sung. But the director insisted that we learn it at the right pitch. Well, when the performance came, some soldiers tossed their caps into the air, others hugged their buddies or waved in excitement, and others stood very still. It had never entered my mind that someday I would become a citizen of their country and call it my homeland."

In early March, 1951, Jacob Hofstee of Berkel, Zuid-Holland, got the word that he and his family would be boarding the *Volendam* in Rotterdam on April 14. That didn't leave them much time for the final preparations of moving a household from one country to another.

"A hectic period followed," recalls his son, John. "Smallpox vaccinations had most of the family reeling for a few days. Some furniture had to be disposed of. And arrangements had to be made to pack and ship those belongings that were to go along to Canada."

Nijman Bros. of Rotterdam, one of the many firms that offered the service, was recruited to supply a crate of eight cubic meters. A smaller trunk would be packed with clothes, linen, pots and pans, and any other items that could be needed in Canada before the arrival of the larger container. The family would have access to the trunk during the boat trip.

"On April 9, Dad celebrated his 40th birthday at the home of his sister-in-law," says John. "Many relatives and friends came to say goodbye. The next morning, the truck of Nijman Bros. arrived with three men and the containers. With a lot of measuring and arranging, all the possessions that were to go along were packed. By 3:30, the customs officer sealed the containers, and the truck left for Rotterdam."

The last suitcases were packed in the morning on April 14. There were a few more goodbyes. At noon, the taxi arrived,

A mother and her daughters arrange their belongings in the sleeping quarters on the Kota Inten.

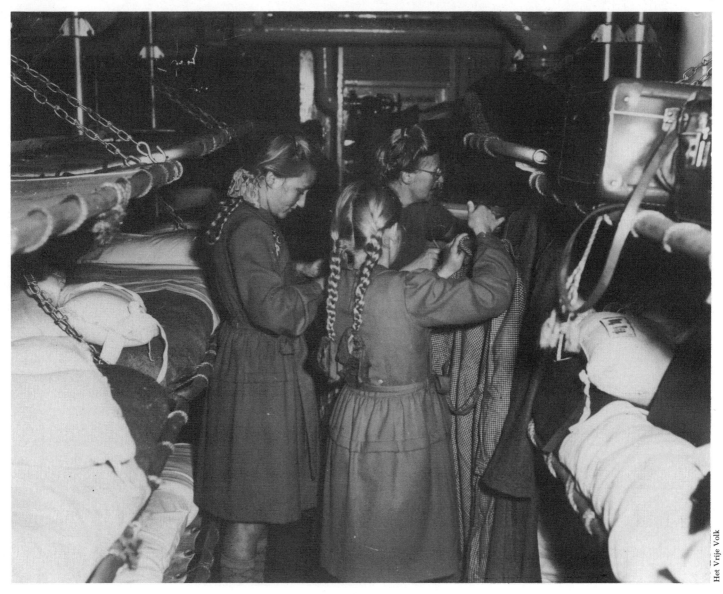

Het Vrije Volk

Passengers gather at the railing after a quick tour of the boat, including their quarters. Relatives mill about on the quay.

Another boatful of emigrants is about to leave.

and the family was on its way to an unknown destination in southwestern Ontario—with a mere $125, which was supposed to last until the first paycheque.

As the years progressed, the various emigration authorities became more adept at making things just a bit easier for those who wanted to leave their homeland.

Days before he was to go to Canada in mid-March, 1955, Jack De Jong of Haarlem, Noord-Holland, went to the camp *Berg en Dal*, located in a forested area near the German border, where a seminar named 'Canada is Calling' was being held. Sponsored by a Roman Catholic organization for young agriculturalists, it was attended by eighty men and women, mostly single, who wanted to learn more about the country they were about to adopt. Most of them were destined for Canada.

De Jong, now of Matsqui, British Columbia, recalls: "Workshops were organized. Some of the speakers—doctors and a nurse—told us about the way of life in Canada, health problems, and the food. A lawyer spoke about buying and selling real estate, cars, insurance, and so on. And a businessman, who had lived in Eastern Canada for ten years, showed slides and movies of everyday life there. The evenings were spent with sing-songs and other entertainment. On the second last day, we were bused to a cemetery near Nijmegen, where thousands of Canadian soldiers, victims of the Second World War, lay buried. A remembrance service was held and wreaths were placed."

A few days later, De Jong was on his way to Canada, for him no longer a mysterious place.

Some emigrants got around the exchange controls by various means, including illegal ones. One honest way was to invest the money which couldn't be taken out of the country in new clothes and furniture. The father of Carl Biel of Meppen, Drenthe, put his money into something different: a motor vehicle.

"It was a used army Jeep, repainted

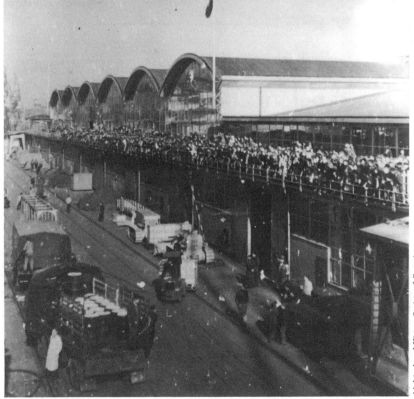

Gerald Prins, a passenger on the Groote Beer *in 1958, waves his hat to relatives on shore. The next photo catches the William Van Oosten family on the* Groote Beer *in 1956. At right is an excellent view of the departure area in Rotterdam.*

Multicultural History Society of Ontario

The Zuiderkruis, *flying the Dutch tri-color at the stern, is about to set sail for Canada. Some of the passengers find a good perch in a lifeboat.*

Tensions Eased Before the Journey

Bob Gosschalk

B.M. (Bob) Gosschalk of Wassenaar, Zuid-Holland, twenty-three and single, knew that he was headed for the right place in 1948. His sponsor, John D. Longworth, a farmer in the Woodstock area, sent him a letter: "We realize this is a big step in your life and do hope you will not be disappointed with Canada and the Canadian people. The Holland family that are with us are very fine people. We like them very much. They are very good citizens, and Canada can be proud of them."

Such kind letters did much to allay the apprehension and anxiety of people who traveled alone to Canada. Somebody would be waiting for them; this assurance must have made them more confident. Some, however, had to keep showing a courage that belied their true feelings. Unfortunately, not everyone received a letter from Canada.

Gosschalk had not been happy working for his father's financial company. He wanted to do something else.

"One of my father's friends had suggested that I go to Canada—I did have some agricultural experience. Sponsorship was arranged through the Canadian Pacific Railway. When my father found out, he didn't talk to me for a couple of weeks. Then he realized he couldn't do anything about it. He bought me a first-class ticket on the *Nieuw Amsterdam*."

Soon he would be working for Longworth for $50 a month and all he could eat—until the oppressive humidity of the Canadian summer and the loneliness of the countryside forced him to move to a fruit farm at Winona in the Niagara Peninsula.

blue with a wooden body built on it," says Carl, now of Guelph, Ontario. "It came along with the furniture about six weeks after our arrival in Canada."

It was a madhouse early in 1952 in the home of Willem Buitenwerf of Uithuizermeeden, in northern Groningen. As soon as word was received that the family could go to a farmer in the St. Catharines, Ontario, area, arrangements were made to get there by means of a still fledgling mode of transportation: the passenger plane. The special flight was to leave at the end of February, some three weeks away. Now it was hurry, hurry, hurry.

Two sales were held: one for the gardening tools and other items related to the business, and one for pieces of furniture, canning jars, and other articles deemed unfit for travel to the new land. New clothes were bought. So were blankets, sheets, pillowcases, a table, and two beds with mattresses. All the belongings, old and new, were packed into two crates for shipment by boat. There was a myriad of other last-minute things—making sure the papers were in order, saying goodbye, and so on.

Then mother, father, and the three children were off to Vlaardingen, Zuid-Holland, to say goodbye to more relatives. From there, they took a taxi to Schiphol, relieved that all the hustle and bustle of the last few weeks were behind them.

"We'll see you in five years," Buitenwerf said cheerfully to a relative who had come along to the airport. He was a bit too optimistic. Sixteen years would elapse before his first trip back to The Netherlands.

Before stepping on board the *Kota Inten* in early 1948, Mrs. Leo Hovius of Grootegast, Groningen, overheard the words of her father: "I'll never see them again."

He was right. He died five years later.

Before Ben and Tina Afman of Baflo, Groningen, made their final decision to emigrate, they informed the authorities that they preferred to be placed in Ontario, as close to the United States border as possible.

"They granted our request," says Mrs. Afman, now of St. Thomas, Ontario, "after asking us for our reason. Ben had explained: 'The only reason I know is that

Boat scenes, top to bottom: passengers practice strapping on life jackets; the children quickly find the swings on the upper deck; the Ryndam *leaves Rotterdam for Canada.*

if we ever want to go back to The Netherlands, it would be closer and cheaper on air fare.' "

They had been informed by a middle-aged man from their village that in many ways Ontario was the best place to locate.

"We often went to his house and asked a lot of questions. When single, he had been in Canada for several years, and he knew more about Ontario than the emigration people. I often wondered why he had come back to The Netherlands. One day, I asked him bluntly."

He explained that he had liked living in Ontario, even though there had been many times when loneliness made him think of going back. Back in The Netherlands for a while, he went for a trip, met a girl, and married her within a few months with the understanding that she would go with him to Canada. When all the forms were ready, she backed out. He had no choice but to stay.

"His testimony gave us a lot of confidence, and we were almost convinced that it couldn't be as bad as some people had told us. He had never seen half-naked Indians with spears in their hands, ready to attack the white people. He had not

even seen them wearing feathers and with their faces painted. All our questions were still not answered, but when we left him, we knew a lot more about Canada than before. This did us a world of good."

There was no room in the van for the fifteen-year-old nephew of Gerald Prins of Kampen, Overijssel. The boy was deeply disappointed. He had been looking forward to going to Rotterdam and waving goodbye to his aunt and uncle and their children. A thought suddenly struck him: he would travel the long distance by bicycle.

"He left early in the morning on that day in April, 1958," recalls Prins, who settled in Renfrew, Ontario (he died early in 1983). "We couldn't help but think of him as we rode in the van to Rotterdam. Would he make it on time?"

He still hadn't arrived when it came time for Prins and his family to board the *Groote Beer*. Everyone was convinced that he would arrive too late. However, minutes before the lines were loosened, Prins spotted the beaming, slightly flushed face among the multitude on the quay.

Ted Smeenk of Voorburg, Zuid-Holland, had visited the dockside in Rotterdam when emigrants were about to leave for a far corner of the world. Later he told his wife: "There's no way we're going to go through that commotion. We're travelling to Canada by plane."

He sold most of his belongings to pay for the air fare for his family of five in 1951.

"I couldn't have cared less," he says. "Going by boat would have been much cheaper. But I avoided Rotterdam. And I was in Canada within eighteen hours."

He also avoided what many immigrants would later look back upon as the most unforgettable experience of the entire process: a voyage across the turbulent Atlantic.

The ship has almost disappeared from sight, but relatives on the pier keep waving. The scene was recorded in April, 1951.

Chapter 6

The Crossing

The Crossing

Like many other emigrants, Geertrui Beldman—who is now Mrs. Trudy Joldersma of Hamilton, Ontario—of Holten, Overijssel, twenty-eight years old and single, kept her diary up to date during the agonizingly long, difficult voyage to Canada. She traveled with the *Beaverbrae* in 1950. Some excerpts:

February 14: "Despite babies crying and mothers pacing up and down, I managed to get some sleep. Infants are lying in their travel beds which are standing in the aisles on the concrete floor. Mothers have fastened their babies' beds to their own beds to keep them from sliding back and forth. Although they block the aisles, there is unfortunately no better way to protect the tykes.

"I'm going to hurry and wash myself, then have some breakfast. I'm hungry.

"In the washroom, I had to forget my sense of modesty completely. It's an open space with a row of fountains against one wall. You're fully exposed. I realize I'm going to have to limit my personal hygiene during the journey. For me, the timing is poor. Mothers with diapered babies have to be very patient. There is nowhere to change diapers and bathe babies except on mother's cot. Our quarters have that dreadful smell of dirty diapers. There is practically no ventilation in that 'sty.' "

February 17: "What did I say about an adventure? What happened to my expectations?

"I'm as sick as a dog. So are many of my fellow passengers. I lie on my cot, groaning. Our quarters smell abominably of filthy diapers and vomit. Crying babies . . . wornout mothers with ashen faces. Fathers coming in to check on their women and children pinch their noses shut and grumble: 'What a stench!'

"We have to keep our own quarters clean. There is even an inspection to see that it's done! Women scurry back and forth with pails and mops to clean up the vomit from the floors and to mop up the washroom. Do all ships make their passengers responsible for cleaning up their own quarters? I'll ask my brothers the minute I see them . . ."

February 19: "I'm so sick now that I can't stand the smell of food, let alone eat it. We're too sick to clean our quarters. We step over the vomit or make a detour

Geertrui Beldman (now Mrs. Trudy Joldersma of Hamilton, Ontario) at the time of her emigration and with her four children.

around it.

"One of the mothers needs a doctor. It looks as if she's dying. She can't even get down from her cot.

"I still try to make it out on deck as often as possible to get some fresh air. But there are never enough deckchairs. Only if I get there early do I have a chance of finding an empty one. But most of the time I'm too late.

"The weather is stormy. Everything swings and rocks back and forth. And I swing with it. Both physically and mentally, I live in continuous disorientation.

"So this is my boat trip . . . !"

February 21: "We have to wade through enormous puddles of water to get to the toilets. Is this because of the storm? We don't know. Actually, we know nothing about what's going on here. Everything is in English, which nobody

As the Seven Seas *of the Europa-Canada Line rides out a storm on the North Atlantic, a huge swell tilts the ship sharply. Above, the* Groote Beer *leaves a long trail as it steams across a calm stretch of ocean in July, 1953. Mrs. Netty Oosterman, now of Lambeth, Ontario, area, enjoys the beautiful weather. At right, Jan Janssens, now of the Watford, Ontario, area, relaxes on the* Scythia *in August, 1949.*

understands. We don't even know whether it's normal for passengers to be held responsible for cleaning up their quarters. Nobody tells us why the toilets suddenly back up. It's still a riddle to us why Germans should be placed in charge of our food lines. We're being treated like inferiors.

"There's a story that one of the Dutch passengers punched one of those hamfisted Germans in the face for ordering people around like they did in the war. Bully for him, I say!"

The passengers on the second boat to ferry across emigrants—the *Tabinta*, in September, 1947—also had a few reminders that the war hadn't been over for very long.

C.M. Hogeterp: "We left Rotterdam at 6:00 p.m. We sailed past the Hook of Holland, and twenty minutes later the boat stopped and was anchored. Of course, everyone wanted to know what was going on. We weren't told officially, but word got around that it was still too dangerous to travel at night because of undiscovered mines left over from the war."

Jerry Rekker: "The next day, while we sailed through the Strait of Dover, we saw the masts of sunken ships, a grim reminder of all the fighting."

Early that morning, Tjasse Heuvel and his two oldest sons were among the first ones on the deck. The sun wasn't up yet.

"It was beautiful weather. Oh, how we enjoyed the sea air after being cooped up in a hall full of people. We had lived only a short distance from the sea, in Uithuizermeeden, Groningen, and that fresh air was still in our nostrils. Later, we

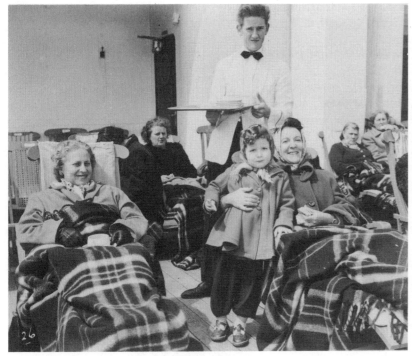

went downstairs to where my wife slept. She was vomiting. She didn't get out of bed during the entire trip. It was different for me and the boys. We ate like ravens. There was real rye bread and lots of chicken. Each morning, we were the first ones on deck to enjoy that beautiful air."

He felt sorry for the women.

"I can still see the ones with small children having to clean all the baby clothes in the wash hall. The pails full of dirty diapers slid from one end to the other when big waves came along. The women just let them go as they grabbed for the posts and hung on."

F.A. Rovers, returning to Canada where he was born of Dutch parents, remembers that some of the passengers grumbled about other things as well.

"Some farmers, used to getting up early, stomped across the steel decks in their wooden shoes, unknowingly making a racket. Of course that didn't sit too well with the people who were sick and those who were trying to catch up on their sleep."

Rovers wasn't among the complainers. He was too busy making money to even notice the noise and some of the other discomforts.

"The ship needed two or three men at $2.00 a day to bring the coffee around. I volunteered. At the end of the trip, I was $24.00 richer. The crew members got a bottle of gin once, and I lined up and got one too. So at the end of the line, the steward was one bottle short!"

When he began to recover from his seasickness, passenger Hogeterp looked up a few of the people he had met on board and talked about the need for a daily devotional period. There was no Protestant chaplain.

"We agreed there should be an *avondsluiting*, an evening devotional. Klaas Mulder and I led these. We read from the Bible and prayed, and everyone—there were usually forty to fifty people present—sang at the top of their lungs. The service lasted about forty-five minutes. The people liked it."

The trip across the ocean on the *Kota Inten* in March, 1948, was like a holiday for Leo and Boukje Hovius.

"Neither of us had ever gone on a long trip before," says Mrs. Hovius. "In Holland, we didn't travel much. So this was quite an outing. The ocean was always a wonderful sight, even when there was a storm. But then, we never got seasick."

But the conditions on board constantly reminded them that they were on a troopship full of poor emigrants, not on a luxury liner hosting tourists with pockets full of money.

"The food was all right. But we couldn't buy any fruit or something extra. Toward the end of the trip, the men were running out of matches. The smokers kept each other happy by passing on a butt to someone who was about to light a cigarette. The toilets were plugged. You can imagine the mess. And sleeping in separate halls didn't sit too well with us—we were newlyweds. Finally, there was no entertainment on board, something that bothered families with children more than it bothered us."

Hovius and his wife tried to ignore the problems and concentrated on their reason for being on the boat. On deck, they became acquainted with people their own age, and together they discussed their reasons for emigrating and their theories on what the future held for them. Never did they lose their sense of humor.

Hovius was standing at the railing during a storm, admiring the waves, when the cap of the fellow next to him flew overboard.

"That one wants to go back to Holland," he laughed.

Later, when people ran about the boat, shouting "Land in sight!" Hovius rushed to the railing. It was bitterly cold. Everything seemed to be coated with ice. A gust of wind came along, and away went his cap. It bobbed on top of a wave and disappeared.

"I hope that one wants to go to Canada," Hovius commented with glee.

Mrs. Koob Kollen, a native of Zwartsluis, Overijssel, and now of St. Catharines, Ontario, kept a detailed diary while the *Kota Inten* sailed for Canada in 1948. Some excerpts:

Wednesday morning: "Yesterday morning we passed innumerable checkpoints, and then arrived on board at two o'clock. We had to lug all our suitcases through the driving rain. At four o'clock, we had to practise putting on our life preservers and reporting to the lifeboats.

Sometimes there was nothing to do but stare at the endless stretch of water.

"I'm sleeping in the upper berth, so I will have some climbing to do. My berth is in the stern, while Koob's berth, also an upper, is in the bow of the ship. I want to see if there's another bed available, because right above my berth there's a naked lightbulb that stays on all night. I wake up practically every other minute, because my berth is also right next to the stairs that go up to the deck. Yesterday we got a warm meal: soup, endive, meat, potatoes, and bread, plus pudding and a sauce. This morning, I was awake at five

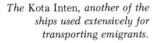

The Kota Inten, *another of the ships used extensively for transporting emigrants.*

thirty and couldn't sleep any more. We also had to move the clock back an hour, so really it was only four thirty. I'd been out on deck for more than an hour when Koob showed up. He had slept much better. We eat cafeteria-style. You are given a tin plate with little compartments and you walk along a counter. This morning, they gave us a tin of porridge, a slice of sausage, cheese, a cube of butter, a spoonful of jam, and three slices of bread. It tasted pretty good, but the corner where we sat smelled of cat urine! Oh yes, I forgot to tell you about the toilets. They are like big jars all neatly in a row, separated by partial partitions with a flimsy curtain in front. Big washtubs too! This morning, I washed with sea water, but that really stings. Tomorrow I will have to find myself a decent tap. Right now, I am in the cafeteria writing. Koob has just picked up the spending money (see letter on page 101). Somebody is playing an accordion. There is a piano here, too, and somebody brought a portable record-player.

"This morning, we passed by the English coast. You could easily see the chalky cliffs.

"The ship's chaplain held a church service, and we sang *Beveel Gerust Uw Wegen* and *Rust Mijn Ziel Uw God Is Koning.*"

Friday morning: "Yesterday and today we saw dolphins jumping out of the waves. Cute to look at, but they were gone in no time. Last night at around three o'clock, we entered the Atlantic Ocean at a point where the currents meet. We were told that the bobbing would get much worse, but until now it's been kind of fun.

"There are a lot of children on board and in my compartment too. They yell and scream, and some of the women are as loud as old Nelly, our neighbor. When I see or hear someone vomiting, I feel like I can hardly keep it down myself. Usually we are sitting or standing around on deck, because below it's unbearable.

"In the cafeteria, you can buy chocolate bars for eighteen cents, a pack of Lucky Strikes for eighty cents, and a tin of fifty

A familiar scene from an ocean crossing: passengers in lifejackets line up near the lifeboats for a mandatory drill. With the aid of a little map in the back of the passenger list, the emigrants could chart the progress of their boat. The one below was kept up to date by J.F. Beckman, now of Beaconsfield, Quebec, while he sailed with the Groote Beer *in October, 1954.*

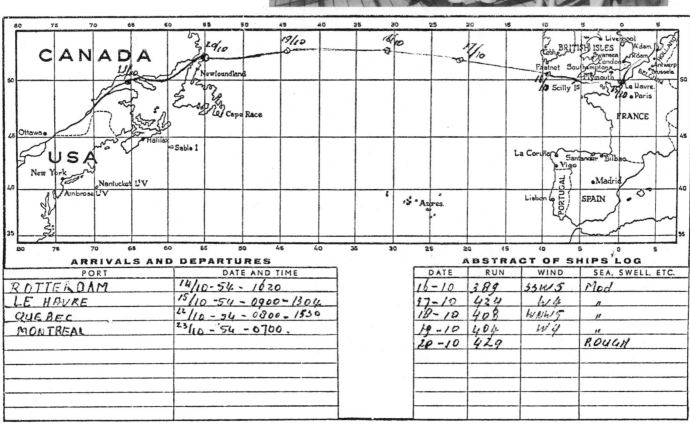

ARRIVALS AND DEPARTURES	
PORT	DATE AND TIME
ROTTERDAM	14/10-54 - 1620
LE HAVRE	15/10 -54 - 0900-1304
QUEBEC	22/10 -54 - 0800 - 1530
MONTREAL	23/10 -'54 - 0700 .

ABSTRACT OF SHIPS LOG			
DATE	RUN	WIND	SEA, SWELL, ETC.
16-10	389	SSW 5	Mod
17-10	434	W 4	"
18-10	408	WNW 5	"
19-10	404	W 4	"
20-10	429		ROUGH

Het Vrije Volk

Netherlanders on the way to Canada enjoy a meal in a ship's dining hall. Mrs. Joyce Damsma of Kitchener, Ontario, explains the photo at right: "That's me in the center, eighteen years old, daughter of Mr. and Mrs. Henry Veenstra, going to Canada on the Volendam in February, 1951. My sister Betty is on my left, and on my right is the girl I became good friends with during the trip." Simon Dykstra of Strathroy, Ontario, says of the other photo: "It was taken on the Volendam in 1950. As a group of single men, we spent a lot of time on deck."

cigarettes for two guilders. Coca-Cola is also available. That's it. There is nothing else to buy. We will use up all of the fifty guilders of spending money.

"There are a lot of foreigners on board: 250 Ukrainians who were carried off to Germany in 1941. The others are still in camps somewhere in Germany. These people have nothing at all. Most of them have relatives in Canada, who sponsored them. For the rest, there are Frenchmen, Poles, Danes, Germans, Britons, and Swedes. There are loudspeakers all over the ship and announcements are made in four languages. Every morning, there is a brief religious service over the speakers, and then fifteen minutes of music. Every evening, Rev. D.J. Scholten holds a church service in the cafeteria. There is also a Roman Catholic priest on board. This afternoon, we had a sing-song on deck for the benefit of some sick women down below. Also this afternoon, some children's games were organized on deck. There is a quiz program in the cafeteria this evening for the men. Tomorrow there will be a quiz for women and on Sunday for both.

"I hung a handtowel in front of the lightbulb and last night I slept right through. All my clothes were lying on the floor this morning. I guess I must have kicked them there. The bow of the ship

N.V. NEDERLANDSCH-AMERIKAANSCHE STOOMVAART-MAATSCHAPPIJ

HOLLAND-AMERIKA LIJN

AFDELING PASSAGE

TELEGRAM-ADRES:
AMERIK.ANO ROTTERDAM
TELEFOON No. 72825
POSTBUS No. 486

M.s. "KOTA INTEN", 12 Maart a/s. van Rotterdam.

In verband met het feit, dat het de passagiers volgens de
huidige deviezenvoorschriften niet is toegestaan Nederlands geld mee aan boord te nemen, hebben wij de volgende regeling getroffen, om passagiers in staat te stellen
hun onkosten aan boord te bestrijden.

Vóór vertrek kan te onzen kantore een bedrag van Fl.25.-
worden gestort per passagier van 10 jaar en ouder. Voor
kinderen van 1 tot 10 jaar mag Fl. 10.- per kind worden
betaald. Van dit geld kunnen de passagiers dus de arti-
kelen, welke aan boord verkrijgbaar zijn, zoals limonade,
rookartikelen en chocolade, betalen.

Passagiers, die van deze gelegenheid gebruik wensen te
maken, worden verzocht het geld te storten bij de agent,
die hun passage behandeld heeft, of dit te doen op de dag
van inscheping op het kantoor van de Holland-Amerika Lijn.

Hoogachtend,

HOLLAND-AMERIKA LIJN

where Koop sleeps bucked so badly yesterday that no one could even stand up. I
didn't have the courage yesterday to wash
myself, because everywhere you went
there was vomit. So I stayed at midship.
We munched dry bread, saved from the
previous meal. We always get porridge in
the morning, but today we also got a
salted fish. Lunch is usually soup and
bread with meat or cheese, and at night
there is a warm meal. People don't drink
tea or coffee.

"The sea is an impressive sight, but it
soon gets monotonous. It doesn't intrigue
me any more and I hope we get some
distraction. You sure get dirty on a ship.
My shoes are scuffed and ruined from all
the times I've stumbled against the iron
railings."

Saturday: "I just cannot imagine that
today is Saturday. Every day is the same.
There are fewer people sick now and most
of them are sitting out on deck. I don't feel
too badly and Koob is not sick either. I
borrowed a few books from the ship's
library, and I already finished one. This
morning, we had a talk with a Lithua-
nian. In 1944, he fled from the Russians
and settled in Germany for awhile. Then
he was wounded and taken to Denmark.
We also talked with a number of Ukrainians. It is just terrible to hear how
these people have suffered and where they
have gone to find refuge. It makes you
wonder that there are still people who
believe that anything good can come from
the Russians and their leaders. It is
remarkable that all these people seek
freedom because of their faith. For them,
there is no freedom of religion in Russia.
They sing so beautifully. It's a joy just
listening to them.

"This afternoon, we got a delicious
salad with our sandwich meal. I went
back for seconds.

"They did the paper work on all the
baggage this morning, using six different
forms. As if we didn't have enough
papers!"

Monday morning: "We had a very intimate Sunday. The church service lasted
well over an hour, and the collection was
for the Ukrainians. Later in the day, there
was music from the portable record-
player. At breakfast, we got an egg and
two slices of raisin bread. For dinner, we
had cauliflower and farina pudding with
sauce. We didn't notice the bobbing at all

*The letter to the passengers
on the* Kota Inten *in March,
1948, says that the exchange
regulations do not permit
Dutch money to be taken on
board. Before departure,
passengers could deposit
twenty-five guilders for each
person above ten years and
ten guilders for each
younger one. This money
would be available on board
to pay for such things as
tobacco products and
chocolate bars. At top, John
Hofstee strikes a typical pose
on board the* Volendam *in
April, 1951. The other
photo, made available by
Jim Bergstra of Shallow
Lake, Ontario, shows a shy
crew member surrounded
by passengers.*

yesterday. We spent most of the day in the cafeteria, because out on deck you get terribly dirty. In the course of the evening, the sea turned rough again and many people threw up. Fortunately, we weren't among them. There was also an international evening of song. First the Ukrainians sang, followed by the Frisians, the Swedes, the French, and the Netherlanders. After that came the Ukrainians and the Swedes again, and they made the place alive. It was very catching, and in the end nobody could stop singing. So we sang a lot of Dutch songs."

Tuesday evening: "The weather started out nice today, but later it turned very cold. The reason was an iceberg at port. Later in the afternoon, we spotted another. We took the long way around it, because most of it was hidden under water. It was a beautiful sight when the sun shone on it. It was just like a huge mountain of salt, forty or fifty meters high. Then you have to multiply that by nine for the part under water. I sent out a couple of telegrams with birthday greetings. They cost only three guilders, fifteen cents. At around four o'clock, we sighted land—Newfoundland. We are now alongside it, and from this distance it looks pretty rocky. I am going to get up early in the morning, because there will probably be lots more to see. Koob spotted some whales, which were being shot at by a fishing boat.

"Dinner tonight was tomato soup, fried cod with a sauce, cucumber, salad, tomatoes, potatoes, and an orange. It was a meal fit for a king, I tell you! If things go

according to plan, we will disembark either on Thursday evening or early Friday morning."

Thursday evening: "Yesterday we thought there would be plenty to see, but that was disappointing. It was foggy on the river all morning—this caused a five-hour delay—and in the afternoon, when the fog had cleared, all we could see was the outline of what looked like an island. We passed the evening in the cafeteria and later went with the chef to his quarters for a nightcap. Afterwards, we went back on deck and spotted two lighthouses. At least it was a sign that there was land.

"I got up at six this morning—mostly because of those screaming kids; there is a woman with five kids right behind me—and spotted land. It was a lovely strip of land, with here and there what looked like dollhouses. A delightful sight, but later we were swallowed up by the mist banks again. The ship had to sound its foghorn and slow down considerably. The water is like glass now. It is simply miraculous. The coastline is very rocky —high cliffs sticking up out of the water, with occasionally a lighthouse or a village. They are like little toys from a distance. Just before noon, a pilot came on board. Shortly after that, we found ourselves among a bunch of islands, proof that a pilot was necessary. We are still close to the right shore of the river, sailing under high cliffs with trees growing high above us. The left shoreline is close enough to be seen, although still far away. Once in awhile, a passenger boat or a freighter passes us. Tomorrow morning, we will disembark. We have to get our papers

It's bingo time on the Nieuw Amsterdam in April, 1951. At right, children play among the dinghies stored on the deck of the Volendam in 1951.

ready. Just now there was an announcement that we would disembark at eight o'clock in the morning."

The Protestant chaplain on board the *Kota Inten*, Rev. D.J. Scholten of Bierum, Groningen, who was on the way to visiting the immigrants in Canada on behalf of the *Gereformeerde Kerk*, wrote about the boat trip upon his return.

"You don't have to be sentimental to be moved when the lines are cast off and the ship edges slowly away from the quay, accompanied by the old familiar sounds of *Het Wilhelmus* roaring out of the ship's loudspeakers . . . I saw not only women and girls but also sturdy men swallow hard or blow their noses as they listened to the melody of the national anthem. The same scene repeated itself when, several hours later, they stood at the ship's railing and watched the coastline of their beloved country recede beyond the horizon. But the Dutch, in general, are too sober to wallow in sentimentality and, besides, they are much too curious. Therefore, they soon began to reconnoitre all the cabins and lounges and the large engine room. At the same time, they tried to find out whether there were any acquaintances or friends of acquaintances among the passengers."

Rev. Scholten found the co-operation of the captain, the head steward, the purser, in fact the entire crew, impeccable.

"I am reminded of the flexibility with which the cafeteria personnel turned their bellywich over to us at specific times for church services and also for the use of the public address system for meditations and spiritual songs. Notably the captain, Mr. Visser, who afterwards became known as *boerenvader*, showed himself to be a man of concern and paid a great deal of attention to the spiritual care of the emigrant company."

The people who were undergoing the highly emotional experience of moving to the unknown needed comfort. For many, the daily devotions, the music, did wonders. They looked upon God to guide them across the unruly waves and to their future homes.

On a Saturday evening in March, 1952, while the *Waterman* kept course for Canada, a few hundred people attended a service. When it was over, they all went to the deck. Their combined voices rang out above the din of the restless Atlantic. Many wiped away a tear as they lustily sang the moving words of a familiar hymn.

> *Wat de toekomst brengen moge,*
> *mij geleidt des Heren hand;*
> *moedig sla ik dus de ogen*
> *naar het onbekende land.*

Rev. Scholten, now of Brantford, Ontario, wrote about his work aboard the *Kota Inten* in 1948: "As a rule, at nine in the morning, there was a morning meditation that came over the intercom and could be heard in all cabins and on all decks. I used this opportunity to play various recordings of Christian hymns. There were also evening devotionals in the large dining room—devotionals that looked very much like a church service. They were attended by many Protestants and by practically every passenger with a positive Christian view of life. On Sunday, a church service was held, attended by part of the crew and the captain. During the afternoon, a kind of Sunday school

A group of young men on the way to Canada with the Groote Beer in late April of 1958. Once, a number of young couples banded together to form what they called the Ocean Choir. One member, Jim Bergstra of Shallow Lake, Ontario, recalls: "It was a good way to fill the time."

"We were on the verge of seasickness and couldn't stand the smell in the eating hall, so we took our food trays to the deck," says Mrs. Adriana Rykes of Anahim Lake, British Columbia. She, her husband, and his brother Peter traveled to Canada with the Beaverbrae in March, 1950. "We ran into a storm that lasted two days. The ship dipped so deeply that the waves washed over the deck. We decided then and there that we would never cross the ocean on a ship again."

was organized for the children. It featured a lot of pictures, books, texts, and, for every attending child, a chocolate bar. One of the tots piped up: 'It's just like Christmas.' In addition, chaplains invited people to come to their cabins for personal discussions. People came for information about submitting church memberships and the whereabouts of the various churches in the areas where they were going."

Rev. Scholten visited the sick. He also spent much time handing out literature. All his booklets and tracts, including the popular *Elisabethbode*, were gone in no time. Several people of non-Christian persuasion came to him for a Bible.

"I should not forget to mention the communal hymn singing which took place during the day on the upper deck, usually directly in front of the entrance to the women's lounge, where quite a few women were suffering from seasickness. At first, there were twenty or thirty in the choir. But once the sheet music had been widely distributed, that number grew considerably. How beautiful that was! Just imagine being out there in the middle of the ocean and hearing the praises of the Lord sung amid the waves and the storms: *Scheepke Onder Jezus' Hoede, Zalig Hij Die In Dit Leven Jacobs God Ter Hulpe Heeft,* and *Ga Niet Alleen Door 't Leven.*"

John Eisen thoroughly enjoyed the trip on the *Volendam* in June, 1949. Seasickness didn't bother him much. He loved playing checkers and shuffleboard with fellow passengers. The days seemed to fly by.

But there was disappointment for the youth from Apeldoorn. "We slept four high in a large room with about ninety other men. I learned quickly that not all people could be trusted. A silver guilder, a farewell present from friends, which I had tucked away in the inside pocket of my coat, was stolen. From then on I watched my possessions more closely. In those days, a silver guilder was a treasure."

Then there was a bit of wry humor.

"A man beside my bunk was really seasick. His ten-year-old son wanted to treat him, and he brought his dad a glass of cold water. His dad thanked him and took a good mouthful. Then he groaned as if in severe pain. It turned out that his son had gone to the wrong tap. Dad had swallowed salt water!"

Willem VanderMolen of the city of Groningen, and now of Chilliwack, British Columbia, remembers: "The trip with the *Volendam* in May, 1951, was beautiful—until there was an awful tragedy. When we woke up one morning, we heard that a German woman had jumped overboard. She didn't want to emigrate with her husband, and she decided to drown herself. Our ship retraced its route for a ways, as required by the laws of the sea, and everyone looked for a trace of the woman. To no avail. We all felt very badly."

"You are so lucky," people told Mrs. Elly Werfhorst before she and her husband boarded the boat for Canada in June, 1951. "You are never seasick."

They knew that she had just completed six years of service with the *Marva* in the Royal Netherlands Navy. She had never been sick on the often turbulent North Sea. Surely the Atlantic wouldn't bother someone who had proved her sealegs long ago. So she looked forward to eight days of looking at the sky and the ocean blue.

She and her husband boarded the Cunard Line's *Scythia* in Le Havre, France. The sea was smooth. But she didn't enjoy the azure sky and the wide horizon. She was seasick!

"The minute good old Europe disappeared from sight, my stomach turned and churned and made me wonder which side was up. The beautiful Atlantic brought no relief. It was smooth as a frozen pond. Not a ripple. All was quiet except for my stomach. I couldn't believe it. I thought: 'What? Me seasick?' "

The queasiness lasted until her arrival in Quebec City. And then her stomach had trouble making the transition from ship to shore. She sat down on a suitcase while her husband hunted for a cup of coffee. The women in flowered hats who doled out refreshments, cookies, and religious material appeared to ignore their presence, concentrating instead on those with children in tow.

The train ride didn't make her feel any better. A banana tasted awful. The butter was salty. The milk was bitter. Even after her arrival in Toronto, the sickness persisted. She and her husband, who had been permitted to take $150.00 each out of The Netherlands, rented a downtown room for $5.00 a day, a lot of money then, and she had visions of a huge doctor's bill.

"My sister arrived from Washington, listened to my complaints, and observed: 'You've never been sick. Why now?' Two days later, she thought she knew, and said: 'Stop complaining! It's obvious: you're expecting!' I cried: 'Not me!' But a doctor confirmed her suspicion. You know, I never lived that down in the family. About all of my pregnancies they would say, 'By golly, she's seasick again.' And my sister would say: 'If I hadn't told her, she still wouldn't know.' "

Mrs. Anna Roefs, who sailed with the *Volendam* in 1951, recalls: "It was an awful boat. It creaked all the time. During our first night at sea, when it was really misty, we nearly collided with a large freighter. Our son, Frans, was on deck at the time and could see the outline of a boat. He said he had never before heard such cursing and foul language. I don't like to think of what would have happened had our boat, crammed with people, been hit by the freighter. But God was with us."

A stiff, chilling breeze hit the *Zuiderkruis* as she sailed past the Hook of Holland and entered the open sea on March 4, 1952. The water was choppy, and it didn't take long for the motion of the ship to take its toll among the passengers, many of them already queasy from all the excitement and emotion of the previous days.

The breeze gradually turned into a full-scale Atlantic storm. Howling winds whipped the waves into a frenzy. One day, the heaving ship did not appear to be making any progress; the next day, while the sea continued to boil, it crept along at half speed.

At the height of the storm, a pan of piping hot soup shifted off a table. Plates and cups smashed onto the dining room floor. Children, and even adults, fell down stairs. The screams at times were frightening. Many feared that the ship would never make it to Canada, that it would disappear under the swirling brine, never to be seen again.

Mrs. Tina Afman of Baflo, Groningen, and now of St. Thomas, Ontario, one of the passengers, wrote to the *Noorder Nieuwsbode*, a weekly newspaper, shortly

The Martin Onderwater family of The Hague sailed on the Sibajak *in 1952. Everyone was given a lifejacket and assigned a lifeboat. Below, Onderwater, now of Abbotsford, British Columbia, enjoys a refreshing cup of coffee.*

The Sibajak *in the 1950s.*

after: "The tables in the nursery were secured to the floor, but the chairs, cribs, and rocking-horses were standing loose. When the ship listed, everything started to shift. The mothers, the children, the nurses, and the stewards were smacked against the wall. We tried to get up on our feet, but another wave came and we were thrown against the other wall. It was terrible."

The children, some with burns from the boiling soup, were taken to the cabins and tied down with belts.

"Several prayer meetings were held," wrote Mrs. Afman. "Nearly everyone attended. Emotion ran high as people called upon God's name and His help among those huge, powerful waves."

After a few days, the wind abated, and the sea became calmer. The people on the *Zuiderkruis* breathed a sigh of relief, although the fear of sinking to the dark depths of the ocean remained with them. The respite, however, was shortlived. The storm picked up again, worse than before. By this time, most of the passengers— eighty per cent, according to one diary—never made it to the eating hall because of seasickness.

"A few days before our arrival in Halifax," wrote Mrs. Afman, "we suddenly heard a tremendous bang. The motors stopped, and the passengers began to panic. Many of them raced to the cabins to get their children out of bed."

It was nine o'clock in the evening. Of

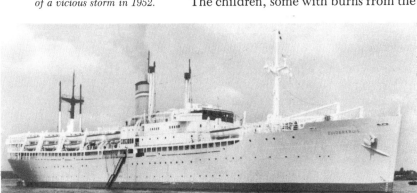

The Zuiderkruis *bore the brunt of a vicious storm in 1952.*

On the Way Over Here

Here are some scenes from the *Veendam* during its crossing in June, 1952. In that year, a record number of Dutch immigrants arrived in Canada: 20,653. Among this multitude were B.W. Prinsen, a bricklayer from Aalten, Gelderland, his wife, and five children. They eventually settled in St. Catharines, Ontario.

"This is a family picture taken during the trip."

"Some people were quite seasick . . ."

". . . The best place to be was on deck if the weather was good."

course, no one tried to go to bed. The wildest rumors made the rounds, and many believed that the ship was doomed.

"The storm had knocked two holes in the bottom of the boat," wrote Mrs. Afman. "We heard the pumps going nonstop. It was the general belief that the sea would become our grave. People began to mutter that it was the captain's fault. The ship, they said, had to be back in Holland on a specific date to pick up more emigrants. Therefore, in view of the stormy weather, corners were cut to make sure it would arrive on time. At 1:30 a.m., a man came by our cabin. He was asking all the men to go with him for a word with the captain. Well, a steward tried his best to calm them down. The situation could be worse, he said, but not better. The captain, after all, was not a rascal, and it was stupid to blame him or any other officer for the bad weather. The lives of the crewmen were as much at stake as those of the passengers. Despite these words, the people on board remained very sober for

the rest of the voyage."

The *Zuiderkruis* chugged along at half power. The passengers kept an anxious eye on its progress, marked daily on a map. Then there were shouts that birds had been spotted, a sign that land was not too far away. People, many of them

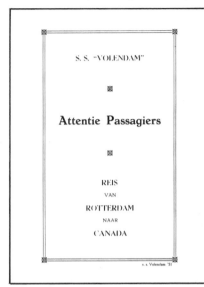

Above: "This mailboat came by after we'd been on the ocean for a few days, picking up mail to take back to Holland. We could let the family back home know how we were making out."

Top left: "Our daughter Jenny (foreground) celebrated her twelfth birthday. One of the family told our steward and he promptly brought a beautiful birthday cake."

Bottom left: "The soup was always ready to perk you up if you could stomach it."

forgetting their ailments, rushed to the deck, as if they had never seen birds before. They peered into the distance, but no land was discernible yet.

Mrs. Afman wrote: "It was on a Thursday afternoon when we saw—a bit hazy at first—the mountains on the horizon. What a magnificent sight! The mountains were covered with snow and ice, and the rays of the sun reflected from the snow onto the water. At the foot of the mountains, there were houses as small as matchboxes. It was like a scene from a fairy-tale. We certainly enjoyed it after such a terrible trip. We stood at the railing until late into the night so as not to miss anything."

The *Zuiderkruis* arrived at Halifax the next day—one and a half days behind schedule. But the passengers, longing to stand on solid ground again, couldn't get off yet—there wouldn't be a train connection until the following day. In the even-

Voyage by Airship

Mrs. Marten Geertsma of Pitt Meadows, British Columbia, explains: "We came to Canada in 1951 on the second emigrant plane. We flew quite by accident; the boat we were supposed to go with was full. It took eighteen hours to fly from Amsterdam to Montreal, with a stopover in Iceland. We put the baby in a net hanging from the ceiling. Our second daughter slept on the floor, and the stewardess offered to look after her."

DC-6 in 1952

Nico De Jong, twenty-two years old, the son of a farmer in the Alphen aan den Rijn area of Zuid-Holland, loved adventure and airplanes. He had always wanted to be a pilot. No wonder that he boarded a DC-6 of the KLM Royal Dutch Airlines in June, 1952, for his trip to Canada. The thought of going by boat had never entered his mind.

"I had to pay the full fare—around $725—myself. There were some eighty-five passengers, mostly single people between twenty and thirty-five. It was like a holiday—we had a riot in that plane. We started dancing, and the pilot said: 'Please, calm down a bit. Don't forget that you're in an airplane.' The flight took eighteen long hours. First the plane landed in Iceland, where the passengers were treated to a dinner—I'm sure it was bear meat—and next it stopped at St. John, Newfoundland, at 4 p.m. That's where I became a landed immigrant. Then on to Montreal."

ing, a Canadian doctor came on board to examine the children with burns and a woman who had received a concussion. He found it necessary to admit them to a hospital in Halifax. That evening, too, the Protestant chaplain, Rev. D.J. Scholten, and his Roman Catholic counterpart held special services of thanksgiving for the safe arrival. Needless to say, the meeting rooms were packed.

Kees and Reina Feyen and their two children had a room of their own when they crossed in 1951. They were on board the *Veendam*, a tourist boat of the Holland-America Line on the way to New York City after picking up passengers in France and England. Few emigrants were on board.

Recalls Mrs. Feyen: "We really had a beautiful trip—good food in a lovely dining room, entertainment every night, and

Quicker by Air

These emigrants look somewhat apprehensive as they prepare to fly to their new country in the early 1950s.

De Spiegel

Frisian Flyers

In early September, 1951, forty-six Frisians from Leeuwarden, Joure, Woudsend, Bakhuizen, Burum, and Tzummarum gathered in front of the travel bureau, Lissone Lindeman, in the provincial capital. A press photographer snapped a picture. Then the group boarded a tour bus and headed for Schiphol. There they received best wishes from the KLM and listened to

the Dutch and Frisian anthems over the loudspeaker. Their aircraft, the Overloon, which the travel bureau had chartered especially for them, stood waiting. "It was a large plane at the time," says Wieger B. Stelpstra of Simcoe, Ontario, one of the passengers. "But now you could just about park it crossways in a 747."

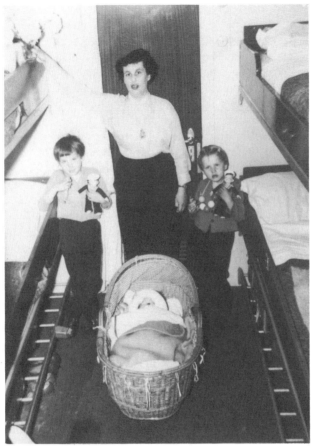

Truus DeVries and her three children, Sonja, Erna, and Anna (in crib), are in cabin 214 of the Zuiderkruis in 1957.

This scene from the Groote Beer in June, 1959, isn't much different from scenes of earlier voyages. Mr. and Mrs. William A. Thysse of Delft, Zuid-Holland, and now of Edmonton, Alberta, relax in the sunshine and study the passenger list.

in the daytime we enjoyed the lounging chairs on deck. There was only one day, during a rough wind, when we experienced a bit of seasickness. We had a bit of excitement, too, when the captain noticed that the boat was going too slowly and, upon investigation, spotted a huge dead whale wrapped around the bow. The boat stopped and backed up to let the whale float free."

Although the trip was enjoyable, the passengers got tired of seeing nothing but water for nine days. No wonder that many of them danced on deck when the Statue of Liberty came into view.

"Even our two little boys were so happy to see land that they were hopping all over the place."

Carl Biel, twenty-one years old when he and his parents left Meppen, Drenthe, in 1949, didn't go over on a boat chartered for emigrants either.

"We travelled with two other families from neighboring villages to the harbor and boarded the boat that was to take us

to Harwich, England. By six o'clock, we were there. A number of us, knowing very little English, left the boat to stroll around the harborfront. But we were sent back by a pair of policemen. The next morning, we took a train to London, boarded a double-decker bus that brought us to another station, and then went on another train to Southampton where the ocean liner *Aquitowa,* third largest in the world, was waiting to take us to Halifax."

The imposing liner, with four large stacks belching smoke, cut through the water swiftly.

"We really enjoyed the trip. The weather was very good. And there was lots of entertainment on board. Some girls in the crowd got us up early on April 1 with shouts that whales were jumping out of the water. We rushed out of our beds, only to be told: 'April Fool!' After five days, twenty-two hours, and a few minutes, we arrived in Canada."

Another *Gereformeerd* minister, Rev. John Van Harmelen of Assen, Drenthe, sailed on the *Groote Beer* in June, 1952, to visit immigrants in Canada on behalf of his church's *Deputaten der Generale Synode voor Emigratie.* By this time, the ships used for ferrying emigrants had been much improved. No less than seven million guilders were spent on modifying the *Groote Beer* before it was pressed into service.

"It was now in fine shape, with easy chairs and beautiful lounges for conversations," the minister wrote later in his church paper, *Kerk en Gezin.* "Actually, it was too much. No emigrant had ever known these luxuries, and no one would find them in the new country. Everything had been taken care of. There were only two small sleeping lounges, and for the rest, the families were assigned cabins. There was a play area for tots, a laundromat, and a room where the women

Below: John Eisen and his mother (at left) are visited by St. Nicholas and his helper while sailing back to The Netherlands with the Maasdam *in December, 1954.*

Above: As the evening sun sparkles upon the sea, a young couple dreams of a future in Canada. Bottom Right: Emigrants on the way to Canada with the Maasdam *in 1966 take part in a hat parade; at the far left is John Mud of Warga, Friesland, and now of Brantford, Ontario. How different these scenes are from those of the first postwar crossings.*

"Look! There's land over there! That must be Canada!"

Passengers line the deck to look at the shoreline as the Maasdam *travels up the St. Lawrence River in 1956.*

The harbor at Halifax comes into view. The photo was taken from the Groote Beer *in the spring of 1958.*

could do the ironing for their families. Also featured was a large dining room, where the emigrants were fed in three successive shifts. Even the 'spiritual consultation room' had not been forgotten."

Recreation was provided for those who wanted a bit of exercise. On deck, a variety of games could be played with wooden and rubber rings. For those who wanted to relax, films were shown in the theatre. But not too many people attended, according to the minister, because "the films were absolutely no good."

As the Protestant chaplain, Rev. Van Harmelen had his hands full. It didn't take him long to break down the 800 or so passengers by their affiliation: 210 were Roman Catholic, 300 were *Gereformeerd*, 100 were *Hervormd*, a number were *Vrijgemaakt Gereformeerden*, *Baptisten*, *Darbisten*, *Hersteld Apostolischen*, *Gereformeerde Gemeente*, *Christelijke Gereformeerden*, and *Vrij Evangelischen*, and three families were "nothing."

"It required intensive work to get to know this seagoing community within a period of seven days. One had to speak with all the parents and get in touch with all of the many single people. Handing out literature was also an important job. Tamma Batjes from Rolde, who was destined for Manitoba, was an invaluable help. He came to be called *De Elisabethbode*, for this circular had to be handed out every day to everyone aboard ship. On Sunday, we handed out *De Spiegel*, while all the women on board were given an issue of *Moeder*. For the rest, there were numerous tracts, and we also sold Bibles and children's literature, made available by the Dutch Bible Society, after every morning dedication."

Not only emigrants were on board. One hundred students were on a trip to the United States. There were also a number of Swedes, Britons, French, and Pakistanis. A string ensemble on the way to New York to pick up a number of American students provided a couple of highly appreciated concerts.

"The journey itself, which many emigrants had been looking forward to with anticipation, was not always enjoyable. The North Atlantic route is often plagued by fog. The monotonous sound of the foghorn reverberated every two minutes and kept many people awake. During the first days, many were seasick and the drug Amosyt, a celebrated cure, was not universally effective. At times, no more than thirty people showed up for breakfast."

During the devotionals, Rev. Van Harmelen made wide use of hymns that were common to both the Dutch and the English language, such as *Abide With Me, The Church's One Foundation,* and *Onward Christian Soldiers.* Piano accompaniment was provided by Frans De Vries of Alphen aan den Rijn, who had made the news when he placed a work-wanted advertisement in the largest daily of San Diego and paid for it with a box of cigars. He had succeeded in drawing American attention to himself, and one American was so interested that he offered to sponsor him for five years. However, he had to wait another eighteen months before being permitted to enter the United States. That was too long for his liking, so he decided to go first to his parents in Sarnia, Ontario.

"Those seven days serving this floating community were unforgettable, especially since I met many of these families later during my trip through Canada," the

The Sibajak *arrives in Halifax on September 29, 1953.*

minister wrote. "Such reunions were always happy occasions."

"It was an awful experience being tossed up and down on the waves, seeing clothes swinging to and fro on the door while bracing yourself with your knees against the wooden bed board," recalls Mrs. Cornelia Sheehy of Ridgetown, Ontario, who traveled on the *Rijndam* in late March, 1955. "Passengers were advised to hang onto heavy ropes fastened along halls and stairways, for a sudden move of the ship could throw you over."

Although she didn't feel much like eating, she decided to sample a meal announced as a Canadian dinner.

"I was horrified to see that guests were served potatoes with the peel still on them. Corn on the cob, something fed to the pigs in Holland, was also on the table. The Canadians and Americans on the boat, who knew how to eat these things, took them in their hands and ate like cannibals gnawing at bones. I asked myself: 'To what wild country am I going?' "

Jerry Rekker of Brampton, Ontario, who sailed on the *Tabinta* in 1947, remembers the collective sigh of relief when the coast of Newfoundland finally came into sight. It was evening, and the headlights of cars and other signs of life brought sheer joy.

He and his son were among the first ones on deck at the break of dawn. "It was a beautiful sight. We were on the St. Lawrence River, and we admired the hills and the colorful houses. When a train disappeared in a tunnel, our eyes nearly popped out. It all was so different from what we had been used to in Friesland."

In the afternoon, the boat docked at Quebec City, a scheduled stop on the way to Montreal. The seawary passengers set foot on shore. The solid ground felt good. Even those who still felt a bit queasy smiled. They were in Canada at last!

"Everyone had to show their papers, but mine had disappeared without a trace. That's why we were the last ones off the boat. There were a few anxious moments. But the most important thing was that we didn't have to go back."

In the evening, the passengers boarded ship again for the last leg of the voyage. When they awoke in the morning, the *Tabinta* was berthed in Montreal.

Passengers line the rails as the Groote Beer approaches the dock in Montreal.

On Solid Ground

Emigrants on the way to Canada—taking the fastest way.

On Solid Ground

After a ten-day voyage aboard an Italian army boat in the spring of 1951, with not much to see besides the coast of England and an endless stretch of water, the weary passengers arrived at Quebec City. Their relief was profound. They were about to set foot on the soil of the country where they would begin a new life. They were finally there.

"It was on a beautiful Sunday morning," recalls Mrs. Peter Brandsma of the Lethbridge, Alberta, area, a teenager then. "We were surprised that there were so many people on board, since we had not seen most of them before; they had been in bed with seasickness. It was standing room only. No one minded it, though, because the view was spectacular. Lovely white houses were scattered between the trees, and on top of a distant hill stood a little white church with a cross on it. I remembered, then, that here in Canada people worshipped the same God we did. That made me feel as if we weren't so far away from Holland after all."

The passengers disembarked—"most of us walked like real seamen already"—and were welcomed by immigration officials in a large building. Hot chocolate milk, cookies, buns, and other goodies were served. For many people, it was the first solid food they had tasted since shortly after the crossing began.

"It was a blessing, especially for the mothers and the little ones, because they had lost a lot of weight."

As the *Volendam* approached Pier 21 in Halifax in 1950, Berend Kraal spotted *Welcome to Canada* painted in big letters on one of the sheds. He then turned his attention to the people gathered on the dock, trying to seek out a particular face.

"There he is," said his father-in-law, Roelof Van Dijk, who was standing next to him. "There's Flinkert."

Van Dijk was obviously relieved. Berend Flinkert, his wartime friend, who had settled on a farm in the Drayton area of Ontario in 1949, had written that he would be in Halifax to help keep the family together. The emigration authorities had decided to send the elder Van Dijks to British Columbia, their daughter and her

husband to Alberta, and the Kraals to Ontario. Of course, this arrangement did not please them.

In The Netherlands, two of their three crates had been addressed in black paint for Ontario. One had a British Columbia address, just to avoid suspicion. Once in Halifax, the family would try to get that crate redirected. Flinkert had promised his aid.

"He waved when he spotted us," recalls Kraal. "We met him right after he cleared through customs. He told us that he hadn't been able to make much headway with the immigration people. They insisted that we had to go to our places of destination. No amount of talking could change their minds. So he told us: 'We'll have to do without their permission then. You're going with me to Ontario.'"

They left the big hall, where everyone was waiting for the train that would take them to points across Canada, and walked to the shed where the crates were standing. After a bit of searching, they found the three belonging to them, including the one marked for British Columbia.

"Flinkert took out his pocket knife and cut the address out of the wood. Only the name remained. Then he tried at the office to get hold of the shipping papers, but without success. The immigration people were directing the people to specific sections of the train, to make sure they would continue on to their destination after their

There were 21 in Jan H. Griffioen's group on arrival in New York from Utrecht on the Nieuw Amsterdam. *Griffioen was headed for a 40-acre farm in Abbotsford, British Columbia. The children ranged in age from 22 years to one-year-old Josie, who is held in the arms of her mother, Sandrina.*

Docking Procedures

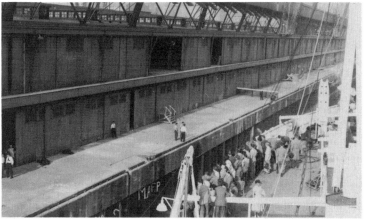

The Waterman *arriving in Montreal in 1955.*

cars had been coupled to other trains along the way. Pretty soon, Flinkert saw that they were keeping an eye on us. He said: 'We'd better get out of here.' Jenny and I stayed, and the others suddenly disappeared. They went to a hotel in the city and left by train for Ontario the next day."

After setting foot in Halifax in 1948, George Eggink was instructed to check if all five of his cases of household effects had arrived with him. That was easier said than done. Dozens of crates were stacked in a hall, and the names printed on the outside were not all visible. So he had no alternative but to crawl here and there and stretch his neck around corners and into dark crevices.

"When I found everything in order, I returned to my wife and children. Some time later, someone tapped me on the shoulder. Two gentlemen stood behind me and asked if I had lost anything. In my broken English, I told them that as far as I knew, I had not. Then they asked me to check my wallet. I had two of them, but that didn't dawn upon me when I felt one in my pocket. No, I said, my wallet wasn't missing. One of the men then produced a wallet from behind his back. I immediately recognized it as mine—one that contained $400, all that I was permitted to take to Canada ($100 for each adult and $50 for each of my four children). It was all that I had. My heart stood still for a moment. 'That belongs to me,' I said. Then they wanted to know what was in it. When I mentioned the $400 and a photo of my family, they gave it to me right away. I offered them a cigarette, but they refused. You know, that experience left me with a good impression of our new compatriots. Generally, over the years, we were not to be disappointed in their cordiality and helpfulness."

Many immigrants weren't too impressed with the Halifax harborfront, or with the city itself. They thought it was a rather dismal-looking place. It certainly was nothing like the bustling world port from which they had set sail.

Even Rimmer Tjalsma, the landing agent in Halifax for the Holland-America Line, found the city so depressing that he looked forward to a "break"—meeting ships in Quebec City or Montreal, the two other major points of disembarkation.

In October, 1954, he wrote an acquaintance in Ontario: "Halifax is still as dull and drab-looking as ever and I'm hoping for an eventual relocation. Any place is better than this hole. I hope it will be Montreal, or Toronto, so that I can return to civilization. As you know, there is nothing doing in Halifax. It's a first-rate place for sailors and people who love fish."

John Snyders, on the way to Alberta, wasn't too impressed with Quebec City.

"When we landed there, we were amazed at the dirtiness and the poverty.

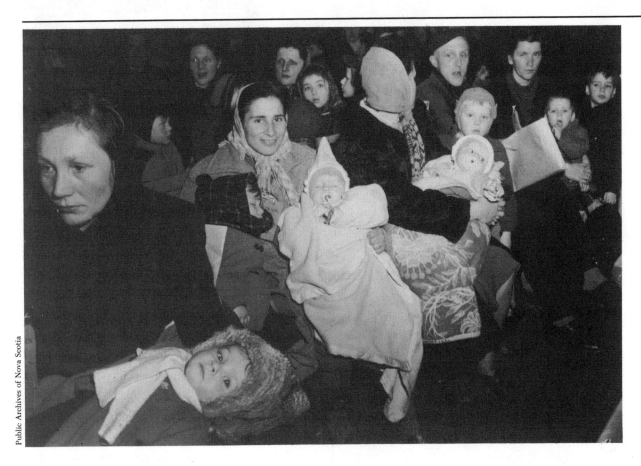

Public Archives of Nova Scotia

Checking In

The large halls at Halifax into which the immigrants were shepherded resembled warehouses. So remarked Rev. H.J. Spier of Rijswijk, Zuid-Holland, who accompanied newcomers aboard the *Waterman* in July, 1953. He wrote about it in *De Spiegel*, the respected Christian weekly.

"The halls were huge, certainly bigger than the space at the Wilhelminakade in Rotterdam. Still, one is able to find his way. He ends up in a bare hall and sits down on a hard bench with other immigrants, waiting for his turn to have his papers inspected."

Rev. Spier told how the customs agents abruptly left the hall at four o'clock, leaving a number of suitcases and other belongings still to be cleared. Many of the immigrants walked about in consternation, asking themselves: "What now? The train won't wait for us!"

"It appeared that the customs people had a break between four and six o'clock.

There really was no reason for anxiety. The first immigrant train wasn't scheduled to leave for Montreal until 7:45. Promptly at six o'clock, the customs people were back on the job, finishing their business with a smile and a helpfulness that seemed to put everyone at ease. I thought of the Canadian soldiers who had to clear S.S.ers out of a factory in Groningen. They stopped the fight when the clock struck at 1 p.m. It was time for lunch! That is Canada: take it easy, and don't worry."

John VanderVliet, the secretary of the Immigration Committee of the Christian Reformed Church, on hand to greet the newcomers, commented to Rev. Spier: "Everything takes care of itself in Canada."

"Indeed," thought the minister. "I've already seen that the pace here is much different than in Holland."

There aren't many happy faces among the immigrants and their small children who have to wait in Halifax. Here they are sitting in the customs building.

An aerial view of the dock and the train station in Halifax.

The Halifax harborfront as seen from George's Island.

Since we had some time before the train left, we went to buy some groceries. We walked along a dirty cinder track. There was nothing growing anywhere. A store stood against a grey and red shale hill, and it was covered on the outside with flattened tin cans that were half rusted. It was a depressing sight. My wife asked: 'John, did they have a war here too?' "

Some immigrants retain bitter memories of the immigration halls: sometimes they were stuck there for days, with little freedom of movement, while officials tried to find them a sponsor somewhere in Canada. One woman recalls that her parents, upset by the cancellation of their original sponsor and their subsequent treatment as virtual prisoners, wrote a letter of protest to Queen Juliana.

Mrs. Anne Hutten of Kentville, Nova Scotia, who arrived in Halifax in 1950 with her parents and eight brothers and sisters, the oldest of whom was eleven and the youngest two months, also has random memories of the immigration building there.

"We had to stay in that hall for two days, because for some reason the authorities had sent another family to the farmer with whom Dad had a contract. So there we were—no job, no destination. Somebody must have scurried around, looking for a farmer who wanted a Dutchman with nine kids, for we suddenly got word at bedtime the second day that we had ten minutes to get on the train. I was in the shower at the time; that was a new experience, after being used to a metal tub on the kitchen floor. I dimly remember other women helping Mom get ready, and being bustled off to the train in the darkness. The station was next to the immigration building and the Hotel Nova Scotian. Until we left, we'd been allowed out of the building only once for a brief walk. The windows had heavy iron bars, as though for criminals, and security was tight. Dad used to talk about that for years—about being shut up like criminals as our welcome to Canada."

Mrs. Hutten, nine years old when she arrived with the *Volendam*, has a few other memories of the time she spent in the immigration hall.

"We were given cornflakes for breakfast, but with very little milk, and my parents complained. A woman finally brought us a jug one evening. We knew absolutely no English other than 'yes' and 'no.' I remember Dad asking a perfect stranger for a match. He had to use gestures, striking an imaginary match, to make himself understood. Gestures got to be a common joke during those first years in Canada. The immigrants used to laugh at themselves and tell stories about how stupid they felt.

Christian and Marie Dobbe, now of Burnaby, British Columbia, would rather forget their first few days in Canada.

Their woes began on board the *Tabinta* in June, 1948, when one of their three young daughters came down with the measles. Before the ship berthed at Quebec City, a second girl was running a fever. The immigration authorities, ever so cautious with cases of communicable disease, ordered Mrs. Dobbe and her three children taken to a hospital by ambulance.

"I was afraid," recalls Mrs. Dobbe, formerly of The Hague. "I didn't know where my husband was. I asked some nurses if they knew, but they couldn't help me. I didn't sleep at all that first night. It was awful."

The next day, her concerned husband showed up at the entrance to the ward with an immigration official. He was not allowed to go beyond the door. He also had had a sleepless night—in the immigration building.

"The girls and I stayed in that hospital for three and a half weeks. The third one had also come down with the measles. My husband came to visit us every day. He said it was just terrible where he was staying. He was being treated like a prisoner for some reason. Whenever he went to the toilet, an official would park himself outside the door."

In the meantime, the authorities steered another newly-arrived family to Dobbe's sponsor, a grain farmer near Nelson, British Columbia. Dobbe, a market gardener in The Netherlands, would have felt a bit at home there. Instead, when the patients were discharged, he was sent to a dairy farmer at Revelstoke. That wouldn't have been too bad, except for one thing: he didn't know anything about dairy farming.

Fred and Coby Prins, who had a sponsor in Ranier, Alberta, also didn't start their immigration happily.

"First, we had troubles going to Canada," he says. "We were expecting our second baby. The *kist* was packed and

A.W. MacKenzie, the minister of agriculture in Nova Scotia, was on hand in Halifax to welcome newly-arrived Dutch immigrants to Canada.

Canapress Photo Service

The Theodorus VanErp family on the roof of Christian Seaman's Home in Hoboken, New Jersey, with the New York skyline in the background. Front to rear they are: Jan, Riekske, Herman, twins Willy and Piet, Maria, Thea, Bernard, Theo, Harry, Gerrit, and Mr. VanErp. Mrs. VanErp holds Nelly. They arrived on the Noordam *and were destined for Windsor, Ontario.*

already on board when Coby had a miscarriage. She was in the hospital for three days of rest—and no visitors. Then she was rushed straight to the boat, and we left. On board, I got a terrible toothache, but there was no dentist on the boat. In Halifax, I was the first one off and to the dentist."

After touring immigrant settlements in Canada in 1952, Rev. John Van Harmelen was ready to go back to The Netherlands to make his report. He accompanied John Vander Vliet, one of the most prominent immigrant helpers who was scheduled to go to Quebec City to meet another throng of newcomers arriving on the *Groote Beer*.

"After saying goodbye at Dundas Street 304 in Trenton, Mr. VanderVliet's home, we took the car to Belleville and the train to Montreal. There we transferred to a sleeper and woke up in Quebec City the next morning. Quebec is a lovely old French city. After finding a hotel room, we went to the harbor, where the *Groote Beer* was moored. A large number of immigrants were just disembarking. Such a bustle! At long last, they were all transferred to either train A or train B. We walked

Ignorant Smugglers

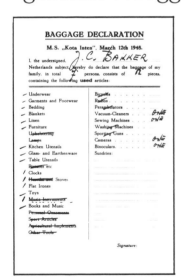

J.C. Bakker filled out this declaration of goods for customs officials in Canada in 1948.

The customs officers were patient with the immigrants, knowing that most of them couldn't understand a word of English or French. But they tended to lose their patience whenever they caught someone trying to smuggle a restricted item into the country. John Eisen, returning from a trip to The Netherlands in 1953, witnessed a few incidents after the *Veendam* had landed at Quebec City.

"An irate officer shouted to a trembling Dutch farmer who tried to import a big box of seed potatoes: 'Don't you know that we have potatoes in Canada?' Out of the suitcase of a young man came a piece of bacon. The officer put his nose to it, and then asked where he had the other half of the pig. The young man tried to explain in Dutch why his mother had packed that piece of bacon into his suitcase. The officer, obviously tired, shook his head, took out the bacon, closed the suitcase, and shouted: 'Next!' A young lady was caught with at least twenty bags of flower seeds.

The officer tried to question her, again with little result."

Smuggling was a well-known word within the Dutch circles. As soon as the government decreed that only so much money could be taken out of the country, people were scheming to circumvent the regulation. And devious ways were devised. Not all of them worked.

In 1951, the Dutch press told the story of an emigrant, whose trip had been subsidized by the government, who tried to get around the exchange controls by investing his money in a new concertina valued at no less than one thousand guilders.

"The man absolutely couldn't play the thing, and that made his musical hobby suspect. The instrument was confiscated forthwith."

Of course, not all smuggling was deliberate. Many of those who had a seed potato or a piece of ham in their luggage were not aware of the restrictions.

through the trains and chatted briefly with many of the new arrivals."

The minister, who returned to Canada permanently soon after, remembers Boukje, a girl from Leeuwarden, Friesland.

"Her fiancé had arranged for her to come over, and was to pay for her expenses. The boat trip had been paid for, but not the train. Boukje, together with some others, had been interned, locked up in the immigration hall, which she felt was a kind of jail. The hall had big doors that were always kept locked. And it had small rooms, like cells, where you had to spend the night. And that Canadian food, she felt, was positively dreadful. She was always escorted by an official of the immigration hall, who kept a careful eye on her. He was responsible for her. Boy, was Boukje nervous."

It was a good thing that VanderVliet was on the scene. He lent her money for the train trip.

"I hope she repaid him. She did look pretty honest. Others were not so. I could tell you a few tales about that. They readily borrowed, but never repaid."

Well, Boukje went back to the immigration hall to pick up her belongings

s.s. Groote Beer

Welcome to Canada

Mogen wij U dit in Uw nieuwe landstaal toewensen nu het ogenblik nadert, waarop U aan land zult gaan in de nieuwe wereld, voor de opbouw waarvan reeds zovele onzer landgenoten eeuwen lang hun beste krachten gegeven hebben en waar ook voor U rijke mogelijkheden openliggen.

Ongetwijfeld denkt U nog met weemoed aan alles, wat U achterliet, Uw familie en vrienden, het land, waar zovele banden U aan binden. Straks zult U het schip verlaten, laatste brokje Nederland, dat U gedurende de zeereis vertrouwd is geworden. En indien U nog enige tijd in Uw haven van aankomst mocht blijven, zoudt U het zien afvaren, terug naar het Vaderland.

Inderdaad, het schip blijft niet, maar laat U achter, doch het zal terugkomen met de vele andere schepen, die in onze dienst varen en zij zullen U steeds weer een groet brengen uit Uw oude Vaderland, post van Uw vrienden die achterbleven, en straks wellicht ook enkele hunner persoonlijk, wanneer zij U in Canada komen opzoeken of zelf als emigranten de overtocht maken.

Wij hopen van harte, dat U een prettige reis hebt gehad en willen U ter herinnering hieraan gaarne dit klein aandenken aanbieden. Het zij U echter méér dan een herinnering, een symbool van de band, die Canada met Nederland verbindt. En al houdt een oneindig grote oceaan deze twee landen gescheiden, dan zult U weten, dat er een schakel is, onderhouden door Uw eigen landgenoten, die als vanouds hun schepen laten varen, niet alléén om U naar het nieuwe land te brengen, maar ook om U straks in omgekeerde richting een bezoek aan Nederland mogelijk te maken.

Wij hebben getracht U bij het regelen van Uw huidige reis zoveel mogelijk behulpzaam te zijn en het zal ons een groot genoegen zijn, dit ook in de toekomst voor U te mogen doen, niet alléén ten behoeve van U zelf en Uw gezin, doch ook voor Uwe vrienden en verwanten.

Indien U er prijs op stelt, voortaan periodiek een berichtje aangaande onze Canada-dienst te ontvangen, verzoeken wij U, bijgesloten kaart, met vermelding van Uw definitieve adres, aan ons kantoor te Montreal te zenden.

Wij wensen U een gezegende toekomst en wachten U in de komende jaren als bezoeker aan Nederland aan boord van onze schepen.

Holland-Amerika Lijn
ROTTERDAM

Printed in the Netherlands

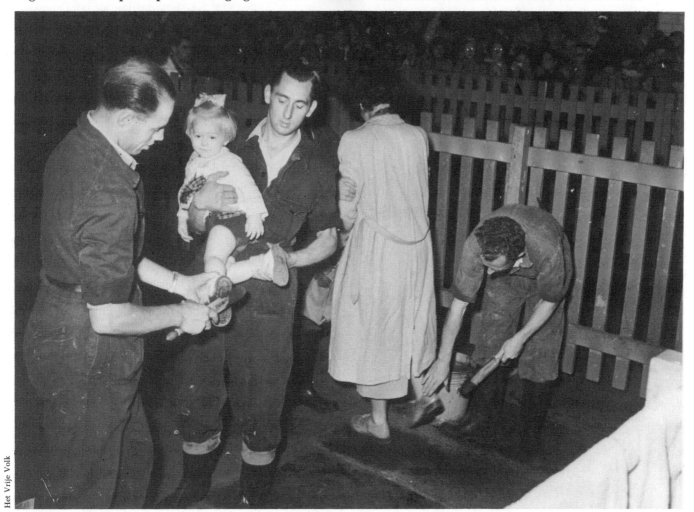

The shoes of emigrants, young and old, were scrubbed free of dirt after a case of foot and mouth disease was discovered in Canada.

Het Vrije Volk

KLM Got Them There

The ones who traveled by airplane in the early 1950s had to go through the same customs procedures, of course. They, too, had to catch a train that would bring them closer to their final destination. The only advantage they had over the boat people was that they got to Canada much more quickly.

John Reinders of Witteveen, Drenthe, decided in 1952 to fly to Canada, rather than go by boat, for two reasons: "In Drenthe, we were pretty far removed from water. You could say we were watershy. But the most important reason was that the farmer who had agreed to sponsor us needed us right away to get things moving for another growing season. We were a bit late already, so we gained quite a bit of time by going with the KLM."

Others went by plane because flying was still a novelty. Most people had never flown before. Some emigrants were troubled by all the publicity about storms, seasickness, and the conditions on some of the ships. And there were some who booked a seat with the KLM simply because it was the most prestigious way to go.

Franx
at Montreal

When the KLM plane landed at Dorval airport near Montreal in the spring of 1953, after a long flight via the Azores, J. Harriet Franx and her husband of Rotterdam were welcomed by the man who had agreed to be their sponsor. They had met him while he was in The Netherlands to visit the grave of his son, a pilot, who had died during the battle of Arnhem in 1944. The man, who held a high position with Imperial Oil, had agreed to guarantee a job and interim accommodation in his own house.

"He and his wife were at the airport with their Cadillac. To simplify matters, they took us to the Mount Stephen Club, a gentlemen's club on Drummond Street. You see, it was Wednesday, ladies' night. The sponsor's wife and I went through a side door, while the men entered through the front. There was a slight problem: my husband was ahead of his time and wore expensive shirts *without* a tie. The frowning steward reached under the counter and produced a ridiculous thing that somehow made the guest acceptable."

John Reinders and his family flew to Montreal in 1952. He says: "We gained quite a bit of time."

and made it back just in time to catch the train for Hamilton, Ontario, where her fiancé would be waiting to pick her up.

Cornelia Annegarn, who came with the *Rijndam* in 1955, couldn't wait to step on shore. But she and the other passengers had to wait for several hours in the Halifax harbor because an Italian immigrant ship had landed just ahead of them.

"Then there was the endless shuffling through halls and corridors where papers had to be checked and rechecked. Some organization gave us a package of cereal at which we marvelled—we could eat it right out of the box. There was the difficult task of trying to find my own belongings in the packed storage rooms and changing all my labels to read Toronto. In Holland, a Canadian immigration officer had told me that I had to go to Winnipeg because Toronto already had all the immigrants it could handle. But I had been assured by a friend: 'Once you are in Canada, you can change your destination.' So that's what I did."

With this done, she could finally step out into the streets of Halifax and breathe deeply the Canadian air, and enjoy the warmth of the sun.

"I was finally on firm ground in the country of my destination. I felt elated. I thought: 'This must be Paradise.' I found a Catholic church, knelt down, and thanked God for the safe trip."

Consternation spread in agricultural circles in Canada in the latter part of 1951. A case of the dreaded foot and mouth disease had surfaced in Saskatchewan—and the finger was being pointed at a young immigrant from West Germany. This was enough to disrupt the best-laid plans of the emigration people in The Netherlands. There was even speculation in the press that Canada, anxious to protect its dairy herds, would restrict the number of newcomers.

A government report stated: "Precautionary steps were taken immediately to prevent the possibility of immigrants bringing the disease to Canada, and all farm immigrants from infected areas in their country of origin were required to submit to disinfection satisfactory to the Department of Agriculture, either prior to embarkation or immediately on arrival in Canada."

When all the fuss died down a bit, it was announced that the Canadian and Dutch governments had reached an agreement that would permit the emigration program to be resumed. But a number of stringent regulations were laid down, particularly for people from the agricultural sector. Emigrants were forbidden to include in their baggage any implements used in the care of animals, such as brooms for cleaning stalls. Work clothes and shoes had to be sent to a disinfection centre. All footwear was to be free of soil, manure and straw. Hay and straw could no longer be used as packing material, something that the authorities had frowned upon for a long time. And so on.

One Dutch newspaper warned: "Evasion of these regulations, upon discovery, could result in another stoppage of the entire emigration to Canada. For the person himself, it could mean no permission to embark or, if discovered in Canada, it could mean immediate expulsion or a long quarantine."

Before stepping on the boat in Rotterdam, the passengers had the soles of their shoes scrubbed clean of soil. But the Canadians didn't take a chance. The new arrivals were welcomed to Canada by having to lift up their feet so that someone could declare that the soles were free of dirt. Others had to slosh through a disinfectant.

The boat travelers were still in the majority in the early '50s. Soon after Jacob Hofstee and his family disembarked at Quebec City on April 25, 1951,

The Seven Seas *is unloaded in Halifax on a wintry day in 1950.*

Members of the John DeJong family from the Groningen area are ready to fly to Montreal in 1952. They would travel on to Picture Butte, Alberta, where DeJong would work on a beef and beet farm.

they started looking for their trunk containing clothes, pots and pans, and other household necessities. They had not had access to it during the voyage as had been promised. A check with the purser had revealed that it had been stored in the main hold with the large containers.

The trunk was found without difficulty. Then, without telling anyone, Hofstee and his son John dragged it to the area where the baggage for the train was stored. They wanted to make sure it would accompany them to their new home—a farmhouse near Chatham, Ontario. The address had been made known to them only after immigration officials had boarded the *Volendam* shortly before its arrival.

When the trunk arrived in Chatham, they found that it had been broken open. A new suit and an older one were missing, as well as some jewelry. Conceivably, the theft had occurred in The Netherlands, and the trunk had been put into the main hold to delay detection.

"There were three or four special trains on the tracks next to the hall," recalls John. "The ones for Western Canada left first, and we were to board the one for Ontario by 3 p.m. Someone who knew a little bit about these things mentioned that there would be no food provided on the train, and that the immigrants should try to get something to eat before leaving Quebec. There was a mad rush across the tracks and the road behind the quay to the little grocery store there. Dad joined the crowd, and came back with a loaf of bread and a pound of butter. That treasure provided sustenance to the family until we arrived in Chatham the next day."

Just off the Volendam *in Quebec City in 1951, Gerard, Hans and Frans VandeWerfhout strike a memorable pose in their pofbroeken.*

Chapter 8

Another Journey

Immigrant children press their faces to the passenger car windows to get a better look at the new, strange country.

Another Journey

One afternoon in late June of 1947, about one hundred and eighty of the weary immigrants who had come with the *Waterman* stepped out of the train at Chatham, Ontario. Most of them were dressed for cold weather on this warm summer day.

One chronicler noted: "The committeemen and others succeeded in getting the small army settled in the waiting buses and, before long, the travelers arrived at the community centre, where they were confronted with tables laden with good things to eat. The Ladies' Aid had exceeded itself in an attempt to welcome friends and relatives from overseas."

John Vellinga, the fieldman of the Christian Reformed Church, kept moving through the babble of adults and the shouts of children, trying to find out whether everyone on his list had arrived. Finally there was a checkmark beside every name.

"In the midst of this gathering of immigrants," the chronicler continued, "the tall figure of Rev. G.J. VanderZiel could be seen as he passed from group to group, patting a child's head or talking to some grownups. His Dutch was not so good—he was from South Dakota. He offered a smile, a word of encouragement, a promise to some downhearted one that everything would be looked after."

One by one, the families and single persons were picked up by their new employers, mostly farmers. Men shook hands, women embraced, and tears were wiped away in the hope that the friendships established on board the *Waterman* and the train would be continued.

When the hall was empty and quiet, Rev. VanderZiel sat down wearily on a bench and murmured: "It will never be the same again. Not for any of us."

Many newcomers had no idea of the immenseness of the new land. They had moved from a small and congested country to the second largest one in the world. Only much later would some learn that Canada was nearly 300 times as big as The Netherlands.

Rev. Harri Zegerius, director of the fledgling Reformed Church in Canada in the early 1950s, recalls boarding an immigrant train in Halifax and being asked

Mr. and Mrs. Dingeman De Leeuw and their children of Piershil, Zuid-Holland, are wearing their tags as the Volendam *approaches Halifax in March, 1951. The couple now lives in Hamilton, Ontario.*

by one of the passengers: "Reverend, will you come and teach catechism in Saskatoon?"

"I had a hard time saying no," he says. "However, I lived in Hamilton, Ontario. You know, those people had no idea of the vast distances in Canada. They came from a country where you could travel from one end to the other in a matter of hours. I had to tell some people who were going to the West that they should stock up on food. They had no idea that they would be stuck in that train for days."

Before the newcomers disembarked from the ship, railway representatives came on board to hand out nametags which also listed destination, name of sponsor, name of terminal or transfer station, and number of the train and the car.

To have to wear a label in a conspicuous way might have felt a bit demeaning. However, the labels prevented many embarrassing moments and mixups. A conductor didn't have to ask the passenger who couldn't understand English where he was going; he merely had to look at the tag.

The railway ticket was usually paid for in advance. The immigrant presented his document to be validated at the station

Tags in place, the passengers are ready to step on shore.   *The map shows the main routes traveled by the immigrant trains.*

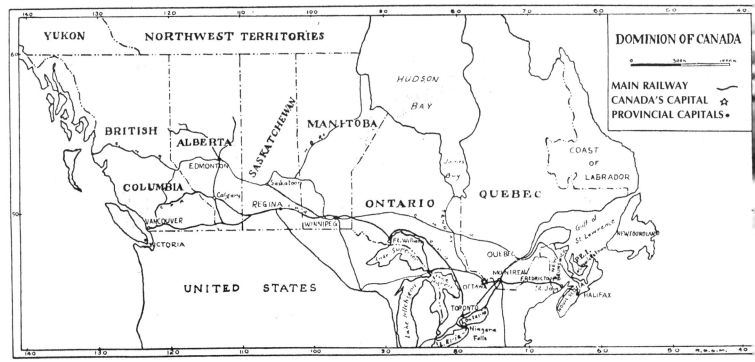

wicket. After this, he could send a telegram to his employer, informing him of the estimated time of arrival.

Once the formalities were completed, the immigrant found a place in the train. Then there was often time enough to head for a store and purchase some food for the journey. Then he settled down, impatient for the locomotive to build up steam and move off toward some place in the interior where he would start his new life.

Representatives of church denominations walked through the aisles, offering advice and words of encouragement. They also handed out literature; Roman Catholics were given their church paper, *Onder Ons*, the ones of the Hervormd faith received the Reformed Church's monthly, *The Pioneer*, and the Gereformeerden were handed the *Calvinist Contact* by a representative of the Christian Reformed Church.

These fieldmen, equipped with lists of all the newcomers, did invaluable work. They were the contact people, the spokesmen. They came to Halifax, Quebec City, and Montreal not only to promote their churches, but to help in whatever way they could.

C.M. Hogeterp, a passenger on the *Tabinta* in 1947, had to wait so long for permission to board a train in Montreal that he decided to take matters into his own hands.

"I gathered together my wife and seven children and shepherded them into a train that was facing west, assuming it was ours. The children, dead tired, soon fell asleep on the hard seats. But in the middle of the night, a train official came on board and told us to go on another train. That one was real dirty. The first thing we did when we arrived in Waterford, Ontario, our destination, was to give the children a thorough washing."

"Three days and three nights in the train—we really hadn't expected that," says Tjasse Heuvel, who headed for Lethbridge, Alberta, in 1947. "The swaying of the train certainly didn't help my wife's motion sickness. At midnight, she had to go to the washroom. After she had struggled to get to it, she couldn't open the door. So she decided to pull on a little rope that was hanging there. Within two minutes the train was motionless; she had pulled the emergency brake! What consternation. The conductor, beside himself

with anger, rushed toward us. We couldn't understand a word of what he was saying, but we were sure there wasn't a kind word among them. It wasn't until an hour later that the train got under way again."

Railway officials distribute passenger tags on board the Sibajak in 1953.

In mid-March of 1952, Ben and Tina Afman of Baflo, Groningen, spent a boring day in Halifax after leaving the *Zuiderkruis* at eight in the morning. Their train wasn't scheduled to leave until the evening. With so many hours to kill, their five children didn't know what to do with themselves. They asked many questions, but their parents didn't have any answers.

The family wandered around the city. They bought bread, butter, and jam, because they had heard that the prices on the train were high. Then they returned to the station, where they chatted with other immigrants.

"On the boat, we had received word that we would be met by a fieldman in Toronto," recalls Mrs. Afman. "We looked for Toronto on the map. We also found the places where our fellow travelers were going and tried to estimate the distances between cities. We thought it would be quite easy to visit each other."

She found the train dirty. Her thoughts wandered back to Groningen, where everything seemed to be so much neater. Surely, she commented to her husband, there must be better train, in Canada. Were the poorest ones reserved for immigrants? If so, why? Immigrants had to pay their fares like anyone else.

The passing scenery was a pleasant diversion. "We journeyed along a beautiful track. Sometimes we traveled between rocks so big that they blocked the sunlight. We saw many summer cottages. In Halifax we had seen so many riches that I couldn't help asking myself why people outside of it lived on rocks. It became dark early, and soon we could see only tiny lights. We were tired and talked-out, so we went to sleep. The seats could be pulled out and used as beds. We didn't need our blankets for the cold, so we could lie on them."

At dawn the next day, she saw mountains.

"When we got closer to Ontario, we were surrounded by flat fields, with snow-capped mountains in the background. It seemed like a fairy tale."

Her husband had only $125 in his pocket when he left The Netherlands. Penny-pinching was the name of the game.

"I'll never know how we ever had the nerve to travel four thousand miles with so little money. We were very careful with what we had, knowing that we probably would not receive a paycheque for a few weeks. We had brought all the way from Baflo a large raisin bread and some cookies packed in foil paper. When we finally needed the bread, we discovered to our dismay that it was moulded. We had tears in our eyes when we threw it out the window. We did save the cookies, and bought just enough on the train to get by on."

The children, not beset by worries about food and the future, romped about. For them, the trip was filled with exciting new experiences. They quickly befriended other immigrant children, and amused themselves in their own little world. Their parents, who were hardly able to smile during the long trip, were relieved when the train approached the Union Station in Toronto and they were told to pack all their belongings and make sure the family was intact. It was 6:45 a.m. when the passengers, feeling stiff-legged and awkward, stepped out.

"In a large hall, we were welcomed by the Red Cross," says Mrs. Afman. "We were treated with milk, coffee, and cookies. The Dutch consul gave a nice speech, welcoming us to Canada and giving us his best wishes for the future. We all had a chance to chat with him, and he gave us some important advice. For one thing, he told us that the rubber boots the

Another view of the dock and railway station in Halifax.

Canadian National Railway

children were wearing would not be warm enough for the Canadian winter. He also asked if we could speak English. We answered that we could speak it a little bit. He told us to keep on talking, Dutch or English—it didn't matter. He said: 'The Canadians are friendly people, and don't ever forget that you know more English than they know Dutch.' We promised to try, and I have to admit that we sure talked a lot of Dutch to the Canadians. They usually just laughed or shrugged their shoulders."

Most of the passengers were picked up by friends, relatives, or their new bosses. Some boarded buses. The Afmans were directed by their fieldman to another train, which would take them to Meaford, on the southern shore of Georgian Bay, where a farming job had been arranged. Everything seemed to be going according to plan. There were long faces, however, when the fieldman said that the train would not be leaving until the next morning.

With time on his hands, Afman decided to check out a tip from another immigrant that a job and accommodation were available at Lindsay, northeast of Toronto. He went by bus, leaving his wife and children on the train.

"It was a long day for us," says Mrs. Afman. "My husband had forgotten to leave the keys for the suitcases. That meant the children's games were locked up. We went for a walk, but all we saw were dirty houses and littered streets. It was so cold and windy that we were glad to be able to get back on a train. The rest of the day we looked out of the windows and waited. At around four o'clock, it started getting dark. And we didn't have any food left . . ."

After four hours in a dark railway car on a lonely stretch of track, mother and children heard a familiar voice talking.

As the Groote Beer *docks at Halifax in June, 1959, the harbor facilities look as dismal as ever.*

Halifax Entry

Scenic Journey in the Offing

The rugged beauty of the ever-changing Canadian countryside left many passengers on the immigrant trains spellbound. How different everything looked from the flat, tidy, crowded country they had said goodbye to. Here there were rolling hills, forests, immense rocks, drab wastelands, endless stretches between settlements, shallow, fast-flowing streams.

Others weren't impressed. They were preoccupied with their young ones and with worries about the unknown. Some people started comparing; in The Netherlands, the cows looked healthier, the houses and barns were much neater, the grass was greener, the cities didn't appear so drab, the trains were more comfortable and considerably cleaner . . .

But most of the passengers realized that Canada couldn't be the same as The Netherlands, that they were in a young country with lots of room and with an obvious need for more manpower. They were excited by the terrain that flashed by.

The trip to the West taxed the immigrants' meagre reserves of patience and strength. How tiring it was to sit on a hard seat for days on end, enduring heat and dust in the summer and cold drafts in the winter. Yet the landscape continued to leave them in awe: the dense forests of northwestern Ontario, the vast stretch of prairie, and the majestic, snow-capped Rocky Mountains. Until such a train ride, few had grasped the natural beauty, the diversity, and the immensity of the country they had decided to adopt.

Boarding the Train

The twins are in harness so they won't get separated or lost during the trip to their new home. The large family below, some of them carrying boxes of sandwiches, boards coach No. 55.

Canadian National Railway

Moments later, a policeman escorted Afman to his family.

"We ate, finishing all the food in the suitcase. I can't even imagine what little Peter was eating at only a year and a half. Certainly no baby food from little jars."

Between bites, Afman informed his wife that neither a job nor a house was waiting for them in Lindsay. They could move in with a Dutch family, and then look for a job, but the uncertainty of that didn't appeal to him. The couple decided to continue on to Meaford.

Many other people who traveled to the West had similar complaints—the monotony and the conditions were depressing. Their boat trip had been difficult, and then having to sit for days in a train—it was almost too much.

Henry and Fredrika Jentink of Grande Prairie, Alberta, recall: "The train ride in 1947 was awful. Four days and four nights on a dirty train. We had very little money, so we bought bread and milk when the train stopped. Sometimes a piece of bread can taste so good, but after

four days, I was so sick of bread, I couldn't even eat it."

Willem VanderMolen, on the way to Coaldale, Alberta, in 1951, remembers: "We ran into a dust storm in Saskatchewan. What a mess in that train. We were eating more dust than food, which we prepared on a little stove."

Mrs. Peter Brandsma, a single girl when she landed with her family at Quebec City in 1951, says: "We spent the day in the city, then boarded a train for the trip to the West. What a trip that was! The engine of our train had quite a pull, and put out a lot of smoke. With a strong wind blowing, can you imagine what we all looked like? Even washing ourselves three times a day, we looked more black than white."

John Eisen, traveling to northwestern Ontario in the summer of 1949, didn't mind the train ride. The shrill whistles sounded before every crossing woke him up more than once during the night; however, during the day, there was always something new to see.

Spending the Night

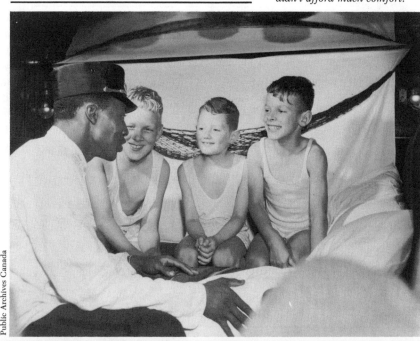

Three youngsters, just off the Waterman in 1947, make friends with a Canadian Pacific employee. But the regular immigrant coaches (below) didn't afford much comfort.

Public Archives Canada

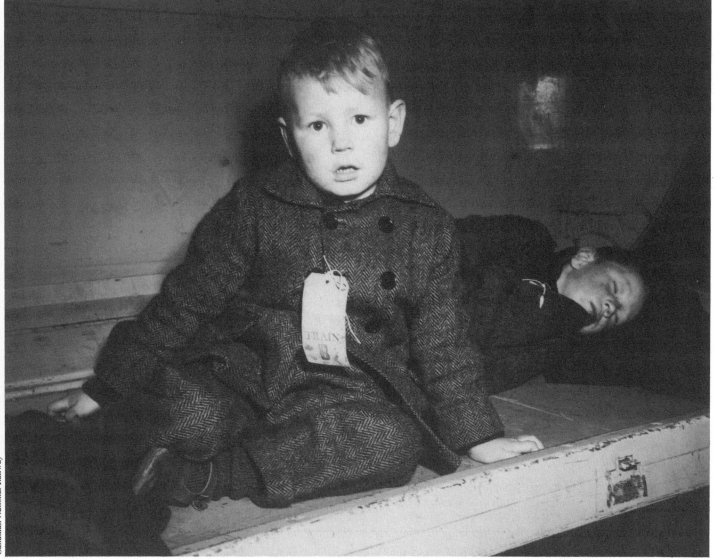

Canadian National Railway

Nova Scotia and New Brunswick

This was the first view of rural Canada for immigrants who left Halifax during the day: rolling pastureland, acres of trees, here and there a house or a barn.

Public Archives of Nova Scotia

"Along the railway line, we could see a lot of small towns, lumber mills, and Indians. The sights added to the great adventure."

The family hadn't bought any food before boarding the train in Quebec City. Eisen recalls: "A tall Negro came by often with a basket full of sandwiches, chocolate bars, and cold drinks. However, my older brother, the keeper of our wallet, often just let him pass. I grumbled about how thirsty I was, but I always got the same answer: 'Go to the tap. There's enough cold water there.' He was a little stingy with the money. No wonder, considering the few dollars we were allowed to take with us to Canada."

The Eisens arrived at the station in Thunder Bay around six in the morning, but had to wait for a connecting train to Stratton until three the next morning. They had no clue what a.m. or p.m. meant. One of the railway employees took John's brother aside, pointed to a big clock, and tried to explain it all to him. Finally the mother and her two sons

Sometimes the Fumes Spoiled Your Appetite

S.P. Knuist and his wife, on the way to Kamloops, British Columbia, early in 1953, settled down for five days of train travel.

"Without a warm meal, we began to feel weak," he says. "The fumes from the train didn't give us much of an appetite. We took a nibble now and then, but found the food was either too sweet or tasteless. We slept on the hard wooden seats, under a single blanket we were lucky to have taken with us. Around Winnipeg, it was so cold that the drinking water froze."

The trip became dreary. There wasn't much to see as the prairie country flashed by.

"To pass the time, we played cards with people who were going to the same area. Now and then, we went for a stroll through the train. We couldn't help but chuckle over the sight of diapers hanging on makeshift clotheslines. At stopovers, we ventured outside for a breath of fresh air. But we didn't dare to go too far, for fear that the train would leave without us."

Mrs. S.P. Knuist tries to relax during the long trip to British Columbia.

understood that they had a lot of time to kill.

"Just outside the station, someone took a picture of me in my *pofbroek* (a popular style of pants for boys)," says John. "That might have been for the local paper. Then we entered a restaurant, because the sandwiches on the train certainly hadn't filled us. Well, to our great surprise, it was a Chinese restaurant. We marvelled at the variety of people we had met so far in Canada—Indian, Negro, Chinese, and what not. Before we ordered, the waiter brought us three big glasses of ice water. We wondered whether ice water was the national drink of Canada. My brother ordered three egg sandwiches. 'Plain or toasted?' the waiter asked. My brother, thinking he had heard the word 'plane,' answered: 'By boat.' Again there was the question: 'Plain or toasted?' This time, we all tried to say: 'No plane.' The Chinese bowed slightly and left. Well, we got lots of toast, butter, eggs, and jam. My mother enjoyed the toast—it was something new —but she lost her appetite for the eggs."

After breakfast, they headed downtown and shopped in a supermarket. Then they strolled to a large park where they enjoyed peanut butter sandwiches and oranges. That night, they watched their first baseball game. After trying to sleep a bit in the open air, they returned to the station to await their train.

"The next night, we arrived in Stratton. Our farmer was waiting for us. He had an old car, with a burned interior. A handshake, a smile, and a few words—and we were on our way to his farm. Suddenly a tremendous thunderstorm struck. It was eerie. For the first time in Canada, I was ill at ease; I wondered where the farmer was taking us. When we arrived at the farmhouse, however, my fears dissolved. The farmer's wife was very talkative and friendly. She had coffee and pie ready for us, and even our beds were made."

Even though she wasn't feeling well, Mrs. Elly Werfhorst found the train ride from Quebec City to Toronto in 1951 an interesting experience.

"In Montreal, an immigrant asked if he could leave the train and go to a bank to cash a cheque for the Bank of Montreal. He thought he could cash it only in Montreal. Of course, the train wasn't held up for him."

She was sitting next to a farm boy. He looked at his hands, and commented:

An immigrant train heads inland.

Passengers leave the train at Moncton, New Brunswick, to stretch their legs.

A view from the train: farmers planting potatoes in New Brunswick.

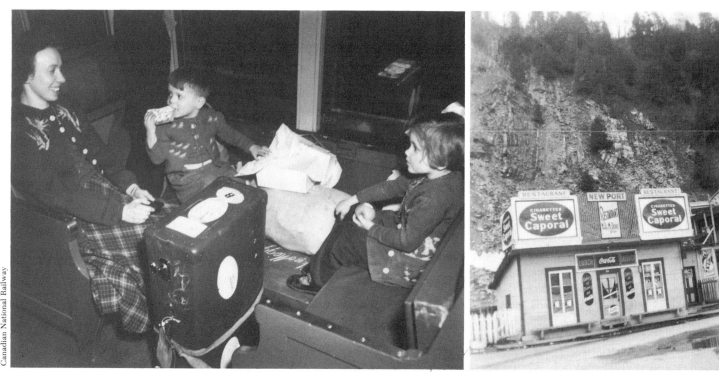

Before getting on the train, many immigrants bought bread and fruit at little stores like the one at Wolfe's Cove, near Quebec City. They had been told that food prices on the train would dent their budgets.

"They're getting soft. Haven't used them for nearly two weeks."

Elly asked him where he was headed. "Kingston." Did he know anybody there? "No." Did he know any English? "No."

"I gave him my little dictionary and showed him how to use it. He studied it for hours. Everyone around us was asleep when we stopped at Kingston. My farm boy disappeared into the night. As far as I could see, no one was there to welcome him at two o'clock in the morning."

Landscape flashed by George Eggink in 1948 as he peered out of the train window. He wasn't impressed. The forests and hills were so unlike the neatly cultivated rural areas he had left behind in The Netherlands.

The stretches of forest seemed endless. What a lot of pioneering one could do in Canada, he thought. Here and there fields were cleared, but the farmhouses and barns were often ramshackle and unpainted. The fields were hilly and scarred with stones. Nothing was growing yet, though in The Netherlands the oats were already sprouting. Even the livestock seemed scrawny.

"I had never seen a Jersey or a Guernsey before. Comparing them with the Holsteins I'd known in Holland, I wasn't very impressed. I was glad that I spotted Holsteins when we arrived at my sponsor's farm near Cornwall."

The vastness and the beauty of rural Ontario left Arie Verduyn spellbound in 1952. He had heard about all the room in Canada—that The Netherlands could fit into southern Ontario with room to spare. Yet the immensity didn't sink in until he had seen it with his own eyes.

There were a number of other things that struck him on his way to Sarnia, Ontario, after he and his family had flown to Montreal. He wrote about them in his book, A Family Chronicle.

"The ever-present, ugly hydro and telephone poles with their transformers and sagging wires were as intruding obstacles, interfering with our attempts to evaluate what architectural merits the mostly look-alike houses had, if any. In The Netherlands, all conductors, except high voltage transmission lines and railroad telegraph lines, were buried so that in villages and cities our eyes could feast on new and old examples of designs by master builders. So far, we had known only clay roof tiles with a retreating dark brown, red or grey color. Here, the large

Quebec Stop and Lunch on the Train

A view of Quebec City from the train.

areas with shingles in a surprising variety of bright colors could not be passed unnoticed. Then there were the roads. With a few exceptions, as in Montreal, they were wide and straight, yet many miles were unpaved, though very useable, gravel roads, which we hardly saw in Holland . . ."

Verduyn, now of Burlington, Ontario, also observed rather quickly the tolerance of Canadians toward different religious views. And he couldn't help but be astounded by an apparent taboo. "I was accustomed to finding a convenient tree or other screen for relieving myself. When I did so behind a column at the construction site of my first job, a fellow worker warned me that this practice could land me in jail."

At the airport in Montreal in 1957, Joe and Kitty Vaessen were told by immigration authorities that they would be bused to the train station, where they could board a train for Toronto at 4:30 p.m.

"I looked at my watch. That meant we had to wait six hours! In Amsterdam, I

Mrs. Dini Hendriksen and her two-year-old son, Henry, stretch their legs while their train stops in Capreol, Ontario, in 1951. Now she lives in Delta, British Columbia.
Below: The train pulls out of Toronto.

Ontario Destinations

was able to catch a train to my home town every hour. From that moment on, we discovered that we had left a comparatively comfortable little country and had come to one that was new and strange in many ways."

Leo Hoens, who boarded a train in Quebec City in 1951, couldn't believe his eyes when he saw adult Canadians pick up newspapers and turn first to the comics section. He had just come from a country where politics was in the forefront of discussion. He thought: "Are people here more interested in the comics than in the news?"

Mrs. Mary Provoost, single when she came here in 1948: "One of my first impressions was one of beauty. Most of the houses were surrounded by neatly-cut lawns, bushes, and flowers. That wasn't the case in Holland or at least not in the country. It was early June, a beautiful time of year in Canada."

Nico De Jong recalls: "While waiting for a train in Montreal in 1952 to take me to the Maritimes, I did a little bit of shopping. Was I pleasantly surprised! A cup of coffee cost ten cents, a package of cigarettes twenty cents, and a bottle of Coca-Cola seven cents."

While the immigrant trains continued to roll across the land, some people cursed the conditions, comparing their situation to what they had left behind. Others were impressed with the natural beauty around them. The various memories are still sharp and clear.

Sid De Haan remembers a moving experience from the time when he and his bride, Alice, were on the way to Edmonton in early May, 1953: "As we pulled into a railway station in a small town, a waitress catapulted out of the coffeeshop and shouted: 'Welcome to Canada!' I can still see her standing there, arms wide open, a broad smile on her face."

Geertrui Beldman noted in her diary in 1950: "A couple of passengers try to

At top left, Adrian and Nelly Verburg step out at Chatham, Ontario, in 1949. In the same year, Dick Both and his family (bottom left) arrive at Owen Sound, Ontario. In 1954, Mrs. J.F. Beckman comes out for a breath of fresh air during a stop. Below, Teunis Schinkel and his family prepare to board at Halifax in 1953.

Above: Johanna Fohkens and her travel crib got a lot of attention in Chatham, Ontario, in 1951.

organize a church service in our compartment. Somebody reads a sermon. But I just can't stay awake. I have a hard time keeping my eyes open during the singing, even though one of the women feels it her duty to keep me awake by poking me in the ribs!"

John Snyders, who headed for Alberta, remembers: "The special trains reserved for the immigrants were dirty, with no dining cars and no heat. I don't think that they had high priority. Sometimes we would pull off on a side track for a long time while we waited for a freight train to pass. During such stops, we would get off to look for wood along the tracks. Then we could start the wood stoves to cook some food and warm ourselves. In Winnipeg, I got off and bought some candles so that we could heat milk for the baby."

A welcoming committee was at the station in Toronto when the train carrying Kees Verburg and his family pulled in. Recalls daughter Ann, then twenty-one years old: "A group of young people took my brother Nick and me to a nice little restaurant, where we were treated to pancakes and our first-ever milkshake. Our parents also were taken somewhere and entertained. We all met again at the station in time to catch our Chatham train. I will never forget the pleasure of that encounter."

One immigrant woman had a harrowing experience while traveling by train to Red Deer, Alberta, in 1959: "My husband and his sister, who had come with us, hurried off the train in Regina to buy some food. They didn't go through the official exit, where they would have been told

At left, a group of immigrants who came on the Waterman *in June of 1947 are waiting at the station in Newmarket, Ontario, for their sponsors to pick them up. Below, Ed DeJong waves to his brother, Harry, who came to pick him up at the station in Hamilton, Ontario, in June, 1949.*

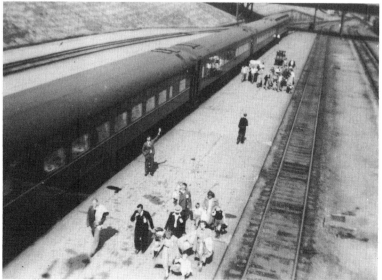

that the stop was only for twenty minutes, instead of the regular forty minutes, because we were behind schedule. So the train left for Moose Jaw before they were back. You can imagine our consternation. My oldest boy begged me to get the conductor to stop the train. Finally I got the children settled for the night, but sleep was out of the question for me. Another passenger assured us that the train would stop for an hour at Moose Jaw and that my husband would be able to catch up with us there. Sure enough, three minutes before the train was to get under way again, they both walked in, laughing and greatly relieved. They had hitch-hiked. The cost: $10."

Once, in 1948, when an immigrant train stopped at a station in New Brunswick and some people got off to do some shopping, they found on returning that the train had left without them. A telegraph operator pounded out a message, requesting the train to wait at the next station. Meanwhile, the stranded people hailed a taxi and sped in pursuit along a road that ran parallel to the tracks. Soon the train passengers looked out their windows to see a honking taxi with its occupants waving wildly at them.

John Visser of Elmhurst, Illinois, who represented *Stichting Landverhuizing Nederland* in Canada in 1948-49, working through the Dutch agricultural attaché in Ottawa, remembers when a passenger on the way to Lacombe, Alberta, was left stranded.

"We were scheduled to make a half-hour stop at Moose Jaw, Saskatchewan, to take on water and coal. Most of the people in the hot, dirty immigrant coaches got off

Jack Dykstra on his way out west at the Nakina station. The sign reads: Winnipeg 503.8 miles; Toronto 704 miles; Montreal 854 miles. Below is one of the northern stations the trains passed through.

Canadian National Railway

and hurried across the road to find the best buys in a grocery store. The dining car at the front of the train was too expensive for them. Well, it turned out that the half-hour stop was shortened to make up time. After the train had been under way for ten minutes, I was informed that a man was missing, and that his wife and nine children were on the train with no money and food. The woman didn't even have the tickets. I thought that this was a dreadful thing to happen to anyone, and I expected to find a woman hysterical and in tears. I dreaded to go to her, feeling a bit guilty myself. When I finally gathered up enough courage to face her, I found her perfectly at ease and not worried at all. She said that her husband was old enough to take care of himself. Other passengers gave her food, and some who were also going to Lacombe lent her money. The conductor issued new tickets. When I visited Lacombe a few months later, I met the lost man. I thought he would be quite angry with me. Far from it. He said he'd had a great time in Moose Jaw. As he had been walking the streets in yellow wooden shoes and with loaves of bread tucked under his arm, an ex-Canadian soldier who had served in Holland had spotted him. When the problem was explained, the stranger took him home for supper and made sure that he got on the next train."

The mixups occurred even in June of 1947. Cor Groenewegen, on the way to a farm at Lefroy on Lake Simcoe in Ontario, put himself in the hands of the people who were at the train station in Toronto to assist the newcomers. After all, the only English words he knew were, "I speak no English."

"People helped the immigrants transfer to different trains," he says. "We got help too. Someone took hold of our travel basket and high-chair and directed us and the five children to a train. When we had traveled for some time, the conductor ex-

A prairie landmark: the grain elevator.

Into the Prairies

There's not much grass for the cattle in the summer heat.

Canadian National Railway

amined our ticket, and said: 'You are on the wrong train!' We didn't understand him. He came back with a translator, who told us that the people in Toronto had put us on the wrong train. We were headed for Brantford instead of Bradford. He advised us to get out in Hamilton, head back to Toronto, and then get the train to Bradford."

That's why he found himself in the midst of a reception in Hamilton given by members of the local Dutch community. The *Hamilton Spectator* recorded it: "Four trains screeched to a stop . . .

Groups of Red Cross Reserve girls ran to the platforms with trays of doughnuts and bottles of milk. In waiting rooms, welcoming parties grouped at doors . . . to give the first welcome in their native tongue to more than two hundred Dutch immigrants who arrived for farm work in this vicinity. Conductors barely got the step in place at the train door when eager, happy, travel-tired and a little bewildered, smiling Hollanders poured out of carriages. Little children, newly-married couples, one Canadian serviceman's fiancée, older people, a sixteen-

Some Western Stops

During a stop on the way to Edmonton in 1953, Mrs. Alice DeHaan takes a stroll to stretch her legs.

The Polets of Leeuwarden, Friesland, on their way to Winnipeg in 1958.

Dutch immigrants arrive at the station in Winnipeg in late May, 1951.

An immigrant train heads farther west.

Another scene from Winnipeg: the first task is to collect the baggage.

year-old boy, a two-month-old baby . . . groups who arrived here were as varied as that."

In mid-October, 1951, immigrant parents got separated from their baby. The child's father, George Fohkens of Sarnia, Ontario, and formerly of Dokkum, Friesland, recalls the details: "We arrived in Toronto at around six in the morning. I left the dining car, where I had been drinking coffee with a friend, and returned to my wife. She had just awakened, and asked sleepily: 'Where have you been?' When I told her, she said she wouldn't mind having a coffee too. So we both went, leaving Johanna, our daughter of six months, asleep in her travel crib. Suddenly we realized with shock that the dining car was being uncoupled from the rest of the train. Our baby and all our baggage were moving away from us! What fright and consternation! Hardly knowing a word of English, we tried with sign language to explain what was happening. Somehow, the person behind the counter understood us. He left to make inquiries, and returned after a few minutes

From a train window: the awesome, fruitful prairies.

Canadian National Railway

Canadian National Railway

A family lines up for the photographer in April of 1950.

Edmonton

June, 1947: an immigrant family, at the end of the road in Edmonton, can still smile at the camera.

The Delleries family arrives in April, 1948.

Above: The train stops in Jasper, Alberta, where the Syrt Wolters family poses (right).
Below: The railway station in Banff, and a magnificent view of the Rockies.

In the Rockies

with the news that everything would be okay. Our section of the train would return, but on another track. We waited on the platform for what seemed like hours. When the train section finally came back, we jumped on board. And there was our baby, still sleeping soundly."

Mrs. Koob Kollen wrote in her diary in 1948: "After the train left Quebec City, we passed through picturesque countryside. The river lay on one side, with forest and rocky terrain on the other. The landscape kept changing. Nearly every house had a car in the driveway. At around eight in the evening, we arrived in Montreal. We crossed a bridge that seemed endless. This is a very large city and well lit. Here's where we said farewell to the first immigrant, a young bachelor who had spent a lot of time with us on the boat. Somebody picked him up, and we waved as he pulled out. Then we went on into the darkness. Once in a while, a waiter would come by with slices of chocolate cake and oranges (twenty-five cents each) and various other foods. When we got sleepy, we simply pulled out the seat so that we could lie down. It was hard, of course, but with something under your head and a coat to cover you, it wasn't too bad. There wasn't much chance of sleeping anyway. The train kept stopping all night, and people kept getting off. At seven-thirty in the morning, we arrived in Toronto, and we all had to get out."

Women from the Red Cross escorted the Kollens to a large waiting room and served them coffee and cake. Then, to their dismay, they learned that their sponsor in Listowel, Ontario, had backed out. A new one had been arranged for them near St. Catharines, Ontario.

"One other couple was heading for St. Catharines, so we resolved not to let this get us down. We were told that everything would work out just fine. When we arrived in St. Catharines, there were people waiting for us, including Rev. Adam Persenaire. It turned out that the man who came to pick us up didn't have the same name that appeared on our card. But he took us along anyway. Instead of a dairy farm, we ended up on a fruit farm. The grower's wife had prepared a table outside, under the trees, and that's where we enjoyed a hearty meal."

Mixups were not uncommon. Sometimes they were unavoidable. But they were the last kind of welcome the weary immigrants needed. Jerry Rekker knows.

"We were so dependent on others. They forgot to let us off at the train station in Belleville, Ontario, so we got out at the next stop, Trenton. It was five o'clock in the morning. Our farmer arrived at the Belleville station, didn't see us, couldn't find anyone who knew anything, and left for home to milk the cows. We waited in that deserted station in Trenton for five hours. Our youngest was ten months, and we didn't have a cradle or a baby-carriage. Did we feel relieved when the farmer showed up at ten o'clock. We must have looked ragged when we arrived at the farm. I can still see the farmer's wife shaking her head."

Young Dutch farmers arrive in Calgary in 1964. The vistas of Western Canada often left Dutch immigrants breathless.

Canadian National Railway

In a rare act of kindness, the farmer gave his new laborer the week off to let him get adjusted to the environment and help his wife organize the household.

Willem Buitenwerf and his family went through the same experience at the train station in St. Catharines in 1952—they were left standing at 10:30 on a frigid February night, even though word of their intended arrival had been sent to the minister, the boss, and a foster brother.

"Nobody was there to pick us up. I was a bit worried, of course, and wondered: 'What's what?' A taxi driver who was there to pick up two persons spotted us and saw that something wasn't right. He came over and asked what the problem was. We couldn't really tell him in English, but I guess he must have understood somehow. He asked where we were going, so we showed him the address. He said 'Come on,' and all five of us piled into the taxi . . ."

To John Booy, it seemed as if nothing could go wrong. His trip across the ocean in August, 1948, had been a joy. On the train from Quebec City to Winnipeg, a courteous fieldman had looked after all their needs, including the sending of a telegram to the sponsor in British Columbia. In Winnipeg, where the train had to stop for five hours, Booy's uncle, who owned a fox and mink ranch, was at the

station to greet him and to show him around a bit. Everything went according to schedule.

Until . . .

"When the train started up again, we were in the British Columbia car. Seven of us sat together—my wife and I, two other couples, and a single girl—and we enjoyed each other's company. At about ten o'clock on Sunday night, when we were well into British Columbia, the train stopped suddenly and we were told to transfer to another car. We didn't even have time to say goodbye to our newfound friends. We sat alone as our train continued on. Close to midnight, it stopped. There we were, not knowing one word of English, and it was pitch-black outside. We thought: 'What have we gotten ourselves into?' There was somebody in the ticket office, but he didn't want to listen to us. We tried again twenty minutes later. Finally he phoned the police. They in turn phoned a taxi, which brought us to the address on our luggage—a farm at Cloverdale. The farmhouse was in total darkness. The taxi driver knocked and the occupant, half asleep, opened up."

The man hung back in the shadows, and mumbled something about their being at the wrong address. He was expecting a couple with one child. The cabbie and the farmer went inside to converse while Booy and his wife waited outside. After a few minutes, the driver left and the farmer brought the suitcases inside.

Then, at last, he asked his guests to come in.

"There sat another wild-west man. He knew a bit of German—his wife was a Romanian—and he was able to tell us that the women had gone to Vancouver to pick us up and that they hadn't come back yet. We could sleep on the couch. Well, were those women surprised to see us lying there when they returned empty-handed."

Booy was so unsettled by the turn of events that he greeted the women with the words, "Bye, bye."

Only a few immigrants were left on the train when it arrived in Charlottetown, Prince Edward Island, one day in 1952. At the station, there was the now familiar scene: the welcoming handshakes by friends or strangers and the quick departure to the new home. Finally, only one immigrant—twenty-two-year-old Nico De Jong—was left.

"You know, I did feel awful then," he recalls. "Here I was, in a strange country, and all the people who had been close to me for days were suddenly gone. All that talk about adventure before I had left Holland seemed a bit hollow now. To make matters worse, I was told that the office would close at 7 p.m., an hour or so before my sponsor was to pick me up. I was a bit confused, and stayed in the office. The man in charge took me by the hand, led me outside, and locked the door. Then it began to rain. Believe me, this was all too much for me, and I had to wipe away tears."

In Halifax, Henry Roefs got a shock when he was informed by immigration officials that work had been arranged for him in Manitoba. He told them that his family had been booked for Ontario—Ajax to be exact—and that a Roman Catholic priest was their sponsor. A couple who had become their friends during the English-language lessons, and who had emigrated a few months earlier, would also be waiting for them.

"We're not going to Manitoba," Roefs said resolutely. "We're going to Ajax. There must be a mixup."

The authorities, however, changed their minds only when they got confirmation from the priest that he was indeed the sponsor and that he was expecting the family.

The priest and the Dutch friends were at the station in Pickering when the train arrived in the early morning hours. It was still a half hour's drive to the home of the friends, where the Roefs would stay for a few days until their own place was ready for occupancy. Everyone was too exhausted to talk.

However, before he said good night, the priest did pass on some information: Roefs would work in a textile factory and the family would move into a house owned by

In many areas of Canada, the early postwar settlers made it a point to get together socially on a regular basis. This fellowship was essential. It ranged from a few people getting together every week to play checkers and chess to more elaborate outings such as the monthly entertainment program for the Dutch people in Edmonton. This photo was taken in June, 1952.

MONTHLY ENTERTAINMENT

The building in Vancouver which once provided temporary lodging for newly-arrived immigrants.

the firm. Even that night, Roefs, a farmer, thought: "I'm not a factory worker. We've got to start saving money right away so that I can buy a farm."

The phone rang at 11 p.m. in the Hamilton home of Rev. Harri Zegerius, director of the Reformed Church in Canada. People were waiting to be picked up at the station. He hurried to his car and sped along the darkened streets, wondering what adventure was awaiting him this night.

Somehow, he got all the people, their suitcases, and other baggage to his home. Then he called the fieldman of the Christian Reformed Church, because some of the immigrants were for his care. Finally, everyone settled down for a good night's rest.

But then at 2 a.m., the phone rang again. An Austrian family had arrived at the station. Would Rev. Zegerius put them up for the night?

Back he went. He took the family to a little hotel and paid for a room. In the morning, he left them in the care of the local immigration authorities.

For those charged with the awesome responsibility of looking after the thousands of people who poured into Canada, the work was never finished.

A truck was waiting at the station when Mr. and Mrs. J.C. Bakker and their five children of Scherpenzeel, Gelderland, arrived in the Niagara Peninsula in 1948. A tarpaulin cover lay crumpled in the back.

"The driver told us that the boss, the owner of a nursery, had instructed him to

pull the cover over us," says Bakker's oldest son, Dave, of St. Catharines, Ontario. "He didn't want people gawking at us. He thought that we would be wearing native costumes and wooden shoes."

The family's house, cramped and dismal, was painted one shade of grey inside and out. The Salvation Army mattresses were soiled. Dave's little sister looked at the stains and asked: "Mommy, when will we be home?" Tears rolled down Mrs. Bakker's cheeks.

The first person to visit the family was a life insurance salesman. Next came a Baptist gospel minister. The third visitor, a Presbyterian minister, prayed and read a passage from the Bible, and received a warmer welcome. Rev. Adam Persenaire, home missionary of the Christian Reformed Church, knocked on the door next. The Bakkers liked him too. For some time, the family went to the Christian Reformed Church in St. Catharines on Sunday mornings and to the Presbyterian church in the evenings.

The next visitor was a prewar immigrant, not from The Netherlands, who brought along groceries and some comforting words: "I know what it feels like to be an immigrant; we were treated like mud. I don't want that to happen to you."

The editor of the weekly *Beamsville Express* also stopped by. Bakker, asked for his first impression of Canada, told him: "As to your country, I'll tell you more in about a year, though I like what I have seen of it. But my first impression is freedom. There is very little freedom in Europe today, and it won't be long before all Europe is taken over by the communists."

Teun Hunse avoided the unpleasant train ride from Halifax to southwestern Ontario in 1950. While the others in the family went by rail, he and two of the other older children went by car—a 1938 Chevy that their father had decided to take along to Canada.

"We just stayed on Highway 2," he recalls. "We figured that we couldn't get lost that way. The going was tough at times; in Quebec, for example, some parts of the highway were still gravel. But we got to see a bit of Canada that way. We slept in the car at night. I can remember my sister being scared, unable to sleep. She imagined bears or other wild animals attacking the car. After four days on the road, we finally arrived in the Niagara Peninsula."

Chapter 9

New Homes

New Homes

John Rupke, who owned a chicken business in Burlington, Ontario, took a one-storey, 20-foot by 20-foot henhouse with him when he joined the first settlers of Holland Marsh, north of Toronto, in the spring of 1934. Dutch families were encouraged to locate in this newly diked-in area, where the black soil was ideal for vegetable growing. In fact, each family received a grant of $600, paid equally by the federal, provincial, and Dutch governments.

Rupke's little henhouse soon became a boarding house for the men who had come to prepare the fertile land and to build homes on cedar poles three feet above the ground in case of a break in the dike. The coop served as a dining room, living room, bedroom, meeting place, and community centre for up to sixteen men.

There were a few double beds for the older men, but most had to find a spot on the floor. Orange-crates doubled as chairs and chests for plates, forks, spoons, and personal belongings. Some of the men were appointed wood-gatherers and hewers while others hauled water from a well a quarter of a mile away. The older men did the housework and prepared the meals of potatoes and lettuce. The cost for room and board: $1.50 a week.

Some of these men went home to their families each weekend, provided there was transportation. Some stayed, and then the little henhouse became a place of worship too, until the first houses were ready and the families took turns hosting the budding congregation.

This was the prewar pioneer period. Many of the immigrants who came later, in the big wave after the war, could not compare their experiences with the pioneers who had carved an existence out of the wilderness.

Nevertheless, some came very close, especially those who ended up in ramshackle shacks in the beetfields of southern Alberta. Even in Ontario and British Columbia, where many of the newcomers concentrated, the housing conditions were often primitive. In some cases, the farmer provided a small building recently vacated by chickens or some other animals, because that was the only accommodation he could offer.

The first homes in Holland Marsh were all of the same, distinctive style.

Ons Tweede Thuis, a publication of the emigration commission of the *Nederlandse Vrouwen Comité*, an organization in The Netherlands, included a letter from a mother of eleven children—ten sons and a daughter—who had arrived in Ontario in May, 1953.

"The farmer picked us up with his truck. There stood our small house—a chicken barn. It contained a big round table and a big chair that was too filthy to sit in. We stood there, dirty and sweaty. The boys helped clean things up a bit, and I took off my slip and swabbed the floor with it. We didn't have a cup to drink out of, not a chair to sit down on, not a pan to cook with. Yes, the farmer had put an old stove in a small annex at the back of the house. We slept on the floor. There were two straw mattresses and two old ones filled with feathers. That's how we slept for six weeks—on the floor—until our *kist* came . . ."

In November, 1951, Mr. and Mrs. Lieuwe Dijkstra and their ten children arrived at a farm near Linwood, northwest of Kitchener, Ontario, and got a shock when they opened the door to their first dwelling in Canada.

Mrs. Dijkstra, now of Beamsville, Ontario, recalls: "That house was terribly dirty. It stank. After I had scrubbed and cleaned for a whole week, it still looked filthy. It was cold outside and there was no wood in the house. Not only that, but the bottom of the stove caved in when we threw in some anthracite. Windows were broken. There was a lot of dog waste in the bedrooms upstairs. I couldn't stand the sight of it, but somehow I got it all cleaned up. When I threw boiled water against the kitchen walls, I saw dirt streaming down. Nothing helped until I got some inexpensive wallpaper and redid the whole thing, including the ceiling. Boy oh boy!"

Little wonder that everyone was jumping with joy when the crate arrived just before Christmas. The curtains, the furniture, and even the blankets added a pleasant touch to the stark surroundings. With everything in place, it looked more like home.

Jacob Hofstee's boss arrived at the train station in Chatham, Ontario, shepherded the entire family into his car, and took them to their new home. The new arrivals walked inside, and then stood there as if in shock. There was nothing in the house—no furniture, no beds, no curtains, no food.

"The boss explained that we would have to buy our own stove," says John, Hofstee's son. "A price of $90 was agreed upon, and Dad had to pay half. The farmer paid the rest, which was to be repaid from the first month's wages. That purchase made a big dent in the money that was left of the original $125 with which we had left Rotterdam."

The family spent the first night on the wooden floor, under their clothes. The next day, the farmer brought some straw. The small trunk, which had been put on the train, also arrived, yielding some blankets and spreads. And before the day was over, a table and some chairs graced the house, courtesy of the farmer.

A dilapidated farmhouse near Wallaceburg, Ontario, inspected by Kees Verburg and family.

Hessel and Wilma Baarda moved into a peach picker's shed at Niagara-on-the-Lake in 1951.

Mrs. Sjaan Hofstee on the back step of her house near Chatham, Ontario.

Klaas Molema of Richmond, British Columbia: "We ended up in this shed when we arrived in Bellevue, Alberta, in August, 1948. It was much worse than it looks on this picture, taken later. There were only two rooms. In one, I made beds for the six of us. The other was the living room. The floors were dirt. Clay and cow manure had been mixed for the lathing in the walls. And there were only three walls—the fourth was the rock against which the shed was built. I had to walk 100 feet to the river to get water, some job in the winter. I had to go down thirty feet, and sometimes I had a hard time getting back up with the water. We stayed in that shed for eleven months." The center photo shows a converted barn in the Niagara Peninsula. In April of 1949, Carl Biel and his family moved in. "We made it real cozy," he says. At bottom: the Lieuwe Dijkstra home near Linwood: "That house was terribly dirty."

Naturally, everyone in the family looked forward to the arrival of the big crate containing household effects. But as the weeks passed and they heard nothing of it, they began to worry. Another Dutch family in the area had received theirs less than a week after their arrival. Several enquiries at the stations in Chatham and Merlin bore no result. Then Kees Wagenaar, an old-time immigrant who lived near them, came to the rescue.

Through his efforts, the crate was located, shipped to Chatham, and brought home with the farmer's tractor and wagon.

"The bill of lading had showed there were two containers for us," says John, "but the railway could find only one. That one container just sat there while a search was being conducted for the other one. The missing one, in fact, was the trunk that we had dragged to the pile of train baggage to make sure that it would follow us immediately to our new home. Well, the railway agent was very happy when we signed for two."

That evening, the house looked more like a home, and the Hofstees were finally able, after nine weeks, to say goodbye to the straw and sleep in their own beds.

Mrs. Netty Oosterman, who came to Canada in 1953, reports: "After one month, we found an apartment in Sparta, in southern Ontario. The outhouse was new to us. It was so far behind the house that I didn't dare go alone at night. There might be bears or wolves; what did I know? Maybe I wasn't the only one who felt that way, for it was one with two holes."

The *kist* hadn't arrived yet, só she and her husband borrowed a mattress and some cooking utensils and improvised a bit.

"I got a chair from the landlady downstairs and my husband sat on the garbage pail. When our belongings finally came after six weeks, we felt rich. My husband tore the crate apart and used the rough wood for making a kitchen table and a coffee table. The lady from downstairs looked on with surprise and amusement. Those tables served us for quite some time, and women visitors were warned to watch their nylons."

When J.A. Grootenboer and his family arrived on a farm five miles west of Portage La Prairie, Manitoba, in the spring of

1948, they moved into a dwelling that was really a section of a former army barracks.

"We fixed it up first on the outside to keep the draft out," he recalls. "Even in the first week of June, the nights were very cold. Our extra blankets were in the *kist*, which hadn't arrived yet. When the outside was finished, we made the place liveable inside. After six weeks, our furniture arrived. When everything was put in place, the house did look a bit comfortable. It gave us a feeling of being at home in a new country."

Even an architect, E. Hendrik Grolle, formerly of Amsterdam, couldn't do much about the deplorable housing that he and his wife, Vera, had to cope with at first. After arriving in Moose Jaw, Saskatchewan, in March, 1953, they and their son lived in a basement where the sewers backed up during heavy rainstorms. Six months later, as new residents of Regina, they moved into a one-room shack with no inside plumbing.

"There was a wooden sidewalk out front and a drafty outhouse in the back," recalls Grolle. "A standpipe on the street corner provided water. It was frequently frozen and would not always budge when I poured boiling water over it. Usually by noon, the thing was operational."

After the first winter, when the temperature plummeted as low as -52 degrees Fahrenheit, Grolle was able to rent a new house. He also bought a good lot from the city for $515, half the actual value, and proceeded to build his own dwelling. Today, after two additions, he still lives in it.

There was a slight overcrowding problem when Arie Verduyn and his family arrived at the house of relatives in the Sarnia, Ontario, area in 1952. Sixteen persons elbowed their way around the place, fought for a chair at dinner time—some had to sit on the stairs—and waited for their turn in the outhouse and in the washtub. The younger ones took turns sleeping on the floor.

"The outhouse for two was the only privacy that existed on the premises," says Verduyn. "Eeke and I cherished its use at night, before going to bed, to discuss the day's happenings and plan strategy just between the two of us."

The tub for the weekly bath was put in the centre of the kitchen and sheets were draped around it. However, the sense of

Mr. and Mrs. Albert DeVries and their son Albert spend a quiet evening in the living room of their home in Cornwall, Ontario, in 1957. Most immigrants brought their furniture with them.

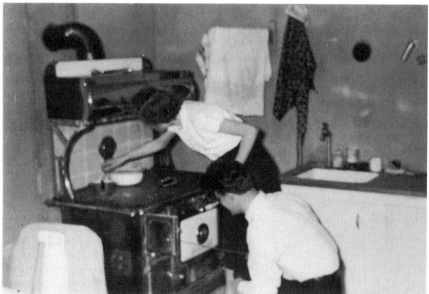

In Mr. and Mrs. John Schreurs' home in Kamloops, British Columbia, the stove was used for cooking and for heating the house.

John Eisen's mother stands in the doorway of her home—part of a barn—in Holland Marsh in 1949. "We used every cardboard box we could find for insulation to keep the wind out."

158   *To All Our Children*

John Kottelenberg and family draw water from the well on a small farm at Coatsworth, Ontario, which he bought in 1954. He now lives at Shelburne.

For more than twenty-six years, this stone barn on the mountain at Hamilton, Ontario, was home for Cor Groenewegen and his family. They first lived in the granary, soon adding other rooms. Until 1965, water was supplied twice a week by the city.

privacy evaporated rapidly when one of the bathers spotted two of the children peeking down from the top of the stairs.

John Snyders: "When we arrived in Brooks, Alberta, a Dutch farmer we had corresponded with drove us to our sponsoring farmer: twenty-five miles of mud roads! There wasn't any pavement within sixty-five miles of Brooks in 1950. The main roads were gravelled, but the others were mud. If it rained, you stayed home. We arrived at the farmer's house and our hearts sank. One bedroom, a kitchen, and a garage. We moved into the bedroom with our three young children, and the farmer, a bachelor, took the garage. There was no water, no plumbing, no electricity. My wife cooked and the farmer became like a boarder. I loved the life and the work, but my wife hated it."

S.P. Knuist recalls: "One year after we arrived in Kamloops, British Columbia, my wife's brother, John Schreurs, decided to get married in Holland and emigrate to Canada. Naturally, they came to Kamloops. We found half of a small house for rent next door to us. It had running water—just cold—from a pipe that stuck out of the counter with an outside tap screwed onto it. A wood-coal stove served double duty: it was used for cooking and for heating the house. In the winter, the landlady provided wood. Sure, the place lacked a few things including an inside toilet, but it was clean, roomy, and cozy."

Mrs. John Olydam of Grande Prairie, Alberta: "We moved to the Peace River country in 1951, to a two-room log house. To make room for all five children, we had to put a chest of drawers on a plank across the foot of one bed. The children didn't need a six-foot bed anyway. Two other dressers were put side by side with a mattress on top, and one of the children slept there. One night in the winter of 1954, when my husband was working in the bush, I woke up. The house was bitterly cold. As I got up in the dark to see if the stove was dead, I bumped into something hard next to it. It was my husband's long underwear—frozen solid!"

Teunis Schinkel's son-in-law, who had been in Canada for a few years, bought an old Roman Catholic schoolhouse near

Amherstburg, Ontario, for about $1,000. Then he fixed it up a bit so that his relatives would have a place to call home right after their arrival in 1953.

"My first impression of our new place wasn't very positive," recalls Schinkel. "It was made out of huge blocks of natural stone, roughly hewn. One day when my wife and I were working in the so-called living room, trying to make it habitable, I let my feeling slip out. In Holland, I said, we lived in a house, and in Canada we were living in a hovel. I thought we had landed in a backward country."

Around the building were tall weeds, and snakes slithered here and there. No one knew that the snakes were quite harmless.

"We noticed a few good things. The hardwood floor was as good as new, the water drawn with a handpump was of excellent quality and there was enough land to plant a garden to help feed a large family."

The son-in-law, a jack of all trades, installed electrical wiring. Now the water didn't have to be pumped by hand. That was one of the last things he was able to do for his in-laws; he died that year of an incurable blood illness at the age of thirty. But that didn't stop the renovations. The old schoolhouse was gradually turned into a comfortable place that was called home for twenty-two years.

Hendrikus and Dini Hendriksen of Nijkerk, Gelderland, who began to work for a farmer somewhere between Chilliwack and Abbotsford, British Columbia, in 1951, recall: "Our first house had a kitchen, but no sink or running water. We also had a wood stove named Wonder, a small table and a couple of boxes. There was a living room, and a bedroom where the rainwater ran down the walls. Our drinking water was stored in a milkcan outside the kitchen door; we drew it from a tap in the barn. When the water stood awhile, the bottom of the pail was covered with sand. The outhouse was behind the farmer's house, quite a ways from our place. The chickens, walking freely in and out, were our neighbors. Once the farmer's wife gave us a sausage. It had so much garlic in it that we couldn't eat it. So we gave it to the chickens. We stayed there six weeks or so, and then moved to Ladner, where we had a nice home with a bathroom."

Of course, not every farmer looked down on his hired help. Far from it. Many

A former rural schoolhouse near Amherstburg, Ontario, became the home of Teunis Schinkel and his family.

Mrs. C.M. Hogeterp and her children at their home near Waterford, Ontario, in 1947.

A two-room log house in Alberta's Peace River area, the home of Mr. and Mrs. John Olydam and their five children in the early 1950s.

Mr. and Mrs. Kees Feyen moved into this house at Prairie Siding, Ontario, in 1951.

Unpacking the crate was quite a chore. On top is Mrs. Willem Buitenwerf, who settled near St. Catharines, Ontario.

On the day in 1950 when the kist *was opened at Portage La Prairie, Manitoba, Peter Heemskerk couldn't wait for the organ to be moved inside.*

farmers went out of their way to welcome the people from The Netherlands, showing kindness and gratitude. Kees and Reina Feyen know. When they arrived at Prairie Siding, eight miles from Chatham, Ontario, in 1951, a two-storey house stood ready for them. Their sponsors, a childless couple in their fifties, had provided furniture, bedding, pots and pans, and dishes.

"They also gave us all kinds of groceries," says Mrs. Feyen. "For the first two days, the farmer's wife brought over a warm dinner, including a baked-bean casserole. My husband was hired for $100 a month, with free housing, utilities, milk, and meat. The farmer had an orchard and a garden, and we were given a share of the crops. When I helped his wife with canning, I could take half of the proceeds home. When I helped with cleaning the house, she paid me by the hour."

C.M. Hogeterp, his brother, and their families got the surprise of their lives when they entered the farmhouse of their sponsor in the Waterford, Ontario, area in 1947. "The table was loaded with cakes and pies—just fantastic! There were seventeen of us and we couldn't eat it all. It was a royal welcome."

In the days that followed, the farmer also went out of his way to make sure that his new employees had a command of the basic English needed on a dairy farm.

"I thought I knew a little bit of English," recalls Hogeterp. "But I soon found out that I didn't. They seemed to talk so fast that I couldn't recognize a word. And what I tried to pronounce didn't make any sense to them."

During slack times, the farmer invited his hired hands to sit down in the stable. He would point to a particular thing, pronounce its name, and ask his pupils to repeat what he had said. Before long, they knew the English words for cow, milk, and so on—not enough to make conversation, but enough to make themselves understood.

The women were taught by a kind lady in the neighborhood, who also brought used clothing for the children now and then.

"The young ones picked up English quickly," says Mrs. Hogeterp. "Of course, they saw other children every day. It wasn't long before they were speaking English without an accent. And before we knew it, they were speaking English to us instead of Dutch."

Hogeterp was impressed by the classless society of Canada. There were none of the "Yes, sir" replies mandatory in the society he had left behind.

"I called my farmer 'boss'. He frowned and said: 'I'm not boss. I'm Bill.' Well, I called him Bill after that and there were no more frowns."

Jacob De Jong, fieldman for the Christian Reformed Church in southern Manitoba, agrees that the housing provided by farmers wasn't always ideal, especially for people who were used to clean and comfortable conditions.

"We had gone through trying times ourselves here in Canada, during the Depression, and so we looked at things differently. But, yes, some of the houses were poor. And some looked poor because they were empty, save for an old table and some bad chairs and beds. It sometimes took quite a while before the furniture from Holland arrived. So there were complaints now and then. But on the whole, it wasn't too bad."

"Our house was small but liveable," says Mrs. Mary Provoost, who came to Ontario in 1948. "I remember my youngest sister sleeping in the closet upstairs. There was no cellar or fridge, so all the groceries and leftovers were stored in a closet in the living room. Our sponsor welcomed us most heartily. We had a very nice supper, with cake and strawberries for dessert. I had never seen so much food on a table."

The furniture crates came about a week later.

"It was so funny to see our boss doubling over with laughter when the potties came out."

Oh, those crates, and the problems they caused. It seems that various freight companies hadn't used proper scales, and some weights had been undervalued. The discrepancies were costly for the immigrants, who had to pay the remainder of the charges upon delivery. More than one immigrant had to arrange for an advance on wages.

William Van Oosten, now of Chatham, Ontario, had experienced another problem: the estimator had ordered too small a crate. When the time came to pack, it wouldn't hold everything that had been earmarked to make the crossing—including a son's scooter. There was much

Jan Knegt, who left Den Hoorn, near Delft, in the spring of 1948, used his kist *as a toolshed. He first worked at a nursery near Beamsville, Ontario.*

The kist *is opened, revealing a wardrobe and a washtub.*

A crate is loaded onto a truck, on its way to the owner.

In 1949, Syrt Wolters bought this cabin at Houston, British Columbia, from a native Canadian for $550. Later, he bought the lot from the government for $15. The other photos show the cabin being renovated into a house and the finished product. The Wolters family later moved to the Victoria area.

grief when it had to be left behind.

Then another problem developed after the *kist* was unpacked in the garage at the family's home in London, Ontario, in 1956. Not all of the items were removed immediately because there simply wasn't any place to put it all.

"One day," recalls Van Oosten, "there was a terrible downpour. As we watched it, all of a sudden we realized that the garage was low-lying and flooding. Oh, what a disaster!"

Rimmer Tjalsma, landing agent in Halifax for the Holland-America Line for a number of years, recalls one instance when the delivery of a crate was delayed intentionally. "Word came from the embassy in Ottawa that a certain crate couldn't be released because its owner had left Holland without settling his tax arrears. Once the taxes were paid, he could have his crate."

The empty crates were put to good use. Some immigrants cut them up and made furniture out of the wood. Others kept them intact and used them for a bedroom or a garage. In any event, they provided ready identification in the early postwar years; the big crates labelled *Groote Beer*, *Waterman*, and *Zuiderkruis* made it easy to pick out the homes of the newly-arrived Dutch.

George Eggink was another immigrant who found the hospitality of his farmer overwhelming. The farmhouse was opened to him and his family for two weeks until their own little house was ready for occupancy. Their Canadian hosts went out of their way to make them comfortable.

"When our crates came, the farmer was a bit surprised. He no doubt thought that we had come from a poor country, one ravaged by war, and that the people there didn't have too many belongings. Otherwise, so many of them wouldn't be applying to go to Canada. But then he saw that although I didn't have too much in my wallet, I had a house full of furniture."

When Hilda Overdijk and her brother and sister arrived at the station in Trenton, Ontario, their sponsor, a distant relative, yelled a greeting in Frisian: "Canada is a land of hard work! Might as well roll up your sleeves!"

He wanted to make sure right from the start that his new charges realized why they were in Canada. He repeated the message the next day: "As long as we have so many rocks in the fields, we can't sit on our fannies. You have to earn your keep."

The new arrivals picked up stones, stones, and more stones. The work was backbreaking. And yet they loved it: the beautiful weather, the fragrance of the lilac bushes, the gorgeous scenery and the total change of environment. There were so many new things to see, so many new experiences, that the sweat didn't matter.

"There were the crickets singing in the evening," recalls Hilda, now surnamed Wielemaker. "And the family privy: two adult-size holes and a lower level with a child-size hole. We noticed the large matchsticks and thought that everything must be big in Canada. Our first Sunday: the charming little wooden church, the friendly minister, the young people who welcomed us—we couldn't understand the sermon or sing the hymns, but we could feel the Christian atmosphere. And the young people's picnic—never before had we experienced such open fellowship, and the hotdogs were a revelation. Even the Saturday evenings were exciting for us. The stores were open until nine o'clock. Everybody shopped, and then congregated in the bowling alleys. After a few games, we usually gathered in a restaurant for a Coke and a few songs from the jukebox."

After two weeks of picking stones and spring cleaning, Hilda and her brother and sister found jobs at the Bata shoe factory in Trenton. They had never intended to stay for long at the farm. They rented a small country house with no plumbing, no electricity, and no insulation. Since the upstairs was too hot, all three slept in one downstairs room.

"No problem for us," says Hilda, "but the visiting minister raised his eyebrows."

John Reinders, who settled near Drayton, Ontario, in 1952, recalls: "As soon as I came here, I saw a good future in Canada for farmers. There was lots of room, lots of good land, and the markets were growing. Mind you, some of the farming methods seemed strange at first. I couldn't understand why some farmers didn't use any fertilizer. I learned later, of course, that conditions here were different: the natural soil and the shorter growing season, for example. But I was still convinced that, with our experience and know-how, we could show the Canadians a few things about farming."

Mrs. Reinders: "The first year was so new for all of us. There were so many

Home, Dutch-style

On the inside, the immigrants' homes looked Dutch. Of course! Most of them had shipped much of their furniture and effects to Canada. These photos show the kitchen (that's a Canadian stove) and the living room of the George Hultink home in the Wallaceburg, Ontario, area in the early 1950s.

Jake Feenstra shovels a path to the outhouse at his home near Woodstock, Ontario. In the photo above, made available by Fred and Tina Feddes of Port Lambton, Ontario, the outhouse is far away in deep snow. The photo at left, supplied by Henry Kroes of St. Ann's, Ontario, shows the popular resting place in another season.

Primitive Rest Rooms

Stories about outhouses abound. The immigrants weren't pleased about their primitive washroom facilities even though they now laugh about them.

The family of Willem Buitenwerf in the St. Catharines, Ontario, area had to share an outhouse with Polish neighbors. It stood some twenty meters from the house, a fair distance even in daylight.

"You can understand that we really didn't like the idea," says Buitenwerf. "The neighbors had four growing sons. Of course, I thought of my wife and daughters."

So he bought a big pail and made a triangular seat out of three pieces of wood. The finished product was put in a nearby shed. Keeping the pail upright while lowering the body upon it was quite an undertaking at first. But soon everyone was quite adept and comfortable.

Returning from a meeting with railway officials and others in Ottawa, Rev. Harri Zegerius of the Reformed Church stopped late at night at the home of an acquaintance in Brockville, Ontario. Nature called, and he politely asked: "Where's the washroom?" An astonished look came across his face at the answer: "In the barn."

"I groped my way through the darkness. I found the toilet in a corner. I sat down—and jumped a few inches. The seat was as cold as ice. Then I knew what was meant by frozen assets."

Mrs. Hilda Wielemaker relates this anecdote: "One evening, while I was hanging out the washing and my brother was working in the garden, an unearthly shriek pierced the air. The door of the privy burst open and a young woman shot out like a cannonball, slacks tangled around her ankles, hands holding her bare buttocks. A swarm of bees was close behind her. We froze. Then, as the hilarity of the situation sank in, we bellowed with laughter. We still hadn't brought ourselves under control when a neighbor, alarmed by all the noise, came running to see whether he could be of help."

stories to tell whenever we immigrants got together after church or during the week. Maybe that's why we laughed so much. One woman said: 'We've never had so many worries, but we've never had so many laughs either.' "

Miss J. Janssen, formerly of Amsterdam and now of Toronto: "For the first few months, I stayed at my sister's place in Lefroy. I helped pick raspberries in her large garden. She put them in little baskets and placed them on a table alongside the road. Those who wanted to buy berries just dropped their money in a can. I was amazed at their honesty. I also remember an incident that took place on the first day. A man walked inside to speak with my brother-in-law. When he heard that I had just arrived in Canada, he pulled a $2 bill from his pocket and handed it to me for good luck. Marvellous!"

S.P. Knuist, who came here in 1953: "Canadians seemed rather unconcerned about the luxuries in life. We didn't think much of their tastes in furniture and clothes. Their lifestyle was simple: a day's work, a few beers, relaxing at home or playing baseball. We were starving for good music and humor. Among the first luxuries we invested in were some classical records."

Tina DeBoer of Drumheller, Alberta: "I just couldn't get used to it at first—from a *gezellige* shopping area in our town in Holland to the wide, dusty streets of a prairie town. The Safeway store stood deserted in the middle of a sunbaked parking lot that was always half empty. Everything was ten times as big as it needed be and a hundred times as lonely."

A fresh layer of snow covered the ground in the bush country near Smithers, British Columbia, on November 15, 1951. John and Margret Bandstra realized right away that this was an ideal time for moving their home, a small cabin, to town, where they would have the conveniences of water and electricity. It had been sitting on stilts for two weeks already, waiting for a few inches of snow. A D4 Cat would pull it along the road to its new location.

"It didn't take us long to get the cabin moving," recalls Bandstra. "In fact, we did so well that at the corner of a planer mill the Cat was pulling only the skids and the cabin was sitting on the roadway. It took us almost all day to get the logs back under the cabin. All the while, nothing could get past us. But people took it in

The House That Moved

Mrs. H.J. Spier—Groen

When Rev. H.J. Spier of Rijswijk, Zuid-Holland, toured Canada in 1953, he saw something in Alberta that was worth a picture: a house being moved from one place to another. A notation on the back of the photo states: "Here comes the new three-room house of the Drost family in Blackfalds."

A Pre-fab

This prefabricated home in Stratford, Ontario, was brought over from The Netherlands in the early 1950s. The Wiersma family, formerly of Hoogeveen, Drenthe, lived in it until 1956.

Home-made

Joseph Winnemuller and two of his sons take advantage of fine weather in Selkirk, Manitoba, in 1954 to build their first house. The family had come from Noordwijkerhout, Zuid-Holland, the year before. Says Winnemuller, who was in nursing most of his life: "It took two years to complete the house. After that, I bought two more lots and built two more houses, which I rented out for many years and then sold. With that money, we had a contractor put up a last beautiful house. The rest of the money we divided among our seven children. After all, we had not forgotten how much the oldest children had helped us in the first difficult years."

Barn Buffs

When Henry Hunse bought a farm at Niagara-on-the-Lake, Ontario, in 1950, the occupant of the house had not moved out yet. So the Hunse family set up house in the barn. But as the days passed, the other family showed no intentions of getting out. Finally, after six weeks, Hunse told him: "If you're not out by tomorrow, we'll throw you in the lake." The house was vacant the next day. That's the same barn in the photo at left, taken later, and then home for hundreds of chickens.

The shed and the kist *were home for the Heeringa family for six weeks. Their new house is taking shape, but it's surrounded by a sea of mud.*

stride. There wasn't any rush in those days. It was close to 5 p.m. before we got moving again."

By 7 p.m., only a ditch separated the cabin from its destination. By then it was dark, and Bandstra decided to leave it on the road and move it in the morning. Besides, he and his wife had to be in Telkwa at eight o'clock for the institution of the 118-member Telkwa-Smithers Christian Reformed Church.

"We went into the cabin to change clothes. But, oh dear, everything was lying on the floor in the middle of the room—books, clothes, dishes, and trinkets. My wife wasn't too happy about that. We didn't have time to straighten up anything; someone was coming to pick us up with his model-T Ford at 7:15. We quickly changed and soon were on our way."

It was late in the evening when the Bandstras returned to their cabin, still standing on the road with just enough room for the cars to go by.

"We decided to sleep in the cabin that night. My wife attached one condition: I had to sleep on the side closest to the traffic. We had a good sleep. And the next morning, we moved the cabin to our lot across the ditch."

Jack Heeringa, an architect in the city of Groningen, brought more than his wife, three children, and a *kist* of belongings to Canada in 1952—he brought along a complete pre-cut house.

He had first put it together behind his house in The Netherlands, using a floor plan he had seen advertised in a copy of the *Saturday Evening Post*. Then he made another one for his brother, who also had emigration plans. The construction drew a lot of attention from neighbors, and even school classes came by to have a look.

The houses were taken apart and packed in crates, to be reassembled on lots in Canada. This was much cheaper than buying a house of similar size here.

"After we arrived in Chatham, Ontario, we lived in a shed," says Heeringa, now of Stoney Creek, Ontario. "Our *kist* came right away, so we used that for a bedroom. Visitors chuckled when they saw our good furniture in that shed. It was kind of primitive at first. But we knew it was only temporary. Our house was on its way."

At night, he and his wife heard noises under the floor, made of old lumber. Then they discovered that something had been at the food in the frying pan. There was no question in Heeringa's mind: the shed was infested with rats.

"That really scared us. I put out some poisoned bait the next night. We could hear the rats fighting over the food. The poison did the trick. We never heard them after that."

Heeringa bought a lot in an undeveloped survey—a former orchard—at Stoney Creek. After six weeks in Canada, he received the good news: the pre-cut house had arrived. Using the wood of the large crate, they built a cabin on the site. This served as home until the basement of the house was ready for occupancy.

"We had the basement finished at the end of November. The rest of the house was completed during the winter."

The house, with three bedrooms, a kitchen, and a living-dining room, was a comfortable place compared with what many other immigrants were calling home in those days. The family sold it in 1970. It is still in use today.

Chapter 10

Earning the Bread

It's time to celebrate the end of harvest on the tobacco farm of Peter VanDyk in the Delhi, Ontario, area in 1949. Eight people in the photo are members of a Dutch immigrant family from Sarnia.

Earning the Bread

Bob Gosschalk was a good tennis player. He spent much of his free time on Saturday afternoons and Sundays swinging a racket at a club in Hamilton, Ontario. It was a good place to meet people his own age and to forget for a while the worries of working on a fruit farm at Winona. Then, one day, he broke his wrist.

"When the farmer saw what had happened, he told me: 'If you can't work, I can't use you. You're fired.' There I stood, with a broken wrist and no job. I picked up my belongings and went to the home of one of the fellows who had driven me back to the farm."

That was his introduction to the sometimes ruthless attitude of Canadian employers. In later years, he heard many more examples of ill treatment. Then he was an insurance agent, visiting hundreds of Dutch immigrants on farms between Niagara Falls and London. A friendly official of the Canadian Immigration Service supplied him with lists of new arrivals and their addresses.

"I became a father figure for many people," he says. "I was often the only Dutch person they had seen for weeks. We traded gossip. I listened to their problems—and there were many. I passed on advice, and found jobs for those who wanted to get away from the farm. And I sold insurance."

Gosschalk, well educated and outspoken, felt his blood pressure rise

Bob Gosschalk in the early 1950s: "I was often the only Dutch person they had seen for weeks."
Below: Syrt Wolters drives a lumber carrier for Houston Planer Company in British Columbia in 1950.

Dutch immigrants near Homewood, Manitoba, bring in the harvest.

whenever he heard someone complain about poor conditions, ill treatment, or simple prejudice. Remembering how he had been kicked off a farm because of a broken wrist, he sympathized with these people.

Traveling along the dusty country roads in his 1949 Austin, purchased by his father in The Netherlands, he would calm down a bit. Certainly all Canadian farmers couldn't be that bad, he thought. He had met many who held Dutch workers in high regard. Maybe some immigrants imagined problems because of differences in work habits, language, and culture. Yet . . .

He had seen with his own eyes a family living in the filth of a dwelling that once housed chickens, the only building the farmer had at his disposal. Somehow, it had been overlooked by the people who were supposed to inspect these things beforehand. He had heard stories about hired hands working dawn to dusk, getting no time off to go to church or to look after other private matters, such as looking for a better job and a better house. He had heard about a farmer who refused to remove a skunk from a well, forcing the immigrant family to haul water from a mile away.

When a reporter of the *Hamilton Spectator* sought him out in 1950, his words were bitter.

The Dutch people, he said, were proud and hard-working, with a culture reaching back centuries before Canada was colonized. They deserved something better than a contract which subjected them to degradation. The ensuing article even described the Dutch immigrant as a "feudal slave," although Gosschalk later claimed that those words were the reporter's. Perhaps, the article implied, officials had led emigrants to expect a country where the streets were paved with gold.

Gosschalk had stirred up a hornet's nest. Canadian immigration officials promised an immediate investigation. So did the emigration people in The Netherlands, who had been informed of the allegations through wire service reports appearing in Dutch papers. According to Gosschalk, the news even reached Queen Juliana. She came here in 1952 and spent most of her time among the immigrants.

The Canadians were indignant. One farmer chased Gosschalk with a pitchfork. The Wentworth County Agricultural Society passed a motion requesting his deportation. Even immigration officials, formerly friendly toward him, began to avoid him.

One farmer, Mrs. Peter Douglas of Ancaster, told *The Spectator:* "Sometimes it is true that a little friction develops, but I feel that this is most often due to the fact that the immigration authorities give these new Canadians a wrong impression of this country. Most of them are excellent people who are willing to work out their contracts and then strike out for themselves. But there are some, as is I suppose inevitable, who arrive with preconceived ideas, who will not accommodate themselves to the customs of a new country. We had one unfortunate experience with a Dutch couple, but the last ones to come to us were more than satisfactory. They were nice people. It is the same with the families to whom they go; some are better than others. But to say that many of these immigrants are treated shamefully is ridiculous."

Gosschalk, who took nothing back despite the backlash, was convinced that the publicity resulted in changes for the better.

"All of a sudden, the rules were relaxed. Emigrants could take more money with them. People could bring in prefabricated

Stoffer VanderMaar of Winnipeg (right) and his brother, Willem, are working on the railroad in the late 1950s. The manure they unloaded was frozen solid and had to be broken up with a pick before it could be shovelled. Willem later returned to The Netherlands.

homes and some farm equipment. I was the one who fought for the little guy. It didn't make me popular. But I was never sorry for having said the things I did."

Some more excerpts from the diary of Geertrui Beldman, now Mrs. Trudy Joldersma of Hamilton, Ontario, who went to a farm in Manitoba in 1950 to do domestic work.

March 5: "One week in Canada. The farmer has called my friends. He's picking me up today. Is it my imagination, or do I detect a note of concern in the eyes of my hostess? The farmer introduces himself. My first impression is a bad one. Are all Canadian farmers so coarse and neglected looking?

"We have to travel about twenty miles. I have no idea how far twenty miles is. It turns out to be a long way . . . If this weren't so serious, I could pretend to be in Switzerland. Banks of snow, some higher than rooftops, on both sides of the road. No landscape visible. It's all one huge platter of snow. I have the feeling that I'm being abducted.

"I meet the farmer's wife; she seems grotesquely stupid, and their one-year-old son looks exactly like his mother. Through a side door shuffles a decrepit, retarded man of about fifty. The farmer's brother, I'm told. Neglected, pitiable. During supper, I get to meet the two boarding hired hands, a couple of leering bachelors approaching sixty, both of whom badly need a bath. Is this the family I'll be staying with night and day? For a whole year? Inside I'm very close to tears . . ."

April 8: "Easter in Canada . . . my first Easter in Canada. Living through icy blizzards in this harsh, merciless landscape, who wouldn't pine for the clear springtime skies of the beloved homeland?

Who would be able to fight back the tears at the memories of that sweet, familiar, most singular place, fondly called home? I'm looking at the photographs for the umpteenth time. Just look at our house underneath that splendid linden. Look at the lush, green pastures surrounded by drainage ditches, ditches with buttercups growing on the banks. This was a part of myself, my world in springtime splendor. This was how it used to be! Why is that little country so full of people; so full that some have to leave to make room for the others? Or isn't that even true? Is it perhaps a hoax that our country is too crowded? Do we come here because . . . indeed, why, really? I ask myself stupidly why I'm here, what drove me to come here to this cold and harsh land of Canada.

"Canada, I'm so terribly disappointed in you. There is nothing gentle, nothing familiar—not in your climate, not in your nature, and not in your inhabitants. No, not even in your people. I find them so ungracious, so superficial.

Farmers attending a Dutch Field Day at Lacombe, Alberta, in June of 1951, listen to a discussion of cereal crops.

The rationing begun during the Second World War was still in effect in Canada when the Waterman arrived in June, 1947.

LETTERS	NUMBERS	Prefix and Serial Number

Name Nom — de Jong, Hert.
Last Name—Nom de famille   First Name—Prénom

Street Address or R.R. No. R.R. # 1
No et rue ou R.R. No.

City or Town Waterloo
Ville ou Village

Province Ont.   **Telephone Number** — Numéro de Téléphone
Province

RATION BOOK 6   CANADA   **CARNET DE RATIONNEMENT 6**

RB-275

Another scene from the Dutch Field Day at Lacombe: hog raising is the topic this time.

"Oh, Holland, you are more cherished than I ever realized. Is this patriotic love? Is this homesickness, a restless yearning for the polders by the sea? Holland, my beloved Holland . . ."

May 14: "Can this really be Sunday? On this Canadian farm in the loneliness of Manitoba? I try in vain to make something of it. How can I create a Sunday atmosphere in these surroundings? The farmer, dressed in his smelly coveralls that stink worse than all the farmers back home combined, is working. An old, lecherous carpenter, who boards here temporarily, has turned the kitchen into a chaotic mess and is busy hammering and sawing as if his life depended on it. It is, I think, a dreadful Sunday.

"And then you have to spend the whole day with the failing hope that another immigrant will come by to pick you up for church. Then, as the day wears on, this hope evaporates too. Then you retreat to your bedroom to read or sleep, or sobbing, make your entries in your diary. Is this immigration? Isn't it hard, unmercifully hard? I'm a prisoner! How could I suspect that living on a Canadian farm meant total isolation? It's more than enough to make me cry! Not even once a week am I allowed to leave this prison, not even to go to church.

"Oh Holland, with your bicycles and bike paths everywhere! To own a two-wheeler and come and go as you please! I have failed to appreciate freedom. What have I done to myself? What am I doing here?"

May 28: "How terribly cruel the life of an immigrant. I want to push back the walls and flee back to my loving mother, to my faithful father, to the only sisters I have. How could I have known this? Must I blame myself for being trapped in this unhappy situation? Simply because I wanted to emigrate? Or is it because I just don't have the ability to adjust? Would other emigrants be able to make something of this situation? Would they adjust? I just don't know any more.

"My caring brothers insisted that I tell the farmer that I'm leaving this summer. That gives him a couple of months' notice to look for new help. But what a scene! For the first time, I was chewed out in an alien language. He was so enraged; it felt like he called me every ugly thing under the sun. A good thing I couldn't understand it all. I wanted to hide—I, who, to some people at least, had always seemed quite heroic. But who can be heroic in this killing isolation?

"I cry nearly every day."

May 29: "I know the farmer had every right to get mad. The year isn't up yet. But what does he know of my situation? How can I make him understand, considering my poor English, that those two old, filthy hired hands of his send chills down my spine? How can I make it clear to him that it's below my dignity to make their grimy beds, empty their smelly chamberpots, and trip over their filthy spittoons? How can I tell him that I've never been barked at by a drunken sot, not until one of those rogues living under the same roof came back from a weekend in the city, soused out of his mind? And how would I dare to tell him I'm fed up with the constant wrangling between him and his feebleminded wife? Oh, I wish I knew more English. I would ask him: 'Must I spend a whole year in this miserable, lonely, isolated place just because you're my sponsor? It's clear to me that you didn't bring me over here as a favor, but simply because a Canadian woman wouldn't degrade herself doing the housework in this dreadful place for a mere pittance? But why should such abominable conditions be good enough for an immigrant? Why should a decent, intelligent young woman put up with the harshness of Canadian farm life? Simply because she comes from another country? But how can you, Canadian farmer, understand a girl from Holland? What do you know about my background? What do you know about the warm, intimate family life I left behind? Your family life has no intimacy. Your world is made up of tractors, ledgers, and nothing else.' "

"Don't kill him! Don't kill him!"
These words still ring clearly in the

mind of Berend Kraal of Moorefield, Ontario, who came to Canada with his wife and in-laws in 1950. They are a reminder of the agony of his introduction to the hard work on the farm and the overbearing attitude of his boss when he learned that Kraal didn't even know how to milk a cow properly.

Kraal, a bailiff with the tax department in Amsterdam after his return from military duty in the Netherlands East Indies in 1947, was so anxious to be admitted to Canada that he assured the emigration service that he was indeed a farmer. During the war, when he was in hiding, he had rewarded his kind host by helping out on the farm. And he gained further experience by quitting his tax job and working a few weeks for a farmer who was about to emigrate to Canada himself. He now knew how to drive a tractor and how to operate a milking machine, and considered himself proficient enough to tackle whatever his sponsor would want done.

He and his wife, Jenny, were picked up at the train station in Moorefield, driven by auto to the farm, and shown to their room upstairs. He immediately took his overalls from a suitcase and reported for work to Johnny, the boss.

"He pointed to the seat of a horse-drawn manure spreader and nodded toward the area where he wanted me to work. I was ready to carry out my first assignment. But I had never spread manure before. It didn't take long for Johnny to discover that I had never been a farmer. There was another fiasco in the

One week after arriving in Houston, British Columbia, in the summer of 1947, Waterman passenger Peter Vriend began to work on the CNR railroad. He's among the crew employed to steer driftwood away from a bridge threatened by high water in 1948. And that's Vriend (below) on a vehicle used for patrolling track.

evening, when I had to milk by hand the few cows whose teats were too large for the milking machine. No matter how I pulled, no milk came out. It seemed as if there was only air in there. I sweated. And I couldn't help but think: these cows must be different from the ones in Holland."

Kraal, physically and emotionally exhausted after the train trip and the trials of the first day of work, couldn't rest yet. It was Saturday night, and he and his wife had to accompany the farmer's family on their ritual journey to town. Most of the people from the area seemed to be there, stocking up on groceries and other supplies, trading gossip, and commenting on the weather.

"Jenny and I would rather have stayed home. Going into one store after another was tiring. People stared at us and said something, but we couldn't say anything back. We came home around midnight."

Convinced that his new employee was useless in farm work, Johnny told him to dig a narrow ditch from the house to the barn for the laying of a waterline. It had to be below the frost line, quite a depth.

"After three days of digging under a blazing sun, I hadn't made much progress. Jenny kept encouraging me. At around six o'clock, she came to tell me that it was time to eat. I put the spade against the wall of the house and sat down for a breather. Just then Johnny's old father, Harry, yelled from the barn door: 'Come here!' I said to Jenny, 'I'm not a dog,' and stayed where I was. He came storming toward me with fire in his eyes. He grabbed my spade. Despite my weariness, I was strong enough to take hold of the handle and press him against the wall. Then he began to yell."

The commotion brought the wives of Johnny and Harry running outside. When they saw the old man being pressed against the house with a spade, they feared the worst, and screamed: "Don't kill him! Don't kill him!"

"I understood the words and let the old man go free. He went inside and began to wash his hands under the pump. I was stupid enough to join him. He snapped at me to wait until he was finished. The food stood ready on the table, and I sat down in my chair opposite Harry. Jenny was still outside, crying. She didn't want to eat. But I was too hungry to let the food pass. When I was finished, we both went to our little room upstairs. There we decided to get away from the farm to avoid another nasty incident."

They walked toward Moorefield, and arrived at the farm where their relatives, with whom they had traveled to Canada, were working. From there, they bicycled to Berend Flinkert's. He had arranged their sponsor; now they told him what had happened and asked his advice. It was straightforward: go back to the farm, stick it out for a month so as to collect the $75 in wages, and look for another place in the meantime.

"Early the next morning, while it was still dark, Jenny and I began to cycle back to the farm. We didn't know the road well, missed a turn, and ended up in Palmerston. By the time we found the farm, it was ten o'clock. Without saying anything, I began to dig where I had left off."

They stayed another ten days. Then, during haying, another argument developed. That evening they were back at Flinkert's place, and he agreed that they should leave right away.

Immigrant life started for teenager John Eisen and his brother and mother one day

after arriving at a farm near Stratton, in northwestern Ontario.

"The food was great," says John, "but the barn work was hazardous. The barn could be reached only with high boots, and the building itself was a mess. Our own house had large piles of garbage in it, and the mice had the time of their lives. Our so-called furniture had to come out of the chicken coop. My brother, a bit fed up, said more than once: 'If the stalls are always this dirty, we won't stay here.' The farmer's wife responded: 'Johan, you have to stay here. We are your sponsors!' But when we were told that we would not be paid for the first month, because we were using some things that belonged to them, we went on strike. The farmer's wife then called up the immigration authorities in Winnipeg to come and tell us to go back to work. We walked to Stratton, some fifteen miles away, to get a truck for taking our meagre possessions to the train station. Well, a truck came along with us. But after speaking to the sponsor for a few minutes, the driver refused to take us to town. We could do nothing but wait for the immigration people. They came the next day, heard both sides, and agreed with us. Before long, we were on our way to Holland Marsh, where we had a good friend."

While John relaxed in the train, his thoughts often wandered back to the farm and the unpleasant two weeks he had spent there.

"One morning, our farmer told us to catch ten chickens and put them in an enclosure. They would be slaughtered at night. We thought he would merely take their heads off. But in Canada, things were done differently. After supper, I was told to get the first one out of the cage. The farmer had a string with a loop hanging in the doorway of a shed. The legs went in the loop and there the chicken hung. The farmer took a knife with a very narrow blade, squeezed the chicken's beak open, and cut its throat. Well, believe me, I nearly fainted. As the blood was dripping out, the chicken was plucked. My job was to get new chickens out of the cage. Well, I made a small hole in the wire—it was old anyway—and two of them got away. The farmer, after counting only eight chickens and finding the hole, didn't suspect anything."

But everything wasn't serene on the train either. A few seats away, a woman was busily kissing a man and keeping his liquor glass full. He was soon fast asleep. The woman took his wallet, and hurried from the train at the next stop.

John, a bit unsettled after watching this incident, hoped that life would be all right in Holland Marsh.

Shortly after stepping off the train in Newmarket, he started working for Holland River Gardens for forty cents an hour. His brother also landed a job with the same pay. Both felt somewhat rich. The good news continued when someone

In 1951 Ed DeJong hauled hay in Aldershot for his brother, Harry. The little girl on this 1948 Chevrolet half-ton pick-up is now Mrs. Kiers of Smithville, Ontario.

Mr. and Mrs. A.J. Van Maren, who came to Canada on the Groote Beer *in June, 1953, pick apples in an orchard at Summerland, British Columbia.*

When there's work to be done, all available hands are employed. Adults and children take a break from field work in Holland Marsh, north of Toronto, in the summer of 1953.

offered the brothers and their mother a quarter of his barn to live in.

"We bought an old Quebec stove and some second-hand furniture and were thankful for God's blessings," says John. "Every cardboard box we got was used for insulation to keep the wind out. In the next winter, we moved to a real house built on poles. There we lived for a few years."

In 1948, Mr. and Mrs. Leo Hovius found their sponsor at work in his barn when they were brought to his farm near Cobden, Ontario, after a disquieting hour-long wait at the train station.

"The boss kept on talking and talking," recalls Mrs. Hovius, "but we didn't understand a word of it. Now and then, he pointed at his watch. We just didn't know what he was trying to tell us. After awhile, we started to look around a bit, anxious to see our house. We had been told that a sponsor was supposed to provide one for married people. Well, there was no house for us. We had to move in with the farmer and his family."

What made matters worse, Mrs. Hovius was expected to clean the entire house. The farmer's wife, a school teacher, wasn't home during the day.

"I didn't look forward to that. I wasn't used to cleaning somebody else's house. My husband got $75 a month, and that included my services. We never got an extra penny for my work."

There were more irritants.

When the *kist* of belongings, including two bicycles, finally arrived, Hovius and wife took to the road once a week to visit new friends, another Dutch couple, some seven miles away. For some reason, the farmer frowned upon these excursions. The door was always locked when the cyclists returned at night.

"It was as if he didn't trust us. But it didn't stop us from leaving the farm to visit our friends. When we got back, we merely shouted until he got out of bed."

Ken Yates, a former Canadian soldier who had been stationed in 's-Hertogenbosch, Noord-Brabant, for half a year during the war, knew the Dutch language reasonably well. He tried his best to cheer things up a bit for the new settlers in the area since he had a soft spot in his heart for the Netherlanders. One day he phoned all the sponsors, telling them that a picnic for the newcomers was set for a certain park and that he expected them to drive their employees there.

"Our farmer never told us anything about that picnic," says Mrs. Hovius. "He and his family went away for the day. We were riding our bikes when Ken came along in his car and asked why we weren't at the picnic. He took us there, but the fun went out of it for us."

When the year's field work was done, Mrs. Hovius, expecting a child in November, had a feeling that the farmer wasn't too pleased about the future. The two small bedrooms he had made available to his charges held no room for a crib—they were filled to the ceiling with the furniture and household goods that had arrived from The Netherlands. Besides, winter was coming, and he made it no secret that no more work was available and that his hired hand should consider leaving.

"He suggested that we buy our own farm. We liked the idea. A nearby farm was for sale for $4,000. But where could we get that much money? We wrote to Ottawa for a loan, but it was refused on

There was lots of horse power on Canadian farms in the late 1940s. In the Chatham, Ontario, area, one of the sons of Adrian Verburg, who left Nederhorst den Berg, Noord-Holland, in June of 1949, drives the horses. In 1951, Verburg got his own farm—and his own tractor.
The women worked hard too. Joyce and Betty Veenstra, who arrived, with their parents in Kitchener, Ontario, in 1951, plant celery.

Young men planning to emigrate attend the camp Berg en Dal *in The Netherlands to learn about life and work in Canada. The camp is mentioned on page 89.*

Mr. and Mrs. Leo Hovius waited at this train station for their boss to show up.

the grounds that we hadn't been in Canada that long."

With the help of others, Hovius found another job. But the struggles weren't over yet for the young family. They had only just begun.

Mrs. Trudy Joldersma recalls: "Before we were married, my husband worked on a farm near Port Dover, Ontario. He was not allowed to use the farmer's washroom. The farmer's son took him to the barn and told him to relieve himself in the gutter behind the cows. After three months of this kind of treatment, he took his complaint to the fieldman, who found him

another job. But he lost his pay for the three months; the farmer never paid a penny for all the hard work. As a single man, far from his family and friends, he must have felt very lonely and rejected because of this demeaning treatment. Really, most of us were treated as second-class citizens in those first years. That made us determined to aim higher."

Canadians didn't like to be told what to do. After all, they were the bosses. What made these immigrants think they knew better anyway?

The average Dutchman, used to different work habits and methods, constantly looked for ways of doing things easier and better. He tried to share his ideas in broken English, but sometimes his efforts backfired.

Rev. John Van Harmelen, minister of the Christian Reformed Church in Brampton, Ontario, in the '50s, remembers one case: "I arranged for a newcomer from Holland, an interior decorator and a very clever man, to be placed in a boat factory. It wasn't long before he was telling other people: 'You shouldn't do it that way. In Holland, we do it this way.' He was told: 'Tomorrow we won't need you any more.' I took him to a carpenter who needed help building kitchens. He told the carpenter that such and such should be done in a certain way. He was at my door fourteen days later, without a job. Figuring that he wasn't going to get along with Canadians, I got him a job with another Hollander, who made ducts for furnaces. That did the trick. He worked there happily."

A Canadian farmer commented to a correspondent for a Dutch newspaper in 1947: "Those Dutch immigrants seem to think that they know everything better than we do. But a farm in Canada is different from a farm in Holland. We can learn a few things from them, but they must also learn quite a few things about how we do things."

Indeed, the immigrants brought many troubles on themselves. Why shouldn't a farmer have gotten angry when he found out that he had been sent an employee who didn't know his job?

One immigrant in the Niagara Peninsula, obviously not a farmer, was so afraid of getting kicked by a cow during milking time that he kept a fence between himself and the animal. Sticking his hands through the railing to get at the teats, he milked her "safely."

Conflicts within the immigrant community didn't promote goodwill either. One immigrant recalls: "When I went to the emigration officials in The Hague, I was told: 'Watch out for your fellow countrymen in Canada. They'll cheat you if they can.' It never happened to me. But it did happen to quite a few people. One man bought a farm from a fellow Dutchman on good faith. The seller said: 'We don't need a lawyer. Just a waste of money.' This man later found out that there was a second mortgage of $2,500 on the place. He was stuck with the payments, so he ended up with a pretty expensive farm."

Word of such transactions got around. In some circles, immigrants got a reputation for being out to get a fast buck. Unfavorable news reports seemed only to aggravate hard feelings.

In the early 1950s, the press in The Netherlands carried an item that alluded to some questionable practices in Montreal. A bureau there placed advertisements in Dutch newspapers, offering 'attractive' jobs for newcomers—for a fee,

of course. One report mentioned four hundred guilders. Dutch authorities in Canada were asked to check into this.

Fopke Jensma, who began work with immigration matters at the Royal Netherlands Embassy in Ottawa in 1948, was close to the situation for years. He knew hundreds of the newcomers—simple, God-fearing, serious, dedicated, and anxious to get ahead—and the problems they encountered.

"It wasn't easy at first," he says. "They didn't have any money. Lack of English made it difficult for them to communicate. The climate was different. And sometimes, because of their different ways of doing and looking at things, they couldn't get along with their sponsors. They worked long and hard for a low wage. The farmers usually regarded the minimum wage as the maximum and didn't bother paying more."

There were many problems over the

Dirk Van Rooyen, formerly of Vleuten de Meern, Utrecht, arrives at a field with his sons to start another day of work. In lower photo, they fork hay up onto a wagon. The family arrived in the Chatham, Ontario, area in 1948.

Members of the Reinders family of Drayton, Ontario, trundle the firewood home in wheelbarrows.

cases did not remain long with his employer and often, apparently, left without cause and without giving his employer any notice. In many cases, the complaints of the farmers were justified, but there have also been instances when the farmer treated the immigrant unfairly. It must be remembered that a labor contract is not legal in Canada, and, under normal conditions, no individual can be forced to remain at any job. It must also be remembered that the immigrants wish to earn money as rapidly as possible and they are leaving farm employment for the same reason that many of our native sons are leaving—to earn more money. On the other hand, it must be borne in mind that the farmer, who agrees to take an immigrant farm worker, agrees to provide work for a year, and he expects the immigrant to stay for a year. Often, an immigrant worker, on arrival, cannot speak English. This, in addition to his lack of experience in Canadian ways, makes him worth little more than his board for the first few months. It is little wonder, then, that farmers are annoyed when the immigrant leaves just when he is beginning to be of some value to his employer."

Jensma, who later served in Winnipeg and Toronto and became the agricultural attaché at the embassy, responsible for immigration matters, is convinced that, despite various problems, the Canadian farmer was pleased with the Dutch worker.

"Sure, a few immigrants were a bit pigheaded now and then and had to learn a few things. But generally, the immigrant knew how to tackle a job. That was appreciated. The early group that came over gave us a good name. They couldn't back out. They had no funds to fall back on. They had the attitude that they had no alternative but to make a go of it. That's why the Canadians liked the Dutch. They still do."

Many of the immigrants, living as frugally as possible, directed every spare cent toward a downpayment for their own piece of land with a barn and a few head of cattle.

"Really, the people from Holland came here at a very good time," says Jensma. "Many farms were vacant and the prices were low. They met with good opportunities. And many were glad that they could take advantage of them."

In the fall of 1947, it was time to get the corn in. The farmers pooled their

contracts which required the farmer to provide work and accommodation for at least one year. Contracts were broken by one side or the other when friction developed. When the parting was by mutual consent, nobody was concerned. But it was a different story when the farmer, at season's end, simply announced that his hired hand had to go because there was no more work or the house had to be used for some other purpose.

"Well, in those cases we tried to find another place for the immigrant. We figured this was the best solution. It wouldn't do any good to force an employer to take back an employee he didn't want. That would have been unpleasant for everyone involved. But finding another job was difficult. The employee usually was let go at the end of the harvest, a time when other farmers didn't have any more work either."

By 1951, there was a noticeable migration of young men from the farms to the cities. The immigrants were enticed by the higher wages paid by industry, the shorter hours of work, and the various benefits such as workmen's compensation and unemployment insurance. The exodus didn't please the farmers.

The 1952 annual report of the Nova Scotia Land Settlement Board stated: "There has been some dissatisfaction among farm employers of immigrant labor, because the immigrant in many

resources; everyone got a hand in harvesting the crop before the onset of wintry weather. Jerry Rekker, a recent arrival, worked long and hard to show his boss that he hadn't come to Canada to play tiddlywinks. Little did he realize that the other farmers were watching his every move.

"My farmer told me about it later. A lot of the farmers were still hesitant to sponsor immigrants, even though they badly needed help, because they weren't sure yet that we could do the work. I was one of the guinea pigs in the Bloomfield-Picton area of Ontario. Well, in January, the farmer's phone began to ring. Other farmers wanted to know whether it'd be worth their while to apply for a worker from Holland. My farmer told me that he had no good reason to inform them that I wasn't an able and willing worker. The result: in the spring, the immigrant population grew by some twenty families."

After the arrival of the first batch of immigrants in 1947, word spread among the farmers in the Waterford, Ontario, area that the ones who were from The Netherlands were hard-working and reliable and knew their business. Suddenly there was a big demand for them.

"The farmers really appreciated us," says Mrs. C.M. Hogeterp. "They knew that we were going to work hard in order to get ahead. And the bigger the families, the better. The children could pick strawberries in the spring and work in the fall harvests."

Farmers asked the Hogeterps to interest prospective immigrants in locating in their area. This wasn't too difficult, for people in The Netherlands had already written of plans to emigrate, asking to have a job and a house arranged for them.

"We would write ten letters a week," says Mrs. Hogeterp. "All we did was encourage the people to go ahead with their emigration plans. We told them that things weren't easy here, but that a good life was possible with God's help and their own determination to succeed. We have since heard stories of how immigrants in other places were poorly treated by farmers. All I can say is that the farmers we dealt with were terrific."

Before many years passed, almost the entire Hogeterp family was in Canada.

After his tour of Canada in 1948, Rev. D.J. Scholten of the *Gereformeerde Kerk*

Het Vrije Volk

wrote an interesting report for prospective emigrants in Groningen.

"First of all, all the fabulous stories about Canada being a land of 'golden mountains' and all the rumors that it costs next to nothing to buy and operate a sizable farm there are indeed highly fictitious. On the contrary, life in Canada means work, work, work! Sometimes people have to work from twelve to fifteen hours a day in tropical heat."

He warned that the social benefits available in The Netherlands were far more than those which had been legislated in Canada.

"The first year is particularly difficult for most immigrant families. The breadwinner has to sign on for a meagre wage, usually one that runs between $50 and $100, the average being $75. And although a dollar has two and a half times the value of the guilder, the price of commodities in Canada is not proportionally

Canadian immigrant farmers will be interested in this photo taken in 1949. A shipment of cattle is being inspected at Rotterdam. The caption reads: "Farmer with dairy herd leaves for America." The rules on what could be imported differed with each country that accepted immigrants.

lower. The price of some articles in dollars is only a little bit less than the price in The Netherlands in guilders. If you also consider that Dutch law requires that any money saved up in The Netherlands be left behind, you will see that it is absolutely necessary to manage one's affairs very carefully."

Rev. Scholten had some positive news too.

"As well as good prospects in trade and industry, it is indeed possible, much more so than in The Netherlands, to buy a farm of respectable acreage, though it requires hard work and careful management. In many cases, such an investment costs no more than a few thousand dollars, and the system of mortgages is very favorable."

In 1949, the immigration people in Ottawa had some satisfying news in their an-

nual report: more than six hundred Dutch families in Canada had already established themselves on their own farms. The immigration program seemed to be working!

A bad case of hay fever made life difficult for Rimmer Tjalsma, who had come to a farm at Watford, Ontario, in 1950. On many days, work was next to impossible. When there was no improvement, his sponsor suggested that he move away from the farm.

"I went to the Canadian immigration office in Sarnia and asked if there was another job somewhere. The official said that there wasn't. Then I asked him what I should do. He replied: 'I suggest you go back to where you came from.' He meant Holland, of course."

Tjalsma looked over the pamphlets that various church representatives had distributed on the boat, and he picked a name at random: Rev. Harri Zegerius of the Reformed Church, based in Hamilton. The minister was understanding when the problem was explained to him over the telephone, saying: "Hop on the earliest train and come and see me. I'm sure we can help you."

Before long, Tjalsma was making $10 a day in the tobacco harvest. His earnings were "terrific," considering he had made only $45 a month at the farm near Watford. There was one big drawback, however: the work was only seasonal.

Jacob Huizinga remembers: "The hardest thing for me to get used to was being

Rimmer Tjalsma primes tobacco at John Hooyer's farm near Nestleton, Ontario. Many immigrants found seasonal employment on tobacco belt farms like the one below.

treated like an idiot. In Holland, I had my own business with ten men working for me. The farmer I worked for had two sons, fifteen and seventeen, who would give me orders. If I didn't understand or if I did something wrong, they'd yell at me: 'No Jake, you can't do it that way.' One day, I grabbed a piece of wood and yelled back and threatened them. Boy oh boy, what a trouble we had over that one. There sure were a lot of things I didn't know anything about, but I didn't know that then. My pride was hurt."

Near Cloverdale, British Columbia, John Booy and his wife thought that pigsties in The Netherlands were cleaner than the little house they had to scrub and dust and make liveable for themselves. The place was empty.

"We didn't have any household goods, but the farmer said we could buy an old stove for $5. We found a pair of old chairs at the dump. We also managed to scrounge up an old table, an old couch, a bed held together with wire, and an old mattress. We had taken three blankets with us from Holland."

Mrs. Booy did an admirable job of painting the interior. They bought linoleum for the floor and hung curtains. After a few weeks, there was electric light. Wow, the place didn't look like a pigsty any more!

There was also something to put on the dinner table. When Mrs. Booy was able to buy a pig's head for five cents, there was soup and meat to last a week.

"But we had to work hard for the two couples who ran the farm," says Booy. "We started milking at 4:30 in the morning. At 10 o'clock, my wife had to join one couple on the combine, and she came home no earlier than 10 p.m. I worked with the other couple, taking in the grain and milking the cows at night. Boy, did those people fight among themselves. One time, I nearly got hit in the head by a flying pail aimed at the other fellow. The pay wasn't much—$60 for both of us during the first month. Two times we got $100, and the last time we were back to $60, because the price of the old stove and other costs had to be taken off. Well, when we left to go to another farm, I threw the lid of the stove into the river to make sure the farmer wouldn't sell it again to someone else."

In early August, 1948, Klaas and Rensje Molema and their four children arrived in Bellevue, Alberta, a coalmining town high in the mountains. Two days later, Molema started work in a mine, earning $10.85 a day. This was very good money for those days, considering that a laborer in a sawmill, for example, was paid $4.50 a day.

"The work in the mine was hard, of course," says Molema, now of Richmond, British Columbia. "But we hardly noticed that in those days. We had to start from scratch, and hard work meant survival,

With a caterpillar diesel tractor, Cecil Aukema plows under corn stalks on Walpole Island, Ontario. Romol Corp., which farmed 2,400 acres on leased Indian reserve land, provided work for varying lengths of time for almost a hundred Dutch immigrants in the 1950s.

At right, fieldworkers take a break for a photo. These men were busy hoeing at C.H. Prudhomme Ltd., a nursery near Beamsville, Ontario. The other scenes are from Holland Marsh, where many early immigrants settled to work the rich soil.

and maybe advancing a bit. After my shift in the mine was over at 3:30 p.m., I worked for another three hours as a plumber-tinsmith at a local hardware store, and I put in a full day there on Saturdays. I got ninety cents an hour for that work."

After eleven months, he quit the mine and started on his own. He had put in a bid for hauling government mail.

"I met the westbound train at 12:45 a.m. and put the mail from two towns (Bellevue and Hillcrest) on board. I delivered the incoming mail to both post offices. At 5:15 a.m., I did the same thing for the eastbound train. This work, six nights a week, paid me an annual salary of $2,600."

Joe Vaessen, just arrived in Toronto and needing a job, was offered help by his brother, an earlier immigrant.

"He told me that his boss wanted to meet me tomorrow and that I should bring a bottle of Bols *Oude Klare* with me. It certainly wouldn't do any harm, he said, because his boss was a former sea captain and certainly must love a nip now and then."

At eight o'clock in the morning, Vaessen waited in the bitter cold at the intersection of Highway 401 and Bathurst Street for his brother, who was to accompany him to the interview.

"Was he ever upset when he saw my unshaven face. I told him I couldn't help it. My equipment—brush, razors, and lather—was packed in my *kist* and still in transit."

The boss hadn't arrived yet and his office had all the equipment necessary to get rid of the unsightly stubble. It was a race against time, but Vaessen succeeded in making himself presentable before the employer showed up.

"I was introduced to him by my brother. Because I didn't understand a thing of what they were talking about, I felt it was a good idea to come forward with my bottle. A big, friendly smile creased the man's face. That same morning, I was working with machines I had never seen before."

In the winter of 1950-51, Pim and George Veeneman got a real taste of the Canadian wilderness. They had landed a cooking and maintenance job in a lumber camp some forty-five miles west of Rocky Mountain House in the Albertan foothills. It was an unlikely place for someone who had come to Canada in 1948 as a farm laborer. But jobs were hard to come by in those days.

A dirt trail carved out of the forested hills by bulldozers served as umbilical cord to the world. Travel on it was precarious at the best of times, and a heavy snowstorm could block it for days. The rectangular bunkhouses, home for up to fifty lumbermen and mill crew, and the sheds for horses and storage had been assembled from logs cut at the site. The kitchen-dining hall and the office-store, both prefabricated, had served in previous camps.

"The kitchen-dining hall was the most important building in the camp," recalls Mrs. Veeneman, now of Simcoe, Ontario. "When the meal was ready, I would grab a hammer and beat a triangle of steel hanging on the outside wall. The men loved to hear that sound. Washed up and with only heavy shirts for coats, they would come dashing through the snow as if competing in the Olympics."

Their wages for working fifteen hours a day for four and a half months would total $800.

"This was a very good salary for winter employment at that time. Besides, we didn't have a chance to spend a penny."

One evening, four students of the Three Hills Bible College, armed with an accordion, knocked on the kitchen door to invite the Veenemans to an evangelical meeting in the largest bunkhouse. Mrs. Veeneman was anxious to go—"it was my first chance to see the quarters of my boarders"—and she left her pots and pans in the care of her husband.

"An oil drum converted into a log-burning heater provided warmth. Lines of damp clothing, from longjohns to parkas, were strung everywhere. There were no chairs, but the iron bedsteads and the night tables made of orange-crates offered adequate seating."

As the evening progressed, she felt the presence of God's Spirit among these rugged men in their crude environment. She asked the students for permission to sing, for she knew a few English hymns by then.

"The men were astonished. They had never met a Christian cook in a lumber camp."

Huibert Van Drunen, who moved to the St. Thomas, Ontario, area after a few years in Ilderton, also had a somewhat unusual job: he worked on a horse farm, grooming and training horses.

Logging: Felling Trees

To get to the sawmill site, Bill Dieleman crosses the Bulkley River (British Columbia) on a raft. At left, Martin Kloostra makes short work of a tree. Horses haul the logs out.

"Several times he raced horses at the fall fairs," recalls his wife. "He didn't go to the big tracks, because he wasn't licensed for that. He enjoyed those years very much and planned to get his licence. However, he decided not to go through with it since his health wasn't too good. Besides, Sunday racing was coming in, and he would have refused to work on that day."

John Versluys, who came to Edmonton, Alberta, in 1953 from Klundert, Noord-Brabant, says: "I left my father's bakery to try my luck in Canada. I worked in Edson for a short time and then was laid off. A friend had written to me and told me to come to Vancouver. There was lots of work for good money, he said. But when I got there, I couldn't find a job, and my English was poor. I was desperate; I had no more money. Finally I got a positive answer to an ad. I took a bus out as far as it went, and then I walked three miles. The farmer came to the door. He was a surly old guy who didn't talk. He yelled. He showed me where I could stay. It was a smelly old bunkhouse littered with mouse droppings. Then he showed me what I would have to do: feed the pigs garbage from restaurants. Thinking of the prodigal son, I said: 'In my father's bakery there are cakes and tarts.' But he didn't understand Dutch."

From Willem VanderMolen, who moved to British Columbia after a bad experience

in Alberta in 1951: "To find work in the middle of winter was not easy. Our oldest son found some evening work in a bowling alley, picking up the pins. He made around seventy-five cents an evening. There was lots of snow that winter, so I knocked on doors and offered to shovel walks and driveways. At one place, I earned $8 and a warm meal. I had wings going home, clutching that money in my hand. We had a feast in our house that day."

The work was hard. And the days were long—sometimes fourteen hours. But when J.A. Grootenboer and his wife returned home from the beetfields near Portage La Prairie, Manitoba, they felt satisfied. They were earning good money. And they were happy.

Their older children looked after the younger ones and prepared the meals. When mother got home, tired and dirty, they listened carefully to instructions for the following day. It was the summer of 1948, and there was no school.

"More families came that summer—about seven in all," says Grootenboer. "On Sundays, we met together for reading services. We took turns being host. The nearest Christian Reformed Church was in Winnipeg, sixty-five miles away. Well, one Sunday we decided to go to church there in a pickup truck. There were four couples—three people in front and five in the back. The driver assured us he knew where he was going, but in Winnipeg he took a wrong turn and we arrived at the church when the sermon was nearly over."

When the work in the beetfields was done, the income stopped. Grootenboer still had a roof over his head, but he had to look elsewhere for money to pay for the groceries. So he went to a Hutterite colony, some thirty-five miles away, and began sawing poplar firewood into four-foot lengths. He stayed there only two weeks, having decided it was no work for a Dutchman. There was lots of snow that winter, and the Canadian National Railway needed extra help to keep the tracks, the vital lifelines, clear.

"I stayed there for ten weeks, shoveling snow and pitching ice for sixty cents an hour. The gaps between the rails and the switches had to be cleared."

He had no car. He couldn't use a bicycle. So every morning, he walked five miles along Highway 1, often in a biting

Even though the women had their hands full with housework and looking after the children, they still helped out with the manual farm work. Mrs. J.A. Grootenboer loads bales of hay on her husband's farm near Murillo, Ontario.

north wind, and arrived at the bunkhouse before 8 a.m. Not another soul was on the road at that hour to offer him a ride. It was a different story after 5 p.m., however. Then there was lots of traffic.

"I got the same job during the second winter. But by that time, I had bought a used half-ton truck. In my spare time, I built a wooden box on the back. Not only could I get to work, but I could take my entire family to church and wherever else we wanted to go."

Like so many of the others who had to struggle during the first years, Grootenboer eventually bought his own farm near Murillo, Ontario.

Melvin Elgersma, who came to Canada in search of land, became his own boss right away. Six hours after stepping out of a train in Hamilton, Ontario, in mid-May, 1947, he was out seeding a 165-acre rented farm near Dundas. His uncle, already in Canada, had made all the arrangements beforehand.

"It was just one of the unusual things we experienced—that everything went so fast," says Mrs. Elgersma. "We arrived just in time to work the fields and plant the corn. Our cousins arrived with their machinery only a few hours after we had moved into our house."

Six years later, Elgersma owned a 300-acre farm, his own dairy operation, and more than fifty Holstein cows. But he refused to stand still. Before long, he and four sons were farming eight hundred acres near Cayuga, Ontario. He beefed up his herd with purebred cattle and made heavy investments in machinery. His farm was quickly regarded as one of the finest dairy operations in the area.

Harold Skinner, the county's agricultural representative, told an interviewer in 1956: "Elgersma's business acumen and his ability to go at things in a big way are responsible for his quick success in this country."

Mrs. Elgersma adds a few more reasons: "We were able to get ahead with the help of our relatives and our children—the oldest was thirteen when we arrived—and with the blessing of God, who gave us good health and the ability to work."

In 1954, after more than one year in Canada, Kees Verburg wrote a letter to a friend, an official of the *Christelijke Emigratie Centrale*, about his impressions of his newly adopted land. He didn't use

Logging: Cutting Logs

When the logs are ready for cutting, George and Orville Markman roll them onto the carriage. The logs are then passed through the saw.

many glowing terms. Some excerpts:

• "The official unemployment figures in Canada are incorrect. Only the people who have an unemployment stamp book and go to the office to ask for work are counted. That does not include the immigrant farm workers: they do not get a book."

• "Almost nobody keeps his hired hand through the winter. Then they call the immigration officer in the spring and get a new family. Contracts are not honored. You may stay in the house for the winter, free of charge, but that is all."

• "Last fall, I worked in construction for a while, all the way in Toronto, 220 miles from here. We made good money. But we had to pay room and board and the gasoline for traveling, so not much was left. We would start out at midnight Sunday to be at work on time in the morning. In December, it started to freeze, and that was the end of the job. From then until April, we were home. It's hard for a farmer to sit at home and do nothing. We weren't the only ones either. Of the eleven

Hollanders on our road, there was only one who had a steady job. Like most of the women, our daughter had a job. She worked in a tobacco factory so that we could make ends meet. Families who didn't have a girl or a woman who could work out often used up all the money they had made in the summer."

• "This spring, we bought a farm of fifty acres for $3,750, with a downpayment of $1,000. Good house and land, but very neglected. We did that so as not to be out of work again. We now have lots of work. But it does not always pay. Last year my boss complained that he received only $1.55 for a bushel of wheat, compared to $1.80 the year before. Now we get only $1.20. If the prices of the products stay low, we may have to sell this place again. I'm not worried about that, though. We have done much to improve the farm, and should not have any problems selling it for a higher price."

Mrs. John Olydam of Grande Prairie, Alberta, recalls: "We worked for four years to save enough money to buy a John Deere tractor with row-crop front wheels and to rent a quarter section. One day, my husband was driving the John Deere across a slippery wooden bridge when the two front wheels got caught on a cross section and swung around. The tractor flipped over and landed in the creek. My husband, who had landed on the bank, walked to the Postma farm and said: 'That's it. We're finished.' A couple of days later, George Postma and his boys got some tractors to pull ours out. It could still run. We were back in business!"

Tony Wielemaker arrived from Koudekerke, Zeeland, in 1951. Working for a farmer in Holloway, Ontario, he became disillusioned with Canadian farming right away. He found the farm buildings shabby, the machinery neglected, and the grounds and fields overgrown with weeds.

Explains his wife, Hilda: "In Holland, he had worked with modern combines and tractors. In Canada, he wasn't even allowed to touch the outdated tractor or the other rusty farm implements, but was kept busy, very busy, at the menial job of scything. After three months, he'd had enough. He left the farm and found a job in construction. He started at seventy-five cents an hour as sweeper and errand boy,

The tobacco harvest in southern Ontario provided fall work for hundreds of immigrants. This photo, showing women at work near the kilns, was made available by Mrs. Mary Provoost of the Aylmer, Ontario, area. In the photo below, a scene from 1948: Melvin Elgersma's wife brings him coffee in the field.

and gradually worked his way up to carpenter. He is now owner of the Wielemaker Construction Company, small but sufficient."

In the spring of 1949, Carl Biel and his family were picked up at the railway station in Beamsville, Ontario, by their sponsor, a nursery grower. With him was a Dutchman who had already worked for the man for a year.

"First we went shopping for groceries," recalls Carl. "A loaf of bread cost nine cents. Then we were taken to a house on the farm near Vineland. The whole family—Dad, my brother, my sisters, and I—worked alongside Dutch immigrants. It was nice to speak Dutch, even though I wanted to learn English as quickly as possible. We worked six days a week, ten hours a day—an hour less on Saturday—at forty cents an hour."

In the fall, their boss looked for a reason to let them go. Most of the field work was finished and winter was around the corner. Carl's father moved to another part of Ontario, worked for a farmer for awhile, and then bought his own farm. Carl got a job on a farm in the Wainfleet area. When the farmer added another single Dutch immigrant to his work force in February, Carl's loneliness dissipated.

"In the spring of 1950, I went home to help my father start farming on our own. We bought some machinery and livestock, and worked the land for the spring seeding. It was tough at first: we had to get used to the Canadian farming methods, so different from the ones in Holland. But Dad was happy to have his own farm again."

John Van Eerden of La Glace, Alberta, remembers: "We had our papers processed through the *Christelijke Emigratie Centrale*. Then our sponsor fell through, and the government found us another one—a rancher southwest of Edmonton, 150 miles away from a Dutch church. We loved the foothills, but in 1953 we decided to go to Peace River. Land was cheap and the stories were great. Thirty miles out of Edmonton, the pavement stopped and the rain started. The mud roads were terrible. At one point where the road was under construction, the crew would wait until eight or ten vehicles were stuck before sending out a tractor and two men to pull everyone out. We bought the homestead because one hundred acres were seeded in

Logging: Finishing Up

The lumber is stacked for transport. At the end of a hard day's work, it's time to unwind. John VanderMeer, Dick Haajema, Clarence Haajema and Jack Reitsma know just how to do that. At left, Harry Bakker stands in a bunkhouse doorway.

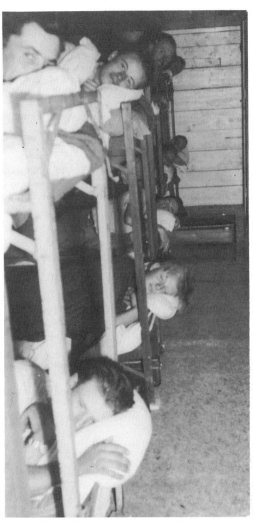

The young men who came from Holland to dig a living out of the soil had to start like most newcomers: as simple laborers. The work was hard, the hours long, and the pay somewhat meagre. But the companionship helped make up for the hardship. These photos, taken on Walpole Island, Ontario, were provided by Fred and Tina Feddes.

fescue, the big money maker in those days. But the fescue was an old crop. It cost us more to combine it than we got for the seed. That was a terrible setback. We were completely broke. But the land was cheap. We rented a school section from the government—160 acres—for $120 a year, and we didn't even have to pay taxes on that. Our machinery was shipped by boxcar from Calgary. On the day it arrived in Sexsmith, we couldn't find our traveler's cheques. They must have been put in the boxcar. But the man at the station insisted that he couldn't open the car until the freight was paid. Finally, we went to the bank and got replacements. We opened the boxcar—no cheques. The next Sunday, I found them in the pocket of my suit!"

In 1959, William Van Oosten was willing to tackle any job. "I did all kinds of things—helping in construction, lawn mowing and gardening, electric wiring, painting at the University of Western Ontario in London. But at the end of the year, no work of any kind was available."

Realizing that his unemployment insurance benefits wouldn't last forever, Van Oosten didn't hesitate one moment when he was offered a position as life in-

surance salesman in London. The irony flashed through his mind: his father had owned an insurance business in Rotterdam, and none of his sons had wanted to take it over.

"I had no choice. I decided to give it an honest try. Later, I wrote my exam for general insurance. I found that building up a business was extremely difficult; the pickings were lean. For two years, I also worked as a verger for an Anglican church to help me over the rough period."

He incorporated his business, and it steadily grew to a turnover of about $250,000 a year. His oldest son joined the firm after completing his university education, and took it over in 1975.

Fred Prins of Brooks, Alberta, recalls: "I was a butcher by trade, so I slaughtered a lot of horses for Dutch people. But when our Canadian friends came, we called it moose meat. We also kept a cow. She supplied more than enough milk for two families. What was left over, we bottled and sold as whole milk. One Victoria Day, John Snyders and I bought one hundred chickens and cleaned them. By noon, we had sold them all. So we went back and bought and cleaned 150 more. By eight o'clock, those were all gone. We didn't have even one left for ourselves. But we made $80 that day, when top wages were $10 a day for a good irrigation man."

John Wannet, also of Brooks, said: "We made extensive preparations for our move to Canada. We studied English. And even though I was a baker by trade, I took courses in welding, drafting, and construction to increase my employability. The day after I arrived in Lethbridge, I had a job as a baker in Bellevue, in the mountains. Two years later, I bought a bakery in a small town of a thousand people on the Alberta-Saskatchewan border. That was the first time we had second thoughts about coming to Canada. We couldn't get used to living on the prairies, and we weren't accepted by the community. After three years, I had the chance to sell the bakery, and we moved to Brooks. I owned the Dutch bakery there for eighteen years, and now I am the town manager."

Two of the sons of Teunis Schinkel had preceded him to Canada. They found work in a slaughtering house at Amherstburg, Ontario, and arranged for his employment there shortly after his arrival in 1953.

"I must confess that I felt humiliated by

Headed for Another Farm

When it was moving time for C.W. VandenHaak of Portage La Prairie, Manitoba, the used furniture crate came in handy. The former resident of Valkenburg, Zuid-Holland, repacked everything into the kist and headed for another farm. He did the same thing in 1952, when the family moved to St. Catharines, Ontario. But the trip did not go smoothly; snow-covered roads and trouble with one of the trailer's axles put them days behind schedule. The family slept in a local jail one night because no other accommodation was available.

Stoney Creek, Ontario, the spring of 1950: Harry DeJong attached boards to a cultivator, inventing a contraption to furrow the soil for the planting of Dutch potatoes. With him are his brothers, Albert and Ed, and his small daughter.

the job. Of course, I had to do the dirtiest work, because I didn't know how to slaughter a cow or a pig. I dragged away the guts of the cows and shook empty the large stomachs. It was a stinking task. Just think, in Utrecht I was neatly dressed in a yellow uniform jacket, selling milk, cheese, and groceries door to door. In Holland, I belonged to the middle class; in Canada, I was just an ordinary laborer. In September of 1954 I landed a more decent job—janitor of an elementary school—which I held until my 70th birthday."

It wasn't unusual for immigrants to change jobs frequently as they tried to move up the ladder to success. George Veeneman of Simcoe, Ontario, for example, moved eleven times since he came to Canada in 1948. He became farm laborer, bull cook, lumberjack, farmer, building contractor, and finally, real estate broker.

There were some who wanted instant success. They didn't find it, of course. Rev. John Van Harmelen tells this story: "A man who used to be a printer in Holland worked on a vegetable farm here. No matter how hard he looked, he couldn't find a job in the printing business. So he went back to Holland, where his old job was still open. I'm sure that if he had stayed in Canada, he would have found a printer's job eventually. If you didn't burn the bridges behind you, you didn't have as much incentive to succeed."

After serving out his one-year contract on a farm in the Cornwall, Ontario, area, George Eggink set his eyes on Hamilton, where some acquaintances from Drenthe had settled. Little did he realize that he was about to enter the toughest period of his immigration: he would be scratching from paycheque to paycheque and moving about like a European gypsy.

In the spring of 1949, he took the train to Hamilton and looked up Peter Turkstra, a long-time immigrant, who landed him a job at a vegetable farm in nearby Burlington. The pay was $90 a month, including free rent and free vegetables. But it was hardly enough to support a family that had grown to seven persons.

"In the fall, there was no more work, and I had to move again. Mr. Turkstra got me a job at a milk factory in Burford. But I couldn't get along with a foreman there and in the spring of 1950 decided to look for something else. Two farmers were interested in hiring me—until they found out that I have five children. Then they came up with excuses: the house was too small, they were afraid children would wreck it, etc. Finally I found a job in a milk factory in Ingersoll. But when we got to the town, we found our house in such a terrible state that my wife didn't even want to set foot in it. No wonder they wouldn't let us see it beforehand. So back we went, with all our household effects loaded on a truck, and ended up with one of our friends in the Hamilton area. You know, I seriously thought then about going back to Holland. My father had a small business there with a new house, and he offered this to me. It was a tough decision, but in the end, we decided to stick it out, come what may, and work hard toward the downpayment for our own farm."

Their perseverance paid off. For $8,500, they were able to buy a 100-acre farm, including four milk cows, two heifers, four horses, some hay, grain, and farm implements, from a farmer in the Jarvis area who wanted to retire. Their struggle wasn't over yet, by any means. But they had a foot in the door, and the thought of returning to The Netherlands never recurred.

John Hofstee, fifteen years old, had been in the Chatham, Ontario, area for only a few days. He and his father were hand-picking corn left over from the previous year's crop. John worked Friday afternoon and Saturday and was told on Monday that there was no more work for him on the farm—none at all.

"Then I worked in the area for a few weeks, cleaning up fields, chopping wood, and the like. Later, I packed my suitcase and hitch-hiked the forty or so miles to Wallaceburg, where I landed a job as a construction worker. I had to carry bricks and blocks and help mix cement. The job was really too heavy for a boy; I was fired after a few weeks."

He returned home and tackled the back-breaking task of thinning rows of sugarbeets. When the strawberry season started, he cycled ten miles, his brother sitting on the crossbar, to get to the berry patch. Later on, they picked cherries. And then it was time for the early potatoes.

The lack of steady work unnerved him a bit. His father, a trucker by trade, was also very unhappy—he couldn't get used to the long hours of farm work for such meagre pay. So they decided to move. Aylmer, in the heart of a tobacco-growing area, seemed a good place. The Hofstees had heard that there was work for everyone in the tobacco fields. Why, children were being paid fifty cents an hour for hoeing!

"Dad and I found work in construction in St. Thomas shortly after we moved to Aylmer," says John. "Every day, we hitch-hiked back and forth until we got our own car in late August. After a few weeks, we quit the construction job in order to prime tobacco. This paid a higher wage—$11 a day. But that job ended after

a few weeks when we refused to work on Sunday."

Other jobs followed in quick succession. Finally, John landed steady work at VioBin Canada, a factory, at fifty cents an hour. His father continued in construction until he was laid off in February, 1952.

"We were poor that winter. It was the only time that Dad and Mom ever accepted money from the deacons of the church. The deacons had to do some persuading, saying that the money had been collected for exactly that purpose."

The story goes on. In 1956, Hofstee got his wish and became a truck driver again, working for National Grocers. John, tired of jumping from job to job and concerned about his future, enrolled in correspondence courses from the Ontario Ministry of Education, later followed banking courses, then business courses at the University of Toronto, and finally obtained his B.A. degree from Wilfrid Laurier University in Waterloo in 1972. He is now head of the business education department of the Listowel District Secondary School.

"If the primary purpose of our family's emigration to Canada was to take advantage of the opportunities for the children, then I guess the goal was reached," says John. "But the road to this accomplishment was very difficult for my father and mother, especially during the first years in Canada."

One day after her arrival in Toronto in 1955, Cornelia Annegarn, a dietician, applied at three hospitals for a job.

"At Toronto Western Hospital, I was accepted right away, but when they heard

Wendell Vanden Hazel takes a rest on his boss's truck at Listowel, Ontario, in 1952.

Mrs. J.R.T. Sheehy (née Annegarn) and her family.

Gerrit Barten, who left Noord-Scharwoude, Noord-Holland, in 1954, packs apples on the farm belonging to Harold Bouter, his sponsor, at Carrying Place, Ontario.

feelings, something she couldn't do with her English-speaking colleagues.

The Dutch nurse with whom she had corresponded before emigration also helped her get adjusted to the Canadian way of life. She took her by car to the majestic Niagara Falls and to picturesque Algonquin Park.

"I became ecstatic about the vastness of the countryside, the rolling hills, the distant horizons. I drank it in with my eyes, uttering one exclamation after another about the beauty of this land."

After fourteen days, Cornelia received her first paycheque. That was a big joy. The five hundred guilders she had received from her father prior to emigration were worth only $125, and half of that was already spent on necessities.

"Having been in the saving habit in The Netherlands in order to go to Canada, I started to save right away to pay back my debts and have money to go back to Holland in case of an emergency. That emergency came too soon. I had $500 saved when my mother sent a telegram that my father, after an operation, was in critical condition. Soon after my arrival, he died."

She returned to Canada, downhearted. Her fellow workers gave her a warm welcome, which helped her to get over her feeling of emptiness. Before long, she started going to clubs and taking courses to get to know more about life in Canada. At one of the clubs, she met the man who would eventually be her husband and the father of four children—J.R.T. Sheehy.

She says now: "I'm glad to be a Canadian. I'm happy in my new country and never regret the move."

that I had arrived only a day or two earlier, they thought it would be better to let me acclimatize a week before starting work."

Although she had read a lot of English and could speak it quite well, Cornelia had great difficulty understanding the spoken tongue. Everyone talked too fast. She found it deadly tiring trying to follow conversations. Her first days in the dietitians' residence were somewhat embarrassing. Little wonder that she loved to visit Dutch friends, where she could speak Dutch freely. There she could speak her mind, express her impressions and her

Ted Smeenk's first job in Canada in 1951 was in the production department of the Kellogg's cereal factory in London, Ontario. It was a new experience for the former office manager, accountant, and owner of a radio and appliance store.

"I had never lifted more than a fountain pen, and here I was lifting 100-pound bags of corn and rice all day. The pay was high: $40 a week, including night-shift bonus. That was because of the rates negotiated by the American Grainmillers' Union. But I still counted every penny."

With temperatures in the factory in the 90s Fahrenheit, he looked forward to his two coffee breaks. A machine in the cafeteria dispensed soft drinks for six cents. That was too much. So his wife, Pauline, packed a teabag with his lunch.

"Hot water was abundant in the factory. In the morning break, I dipped my teabag, squeezed it, and carefully put it back in the piece of waxed paper. I did it again at lunch and in the afternoon, and I had three cups of tea for less than half a cent. When summer temperatures reached ninety degrees outside, I would go home on my bicycle and count my pennies, hoping I could spare thirty cents for a brick of ice-cream for the family in the hot upstairs apartment."

By October, production slackened, and Smeenk faced another new experience.

"I was laid off! I had never heard of a layoff when I was in Holland. As far as I knew, people were always employed full-time. Plants and machines were too costly to leave idle for part of the year. Seasonal manufacturing was augmented by diversified product lines which operated in the off-season. Now I didn't qualify for unemployment benefits. No more income! After pleading that I could not feed my family, I was hired back as a floor sweeper for ninety-seven cents an hour. I swept floors, washed walls, and crept on my belly under machines to scrape the grease off the floors. A month later, the whole factory was spick and span. That was the end of my factory job. I was laid off again . . .

With his back against the wall, he was ready to tackle anything. He remembered the new peeling knives he had bought at an auction sale in The Netherlands and had brought with him to Canada.

"I put some knives in one pocket, some potatoes in another, and went from door to door, demonstrating to my Canadian neighbors how to use a quick-peeler. Each sale brought a quarter, and each quarter bought two day-old loaves of bread at the A & P store."

Almost daily he went to the unemployment office to look for work. But unemployment was rampant that winter. Finally, the director called to say a sales job was available.

"Another unemployed man was making paper maché candy cane decorations in his basement. He gave me three samples. Each one sold would give him twenty-five cents for materials, twenty-five cents profit, and there would be twenty-five cents for me. After walking for two days and earning twenty-five cents, I threw away the samples and faced the bleak future."

Before the layoff, Smeenk had used his penny savings—$600—as a deposit to buy an old house. The owner, an elderly woman, had been admitted to a mental hospital the year before. The dwelling had been neglected for ten years.

"The toilet was broken and backing up. The plumbing was leaking, and when we turned on the water, the ceilings came down one by one from the leaks. The floors were covered with two inches of dirt. Rags filled the holes in the windows."

On moving day, Smeenk discovered that the hydro and water had not been turned on as requested. Late at night, in the darkness, the exhausted couple spread a mattress on the filthy floor and fell asleep instantly. The following morning, it being Sunday, Smeenk went to see one of the priests at the Redemptorist church next door and asked to borrow some lightbulbs, a ladder, a pail, and a sponge. The priest said: "But this is Sunday!" Smeenk then asked if he knew the story of Christ saying it was all right for a man to rescue his donkey from a well on the Sabbath, adding: "Father, my donkey is in the well, and I only have today to get it out." The priest gave him his blessing and all the cleaning supplies that had been requested. It took a whole day to clean one room, even with the help of cousin Corrie Bontje, the housekeeper of Bishop John C. Brody.

Necessary repairs to the plumbing, drain, and toilet put Smeenk $400 in debt. There were payments to be made on a $1,500 loan from the Catholic credit union and on a $5,000 mortgage. And he had mouths to feed. Little wonder that he was eager to tackle any job that came along.

Bachelors would often visit the Smeenk home for a game of cards or a solid Dutch meal. One of them, Joe VanderWerf, a landscaper for General Motors, mentioned one day that two men from London Life had offered him a job selling insurance to immigrants. Joe, who wasn't interested, asked if Smeenk wanted the job. The reply: "I'll do anything. We have to eat, you know."

Smeenk called at the wrong firm. It was the manager of North American Life who was looking for someone to call on immigrants. Smeenk was hired, but only after a struggle. The head office was against hiring someone who hardly knew a street or a soul in his community and who spoke English with difficulty. The manager put him on staff nevertheless, guaranteeing $225 a month advance on commission out of his own salary.

"I trained with a dictionary, translating unusual words of the application form

Having put all his money into the purchase of the farm, Wolter Hummel had to use horses for the first two years. The work became easier when he bought a tractor.

and medical questions. Later, I kept studying company courses, tax laws, etc."

After more than thirty years, Smeenk is still with North American Life, although he has been on disability leave since 1979 when he suffered a ruptured aorta and required heart surgery.

Wolter Hummel and his wife, formerly of Haren, Groningen, were somewhat unusual passengers on the *Waterman* in June, 1947. They were headed for Canada, but not as emigrants. They intended to visit friends in Parkland, Alberta, and then return to The Netherlands.

But Wolter soon became convinced that Canada was the best place for an enterprising farmer to be. Forty-eight years old, he applied for immigrant status and stayed in Alberta for a few years to get experience in Canadian farming methods. Then he bought a dairy farm at Tatamagouche, Nova Scotia, using the proceeds from the sale of his house in The Netherlands. Within a few years, he bought two neighboring farms and combined all three into one unit.

After eight years in Nova Scotia, the property was sold and the couple moved to Truro, where Mrs. Hummel resumed her profession as a teacher for the deaf. But when her husband found retirement boring, he bought new acreage.

When they felt it was time to retire for a second time, he and his wife moved to Calgary, Alberta. They stayed there for nine years before deciding to head for Brantford, Ontario, where a relative lived.

"We lived there for three months, decided we didn't like it, and went back to Calgary," says Mrs. Hummel. "Still, we wanted to be close to the family, so we're back in Brantford again . . ."

Mrs. Hummel's mother, Aaltje Beukema, came to Canada to stay after the death of her husband. She died at the age of eighty-four in 1961, and was buried at Tatamagouche. The Hummels (above) now live in Brantford, Ontario.

In the Beetfields and Elsewhere

G. Kuik

In the Beetfields and Elsewhere

"Alberta needs approximately a thousand sugarbeet workers," stated *De Gids*, a guide for prospective emigrants published by the Christian Reformed Church. "The farmers are asking for Hollanders. One can have a contract per acre or per hour. Included are a free house, a stall for a cow, and a garden. Most of those who tackle their work with diligence can have their own land within a few years and make a good living. However, one has to be a beet worker to do this work. Families with children will have no difficulty being placed."

Willem VanderMolen will never forget stepping out of the train at Coaldale, Alberta, in the spring of 1951.

"Farmers were waiting to pick up their help. Some were laughing. Other were scowling. I thought: 'Which one is ours?' Then a tall, husky man with a dark frown found out that we were the ones he had sponsored. Suddenly it seemed as if the clock had been put back. It seemed he thought we were his slaves."

The family piled into an open truck. The first stop was a little store, where they bought food and household items. Then they continued on over three miles of back roads until they came to a dilapidated farmhouse.

"I thought at first that this was our house. But it turned out that the farmer lived there. Our place stood a hundred feet back in the field, near an irrigation ditch—a former chicken coop, twenty-four feet by twenty-four feet. Behind it was a little outhouse. Since we were anxious to see our new home, the farmer opened the door. What we saw was not impressive. A small space combined as a living room and kitchen. A rusty cooking-heating stove stood on one end of it. Behind a wall we found two small bedrooms, six feet by six feet, each nearly filled by a bunkbed. Here we had to live with a family of eight. We were too tired to grasp our situation. We unpacked the few belongings we had taken with us—the rest would come later—and went to bed early."

During the night, constant howling kept most of the family awake for hours. No one knew what was making the eerie

noise. The next day, they learned that a pack of coyotes, or prairie wolves, had decided to sing them a welcome. The VanderMolens were advised to stay away from the animals.

It took some time for the recent arrivals from one of the most congested countries in the world to fathom the vast distances of southern Alberta. Their nearest neighbor lived one mile away. And the nearest public school was three miles away; the children had to be picked up and brought home each day by bus. There was another big surprise one June morning: a snowfall had completely covered the sugarbeet plants.

As he looked out at the snow, Vander Molen feared the worst. His farmer seemed to have been born in a bad mood; he would surely take out his frustrations on the workers. Even after the snow melted, the slippery mud would keep workers from the fields. Valuable days would be lost.

Sure enough, the farmer's scowl grew blacker each day. He saw the weeds outgrow his plants. When the soil was firm again, VanderMolen and his wife began to hack out the weeds carefully, making sure the plants were left untouched. But the boss became impatient. He

Under a hot July sun, members of the J.P. Kolk family hoe beets near Iron Springs, Alberta.

Mr. and Mrs. Willem Vander Molen celebrate their 50th wedding anniversary.

But VanderMolen was behind in his work. The farmer let him know that more than once.

"My wife worked in the fields just as long as I did. Then she still had to make a warm meal, clean the house, do the wash, look after the kids, and so on. Many, many times we were so tired that we lay down on the bed fully clothed and fell asleep. Still, when we heard the whistle of the train in the distance, we thought: 'Don't stop for us! We want to stay here!' "

The work got done. At last the fields were clean and the beets could have a chance to grow. Then Mother Nature got in the way again: an extremely dry summer stunted their growth. But regardless of their size, the beets had to be harvested in the fall. That was the next big task.

Wielding a large beetknife, Vander-Molen chopped off the tops of the beets that had been rooted out of the ground. The work wasn't easy, but it didn't take long to get used to it. Things went wrong again when it started snowing on October 8, VanderMolen's birthday. When the storm was over and only the top of the beets were visible, all work had ground to a halt.

"Many farmers believed that the snow would stay. Some even gave their workers permission to move on if they wanted to. But our farmer wouldn't hear of it. The snow melted slowly, and the work resumed. In the middle of the night, you could hear the neighbors' tractors working the fields. That was the best time, really. When the sun came up, everything got muddy and slippery."

VanderMolen was irked that his farmer never started work earlier than five or six o'clock. One day when there were no more beets to be topped, he decided to explain to the farmer how he could get the harvest in more quickly.

"I biked out to where he was working in the field. I asked him kindly if he could dig up more beets in a day. Quite angry, he said no, that was impossible. I then made the mistake of telling him that other farmers started much earlier than he did, and that they were making better progress. He suddenly became so angry that he smashed his big fist into my face. Blood came streaming out. I spotted a hammer and tried to hide it, afraid that he might use it. But he thought I had other intentions and another wicked blow followed. You know, the thought of striking back never crossed my mind. I knew it had been building up to this since our refusal to work on Sunday. I thank God that no

wanted his help to work on Sundays to make up for lost time.

"Well, we wouldn't work on Sunday. Our farmer was very, very angry. He said that his former employees had worked seven days a week. But I told him that for us it was a day of worship. Other immigrants who had been here for some years made sure we had a ride to church in Coaldale each Sunday."

Relations deteriorated further when some of VanderMolen's children contracted scarlet fever. "The doctor ordered all of us to stay at home and not mix with other people. No one was allowed to visit us, and my wife and I couldn't go out to work. This lasted a number of weeks, and of course it meant trouble with our farmer. He cut off our free milk and eggs. And when he bought our groceries on Saturday, he often kept them in his house until Monday. We were told by other immigrants that we were unfortunate to have a difficult boss, that all of them weren't like that. Well, that didn't help us then."

One Sunday when the family came home from church, a supply of milk, eggs, and other food stood on the kitchen table. The mystery donor never identified himself. Then the rest of the family's belongings arrived. There was a feast to celebrate the occasion. Their pedal-organ was played as never before, and the entire family, forgetting for a while their difficulties, sang hymns and praised the Lord.

Provincial Archives of Alberta

A farm worker checks the irriga-tion in a southern Alberta beet-field.

hatred came into my head then."

When Mrs. VanderMolen saw her bloodied husband, she knew right away what had happened. Her mind was made up—they would leave this farm as soon as she could make an arrangement with another farmer, whose help had moved to British Columbia when the snow fell. They made an agreement to break the contract. The wages still owing would not be paid.

"We moved that very afternoon," says Mr. VanderMolen. "Our new house was one big room—no kitchen, no living room, no bedrooms. An area set aside for sleeping was marked off with drapes. Still, this farmer wanted to please us. It seemed as if we had moved from night in-to day."

When the harvest was done, the family quickly moved to the other side of the Rocky Mountains, far away from the beets and the bitter memories.

In an article published in the United States in the late 1940s, Rev. John De Jong, home missionary in southern Alber-ta for the Christian Reformed Church, wrote: "The immigrant suffers many physical privations. Imagine yourself in a little, dirty, cold shack way off somewhere on the prairie, on a road which is inaccessible part of the time due to snowdrifts and mud, and with little contact with the outside world. Your kit-chen stove may be the only source of heat. There may be another room which must serve as bedroom for the family, but some shacks do not even have two rooms. I remember a home where the visitors have to sit on the bed next to the table and the stove. Another family of fourteen has two little houses of two rooms each, small rooms at that, with no modern conve-niences whatever. Water must be carried from a distance, if snow cannot be melted. An oil lamp provides the only light. Dur-ing our recent forty- to fifty-below temperatures, the windows were so thick-ly frosted that they were about an inch thick, admitting hardly any light at all—this was in the kitchen, due to the steam from cooking. These people had owned a fine home in the Old Country, with every convenience. Never, however, have I heard a note of complaint from them. Their lamp of hope burns brightly. We need not wonder, however, that some immigrants become discouraged and despondent. Ask yourself: how would I react under such conditions?"

Another minister, Rev. J.M. VandeKieft, wrote in the *Banner*, a publication of the Christian Reformed Church, in 1951: "I was invited to come in and see one of their homes. It was an elongated chicken coop, redecorated and made to look homey and cozy in real Dutch style, clean, and with furniture neatly arranged. They took some pride in the way they had transformed the old coop into their first home in Canada. There was a sparkle in the mother's eyes as she led us to a tiny bedroom with two double-deck bunks, a box cradle, and a little corner floor-bed, and said: '*Hier liggen onze schatten* (this is where our little ones sleep).' An even half dozen, aged from less than one year to almost eight, and all in *prima* health. Their only complaint was that the rent—$30 a month— was rather high, since another immigrant family was occupying the other end of the coop and paying the same amount. And there was neither water, gas, nor electricity—in fact, no conveniences of any kind. Yet these people were contented and

cheerful, working hard, and trusting their covenant God to provide for them and their family as they were seeking His kingdom first and foremost."

Mrs. Peter Brandsma, who came with her parents to southern Alberta in 1951, recalls the first day: "Our new home seemed to be in the middle of nowhere. One oil lamp stood on the table and two mattresses were on the floor. With the ten of us, the question was: who was going to sleep where? Luckily, we had enough blankets with us, so most of us rolled ourselves in. With the words of our fieldman still in our ears—'Well, you are in Canada'—we fell asleep."

Dick De Klerk, another immigrant, remembers: "We had a house on the farm which was more fit for a bachelor than for a family of eleven children. It included a small porch which we used as a kitchen, a living room, and two small bedrooms. The bedrooms were so small that we had to saw off one bed in order to get it in. When the farmer saw this, he asked: 'What are you doing now?' I replied: 'Do you want me to push the bed through the wall?' We were lucky that our crates were big enough for us to make them into a bedroom for some of the children. That was all right during the summer. But in the fall, the temperature dropped down to

A typical beetshack. Jetty Poelstra, who supplied the photo, notes: "This was our first home in Canada. The porch was really our kist. *My mom did her washing there, hauling water out of the ditch and heating it on a coal stove. There was no washing machine. We carried drinking water in a pail from a little well, a fourteen-minute round trip."*

thirty below Fahrenheit, and in the morning the blankets were frozen stiff on the beds."

A welcoming party was waiting in Lethbridge when Tjasse Heuvel and family arrived in September, 1947: his wife's relatives, who had been in Canada since 1926, Rev. P.J. Hoekstra, one of the pillars of the Christian Reformed Church in Western Canada, Bernard Nieboer, the fieldman, and others just curious to see new faces from the old fatherland. There were dozens of questions: about the train trip, the boat trip, life in The Netherlands, the five-year German occupation.

"Finally, we stepped into a 1936 Buick belonging to one of my wife's brothers and drove fifteen miles, first along a main road, then on clay roads muddied by a recent snowfall. We were sliding from one side to the other, and I wondered whether we would end up in the ditch. But we arrived in one piece and were given a warm welcome by my sister-in-law and her seven children. We had a party that night, and we talked until the wee hours of the morning. There was so much to say to each other. Then we went to our shack,

twenty feet by twenty feet, where our beds stood ready. We were soundly asleep in minutes."

When Heuvel woke up in the morning, his nose caught a strange, obnoxious odor which seemed to be coming from under the floor.

"Oh, we had a few skunks under the

The Heuvel family—all but mother, who took the photo. At bottom, John Pater and family, 1951 immigrants from Joure, Friesland, top beets near Taber, Alberta.

Durk Senneker, working in the beets near Iron Springs, Alberta, in 1950.

and the Heuvels had $550 in their pocket—really not much, even in those days, to last a growing family through the long Canadian winter.

"We had help from a lot of the old immigrants, because we were among the first ones there after the war," says Heuvel. "They came with chickens, turkeys, half a pig, and an abundance of home-canned vegetables. Tremendous!"

The transportation problem—not everyone could squeeze into the Buick at one time—was solved when another long-time immigrant offered to sell his 1927 Chevrolet for $150. The terms were generous: payment could be made the next year or, if difficulties arose, ignored altogether. The car was paid for on time.

When winter storms piled the snow unbelievably high, a car didn't help much. There were times when nobody could get in or out. One stormy Sunday, when the family was just idling away the hours, some unexpected visitors arrived—two hundred pigs, big and small, the property of a neighbor. They rummaged with their snouts under the house, no doubt looking for sugarbeet tops, a delicacy for them. They actually shook the house. Many farm animals were unfenced. Another time, the Heuvels were surprised to see fifty horses alongside the road.

The next year, at the new farm, father, mother, and the two oldest sons worked forty-six acres and earned $1,800. They bought some furniture, a cow, and even a saddle poney for the youngest son. It was a start. They were on their way to getting established in the new country. Life would never be easy: when they lived on a ranch later on, Mrs. Heuvel had to do her wash in a fast-flowing river. And in the bitter cold of winter, dried cow dung, picked up from the pastures, was used to start the coal stove. The children had to take their Saturday night bath in a tub placed behind the stove, with a blanket as a screen.

"We never complained," says Heuvel. "We really had it good. We liked Canada."

house," explained his brother-in-law, "and we thought we'd get rid of them before you arrived. We shot 'em, but they let their stink bombs go off."

Rev. Hoekstra and his wife visited the shack a few days later. They, too, noticed the lingering smell. The Heuvels looked a bit awkward. But the minister quickly put them at ease, saying: "That's such a healthy smell."

In March, 1948, the family moved to another farm. The floor of the shack, covered with a thick layer of mud, was cleaned just in time for a visit by Rev. and Mrs. Hoekstra.

"And how are things?" the minister inquired.

"We're in excellent health," replied Mrs. Heuvel, a twinkle in her eye. "You see, we've got skunks under this house too."

Back to the fall of 1947. A day after their arrival, Heuvel and his wife went to work the beetfields. The work was hard: at the end of the day, their fingers felt swollen to twice their size. But the beets had to be gotten out of the ground. And the family badly needed the dollars, with winter around the corner and with the prospects of further work slim. Fifteen acres of beets were harvested in ten days,

Bernard Nieboer, the energetic fieldman, knew what the immigrants were up against. When he came to Canada in 1926 as a fourteen-year-old, he lived at first with his large family in a one-room shack. He later became a beet farmer himself.

Someone wrote about him in 1950: "He does not baby them along, but fights hard

The Work Was Done on Time

Also in 1947, fieldman Bernard Nieboer was in Winnipeg to meet Henry and Frederika Jentink. He passed on some unexpected news: the sponsor had taken another family. Jentink thought: "Boy, oh boy, out of a job before you even get there."

That summer, the Jentinks worked for a sugarbeet farmer in Picture Butte, Alberta.

"We lived in a beet workers' shack that was like a chicken coop. Mr. Nieboer came on Saturday to see if we were settled in. We asked him: 'Where's the church?' He told us it was in Nobleford. 'Can we go there on the bikes?' He answered: 'No, you can't. It's twenty miles away.' Later, we arranged for people to pick us up. Our farmer wanted us to work on Sundays. It was a big problem for us. We didn't know the language, but we knew that we couldn't work on Sundays. The farmer told us that the Japanese who had worked here before always worked on Sunday, and that we'd never finish before winter. But we never worked on Sunday and still finished. The farmer even gave us a good bonus. That first year, I lived for Sunday. We needed the church, but we needed the company of the people even more. We were all immigrants and nobody had much, but we felt so together in it. The Sundays were what kept me going."

When the beet work was finished, Jentink and his oldest boy left home to work in the bush. Many immigrants did that in the early years, earning enough money to carry them through to the end of winter and into spring.

"The work was very strange and hard for them," says Mrs. Jentink, "but the worst was the living conditions. Rough, tough men—many of them foul-mouthed and bad-tempered. In some camps, there was a lot of drinking and gambling, and our men had to take a lot of abuse for not going along with that business. They slept in these rough bush camps—sometimes thirty or forty men crowded in bunks in one shack. And some of these guys weren't the cleanest. The women and children suffered too. Alone all winter, and few neighbors. We didn't know the language and the customs. Many of us didn't know how to drive. And the prairie winters are

Henry and Frederika Jentink join the beet workers at Picture Butte, Alberta.

Jentinks recall: "We lived in a beetshack that was like a chicken coop.

so long and cold. Oh, the loneliness! We sure prayed that our men would get back safe."

One day, her little boy was sick and craved for an orange.

"I walked to Picture Butte through knee-deep snow. I got some groceries and started back. Then I got a ride. So you always got a little help when you needed it."

The top photo, dated 1956, shows a Dutch family topping the sugarbeet crop at Coaldale, Alberta.
The beets went to processing plants such as this one at Picture Butte.

to see that good living quarters are supplied to them by farmers, and that there is no exploitation. He constantly rails against such things as the obsolete colonist cars into which the new arrivals are crowded for their long journey west, often with only the barest amenities, and says heatedly: 'These people are not cattle. They are immigrants who have paid their own way to this country, and sometimes the welcome is not even the least that they might expect.' "

At his home in Iron Springs, Nieboer recalls his unenthusiastic response when he was asked by Rev. P.J. Hoekstra to take on the job of fieldman. He had no training. And he foresaw hectic days and nights, lots of paper work, scrambles to meet the demands of strangers, and extra efforts to keep his farm from falling into neglect. Yet he couldn't say no.

His fears of working long hours and of putting up with complaints were certainly realized.

"My telephone rang all the time. Filling out all the forms and keeping the records straight took a lot of time. The dossier on each family was reviewed and matched with a sponsoring farmer. When farmers changed their minds, or hired other people, we opened up our home. Sometimes up to four families stayed at our farm at one time. None of the immigrants under my care stayed in hotels or ended up as wards of the government."

There were times when he felt like quitting. He got upset when newcomers complained about housing and working conditions, not offering one kind word for the help they were given. He remembered the Alberta he had come to: no roads, no houses, no electricity, no telephone, no welcoming committees. Did he really have to go into long explanations that the beet farmers didn't have luxurious dwellings for their itinerant help? Sometimes he tried, but it didn't help. One family, when shown their house, reacted critically: "That's not a house! That's a chicken coop!" Nieboer retorted: "Then you should know that chickens go to roost at sundown. See you later."

Despite such letdowns, he grew to like his job. And as time went on, he became more proficient. He went to Winnipeg one day to meet a train which was carrying 267 immigrants from Halifax to Lethbridge. He tried to make sure that everything was in order before the people would step out of the train. The sponsors were notified by telegram of the pending arrival. Upon arrival at Lethbridge, all the immigrants were dispersed within forty-five minutes. Such co-ordination was the result of long hours spent at the kitchen table of the Iron Springs farmhouse.

There was also time now and then for a good laugh. One night, while on the road, Nieboer and Rev. Frans Verhagen of the Roman Catholic Church had to share a bed. Father Verhagen commented jovially: "It's only possible in Canada that a Dutch Catholic priest and a Dutch Reformed brother can sleep together in the same bed."

In his fourteen years as fieldman, Nieboer placed more than five thousand immigrants and met thousands more—no small feat for someone who was reluctant, at first, to give his heart to the work. But the results can be seen even in black and white: in 1947, there was a handful of Christian Reformed congregations in Alberta; in 1983, there were forty-three.

At the other end of Canada, in Nova Scotia, Dutch immigrants were making their presence felt too. In 1947, the province welcomed 121 individuals from The Netherlands—twenty-eight families and twenty single men.

The province's Land Settlement Board, which did much over the years to ease the financial strain for those who wanted to buy their own farms, stated in its annual report: "These immigrants have, in the main, proven to be satisfactory citizens. Although they find conditions considerably different here, they are rapidly adapting themselves to Canadian practices . . . The movement of twenty-eight Dutch families into the province has filled the long-standing need for married men

Alberta, 1950: Dutch immigrants take a break from hard work in the beetfields.

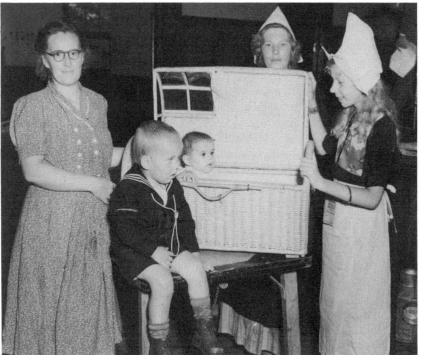

Dutch settlers in Nova Scotia were brought together by the province's settlement board for a social program in 1951. One mother brought her baby along in the travel crib purchased for the boat trip.

on farms. It is anticipated that there will be a larger movement of Dutch families into Nova Scotia this coming year, although the limiting factor is housing accommodation. Not many farmers have extra living accommodation for married men."

In its report the following year, the board noted that two married Dutch immigrants purchased farms with the aid of loans. "Both cases necessitated considerable downpayments. In one case, the immigrant had a large family, with several capable of earning money, and he paid the full amount of the downpayment to the board himself. In the other case, the immigrant's former employer assisted by lending him sufficient money to qualify for a loan from the board. Other Dutch immigrants would like to purchase farms of their own, but are finding it difficult to save much money. Some of them are over-anxious, and have applied for loans on very cheap farms. They were turned down by the board with the advice that it would be much better to work as farm laborers for another year or more to earn enough money to qualify for a loan on a better farm."

The board later concluded an unusual agreement with the Netherlands government which backed low-cost, long-term loans for Dutch settlers.

There's another interesting story from Nova Scotia. It's told by Dirk C. Geense of Truro area, former loan officer with the settlement board.

Theo Verstraten was born in St. Oedenrode, Noord-Brabant, where his father operated a small farm. Being a

Young Dutch farmers look over a map of Nova Scotia during a meeting arranged by the land settlement board.

farmer at heart, and seeing no chance to start on his own, Theo decided, when twenty-seven years old, to try his luck in Canada. He came to Forest, Ontario, in 1951, and was employed by a cash crop farmer during the summer and by a neighboring dairy farmer during the winter. After one year, he concluded that with a wage of $55 a month he would never be able to buy his own farm. So the next spring he started to work in the construction industry, where he could earn more money.

"During an evening Theo spent with a friend," says Geense, "the latter showed him a family picture in which he noticed a very attractive young woman. After some correspondence, Theo wanted to get better acquainted with Antoinette. So he used the greater part of his hard-earned money to meet her personally. Their feelings appeared mutual, and they got married in 1954."

By 1959, the couple had saved enough money to buy some cows and sows. They rented a 100-acre farm, selling manufactured milk and weanling pigs. The income from the farm was limited, however, so Theo had to continue working in construction. He didn't like that. After all, he had come to Canada to be a full-time farmer. He looked around for a farm that

would support his family, and soon concluded that the cost of a fluid-milk operation was beyond his reach.

"A friend named Lambert Vissers had brought back from Nova Scotia enthusiastic stories about the opportunities in that province. Fluid-milk farms could be obtained at considerably lower prices than in Ontario. In addition, there were the incentives offered by the farm loan board."

Theo was one of the several Dutch immigrants in Ontario who decided to start full-time farming in Nova Scotia. In 1961, he bought a 130-acre farm near Collingwood. Ninety acres were under cultivation and the rest was woodland. He bought an additional thirty acres two years later. In 1966, he leased another 100-acre tract, which he bought outright at a later date. He was an immigrant farmer on the move. The barn on his home farm could stable only forty-three head of cattle. So Theo built a farrowing barn for sixty sows. He figured that this addition, along with the fluid milk, would assure a good future for his family, which by that time—1967—had grown to nine children.

"Everything looked promising. But then, unfortunately, Theo became ill with a disease, which eventually affected seventy percent of his kidneys. He was unable to work. The children were still very young—the oldest son was only twelve—and did not seem very interested in farming. Needless to say, Theo and Antoinette suffered some sleepless nights. Under the circumstances, it seemed almost impossible to continue farming."

However, other people came to their aid, among them John Van Vulpen, whose father had been buying their weanling pigs. With the help of friends, they struggled on. Fortunately, the two

oldest sons became more interested in the farm and started to do most of the work while not neglecting their high school education.

"Theo's health had not improved very much," says Geense. "To make matters worse, he underwent open heart surgery in 1976 and again in 1978. After the operations, he was able to get around and manage the farm. During his illness, they decided to sell the sows and remodel the farrowing barn into one for cattle. They increased their dairy herd to fifty cows

---

Roefs: From Textiles in Ontario to Nova Scotia Agriculture

In the summer of 1951, someone from the Nova Scotia Land Settlement Board came to Ontario to interest Dutch immigrants in the farming opportunities available on the East Coast. The message that farms were relatively cheap in Nova Scotia caught the ear of Henry Roefs of Ajax, a long-time farmer who was now working in a textile factory. He missed the cows and the farm life. His aim was to get his own farm again. And why not in Nova Scotia?

"The oldest son of our Dutch friends in Ajax had bought a farm there," recalls Mrs. Roefs, "so his mother and I decided to take a train trip and see what was what. We didn't learn much. Our impression was that farming was very primitive there—for example, everyone still seemed to be using horse and wagon. Anyway, we had seen Nova Scotia and we would await developments."

At far right: Mr. and Mrs. Henry Roefs in the winter of 1962. Below: The Roefs' first farmhouse in Nova Scotia.

Now it was the men's turn. In February, the heart of Canadian winter, Roefs and his oldest son decided to travel by car to Nova Scotia. With them were the fiancé of Roef's oldest daughter and the heads of two other Dutch families. None of them knew about the deep snow in Quebec and beyond. In fact, they thought that the crocuses might be in bloom along the coast.

"Two days after they left, there was a knock on our door in the middle of the night. There stood our Frans and Cor, our daughter's fiancé, cold, hungry, and dirty. The car had gotten stuck in Quebec between two walls of snow. Unable to go farther, the men had pooled their money. Two would go back with the car and the other three would continue on the train. The two had just enough money to get home, but without a bite to eat."

The men obviously came back impressed by what they had seen and heard. Two

and seventy head of young stock. Over the years, the fluid milk quota was increased to 850 litres a day. Their herd became a top producer. Despite Theo's illness, the farm progressed well. The perseverance and determination of the entire family paid off."

Eventually Theo and his wife built a new house in the village and sold their farm to two of their eleven children, Francis and Joe.

After three and a half years in Canada, J.A. Grootenboer traveled by train from Portage La Prairie, Manitoba, to the Ontario township of Oliver, sixteen miles west of Fort William, with the intention of using his carefully-saved dollars to buy a farm. After all, wasn't this the reason he had come to Canada?

"The farm was 240 acres, with a house and other buildings in very good shape. I bought it. At the end of July in 1951, we traveled the five hundred or so miles by truck, and became the first Dutch immigrant family in Oliver township. We

of the families moved to Nova Scotia in the spring of 1952. Roefs and his following planned to go in the fall.

"I spent the summer in the cellar, packing for our move," says his wife. "It seemed as if we were emigrating all over again. Frans, our son, didn't like the idea. He had spoken to a number of people who had moved to Ontario from Nova Scotia. They had told him that there was no work there, that young people would be better off in Ontario. Frans said to us: 'I'm not planning to farm anyway, so don't hold back because of me. I'm going with you, but if things don't suit me, I'll return to Ontario.' "

Mrs. Roefs, her oldest daughter, and her two youngest sons went by train. So did the belongings. Roefs, Frans, and the rest went by car, which puttered along somehow and got them to Cape Breton Island without trouble.

"Our farm had two horses, a number of horse-drawn implements, six cows, and some calves. The barn was new. There was also an older barn, which wasn't too good. The house looked all right, but it turned out to be very cold in winter. We had only a wood stove, and it was burning all the time. Even so, sometimes it was so cold that a sheet of ice formed over the water in the kitchen."

The first years on the farm were rough. There seemed to be no organization in the farming community. The Roefs' neighbors merely farmed as they had for generations. This didn't make it easy for the farmers from The Netherlands, who were used to different methods and wanted to improve things.

"If they had put us all on the best farms,

it would have been another story. But they must have figured that a Hollander could make a good farm out of a bad one. Well, it was our own fault. There were lots of times when we thought that we should have looked around more and found out a few more things before we headed for Nova Scotia."

But there was no turning back. They all had to roll up their sleeves and work like they'd never worked before. Eventually, they bought more cows, cleared more land, and the Roefs were able to squeeze out a living.

"In the first year, our milk cheque was between $40 and $50 a month. In the second year it grew to $100. It wasn't easy to pay all our bills from that. But with our children working, and with us making some extra money by cutting wood, we managed to get by. After twenty-three years, in 1975, when we sold our farm, our income was around $4,000 a month. That's quite a difference. Believe me, that was the result of a lot of hard work."

The Roefs toast Mrs. Roefs' 82nd birthday in 1983.

Resettlement in the New Land

An immigrant family on the move again.

Many immigrants moved here and there during their first years in Canada, trying desperately to find the right place. Quite often, they were moving to find a suitable job. Sometimes just a good word spoken by other immigrants sealed the choice. And then there were some who piled their belongings into a vehicle and started moving without knowing where they would end up.

One morning, a moving van pulled up outside the Hamilton, Ontario, home of Rev. Harri Zegerius. No fewer than fifty people came out of it. The minister didn't know what was up. He had received no advance notice of the arrival of such a large group.

"I soon learned their story," he says. "After their arrival in Canada, they were scattered in Quebec and felt quite lonely. So they contacted each other and made plans to move to Ontario. They rented a van, packed their furniture, climbed in, and moved west. They ended up at my house, the Reformed Church office in those days, seeking help."

The coffee kettle was put on and sandwiches were made. In this cordial atmosphere, plans were discussed. The gathering ended with devotions.

"I could see that they were refreshed. They looked like different people. Well, we set to work immediately, and all the families got distributed."

The loneliness of farm life in Prince Edward Island was too much for bachelor Nico De Jong. So he made plans to travel by bus to Toronto. In his pocket was the address of a Dutch church there. That's really all he needed to get in touch with a Dutchman willing to provide him with room and board and possibly a job.

"I wasn't too impressed with Toronto when I got there. I noticed the old-fashioned streetcars and telephone booths, and the curved wooden poles for cables and lights—quite a contrast with Amsterdam or Utrecht. But it was still better than being in the wilderness."

At seven o'clock on a Sunday morning, he was on the empty streets of Toronto, searching for the street on which the Dutch church was located. He found it an hour later, but he couldn't find a church building. So he walked around the neighborhood, waiting for people who looked Dutch in appearance to assemble in front of one of the doors. This eventually happened.

"I tried to mix a bit and get a conversation going. I said who I was and where I came from, but no one was impressed and no one seemed to understand that I was trying to make contact with someone. After the service, the same thing happened. I must have looked pretty desperate, because a woman came up to me and started to talk. One thing led to another, and I was invited to go for supper with her and her husband and to talk about plans for my immediate future."

Nico never regretted grabbing that opportunity. He stayed as a boarder and found work in a factory the very next day.

One year after his arrival in the Wallaceburg, Ontario, area, Kees Verburg bought a small farm. Twelve months later, he sold it and acquired a bigger one. After buying and selling two more farms, he finally settled down.

"My mother told him that after thirty-five years of marriage and fixing up nine houses, she'd had enough," says daughter Anne. "My brother took over the farm some years later and my parents moved next door, fixing up yet another house. You know what they were doing on their 50th wedding anniversary? Fixing up another house—their winter home in Florida."

started with one thousand chickens and grew from fifteen to twenty acres of potatoes, barley, and oats, and enough hay for up to twenty head of Holstein milking cows.

He and his family worked long and hard during the following years to make the farm a profitable operation. They built up the milk quota, raised calves for breeding and veal purposes, cleared a 100-acre bush and thus got more workable land, repaired fences, and replaced old buildings. Somehow, they found time to do a few other things on the side.

When there was no demand for industrial milk, Mrs. Grootenboer made butter. Her husband didn't let any milk go to waste either—he learned how to make cheese from a young immigrant whose father was a cheesemaker on a farm at Bodegraven, Zuid-Holland.

"I sold butter and cheese for fifty cents a pound to private customers in the cities of Port Arthur and Fort William (since renamed Thunder Bay)," he says. "I also sold eggs, potatoes, and vegetables to stores and private customers. To supply them, I had to go there twice and sometimes three times a week. I was more than once in the jail too—to deliver a load of potatoes. The price for a 75-pound bag of grade A ones, delivered, was $1.75."

And that's how this family got ahead. That's how a lot of immigrant families got ahead.

Dutch immigrants also settled on Wolfe Island, a fertile piece of land twenty-seven miles long and twelve miles wide in the St. Lawrence River opposite Kingston, Ontario. The isolation of island life, especially in winter when the ferry, *Wolfe Islander*, was laid up, had caused many of the Canadians there to abandon their farms and move to the industrial mainland. So the Dutch moved in, finding

A proud moment for Mr. and Mrs. J.A. Grootenboer. The Ontario agriculture minister, W.A. Stewart, presents a plaque and a cheque for winning eighth place in a Canada Centennial farm improvement competition. More than 4,000 Ontario farms were entered.

flat land and good soil on relatively cheap farms.

With typical perseverence, they brought the land back into shape, repaired buildings, and built new ones. The island began to take on a new appearance, and its economy prospered.

"When we came here in May of 1948, I was able to get eight cows and rent a hundred acres," Ben Vollering told an interviewer in 1952. "Today, I own my own 100-acre farm and have forty cows and two hundred hogs. There's good land here."

Now, more than three decades later, the Dutch are still on Wolfe Island, though in diminished numbers. There were a number of reasons for the decline. Even though a year-round ferry service to Kingston was established, life was still isolated. Some of the immigrants didn't feel at home in a place that lacked a Dutch church. Also, the naturally restricted acreage lessened the chances for growth and for keeping children on farms' close to home.

The ones who did stay seemed to become completely integrated into the Canadian way of life. They began to attend the United Church, for example, and became involved in community events. They figured that they could be both Dutch and a part of the Canadian fellowship.

In August, 1949, two principal members of the Immigration Committee of the Christian Reformed Church, John VanderVliet and John Vellinga, traveled to Cochrane, a town in Ontario's north-land where mining, lumber, and pulp were the mainstays of the local economy. But they weren't interested in gold or timber. They had come to explore the possibility of directing Dutch farmers to the area.

Farming in the North? Many said it couldn't be done. It had been tried before. The result: hundreds of farms were abandoned outright or were falling into disrepair. Two mass colonization schemes had failed miserably, mainly because the North was too sparsely populated to provide a market for the farmers' produce.

However, the scouts were impressed with the possibilities. They were sure that some enterprising immigrants, anxious to have a farm of their own, would be interested in acquiring the cheap, fertile land.

Two busloads of farmers visited the area in early fall. They tramped through unplowed fields, studied ramshackle houses, and conferred in Dutch. They, too, saw the possibilities. And some of them returned, bought or rented land, and began the difficult task of restoration.

This group of pioneers was led by Arie

Mrs. Harm Middel stands on the porch of her home in Cochrane. The porch was enclosed with boards from the kist; even the door was home-made.

Harm Middel stacks hay on his farm at Cochrane, Ontario, in 1953. The farmer from Siegerswoude, Friesland, liked the area, even though the winters were long and harsh. But his children felt otherwise and moved away. Eventually their parents decided to follow them to southern Ontario.

Struyk, father of eight sons and three daughters, who had come to Holland Marsh in March of 1949 after deciding there was no future on the family farm near Rijssen, Overijssel, or anywhere in The Netherlands. For $1,800, he became owner of one hundred and fifty acres and a rather good set of buildings. By the time the family got settled in their new home, their cash reserves had dwindled to a mere $17. However, they never got discouraged.

Arie and his oldest sons spent all winter in the bush, cutting pulpwood. By summer, their savings amounted to more than $3,000. This money paid for cattle, machinery, a tractor, a car, and other necessities. The Struyks had something going. And so did the other members of the burgeoning Dutch settlement.

"I sold $1,000 worth of potatoes last summer," Struyk told an interviewer in 1952. "We knock down trees and more land becomes available for more potatoes. No wonder we like it here. The soil is rich, rain falls when we need it, and we're working land that nobody wanted."

J.P.S. Ballantyne, commissioner of agriculture for Northern Ontario, commented: "Their arrival has been a spur to the community. We need more of them here. In fact, we expect more next spring.

This could mean a return to the golden era of farming."

But it was not to be. Although the community seemed to be prospering and growing, certain factors were at work that would eventually lead to its virtual downfall. There were internal disagreements. Jealousy surfaced. The hardships of starting from scratch on an abandoned farm in the isolated North with its long, cold winters caused some to long to return to the south.

In May of 1953, Struyk and his wife traveled to southern Ontario. Soon they had bought a farm near Mount Hope, in the Hamilton area. With the leader gone, the community began to disintegrate. One by one, the families moved away.

There are still a number of Dutch immigrants in the area, including one of Struyk's sons. They obviously like it there. So does Struyk, really. After all, that's where he got his start and built up enough capital to buy a farm in the south.

"I don't understand why more people don't settle in the Cochrane area," he says. "It's easier starting there than anywhere else, and there isn't better soil anywhere. We grew rye six feet tall, so tall it wouldn't even go through the binder. We had a beautiful time in Cochrane."

Arie Struyk made enough money cutting wood during the winter to buy farm machinery, cattle, a tractor and a car.

The Van Ewijk children haul in the hay with a horse and sled.

The Canadian farmers who sponsored and met the Dutch immigrants were sometimes callous or arrogant. Even in Prince Edward Island, where quite a few Dutchmen settled, poor treatment was a fact of life on some farms. Aart Van Ewijk knows.

He left his small farm near Nijkerk, Gelderland, and sailed to Canada on the *Zuiderkruis* in February, 1952, with his wife and eight children, the oldest of whom was fifteen. They arrived at the station in Souris, Prince Edward Island, at seven o'clock in the evening. The station master was the only person there. He consoled: "Oh, there'll be someone here soon. Just wait and see."

The sponsoring farmer and a neighbor finally came with two horse-drawn sleds and began to take the family of ten to a farm a few kilometres away. Then Van Ewijk suddenly discovered that some of the trunks had been left at the station. With great difficulty, he managed to make the farmer understand his plight. So back to the station went the farmer, Van Ewijk, and his oldest son. Before they got there, the farmer decided to stop at an establishment for a drink to warm up his limbs numbed by the frigid night air. The boy stayed outside to look after the horse. It was ten o'clock when the sled finally pulled up at the station. But the farmer, who obviously loved his bottle, went inside and resumed his imbibing. After midnight, he was ready to hit the road again.

"I had to make sure all the time that I didn't lose my boss, because he was too drunk to sit up," says Van Ewijk. "Either the horse knew the way or the Lord guided us home. I certainly didn't know where to go. Everything was white, white, white."

The next day, the family was shown the house that had been set aside for them. They were shocked to find a cold wind blowing through it. The stove, with no pipes on it, was somewhere outside. So back they went to the farmhouse, where they could have two bedrooms.

Van Ewijk's stomach turned over when the farmer grabbed an axe one day, selected a cow, let it to the barn, and felled it with a few sharp blows. He then went for a drink, leaving his hired hands to do the slaughtering. A few days later, the same thing happened to a pig. Van Ewijk, sickened, felt like going back to The Netherlands.

After three and a half months of work, the Dutchman had not received any pay, even though the agreement stipulated $75 a month. His family, however, did get food: meat, potatoes, eggs, milk. Whenever he broached the subject in his broken English, the farmer indicated he didn't understand what was being said.

In frustration, Van Ewijk went to the immigration people, but he was told: "Be patient. Your farmer is a good man. It'll come in due time." So he had to barter for himself. The farmer eventually did start paying, but in inconsistent amounts and never as much as his employee was entitled to.

After eight months, Van Ewijk decided to buy a farm at Breadalbane for $3,300, with $500 down. When it was time to leave, he demanded that the farmer at Souris pay the wages owing. In turn, the farmer presented a foot-long list of what his hired hand allegedly owed him: the cost of two trips to the station, trips to Charlottetown when Mrs. Van Ewijk accompanied the farmer's wife to buy groceries; the cost of eggs, potatoes, meats and so on. Finally, in the middle of a field, the two men ended the stalemate; Van Ewijk would get a cow. A neighbor trucked it to Breadalbane before the farmer could change his mind.

Chapter 12

Homesickness

A vicious hail storm broke windows in the Alberta
home of Mrs. Frank Zee. She was already deeply
homesick, and the weather was no encouragement.

Homesickness

Mrs. Frank Zee was not happy to be working in the sugarbeet fields of southern Alberta. Fifty-five years old, she had decided to come to Canada to keep her family together. Two daughters and some other relatives had gone before, and her eldest son had made up his mind that he would join them. So she and her husband also took the big step, not wanting to be left behind.

Mrs. Zee hadn't known that an immigrant woman would have to work just as hard and long as her husband. Already she had spent most of her lifetime raising a family. And she had survived trying times during the German occupation.

Slaving in the field under a blazing sun, she often wondered why she was doing it. Hadn't she done enough in her life? And there was nobody to talk to, only endless rows of beets. There was nobody to listen to her concerns, nobody to offer her some encouragement.

"It was a difficult time for her," recalls her husband, who came to Canada from the small community of Andijk, Noord-Holland, in 1949. "I remember her writing gloomy letters to Holland and saying that she wanted to go back. Well, we got letters in return that told us never to come back. If we did, we would be left stranded in Rotterdam. They were trying to give us a helpful message, I guess. They wanted us to stick it out."

Zee and the children noticed the terrible effort she made each day to act as if things were normal. But her heart was still in The Netherlands. She felt alien to Canada, to its vastness, its people, its harshness.

Zee could do nothing but prepare to return to The Netherlands. He asked the fieldman for that area, Bernard Nieboer, to arrange the bookings. This man, who was expected to be a jack of all trades, took it in stride and promised to look after the details. The return was set for December 19, 1949.

"December came, but we didn't hear anything about the trip back," says Zee. "Finally, I asked Bernard where things stood. He knew very well that the children and I preferred to stay in Canada and that everything revolved around mother's welfare. He replied: 'Frank, I didn't do anything. To put it plainly, I thought it'd

be better to have the wife *kapot* than the whole family *kapot*.' You know, I still have a deep place in my heart for Bernard. He was a wise man."

Mrs. Zee struggled on. It wasn't easy. But, like so many of the other wives who had been uprooted and replanted in strange soil, she persevered. And when the family moved to Red Deer in 1952, away from the sugarbeet fields, they noticed an immediate improvement in her outlook.

In southern Ontario, Rev. John Van Harmelen of the Christian Reformed Church remembers counselling many women afflicted by that common malady—homesickness.

"While their husbands worked long hours trying to scrape together a few

Immigrants were eager for letters from The Netherlands. Alie Hunse ponders a letter at her father's home near Niagara-on-the-Lake, Ontario, in 1950.

dollars, the women were confined to their little homes, looking after their young ones."

Television was a rarity in the early 1950s. A radio wasn't of much use unless a musical program was on. If it hadn't been for relatives who forwarded, by boat, copies of *De Spiegel* and a variety of women's magazines and church papers, there would have been little to read. Little wonder that the women, in their strange and lonely environment, often felt like going back to The Netherlands on the next boat.

"In the winter when ice covered the windows, the young wife of one immigrant used to sit for hours breathing a hole in the ice so that she wouldn't lose sight of him. He was working not too far away. And when he finally came in, oh boy, you should have seen that smile."

There wasn't much doubt in the mind of George Eggink that his wife was homesick. All he had to do was read the letters that she was sending to her mother in The Netherlands.

"My mother-in-law wrote back, saying that it would be better for her to return to Beilen, Drenthe, if things didn't suit her in Canada. As this sort of writing continued for several months, my wife became more and more disheartened. Well, without my wife's knowledge, I wrote to her parents, telling them about the consequences of their letters. Fortunately, they interpreted this correctly, and the following letters were more cheerful. This benefitted all of us."

Mrs. Eggink still lives happily on a farm in the area of Jarvis, Ontario.

Pat Rykes reads a letter from The Netherlands on December 25, 1950, his first Christmas in Canada. He was living near Pine Falls, Manitoba, then. Later the family moved to British Columbia.

Mrs. Reina Feyen of Chatham, Ontario, also wrote many letters to relatives in Smilde, Drenthe, and elsewhere to make time pass and to keep in touch. She always looked forward to the arrival of the mailman—maybe he had something from The Netherlands.

"We wrote letters to my parents every week—his were dead—and to the brothers and sisters from both sides of the family on their birthdays. That was quite a chore, as Kees had ten brothers and sisters, all married, and I still had eight brothers and sisters in Holland."

Homesickness wasn't restricted to women. Martin DeVos, a former fieldman for the Reformed Church, remembers a man near Brockville, Ontario, who just couldn't get used to the new land, even though he was surrounded by loved ones. He ate little and spoke hardly at all. His drawn face and expressionless eyes showed that his thoughts were far away—in The Netherlands.

His wife asked DeVos one day: "What can I do? He seems to be getting worse each day."

DeVos asked: "Have you got any money saved up?"

"Yes," answered the woman.

"Well, send him back to Holland," the fieldman said forthrightly. "And if you don't want to go with him, stay here. Then see what happens. As far as I'm concerned, that's the best remedy. You'll find him back in Canada before long."

The man went back to The Netherlands—alone. He stayed for a few months, didn't like it there either, and returned to Canada "completely cured."

Mrs. Netty Oosterman of Lambeth, Ontario, who came to Canada in 1953 from Rijnsburg, Zuid-Holland, recalls: "When the first of my four sons was born, eleven months after our arrival, I experienced my most difficult time in Canada. It was so different from the joyful events in Holland, where babies were born at home and relatives are near. I entered the hospital in St. Thomas on a Thursday night, but the baby wasn't born until early Saturday. It was a difficult birth. I woke up crying—no baby in sight, no husband. I kept asking to see my baby, but they said there was no time. I did not know enough English to tell them off. Finally, at four in the afternoon, they came and showed him for one minute. I did not hold him, and did not see him again until the next morning. My hus-

band, who had to work, learned that he was a father when he came to the hospital at seven."

Mrs. Oosterman was happy with her son, of course. But she missed sharing the joy with relatives. After two months, the new mother realized she was homesick. She couldn't even eat.

"We figured that outdoor work would do wonders for me. You know, fresh air, thoughts elsewhere. So, while friends looked after the baby, I began sorting pears. I was on my feet all day and came close to fainting. But I stayed on and my appetite increased. And when the work was finished, I felt much better. Then I went home to the baby and faced our immigrant existence again."

Yes, homesickness did drive some people back to The Netherlands. Sometimes

"homesickness" was a word to cover simple failure, or for disappointment in not finding instant success. A few times the return was the result of marital discord. But most of the time it was genuine homesickness—a desire to return to all that was familiar.

The loneliness was overwhelming. No relatives ever dropped over for a visit. It took so long to get a letter from The Netherlands. And when one did arrive, it only awakened one's longing to be back in the Old Country. English seemed nothing but gibberish, and the women isolated in the country had no opportunity to learn the language. Many of them felt that they had been misled, given the wrong information about Canada.

In Bradner, British Columbia, in 1953, fifteen-year-old Piet Madderom noticed that there was something amiss with his mother. She hadn't been herself since the

Immigrants who came to Alberta faced this kind of prairie town, stark contrast to the familiar scenes of The Netherlands.

family had left the village of Sint Pancras to join a close relative who had written: "It's a beautiful country. Why not come?"

Recalls Piet: "Mother loved to sing. But she didn't sing any more, and we knew that something was wrong. She would sit by herself, staring with reddened eyes out of the window. At first, we all figured that the homesickness would pass with time. However, it grew worse. Her hair became grey and she hardly said a word. We feared that we might lose her if she did not go back to Holland."

After two years in Canada, Father Madderom, who had dreams of starting up his own flower bulb business, made a hard decision: the family would go back. They borrowed money for the return trip of mother and the four children. He would stay behind to pay off the debt by working at a gardening center in Vancouver.

Piet, who had wanted to stay in British Columbia and become a teacher, says: "We traveled by Greyhound bus from Seattle, Washington, to New York City. There we boarded the *Sibajak* for the trip to Holland. Already we noticed a difference in mother's behavior. She became livelier, more open. She said that she'd had no idea of what Canada would mean to her. She had missed her relatives, the village . . ."

From a Psychological Perspective

Dr. Harry VanBelle

Dr. Harry VanBelle, professor of psychology at Redeemer College in Hamilton, Ontario, is himself an immigrant. He says that the amazing thing about the early postwar settlers is that not more of them became homesick and depressed, and that so few returned to their native land.

"Psychologists have long known that depression is frequently caused by stress, and early Dutch immigrant life was certainly highly stressful. Factors involved in stress include newness, strangeness, social isolation, uncertainty, and especially a personal inability to do anything about the situation. A person under stress is in limbo. There are excessive demands on him to change, which overtax his ability to adapt. The common reaction to such a situation is to become immobile, to give up and do nothing, to sit and stare—to become depressed, in short."

From that psychological perspective, says Dr. VanBelle, one has to admire the enormous emotional resilience of the many immigrants who did not succumb to homesickness.

"In my own immigrant experience, the psychological effects of immigration would have been much more extensive and longer lasting had it not been for the support and the hospitality of the American Christian Reformed Church. It provided the Dutch Christian immigrants from several Reformed denominations with a church community in which they could celebrate their faith. It cushioned the inevitable culture shock of immigration by providing the immigrants with a social structure that became their bridge out of their Dutch-European culture into the Canadian-North American culture. The Canadian Christian Reformed Church, made up largely of Dutch-Canadian immigrants, owes a great debt to its counterpart in the United States. It is especially indebted to the home missionaries, who during the early years did so much to gather Dutch immigrants into thriving church communities. They are the unsung heroes of the Canadian Christian Reformed Church. Without them, many more immigrants might have become depressed and returned to their homeland, disillusioned."

PLAY GROUNDS SPEED 15 M.P.H.

Adrie Wagenaar-Madderom, seven years old at the time of emigration, recalled the homecoming in an article in the magazine of *Wereld Contact*, the travel organization with which Piet is closely connected.

"Relatives waving on the quay—it was like a repeat of two years earlier, when we slowly sailed away. Weeping aunts waving handkerchiefs. The only difference was that this time we were moving closer. 'I see Zus!' shouted my mother, and she began to wave with both arms. Zus yelled from the quay: 'Es has twins!' 'Twins,' said my mother, and began to cry. I wondered who Es was. Once on shore, we were enthusiastically kissed and embraced by everyone. I said to a niece in English: 'I like your dress.' 'Shame on you,' said an aunt, clasping her hands. 'Child, you're home now, so just talk like the rest of us.' "

Without a home, the Madderoms had to stay with relatives. In the meantime, the father worked long and hard to pay off

his debts and save enough for his own return fare. When the Suez Canal crisis broke and fears of a wider conflict were widespread, he didn't want to risk being stranded in Canada; he booked a seat on an airplane and returned to his family.

"Father and mother went back to Canada once for a visit to see if they had really made the right decision," says Piet, now of Zuid-Scharwoude, Noord-Holland. "When they came back, they said: 'We've seen it again, and we're convinced that we had made the right decision.' "

Oddly, culture shock can be felt more acutely now than ever before, especially among elderly widows. Often they feel that they have never become part of the country. After all these years, they suffer loneliness in what still seems an unfamiliar land.

Mrs. Elly Lucas of Burnaby, British

Mrs. William Thysse draws water a block and a half from her home in Regina, Saskatchewan, in the winter of 1959-1960. Says her husband, now of Edmonton: "She took it all in stride. I never saw a tear, and she was happy in Canada from the first day. I had heimwee for a long, long time."

Columbia, a psychiatric nurse who left Makkum, Friesland, in 1954, has observed this phenomenon closely. Through her work at an out-patient mental health clinic, she has come to know many people with psychological scars attributable to the immigration experience. And the Dutch people aren't unusual. The elderly of other ethnic backgrounds, such as Germans, Italians, and groups from Eastern Europe, also continue to suffer dislocation and alienation.

"It's a fact that many women came along to Canada reluctantly," says Mrs. Lucas. "Their husbands wanted to go, so they consented dutifully. They were never in the limelight. But they were a pillar of strength. Over the years, while they looked after their families and their households, they never really got a chance to integrate into the community and society. Their social contact was restricted to the weekly Ladies' Aid meeting at the church or a Sunday visit to immigrant friends. Now, when they are on their own, they seem lost."

The establishment of homes for the aged, which provide companionship and professional help, has lessened the problems somewhat. But these institutions are limited to certain areas. In many towns and villages across Canada, elderly people continue to live in loneliness.

"The older the immigrants get, the more they want to return to their original language," says Mrs. Lucas. "After a while, the little English they knew has been forgotten. Many of them now know only 'yes' and 'no.' They can't converse. They're outside of the mainstream of life. When some of the women go shopping, they want a daughter along because they don't feel sure of themselves. Some can't even write a cheque. They are becoming very dependent on their children. Of course, such situations are an emotional strain on a lot of people."

Bitter words about Canada, about the *rimboe*, about the backward conditions, about its people, were inevitable whenever a boat with returnees among its passengers docked at Rotterdam.

"Canada turned out to be a big disappointment for us," said a woman from Lichtenvoorde, Gelderland, after stepping off the *Veendam* in 1950. She and her husband, disillusioned, had decided to return to The Netherlands with their nine children.

"When you drive with a car through Canada, yes, then it's beautiful. They call that the hills. But if you have to work in those nice hills, well . . . just ask my husband. That house we were put in . . . a cow stall here is better than that. No one had lived in it for thirty years. Maybe we haven't got the real pioneer blood. There are hundreds of Hollanders who are able to adjust and who don't want to come back for love or money."

Her husband added: "Good soil there. But to live with a family in such a wilderness . . ."

Another woman, from Gemert, Noord-Brabant, commented: "It's a different kind of life there. It isn't easy in the winter. We had it better here than in Canada, and I'm not afraid to come out and say that I was homesick. I missed my grandfather, my brothers and my birthplace. A family with small children shouldn't emigrate. They're asking for poverty. We know."

Even in later years, when most immigrants were enjoying the challenge of adapting to Canadian society, there were people who decided to return to The Netherlands. In many cases, they had dreamed of making it big in the new land, only to find themselves without jobs or with jobs so menial that they felt humiliated.

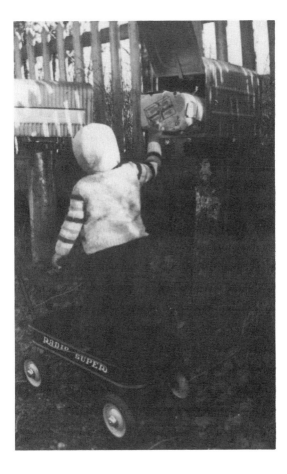

A parcel has arrived from The Netherlands! Bernie, the son of Mr. and Mrs. A.J. Van Maren, made the discovery at his home in Summerland, British Columbia, while making his rounds one day in 1954.

There were difficult times in Canada in the late 1950s and early 1960s. Unemployment was high. This situation certainly didn't help the newly-arrived immigrant, who had left a good job in The Netherlands to seek advancement in Canada. Emigration bureaus maintained that people with technical skills were more than welcome in Canada. What many emigrants didn't know was that Canadian enthusiasm could dry up pretty quickly when their own economic situation turned a bit sour.

In 1960, P. Hofhuis of Bussum, just north of Hilversum, returned to The Netherlands disillusioned and somewhat angry. The press carried the story. A few years earlier, he had visited Canada as a representative for *Maatschappij Nederland*. He had been impressed with the country, particularly Vancouver. Not only that, he had been assured by a number of business contacts that a job would be waiting for him should he ever decide to pull up stakes. Back in The Netherlands, he had had no trouble convincing his wife to make the big jump.

"When we arrived, the people were astonished and asked us why we had come. Go back right away, they said, because there isn't any work. We laughed at first. But after a few weeks, we knew that they were right. The businesses where I had been promised a job were lay-ing off hundreds. There was no work any more."

He applied in Vancouver, in the surrounding area, and even in places far away. Most of his letters weren't even answered. Finally he gave up trying to find a job in his field. But even then there was little else available. Once he saw a newspaper advertisement asking for someone to sell programs for a fair in Vancouver. When he checked into this, he found that no fewer than three thousand persons had submitted a written application.

One time, he was successful. He got a job as a pinboy in a bowling alley. But it came to an abrupt end when the league ended its season.

Here's an anecdote told by Rev. D.J. Scholten of the Christian Reformed Church: "In my congregation in Lethbridge, Alberta, there was a woman who longed to see her relatives in Friesland. Her husband told me: 'Reverend, that seems to be the only thing on her mind. I don't mind her going, but I just haven't got the money to pay for a trip.' Later, this man came to me with a big smile on his face and said: 'My wife told me she had a dream and that she had seen all her relatives. Well, I told her to forget about that trip to Friesland. She didn't need it any more.'"

There wasn't much counter space in Mrs. William Thysse's kitchen. Meals were prepared on the hotplate. The handpump beside the sink didn't work.

The other Protestant denominations and the Roman Catholic Church also had their unsung heroes, early and late in the history of the Dutch immigration. Many of these ministers and priests were called on to counsel and guide distraught people who just couldn't cope in their new environment, no matter how hard they tried.

Rev. Willem DeWitte of Ottawa, a member of the Priests of the Sacred Heart who served in the London diocese in the late 1950s, found that the best remedy was the advice: go home for a visit. After a few weeks in The Netherlands, the homesick person would begin to long to return to the family in Canada.

Father DeWitte also found that homesickness was felt more keenly by people who had left behind a trade or business in The Netherlands and who now were working at unfamiliar and often demeaning jobs just to put food on the table. These people, greatly disappointed, often asked him bitterly, "Why did I come here?"

"In two years, I visited around 830 families in the diocese, most of them hardworking farmers. The incidence of homesickness among these rural people was very low. They had come to Canada to farm, and that's what they were happily doing."

Some of the people who couldn't adjust were still deeply attached to the city, town or village where they were born. For them, the only solution was to return permanently to their relatives and their friends in the old surroundings.

Father DeWitte remembers hardly any severe homesickness among young people and those who were married shortly after their emigration. Not yet set in their ways, they were able to adapt more easily than older immigrants.

All in all, the number of people who returned to The Netherlands either because of homesickness or dissatisfaction was small. Says Father DeWitte: "I remember a discussion at which it was mentioned that the proportion of failed immigrants at that time—the late '50s—stood at one percent."

The children of Gijs and Marie Berkelaar of Clandeboy, Ontario, pick up mail from The Netherlands, including a copy of De Spiegel. *They are (left to right) Ria, Corrie, Cobi, Sim and Magda. The photo was taken in 1951.*

Chapter 13

Everything Was So Different

Everything Was So Different

Deep snow blanketed the countryside around Linwood, a small community northwest of Kitchener, Ontario, during the winter of 1951-52. Snowplows often operated around the clock in a losing battle to keep the rural roads in this snowbelt area cleared. Fresh snowfalls and heavy drifting made travel risky and often impossible.

"There was so much snow that we couldn't go to the Christian Reformed Church in Kitchener on Sundays," recalls Mrs. Maaike Dijkstra, who had left Leeuwarden, Friesland, in November, 1951. "A number of other immigrants in the area were in the same predicament. We couldn't do without church services, of course. So we arranged to use the United Church at Linwood at 2 p.m. on Sundays. There was no charge—the only thing we had to do was clean the church."

For the five families, getting to the United Church wasn't easy either. They found that the best way to travel over the snowy roads was by horse-drawn sled.

"We had a sled too," says Mrs. Dijkstra, now of Beamsville, Ontario. "During the week, it was used for hauling cow manure from the barn. On Saturday, my husband, Lieuwe, scrubbed it clean. In the morn-

ing, we placed chairs on it for our ten children, put the horse in front, and off we went."

The men took turns reading the sermon. A collection was held to make everything as authentic as possible; the money was turned over to the Kitchener church. And after the service, Sunday School lessons were led by Peter Vos. When the snow melted in the spring, and the roads became passable again, the families rejoined the congregation in Kitchener.

The Dijkstra family began to make plans for a special dinner as their first Christmas in Canada approached. The boys had their eyes on a flock of wild pigeons roosting in the barn. With their parents' consent, they captured about a dozen and got them ready for the soup pot.

"Just then the boss came with a big box. It held a big turkey and neatly-wrapped toys for the kids. What a surprise! We felt so sorry then that we had killed those birds."

The Dijkstras later got another surprise from the farmer—a bag of potatoes.

"He figured it should last us three or four months. But we had a big family and the boys ate a lot and the potatoes were

Reind Wikkering discovered Canadian winters the hard way when his car got stuck in a driveway near Acton, Ontario. There was nothing to do but dig.

gone in a week. Then we went back to pancakes and brown beans. When the farmer learned that we didn't have any potatoes left, he couldn't believe it."

The Dijkstras had been at the farm near Linwood for only a few days when an old car pulled up in front of the house, and a large family piled out. The visitors, also Dutch, explained that they had heard newcomers had arrived in their neighborhood, and they wanted to get acquainted.

"We welcomed them with open arms," says Mrs. Dijkstra. "How we loved to see other people from Holland. There was so much we could talk about. We had enough coffee in the house, but not enough cups to go around. So the next time they came, they brought their own cups along. The early immigrants sought each other out for companionship. Friendships were formed that still exist today."

The immigrants took along all their children on these visits, usually on Saturday nights or Sunday afternoons. When the Dijkstras finally got their own car, all of them—ten children were born in The Netherlands and five more were added

When the church service in a basement in Kitchener ended, it was time to chat. In the summer, the Dijkstras drove a Mennonite buggy to town.

later in Canada—somehow squeezed in. And off they went, happy to be going somewhere for much-needed fellowship.

"Quite often, we made arrangements after the morning church service. We loved to stand there as long as an hour and in all kinds of weather, chatting with people we hadn't seen for a whole week. There were a lot of us Frisians who would start speaking in Frisian to each other. I can remember one person from Zuid-Holland complaining: 'The whole week long, I can't understand what the Canadians are saying. And now, among my countrymen, I can't understand anything either.' Anyway, it was good to see each other, and we usually invited someone over for coffee."

Winter wasn't the only time a horse was used for transportation. Before her husband was able to scrape together enough money to buy that used car, Mrs. Dijkstra went to town, some three miles away, in an old Mennonite buggy pulled by an aging racehorse.

"The first time we put it in front of the buggy, the horse ran for five minutes. We couldn't get it to stop. One time, I went to Linwood by myself, and the harness broke. I bought some rope in a store and tied a few knots. Surprisingly everything held until I got home. Oh my, we can laugh about it now, but at the time the palms of my hands were sweating."

John Reinders, who settled near Drayton, Ontario, in 1952, can't forget his first winter in Canada. He kept wondering: What next? When he woke up on October 14, he found the world, including his beet crop, covered with snow. With consternation, he wondered: "How can we get through this winter?" But when the sun rose and the snow began to melt, he realized that it had been one of those freak Canadian storms he had heard about; winter could still be weeks away.

When the cold weather finally arrived, more new experiences awaited the Reinders clan. There were many mornings when the model-T Ford, bought for $120, refused to budge. Sometimes the laneway would be blocked by a heavy snowfall or waist-high drifts. Walking the short distance from the house to the barn could be a major excursion. As the howling, biting wind crept through the cracks of the poorly-insulated dwelling, the wood-burning stove burned round the clock and the inhabitants wore their woollen socks to bed.

One day, after a severe storm, Mrs. Reinders looked in vain for her roadside mailbox. It had been buried completely by a snowplow. As she walked back to the house, trying to step in her own deep tracks, she thought about the extremes in Canadian weather: from the oppressive heat of summer, when the grass dried up and a good night's sleep was impossible to find, to the bitter cold of the winter, which seemed never to end.

Up he went, one hand firmly grasping the ice-cold steel and the other a grease gun and oil can. He positioned himself on the little platform and went about his work, getting rid of the irksome squeak and making a few adjustments.

Jacob Huizinga, who had emigrated from Zwaagwesteinde, Friesland, in 1948, was making sure the little windmill outside his house at Dobbinton, Ontario, was in good working order. He depended on it to supply his family with clear water drawn from a deep well. Most farmhouses had one of these contraptions nearby.

Son Melle was close on his father's heels, ready to hand up a wrench or a screwdriver at a moment's notice.

John Snyders of Brooks, Alberta, remembers vividly his first winter in Canada—the 1950-51 one. There were three blizzards. "One stormy Sunday morning, our Dutch neighbor came to pick us up for church. I went, but my wife and children stayed home. After the first service, the minister told us to go home. Halfway between Brooks and Castles, we got stuck. It was -15 Fahrenheit. The wind was howling. We walked a mile and a half to a farmhouse. We had frost-bitten fingers, faces and noses. The next day, we went to Brooks by train and then we had to stay there in the hotel for two days. We got home on Thursday evening. In a blizzard, you get a fine powdery snow, and the wind drives it through every crack. My wife stuffed rags into cracks and hung blankets over the windows. On our porch, there was one large nail hole. The wind blew enough snow through that hole to fill half the porch. There was still snow in the willows in July that year."

"How are Dutch immigrants to Canada faring, especially in regard to adjusting to Canadian life? Generally speaking, the answer is, fortunately: good."

Mrs. John Reinders checks her mailbox at her home near Drayton, Ontario, on a wintry day in 1957, and then poses for a photo to be sent to relatives in The Netherlands.

The windmill needs some maintenance.

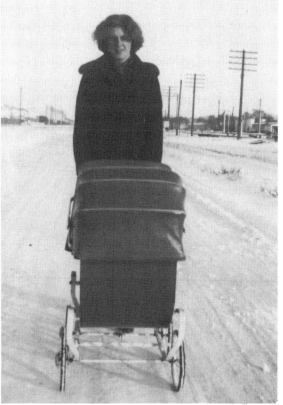

Mrs. Cor Knegt hangs her wash outside her home in Beamsville, Ontario, in the winter of 1948-1949.

Chris and Trix Linzel use a horse and cart to get through the deep snow in Prince Edward Island.

Joseph Winnemuller's oldest son brings home a meal after an afternoon of hunting near Selkirk, Manitoba, in 1954.

Immigrants cut firewood near Onion Lake, Saskatchewan, in 1949.

Mrs. Truus Heemskerk takes her baby for a stroll in Portage La Prairie, Manitoba, in 1951.

Winter

In early 1961, children play hockey on the outdoor skating rink at Dingeman De Leeuw's farm at Millgrove, Ontario.

The snow doesn't keep Joe Wiersma from riding his Dutch bike in Stratford, Ontario, in early 1952.

After a three-day blizzard, the children of Mr. and Mrs. Marinus C. Mol had a super snowslide. The Mols lived in Prince Edward Island for two years.

Alice Prins finds the snow piled high in Renfrew, Ontario, in 1959.

The Reinders children of Drayton, Ontario, get ready for a snowball fight.

Jan Heersink, the mayor of Steenderen, Gelderland, who was in Canada to work for the immigration committee of the Reformed Church—more on that later—was speaking to the people in The Netherlands over the *Wereldomroep* network in December, 1952.

"Usually several years pass before people feel at home and at ease in their new country. Everyone needs some time to adjust, especially when the transition is sudden. One person adjusts more easily than another and there are some who never adjust completely. Adjustment is a very personal matter. Things that to some are trivial become serious obstacles for others."

One of the big problems was the language.

"Despite all warnings, most immigrants arrive without sufficient knowledge of English. They have all kinds of excuses for not having taken English lessons. But excuses don't help. The reality hits home as soon as one arrives in Halifax and it appears that customs officials speak nothing but English. The presumptuous immigrant who then orders *twee ranja* in the cafeteria can't seem to understand why he doesn't get what he wants. An older immigrant recently told me that he had given up trying to learn English and was now trying to teach his Canadian

JoAnn VanDyk, daughter of Mr.and Mrs. Peter VanDyk, got in the act when her father shot a pair of ducks at the farm near Delhi, Ontario, in 1950. She's now Mrs. Ed DeConinck.

employer Dutch, but without much success. We have to make sure that immigrants learn to dream in English while still in The Netherlands!"

The younger the immigrant, according to Heersink, the more easily he adjusts.

"He is not so deeply rooted in the Old Country, nor does he leave much behind. Older people have their achievements and perhaps have moved up the social ladder. But in Canada, they have to start all over again. The greater their achievements in The Netherlands, the greater the drop to the bottom."

Heersink had a few other observations to pass on:

● "Readings or discussions about Canada give people certain ideas about the country. The reality is often very different, which means, in the beginning at least, some disillusioning setbacks. They can be discouraging, but Canada is not responsible for the setbacks; the problem is that too many people go there with preconceived notions."

● "Family life is also subject to numerous tensions unknown in the Old Country. The spiritual nurture of children requires a great deal of love and attention, more than it did in The Netherlands where the children grew up in the protection of familiar surroundings. Much of this nurture is left to the mother. In addition to her own difficulties, she has to bear those of the entire family."

● "The purchasing power of the dollar is equivalent to at least two Dutch guilders. Small wonder then that the man who earned forty-five guilders a week in The Netherlands and now earns forty-five dollars a week figures that he has it made in Canada, for now his purchasing power is twice as high."

● "Transition to Canadian schools presents few problems. Children can learn the language, depending on their age, in a few months. Education in The Netherlands is much deeper, but in Canada it is much broader. Elementary schools have the following subjects in their curriculum: team spirit, health, music, art, literature, public speaking, social studies, and a few others. It is a credit to the Canadian educational system that it tries to make Canadians out of the various ethnic groups represented."

Just before this book went to press the sad news reached us that Jan Heersink had died.

There were Canadians who looked upon the Dutch immigrants—or any other newcomer from Europe, for that matter—with some disdain. They believed that foreigners robbed them of the few jobs available. If they had their way, the country's borders would be closed.

Such bitter feelings surfaced now and then. There were harsh words and name-calling. There were fistfights and incidents of pure vandalism. Then there was simple silence, an attempt to ignore the presence of immigrants, perhaps the deepest insult of all.

Leo Hovius, who had found a job with a big dairy operation at Georgetown, Ontario, came face to face with this form of discrimination.

"We lived in a large house with two other families—one Dutch, one Canadian," says his wife. "We shared one bathroom and we each took turns cleaning it a week at a time. Our Canadian neighbors remained strangers. They completely ignored us; it was as if they didn't want us there. And we had no contact with any of the other workers on the farm. They just ignored us."

As the weeks went by, the situation worsened. The workers began to tease Hovius and his wife mercilessly.

"The wife of our Canadian neighbor kept on plugging the toilet. And when it was her turn to clean it up, she didn't, of course. She also let the heating go off. When we ignored this pestering, they started fooling around with our car. Leo was just on his way to town one morning when he discovered that someone had drained the radiator. Soon after that, he found that someone had scratched the paint with a sharp object. And so the nonsense continued."

If the workers intended to get Hovius and his wife to leave the farm, they succeeded. The Dutch couple said they'd had enough and moved on.

The early immigrants brought along a few eye-catching habits—such as wearing wooden shoes. These were common footwear for young and old in the rural areas of The Netherlands. Even today, wooden shoes are still popular, especially among some of the old-timers in Canada.

In the late 1940s, Dick DeJong, a wooden shoe maker by trade, set up a little shop behind his home near Flamboro, Ontario, and began producing one of the products which had made The Netherlands famous.

"Working alone, I turn out ten pairs a day," he said then. "I sell them to the Dutch people at Holland Marsh and on farms in other places. They all want them, for they are a lot better than the boots Canadian farmers wear. As a matter of fact, some Canadian-born people are now buying and wearing them."

He sold the largest sizes for men and women at $1.50 a pair. Children's sizes went for a dollar.

He had some good advice for future Canadian customers: "We don't wear them in the house; we leave them at the back door when we go inside. That way, we never carry mud and dirt into the house."

One young woman wrote to her mother in The Netherlands: "Yesterday we were invited for dinner by the farmer. Mother, you should have seen what was on the table. There were baked potatoes with the peel still on them, cooked corn (the stuff

Mrs. William Thysse goes grocery shopping soon after her arrival in Regina, Saskatchewan, in 1959. Her bill amounted to $34.

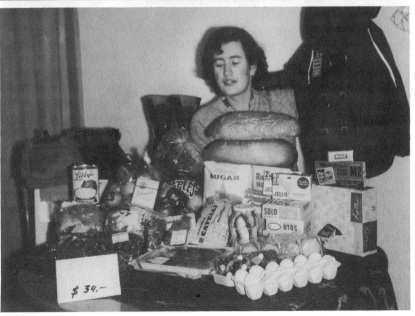

Henry Hendriksen, three years old in the fall of 1951, holds onto his friends after a good frolic in the mud. He and his family lived in Ladner, British Columbia.

A lot of work went into the large garden at the home of Mr. and Mrs. Henry Kuiperij at Acton, Ontario. The children helped by pulling weeds between the endive, onions, and potatoes.

we feed to the chickens), and celery sticks. Well, I took one potato and a little corn and that was it. You should have seen the Canadians. They ate those green stalks of celery like candy cane. Anyway, the pie with ice cream for dessert was delicious. I don't know, mother, if we will ever become Canadians."

She eventually acquired a taste for these foods. And, yes, she became a Canadian.

A young farmhand took his wife to town on a Saturday afternoon. They shopped a bit, and then ordered coffee and apple pie in a restaurant. A sign on the wall said, "Hot dogs 20 cents," and they wondered what was being offered.

At home, the farmhand looked up the word dog in his little English-Dutch dictionary and exclaimed: "Exactly what I thought! They eat dog meat in this country!"

A few weeks later, the farmer took his employee to town for a few errands. They ended up at the same restaurant. The farmer, thinking he was doing something kind, ordered two cups of coffee and two hot dogs. The Dutchman's stomach recoiled. But he hardly knew a word of English and couldn't tell his boss that he had no appetite.

Oh yes, he also became a Canadian. But he never did like hot dogs.

Mrs. Mary Provoost of Aylmer, Ontario, recalls: "The food was awful at first. The onions and eggs were sweet and the potatoes watery. I don't know how we ever got used to all that."

The newcomers did miss the food they had been used to in The Netherlands. Many items in their daily diet were not available here. And they often regarded with a critical eye the items on the shelves of the grocery store.

Some began growing their own potatoes. Kale, soft lettuce, endive, and a wide variety of beans, particularly the slicing kind, also grew well, and are still cultivated in many garden plots today.

Arie VanderKooij, putting years of experience to use, planted one of his favorite crops in the black, fertile soil of Holland Marsh in 1947. It was *witlof*, chicory, not a common root vegetable in Canada.

But the Netherlands ambassador in Canada, Dr. J.H. Van Royen, certainly knew that he had delicious meals awaiting him when he was informed in mid-November that a basket of *witlof* had arrived at his door in Ottawa. He was with the Netherlands delegation at the United Nations in New York City at the time.

VanderKooij was continuing a practice he had started during the German occupation. Queen Wilhelmina, in exile in England, had been the happy recipient of a regular shipment of his home-grown grapes smuggled out of The Netherlands by an *Engelandvaarder,* one who carried messages back and forth across the North Sea.

The Dutch appetite for things Dutch did not go unnoticed among business people. Importers set up shop, selling their wares to people who peddled them by car or truck to the immigrant families. Later, Dutch stores sprang up in many communities. So did Dutch butcher and bakery shops.

In Renfrew, north of Ottawa, John Eisen, afflicted with a crippling disease, decided to set up a store in his living room to serve the Dutch community. He and his wife ordered $150 worth of goods from Holtzheuser Bros., a large importer in Toronto. They stocked up on peppermints, bouillon cubes, lemonade, and so on, and opened their door to customers.

"We were given one month to pay the bill," recalls Eisen. "We managed to pay on time. But we soon found out that there weren't enough customers in Renfrew for us to turn a profit. Se we decided to take our Volkswagen bug and go to the Dutch people in Pembroke for more business."

That job was delegated to Mrs. Eisen. One family referred her to the next. And soon she had customers in a number of communities, often traveling a hundred miles a day to peddle such goods as rusk, licorice, soup, cheese, cold cuts, cookies, underwear, spoons, cigars, cards, wooden shoes, table cloths, and tea towels. It wasn't long before a van was pressed into service.

"People, in general, appreciated her coming to the homes and farms. She became almost a necessity for many families. Many women in those days, especially the ones on the farm, were still kind of isolated. They offered a cup of coffee or a cool drink or *een bordje soep.* In the ten years that my wife was on the road, very few customers did not appreciate her coming."

There was one memorable exception. One day, she arrived in the midst of a boisterous argument between spouses. Despite the objections of the husband, who appeared a bit tipsy, the wife ordered groceries. Mrs. Eisen got the items from the van and placed them on the kitchen table. That was too much for the husband. He cleared the table with one sweep

Kale, *or* boerekool, *is a cold-weather favorite of many immigrants. These healthy plants are growing in the backyard garden of Mr. and Mrs. Gerrit Barten of Brampton, Ontario.*

Arie VanderKooij displays some of the witlof *that he grew in Holland Marsh in 1947.*

Mrs. John Eisen was on the road selling Dutch products for ten years. Then her son John took over.

of his powerful arm.

"Groceries flew everywhere. The wife sobbed as she started to pick up the pieces. The husband pulled out his wallet, paid my wife, and then told her to get lost."

At the army base at Petawawa, where some Dutch families lived, Mrs. Eisen was a welcome visitor.

"One evening, my wife came home with the news that one family at the base was going to leave for Germany. Of course, that happened all the time. But this family had a 1½-year-old purebred German shepherd for which they were trying to find a home. Well, we decided to buy him for $50 in groceries."

Mrs. Eisen would usually fill up the van in the morning and leave in the afternoon. Sometimes she wouldn't be home until midnight.

Jack Thalen's second truck.

Catering to Dutch Immigrants

The Thalens in traditional dress, 1964.

Behind the counter in the little store in Guelph, 1960.

"One time, sometime in November, a big black bear crossed the road a few feet in front of the van. Another time, she came home with a blue shoulder—she got stuck in a snowdrift and had to push herself out. Our Lord always brought her home safely."

While Mrs. Eisen was on the road, the store was looked after by her husband, confined to a wheelchair, their son, John, and their dog, Knight. The store still exists, in larger quarters. But in the last few years, the Eisens have noticed a rapid drop in the sale of Dutch goods. Now they focus on selling Bibles, plaques, and Sunday School supplies.

In others areas of Canada, however, especially where Dutch-Canadians are clustered, the Dutch shops are as popular as ever, offering everything from salted herring to Frisian clocks.

Wherever Dutch products are readily available, their consumption has become habit-forming unto the second and third generations. The children and grandchildren of immigrants often still prefer the Dutch cheeses and luncheon meats to similar Canadian food. In the cities, where there are more immigrants with an urban background, the Dutch have developed a strong dependency on the weekly trip to the specialty shop. On the other hand, the earlier, rural immigrants, besides being more cost-conscious, are more accustomed to Canadian-style food because at the time of their immigration little else was available.

"We have our faithful clientele," says Bastiaan De Haas, operator of the Holland Shopping Center in New

One merchant who shares the view that Dutch stores must diversify to remain viable is Jack Thalen, who with his son Harry operates the Dutch Toko stores in Guelph and Hamilton, Ontario.

"Our business has drastically turned toward the Canadian market," he says. "We wouldn't be able to make it if it hadn't. We are still strictly in European goods, but they are aimed at a wider public. We have to look to the future. But of course, the Dutch remain a vital part of our business."

Thalen, a former resident of Drenthe, and the Wieringermeer, came to Canada in 1950 and settled at Freelton. He first went door to door from Smithville to Fergus selling fruit and vegetables from his father's farm.

"I called on everyone, including Canadians. But I eventually ended up with mostly Dutch customers. Then I came across a little store that was for sale in Guelph. I bought it and enlarged it. When my son came into the business, I also took over the store in Hamilton."

His shops, and the many others across Canada, do more than offer epicurean delights for the sweet tooth. During busy periods, they're a social center where customers can chat in Dutch. The weekly visit gives them the touch of the Old Country they still cherish.

Thalen spends much of his time for the Back to God Hour *radio program and his son Harry, shown above in the Hamilton store, has taken over much of the business. The other photo shows the store in its old location.*

Mrs. H.I. Roeleveld of North York, Ontario: "This is a picture, taken in my kitchen, of Dirk Paul who sold Dutch groceries door to door in 1958. He had two cardboard boxes of van alles wat (a little bit of everything)."

Mr. and Mrs. J. Olivier put things in order before opening their Dutch shop in Victoria, British Columbia, for another day of business in 1958. Olivier started the store in his living room and is now in his third location.

Westminster, British Columbia. "Some people have come here every week since my father opened the store twenty-five years ago."

They spend up to $25 a week on items that have satisfied their palates since they were young: cheese, tea-rusk, spice cake, smoked beef and other luncheon meats, peppermints, soup, fish, and so on. Gift items, such as Dutch clocks, tablecloths, and records featuring Christian music, are also popular.

"Despite what some people think, our type of business isn't dying off," says De Haas, formerly of The Hague. "The children have learned the tastes and habits of their parents. We're as busy now as we've ever been. The cheese is a real big seller. We ship it throughout British Columbia."

His father, John, launched the business in 1952 in the way so many owners of Dutch stores got their start: going door to door with products that the taste-conscious immigrants couldn't buy in most grocery stores.

Gerrit Te Nyenhuis runs the Dutch Canadian Shoppe in a mall at New Minas, Nova Scotia. A newcomer to the ethnic food business, he is shoring up his future by catering to Canadians as well.

Mr. and Mrs. John De Haas, with their son Bas and his wife Alice. Bas and Alice took over the store, the Holland Shopping Center, in October of 1982.

"A lot of Dutch people come in for cheese, cookies, meats, and gifts," he says. "But I do things to get the Canadian traffic too. For example, I stock products from Switzerland and Germany. Because I'm in a mall, I try to cater to everybody. When I first opened in the fall of 1980, my customers were sixty per cent Dutch and forty per cent Canadian. That's vice-versa now. This approach seems to work; I've recorded a twenty per cent increase in sales every year."

Te Nyenhuis was 13½ years old when he emigrated with his parents and seven brothers and sisters from Emmen, Drenthe, in 1958. His family settled in Canning, Nova Scotia, where he went to school for one year. Then due to his problem with the language, he was given permission to go to work.

"When we moved to Kentville the next year, I got a clerk's job in one of the grocery stores. Through the next nine years, I worked myself up to management positions in various companies and towns, but always in the grocery business. I worked as a cookie distributor near the Annapolis Valley for four years, starting in 1977. In 1980, I began to think of opening a Dutch shop. Since the valley had quite a number of Dutch people, it seemed a likely place to start."

His shelves are stocked with brass, copper, pewter, tablecloths, Christian books, jewelry, spoons, a wide range of Dutch and Indonesian items, and . . . maple sugar.

The voracious appetites of the growing immigrant boys kept mothers busy in the kitchen and fathers working hard to make sure there would be enough on the table each day. The boys put away food as if there was no tomorrow. And the food didn't have to be fancy. A plateful of steaming potatoes wetted down with thin gravy pacified many growling stomachs.

Rev. Harri Zegerius tells a story of sharing a noon dinner with a farm family near London, Ontario. The family had invited him over to inspect a farm they were planning to buy.

"But first, of course, we had to eat," recalls the minister. "You can't hit the road on an empty stomach. And a good dinner it was—a big pan of boiled potatoes, heaps of fresh peas from the garden, and delicious meatballs with gravy. A good deep plateful just about filled me up. But the fourteen-year-old son, who had worked in the garden all morning, went on and on. He put away four plates full without blinking an eye. Then it was pudding time—vanilla pudding liberally covered with fresh raspberries. I felt like smacking my lips when I finished my plate. But the son had another plateful, and another. I began to wonder where he put it all."

But that wasn't the end. While his mother was devotedly reading a long chapter from the Dutch-language Bible, the son was surreptitiously forking potatoes from the pan and quietly and quickly putting them away. Apparently the mother never noticed.

"Let me tell you," says Rev. Zegerius, "it was an almost unbelievable performance."

At Trenton, Ontario, Tony Wielemaker was on the road in his 1951 Prefect early one Saturday morning to pick up his girlfriend, Hilda Overdijk, for a day's outing. He hit and killed a rabbit. Most people would have left it for the scavengers. But not Tony. With typical

A new arrival from The Netherlands has gotten some help from her neighbor in learning to bake. A lemon-meringue pie comes fresh from a wood-stove oven.

Dutch efficiency, he picked it up and threw it in the trunk.

Says Hilda, now his wife: "At my place he cut its throat, hung it in the tree in front of the house, and hoped that my brother would find it when he woke up and skin it for Sunday dinner. Well, my brother did find it. But he smelled a joke, and buried the beast. So much for our rabbit stew."

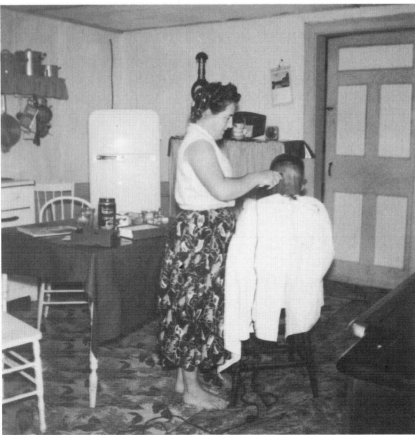

Ralph DeJong of Williamsburg, Ontario, steps off the bus in 1950 with ten loaves of rye bread, one for each newly-arrived immigrant family in Cornwall. He had attended an immigration meeting in Hamilton.

When immigrants counted every penny, going to the barber was out of the question. Mom or Dad hauled the scissors out of a kitchen drawer and started snipping away. Often the result didn't look very professional, but that didn't matter.

Mrs. Gerrit Barten, formerly of Noord-Scharwoude, Noord-Holland, now of Brampton, Ontario, stands in the kitchen of her home at Carrying Place, Ontario.

An unpleasant aspect of early immigrant life was the deep jealousy that often came between immigrants. Rev. John Van Harmelen detected it when he visited Canada in 1952, and he wrote about it in *Kerk en Gezin*, the organ of the *Gereformeerde Kerk* in Assen.

"A and B emigrated to Canada at the same time, met each other on the boat, and went to the same destination. Ideal, one would think! But several years later A bought a beautiful farm and managed it well. B, however, was not so richly blessed and didn't make much headway, although he had done reasonably well. When I spoke to B, it was apparent that he was jealous of A. They had come to Canada at the same time, and look at the difference now! He could not endure the fact that God had blessed A more richly than himself. This was an immense cross for him to bear . . ."

Rev. Van Harmelen found that immigrants were very different from each other.

"One saves his money for the future; he buys only the essentials, and the rest goes to the bank. Another buys all the luxuries available in Canada. Making the most of his money, he owns practically everything. But if you inquire about his arrangements for the future, the picture is less rosy. He has been in Canada for five years already, but he has no long-term security."

He also found that more than one immigrant ended up deep in debt because of easy credit.

"The credit system is an insidious temptation for those with a weaker nature. You can get everything on credit—a house, a washer, a fridge, a radio, a television, a car, etc. In fact, a salesman would faint dead away if you offered to pay for everything in cash. He is likely to say: 'You could have enjoyed these things long ago.' "

There were so many others things the immigrants had to adjust to. For example:

● Mrs. Mary Provoost of Aylmer, Ontario: "Once, while sitting on one of the beautiful hills behind our place, we were approached by a cute little animal. We coaxed it along for awhile, until all of a sudden we realized it was something we already had heard a lot about—a skunk. We ran for our lives."

● Carl Biel of Guelph, Ontario, twenty-one years old when he emigrated in 1949: "A drawback was that there was a shortage of girls my age for the first eight to ten years. Most immigrants were

...e Dijkstra children didn't have to take turns bathing when they lived near Linwood, Ontario. There was room for them all in the horse trough.

...rence Feddes of the Port Lambton, Ontario, ...a takes his Saturday bath.

Space was at a premium in most of the immigrant homes.

Ann Grootenboer feeds the cats at Murillo, Ontario.

...e Reinders children of the Drayton, Ontario, area took their weekly baths in an assortment of tubs.

Chris Grootenboer gives a helping hand.

Children in a strange land: everything seemed different to them too. The children of John Kap play in the mud near Sarnia, Ontario, in the late 1940s. The spring thaw in 1953 turned a rutted rural road at Spencerville, Ontario, into a play area for the children of Gijs Berkelaar. Just before Easter, the children of Henry Kuiperij of Acton, Ontario, were allowed to dye boiled eggs in pretty colors. But then they had to eat them all too.

young families. Yes, there were many lonely months for the boys. We didn't associate with Canadian girls."

● Mrs. Elizabeth Hryciw of Calgary, Alberta: "The first year in Canada was a most difficult one for all of us; Dad's work was not secure and we were very poor. We were isolated in the country near Springfield, Ontario, and the winter was very harsh. We did not qualify for medicare until we'd been in Canada for a year, so when Mom was in the hospital with a miscarriage, the bill seemed monumental. Not once did my parents request social assistance, and by careful saving and spending they managed to keep out of debt."

● John Hofstee of Listowel, Ontario: "On the first Sunday in Canada, we got the boss to drive us to Chatham, to the Christian Reformed Church, which had a Dutch service in the early afternoon. It turned out that Chatham had gone to Daylight Saving Time that day while the countryside had not, and as a result we arrived at church an hour late. After the service, the minister took us to his home for tea, and he later drove us home."

● Mrs. Provoost: "I remember a certain shopping trip. We needed a brassiere and went to a five-and-ten-cent store. The lady pointed to a bracelet. Oh well, it would have been more embarrassing the other way around."

● Rudy Knite of Tangent, Alberta: "When our oldest daughter was a baby, my wife and I used to put her in a cardboard box while we worked clearing the land. One day, while clearing a 100-acre field, we put the box under the trees at the edge of the bush. In the afternoon, my wife was on the tractor, harrowing the far side, while I was picking roots about a hundred yards away. Suddenly, I saw a big male black bear coming out of the bush next to the cardboard box. I froze. The bear sniffed at the box for a while and then ambled on. It was about two minutes before I could move. We didn't work any more that day."

● Piet Sybrandy of Toppenish, Washington: "Many of our immigrants became money hungry. When I lived near Holland Marsh, I walked thirteen miles to church and thirteen miles back rather than pay $1 one-way gas money. The people who offered me a ride figured I could pay the entire cost. Not me. I walked instead."

● Leo Hoens of Vancouver, British Columbia: "I found it difficult to adjust to the Sunday lifestyle of the typical Cana-

Mrs. G.J. Ferwerda of London, Ontario, says of the photo at top left: "Soon after I started to work at the hospital, I bought this bicycle to pedal to and from work. People stared and sometimes yelled after me. In those days, only children biked!" Some immigrants brought with them their sturdy Dutch bicycles. Ted Smeenk of Voorburg, Zuid-Holland, owned one powered by a small diesel engine. He is shown in London in 1951 with wife Pauline and children Frank, Robbie, and Josie. At left, the five young daughters of Cornelis Verkerk have a lot of fun with the stone-boat on the Percy Mac-Donald farm at Fergus, Ontario, in 1950.

dian. A Sunday afternoon in Holland had been more relaxed. For me, it had been a question of either watching a handball game, visiting a friend, or staying home to listen to records. Here it was a day of hard work around the house—working in the garden, cutting the grass, painting . . ."

● Ted Smeenk of London, Ontario: "Our three babies born in Holland were delivered at home by midwives, so when our fourth one was due in March, 1952, my wife didn't want to go into the hospital. She didn't speak English, and felt that everything would go much more smoothly if the baby were delivered at home. However, when my wife went into labor, our doctor was enjoying his day off at Grand Bend on Lake Huron. I started phoning other doctors, but no one else was willing to do the delivery at home. After

Mrs. Lena Van Spengen goes shopping in Saskatoon, Saskatchewan, in 1952 with son Karel and daughter Alida. Immigrants found many goods cheaper than similar goods in The Netherlands. At top right, Jake Feenstra (right), hired hand on a dairy farm near Trenton, Ontario, came across something new in the fall of 1948. His farmer killed four pigs for his own use, and then suspended them from tall tripods for the butchering. At right, Mrs. John DeJong, who settled in Picture Butte, Alberta, in 1952, is visited by her daughter, Margaret Oosterhof. Tina pours the coffee. While they chat, both women are busily crocheting and knitting.

It's a beautiful Sunday afternoon in the summer of 1952. Three families out for a drive stop for some fresh air and an impromptu picnic along a road in the Niagara area.

Left: Many immigrant families enjoyed sightseeing. Traveling from the Niagara Peninsula to Manitoulin Island in 1959, Peter Heemskerk stopped to take a photo.

Above: Most immigrants had to adjust to living thousands of miles away from their relatives. Family get-togethers, an integral part of social life in The Netherlands, were rare occurrences in the early days. But there were exceptions—when more than one in the family emigrated. C.M. Hogeterp wrote so many enthusiastic letters that most of his family ended up here. Once a year, they got together for a picnic in southern Ontario.

Families sometimes took to the road to visit people they had known in The Netherlands. A butcher and two bakers who had lived on the same street in Hooge-veen, Drenthe, meet again in Ontario in 1951. They are Karl Prins, John Swijting, and Riemer Wiersma, all immigrants. Wiersma's sons, Joe and Jake, now operate their father's bakery in Chatham, Ontario.

twenty-five calls, I found an elderly doctor who agreed to come, provided I had someone from the Victorian Order of Nurses there. Those were hectic hours. Fortunately, everything went all right."

Once they got their cars, the immigrants loved to travel. There was so much to see. There was so much to tell the folks back home. And it was good therapy for the immigrant to take himself out of his confines briefly. A day trip to Niagara Falls, a ferry ride to Vancouver Island, a walk in the northern bush, a roadside picnic—such outings did wonders psychologically.

Despite their rather meagre existence in the beetfields of southern Alberta, Tjasse Heuvel and his wife, Agtje, scraped together time and money for a bit of sightseeing. Having traveled thousands of miles by boat and train, they weren't satisfied with just taking in the endless stretches of their own countryside. There was much more to be seen in the New World.

"In 1950, we went to see relatives in Montana, across the border," says Heuvel. "We traveled through mountains. What a wilderness. Big bears walked around the farmhouses. It was nice to see, but we certainly didn't want to live there."

They also traveled north to Neerlandia, a community founded by Dutch settlers.

"We stopped to visit friends who had trekked to the area in 1926. They had cleared 164 acres with the axe and had first lived in a hollow in the ground. That was real pioneer life."

Members of the Klaas Terpstra family, now of Hamilton, Ontario, meet a resident of Algonquin Park.

Mrs. Gijs Berkelaar works at her Dutch sewing machine on the veranda of her home at Spencerville, Ontario, on a warm summer day in the early 1950s.

Chapter 14

The Language Barrier

The Language Barrier

A customs official in Quebec City looked at the baggage of the Gerald Prins family, pointed to a small wooden crate and asked: "What's in there?"

Prins had to think for a moment. His knowledge of English was limited. He seemed to have forgotten most of the words that his brother, a teacher, had taught him. Suddenly, something clicked in his brain. He answered: "My tools. Me a carpenter."

The official, quite satisfied, moved on.

Prins's seventeen-year-old daughter, who had been taught English as part of her school curriculum, looked at her father with astonishment and asked: "What did that man say?" Prins told her, and beamed with inner satisfaction.

This first successful encounter with the English language didn't mean that he had mastered it. Far from it. For two winters, he went to night school to get a better grip on it. But even then he found it difficult to follow someone who talked fast, and so he tried to avoid conversations. A Canadian once remarked to a fellow worker: "That Dutchman doesn't say a lot." Prins thought: "Of course not. I was hired to do carpentry work, not to talk." But deep down he knew that his one or two-word sentences were simply a result of a language problem.

"This slowly changed," he says. "But it wasn't easy. How could it be for someone who starts learning a new language at age 45?"

"Learn English!" That message was drilled home repeatedly in The Netherlands. But it was easier said than done.

John Reinders, fifty-nine years old when he flew to his new country in 1952, knew that old habits were hard to break. He had tried hard to learn a bit of English. But he went to Canada hardly knowing a word.

"I went to a teacher in our neighborhood in Drenthe," he recalls. "It sounded easy. But when I woke up in the morning, I couldn't remember anything. Really, it's no wonder, what with all I had on my mind in those days. I had a lot more things to worry about than English lessons. I'm sure my age didn't make it any easier. I tried, but it didn't work."

Reinders took a bit of comfort in that he was traveling with ten other families from Drenthe, all of whom intended to settle in the Drayton, Ontario, area. He would be able to continue speaking Dutch. And if English were required on occasion, someone from the group could look after that.

Over the years, he learned enough English to know what people were talking about. But he still feels himself an outsider when he is required to speak in English. Fortunately, there aren't too many occasions which make him tongue-tied.

"Within our family circle, we spoke Dutch. We spoke Dutch with the other immigrants. The church service was in Dutch. You know, they say that in the Drayton area one out of every three persons you meet is a Hollander. When I go to the bank or to the store, there's usually

Dutch-Canadian Dialect

Many of the first-generation Dutch in Canada now speak a unique combination of both languages, as Ted Smeenk of London, Ontario, illustrated in a letter to the editor of *Hollandia News*, a bi-weekly newspaper: "We talk Dutch about as follows: Doe you like mijn nieuwe jas? Ik had met die andere een accident gehad. Er was een hole in de sleeve gebrand, toen ik te dicht bij de stove had gezeten. Ik hated die reddish color anyway. Vind je deze navy kleur niet veel nicer? En toch was die niet expensive. We dreven toevallig met de car voorbij dat storetje en daar was een grote sale aan en ik zeg tegen Sjon laten we daar es effe kijke. En laat ik daar nou net die navy coat vinden in mijn size. Nou we wat meer gesettled zijn hoef ik niet meer met een ouwe coat te lopen met een gefikste mouw. Laat de armoe de pes maar krijge. Ik ben er echt happy mee."

When such people go to The Netherlands and speak Dutch to their relatives and friends, smiles and chuckles are not an unusual reaction.

Dad's English Was Mostly Body Language

Mr. Beldman stands at the far left in this group of new arrivals in London, Ontario.

The Beldmans, parents of Mrs. Trudy Joldersma, came to Canada from Holten, Overijssel, in their mid-60s because their eight children had decided to emigrate. Once a week, the entire family went to the grocery store in Jarvis, Ontario. That place became familiar to most immigrants, and the store clerks knew many of them by name.

"Dad, who never did learn English, used exaggerated sign and body language to show what he wanted or needed," says Mrs. Joldersma. "My mother, slightly embarrassed, softly exhorted him to more acceptable behavior: 'Willem, what must those people be thinking.' Dad never suffered feelings of inferiority because he lacked English, nor did he apologize for this deficiency. On occasion, he would go on his own to the village store, riding his bicycle. He took delight in drawing pictures of the desired items on a piece of paper and having the store clerks run around making sure he got what he wanted."

He demanded of his grandchildren that they speak Dutch to him. *"Hollands praten,"* he would say. There was never a language barrier between them.

Mrs. Joldersma, who shared a house with her parents for thirteen years, says: "I believe that my parents were instrumental in giving their grandchildren the heritage of understanding and speaking a second language. Their presence forced all of us to maintain Dutch in our homes much longer than in the homes of those families who had left their elders behind and whose children knew their grandparents only from pictures. All twenty-nine grandchildren in our clan understand Dutch perfectly and most of them speak it as well. This is an amazing fact, considering that the oldest grandchild of the nine born in Holland was only six upon arrival here and that the remaining twenty were born in Canada."

Although he insisted that people speak Dutch in his presence, Mrs. Joldersma's father supported the changeover to English-language services at the church in Jarvis. He would tell others: "We have to do it to keep the young. We need English in the church as soon as possible."

His wife was of a different mind, always busy deciphering the newspaper, listening to the radio, or discussing the English sermons after church. Because she loved singing, the hymns became for her a source of learning material.

a person there who can understand me. There's no need to learn English."

He keeps up on world events by faithfully tuning in each evening to the Dutch-language *Wereldomroep* sent over the shortwave from The Netherlands.

Mrs. Elizabeth Hryciw of Calgary, Alberta, tells how her mother was determined to learn English, partly to fight off the isolation and loneliness of being at home all day.

"She had us bring children's books from the library and she would read them with her Dutch-English dictionary in one hand and notepaper and pen in the other. She encouraged us to speak English at home so that she would learn it more quickly, and we were to correct her mistakes when she spoke. As a result, we spoke very little Dutch."

When the mother made her first trip back to The Netherlands in 1961, she was so excited at seeing her sisters waiting for her behind the glass partition that she unknowingly began to speak English to the customs officer. He sniffed his nose and haughtily enquired in Dutch: "Have you forgotten your mother tongue already?" The poor woman was embarrassed.

"When we came to Canada as children, we were fortunate to have two teachers who were anxious to give us instruction in English," says Mrs. Hryciw. "They would keep us after school on their own time to teach us grammar. By the end of our first school year, we were getting perfect marks in spelling and reading."

The two younger children of Arie Verduyn were sent to a small country school near Sarnia, Ontario, where the teachers did their best to get them adjusted to their new environment. But it was a different story for the two older children, who were sent to the high school in Sarnia.

"The staff was completely unprepared to teach teenagers who did not speak their language," says Verduyn. "Most of the time, they were left all by themselves in a small room, a frustrating experience for

Children Learned It Quickly

Colin Campbell, who taught Grades 5,6, 7 and 8 at the public school in Port Lambton, Ontario, in the late 1950s, felt some concern when he was told that he would soon be getting pupils from a large family recently arrived from The Netherlands. He hadn't been a teacher that long. His class already had forty pupils. He could foresee difficulties teaching children who didn't know the language.

"Well, the children proved to be a delightful addition to the school," he recalls. "They came from a Christian home where there was much love and the wise discipline which is the product of true parental love. They were diligent, well-motivated and co-operative, with the cheerful friendliness which comes from emotional stability. Their fellow pupils and their teacher enjoyed them very much."

Problems with English? Sure, they had an accent at first and their vocabulary was limited. But children learn fast. And before long, they had no apparent deficiencies.

Educational authorities placed newly-arrived immigrant children in lower grades than their ages warranted. This policy disturbed Campbell, for he knew that in many respects these children were ahead of their Canadian counterparts. Lack of English—a temporary impairment—was no reason for moving the child back a grade or two and assigning him mathematical equations he had mastered long ago. So when he heard that Keith, who had completed his eighth grade in The Netherlands, would enter his class instead of starting high school, he decided to do something about it.

"A neighbor who had come to know the immigrant children came to me before school opened in September to tell me that he considered it a shame that Keith should be placed in Grade 8. When I talked to the principal of Wallaceburg High School, he agreed at once, saying that it would be far better for the boy to spend the year in Grade 9, even though he might not make the year."

Keith proved to be an outstanding student throughout high school and went on to earn a doctorate degree.

youngsters eager to learn. When it became clear that we, ourselves, had to do something about it, we engaged the teenage daughter of a minister to give lessons in English. One of the first things we asked her was: 'How does one politely greet a stranger?' To our surprise, she insisted that it was merely the familiar 'Hi' . . ."

"It was a handicap at first, not being able to talk with people," says J.A. Grootenboer, who arrived near Portage La Prairie, Manitoba, in 1949. "My English was limited to yes and no. Right away we got the daily paper from the boss and I tried to read it with the pocket dictionary beside me. I spent most of my spare time doing that. Before we had left Holland, we had cancelled every subscription we had to Dutch-language publications. We burned all our ships behind us. For this reason, and because of all the energy we spent on learning, we were able to help ourselves within a short time."

Nevertheless, when Grootenboer and his wife went to town for some shopping, they carried that little dictionary with them, not leaving anything to chance.

Mrs. Huibert Van Drunen of Stratford, Ontario, remembers her surprise when she and her husband arrived in Ilderton, Ontario, in the summer of 1950.

"A married hand was to receive $75 a month, plus fuel, milk and a house—but our farmer did not have a house for us yet. So for four months we lived in with the Canadian farmer. Of course, we were disappointed. But there were advantages."

Van Drunen did not have to buy groceries, not even food for the baby. With the money he saved, he was able to buy a 1929-model car after three months. And their stay with English-speaking people enabled them to learn a bit of the language.

The Accent Can Linger Decades Later

Bas Korstanje at work in his newspaper office.

Many immigrants, especially the older ones, will continue to speak with distinct accents, no matter how fluent they become in English. Even if they changed their names, their speech would betray them.

Bas Korstanje, editor of the editorial page of *The Spectator* in Hamilton, Ontario, who came to Canada in 1956 after working ten years for the *Rotterdamsch Nieuwsblad*, wrote a column in January of 1983 about his lingering accent.

This year it is going to happen. I'm going to hit the half-way mark—27 years . . .

Now that may seem a peculiar half-way to anywhere, but in my case it's undeniably a milestone. I will reach the point where, for one brief, shining moment, two cultures will clash like cymbals somewhere deep inside me.

The outcome of that collision can only be awaited with considerable trepidation because it could easily complicate, if not severely hurt, my reputation as a linguist of sorts.

Until now, you see, I have always

"It was difficult at first," says Mrs. Van Drunen. "I remember thinking at meal times: 'I hope they don't start up a conversation with us.' Of course, they always did. Fourteen-year-old Terry, the farmer's youngest son, was our English teacher. He corrected us when we made mistakes. The other family members were too polite to do this. Except once. I came in and greeted everybody with 'Goodbye.' The farmer laughed and said: 'Already?' "

One of the postwar pioneers, Arie VanderKooij, ran into the language gap before he was officially an immigrant.

"I wanted to post a letter when the *Waterman* stopped at Quebec City on its way to Montreal in 1947. I needed a stamp. But I didn't have a clue what the word was. So I took a Dutch stamp out of my wallet, licked it and pretended to put it on the envelope. The clerk, of course, knew right away what I wanted."

Despite the hurried lessons, most immigrants were stuck when it came to the nitty-gritty. Even a former kindergarten school teacher in Amersfoort, Mrs. Trudy Smit of Brossard, Quebec, went job hunting in Toronto in 1956 with some insecurity. "I had taken some English courses in Holland," she says, "but not enough. A day or so after my arrival in the city, I found work in the diet kitchen of one of the big hospitals. They told me: 'There's a Dutch girl here who can help you get started.' On my first day at work, she was on vacation. So they told an Irish girl to instruct me. I hadn't a clue about what she was saying."

Piet Sybrandy, who came to Holland Marsh as a fifteen-year-old from Sneek, Friesland, in 1951, was anxious to master a few words so that he could communicate with the girls. "Come Saturday night, finished with work early, I washed up and walked to Bradford and entered one of those general stores with a soda bar. It served a delicious vanilla milkshake for ten cents. And a very understanding lady

managed to get away with mispronunciation of certain words by shamelessly playing up the fact that I was not born here.

If someone draws attention to the verbal liberties I take with the language every so often, I admit with a helpless and disarming smile: "I can't hellup it if I hef an axent. I nefer vent to skool here."

That usually fills any critic with deep remorse and great admiration. Often they immediately go out of their way to praise my command of the language. They call up dark visions of how terror-stricken and tongue-tied they would be if, at any time and heaven forbid, they would find themselves in the unfortunate position of having to fill my wooden shoes in Holland and speak Dutch.

"You vould kwikly lurn," I flatter them.

It's amazing how long even close friends will allow you to play that kind of fraudulent game.

But now there's that half-way mark looming on the not too distant horizon—the point where I will have been a Canadian exactly as long as I was once a Dutchman.

Now what do I tell anybody who  *detects an accent? I've been here only 27 years? Ridiculous! That's half of my life so far.*

And since it took me a few years after birth before I learned how to say Mama and Papa—not to mention Schiedamsche-singel, schaterlachen, Scheveningse scharretjes or sluizen van IJmuiden— I have been speaking English for the longer and probably also more productive part of my life.

And still . . .

Before I go on, let me hasten to point out that Schiedamschesingel is the name of a street, schaterlachen is to roar with laughter, Scheveningse scharretjes are fish smoked in the fishing village of Scheveningen and the sluizen van IJmuiden are akin to the Welland canal locks. No naughty words at all.

The trouble is that everybody has been far too kind to me over the years, including my own family.

After knowing me for a while and getting used to my faulty baritone which merrily misses the fine distinction between bed, bat and bad, or red, rat, and read, they don't even notice anymore. What accent? It's just the way he talks. It has

worked there. When she wasn't busy, I would point out various items such as sugar and flour and say the names in Dutch. Then she would tell me the English words and correct my pronunciation until it sounded about right. I believe the customers lingered at the soda fountain just to take in the free entertainment."

S.P. Knuist, formerly of Kamloops, British Columbia, and now of London, Ontario, didn't take it all too seriously.

"We met many people from Holland who were in the same position: just married, trying to make a go of it. We helped each other in many ways. It just so happened that many of us went to the same church and came from the same province in Holland. So we had many things in common. We weren't ashamed of our poor English; we talked a mixture of Dutch and English and laughed at the comical expressions. We had a lot of fun."

Then there was Hilda Overdijk's future husband, Tony Wielemaker, who left Koudekerke, Zeeland, in 1951, came to the Trenton area and immediately stumbled upon a big language problem: during the week he had trouble with the English which his co-workers spoke, and during the weekends with the Frisian which most of the people in his congregation spoke.

"He was smarter than some," says Hilda. "He figured that if you can't beat them, join them. He soon learned to understand Frisian as well as English."

A minister from The Netherlands had usually had some education in the English language. That came in handy for mediating employee-employer disputes or accompanying members for job interviews. But it was another matter to prepare an English-language service from beginning to end, including the sermon.

"Yes, it was a bit awkward," says Rev.

The Accent Lingers

reached the point where, at a party, a roomful of born Canadians under my direction will lustily sing "Ven I'm vashing vindows." The late George Formby would break his ukulele over their heads if he could hear them massacre his "When I'm cleaning windows."

What frightens me is that it may be too late. I've always told myself that I could do much better if I wanted to. If I were introduced to the Queen, I would watch my tongue and sound like a BBC newsreader, I smugly believed.

Not anymore! The other day I tried it on a daughter-in-law who was knitting baby booties.

"What a Wonderful Way to While aWay a feW empty hours on a Windy Weekend," I said, carefully measuring my Ws.

She didn't jump up to shout "By George, he's got it," but then I'm not exactly My Fair Lady.

Instead she looked up and her eyes were filled with concern. "Are you all right, Dad?" she asked. "You don't sound like yourself."

Well, I thought, at least you don't write with an accent.

Wrong!

After gleefully reprimanding one editorial writer the other day for spelling dilemma as "dilemna" and another for trying to substitute "wierd" for weird, I delivered myself of the following gripping sentence: "Dark clouds are stapling over Poland . . ."

I heard them discussing it when the proof came up for corrections. No longer really sure of anything I do with or to the language, they were taking no chances but checked and double-checked.

Finally, they reluctantly asked how one "staples" clouds or how clouds "staple" anything for that matter.

In Dutch "stapelen" is to pile one thing on top of the other and . . .

Well, you see what I mean.

The first 27 years were easy, but the road ahead looks a little rough.

Call it culture shock.

D.J. Scholten, minister of the Christian Reformed Church in Lethbridge, Alberta, in 1953. "Many ministers had to work with dictionaries—me included. We must have translated a word incorrectly now and then."

He shouldn't feel too badly though. The preachers who came to Canada from the United States to minister to the early postwar settlers had problems too.

Rev. Henry Venema, whose Dutch was not the best, practised at home with his wife. One Sunday, shortly after their arrival, he had to go to a small country church to preach his first Dutch sermon. When he returned home, his wife anxiously asked him in Dutch: "Well, how did it go?" He replied: *"Best. Al de banken waren bezeten."* But he should have used the word *bezet* (filled) instead of *bezeten* (possessed).

Pronunciation of English is difficult for many immigrants even today. They can never twist their tongues far enough for the "th" to come out. One classic story concerns a man who is asked his age. His reply: "I am dirty, and my wife is dirty too."

The new Canadians, using a mixture of both languages in their conversations, created a vocabulary of their own. One woman in the southern Alberta beet country misused the Dutch word for baptism—*doop*. She drew her daughter's attention to Rev. Scholten and said: "Look, here's the minister who doped you."

Shaking with laughter, the minister commented: "And I didn't even use a drug!"

Mrs. Frank Tolsma of Vauxhall, Alberta, laughs over another incident: "I once needed corn starch to make a pudding. Well, we went to the store and found starch. But it turned out to be starch for clothes. That didn't taste too good."

Melle Huizinga of Edmonton, Alberta, chuckles over this one: "A man called Dirk figured himself to be a great singer. Well, he sure could sing loud. When we had our Farm Forum meetings, we would always start with singing 'The King.' Most of the Canadians sort of mumbled along with the piano. But not Dirk. With Frisian lustiness, he would always bellow out: 'God shave our noble King. God shave our gracious King.' The Canadians never twitched a muscle. But, as young boys, we would really crack up and get dirty looks from our parents."

The humorous stories are endless . . .

about the immigrant who saw the sign 'Rooms' (it's the Dutch word for Catholic) in the window of a rooming house and wondered if the Protestants did similar advertising . . . about the man who asked the service station attendant to put some "sky" in his tire . . . about the woman who told the dentist her "upstairs" tooth hurt . . . about the Dutchman who ordered a piece of "pee" in a restaurant when he wanted some pie . . .

Carl Biel of Guelph, Ontario, who came from Meppen, Drenthe, as a twenty-one-year-old in 1949, did the right thing: even though he knew enough English to get by, he took formal lessons to get to know it better.

"I went to night classes—and took my mother along. My friend figured my English was good enough and laughed at me for going to those lessons. But I never regretted it. Going to those classes helped me very much in learning how to pronounce words properly and to write formal letters."

Biel was far ahead of many people. Some hardly knew a word of English, to

100% English

In Oshawa, Ontario, Jane Span, who is now Mrs. Frank Roorda of Kitchener, Ontario, was all smiles when she learned in 1957 that she had scored a perfect mark in her English examination. Over a four-year period, twenty-seven perfect papers in English and citizenship had been written by new Canadians in Ontario.

J.B. Wallace, citizenship adviser of the community programs branch of the Ontario Department of Education, wrote: "When one of our markers rates either half of the examination paper at 100 per cent or close to it, we always re-read the paper here in the office, and if we can find a single unacceptable answer in it, we record it at 99 per cent or less. In your case, we did not find any place at all where we could call an answer wrong, incomplete, or unsatisfactory. And so, we have no choice but to award you 100 per cent, and with fifty good reasons for doing so . . . It is very pleasing to us native old-timers to see a newcomer do so well at learning our language."

their own embarrassment. One settler in the Niagara Peninsula was told by his boss to prune the cherry trees. The man didn't know what cherries were, and he didn't know enough English to ask. So he guessed—and began to prune the maple trees.

Not knowing the language also left many immigrants with an insecure feeling. Says Coby Prins of Ranier, Alberta: "We were living on the farm, and that was scary. When the men left, I was alone with the children. And I didn't know English. I used to think about what I would do if a strange man came. Then, one day, this dirty man with a week's growth of beard came. I was terrified. I locked the door and didn't answer when he knocked. Finally, he called in Dutch: 'It's all right. I'm a Dutchman.'"

Phew!

Chapter 15

The First Car

Martin VanderWesten, who had owned a moving company in The Hague, became the proud owner of a second hand hearse in Canada. It was a bargain, and that's what mattered. For years, it brought him to work at Coleman's Meatpackers in London, Ontario.

The First Car

It didn't take long for S.P. Knuist of Kamloops, British Columbia, to realize that walking and bicycling in Canada were nothing like those modes of travel in The Netherlands, where the distances were relatively short and the land was as flat as a pancake.

"Every day while going to work, I would pass a car dealership and look wistfully at the second-hand cars. I would have liked to go in and ask for more details about some of them. But I was afraid that with my limited knowledge of English, I would be taken to the cleaners. I didn't trust car dealers then any more than I do now."

One day an old car on the lot—a 1929 Ford convertible—caught his eye. So did the $50 price tag prominently displayed on the front window.

"I wasn't sure if the $50 was the full price or a downpayment. And I certainly didn't know much about the mechanics of cars. Did it run? Well, I went to look at it more closely and it didn't take long for a friendly salesman to show up. Yes, the total was $50. Yes, it ran. He said: 'Go ahead, start it up and take it for a spin.' I didn't want to tell him that I didn't know how to start it, let alone drive it. He must have noticed my hesitation, for he slid in behind the wheel and showed me the manual choke and a few other things. I bought it and asked him to drive it home for me."

Without a driver's permit, Knuist drove around the neighborhood every evening. When he thought he was ready for a licence test, he went to the examiner. The gentleman looked at the car, frowned and asked if it was insured. When the answer was no, he declined to go for the test. The Dutchman went home, bitterly disappointed.

"I drove around in the car for awhile. Then someone asked me if it was for sale. I said: 'Sure, for $75.' He took it. I added another $75 and bought myself a 1948 Chevrolet, went back to the licence bureau and got my driver's permit with no trouble at all."

A car was usually an immigrant's first big expense, and he had to scrape together a few dollars to buy something cheap on the used car lot. He really didn't care what it looked like, as long as it could transport his family to the store, the church, the homes of friends, and the sightseeing spots in the area.

S.P. Knuist gets ready to take his wife for a spin.

Albert DeVries and his daughter Trynie polish their Hillman in Cornwall, in 1957.

Jake Feenstra drove this Ford around Woodstock, Ontario, in 1949.

Dirk Van Rooyen snapped this photo of his family and car near Chatham, Ontario.

Two families—Graaskamp and Prinsen—celebrate the joint purchase of a truck at Chippawa, Ontario, in June of 1952.

Not long after Luke DeVries of Cornwall, Ontario, posed with his car in 1957, it was demolished in an accident.

When the immigrant wrote to his relatives in The Netherlands about the big acquisition, images of newly-found wealth must have sprung to their minds. What they often didn't know was that the vast distances in Canada made a car a virtual necessity. Most people had one. It wasn't a status symbol, or something reserved for the well-to-do.

"Coming from a country where very few people owned a car, it was really something to buy one four weeks after arrival," says Aart Oosterman, who settled at first near St. Thomas, Ontario. "It needed fixing every other night, but that wasn't a problem. I had learned some basic mechanics while in the army."

The old Ford, bought from a friend for $50, certainly did present some challenges.

"While I was driving at night, sometimes all the lights went out. So I would stop, kick the fender, and on would come the lights for awhile. Once, while driving on a gravel road, I noticed a truck behind me and then felt a bang. I thought the truck had hit me. But it hadn't—my back wheel had come off, as I realized when I saw it passing me down the hill. Since I had to concentrate on keeping the car on the road, I didn't see where the wheel ended up. I came back later with friends, but we never found it. On another day, I felt the car sliding farther and farther to the left and saw people shaking their heads. A quick inspection told me that the bolt that held the body on the springs had broken off. So there I was, my wheels going straight but the rest of

Some immigrants bought a truck. This photo from the Peace River area of Alberta shows two of John Olydam's children doing a bit of cleaning.

J.C. Bakker, a 1948 arrival, used this relic, a model-T Ford, to travel around the St. Catharines, Ontario, area.

the car at an angle. Well, I had to fix that. I hung the car with block and tackle on a big tree and inserted another bolt. It wasn't quite long enough, so I cut the springs down. Then my wife and a bunch of kids had to go in the back and jump up and down so that I could fasten the nut on the bolt."

Dick Both, who lives near Owen Sound, Ontario, tells of his experience with a Model-A Ford which belonged to a friend.

"When we didn't have a car yet, we were picked up and taken to church. Seven people crowded into that car somehow. One Sunday, after traveling a little ways, we got a flat tire. The spare one was put on all right, but it turned out to be a few sizes larger than the other three. No matter. We continued on to church, sitting at a slight angle."

Both later bought his own car, a 1938 Dodge, and taught himself to drive it by taking it up and down the laneway, across the grassy area near the barn and over the ruts in the fields.

C.M. Hogeterp used the barnyard for driver training.

Dick Both's 1938 Dodge.

Another immigrant who took a few dry runs on the farm was C.M. Hogeterp. By his own admission, he wasn't much of a driver. But he got up enough courage one day to go to Hagersville, Ontario, for his permit.

The part-time examiner frowned when he learned that the immigrant couldn't speak or understand much English. But Hogeterp's sponsor, who was present, came to the rescue by saying: "Listen, he won't do any harm. The only driving he'll do is to the grocery store on Saturday and to the church on Sunday. Nothing to worry about."

Hogeterp got his licence.

Another truck owner: Frank Tolsma, who settled near Fort Macleod, Alberta, in 1951.

Klaas Terpstra sold cars in Brockville, Ontario.

One day, he awkwardly steered his 1934 Chevrolet, bought for $135, to the nearest pump and ordered thirty-five cents worth of gasoline. His brother, whose family asked for rides now and then, chipped in half the amount. That was in the days when every penny counted.

Jake Feenstra and his brother Henry had good times with their proud possession—an ancient Ford bought for $200. On New Year's Eve in 1949, they drove it to a house party outside Woodstock, Ontario.

"We were having a lot of fun," says Jake, formerly of Bolsward, Friesland. "At two o'clock in the morning, my brother decided it was time to go home. He thought I was already in the car, so he drove off. But I was somewhere in the house. When he finally discovered that he was driving by himself, he quickly headed back to pick me up."

Later that morning, when it was daylight, the brothers came across a young immigrant they knew. He was standing alongside the road, clutching a suitcase.

"He was not a hundred per cent and should never have come here," says Jake. "He was kicked off the farm and had nowhere to go. So we opened up the trunk and gave him a ride to our place. We took care of him and saw that he went back to Holland."

For Ted Smeenk of London, Ontario, owning a car was a key to success. In the early 1950s, he began to sell life insurance, walking the streets and hitchhiking in rain and snow. Late at night, out in the country, he often had to ask for a ride home. Sometimes he worked with fellow agents who had cars, but then he had to split the profits of his sales.

"I was sure there had to be a better way," he recalls. "An unemployed Dutchman owned an old car—I hired him for a dollar an hour and the cost of the gas."

Within three months, all his bills were paid, and he had bought his very first car: a 1936 Dodge coupé for $900.

"How proud I was. And my neighbors were jealous. On Sundays, after mass, I loaded my three little ones in the back seat and delivered policies. In the first year, I sold $750,000 worth of business, was the leader of the London agency, and my production won the general manager's cup for my branch."

Jerry Rekker, at work on a farm near Bloomfield, Ontario, didn't know how to drive a car either. But that didn't stop him from dipping into his hard-earned savings and buying a 1930 Chevy for $125. He didn't want to be isolated.

"My farmer was a cautious man. He didn't dare give me lessons. So I had to manage by myself. Four weeks later, the examiner gave me the licence with the advice not to travel in the city too much."

Rekker put on most of the mileage on Sundays, driving people to and from church.

Klaas Terpstra, who emigrated from Leeuwarden, Friesland, in 1951, knew that a car had four tires and a steering wheel, and ran on gasoline. But that was the extent of his automotive knowledge. Nevertheless, he decided to become a car salesman, come what may.

"Having worked and failed gloriously as a farm hand, I thought anything would be better than that hard labor," he recalls.

The General Motors dealer in Brockville, Ontario, eyed the influx of the Dutch in the area and decided to add a Dutch-speaking salesman to his sales force of seven. Terpstra got the job.

"In 1952, minimum wage for the average worker was approximately ninety cents an hour, or $35 to $40 a week; we agreed on a weekly salary of $35. To make the position more attractive, the dealer offered a one per cent commission on every transaction. Fringe benefits were out of the question. I was given no training, but the advice: 'You don't have to lie; just don't tell everything you know.' That was no problem for me, because I knew next to nothing about the product I was going to sell."

He soon learned that many of his clients didn't know anything about cars either. They raised hoods, but the workings of an engine remained a mystery. They opened and closed doors, but that was no proof of quality. They kicked tires, but didn't know why. Many were not even concerned about the total price of the vehicle; they seemed more anxious to know about the monthly payments.

"Some didn't even have the downpayment," says Terpstra, now of Hamilton, Ontario. "But in a town with two finance companies, that problem was solved in no time. They would go to one and borrow the downpayment and then to the other for the remainder, and arrange payments."

Terpstra wasn't satisfied with sitting in the showroom, waiting for people to come in. He hustled from morning until late at night, even on holidays. On Friday nights, when people came to town to shop, he walked up and down the main street, looked for familiar faces, and invited people to visit the showroom and the used car lot.

"One of the first deals I made was with Peter, a carpenter, who with his brother Henk, an electrician, bought a 1931 Oldsmobile for $300, providing me with an extra income of $3 that week. I also remember when my barber Bill's car stalled right in front of my house. The old 1932 Plymouth had come to the end of the road. That evening, I sold him a 1941 Plymouth, and during my two years in the automobile business, he bought four more cars, ending up with a 1953 Buick for $2,495. He was a happy customer."

There were unhappy ones too.

"I recall a farmer who bought a 1938 Hudson for $250, with $75 down. Unfortunately, it was using more oil than gas, so he replaced it with a 1941 Ford. Not long after, he called me in because the battery was dead and the transmission didn't seem to work properly. Going up the driveway, I saw three of his five kids inside the car and the other two on top. The ones inside were having a great time turning on the ignition key, blowing the horn, and trying out the gearshift without using the clutch. The ones on top were hammering away,

Willem Buitenwerf and members of his family show off their 1934 Plymouth, bought for $225.

Rather an embarrassing moment! Gies Van Donkersgoed's pick-up was parked on a slope near Iron Springs, Alberta, in 1950 when it sprung out of gear and plunged into a ravine.

These boys in the Wallaceburg, Ontario, area seem pleased with Dad's acquisition.

The First Car 267

Ted Smeenk's 1936 Dodge.

Oh dear, a flat tire! And on a Sunday, when everyone's dressed in his best. These men are changing the flat in Fortwick, Ontario, in 1952, after attending a church service in Listowel.

trying to get the attention of the others. I tried to tell the farmer why his battery went dead so often and why he had transmission trouble, but he felt that a good solid car should be able to take such abuse. I suggested he go to the army and buy a tank. He settled for a Jeep."

Only a few people bought new cars, then selling for $2,300 to $2,500. Most settled for used cars in the $600 to $1,000 range. Many immigrants, buying a used car for the first time in their lives, did not realize that they were inheriting someone else's troubles.

"At times it was very frustrating. I'll never forget the man who came to me on the last day of 1953, and rattled off a list of what was wrong with his 1931 Chevrolet. He wanted a better and more reliable auto for approximately $700. I thought: 'Is there anything dependable for

$700?' I consulted my sales manager, telling him that I had a customer whom I respected and that under no circumstances would I betray his confidence in me. The boss suggested a 1947 model with an overhauled engine, ready to go. My client took the car without asking questions. When he didn't show up at the church service on New Year's morning—he never missed a service—I began to feel uncomfortable. Indeed, the car had refused to start, but so had many new ones on that cold winter day. We solved the problem, but the man's pious brother-in-law felt it his duty to give me a lecture on godliness, honesty and Christianity. His interference left a bad taste with me."

Although he doesn't defend shady dealings, Terpstra is quick to point out that members of the public wouldn't think of telling the whole truth about a car they were trading in.

"They'd think it was stupid to tell the salesman about the worn-out transmission, heavy oil consumption, and the almost dead battery. People don't care about a car dealer being stuck with a piece of junk or a car needing hundreds of dollars of repairs, as long as the salesman didn't give them the same medicine."

One unforgettable and unfortunate trip to church made Willem Buitenwerf of St. Catharines, Ontario, decide to buy his own car.

"We were picked up by someone who would take us to the 5 p.m. Dutch-language service of the Christian Reformed Church. We sat on crates in the back of a pickup truck, under a canvas. My wife tore her new dress on one of those crates. Then we nearly froze—the temperature was 13 degrees Fahrenheit and we didn't have any boots yet. We didn't want to go through that again."

Buitenwerf promptly bought a 1934 Plymouth for $225 and drove along rural roads to get some experience. His son, Wim, also enjoyed the novelty of sitting behind the wheel.

"One day, Wim decided to drive by himself. He thought: 'Everything's going fine.' But before he knew it, the car was in the ditch. No matter how hard he tried, he couldn't get it out. A Canada Bread truck came along, and the driver offered to give the car a pull. They got it out all right, but in the process the bumper came off. Wim came home with tears in his eyes. Well, we put the bumper back where it belonged, and then everyone could laugh over the incident."

Chapter 16

One Family's Dream Come True

Malak, Ottawa

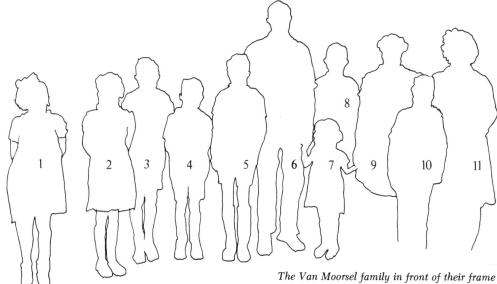

The Van Moorsel family in front of their frame house at Rockland, Ontario in 1948: Toni (1), Rita (2), Arnold (3), Bill (4), Harry (5), John Sr. (6), Liz (7), Albert (8), Mother Petronella (9), John Jr. (10), and Lena (11). Daughter Nelda was away when the picture was taken.

One Family's Dream Come True

Malak, Ottawa

Like so many others, Mr. and Mrs. John Van Moorsel decided to emigrate to Canada for the sake of their children. They had ten children, five sons and five daughters.

Van Moorsel knew only too well that his small farm at Boerdonk, Noord-Brabant, couldn't provide a future for them all. Buying or renting additional land was impossible. With the outlook so bleak at home, he set his sights and hopes on spacious Canada.

He found a sponsor—J.R. Mahoney, a farmer at Rockland, Ontario, not far from Ottawa. Soon after that, in the spring of 1948, the family was on the *Tabinta*, heading for the country of their hopes and dreams.

They found their new home, a frame structure, large enough for comfort. Father was paid $75 a month, which didn't seem like much for all the hours he put in. But they got by. And they realized that the longer they stuck it out, the closer their dream of owning their own farm in the New World would become.

Two years later, with the help of Mahoney, who lent some money, the family moved to a rented farm overlooking the St. Lawrence River near Morrisburg. Father was now his own boss. Hard work and thrifty living were paying off.

Van Moorsel was the proud owner of a used car, a tractor and some other farm machinery. His older sons helped him in

With all those hungry mouths to feed, mother and daughters were constantly in the kitchen. Five loaves didn't last long.

Not all the early immigrants had a kitchen big enough to comfortably seat a family the size of John Van Moorsel's.

School was difficult at first for the Van Moorsel children because they didn't know the language. But it wasn't long before they understood what was being said.

The garden has yielded a bountiful crop. So why not make some money by selling the surplus at the roadside?

Dressed in their Sunday best, the Van Moorsels set out to attend mass.

Father Van Moorsel gets competent help from his sons at haying time.

The children give the family car a good polish.

the fields and barns. The older girls brought home earnings from working as domestics in the homes of Canadians. And mother, also a real workhorse, had her hands full looking after the many needs of her house and family.

In 1953, Van Moorsel was ready to buy his own farm. He looked around Ontario and finally selected acreage near Mitchell, northwest of Stratford. In the ensuing years, everyone continued to work hard, so hard, in fact, that eventually the family was able to buy two more farms.

All of Van Moorsel's children are married now. One owns a flower store and nursery and another is in the real estate business. And the other eight? Well, they all have their own farms.

The dream came true.

Above: Mrs. Van Moorsel in 1983 with her ten children.
Right: Mr. and Mrs. John Van Moorsel on their 45th wedding anniversary. Mr. Van Moorsel died in August, 1979.
Below: The sons and daughters of Mother Petronella, their spouses, and some of the grandchildren.

One of the sons, Harry, owns a cash crop farm and an insulation business near Mitchell, Ontario. With him in the field of soya beans are his children, Brent, Darryl, and Pamela.

John Van Moorsel Jr., with his two sons, David and Kevin.

Hard labor and determination to get ahead also paid off for Ralph and Anna DeJong, who headed for Canada aboard the Tabinta in 1948 after farming for nine years in Eernewoude, Friesland. Their sponsor lived at Glen Walter, east of Cornwall, Ontario. In 1951, they bought a 150-acre, deserted farm at Aultsville and started with three cows and some calves. The barn roof leaked so badly that De Jong had to wear a raincoat during the milking. In six years, the farm boosted twenty-five milking cows and a milking machine. Times were hard. One of the children cut up a $2 bill in twenty pieces so that Mommy and Daddy would have more money.

The family had to move because of the St. Lawrence Seaway project and in March, 1957, settled on a 100-acre farm at Williamsburg. It has since grown to three hundred acres. Within five years of DeJong's immigration, four brothers also came to Canada with their families. The latest count of children and grandchildren stood at 145.

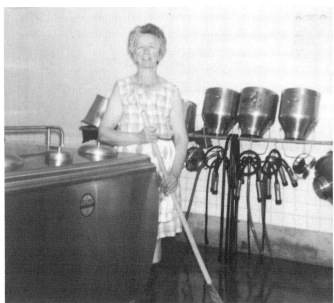

Chapter 17

Immigrants of All Kinds

Immigrants of All Kinds

Dr. A.H.J. Lovink, chief envoy of The Netherlands in Canada for two terms, liked this country so well that he decided to settle here after his retirement. He bought a property overlooking the Ottawa River on the west side of the capital city and hired a Dutch builder to erect a beautiful home on the spot. The view from his study is breathtaking.

Canada's natural beauty had fascinated Dr. Lovink, a devout outdoorsman, since he first set foot in the country. In 1952, he and several other men completed the first of seven 500-mile canoe trips, retracing without guides the old trade routes of the voyageurs from Montreal to the Arctic. His love affair with the rugged landscape never faded. He is now a director of the Royal Canadian Geographic Society, which devotes most of its efforts to publishing a monthly magazine of superb quality.

"There were other reasons why we decided to stay in Canada," he says. "We made a lot of friends here over the years. Had we gone back to Holland, we would have broken many ties. More important than anything, though, was the fact that all our children were here. I could just picture my wife hopping on an airplane every few months just to see the children. So we stayed. And we have no regrets that we did. We have made it a point to visit Holland every two years so as not to lose contact."

Dr. Lovink, who was the ambassador here during the big influx, is proud of the way the immigrants overcame their hardships, adapted themselves to their new surroundings, and became established as solid citizens. All of the immigrants, he says, brought something that wasn't already here. "They enriched the country very much. With their will power, they contributed tremendously, and gave back a bit of what they owed Canada from the war."

As the top Netherlands official in Canada, Lovink was deeply involved with immigration matters. He traveled extensively to talk with newcomers and to find out, first-hand, how they were coping. "The main problem was economical—the cost of this and the cost of that."

What about allegations that Canadians took advantage of the newcomers, and

Dr. and Mrs. A.H.J. Lovink

that working conditions here left something to be desired?

"People who leave their country voluntarily can hardly arrive somewhere else with a long list of demands. Perhaps they do have to take a rotten job at first. But don't you think it's important that they show their talents and prove what they're worth?"

Dr. Lovink, ambassador here from 1950 to 1957 and from 1960 to 1968, accompanied Queen Juliana during her visits to the immigrants. He was with her in 1952 when word got around that she had come to Canada solely to check into reports that her fellow countrymen were

The Lovinks (at right) at an official function in Ottawa.

Many immigrants have been visited in Canada by relatives from The Netherlands. One happy reunion after twenty years took place on September 3, 1947, in Edmonton, involving the Schelling family. They are Mary Schelling, Mr. Rothe (her father), and Mr. and Mrs. Henry Schelling.

at the Theodorus Niemeyer pipe tobacco plant in Brantford, Ontario, to meet with twenty selected couples of Dutch origin, a crowd of several hundred cheered when she stepped from her limousine.

"She turned to the crowd to acknowledge her welcome," the local paper reported. "The crowd broke through police cordons to surround her car . . . At the top of the steps leading to the plant, the queen turned and waved at the people, who began to sing the Dutch national anthem."

Dr. Lovink remembers one heart-warming incident in Winnipeg, Manitoba. "The queen wanted to speak to the immigrants. So she stood on a small platform in the middle of a field and talked. When she was finished, we went back to the plane. I had noticed a man standing there with a small boy, whose leg was in a cast. The queen was already in the plane when I said to her: 'There's someone outside who's been hoping for a chance to meet you.' She went down the steps, walked over to the boy, and signed his cast with her name, the date, and the word '*beterschap*.' "

being mistreated. He denies that this was her purpose.

"She wanted to meet with as many immigrants as possible. She was always interested in their welfare. She wanted to see for herself how they were doing in their new land. She spoke privately and personally with many of them at each stop. It seemed to me that she was happy with what she saw and heard."

The pull of the House of Orange remained strong among the immigrant community. Many came from miles away just to catch a glimpse of the queen. Some tried to get as close to her as possible, hoping for a chance to touch her.

The appeal never diminished, even in later years. In 1967, when Juliana stopped

"Netherlands woman charters KLM airplane for her entire farm." This startling headline appeared in a Dutch newspaper in the mid-1950s. It wasn't too far from the truth. Indeed, a woman, Jacoba Bregman, forty-seven years old, flew across on a Skymaster with rolls of chicken-wire, furniture, books, a tractor, a record-player and . . . twenty-three dogs, many of the Afghan breed. Her pony, donkey, and three horses, all subject to stricter controls, were coming by boat. Her cows had been sold.

Before she left her *Uilenhof* farm at Garderen, near Apeldoorn, one of The Netherlands' most notorious emigrants commented: "There are no possibilities for me any more on this farm. I want to get away from this country. I'm getting fed up with all those regulations and the red tape. And who is making any money? I can't make one cent of profit any more. And what about the future? Money for this and money for that. You won't be able to be your own boss any more . . . Not that I'm so crazy about Canada. I would rather stay here. But I can't stay. They've made it impossible for me and whoever else used to enjoy a little bit of freedom."

She received more than one hundred letters from people who wanted to fly with her, including a family of ten per-

Knapen: Priest Missionary at Peace in a Foreign Land

Rev. Christiaan Knapen of Grouard, Alberta, a Roman Catholic priest, came to Canada in 1946 to serve as a missionary among the native people in the cold, lonely stretches of the Far North.

"I was ordained into the priesthood in 1942," he says, "and four years later I was sent as a missionary to the north of Lesser Slave Lake in northwestern Alberta. Some things have changed since then. Now we have roads, radios, and snowmobiles. Other things have remained the same: poor housing, limited educational opportunities, the difficulty of communication. I arrived on August 15, 1946, to a vast whiteness. Eight inches of snow covered the ground. It was a terrible year. I didn't know any English or Cree, so communication was difficult. But I stayed—thirty-six years now. The people accepted me. What more can I say? I kept the vows I made when I became a missionary."

Above: Rev. Christiaan Knapen (right) is on his way to Canada in 1946.
Below: The church Knapen serves in north-western Alberta.

sons. But she didn't have any room left. Besides, she had no intentions of starting a colony. She merely wanted to farm by herself somewhere in Nova Scotia.

With her hair cut short, and dressed in riding pants, a blue sportsjacket and rubber boots, Jacoba was the center of attraction at Schiphol airport. "Do a good job," someone shouted. Another commented: "She's got too much spirit to stay here."

More than two thousand curious people thronged the airfield at Sydney, Nova Scotia, to catch a glimpse of the eccentric immigrant. Two Canadian veterinarians were also on hand to make sure her dogs weren't bringing any unwanted diseases with them. The blue and white aircraft was barely at a standstill when Jacoba hurried down the steps to get all the customs and immigration formalities out of the way. Then she and two of her dogs hopped onto the back of a truck and headed for her farm at Millville.

"It's big," she said, her eyes roving over the wide countryside.

We next heard of Jacoba two years later. The administration of the zoo *De Havenberg* at Amerongen received a letter in which she complained that things weren't going too great in Canada. In fact, she was exploring ways of getting her animals back to The Netherlands.

She had bought the farm on the basis of photographs. But it hadn't taken her long to discover that she had paid too much money for it. The buildings had been in a dilapidated condition and she had needed considerable capital to put everything in working order. She had spent so much money, she explained, that now she had to sell the farm.

The last we heard of Jacoba was this press item from The Netherlands: "Miss Jacoba Bregman, who emigrated to Canada in 1955 with her twenty-three dogs and tons of farm material, is on the way to the southern part of Ontario. She is traveling in a cattle van with sixteen dogs, four horses, a donkey, and a pony. Her plan is to stay with friends, but she won't say who they are. Reporters who asked her if she really had a million dollars got this reply: 'Why don't you make it two million? I've got lots of money. I'm swimming in it. I've got a couple of suitcases with me that are chock-full of the stuff . . .' "

Jan Heersink had the world by the tail.

In April of 1945, less than two weeks after the Germans had been routed from Steenderen, a community of four thousand in the Achterhoek district of Gelderland, he was appointed its interim mayor. That wasn't an easy task at a time when everything was a mess—municipal services, streets, houses, and personal lives. But he tackled his job of getting Steenderen on its feet again with youthful

Mayor Jan Heersink says farewell at a special meeting of the municipal council of Steenderen, Gelderland, in April, 1954.

vigor. The authorities in The Hague must have noticed. The following February, he was confirmed as *burgemeester*, the youngest one in the land.

The next few years were difficult and challenging. Reconstruction took much time and capital. Yet it was a great opportunity to get many needed projects under way. Much was accomplished in Steenderen.

But inwardly, Heersink, whose future seemed so secure, wasn't happy. There was something about postwar Netherlands that disturbed him. He often thought of moving lock, stock and barrel to the New World, where many of his relatives had established themselves before the war. They obviously were satisfied. So why couldn't he move there with his wife and four young sons and be successful and happy too?

First he went to take a look. One of his many functions during his tenure as mayor was to serve as a member of the emigration committee of the *Hervormde Kerk*. On its behalf, he visited Canada from December, 1950, to March, 1951, to see what was what. By that time, the Reformed Church of America was doing a good job of looking after the needs of the *Hervormden*. Heersink liked what he saw. He was more deeply convinced that this was the land of his future.

He went back to Steenderen, but he didn't stay there long. The Reformed Church had asked him to help set up an immigration committee in Hamilton and to be its director of immigration. The stream of immigrants was swelling to a flood. So he arranged a leave of absence from Steenderen and went to Canada with his family in September. He stayed there for two years, working among the immigrants and dealing with the many problems associated with the influx of so many people.

Then he went back to Steenderen again, this time to say farewell.

One newspaper wrote: "He is the son of a farmer in nearby Hummelo and his wife, Mieneke, is also a native of the *Gelderse Achterhoek*. By nature, people from that area are loathe to change. Preferring to stay where they are, they seem innately shy in a strange environment. But now that the head of their community is leading the way, it's likely that others will follow him."

A reporter asked one resident: "Don't you find it sad that your mayor is leaving?"

"Not at all," replied Harm Otten, a

mason, "because I'm going with him. And my wife and my three daughters are going too. So is Pruim, the greengrocer."

Still, there were people who shook their heads in unbelief and asked: "Why?"

"I feel that I can do more useful work in Canada than in Holland," Heersink told a reporter for *De Graafschap-Bode.* "I'm more or less worked-out in Steenderen, while in Canada there is still so much to organize. Moreover, I have four boys. The future is more promising for them in Canada."

Heersink, the Dutch vice-consul in Burlington, Ontario, and an investment adviser, believes he made the right decision. Inwardly, he often compares The Netherlands with Canada, and his adopted country always comes out on top.

"Why is Canada better? There are a number of reasons. All the room that we have here influences the way we live. There doesn't seem to be the hurry-hurry feeling. Traffic, for example, moves along at its own pace. People can be more themselves. Nobody tells you who your friends should be. Furthermore, the Canadian is not a braggart. He is friendly toward the Dutch. Canada is a good place to bring up a family. It's a nice country, really. It's like one big park. Want to hear more?"

When Jan M.J. Rademaker came to Canada in 1955 at the age of thirty, he had no idea that some day he would be a Roman Catholic priest, ministering to people in many parts of Canada.

In The Netherlands, he had worked in offices. Terribly bored and wanting a change, he took a 'retraining' course before emigrating, to gain a bit of experience in outdoor work. After all, many of the jobs in Canada were to be found in the open air.

"I landed on a farm near Ottawa. It was a very bad experience. I stayed only about a month. I was able to leave because I had paid my own fare coming over and had a little money left. I do wonder what would have happened if I'd had to stay, like so many others. The retraining course had proved useless and the farm selection very bad. And there had been little or no help from anyone."

Rademaker then worked for two months at whatever came to hand, living in a boarding house in Ottawa. Suddenly, everything turned around for the better: he found a good position as a bookkeeper, and a Canadian family of Scottish-Irish extraction took him in.

"I changed jobs in 1961 and went to an isolated power plant near Yellowknife in the North West Territories. I liked it very much. In 1962, I was transferred to Inuvik, and in 1963 to Moose Factory, On-

Vice-consul Jan Heersink meets Juliana, once again a princess, during her visit to Canada in 1981. The other women are Mrs. A. Klein and Mrs. Heersink.

The Clan Moved en Masse

The photos on these two pages, taken in 1950, show the five family units of the Van Donkersgoed clan that settled in Canada.

Toward the end of the war, when the Germans knew that defeat was near, their reign of terror escalated dramatically. The Dutch underground, becoming bolder, struck left and right at prime targets.

One night, bullets ripped through a German staff car on a lonely stretch of road, causing casualties. This bold attack infuriated the German command, and they decided to take revenge on Putten, a village between Amersfoort and Apeldoorn. The residents were routed from their homes and herded into a church. Their houses were set on fire. Then, 650 of the men were shipped away as hostages to concentration camps. Most of them did not return.

From that ravaged area came one of Canada's best-known immigrant clans—the Van Donkersgoeds. The announcement in the late 1940s that six closely-tied families of the group, some fifty-seven persons in all, wanted to settle

in Canada, caused quite a stir. They wished to go together and work as a group on one farm.

Officials were embarrassed. They had no choice but to explain to them that not even in Canada, so huge on the map, was there a farmer capable of permanently hiring so many people. The Van Donkersgoeds finally agreed to emigrate as separate family units.

The first family to arrive in Canada was headed by Klaas Van Donkersgoed. They settled in the Iron Springs district of Alberta, and in the fall of 1948 earned $2,000 harvesting sugarbeets and grain. In the winter, the girls worked as domestics and the boys made some money on the railroad. Then, in 1949, they completed a contract to work sixty acres of beets at $41 an acre.

By this time, the other families had arrived, three to settle around Iron Springs and Picture Butte and one on a farm near Brandon, Manitoba. The sixth family, the

The boys will have to do that for me.' "

And that's what the boys, and the girls, did. The sponsoring farmer at Iron Springs gave them a contract which required the family to grow and harvest a specific number of acres of beets. Vanden Hazel helped a bit, but he didn't over-exert himself. His children worked hard to make sure that the contract was honored.

"Life wasn't too bad in Alberta. We felt at home among the Hollanders there. We were all on an equal level, and we looked after each other. However, we saw no chance of buying a farm in Alberta. So we moved to Ontario, in the area of Drayton, where most of the family settled. I had to keep my sons in mind. And I really couldn't stop working myself yet. I couldn't get a pension unless I was seventy years old and had been here for at least ten years. And that was only $40 a month, not much even in those days."

Despite his age and initial misgivings, he readily adjusted to life in his new country.

"My expectations weren't that high. One immigrant always saw Canada differently than another one did. I have no complaints. There was one thing that did bother me though: the misinformation about Canada that I had received in Holland. I found out the truth about things when I got here. I won't go into specifics, but I'm convinced the authorities in Holland could have done a better job in letting people know what to expect. Someone once asked me what I thought of Canada after all these years. I told her: 'Canada is good for everyone, but I'm not so sure that everyone is good for Canada.' I still believe that."

Vanden Hazel, now approaching his mid-90s, remembers well the dark days of Putten. His wife, Johanna, was cycling to relatives in the village when someone told her to go back because the Germans were about to carry out a bicycle *razzia*, confiscating all two-wheelers for their own use. She heeded the warning.

"She was lucky. If she would have kept on going, she would have ended up in that church. But the tragedy didn't escape our immediate family. My brother, Dirk, never came back. Neither did three brothers on my wife's side . . ."

smallest, had to stay in The Netherlands because the father was unable to pass the medical exam.

Local farmers were enthusiastic about their new neighbors. They called them industrious workers and fine people. Said farmer Edmund Green of Iron Springs: "I've never seen better. Canada is sure lucky to get people like that."

The adults never regretted having moved away from Putten. One of them, Wienik Vanden Hazel, whose wife was a Van Donkersgoed, said once: "The everyday life is harder here. The winters are oh so cold. But the young people are adaptable, and they are enjoying the adventure. If all goes well for our children, then that is our real and abiding pleasure."

He was nearly sixty years old when the *Tabinta* brought him to Canada in 1949.

"I was really too old to move to another country," he recalls. "I had a farm at Voorthuizen, not far from Putten, which I had built up with lots of sweat. I really didn't want to go. But my wife kept on insisting. The Van Donkersgoeds were really family-minded, and she couldn't stand the thought of staying behind in Holland. She actually got homesick at the thought. So we decided to go, too, with our three sons and two daughters. I told them: 'I'll go to Canada, but not to do any hard work.

Wienik Vanden Hazel, in
wooden shoes, looks on as his
children take a break from hard
work in the beetfields.

tario. The North is beautiful and I have
many good memories of people and places
there."

So he should. It was in the North that
he met the Obloate Fathers and started to
help out around the church. He became so
involved that he decided to join them.

"Because of my non-Canadian educa-
tion and advanced age, I was sent to
Rome, Italy, to a special English college. I
was ordained to the priesthood in
December, 1969. I was back in Canada in
the summer of 1970, served four years in
Flin Flon, Manitoba, a mining town, half
a year in Halifax, a year and a half in
Thunder Bay, Ontario, four years in
Shubenacadie—eight hundred square
miles of farms with a good number of
Dutch farmers—and am now at Sacred
Heart Church in Sioux Lookout, Ontario,
a railroad town. In all these places, I have
found that being an immigrant myself is a
very definite asset. Having seen a lot of
Canada through work and vacations, I
really think this is a fantastic country. I
have never really regretted coming
here—after the first few weeks. I've been
back to Holland several times, and find I
don't belong there any more. To be un-

married with no close relatives nearby is
sometimes difficult, but good friends
make up for it. I feel that I'm definitely a
Canadian, but some people still think of
me as Dutch, which I find hard to accept.
If I had to start all over, I certainly would
come here again—but sooner."

Another Dutch priest in a remote area of
Northern Canada is Rev. Henk Huybers.
He was once one of the members of the
underground legion who assisted downed
Allied pilots and people in hiding during
the German occupation. He chose to come
to Canada in 1948, and headed for the
Mayor area in the Yukon, just below the
Arctic Circle. He's been there ever since.

On November 29, 1982, he wrote to acquaintances: "Last winter was mild, with
only a minus 20 until Boxing Day. Then
the temperature dropped and it stayed
cold until February. So I hope that this
winter will be mild, so that I can visit my
people in the bush and the little communities along the highway regularly. We
say mass for them and give instructions for
children and adults. Our homilies and instructions have to be prepared for a few as
if it were for a few dozen. After praying

for our people, this is our first duty."

Father Huyberts spoke with joy about a six-week visit by his younger sister, Gerda, and her husband, Zef, from The Netherlands. He had met them at the airport in Whitehorse, three hundred miles to the south, and had taken them along on his regular mission trips, and also to the Arctic Circle and to Alaska.

"They were very impressed, not only by the ruggedness of the mountains and beautiful valleys, but also by the miles and miles of tundra. They admired the flowers, birds, and animals. They were amazed by the glaciers and the rivers. They really enjoyed their trip."

Rev. John Van Harmelen of the Christian Reformed Church remembers a young man from Assen, Drenthe, who seemed somewhat introverted—he stayed by himself, shunned companionship and hung onto every cent he made.

"Only later did I learn that his father and mother in Holland went to a notary and, with the dollars received from their son, paid off their entire mortgage."

There was a similar case in Georgetown, Ontario. The three oldest sons of an immigrant went to work with the vowed intention of giving their earnings of the first five years to their father. They figured he needed it more than they to get his feet on the ground again.

Dr. A.J. Verster of Beamsville, Ontario, a physician and surgeon, cites a number of reasons for his decision to emigrate.

"The *ziekenfondspraktijk* in Holland was not very satisfactory. I practised in The Hague for seven years, and remember forty people in a waiting room, and thirty to forty house calls a day. You were more or less forced to refer anything that took more than five minutes to a specialist. It was really a form of slave labor."

Three years of army service in Indonesia had awakened restlessness in him, and the tense political situation in Europe in 1957 (Suez, Hungary) also made it easier to leave.

"The emigration itself was not too difficult, but in order to practise medicine, I had to do a year's internship and then write the exam of the Medical Council of Canada. It is much more difficult now. I interned in Halifax. It was an interesting but rough year—hard work, on call every other night. The pay was $50 a month.

The fact that I had a wife and three children did not make it any easier. But I still think that it was worth it. During the intern year, you learn the language, which is not exactly the same as the English you've learned in school. You also become familiar with the medical customs of the country, the different names for drugs, and so forth."

After passing his exam, he moved to Beamsville, where he took over a small practice from an old doctor. The first few years were difficult, even though the area had a large Dutch community.

"After a year or two, the Canadian part of the practice started growing, too, and we were able to live on our income. In 1965, after practising solo for seven years, I joined a group practice in Grimsby, and I am still a member of the group. This move took the pressure of the practice out of the house. I still remember our first meal without the telephone ringing. I

Some parents of immigrants got to like Canada so well during visits that they later decided to move here permanently. Mr. and Mrs. Theo DeVries moved to Mount Hope, Ontario, in 1982 to be close to their son. They bought his house and he moved into another. The mother of Mrs. DeVries (center) came over for a visit in May of 1983.

can say that my life as a family physician in Canada has been very rewarding, much more so than I ever could have expected in Holland. Financially, I would have been better off if I had stayed there. I would not have lost the year of internship and the first few years of building up a practice. Also, the income of the physicians in Holland is considerably higher at present than it is here."

But he likes this country. And he has decided to stay.

"As a first-generation immigrant, you always stay somewhat mid-Atlantic. Here you have an accent, and in Holland they think that you talk funny. But my life is here, my family is here, I am happy here. I can get excited about Canadian politics. I get upset when someone talks this country down. The last time I was in Holland, it looked a little bit like a foreign country."

At right, Tony and Jean Koning in 1943. Today, the Konings (below) serve the Anglican church.

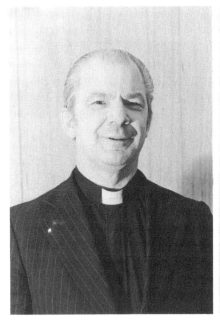

Tony Koning fell in love with Canada while stationed at The Netherlands army recruiting center in Stratford, Ontario during the war. He also fell in love with a Canadian girl. Little wonder that he is still in Canada—not as a soldier, by the way, but as a rector of the Anglican Church.

His wife, Jean, recalls walking with her friends toward the Stratford Collegiate Vocational Institute in January of 1941, talking happily about the arrival of Dutch soldiers in the town. She was eighteen years old and in her final year of high school.

"I remember saying: 'Well, I know one Dutch word—*ja*.' Little did I know then that on August 22, 1942, I would be saying *ja* in St. James' Church in Stratford to become Tony Koning's bride."

She didn't meet Tony, however, until September of 1941. A friend of hers was going to the Stratford Fall Fair with Sergeant-Major Pieter Roos, another Dutchman, and she said: "I'll ask him to bring a blind date for you, Jean." That date turned out to be Tony.

When Hitler unleashed his war in May of 1940, striking neutral Holland despite solemn pledges to the contrary, Tony had been working as sergeant-administrator at regimental headquarters near Eindhoven. The Germans became the masters of The Netherlands after five days of vicious warfare. Tony was able to stay out of their clutches, and ended up in England.

"There was talk about setting up a recruiting center in Canada," he recalls.

think that in the group I work just as hard, if not harder, but when I'm off, I'm off."

Looking back, Dr. Verster is convinced that the decision to come to Canada was the right one. The practice of family medicine here was, and still is, to a great extent more complete.

"I can follow my patients when they are in hospital, assist in surgery, look at x-rays, talk with the specialists, etc. We still have some time to spend with our patients. The system of more or less compulsory post-graduate study and courses keeps the doctor up to date. Altogether, I

"In fact, the contingent had already been chosen. The captain in whose office I worked was in charge of it. At the last moment, one member, also a sergeant-administrator, was taken to hospital with a serious illness. When the captain told me of his predicament, I said: 'I'll go.' The paperwork was done in a hurry, and in December, 1940, the contingent joined a convoy which was to leave from Greenoch for the African front. In the middle of the Atlantic, the convoy turned south and our ship, with one cruiser ahead of us, sailed to Halifax."

In January, the officers arrived in Stratford and were billeted in the barracks, a former furniture factory, vacated by the Perth Regiment. The Dutch flag and the Union Jack were hoisted, and the *Prinses Juliana Kazerne* was ready to sign up recruits and train them for the vital battles to restore freedom to The Netherlands and other oppressed areas.

After their meeting at the 1941 fall fair, Tony and Jean dated regularly. They fell in love. And they decided to get married, although no date was set. By August,

1942, Tony received word that his unit would be moving to England in five weeks.

"Either you marry me now," he said, "or we'll never see each other again."

Recalls Jean: "I thought about it all that weekend. My parents wisely said: 'You'll have to make up your own mind.' I was only nineteen and didn't think I wanted to settle down to marriage, but I couldn't bear the thought of never seeing Tony again. So I decided to say yes."

While on a one-week honeymoon in Montreal, Tony got a telegram from his commanding officer. The plans had been changed. The unit would be moving to new quarters in Guelph, Ontario, instead of England. So the Konings moved to Guelph. It wasn't until September, 1943, that the whole unit moved back to England, and Jean and many other wives were left behind in Canada.

"When I married Tony, I lost my Canadian citizenship and had to apply for, and was granted, a Netherlands passport and citizenship. That law, by the way, was changed after the war. When the fighting

On June 27, 1947, thirty-five passengers of the Waterman *were met at the train station in Kitchener, Ontario, by a number of Dutch war brides. These women went out of their way to make the newcomers feel welcome, and gave out chocolate bars to everyone.*

Gerald and Janke Jones met in Zeist after the war and now live near New Minas, Nova Scotia.

a priest. He now lives at Thedford, Ontario.

"Trees heeft een Canadees . . ."

This ditty about courtship between Dutch girls and Canadian soldiers became popular after liberation. After all, as the war ended, the smooching began. Many of these friendships remained platonic. Others contributed to an increase in the number of illegitimate births; after five years of oppression, morals were a bit loose. However, many serious relationships also were formed after the restoration of peace—romances which resulted in marriage and wives who moved to Canada to join their repatriated husbands. The Canadian government paid for the passage of nearly two thousand brides and more than four hundred children. These war brides were the forerunners of the postwar influx. They helped to cement strong bonds of friendship between the two countries. The emigrants followed in their footsteps— and so did more war brides.

One of the later ones, Mrs. Janke Jones, arrived in Canada in 1948. She and her husband, Gerald, live on a small farm outside of New Minas, Nova Scotia, next to Kentville. The two met on her family's estate in Zeist, just east of Utrecht. Janke and a sister had just returned from relatives in Friesland with whom they had stayed during the last months of the war.

"My sister and I were walking around the estate with some kid goats. Gerald, on duty for his company, happened to be outside, and we started talking. That's how I first met him. His line was that he'd like to buy the goats. From then on, we saw each other almost every day. However, my father, who was very strict, didn't really like me going out with a Canadian soldier. He was very worried about his daughter, especially because of the problems that some of the girls ran into."

Janke and her soldier friend, six years her senior, fell in love. They made plans to get married before his scheduled departure on October 21. But her father wouldn't give his permission, saying: "If he's really serious and if he wants to come back in two years to marry you, then I would give my consent."

Letters were exchanged regularly. Once, Gerald didn't write for six weeks, and Janke thought: "This is the end!" She was relieved when he finally wrote that he had cut his thumb and hadn't been able to write.

"I went to night school to learn more

was over, I applied to go to Holland to rejoin Tony. Boat passage was at a premium, but I was finally able to sail at the end of October on an old tramp freighter. As it neared the English Channel, some two weeks later, a watch was posted to keep a lookout for floating mines. In Amsterdam, I went through the same repatriation process as native-born Netherlands citizens returning home after the war, although I had never been in Holland before."

The damp climate in The Netherlands didn't suit Tony at all. He was sick often. The doctor wholeheartedly agreed with his plan to emigrate to Canada, where the drier climate would be better for his health.

"My parents sponsored us," says Jean, "and we arrived back in Canada in 1946. Tony's sister came out the following year and his parents the year after that."

Tony got a job as a bookkeeper at a furniture factory in Stratford for $25 a week. A few years later, he became an office manager at a factory in London. In the meantime, he studied by correspondence for a certified general accountant's degree. In 1954, the family moved to Huntsville, where he set up his own accounting business. In that town, he became more and more involved in the lay ministry of the Anglican Church.

His connection with that denomination dated back to the days when he was with the army in Stratford and an Anglican chaplain had often visited the barracks. In June of 1966, after much study, Tony was ordained deacon and posted to Manitowaning on Manitoulin Island. Later that year, he became

English. Toward the end of 1947, a telegram arrived at our house. My mother got it, and she wrapped it up as a present for *Sinterklaas*. And there it was: Gerald would be arriving on December 12. I met him on the estate where we lived. We were going to get married, and I was going to go back with him."

The ceremony took place in January. Everyone was happy—until the newlyweds learned that Janke couldn't emigrate to Canada until her husband had obtained papers showing that he had a job and a house.

"I had to stay in Holland for another five months while he got all those papers organized. Finally, the papers came through. Then I had to follow the same procedure as any emigrant of 1948. They didn't consider me a war bride because of a special rule: anyone not married to a Canadian by January, 1947, was on her own if she wanted to go to Canada. Because I had married a Canadian, I was no longer considered Dutch, and yet I wasn't automatically a Canadian because of that cutoff date."

Janke sailed on the *Tabinta*. She took the train from Quebec City to Halifax, where her husband was waiting.

"He took me to the Forties—way, way back in the woods somewhere. His family was just fantastic. I stayed with his sister because he was away most of the time, driving a grocery truck. I'd see him just on Saturday night; on Sunday, he had to leave again. This went on for about four months. I had to get used to the Canadian way of living. I couldn't believe the wildness of the surroundings. You could pick everything for free—raspberries, wild strawberries, blueberries. The houses were totally different from what I had been used to. There was a wood stove—and it was already so hot in the summer. The amount of cooking the women did surprised me. I had to learn to cook the Canadian way, make pies, make bread. Thank goodness, Gerald's sister helped me a great deal. I also was impressed with the friendliness of the people. They cared; they were tremendous. They held two wedding showers for us, and we were given many nice gifts. Everybody made me feel at home."

After staying with another family member for a while, Gerald and Janke moved to a little bunkhouse intended for summer use only.

"It was our own, and that was what I needed: to be by myself. We fixed it all up, to make it as homey as possible. Then something awful happened: I became very, very homesick. I cried a lot. Looking back, I'm amazed at his patience; sometimes he would sit with me and talk to me until four o'clock in the morning even though he had to go to work early—he worked in the woods at that time. I didn't know what was wrong with me, that it was homesickness. I guess it must have been a tremendous culture shock. Besides, we lived way back in the woods. There was no mail for weeks on end when we were snowed in. No electricity. No indoor toilet. We had to haul the water by bucket. Everything had to be done by hand, including the washing."

The homesickness began to pass after a year or so. When her first child was born, and she had someone to care for all the time, she thought less of her relatives in

Samuel and Sophia Marchent on their wedding day in Amsterdam in 1946.

Three Dutch war brides—Sophia Marchent, Elizabeth Bailey, and Bep Chapman—visit Jasper National Park in 1947.

Sophia and her second husband, Dr. Anthony Peers, whom she married in 1959.

Europe. She considered herself cured when she went back to Zeist for a visit four years later and didn't have any qualms about returning to Canada.

Like many war brides, Janke was confronted with differences in religious viewpoints. She was *Hervormd*, raised to believe that one should not even ride a bicycle on Sunday. Gerald was Baptist. In Canada people drove a car to church on Sunday or to anywhere, for that matter. After a bit of soul-searching, most newcomers adopted the Canadian way. After all, most churches weren't within walking distance.

Gerald and Janke's first three children were baptized at the Christian Reformed Church which they attended. But Gerald felt out of place there. Janke eventually decided to join the Baptist church.

"I felt that I should go with him. So our last girl wasn't baptized as a baby. I wasn't completely upset by that. I had to make a choice, and that was the best choice for our family. We couldn't go to two different churches."

To everyone's delight, the youngest daughter, Marina Joy, chose to be baptized at the age of twenty.

Among the first war brides to arrive in Canada was Mrs. Sophia Peers of Edmonton, who came in 1946, before the troopships started ferrying emigrants across. She arrived as the twenty-year-old wife of Samuel Marchent, now deceased.

She and her family had to leave The Hague when an Allied raid on V-2 rocket installations at nearby Wassenaar wiped out a residential section of the city, including their house. She went to stay with relatives in Nijkerk, Gelderland.

"I got itchy feet when the war was over and became an interpreter for the Canadian Provost Corps, for I had a good command of English. That's how I met Samuel. He was in charge of the office. When he proposed to me, I said yes. We were married in March, 1946, in Amsterdam. We first went to England, where he had relatives, and then traveled to Canada."

At first she felt lonely in the strange environment; however, her bout with homesickness didn't last long.

"When I thought about the rotten times we had during the war, then I considered myself very lucky to be in Canada."

The loneliness was lessened when other Dutch immigrants arrived in Edmonton in 1947. One of them was another war bride, Mrs. Elizabeth Hall, now of

Westport, Ontario. She had met Jack Bailey, a Canadian serviceman, in Amsterdam after the war, and had married him in Canada. Mr. Bailey is also deceased.

The two women have remained friends since their first meeting. Even though they live many miles apart, they continue to visit each other. They had so much in common in those early years in Canada that a deep and lasting friendship was established.

E. Hendrik Grolle, an architect from Amsterdam, found out when he arrived in Saskatchewan in 1953 that he could not pursue his profession. Saskatchewan law required architects to be British subjects.

"I went to see the minister of education, Woodrow Lloyd, and complained about discrimination. Half a year later, the act was changed."

At first, he detected resentment among the closely-knit architectural community. All such nonsense seems to have vanished now.

On June 26, 1942, the Germans informed the Jewish Council in occupied The Netherlands of a momentous decision: by order of the police, all Jewish men and women between sixteen and forty years were to be sent to labor assignment in Germany.

Summons were sent out for the departure of four thousand people on July 15. Margot, the sixteen-year-old daughter of Otto Frank, who ran a small spice importing business at Prinsengracht 263 in Amsterdam, received hers on July 4. This was the sign for the Franks and another family, the Van Daans, to go into hiding in a secret annex at the back of the Frank house.

The rest of the story is well known. The people in the annex lived in constant fear of being caught by the ever-present Gestapo. After two years, their luck ran out. The German police, tipped off by a Dutch informer, suddenly appeared at the house on August 4, 1944, made straight for the bookcase which hid the entrance to the annex, arrested the eight occupants, and shipped them off to a concentration camp. Only Otto Frank survived. When

Anne Frank

Canada as a New Playground

The headline in the Dutch paper read: "He's blowing his way to Canada." And so he was, as were many others. They became rather unusual immigrants. In the early 1950s, the Canadian government looked overseas for qualified musicians to strengthen its military bands. This was an excellent opportunity for those with a taste for adventure or those who had been toying with the notion of emigrating.

One of them, John VanderSpek of Burlington, Ontario, had belonged to the *Residentieorkest* in The Hague and a number of other musical groups. He was recruited in 1954, played French horn in the Royal Canadian Regimental Band in London, Ontario, and stayed to become a citizen of this country.

"Initially," he says, "I was disappointed in the low grade of military music here. We were used to the high calibre of military bands in Europe."

But his stay in the army was far from boring. He played for Haile Selassie, Prince Philip, Charles De Gaulle, and Nelson Rockefeller, among others. His travels brought him to many points in Canada and the United States, and he also went to Europe a number of times.

John VanderSpek

he returned to the house a year after he was freed, his eyes spotted the diary of his younger daughter, Anne, lying on the floor. Her thoughts and feelings recorded there were later to make millions smile and weep.

What many do not know is that an immigrant who lived for years in relative obscurity in Weston, Ontario, played an important role in the attempt made by the Franks and the others in the annex to avoid the clutches of the Gestapo.

Austrian-born Victor Kugler was working with Frank when the Germans, after months of harassing Jews, decided to issue the summons through the Jewish Council. He realized, too, that the writing was on the wall for the Jews. Once he spoke about the day when Frank decided that the time had come to go into hiding: "It was a warm day. I went to work as usual. But to my surprise, Otto was waiting for me at the door. He said: 'The time has arrived to go into hiding.' Well, I knew that Otto had made the right decision. He had lived in Germany during the 1930s and had seen first-hand how Jews had believed the Nazi promises, the empty promises, and had left for places from which they would never return. He had begun preparations long ago—with the help of me and a few others in the shop—for his inevitable move."

It was Kugler to whom a letter was sent, postmarked from a border town, giving the information that the family had left The Netherlands. And it was Kugler who made sure that there was enough food to sustain the ones behind the bookcase. And then, as it turned out, everyone's efforts ended in tragedy anyway.

More than 140,000 Jews were living in The Netherlands when the war broke out. When peace was restored, more than 100,000 of them were dead. Little wonder that there are few Jews among the Dutch immigrants.

The Canadian immigration authorities didn't want to admit anyone who might become a burden on their fledgling social welfare system. This usually meant that older people, regardless of good health, were rejected outright.

Some of the older applicants had no intention whatsoever of working in Canada. they wanted to come along to keep the family together, or they didn't want their line of support to be broken.

Nan Mulder constructs a duck nest out of white top grass.

Calling All Ducks

Nan Mulder came to Canada in 1949 intending to farm. Of course! Otherwise he would never have been let into the country. But deep in his heart, he knew that his farming career wouldn't last too long. He was anxious to get back to his first love: running a duck decoy.

He and his brother, Marinus, had carried on a family tradition that dated back more than one hundred years—decoying ducks into a trap and selling them on the market. They had a pond and some surrounding land at Hippolytushoef, near the Waddenzee, an area rich with wildlife. But the income did not justify the long hours, even when added to the slim earnings of a small farm the brothers also

Nan Mulder first lived in the Saskatchewan log house shown at left. His dog, Honey, helped him in his work.

An aerial photo, taken in 1952, of the Delta Waterfowl Research Station on Lake Manitoba.

operated. They could foresee no future in decoying in The Netherlands.

Nan, his wife and three sons first settled in a log house on a farm near Lloydminster, Saskatchewan. "He was a nice fellow, my boss, but too close with his money. So I got another farm job." This next move took the family halfway back across the country, to a dairy farm in southern Quebec. They liked it there. But Nan missed his ducks.

"When it came time for leaving the farm, I started writing letters. And what do you think? There was only one duck decoy in Canada! It had been built at a waterfowl research station in Manitoba. My wife didn't want to go back nearly the whole distance again, so I went by myself to see how I liked it. She came later with the boys."

The Delta Waterfowl Research Station on the southern shore of Lake Manitoba was established by a wealthy American industrialist when it looked for a while as if the continent's duck population might be wiped out. Over the years, it gained widespread recognition for its research work and conservation measures. The banding of ducks was an important part of this work, and the person put in charge of it was the soft-spoken immigrant from The Netherlands, whose motto was: "Look, listen and learn."

Nan immediately applied his own knowledge by building an improved decoy, a long reed-camouflaged tunnel which opened on a pond where ducks were encouraged to feed and nest. Frequently, a dog would be used to entice ducks into the tunnel. After appearing near the opening, it would dart behind the first of a series of reed fences. The curious ducks couldn't resist paddling warily forward to find out where the dog had gone. They were lured far enough to be caught and banded for study.

Nan, who later got a game warden's job to keep him occupied during the months when the ducks weren't around, remembers well his first morning at the Delta Marsh. He was awakened by a quacking noise, jumped out of bed, and saw a flock of Canada geese flying low overhead.

"I will never forget that sight and that noise. It made me feel right at home. I stayed."

John Kap, who ran a flower shop in Maassluis, just west of Rotterdam, ran into an awkward situation when his mother-in-law, seventy-four years old, wanted to come along to Canada. She had been living in his home for eight years and didn't want to be left behind to fend for herself. The Canadian authorities, after the required checkup, said no. She was too old to be of any use. No consideration was given to the circumstances—that her only daughter, on whom she depended totally, would be leaving her.

Well, the Kap family didn't take that sitting down. John went to Canada by himself, on board the *Waterman* in 1947, and began establishing roots in Sarnia, Ontario. His pregnant wife couldn't go with him because there was no doctor on board, but she and his children would join him after the birth. In the meantime, an effort was launched in The Netherlands to get the authorities to change their minds about the grandmother.

A letter signed by Mrs. Kap was sent to Princess Juliana, herself an only daughter. It read in part: "To leave my mother behind seems worse than to mourn her death. I'm her only child. She lives with us and is part of the family. I tried to convey this at the consulate and was told that in London, apparently the location of the head office, another attempt would be made to grant permission. I fear that too

A New Country with a Different Style and Class

Another unusual immigrant was Dr. Paul Hoeberechts, a practising neurosurgeon in Nijmegen, a city torn by warfare. He was at the top of his profession and well respected. Why did he want to leave The Netherlands and start all over again here—after that year of internship?

"Leaving our friends behind us was the hardest part," the doctor told an interviewer in Toronto in the early 1950s. "At our age, you do not make a close friend so easily. Our three children were the deciding factor. We saw that they would have to leave Holland eventually, so we thought it would be better to leave when we could go with them. Canada is a wonderful country for the children. In Holland, all they do at school is study, but here they have sports, music, plays, public speaking. They have a much better time than we did."

Dr. Hoeberechts and his wife passed on some interesting observations about the customs of the two countries:

• "We were surprised at the way people change jobs here. In Holland, the competition is so keen that if you have a job, you stay in it and you save your money for your old age, because you know that by that time, you will likely be replaced by somebody younger."

• "In Holland, people spend much more time in their homes than they do here. So they gather good things around them—good paintings, good books—and in time these things become almost like old friends. It is hard to part with them."

• "There are very few young marriages in Holland. Dutch people save up, buy furniture, and are ready to start housekeeping when they get married. Engagements of five, six or seven years are not unusual. You would never see a grandmother forty-four years old in Holland as you do here."

• "Immigration for the professional man is a far more risky procedure than for the laborer. A laborer will very soon have a higher standard of living here than he had in Europe."

• "I was fortunate to have good neighbors. They corrected my English, and when they saw that I wasn't going out, they told me it was about time I did—so they babysat for me."

• "I was surprised by the number of people who painted or remodeled their own homes. In Holland, we wouldn't think of doing our own painting or gardening. These are very specialized jobs. Here everybody is painting or fixing something."

• "It used to amuse me to see a lady with high heels, the very latest in hats, well-dressed, carrying two huge paper bags full of groceries. Here the women are much better dressed than in Holland, but in Holland you would never see a well-dressed woman carrying groceries."

Ada Boulogne leaves The Netherlands in July in a light winter coat. Her sister, Diny, waits pensively with her father at Schiphol airport. The father first taught at the Christian school at Lacombe, Alberta.

The Daughters Came First

Bastiaan Boulogne, a teacher in the Christian primary school of Den Burg on the island of Texel, wanted to emigrate to Canada. After spending twelve years with his family in the Dutch East Indies, he was finding life in The Netherlands too restrictive. Unfortunately, he didn't have any agricultural experience, one of the main requirements in the early days for getting a visa to enter Canada. Only farmers, gardeners, domestics, and miners were being welcomed with open arms.

John VanderVliet of Trenton came to the rescue. He advised Boulogne to send his two older daughters ahead to Canada, where he would find them jobs as domestics. Once established, the daughters could sponsor the rest of the family.

Ada, nineteen years old, left for Canada in July of 1951. Her sister, Diny, twenty-one years old, went the following month. Both had agreed to take jobs in Belleville, Ontario as live-in maids-babysitters for $40 a month, and to stay for at least one year.

"I was dressed in a light winter coat when I boarded the plane at Schiphol," recalls Ada, now Mrs. Piet Roeper of the Stirling, Ontario, area. "It was rather cool in Holland, and I had always thought that Canada was a cold country. What a surprise to land in Montreal and be greeted by a heatwave."

Both she and Diny worked for a Jewish family. Many of the new customs they encountered, which they took for Canadian customs, were actually Jewish ones.

From their $40 pay, they reimbursed their parents $20 each month for the plane trip. Their living style in those days was so frugal that they still managed to have money left over to put in the bank.

"There were quite a few single girls in Belleville," says Ada, "and we soon found out that there was continual 'open house' at the farm home of the Jacob Westerhof family. Every Sunday and holiday, a group of girls flocked to their place. They had five boys of their own. We often turned the house upside down. I now sometimes wonder how Heit and Mem could have fed us all the time on their $75-a-month wage."

The rest of the Boulogne family —mother, father, Leviny, and Jack —arrived in Belleville in late October. Boulogne tried to get into the public school system, but without success. He worked as a salesman for the Fuller Brush company for three months. Then he found a position as a teacher in the Christian elementary school in Lacombe, Alberta, one of the first Christian schools in Canada.

To become acquainted with the school system in Alberta, he taught in a public junior high school—Grades 7, 8, and 9—until the end of the school year. He was also required to take some summer courses at the University of Edmonton. In September, 1952, he began work as principal-teacher of the school in Lacombe, responsible for the higher grades.

John Kap's mother-in-law was allowed to emigrate to Canada with her daughter.

much time will elapse with no favorable results. The short time between now and the date of departure demands an immediate decision. That's why I am asking you to use your influence to get assent for my mother. As the only child of a loved mother, you certainly must feel the bond that is now being threatened . . ."

The letter wasn't thrown in the wastepaper basket. Before long, there was a communication from the immigration office at the Canadian Embassy: "The matter of your mother's admission to Canada is now receiving the careful and sympathetic attention of the Canadian immigration authorities and we are hopeful that a favorable decision will be reached in the near future."

One day before the departure of Mrs. Kap and her five children on the *Veendam* in March, 1948, a telegram arrived. Her hands shook so much that she had a hard time opening it. As she read it, her eyes lit up. Nobody had to ask her what it was all about. Her mother could go, provided there was assurance she would not become a burden on the state.

Kap, who had been anxiously awaiting developments, was understandably elated when he heard that the entire family was on the way to Canada. He immediately wrote to his wife, in care of the *Veendam*. She would get the letter when she arrived in New York City.

"I am the luckiest man in Canada," he wrote. "I went right away to my bedroom and thanked God that mother was able to come too . . ."

Rudi Mahler was born in the Dutch East Indies, the Asian archipelago now known as Indonesia. With the Dutch army, he fought against the Japanese invaders in 1942. After the capitulation, he was made a prisoner of war, and spent the next three and a half years in the hell of various Japanese camps.

The end of the war in the Pacific in 1945 did not mean the end of hostilities. Nationalists, who had been active throughout the Japanese occupation, established the Republic of Indonesia, which claimed rule over Java, Madura, and Sumatra. Dutch opposition led to warfare. After a conference mediated by the United Nations, Indonesia finally became a sovereign country on December 28, 1949.

During this post-war turmoil, many residents of the islands who held Dutch citizenship headed for the European part of the kingdom. They found life in Europe much different from what they had been used to; sometimes the congestion was unbearable. So it wasn't surprising that many of them moved across another ocean—to spacious Canada.

Mahler, a native of Jakarta, arrived in The Netherlands in 1962. It took him two years to get his Dutch passport back, a bureaucratic nightmare which still troubles him. Although he eventually ended up with a good job as a construction coordinator, he wasn't happy.

"I could see no future there for my children. And there was no elbow room. So in 1969 I emigrated to the West Coast of Canada."

He discovered that many other people who once lived in Indonesia had done the same thing. Some had bypassed The Netherlands, moving directly to the Vancouver area. They still keep up social contact, with the help of the Canadian Indonesian Society.

Joseph Winnemuller of Selkirk, Manitoba, was one of the Netherlanders who returned from the East Indies in 1948.

He, too, had been a prisoner of war, doing forced labor on the Burma Road, which was to be a 400-kilometre railway line from Bangkok to Rangoon. The murderously hot climate, tropical diseases, and the rugged terrain claimed twelve thousand lives. Winnemuller survived, and later worked in a factory in Japan. His wife, with three small children, spent the war years in camps in Java.

"Back in our small country," he says, "we became worried. We decided to move on to Canada; perhaps there would be a better future there for our children. We left in 1953. The first years here were difficult. Now, after thirty years, we still think and talk about those times. But this great country and its people have been good to us."

Mr. and Mrs. Joseph Winnemuller were married forty-five years in 1983.

Chapter 18

Keeping the Faith

The Christian Reformed congregation in Stratford, Ontario, met at first in the YMCA building. The photo on the preceding page was taken on Christmas Day, 1952.

On July 1, 1955, 4,200 young men and women packed into the Brampton Memorial Arena for the first all-Ontario youth rally of the Christian Reformed Church.

Keeping the Faith

Shortly after the turn of the century, John Postman decided to emigrate to Canada, many parts of which were still virgin territory waiting for settlers. The country was in an early stage of development, and needed people with ambition and agricultural know-how.

Postman, his wife, and ten children were just such a hardy, ambitious family. First they settled in southern Alberta, near Monarch, and life was not easy. Long hours of hard work constructing bridges hardly seemed worth the effort when they counted the money in the pay envelope. Yet the couple knew that their lives in The Netherlands would have been hard, too, and that their own future and the future of their children lay in this rugged, empty, and seemingly unfriendly land. Besides, they had a profound belief that God would look after them and make things work out for the better.

In 1913, with plans to farm and with a pioneer's desire for the unknown, the entire family moved to La Glace, an isolated community in the North. Machinery and livestock were put on the freight train and transported to Edson, to the end of the

Church is out, and it's time to socialize. This photo was taken in the early 1950s at the Christian Reformed Church at Cochrane, Ontario.

the land themselves. Much of the property the Postmans acquired was later sold to other Dutch settlers; thus, a small community of the Reformed faith came to be established in the area.

This nucleus grew into a sizeable number after the postwar influx began. In September of 1949, Hen:y, one of Postman's sons, invited Rev. P.J. Hoekstra and fieldman Herman Wieringa to the La Glace area to discuss ways of establishing a Christian Reformed Church and encouraging more strong Christian immigrants to settle there. Not much came of the meeting. It wasn't until a year later that Rev. John Hanenburg, home missionary, traveled from Edmonton to conduct the first service in a hall at Grande Prairie, not far from La Glace.

John Postman launched the congregation when he moved his large family to the area in 1913. He didn't live long enough to see it become officially recognized in 1955, but if he had, he would have been proud.

The Christian Reformed Church, the largest of the Calvinistic denominations in Canada, was established in 1857 by a group of Dutch immigrants living in western Michigan. It spread throughout America, but it didn't cross the Canadian border until 1905, when a group of Dutch immigrant farmers moved from Montana to southern Alberta, settling around Nobleford and Granum. Other congregations were formed—in Winnipeg in 1908, Edmonton in 1910, Burdett in 1911, and Neerlandia in 1915. During the 1920s, home missionaries sent from the United States helped to organize churches among Dutch immigrants in the Ontario cities of Chatham, Hamilton, Windsor, and Sarnia. Similar work was done on the West Coast, in Vancouver, the Fraser delta, and the Bulkley Valley. The Holland Marsh church was organized in 1938. By 1947, when the *Waterman* docked at Montreal, there were fourteen congregations scattered across British Columbia, Alberta, Manitoba, and Ontario.

The early immigrants did much to help the newcomers get settled, as the next chapter will show. Local immigration societies were set up under the umbrella of the church's Immigration Committee for Canada, which promoted a vigorous drive to get immigrants of various Reformed persuasion to join the membership. The church never looked back. Today the Christian Reformed Church has 18,521

The photo above, taken in August of 1952, shows members of the Canadian Reformed Church in the Homewood and Carman areas of Manitoba outside their place of worship—an old Anglican church. The photo below was taken at the Christian Reformed Church in Vancouver.

Home Base
During the First Years

Worshippers leave a large house in Pembroke, Ontario, used by the Christian Reformed Church for services in the early 1950s.

Members of the Canadian Reformed Church in Hamilton, Ontario, first met at the Labor Temple in the city in the early 1950s. They were assisted by the Protestant Reformed Church of the United States.

Immigrants catch up on the news after a service at the Christian Reformed Church in Iron Springs, Alberta, in 1955.

In 1947, newly-arrived immigrants in Kitchener, Ontario, met at first in a Presbyterian church. A congregation of the Christian Reformed Church was later instituted in the city.

This Christian Reformed church in Essex, Ontario, was once a warehouse.

families, or 82,738 members, in 193 congregations in Canada.

The Reformed Church in Canada, an extension of the oldest organized Protestant church in North America, is not quite as large. Congregations were not organized at once for former members of the *Hervormde Kerk* in The Netherlands; they were advised to join the United Church of Canada at first. Not until the Reformed Church in America sent an investigative commission to Canada were churches organized—in Hamilton on October 10, 1949, and in Chatham the next day. Both requested the RCA to accept them.

Reformed Church statistics show 2,159 families, or 6,933 baptized members, in twenty-eighty congregations. Five more congregations were in the process of being organized. A church centre has been established at Camp Shalom, a 135-acre retreat between Cambridge and Paris, Ontario, where the summer program includes varied activities for young and old.

Another denomination, the Canadian Reformed Churches, was organized for immigrants who belonged to the *Gereformeerde Kerken, onderhoudende Art. 31 K.O.* in The Netherlands. The first was instituted in Lethbridge, Alberta, in 1950. Since then, the word has been growth. There are now around ten thousand members in thirty-two congregations in several provinces.

Two smaller Calvinistic denominations, both strictly orthodox, were established out of various splinter groups during the 1950s.

The Free Reformed Church was organized for people who belonged to the *Christelijk Gereformeerde Kerk*. It also included members of the *Oude Gereformeerde Kerk* and the orthodox wing of the *Hervormde Kerk*. The first congregation was established in Dundas, Ontario, in 1950. There now are eleven of them in Canada, with a total membership of 2,529. The Netherlands Reformed Congregations, made up primarily of members of the *Gereformeerde Gemeente*, has its Canadian roots in Norwich, Ontario, where a congregation was

The children at left attended the daily vacation Bible school at the Christian Reformed Church in Renfrew, Ontario, in the summer of 1958.

The Christian Reformed congregation in Chatham, Ontario, swelled during the postwar influx. A new church was built in 1950; on its steps stands the Dirk VanRooyen family (left). At right, Ralph and Anne DeJong are photographed with their sponsors in the Cornwall, Ontario, area on their first Sunday in Canada. They now live at Williamsburg.

established in 1950. This denomination now has ten churches in Canada and fourteen in the United States, with a total membership of 8,552. Other denominations include the Reformed Congregations in North America and the Orthodox Christian Reformed Church.

The many Roman Catholic immigrants, most of them from Noord-Brabant, usually became members of existing parishes. Some priests came from The Netherlands to assist them, and so groups of Dutch Roman Catholics became established in southern Alberta and southwestern Ontario.

Many other immigrants, for reasons of necessity, convenience, dissatisfaction, or conviction, joined established Canadian churches: Presbyterian, Baptist, Anglican, and United, to name a few. Clergymen of Dutch background also serve in many of these congregations.

Isolated on a farm at Mount Elgin, a village near Woodstock, Ontario, Mr. and Mrs. J. Hugo De Wit missed going to church. The Sundays passed uneventful-

ly, leaving a profound emptiness. The couple, who had emigrated on the *Waterman* in 1947, longed for spiritual fulfillment and companionship with people who spoke their language. Finally they wrote a letter to the First Christian Reformed Church in Hamilton, requesting a visit from one of the elders.

The clerk, Ralph De Boer, wrote back: "With the arrival of so many new immigrants, it is nearly impossible to visit each one right away . . . One or more missionaries will be appointed soon, and they will visit regularly and hold services where needed." De Wit was invited to attend the next Sunday's services at the Hamilton church. "You can then get acquainted with the many Hollanders who live here . . . Presumably there is a bus service from Mount Elgin that will get you here on time."

There was another letter from De Boer on September 10: "The consistory of the Christian Reformed Church in Hamilton has decided to pick you up for the Lord's Supper which will be celebrated on Sunday, September 14. You are requested to

Members of the Emmanuel Community Reformed Church in Edmonton turned out in full force to pull the plow and break the ground for their new sanctuary in the mid-1960s. Raising funds for new church buildings often meant sacrifice. The young farmer donated six handsome roosters for the building fund of the Reformed Church at Drayton, Ontario. In 1948, the group of Christian Reformed Church members shown above first held church services in Allan Zietma's home, a farm near Seaforth, Ontario. Later they found a larger meeting place, the Presbyterian church in Clinton.

take along your lunch. You can eat in the basement of the church, where the Ladies' Aid will serve coffee to the adults and milk to the children. Wilfred Turkstra will pick you up. As more families will depend on Turkstra for a ride, you are asked to be ready at an early time. Turkstra can't wait. Otherwise, some people won't get to church on time."

The driver intended to leave Hamilton at 5:30 a.m., pick up the first family by 7 a.m., and have all of his passengers arrive in time for the 11 a.m. service.

Even though there was no church in his area that he could readily identify with, C.M. Hogeterp, a deeply religious man, didn't want to miss a Sunday of worship. And so, on the first Sunday after their arrival in 1947, the Hogeterp family found themselves in the Baptist church in the village of Villa Nova, Ontario.

"It was so lovely," recalls Hogeterp. "The people spoke to us, but we couldn't understand them or respond. Yet we knew in our hearts what they were saying. We didn't get much out of the sermon, of course. But the singing went all right because we knew some of the melodies."

A week later, John VanderVliet, already a busy man in the immigration field, came from Hamilton to say hello. He promised the new arrivals that arrangements would be made so that they could go to church in Hamilton.

The arrangements were somewhat complicated. Hogeterp's farmer brought the family to Hagersville, where they boarded a bus to Hamilton. Someone from the church picked them up at the bus station and took them to church. Another volunteer drove them home after the service.

By March of 1948, there were enough families in the area to warrant services being held in the basement of the Presbyterian church in Hagersville. Rev. Adam Persenaire, the home missionary, was their mentor. Later, when the group had grown to some forty-five people, they rented a rural church. On November 28, the congregation was officially organized with the election of two elders and two deacons. Hogeterp was one of the elders.

"Immigrants were starting to flock to the area, and even the Stone Church, the one we rented, became too small to hold us all. Rev. Persenaire gave us some advice: start looking for your own piece of land, your own building. One morning early in 1950, I got a phone call from him.

He said some land was available near Jarvis. We went out and talked to the farmer. He was willing to sever three acres and sell them to us for $300. To make a long story short, Rev. Persenaire paid by cheque, we went to a lawyer to get everything in order, and then we told the congregation. Fund-raising for a new church started. We talked to Peter Turkstra, a building contractor in Hamilton, and he agreed to build a church for $25,000."

The building was put into use in 1951.

"We were so happy to be in our own church that we couldn't wait for it to be finished," recalls Mrs. Hogeterp. "We sat on boards across orange crates. And when it rained, we had to move everything over a bit to keep from getting wet. There wasn't even glass in the windows when we first started using it."

George Eggink, working on a farm near Cornwall, Ontario, in 1948, was surprised one day to see his wife come running into the field. He feared the worst. But then he noticed the big smile on her face.

"She told me that a Dutch-speaking minister was at our house and that he was anxious to talk with us. The farmer gave me permission to leave my work. And there was Rev. Adam Persenaire. Boy, were we happy to meet him. He was the first Dutch-speaking person we had met

since coming to Canada six weeks earlier. We talked for a long time about many things. We sure felt good after that."

The farmer had urged the Egginks to accompany him to the United Church. They had done so a number of times, but they hadn't felt at home there.

A bucket and broom brigade is ready for an afternoon of work in the spring of 1953. The women regularly cleaned the John Knox Presbyterian Church in Exeter, Ontario, which the Christian Reformed congregation used every Sunday afternoon.

A Denomination New on the Canadian Scene

Two weeks after he arrived in the Bloomfield-Picton area of Ontario in 1947, Jerry Rekker was approached by a minister of the United Church, who expressed the hope that the immigrant family would join his congregation. Rekker appreciated the welcome very much. But he told the good man that he intended to join the Christian Reformed Church.

"He had never heard of that church," recalls Rekker. "That stunned me. He suggested that the church must be pretty far away and that it would be hard for us to link up with it. Well, he was right. The nearest congregations were in Holland Marsh and Hamilton."

The few Dutch families in the area first met in the basement of a home. A missionary visited now and then to see how things were going. Word got around the Canadian community that these im-

migrants loved to sing, and could do it well. Rekker and his family were even invited to sing at the annual meeting of the United Church. The Canadians were thrilled.

"There wasn't always peace between the farmer's wife and me," says Rekker. "She couldn't understand why we wanted to form our own congregation. She once asked me: 'Are you saying that our church is not as good as yours?' I asked her: 'What does your church teach—that the Bible is God's written word or that God's word is in the Bible and that it is a very educational book?' She said, 'I don't want to discuss that,' and walked away angry."

By the summer of 1948, the immigrants were using a little Quaker church that had been used only once a year. They eventually bought the church, tore it down, and built a new church on the site.

Numerical and Percentage Distribution of Religions for the Dutch

Canada, 1971

	No.	Total %
Total Dutch in Canada, 1971	425,900	100.0
Anglican	24,600	5.8
Baptist	15,500	3.6
Christian Reformed	77,600	10.2
Confucian and Buddhist	200	-
Greek Orthodox	300	-
Jehovah's Witness	5,200	1.2
Lutheran	8,000	1.9
Pentecostal	5,300	1.2
Presbyterian	20,300	4.8
Roman Catholic	98,100	23.0
Salvation Army	1,300	.3
Ukrainian Catholic	200	-
United Church	79,700	18.7
No Religion	34,700	8.1

In the 1971 Census, Canadians whose heritage was Dutch only and Canadians whose heritage was of multiple foreign origins were included for the totals listed here. 1981 census statistics did not include both.

Source: Statistics Canada, Table 22 in Kralt, **Ethnic Origins of Canadians**, *p. 58-59.*

The United Church Observer *gave the Dutch presence in Canada front page coverage in November, 1949. Many immigrants joined that denomination.*

"We were thankful that God sent Rev. Persenaire our way. The following Sunday, he picked us up and took us to a farm where a number of immigrants were gathered for a church service. We felt completely at home among them. We realized right away that this was where we belonged."

In Portage La Prairie, Manitoba, members of the burgeoning Christian Reformed Church met in an old government barracks used during the week for the overflow of pupils in the rural school. For the services, the school seats were shoved to the sides and some wooden benches were lined up in the centre. An old table with a cloth-covered box on top served as the pulpit.

Mrs. M. Dornbush, the minister's wife, wrote at the time: "The stoker furnace is in the back of the room and makes considerable noise. In spite of this distraction, the audience is very quiet and attentive during the service. It makes one realize that, after all, these things are only the externals. Worship is the central thing, and all these other things fade into the distant background."

When he toured Canada in 1948, Rev. D.J. Scholten noted down some ways in which church services in Canada differed from those in The Netherlands. It was interesting information for the people back home. In Canada, he said, the congregation often had to stand up for the singing of hymns. Open collection plates, instead of bags, were used. The hymn book contained no fewer than 468 selections. And bulletins were handed out each Sunday, containing the liturgy, information about the church's organizational activities, and personal items.

Some other observations:

● "The word of the Lord is being administered faithfully, and our brothers and sisters receive the same gospel as they did in The Netherlands."

● "The immigrants pay a great deal of attention to one another. Families who live far away from the church are picked up by bus and then brought home again. The whole family makes the trip."

● "What happens to the little children? In each congregation, there are usually a number of efficient young ladies who volunteer to babysit in the basement. What is a basement, you ask? That is the space usually reserved for meetings, under the church sanctuary itself."

● "Each church also features a service in the Dutch language, which is deeply appreciated by our brothers and sisters, for the transition to English is far from simple. Yet immigrants who are living in Canada permanently must adjust to the language as quickly as possible. The Canadian government does not intend to have foreigners organize separate ethnic groups. They want new Canadians to immerse themselves in Canadian life. The slogan is: 'They must become Canadians!' I urge future immigrants to do the following: learn English, learn English, learn English! Start organizing conversation clubs now. You can spare yourself much disappointment later. Many times I have heard people sigh: 'I wish I had learned more English, and sooner.' "

The life of those charged with ministering to the new arrivals in the late 1940s wasn't enviable. The church facilities were often primitive, the distances they had to travel were daunting, and their problems were numerous. Yet they tackled their task with enthusiasm and dedication, knowing that many people relied on them for spiritual strength to carry them through difficult and uncertain times.

Mrs. S.G. Brondsema, whose husband served three Christian Reformed groups at one time—Toronto, Brampton, and Dixie—describes a typical Sunday in a booklet called "Canadian Challenge," which was published by the Women's Missionary Union of the church in Grand Rapids, Michigan.

"As we have three groups of immigrants to minister to and preach to every Sunday, it is necessary to leave the house early on Sunday morning. So the 'Sunday bag' is packed, and at about 9 a.m. we leave. After dropping me off at the meeting place in Toronto, my husband goes on for fifteen miles to get another family. In the meantime, I straighten the chairs, dust the piano and desks, get out the psalters and collection plates, etc., and soon the people start coming by bus, streetcar, Jeep, taxi, and car. At ten o'clock, the minister is back with his load and the service, mostly in Dutch, begins . . . This meeting place is not large, and when fifty or more are present, they are packed like sardines."

After the service, most of the people linger awhile to exchange pleasantries and to catch up on the news. But Rev. Brond-

sema has to leave immediately, first to return his passengers and then to drive another thirty miles, to Brampton, for his next service.

"We drop in at a little café where we are expected, and we are served at once with coffee, sandwiches, and pie. Then we dash on again along Ontario's fine highways and usually arrive just in time

Top: The sign is up, welcoming everyone to the services. Middle: In the early 1950s, a Christian Reformed congregation meets in a hall in Forest, Ontario. Bottom: The first Netherlands Reformed Congregation in Canada was organized in Norwich, Ontario. A school shares the site.

for the one o'clock service. Here the large group of 170 people meet in the Presbyterian church, and are noisily awaiting the pastor. This group, just a year old, is already organized into a congregation. After the hour and a quarter service, two of the ladies conduct Sunday School, and the pastor and his wife have a few minutes to talk. One of the ladies says: '*Mevrouw*, will you ask the *dominee* if he can drop in this week and help us? Our boss is so demanding.' 'All right,' I answer, and tie a knot in my hankie so as to remember to tell my husband. One of the Sunday School teachers says: 'We are out of little Sunday School cards. Will you tell the *dominee*? I see he's busy with so many others.' 'O.K.,' I say, and another knot goes in my hankie."

Rev. Brondsema, a bit tired by now, arrives at a little Presbyterian church in Dixie just in time for the three o'clock service. About sixty people are waiting.

"After the service, a small Sunday School meets and my husband confers with the board—there's no consistory yet. I'm told that one of the members was taken to hospital, and another knot goes in the hankie. Then fond goodbyes are said, and we usually receive an invitation to have a cup of coffee with one of the families, which is gratefully and thirstily accepted. Then we leave for home, sweet home, where we arrive between six and seven o'clock. How good it seems, for my husband's throat is sore from preaching and my jaw is tired from talking Dutch all day."

He lights a cozy fireplace, and she prepares a hot meal. After dinner, the minister relaxes with a book. His wife washes the dishes, and then catches an hour's sleep on the couch.

"Suddenly I remember. I tell him: 'I have three knots in my hankie this time, but I can recall only two of the matters I had to tell you.' 'Oh,' he says, 'sleep on it tonight, and tomorrow you will

Didn't Fit In, so They Started on Their Own

They began to meet for separate church services in Cobden, Ontario, in 1948.

When Mr. and Mrs. Leo Hovius came to Cobden, a village north of Renfrew, Ontario, in 1948, they accompanied their sponsor to the Presbyterian church. The minister, Rev. Henry P. Baak, knew their language.

"He knew we were there," says Mrs. Hovius, "and he put in a bit of Dutch here and there for our benefit. Some members of the congregation must have wondered what was going on. But the minister's effort didn't really help us—we couldn't understand the sermon."

When more Netherlanders arrived in the area, they decided together to meet separately.

"At that time, most of us didn't know English yet, so we needed services in the Dutch language. I don't know if other people had taken copies of sermons with them to Canada, but we had been given a stack. Rev. Baak thought a separate service was a superb idea. He arranged with his board of elders for us to meet in their church on Sunday afternoons. The married men had to take turns reading the sermon. My husband didn't think too much of the idea—he was a bit nervous, you see. But we women thought everything went fine. We sang those Dutch psalms *uit volle borst* (at the top of our voices)."

Then the missionaries from the United States came. And there were a few sighs of relief—from the married men.

remember.' So another Sunday for the immigrant minister has come to a close."

The Edmonton Christian Reformed Church was among the first of that denomination in Canada. A certain pioneering spirit remained even after the Second World War. Its immigration committee, organized in 1946, helped many immigrants get settled in that area, now among the most prosperous in Canada. A second Christian Reformed congregation was established in 1951, and more churches were organized later. The immigrants also set up a credit union, a burial fund, three elementary Christian schools and one Christian high school, and a home for senior citizens.

The roots of the first congregation have been traced back to the spring of 1906 when Fred Baron and his family settled in the Edmonton area. They were joined in 1910 by a number of families from The Netherlands, including a Mr. and Mrs. Kippers. Shortly after the Kippers' arrival, tragedy struck; two of their children died of typhoid fever. When the other Dutch immigrants read their names and the address in the newspaper, they went to offer their condolences. Eventually, the Kippers invited all these people to get together to discuss their religious problems. As the leader of this group, Mr. Kippers was asked to attend a meeting of Classis Pacific of the Christian Reformed Church in Lynden, Washington, and request financial aid for the establishment of a congregation in Edmonton.

Everything went smoothly, and in October, 1910, the church came into being in the home of the Kippers. There were nine families, including twenty-three children, and one single person. Kippers and Baron were elected elders, and another immigrant named Rooseboom became the deacon.

After paying for their incorporation, the little congregation had only thirty cents left. That didn't daunt their plans for a meeting place. The proceeds of a special offering were used to purchase a tent, which was placed on the present site of the Canadian Pacific station. When the weather turned cold, the services were held in the homes of members. In the spring of 1911, they rented the second floor of a furniture building.

Kippers was an energetic man. He wrote a number of articles for church periodicals in The Netherlands and the United States, expounding the oppor-

tunities in the new land. People took note. A number of families and single people, more than sixty persons all together arrived in the area. Because of this growth, the church needed a minister. Before the year was out, Rev. T. Jongbloed had been installed as the pastor.

In 1914 there was a devastating crop failure in Alberta, resulting in much unemployment. It was also the year when the First World War began, and The Netherlands, although neutral, demanded that several of the young men return. A number of families left the province. Church membership dwindled to twenty-five. When a congregational meeting was held in 1923 to call a minister, only fifteen members attended.

But a few years later, the numbers increased again as new families moved into the area. And the growth never stopped. In 1947, when the postwar influx began in earnest, a church building was erected. The second Christian Reformed church was established in 1951, the third in 1952, followed over the years by seven others; today the combined membership totals 4,790.

Mr. and Mrs. B. Sterenberg of Lethbridge, Alberta, who arrived in

The vehicle on the left is a school bus which was used to transport members of the Canadian Reformed congregation at Lethbridge to and from the services. The other photo shows a group of immigrants gathered for a church service in Ruthven, a village near Leamington, Ontario, in late 1947. The congregation was organized by the Christian Reformed Church in Windsor.

Jacob Kuik of Enschede, near the German border, requested the emigration society in Utrecht to arrange a placement in southern Alberta, preferably Lethbridge, where a small group of members of the Canadian Reformed Churches had settled. To him, it was important that he be among people of his own faith. That would make adjustment much easier.

In July, 1950, he and his wife and six children, including twenty-six-year-old Gerry, who was married, boarded the *Volendam* after only a few days' notice, expecting to go to Lethbridge. But other people had other plans.

Recalls Gerry, now of Winnipeg, Manitoba: "When we arrived in Halifax, we were told that we were sponsored by a farmer in Homewood, Manitoba. If they had said we were going somewhere on the moon, I don't think it would have made much difference. Ask any Manitoban outside of this area where Homewood is, and ninety-nine out of a hundred wouldn't know, let alone a group of immigrants with only enough knowledge of English to know when to say yes or no."

The sponsor picked them up. Father and mother sat in the cab with the driver and the seven others squeezed among the suitcases and boxes in the back. Everyone thought the trip to the farm would be short. Instead, the pick-up jolted across one hundred kilometers of gravel and dirt roads.

"When we finally reached the farmer's house, they asked if we wanted something to drink," says Gerry. "We thought a cup of tea would be just dandy. What we got, however, was a pail of water with a big soup ladle in it. You can imagine our amazement. No great welcome; no red carpet. We were just poor immigrants!"

It took a few days for the family to realize just where they were living and that they were some 1,200 kilometers from their desired location. This distance was almost incomprehensible for people who had just come from a tiny, congested country.

On Sunday, the farmer's son took the family to the Christian Reformed Church in Winnipeg.

"However," says Gerry, "we didn't feel at home there. It became quite clear that we were completely isolated church-wise. We started sermon-reading in our home on Sundays—certainly not an encourag-

ing undertaking. We were joined by two *Hervormde* families who came on a somewhat regular basis. Sometimes, some of us would attend the Christian Reformed Church in Winnipeg. On one of those trips, the car ended up in the ditch —a novice driver's mistake. Dad and my brother John were shaken up, but there were no injuries."

The family once again thought of moving to Lethbridge, just so they wouldn't be so isolated. Gerry would go there first on a scouting mission and to make ar-

Top: Homewood, Manitoba: "If they had said we were going to somewhere on the moon, I don't think it would have made much difference."
Bottom: The Kuik family is shown on board the Volendam *in the summer of 1950.*

Services Prairies

rangements for the family's possible settlement there the following year.

"It was quite an experience," he recalls. "If our accommodation we had in Homewood wasn't wonderful, compared to Lethbridge, we had nothing to complain about. Also, the winter work situation for our young men and women was much better. In discussions with many people in Lethbridge, the advice I heard was unanimous: stay where you are and continue what you are doing."

Gerry returned home to give this

At first church services were held in the Kuik home at Homewood.

message—but before he could open his mouth, he was told that he had been a father for three days. The baby, scheduled to arrive in mid-January, had decided to make an appearance on Christmas Day.

"It didn't take long before things started to change," says Gerry. "In the spring of 1951, six families and a few single persons arrived. With all these additional people, our house became too small for our Sunday sermon-reading gatherings. So we moved to the United Church in Homewood. With further growth, the matter of church institution came up. At a meeting on July 5, 1951, under the chairmanship of the late J. Tiggelaar Sr., we decided to ask the church at Edmonton, which at that time already had a minister, Rev. J.T. Van Popta, to assist us in instituting our church."

Since not all those at the inaugural meeting belonged to a given denomination, Van Popta drew up a confession based on the three forms of unity. During the evening, two elders and one deacon were elected.

Sunday, August 12, was a busy day. Rev. Van Popta installed the office-bearers, celebrated the Lord's Supper, and baptized Gerry's child.

"All kinds of questions and problems arose: which classis do we join, the one in the West, consisting of the churches in Alberta and British Columbia, or the one in Ontario? What about weekly or monthly contributions? There were problems with heating the building, an old Anglican church, with the gas lamps (there was no electricity), and with transportation to and from church. Fortunately, for the first year or two, our farmer boss, Dave Froebe, lent us his half-ton truck every Sunday. Every Saturday, he made sure that the tank was full of gas. Every Sunday, we picked up the truck at 7:30 a.m., used it all day, and brought it back again at night."

The arrival of new immigrants in the Homewood and Carman areas meant a growth in the church membership. In 1953, there was income enough for the congregation to call its first minister. Some families moved to Winnipeg, resulting in the institution of a Canadian Reformed congregation there. Both churches enjoyed steady growth in the following years. Today there is a combined membership of around six hundred.

The Reformed Church sent a trailer to Canada for welcoming the immigrants. Neil Eelman plays his famous organ.

Nobleford in 1927 and 1930, respectively, recall changes when the postwar immigrants began to settle in the area: "For the church in Nobleford, the immigrants were a boon. We needed new blood. And yet both sides had some difficulties ad-

The CHURCH HERALD

A CHRISTIAN WEEKLY SERVING THE REFORMED CHURCH IN AMERICA

GRAND RAPIDS, MICHIGAN   MARCH 31, 1950

Contingent for Our Canadian Work

Four of our new workers in Canada standing in front of a trailer-home which will be used by Mr. N. Eelman and Mr. J. Van Oyen to meet incoming ships with a welcome from the Reformed Church. Left to right, the Rev. Harri Zegerius, Mr. N. Eelman, the Rev. Walter Teeuwissen, and Mr. J. Van Oyen.

➤{ In This Issue }◄

justing. We old-timers had been more isolated and were more old-fashioned. The new immigrants were freer. They would go to a stampede or a fair; they would drink—things we never felt good about doing. There was also the language problem. We had kept the Dutch language for a long time, but by 1948 our services were mainly English. Then we had to have more Dutch again. So we settled on half Dutch. Our young people didn't like that very much, but we compromised. Everybody learned from the others. We think the experience was good for both the earlier and the later immigrants."

A shade of bitterness appears when former fieldman Martin DeVos of Dunnville, Ontario, talks about the early days of the Reformed Church in Canada. He believes that his denomination in The Netherlands, the *Hervormde Kerk*, missed the boat by not giving proper advice to emigrants about church affiliation and by failing to organize churches for its members in the new land.

"The Christian Reformed Church was more active and better organized when I came in 1949," he says. "The Reformed Church hadn't done a thing yet. Our people were being advised to join the United Church. That upset me deeply."

Rev. Leon Bruyn, under the employ of the *Hervormde Kerk*, worked among the immigrants, ministering to their many needs and steering them to the United Church as church policy would have it. Traveling in his small car between Chatham and Ottawa, he conducted services for clusters of immigrants and looked after hardship cases.

The Christian Reformed Church extended an invitation to the *Hervormden*. Some people accepted it. But others grouped together and held worship services in their homes, still hoping that their denomination would be established in Canada.

The Reformed Church in America was stirred to action by a letter from brothers Arend and Geert Dunnink of Waterdown, Ontario: "Come and help us. After all, we are your own people and church. Thousands of *Hervormden* are walking around in Canada like lost sheep . . ."

An investigative commission consisting of four ministers, including Rev. Harri Zegerius of Grand Rapids, Michigan, was sent to Canada. It visited groups in Chatham and Hamilton, both vehemently opposed to joining the United Church, and made contact with immigration authorities in Toronto and Ottawa. The conclusion: "Tremendous work is already under way, but much more needs to be done. We have to start working. Five men are needed immediately to get things going."

Before long, the first ministers and lay workers began to arrive. Three crossed the border in February, 1950, in a house trailer with the words *Welkom Immigranten* written on the sides. Neil Eelman, a layman from Grand Rapids, intended to take it to Nova Scotia, for meeting incoming immigrant boats.

"In Quebec, it ran into difficulties," says Rev. Zegerius, the first director of the church's mission work in Canada, based in Hamilton. "It got stuck in the deep snow. Then the police came along and made threatening noises. They said they were against any evangelism preaching. Well, the trailer was pulled free and hidden for the rest of the winter. In the spring, we put it on the road again."

Eelman, who traveled hither and yon to assist immigrants, became known for the little organ he carried along. No matter what the occasion, he would play the familiar heart-warming tunes. And the people would join in song, smile, and feel spiritually refreshed.

The early ministers were overburdened. When the stream of immigrants grew and more groups of worshippers began to meet, they served two, and sometimes three, congregations. Later, fieldmen took over quite a bit of the work. And the arrival of six ministers from The Netherlands eased the load even more. But the work remained difficult. Each day brought new challenges.

"People came from different parts of Holland, and from both cities and villages," says Rev. Zegerius, who himself had emigrated to the United States at the age of thirteen. "One wanted things done one way, another differently. I tried to stay close to the RCA way."

His home at 30 Beulah Avenue in Hamilton doubled as the church office for two years. Many new immigrants ate and slept there. During the first month, his wife served three hundred free meals. After that, everyone was too busy to keep count.

"We didn't have much privacy," he says. "Sometimes people were waiting in the front hall and in the living room, a fieldman was doing paper work on the dining room table, and I was upstairs counselling a family. There wasn't any room for my wife any more. Finally, we decided to move the church office to the upstairs of another house."

A tribute to Mrs. Zegerius appeared years later in *The Pioneer*, the church's monthly magazine in Canada: "Sometimes your house, from cellar to attic, was overcrowded with new families and many meals had to be prepared. We thank you for all the work you took upon yourself. Then came the time that new groups had to be organized, and many hours which your husband should have spent in the family circle were used on the road or in meetings. For our sake, you must have felt lonely very often. We think of your children, who must have missed their father all too often. We wish to thank you for all you did and all you sacrificed for the sake of the Dutch immigrants."

The early Roman Catholic immigrants found a church waiting for them almost everywhere they settled in Canada. They could worship according to familiar patterns; the Latin mass was the same in both countries. Yet there seemed to be something lacking.

The biggest difficulty at first was the language barrier. The church attracted people of many nationalities, which made social communication very difficult. Furthermore, many of the newcomers didn't understand or appreciate the customs and attitudes of other ethnic groups. It was obvious that something needed to be done

"Finally, we decided to move the church office to the upstairs of another house."

to assist these people during a transition period.

In London, Ontario, Bishop John C. Cody was convinced that ethnic priests were the answer. He encouraged their coming to Canada to work among the immigrants. With the emigration movement in The Netherlands escalating, he recommended that particular attention be paid to this group.

Many of the Catholic families came from rural Noord-Brabant and had many children. The parents devotedly followed the church's teachings that birth control in any form was sinful and that a large number of offspring was a rich blessing from God. When the farmers of Noord-Brabant took up the challenge of immigration in increasing numbers, priests from their province decided to follow to keep their sheep in the fold. Some of these priests had actively advocated emigration, particularly among the young single men who looked forward to a future in farming.

Members of the religious order of Society of the Sacred Heart (S.C.J.) from Asten, Noord-Brabant, came to Canada to investigate the possibility of staying here and working among their countrymen. Soon they discovered that they were, indeed, needed.

The story is told that some of the priests who reported to Bishop Cody's jurisdiction were advised by Sibert Graat, a prewar immigrant from Limburg, to purchase a large rural estate reputedly owned

Rev. Martin Grootscholten talks with a newcomer in Canada—Kees Nuiten of Lage Zwaluwe, Noord-Brabant. The young farmer came to Ontario to learn Canadian farming methods.
At Right: Dutch immigrants of the Roman Catholic faith gather in front of the seminary of the Sacred Heart Fathers in Delaware, Ontario, for a mass prior to the first all-day picnic in 1951. The event, organized by Rev. Jan Van Wezel, gave the immigrants a chance to exchange stories of their settlement experiences.

by a Canadian senator. As strong anti-Catholic sentiments still lingered in rural Ontario in those years, the reverend fathers were counselled to doff their black soutanes and white collars and step into farmer's overalls before heading for the farm to make a deal.

The farm home at Delaware, near London, became a convent of the Sacred Heart priests. Later it was turned into a junior seminary, a Dutch innovation in the London diocese. At first it attracted some of the sons of Dutch immigrants and a few Canadians, but it never really succeeded and was eventually converted to other uses. Bishop Cody, however, had been so taken by the junior seminary idea that he had a large, costly seminary built between London and St. Thomas. Named Regina Mundi, it later was turned into an exclusive boarding school for foreign and Canadian students.

Among the priests in the London area was Rev. Jan Van Wezel, an energetic leader who was one of the pillars of strength for the early immigrants. Bishop Cody soon appointed him associate director of immigration for the diocese. By this time, boatload after boatload of immigrants were arriving at Canadian ports. These people needed help in getting settled, and that was part of Father Van Wezel's task.

"Many of the newcomers found the Canadians cool towards them—they were kept at a distance," he says. "This was mostly because of the language, but there were other reasons as well. Further, there was no organization to help the Roman Catholic immigrants. They were strictly on their own. Many of them, particularly the single people, struggled with loneliness. They found it very hard to form friendships with Canadians of their age."

Father Van Wezel filled this need by organizing several youth clubs. Young people drove for miles to come together and enjoy each other's company. Many friendships were formed, and the loneliness seemed to disappear.

Word of this reception given to Catholic immigrants spread throughout Canada. Many families, not satisfied with their jobs and surroundings, packed their bags and headed for London, sometimes traveling in vehicles not fit for the road. They were met by Rev. Martin Grootscholten, who had set up an office in London to assist the newcomers.

In the meantime, Father Van Wezel had been transferred to Ottawa to set up a national bureau for immigrants. He succeeded in setting up a hostel where newcomers could stay temporarily for a nominal fee. He was given an assistant, who eased his workload a bit. But it became obvious that he needed more help if a proper job was to be done across Canada. In 1953, he went to The Netherlands, seeking priests who could serve as social workers among the immigrants. Twelve were recruited, and more came later.

"With their considerable numbers, the immigrants rejuvenated parishes in southwestern Ontario," says Father Van Wezel, who now lives in retirement in Noord-Brabant. "Their children refilled classrooms and even saved some separate schools that were being threatened with

Rev. John Van Harmelen (center) visits the Christian Reformed Church in Sarnia, Ontario, in 1952. He toured Canada on behalf of the Gereformeerde Kerk. He and his family, shown examining literature about Canada, emigrated in 1953.

closure because of declining enrolments."

Another Dutch priest comments: "The Dutch Catholics retained their convictions. They became good Canadian Catholics. In those days, only a few drifted away from the church."

Above: Rev. and Mrs. John Van Harmelen enjoy retirement.

At Right: In 1950, Rev. and Mrs. John Rubingh of the Christian Reformed Church in Renfrew, Ontario, share their backyard with a few of the many young visitors who spent Sundays with them.

Below: The Christian Reformed Church on Church Street in Brampton, Ontario, was opened in 1954.

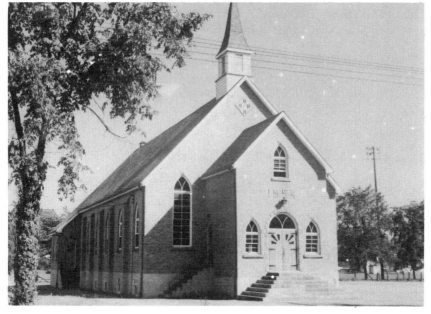

The Sacred Heart fathers are still at Delaware and a number of other Canadian centers, including Ottawa and Winnipeg. They have proved to be longer-lasting than a group of nuns from Noord-Brabant, the Sisters of Bethanie, who came to Canada with the intention of working among wayward girls. They labored on a farm at Lambeth, Ontario. When their goal did not materialize, they returned to The Netherlands.

When Rev. John Van Harmelen visited Canada in 1952, he made observations about Christian Reformed congregations. Like Rev. D.J. Scholten did in 1948, he passed his impressions on to the people in The Netherlands when he returned.

Here are a few:

● "After church, the people all gather around to talk to one another. No one seems to be in a hurry to get away. In The Netherlands, people can't seem to wait until the minister steps from the pulpit before they make a rush for the door. In many congregations here, the minister stands at the door and shakes each parishioner's hand. He enquires about how things are going at home, and he gets news that may be important to him for his work during the coming week."

● "Most churches here have a basement, which serves as a meeting place for the young people's societies and the men's and women's societies. In fact, it is designed precisely for this use. If the congregation doesn't have enough money to build a complete church, it first makes do with the basement, using that for a sanctuary until there is enough money to finish the building. This method is also used in house construction. Various immigrants I visited lived in basements."

● "I also attended a number of young people's society meetings that were held in the basement. Usually, the young men and young women meet on the same evening, though in separate rooms. The meetings take place on the same evening because members often come from the same family and thus they have to make only one trip with the car from what often are considerable distances."

Before Rev. Van Harmelen sailed with the *Groote Beer* to Canada, a notice in the *Friesch Dagblad* caught the eye of a seventy-year-old Mr. Zijlstra in Franeker. It mentioned that the minister from Assen would be chaplain on the boat and would visit among the immigrants. It even gave his address: Molenstraat 14.

The man cycled all the way to Assen, found Rev. Van Harmelen at home, and blurted out a request: "If you come across my son in Canada, tell him to write his old father. I haven't heard from him in six months."

The minister made note of the name and address—Millbrook, in Ontario—and promised to enquire about the son. When he arrived in Trenton, at the home of John VanderVliet, he was told: "You'll meet a lot of new immigrants this Sunday. You're requested to preach at 10 a.m. in Peterborough, at 1 p.m. in Campbellford, and at 7 p.m. in Trenton." Little did he realize that he would meet up with the son during his first Sunday in Canada.

"After the service in Peterborough, we shook hands with all the people who were in the church. A young fellow said to me in the Frisian language: 'I'm Zijlstra from Franeker.' I asked him: 'Do you live in Millbrook?' He said: 'I sure do.' I said: 'You'd better sit down this afternoon and write a long letter to your father.' I chatted with him for awhile, and he promised to keep regular contact with his family in Friesland."

A man from Smilde, near Assen, had also come to the parsonage. He had asked the minister to present a gold watch, obviously a family heirloom, to his oldest son, who was working for a farmer in the Trenton area. The request was fulfilled in

Off to the Sunday Service

In the early 1950s, George Tigchelaar of the Campbellville, Ontario, area used his stake truck to take fellow immigrants to the Christian Reformed Church in Hamilton. The Rustenburg family has just been picked up at their home near Millgrove. Above, Harm Brouwer takes his family to church at Rocky Mountain House in a farm wagon during the winter of 1950-51. When the snow was high, he replaced the wheels with runners. At left, the families Kikstra and Veeneman travel to the same church in 1950.

Campbellford, the second stop during the minister's first Sunday among the immigrants.

"We met the son in the consistory room. After the service, I surprised him with the watch. We visited him at his home and had lunch there. Boy, was he happy!"

Everywhere Rev. Van Harmelen preached, people came to him and said: "Why don't you come to Canada to stay? We need Dutch ministers here."

Recalls the minister: "They deeply appreciated the ministers from the United States, but they had been used to a different kind of preaching in The Netherlands. There was no question about

it: they wanted Dutch ministers to come here. I remember telling my wife upon my return: 'If I ever get a call to Canada, let's go. I feel that I can be of real service to the people there.' "

Well, he did go to Canada—in 1953. His first charge was the Christian Reformed Church in Brampton, Ontario. There he quickly learned that a minister serving an immigrant church had to keep together people from different branches of the Christian faith. Many times he had to walk a middle road so as not to offend any one segment of the people.

"When I arrived in Brampton, I discovered that the members of the Im-

It Got Them to the Church on Time

There's room for the whole family on Albert Eisses' motorbike.

Some people must have blinked twice when they saw a motorbike with two adults and three children on it, roaring along the highway south of Barrie, Ontario, on a Sunday morning in 1949. Mr. and Mrs. Albert Eisses, who lived on a farm near Stroud, were on their way to church in Holland Marsh. They dropped off their children at the house of friends in Churchill, a small community on the way, and then continued on to the service.

One Sunday, Mrs. Eisses and her five-year-old son, John, headed for the Marsh themselves. She rode her bicycle over three miles of gravel road, left it at a house near the highway, and began hitch-hiking the twenty-five miles to the church.

"The third car picked us up," she recalls. "The driver asked: 'Where do you have to go?' I said: 'To the church in

Holland Marsh.' He said he was going only as far as Churchill. I told him that was okay. I was confident that the Lord would get us to the church. At Churchill, we started walking along the highway. Near the bottom of a hill, a car stopped, and the driver offered us a ride. We got out at the bridge in Bradford, and began to walk again—in the wrong direction. I asked a man how to get to the church, and he told us to follow a ditch across the fields. The ground was so soft that I wondered whether we would make it. Finally, after walking quite a distance, we came within sight of the church."

The deacons were collecting the offering and the congregation was singing *Geloofd Zij God Met Diepst Ontzag* when mother and son, their shoes covered with muck, entered. They sat down in a vacant pew. When someone quickly whispered that the places belonged to the deacons, they squeezed in another pew.

"After the service, I looked around for people from Bradford. I wanted to ask them if they would take us back to the highway. But I couldn't find anyone who went that way. A couple who lived next to the church took us home for coffee. It turned out that they also used to live in Assen, Drenthe. We had a pleasant talk. Their son drove us back to where we had left the bicycle. We were home at two o'clock."

Mrs. Eisses hitch-hiked two more times, and then stopped when someone told her it was a dangerous practice. Then the motorbike began to disrupt the Sunday morning silence again.

manuel Christian Reformed Church had belonged to five different denominations in The Netherlands. I said to myself: 'If we can keep them together for five years, we will have won the battle for unity. Then there'll be no need for all these separate churches.' When an opening for an elder came up, for example, I recommended to the consistory that we nominate persons who attended the *Hervormde Kerk* or the *Christelijk Gereformeerde Kerk* in the past. And if a Dutch sermon had to be read, I always checked it for words which referred to a special audience, such as *Hervormden* or *Gereformeerden* and changed these to Bible *believers*. During the service, I announced only those hymns which could be found in both Dutch hymnals we used. I wanted to keep the immigrants together, not let them drift off in different directions. You know, I think you'll find two strong Christian Reformed Churches in Brampton. Brothers and sisters of one faith found one another."

He found out other things. Funerals were a rarity. During the first five years, he did not bury one member of his congregation. Sickness and old age claimed

very few immigrants in the early years. And a minister had to be ready for the unexpected. One day, he got a postcard from Sydney, Nova Scotia: "We've packed everything in our old crate and put your address on the outside. We're leaving by car. Please look after us. I'm a baker . . ."

In 1953, Rev. D.J. Scholten also came to Canada to stay. He went to Lethbridge,

Some congregations organized after the war met in basements. This one was used by the Christian Reformed Church at Cornwall, Ontario.

Top: The funeral chapel served for five years as home for the First Christian Reformed Church of Lethbridge.
Below: The church building was officially opened in 1956.

Rev. D.J. Scholten greets the people who came to the station in Lethbridge to welcome him and his family.

Alberta, the heart of beet-growing country, to be the congregation's first full-time minister. Most of the members were at the train station to welcome him and his family. Rev. Scholten threw up his hands and said: "There are too many of you to shake hands with. So I greet all of you at once."

He recalls: "That welcome was unforgettable. The entire group went to the church—a former funeral chapel. A funeral chapel? Well, the most striking and moving thought was that in this house of the dead, the living word of God was preached."

The congregation's first service had been held on March 13, 1949, in the YMCA building. Soon after, the funeral home had been purchased for $14,000.

Rev. Scholten found conditions a bit primitive.

"When I arrived, there was no babysitting hall. I rubbed my eyes at the mothers who had stayed over for both services and were feeding their babies and listening to me at the same time."

It was good for morale to have a minister with a sense of humor. After three or four baptisms in quick succession,

Young People Used the Church for Social Activities

Above, young people of the Christian Reformed Church relax during a break at a leaders' conference in Guelph, Ontario, in 1956. The other photo, dated 1950, shows the first young people's society of the Christian Reformed Church in Drayton, Ontario.

Rev. Scholten printed this message in the bulletin: "Everyone should write to relatives and friends in Holland to say that Canada is a fertile country."

The church also grew through the constant arrival of new families.

"Several members of our congregation always went to the railway station to meet the immigrant trains," recalls Rev. Scholten. "For the night trains, the clergy took turns: for instance, I picked up the people for Father Verhagen of the Roman Catholic church and for Rev. Karel Hanhart of the Reformed Church. It even happened that members of our Protestant churches slept overnight in the Roman Catholic manse—ecumenical cooperation 1953 style."

There was more of that co-operation when *Sinterklaas*, the Dutch Santa, made his rounds. A woman visitor to Lethbridge had brought a surprise—a *Sinterklaas* costume. So all the immigrants got together for an evening of fun. Rev. Hanhart was the good saint, Rev. Scholten, with shoepolish smeared on his face, was *Zwarte Piet*, the Moorish aide, and Father Verhagen was master of ceremonies.

At left, a youth group gathers at Neerlandia, in northern Alberta, for a rally in 1962.

Above: An outing for a Christian Reformed young people's group. They all wear their Sunday best. At left, a group of young people from the Christian Reformed Church in Listowel, Ontario, visit Niagara Falls in 1952.

Rev. H.J. Spier of Rijswijk, Zuid-Holland, shared with the readers of *De Spiegel* his impressions of church life in one community in Nova Scotia in 1953: "In April, there were only thirteen persons; around the middle of July, there were close to a hundred. Together they are building up a church community, even if it's in a barn with lots of chinks. The rough wooden benches were covered with newspapers to protect clothing, especially nylons. It was so full on that second Sunday in July that a number of young people had to sit in the hayloft. However, they weren't out of reach of the person taking the collection. Herman Lam, the fieldman, turned out to be an excellent organist. It was important that new immigrants went to a centre where they could build up a church community with others. I heard someone sigh: 'If there were no church here, I certainly wouldn't have stayed.' "

Here are some more comments from immigrants:

Anno Slomp of Nobleford, Alberta, who had arrived in Iron Springs in 1954: "For us, immigration wasn't such a bad move because church was a constant. When my father passed on, we really felt the comfort of the church and the interest people had in us. As people, we really grew because of the church. We have been richly blessed in Canada, and not only in material things. We found a community, good friends, Christian schools for our children, and many more things that bring happiness."

L. Reedyk of Lethbridge: "I had been very active in choirs in Holland, having sung tenor for years. At the farewell party of the choir there, I promised: 'In Canada, I'll become a member of a choir even if there is only one in all Canada.' Traveling from Quebec City to Lethbridge, I wondered if I had been

A 1949 newspaper advertisement announces a church service to be held at the YMCA in Lethbridge, Alberta. Members of the Christian Reformed Church in Iron Springs, Alberta, first met in a dance hall. Bottom: A large crowd gathered to witness the cornerstone of the new church laid.

Attention Dutch Immigrants!

BEKENDMAKING!

Er zal een dienst gehouden worden in de Nederlandsche taal a.s. Zondag morgen om 10 uur in net Y.M.C.A. Gebouw door. Ds John De Jong.

ST. AUGUSTIN'S PARISH CHURCH

Multicultural History Society of Ontario

Multicultural History Society of Ontario

wise to make that rash promise. When we arrived in Lethbridge, I asked some Dutch people: 'Do you have a choir here?' They answered: 'Yes, we had a meeting last Monday to organize one.' That was the day we had landed in Quebec. Naturally, I had to join."

Peter Meliefste of Coaldale, Alberta: "Rev. G.Ph. Pieffers was called from Holland to be minister of the Canadian Reformed Church in Coaldale. He and his family arrived at the train station at 9:30 on a Sunday morning, dirty, hot, and tired. At 2:30 that afternoon, he preached his first sermon in Canada. What a man!"

H.C. Barthel Sr. of Lethbridge, Alberta: "At first, we hired a school bus and driver to take us to church. After some weeks, we decided that we needed our own transportation. So, with Rev. P.J. Hoekstra's guidance, we bought an old ambulance for $180. It had been used as a dog catcher's van and badly needed cleaning. We spent another $40 to fix and clean it. With this, we were able to transport sixteen people. Sometimes the trip took longer than expected—one Sunday morning, the service was delayed half an hour because we arrived late."

William Van Oosten of Chatham, Ontario, who had arrived in London, Ontario in 1956: "The people of the Christian Reformed Church gave us a warm welcome. The pastor, John Gritter, was like a father to us. Whenever a family arrived in London and the station master had difficulty understanding them, he would call Rev. Gritter. Even in the middle of the night, he would get up to go to the station. Before he left the house, he would tell his family that they were going to have guests. Sometimes, the new arrivals, after finding out that their host was a minister, would protest: 'We're not church members at all.' He would reply:

The Ontario Christian Reformed Churches' festival of choirs was held near Elora in 1959.

A Permanent Home

Left: The Willem VanderMolen home in New Westminster, British Columbia—"more or less the center of our church."
Above: The Christian Reformed church and parsonage at Charlottetown, Prince Edward Island, in process (1965), and completed.

A church in Holland Marsh in 1947, just after the postwar influx had begun. The band of the Christian Reformed Church (below) in Fort William (now Thunder Bay), Ontario, photographed in 1955.
Bottom: Rev. Ralph J. Bos with an immigrant congregation in front of the Sons of Temperance Hall in Port Williams, Nova Scotia, in November of 1953.

'Never mind. You are tired and hungry. Here is food and a bed.' "

Willem VanderMolen of Chilliwack, British Columbia: "We had lots of room in our large frame home, bought for $6,500 with $500 down. It became the focal point of the activities of the Canadian Reformed Church in our area. We rented the Seventh-Day Adventist Church building in New Westminster for the services. But on many Sundays, in addition to our family of nine, up to twenty people would sit around our table for dinner between services. Our home was used also for regular school board meetings and even for full membership gatherings. The boys and girls used to meet there too. It was more or less the centre of our church."

Carl Biel of Guelph, Ontario: "On Sundays, we all went to church in St. Catharines in a so-called church truck. Someone drove this truck along a route to the church and picked up all the immigrants along the way. We very much enjoyed this togetherness. I believe it kept us from getting homesick."

All across the land, church groups continued to be organized wherever the clusters of immigrants were large enough to support them. The first attempts to

establish some degree of organized church life among the Protestant immigrants in the Annapolis Valley of Nova Scotia were made in the fall of 1952. Rev. H. Moes, who had spent a few months in the Maritimes for the home missions board of the Christian Reformed Church, intending to form church groups, held a number of services in the hall of the Kentville United Church. Seventy people attended the first one. After each service, the church's ladies' auxiliary served refreshments.

Rev. Moes also conducted a few services at a home in Middleton for those living in the western end of the valley. However, it wasn't until the following spring that steps were taken to form a church society. The first service, attended by twenty-six people, was held at a home in Victoria Harbor. The next one, nearly a month later, was held at another home in Starr's Point, near Port Williams. After that, services were held more regularly. And the living rooms were exchanged for the more spacious Sons of Temperance Hall in Port Williams. The rent was $2 a Sunday. In the fall, Rev. Ralph J. Bos, newly-appointed home missionary for the Maritimes, arrived in Truro from Ontario, and came every third Sunday to conduct the service.

"Although you were not all of the same background, you soon developed a spirit of unity," he said later in a message to the congregation. "You were soon willing to help those of your number who had special needs. Because of distance, I could not always be present immediately, but I knew that someone would be there to help those who had critical needs."

Following the institution of the church in June, 1955, the congregation didn't waste any time moving into a vacant Baptist church in Lower Canard. The first year's rent was $25. In December, the consistory set up a building fund with $200 raised by the ladies' society at its fall bazaar. In 1958, a 2½ acre site in Kentville was purchased for $3,000. A church was built there a few years later.

When Rev. Harri Zegerius stepped out of the train in Toronto early one morning after a trip from Ottawa, his somewhat bleary eyes spotted a Dutch suitcase—green, wooden, rather battered, with dull brass corners. It belonged to a middle-aged couple, much wrinkled and weary, who had just ended a two-day trip from Saskatchewan.

"A cup of coffee soon loosened their tongues. They had been in the boondocks —way out, really—for sixteen months. In that time, they'd heard many pro-

The first wedding in the First Christian Reformed Church at Rocky Mountain House, Alberta, took place on May 7, 1952. The happy couple: Klaas and Lies Kikstra.

Ah, the Church Picnic, the Social Event of the Year

No early immigrant would miss the annual summer picnic.

Rev. John Van Harmelen told the people in The Netherlands about it in 1952: "July 1 is the big Canadian national holiday. Nearly everyone is off work. And nearly all members of the congregation use this day to reinforce the ties among them. Wherever I went in Canada, I was shown photographs of congregations picnicking. The women start baking for this picnic several days in advance. Large quantities of cake, doughnuts, pies, and hot dogs are available. There is lots of lemonade and ice cream. These items are sold at a very reasonable price to give everyone a chance to buy something and to increase the kitty of the church."

By 11 a.m., nearly everyone has arrived at the park. The minister opens with prayer. There are a few hymns, followed by welcoming remarks, which include a warning about touching poison ivy. Then the eating starts.

"After lunch, one can go swimming in the lake or play various games, including pitching horseshoes, something we don't do in The Netherlands."

Mrs. Reina Feyen, a member of the Christian Reformed Church in Chatham, Ontario: "The church provided all our social life. Vacations were unheard of during the first years in Canada, so the only outing was the church picnic at Rondeau Park on Lake Erie. It was held on Labor Day, a national holiday, when most people would be able to attend. The lunch, the chitchat, the games for the children and the adults, and the refreshing dip in the water amounted to a real treat for the entire family. It was an important day for all of us."

An immigrant's farm near Woodstock, Ontario, was the setting for the picnic of that city's fledgling Christian Reformed congregation in the late 1940s.

Rev. Cornelius Witt welcomes picnickers as members of the Christian Reformed Church gath under the trees in Trenton, Ontario, in 1952. That's an organ on the back of the truck.

A scene from the church picnic held in 1949 by the Christian Reformed Church of Jarvis, Ontario.

Multicultural History Society of Ontario

ung people from Smithers and Telkwa, British Columbia, gathered
Moricetown on July 1, 1952, for a picnic. One popular event was
gsteken. George Koopmans, riding a bike, has to put a stick through
e hole or get dunked.

Tug-of-war, a major event at the 1954 picnic of the Christian Reformed Church
at Fort William, Ontario. Below, members of the Canadian Reformed Church
in Smithville, Ontario, enjoy some good food and fellowship on Labor Day in
1960.

ne two lower photos, made available by Mrs. F. Huizinga of Sarnia,
ntario, were taken at a church picnic in Owen Sound, Ontario, in
48.

mises, but not once had they been taken to a church service. Now they were looking for spiritual help. They said: 'We'll let you know when we've settled down. Will you come and hold a service for us then?' I sealed that promise with a prayer."

Some months later, in early 1951, a letter came from St. Catharines, Ontario, signed by eight families, including the couple from Saskatchewan. Fieldman Martin DeVos led the first service. Before long, St. Catharines had a thriving Reformed congregation.

"When we celebrated the 25th anniversary of that congregation," says Rev. Zegerius, "there were many reasons to be grateful to God. And right on the platform, to remind us of God's providential ways with us, was that old green suitcase that helped to start it all."

Why have so many of the Dutch immigrants joined the United Church, as shown in the statistical chart earlier in this chapter?

Rev. William VanderVeeken of Bedford Park United Church in Toronto, a native of Ontario, believes there are two main reasons: first, there was the decision of the *Hervormde Kerk* to steer its members to the United Church during the first years; second, there was a feeling among a certain segment of the immigrant community that the Reformed churches here were too static and unwilling to change their outlook consistent with the times.

"Many people felt that their church in Canada didn't change too much, that it didn't keep up with the changing times. So they joined the United Church. We believe that the church is a growing thing, that it should be flexible in its understanding of how it should fulfill its ministry in the world."

There were other reasons. Some people joined the United Church because it was conveniently located in the neighborhood. Others, for various reasons, didn't want to belong to a Dutch-oriented fellowship. Some simply wanted a change.

Of course, the United Church wasn't the only available alternative place for worship. The Presbyterian Church also attracted many from the immigrant community.

Dr. James Sauer, director of church growth for the Presbyterians, once commented: "The Dutch are very active and great supporters in the local congregations. The men often become elders . . . They are a visible minority."

The Jan Knegt family and other immigrants rode in this truck to the Christian Reformed Church in St. Catharines, Ontario, in the late 1940s. Some time later, the Knegt family rode inside Cor Groenewegen's truck on the way to the Sunday services at the Canadian Reformed Church in Hamilton.

Chapter 19

Helping Hands

Helping Hands

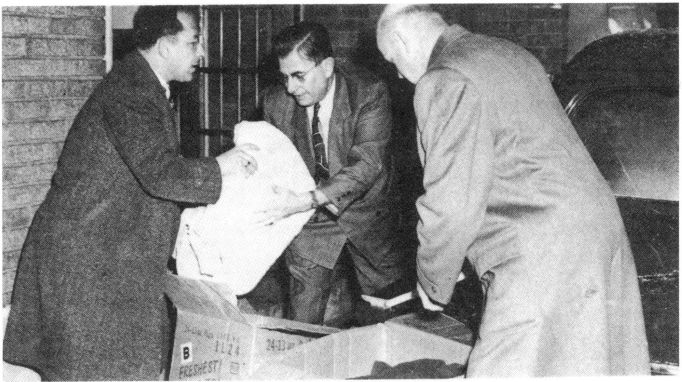

The station-wagon was stuffed full of bundles and boxes of used clothing and the man behind the wheel looked a little used himself. He wore a pair of coveralls and an old hat. Beads of sweat stood on his brow, his shoulders sagged with fatigue and yet his eyes glistened with anticipation.

He was none other than Rev. Harri Zegerius, returning to Canada with another load of clothing donated by Reformed Church groups in the United States and destined for hard-pressed immigrant families. He enjoyed this work. It was rewarding to see the relief in the eyes of a mother who couldn't afford to buy clothes for her growing children or a Sunday dress for herself.

Used overcoats sometimes served as extra blankets during the winter. Many houses, heated by a wood-burning kitchen stove, were ice-cold long before morning. Arguments over who was entitled to an extra coat for the bed or a hot water bottle were not uncommon.

Rev. Zegerius got so involved with his work that occasionally some part of his wardrobe became lost.

"One day, I couldn't find my suit jacket. I looked all over the place. Finally,

Used clothing is being packed into boxes for shipment to Canada. At left is Rev. Harri Zegerius, the Reformed Church's first director of Canadian work. The photo below shows a loaded trailer about to leave Grand Rapids, Michigan.

I concluded that it must have gotten gathered into a bundle of used clothing. When I was in Halifax once, meeting an immigrant boat, I spotted an old man shaking from the cold. He was dressed only in a suit. I said to him: 'Here, take my overcoat. I don't need it back. I'll find something for myself in the bundle."

There are more memories:

● "We once had a flat tire on the way to Canada. We looked all over for the spare. Finally, we deduced that it was

They Went Out of Their Way to Help

John and Alida VanderVliet

Hundreds of people across Canada stood ready day and night to lend a helping hand to the newcomers. Most often, they were immigrants themselves—ones who had come before the war and knew hardship from experience. They wanted to ease the burden.

One who stood tall among this small army was John VanderVliet, the amiable, sincere, and energetic executive secretary of the Immigration Committee for Canada of the Christian Reformed Church. He helped organize the placement of the first postwar arrivals. He did field work himself. And during the ensuing years, when the trickle became a flood, he seemed to be everywhere—meeting boats in Halifax, visiting with newly-arrived families in rural areas, meeting with Canadian officials, and looking after the affairs of the committee. He also found time to edit *Calvinist Contact*, a Christian newspaper aimed at the immigrant community.

VanderVliet knew what immigration was all about. He had come to Canada in 1926, when few people were around to

help him get adjusted to the strange surroundings and way of life. He had to fend for himself. His determination to show his relatives in The Netherlands that he had not taken the big step for naught had helped him keep his head above water.

He and his wife Alida—they were married in Beverwijk, Noord-Holland, in 1923—worked hard to become Canadian citizens. But on the day they got their citizenship papers, he took sick and was taken to hospital. The doctor had bad news: tuberculosis. To make matters worse, one of VanderVliet's daughters also contracted the dreaded disease. During these trying times, Mrs. VanderVliet never lost hope or courage. Each Saturday, she delivered eggs, making a profit of five cents on a dozen.

VanderVliet recovered, and so did his daughter. Then a big task awaited the former teacher and soldier.

Recalls one of his three daughters, Mrs. Leonard Voskamp of Carrying Place, Ontario: "My father was appointed by the Christian Reformed Church in 1946 to work in immigration. Since we lived in Hamilton at that time, and there were several organized Christian Reformed congregations in that area, it seemed wise to move away from that area and try to begin new churches in Ontario. We moved to Trenton in December of 1947, and my father opened up an immigration office there. After immigration really started rolling, I helped him in the office for five years, doing secretarial work. During that time, my father kept himself busy with attending meetings with immigration officials in the province, with committee meetings, and with placing immigrant families and single persons with sponsors. He also received a lot of correspondence from future immigrants, who wanted to know all kinds of things about this country and their sponsors. He spent a lot of time solving problems as they arose. He also tried to meet every immigrant boat that arrived in Halifax and Montreal,

under all the clothes. Well, we didn't feel like taking them out. So we did the simplest thing: bought a new tire."

● "At the border, we had to meet a two-ton truck full of loose clothes and transfer the entire cargo to our own truck.

That was a lot of work. Then we had some explaining to do to the police. Boy, did we sweat that day."

The home missionaries of the Christian Reformed Church often returned from a visit to the United States with a carload of

greeting each family head, and traveling along on the immigrant trains."

VanderVliet tried to make sure that the immigrants weren't clustered together. He believed it was essential that they have contact during the week with Canadians, so that they could learn the language and customs and ease themselves into the society of their new land. But this didn't mean that the desires of individual immigrants were ignored.

"If a certain family in Holland wanted to go to a certain area in Ontario, the fieldman was informed of this and every effort was made to go along with the immigrant's wishes," says Mrs. Voskamp.

VanderVliet's wife was also an invaluable help. She never knew when her husband would be home, and when he opened the door of their house at 304 Dundas Street West, she wouldn't know how many people he had with him. Sometimes there would be as many as twenty people needing food and accommodation.

"If there had been some mistake, or if a sponsor backed out at the last minute, then the family or families were set off at Trenton," says Mrs. Voskamp. "We were asked to keep these people at our house for sometimes up to three or four weeks until other employment was found for them. Fortunately, we had a large house."

Over the years, Mrs. VanderVliet and her daughters made thousands of cups of coffee and prepared hundreds of meals for visitors, many of them unexpected. They made them feel at home. In fact, some were reluctant to leave when a job and accommodation were found.

For his service to the immigrants, VanderVliet was awarded the prestigious Olivier Van Noort medallion by the *Nederlandse Emigratie Fonds.* Another recipient of the award, Jan Heersink, who worked among the immigrants on behalf of the Reformed Church, says of his former colleague: "He was very fair, hard-working, and well-liked by

Rev. P.J. Hoekstra

everyone. He was the opposite of the bureaucratic type. There's no question about it: he did a lot for the people."

There were other stalwarts—for example, Rev. Paul De Koekkoek, H.A. Wierenga, and Bernard Nieboer in the West, and John Vellinga in Ontario. And there was another recipient of the Olivier Van Noort award—Rev. Peter J. Hoekstra, home missionary in Western Canada and president of the Immigration Committee.

He went to Vancouver in 1927, serving as a home missionary. Following an eight-year pastorate in Sultan and Duvall, Washington, he served the church at Nobleford, Alberta, from 1944 to 1949. From that date until his retirement in 1962, he was a home missionary in Alberta, working among the many immigrants there. During the years he spent in Lethbridge, his home was the second floor of a former funeral chapel used by the congregation for church services.

Rev. John Gritter wrote in 1966: "His appointment as head of the committee was a natural one. With great knowledge of immigrant life, with a broad acquaintance with immigration officials and railroad leaders, with intimate understanding especially of life in Western Canada, with fairness, firmness, and congeniality, he guided the committee through these important years."

People concerned with the settlement of Dutch immigrants traveled far and wide to find suitable areas. Conferring near Lethbridge, Alberta, in 1948 were John Visser, Bernard Nieboer, Dr. Prins of Groningen, Rev. P.J. Hoekstra, and Rev. John DeJong.

A 1949 scouting mission to the Rocky Mountain House area of Alberta turned up a dilapidated house and farm for sale.

The group discusses settlement possibilities with a farmer in northern Alberta.

Members of the group walk across a plowed field. The road had come to an abrupt end.

used clothing. Their wives usually assisted with the distribution.

Mrs. John Gritter, one of those wives in the late 1940s, whose husband ministered in the Aylmer, Ontario, area, wrote once: "She searches through the boxes, finds underwear for this one, a coat or dress for that one, and socks or shoes for another. Hearts are made glad and the Lord is thanked for the evidence of Christian thoughtfulness. Just two days ago, I had occasion to gladden a family with a donated quilt. The mother was ill, but had given one of her blankets to her little fellow, who cried at night because he was cold. I had taken that quilt just in case someone should need it, so I went to the car and brought it in. The mother looked as if it was an answer from Heaven. The next day, when we visited her, she said: '*Hij heeft vannacht lekker warm geslapen.*' " (He finally had a good night's rest in a warm bed.)

In The Netherlands, one of the emigrant's best friends was an amiable, fatherly figure who used to be head of the Christian junior agricultural school in Hoogeveen, Drenthe. G.W. Kaemingk, a member of the governing board of the *Christelijke Emigratie Centrale*, went out of his way to counsel applicants, drawing on his wide knowledge of life in Canada, Australia, Brazil, and South Africa.

When this advocate of emigration who called a spade a spade made one of his visits to Canada, a chronicler wrote: "He wasn't afraid to disagree with opinions held by his colleagues and his own board. He dared to plant fifty families as a new colony in faraway Brazil and visit them later despite the warning from someone that 'they'll murder you.' They didn't kill him. Accompanied by Mrs. Kaemingk, he was received as their father and priest."

John Visser, who came to Canada in 1948 as a representative of *Stichting Landverhuizing Nederland*, the quasi-governmental umbrella organization for the emigration movement, traveled almost continuously throughout Western Canada. He accompanied immigrant trains from Thunder Bay, Ontario (then Fort William and Port Arthur), or Winnipeg, Manitoba, to points west, and he visited immigrants across that vast region, often in very isolated places. The Dutch embassy in Ottawa often gave him names of people, mostly Roman Catholics, who

John Visser of Stichting Landverhuizing Nederland *(left) meets A. DeJong, fieldman in British Columbia, in Vancouver in 1948. Below: Bernard Nieboer, fieldman in Alberta, visiting a band of native Canadians near the Athabasca River north of Edmonton, and Nieboer today with his wife Mary at home in Iron Springs, Alberta.*

Christian Reformed Church

Uitgegeven door
De Commissie voor Inwendige Zending en de
Immigratie-commissie voor Canada
van de Christian Reformed Church

*The denominations
distributed pamphlets to
emigrants.*

needed assistance or special attention.

Visser, now of Elmhurst, Illinois, stayed in the job until mid-1949, when he and his wife concluded that he had been away from home too long. So he began to farm on a sharecropping basis. But he had been in his immigration post long enough to know how difficult life could be for the early settlers of the West.

He remembers being notified of a Roman Catholic family from Noord-Brabant—mother, father, and eleven young children—which had been granted a visa on the assumption that a sponsor could be found. Soon they would be arriving by train in Winnipeg.

"It was just impossible to find a farmer willing to accept such a large family. As the time came closer, I made a quick trip to Regina, Saskatchewan. I had been summoned there one time by the minister of

agriculture, who asked me why his province did not get as many immigrants as Alberta and British Columbia did. I thought that this would be a good time to see him and find a place for this family. After I explained my difficulty, he told me not to worry; I could just send them over. I didn't want to question a person as important as the minister of agriculture; much relieved, I just waited for the family to arrive in Winnipeg. When that day came, I found a mother with eleven children, each as neat as a pin. Anyone knowing the conditions on those old immigrant trains will know how utterly impossible this seemed to me. The father, who didn't seem to be worried about anything, was smoking good Dutch cigars. It turned out that he was a horse dealer. Before we stepped on the train to Regina, I telegraphed ahead to the Red Cross, asking that lodging for the family be arranged. Representatives were waiting at the station when we arrived there late the next evening, and they put the family up in a good hotel. I found out that the minister of agriculture had kept his word; the family was to take a train the next morning to Swift Current, Saskatchewan, where the government was working on an irrigation project. I went along, and nearly fainted when I saw the place where they had to live, about a mile from town. Again I heard no complaints—only appreciation for what I had done for them. The mother, who was expecting again, was totally exhausted. I still do not know how she managed to keep all her children so spotless. Anyway, I received a letter two months later, saying they had decided to go to relatives in Ontario. I was not surprised."

One day, Ottawa gave Visser the name and address of a member of the British Columbia legislature, a native Netherlander, with the suggestion that he find out whether this person could be of assistance to immigrants. While traveling home from a visit to the Vancouver area, he decided to look the man up.

"I looked at the map, and it seemed simple. The town was on the Arrow lakes, about halfway between Revelstoke and Nelson. I found out that CPR steamers traveled the lakes and that I could use my free rail pass on them. From Revelstoke, I took a local train to get to the place where I could board a boat, one of the rear-paddle-wheel type. I boarded on a Friday night. The sleeping accommodations were excellent and the meals were sumptuous. We traveled on the long, narrow lakes all day Saturday, making stops on both shores to take on passengers and cargo. All this took much time; nobody seemed in a hurry. In the evening, we arrived at Nakusp, and the passengers were told to disembark; the boat would not go on until Monday morning. I found a hotel and spent Sunday there. The crew took the boat out on the lake and went fishing. I was only fifteen miles from my destination, but I had no other way of getting there."

When the boat finally stopped at the legislator's home town on Monday, Visser heard disappointing news: the man he wanted to see was at his office in Victoria. Determined that the trip not be a waste of time, he talked at length with some of the local people and took in the surroundings.

"Here was a narrow valley, two or three miles wide and maybe ten miles long, with the lake on one side and high mountains on the other. There was only one road. The people were Hollanders, and I believe all of them had come from the city; among them were a locksmith and a streetcar conductor from Amsterdam. They had been there some twenty years, dumped by the CPR to hack their living out of a wilderness. To their credit, they had survived, and owned small farms and livestock. After the war, they had managed to get a cheese-maker from Holland to run a small cheese factory for them. I took the next boat back. When I got to Revelstoke, nearly a week had elapsed. I reported on this visit, but never felt free to direct new immigrants there."

Visser also recalls a memorable train trip.

"On the way from Edmonton to Vancouver with the CNR, I wanted to stop over at a lumber camp in the mountains to see a young couple. Ottawa was concerned and wanted to know how they were making out. Only local trains stopped there, so I planned to take the one from Kamloops to Vancouver. I would spend the night at the camp and take the following day's train back out. It would bring me to Vancouver on Saturday, and I would spend Sunday there with Mr. De Jong, a fieldman in British Columbia for the Christian Reformed Church. I asked for the local train in Kamloops, and I was told where to board. I was early, so I made myself comfortable and started reading. The train left on time, and I felt things were just going fine—until the conductor came to check the tickets. I showed my pass and told him I was going to Vancouver. 'I've got bad news for you,' he

Real Heroes

The full-time and part-time fieldmen appointed by the various denominations took on a difficult job. They bore the brunt of frustrated criticism when people blamed them for poor placements. Even today, some immigrants cling to the belief that the fieldmen pocketed money in return for finding someone a good house or a good employer. Not all criticism can be dismissed outright, of course, but a few faults or mistakes cannot detract from the superb work done by most of the fieldmen, working under difficult conditions. Harry Cunliffe of Ottawa, Canada's chief immigration official in The Hague for a number of years, offers this comment: "The fieldmen should be the real heroes of this book. Coping so successfully, and simultaneously, with Canadian and Dutch officialdom, Canadian farmers, their own support groups, and the newly-arrived immigrants and their families as well, could not have been an easy task."

said. 'We're going to Edmonton.' Boy, I was upset. I told him I didn't want to go that way. 'Okay,' he said, 'we'll let you off right here.' The train stopped and I got off. I was ten miles from Kamloops. I soon came to a road, and got a ride with a Japanese market gardener back to the station. There I learned that two trains had been sitting back to back and that I had stepped into the last coach of the train to Edmonton. My troubles weren't over yet. The Vancouver train had left and I was stranded, facing a weekend in the wilderness. I went to the station-master and convinced him that I was rather important—I showed my pass—and that my mission bore real consequences. Well, he found out that a freight train was leaving shortly. Although it was against regulations, he convinced the engineer that I could travel in the caboose. At the lumber camp, the train was slowed down enough to enable me to jump off safely. I found the young couple was doing really well. They gave me a bed for the night and a good breakfast in the morning."

Visser concludes: "Personally, I like Western Canada very much—even more than I do Ontario. There are good people there."

Like many others, Visser has profound respect for Bernard Nieboer, and for his persuasiveness. "It's been said that Nieboer could sell refrigerators to Eskimos, and I believe he could."

Martin DeVos, a fieldman in Ontario in the early 1950s for the Reformed Church, knew what the immigrants were talking about when they came to him with complaints about inadequate housing and low wages. He had gone through all that himself after he and his young wife had arrived in New York City aboard the *Veendam* in March, 1949. He had started working for a vegetable grower in the Burlington area for $22.50 a week.

"A free house was included," he says, "but it was just a shack. Indians had lived in it for a number of years. What a mess! You could see daylight through the walls."

He left the farm when an agreement couldn't be reached on the second year's wages. He figured he needed more money, especially after his first child was born in February. But the farmer thought otherwise. DeVos, in his mid-twenties, then worked for a while in Copetown and Waterdown before Rev. Harri Zegerius asked him to become a fieldman.

"Local immigration committees had been set up to look after the new arrivals and their problems," says DeVos. "But in the early 1950s, there was such a flood of immigrants that the work became too much for volunteers. It was apparent that full-time help was required. Why was I selected? I don't really know. Maybe it was because I had organized a young people's group and was active in other church work."

He was on the road much of the week, quite often until late at night. His wife and child didn't see too much of him. There was lots to keep him on the go: staying in touch with immigration officials in Toronto, Niagara Falls, and Fort Erie, passing on information to farmers about families who wanted to come to Canada, checking out the housing for immigrants, assisting the immigrants when they arrived, and being an ombudsman to sort out problems between employee and employer.

"There was always something. People lost their baggage, and it would be up to me to track it down. And when it finally arrived at the station, I was the one who had to get it. When people got sick, I sometimes had to arrange for a doctor. Not only that, I had to act as interpreter, translating personal questions and answers. When I worked in the Prescott area, I was asked to translate when a young Dutch immigrant was picked up at the border with a bag full of pornographic material he had acquired in the United States. His room was searched and it was full of all kinds of smut, something that

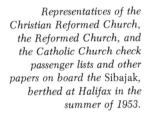

Representatives of the Christian Reformed Church, the Reformed Church, and the Catholic Church check passenger lists and other papers on board the Sibajak, *berthed at Halifax in the summer of 1953.*

was really frowned upon in those days. Arrangements had to be made to send the fellow back to Holland."

An immigrant at Gananoque, near Kingston, complained that he had been promised good accommodation, but had landed in a shack instead. His wife, who had lived in a decent place in The Netherlands, couldn't get used to this backward step and was crying her heart out. DeVos, knowing there was nothing he could do to make things right on that farm, asked the woman: "How long will it take you to pack?"

"Ten minutes," she replied.

He then found her husband in the barn, and told him: "Go in the house and help your wife pack. I'm taking you out of here. I'll get another job for you." The farmer was beside himself with rage when told that his hired hand would be leaving within minutes. Naturally, he blamed DeVos for this development.

"The farmers had legitimate complaints too. There was more than one case of a farmer discovering to his dismay that his employee didn't even know how to milk a cow by hand. These immigrants had lied through their teeth to get into Canada, telling the authorities they were qualified farmers when in fact they were not. In these cases, I was on the firing line. I had no alternative but to take the person away and bring the farmer another one."

It wasn't unusual to see DeVos at the train station in Brockville at 3:30 or 4:30 a.m. to pick up new arrivals. Sometimes there were six or seven families to take care of. He had instructions from the Reformed Church to help everyone, regardless of their church affiliation. Roman Catholics and non-churched people often slept at his house, or were put up temporarily in sparsely-furnished homes the church had rented specifically for that purpose. When accommodation was in short supply, other Dutch immigrants opened their doors.

"I have fond memories of how everyone was so anxious to help each other. I haven't experienced that since. I guess times have changed. What people did for each other then was just tremendous."

He often conducted church services on Sundays, either in someone's home or in rented quarters. Preaching meant considerable preparation in the few spare hours he could call his own. There was no extra pay for this. It was considered part of the mission work to which a fieldman had committed himself.

"The pay wasn't much—$100 a month plus mileage and expenses. A lot of people were under the impression that a fieldman made a lot of money. The story got around that we got $25 for every person we placed. Some even think that today. Well, it's not true. When I was a fieldman, I had a hard time making ends meet. My wife had saved up $100 in a drawer when Rev. Zegerius asked me to take on the task. Three years later, we were $1,400 in debt. Having regarded the job as a calling, I had stuck it out. But after three years, I couldn't take it any more."

Still, he has pleasant memories of those years. He knows that he and the other fieldmen provided an invaluable service, and one that has not been forgotten.

Jan Heersink (left) of the Reformed Church and Herman Lam, fieldman of the Christian Reformed Church in Nova Scotia, wait together to meet an immigrant boat in Halifax.

"A few years ago, I was flying back to Holland. I started talking with the fellow in the seat next to me, and he mentioned that he had arrived in Whitby in 1951. I asked him: 'Who met you?' he said: 'Mr. DeVos, a fieldman. He did so much for me then, I'm still grateful.' I turned toward him, extended my hand, and said: 'Let me shake your hand. I'm glad to meet you again.' "

In 1952, when the influx of immigrants peaked, Rimmer Tjalsma, another fieldman of the Reformed Church, made the thirty-six-hour train trip to Halifax once a week to greet new immigrants, particularly those who had been allowed into Canada without a sponsor. His job was to lead these people to the Whitby, Ontario, area, where jobs were waiting and where efforts were under way to establish a church.

He had put an ad in the local newspaper, asking for jobs on farms or in trades. By that time, Canada had relaxed its rules concerning sponsorship and had opened its doors to non-agriculturalists as well.

The trip to Halifax would have been extremely boring had it not been for the company of friends and co-workers—John VanderVliet and John Vellinga, for example. These men, traveling with free passes supplied by the railway, always had a lot to talk about.

But they didn't see much of each other on the way back. They had their hands full looking after the hundreds of weary, irritable, excited, apprehensive immigrants crammed into the train for the next leg of their journey. Somebody had to make sure they got out at the right stop.

"The tags which every immigrant wore made things simpler," says Tjalsma. "When the conductor announced the next stop, I went up and down the aisle to alert those who had to get out. Sometimes that was at three o'clock in the morning. Then the station would be locked, and there would be nobody waiting to pick up the immigrant family. The conductor would unlock the door with a master key and say adieu. The train would be under way within five minutes, leaving the family behind in the dark. The people would have to wait until the station master arrived at seven o'clock, read their tags, and called their sponsor. I always felt sorry for the ones who received this kind of reception."

It was close to midnight when a train carrying a young couple from Nova Scotia pulled into the station at Hamilton. They were welcomed by officials of the Reformed Church, including Neil Eelman, a lay preacher, who had been responsible for steering them to southern Ontario. They all went to the home of Rev. Harri Zegerius and bedded down for a restful sleep.

But what a night it turned out to be!

"At four a.m., instead of the soft breathing of exhausted travelers, we heard a great rumble and stomping upstairs," recalls the minister. "Oh my, a baby was about to be born. Mr. Eelman

Neil Eelman (right) talks over immigration business with Jan Heersink in the Reformed Church office.

Mr. and Mrs. John Langeraap and their children near Dunnville, Ontario. The Langeraaps opened their home to many newcomers.

and I stepped into our clothes and rushed the couple to a hospital on the mountain. We got there on time. A fine baby daughter was born."

Not everything went smoothly, however. Eelman, still single, was so excited that he slammed the door of his Jeep shut and left the keys inside.

"How we struggled on that icy-cold night to get that vehicle open. Fortunately, a policeman came along to help before we froze to death. Then back to Beulah Avenue for some much-needed sleep."

There's more to the story. Twenty-five years later, in 1975, the couple invited Rev. Zegerius and his wife to dinner. The immigrant, Jaap, had farmed south of Hamilton and had worked in a gypsum mine to make some extra cash. After selling the farm, they had built a fine ranch-style home on some acreage where he and his wife now lived comfortably in semi-retirement.

"The startling surprise of it all was this: here, at the dinner, was the daughter who was almost born at our house. And with her was her own little family, including a baby daughter born just two weeks previously. There was lots of food, talk, and laughter—and maybe a tear in remembrance."

One Sunday morning, Christopher Steenhof, a fieldman of the Christian Reformed Church in the Toronto area, arrived at the church building on Glen Forest Road with thirty-five immigrants in tow. For a moment, the subdued,

uncertain group stood on the path in the churchyard and listened. They heard people singing—in Dutch. For the first time since their arrival at Union Station, they smiled.

Steenhof led them into the church hall, and explained that he had nowhere to put them. The immigrant reception homes were packed, and all other available accommodation was full. But that's why he had brought them to church.

Before Toronto folk sat down to their Sunday dinner, the thirty-five immigrants had found temporary homes in the city. Said one churchgoer as he welcomed a family of four: "Before we met, I was singing a hymn of thanksgiving for our new life in Canada. This is one time I can show my thanks in a practical way."

Rev. John Van Harmelen was awakened at 1 a.m. one night by a telephone call from the station master in Brampton, Ontario. A family was waiting to be picked up—by anybody. He assumed they were Dutch because the surname began with the letters *Van.*

"I picked them up," says the minister. "I told them: 'Let's go to bed first, and we'll talk in the morning.' When we sat down for breakfast, I noticed that they crossed themselves. Somewhat surprised, I asked: 'Are you Roman Catholic?' They were."

When breakfast was finished, he phoned the priest in town.

"The first thing he said was: 'Ask them how much money they have with them.' I did, and they said there was only $5 or so left. When I conveyed this to the priest, he said: 'You'd better take care of them, John.' I couldn't believe it. I turned to the family and said: 'You are Dutch and I am Dutch and I am going to help you. Today we're going to look for a house.' "

They found one for $45 a month. The minister paid the advance, knowing he'd be repaid in due time. The next day, he got the man a job with a flower grower.

"The family came to church regularly. They put their offerings in an envelope, like most other people. Yet I sensed that they didn't feel at home. One day, the man came to me and said: 'Would you mind if we went back to the Catholic church? Mother wrote that we can't stay away from there just because of one rotten priest. She is right. We can't.' "

Rev. Van Harmelen didn't feel sad when the family left. He knew that he had gone

Temporary Accommodation Allowed Some Breathin

Many immigrants, mostly non-farmers, found temporary lodging in houses rented by the churches.

The Reformed Church ran an immigration house at Winona, near Hamilton, Ontario. The rent was $2 a week per room for those able to pay. For those with nothing to spare, the fee was waived. When a reasonable length of time had elapsed, the immigrant's rent was doubled. This was merely to prod him into finding his own accommodation and thus

A barn near Burlington, Ontario, and a house in Chatham, Ontario, provided temporary accommodation for immigrants.

make room for other newcomers.

One family found a house and employment, packed their belongings in the fieldman's car, and then said goodbye to the other immigrants left behind. As they drove off, the fieldman heard weeping from the back seat and murmurs of "We'll never forget this."

When John Langeraap and his family moved out of the large farmhouse near Dunnville that had sheltered so many immigrant families, it was turned into a reception center. The owner, who lived in a new house next door, didn't mind. The house was in use, somebody paid the rent, and a useful service was provided.

"It became a shelter for sometimes two or three families at a time," says Rev. Harri Zegerius. "For much of the year, I brought a family there now and then."

Rev. W.W.J. VanOene of the Canadian Reformed Churches makes references in his book, *Inheritance Preserved*, to an immigrant hostel near Burlington, Ontario. The local newspaper of May 5, 1960, wrote: "A large barn was acquired on Utter's farm, situated on the Guelph Line, just below No. 5 Highway. This barn has been converted in a very workmanlike manner into apartments. Almost ten immigrant families stay there for $29 a month for varying periods of time."

The Christian Reformed Church also operated a number of reception centers. In early 1952, Christopher Steenhof, fieldman of the Christian Reformed Church, presented a glowing report about a ten-room house in Weston, Ontario, that was being rented by the local immigration society for $125 a month. Other centers were set up in areas where the housing shortage was acute.

In Vancouver, the Christian Reformed

out of his way to help them, and he knew that they were happy.

Immigrant John Langeraap had known difficult times. He came to Canada in the spring of 1948 aboard the *Tabinta*, and was placed with a farmer in the Tilbury, Ontario, area. The placement was a shock: there wasn't even a house for the family. Mother, father and two children had to share one bedroom in the farmer's house. It held only a single bed and a cot. Not only that, the food was terrible. Says Mrs. Langeraap, now of St. Catharines, Ontario: "During the war, we never suffered hunger. But in this country of plenty, we were given only enough to survive."

The experience made the couple determined to help those who would come after them. They knew that a little compassion

Space

Church established and operated an immigration house in an older section of town near the waterfront. Families and single people could board there for $1 a day until, either on their own or with a fieldman's help, they had found a job and another place to stay. Sometimes that took more than a week.

They were looked after by Mrs. Magdalene Ydenberg (her first husband, surnamed Selles, died in 1963), formerly of Kampen, Overijssel, who had emigrated in 1951. She prepared meals for as many as five families at a time, and some of them with ten or more children. She kept the place tidy, listened to problems, and gave advice. And sometimes she even played the part of fieldman, suggesting to people where they might look for a job.

"I sometimes felt like a real mother," she recalls. Not that she wasn't one already. She and her husband had four children of their own. The family lived in the rooming house free of charge in exchange for Mrs. Ydenberg's work. Her husband, who also had a day job, helped out at night. He even built little rooms in the basement for the bachelors.

"We began this work in February, 1952," says Mrs. Ydenberg. "It was a dirty house until ladies from the church cleaned it. They also donated mattresses, forks, knives, plates, and so on. It was terrific to see how people put themselves out in those days to help others. The old house wasn't in a nice section of the city. In a way, that was a good thing. Sometimes there were two dozen children who wanted to play outside. I'm sure there would have been complaints if the house had been on a nice street."

When there was room, the fieldman also brought to the house people who did not belong to the Christian Reformed Church. "I took them to church on Sundays," says Mrs. Ydenberg. "It was my small contribution to the evangelical program. Oh, there were so many things that happened during the five years or so that we ran the house. Now I feel sorry that I didn't keep a diary. I was too busy, I guess. I could have written interesting stories about the hundreds of families who passed through the door. Now I've forgotten most of their names . . ."

Other temporary homes for immigrants: at top, the former Langeraap farmhouse near Dunnville, Ontario; at left, a house in Winona, Ontario.

and a helping hand could go a long way in making newcomers feel at home. The opportunity finally came when they settled on a rented farm in the Dunnville area.

"In the three years we stayed there, my husband and I sponsored around one hundred and fifty families. That was a busy period for us. We looked after a lot of people. I'm sure I wouldn't recognize many of them if we crossed paths. Yes, we had to count our pennies in those days. Fortunately, we always had enough to eat."

The Langeraaps often traveled to the train stations in Dunnville and Hamilton to meet the people they had sponsored.

"We had to look closely and ask: 'Are you so and so?' The people all looked lost. You could see the relief on their faces when they met someone who would give them food, a place to sleep, and help in looking for a job."

One immigrant family came prepared to bed down in the woods. They intended to roll out sleeping bags between the trees and huddle closely for warmth. To their surprise, they were able to enjoy the comforts of a bedroom.

"In my childhood, I never knew a time when there weren't a lot of strangers around our table," recalls Gaye, Langeraap's oldest daughter. "Even at Christmas and New Year's, we were never alone as Mom, Dad, and the kids. Sometimes there were three or four families. Well, we peeled a few extra potatoes and cleaned a few more beans. Nothing fancy. There was always something for everyone."

It's a fact, though, that the Langeraaps—and there were others like them throughout Canada—sacrificed a lot to help total strangers.

"I remember that my mother wanted a new dress so desperately. She was tired of patching up the ones she had. But Dad said there was no money for a new dress. He

A Volunteer Army Was Always Ready to Receive the Newcomers

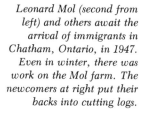

Leonard Mol (second from left) and others await the arrival of immigrants in Chatham, Ontario, in 1947. Even in winter, there was work on the Mol farm. The newcomers at right put their backs into cutting logs.

A delegation of Dutch people came to the station in Winnipeg to give a new family a hearty welcome. There were smiles and handshakes. But there was also some bad news: the sponsor had backed out and no immediate replacement had been found. The family had no place to go.

Fieldman Jacob DeJong of the Christian Reformed Church recalls: "We asked: Who could take them home and give them lodging for a few days? Nobody answered. So then I told the family—father, mother, and three small children—that they could stay with me. We sure had a house full for

about two weeks. I had six children of my own, and my place wasn't that big."

Fortunately for the newcomers, not everyone kept their doors closed. In Chatham, Ontario, for example, a small volunteer army stood ready to lend assistance. Among them were such stalwarts as Peter Lugtigheid, John Vellinga, Leonard Mol, and his sons, Marinus and Stanley.

The Mols had come to Canada in 1939, just before the outbreak of the war. When the immigrants began to arrive in 1947, they were farming their own three hun-

needed the little bit that was left over every month for helping the immigrants. You know, when no car was available for visiting the people, he went with the tractor. When there was not enough bread, he thought nothing of killing a pig . . ."

Mrs. Langeraap, formerly of IJlst, Friesland, would like to forget her experiences with one family. But she can't.

"It was a difficult case. A family with four children first went to Winnipeg. Then they returned to Ontario. No work. They ended up at the Salvation Army, which got them in touch with Rev. Zegerius. He came to us: 'Would you mind looking after them for the time being?' Well, we did so, and were reimbursed $10 a week by the Reformed Church It wasn't a pleasant time. The people were so despondent that they became ill."

When the Salvation Army had called Rev. Zegerius, he had learned that the family hadn't eaten for two days. Their

An information pamphlet was given to Roman Catholic immigrants when they arrived in Vancouver.

dred acres. By August, they had four young immigrant men in their employ, including three brothers from Slootdorp, Noord-Holland.

A reporter from the United States, who visited the farm, wrote later: "Sometimes there are visitors in the evening—boys and girls of Dutch background from the district. They sit on the grass and are served cake and lemonade. They sing Dutch songs, and some try a bit of flirting. Mother Mol is a firm chaperone and tells the visitors when it's time to go home. After all, work starts again at six in the morning."

The Mols were often in the thick of things when the immigrant trains pulled into the station at Chatham.

"Many people came and went," says Marinus, now of Brampton, Ontario. "Quite a few needed help, and it was mostly volunteer help. For example, transportation was given to anyone who wanted to go to church on Sunday. Members of our church picked up people here and there with their cars. Peter Lugtigheid, my brother Stanley, and I also used our own stake trucks. To make sure no one was left stranded, a schedule was drawn up. This all took a bit of organizing, but everything went smoothly."

Usually at their own expense the Mols and others of the local immigration society also made exploratory trips to areas which might be suitable for settlement. One such trip in 1949 took them to the Fort Frances-Rainy River area of Northern Ontario, where arable land was selling for $10 an acre.

"My father and other persons also made an extensive trip to the Maritime provinces in the early 1950s for the same purpose," says Marinus.

On their way to Rainy River, Ontario, and waiting for a ferry, Harry Vellinga and Stanley Mol talk with a native Canadian.

crate with furniture and other belongings stood unclaimed in Aylmer, and officials were making all kinds of threatening noises.

"I took a flat-bed truck and went to Aylmer by myself to get the *kist*," he says. "I paid $100 out of my pocket, loaded the thing, and took it to the Langeraaps. There it stood outside, unopened. I guess that family really wanted to go back to Holland."

After ten weeks, they did go back, with the assistance of the Canadian government.

A list kept for volunteer drivers of the Christian Reformed Church in Chatham, Ontario.

There were different ways in which people extended a helping hand. The Langeraaps weren't the only ones who sponsored other immigrants. Bert Van Loon, a tobacco farmer near Vittoria, Ontario, who emigrated to Canada in 1927, signed for some twenty-five families, including one from Leiden, Zuid-Holland, with eighteen members. Dozens of other prewar immigrants did the same thing.

In Stoney Creek, Ontario, immigrant Dr. H.L. Van Vierssen Trip set up a maternity clinic.

"There were many Dutch immigrants in that area," says his wife. "However, about the only time they needed a doctor was for childbirth. So we started a maternity clinic in our residence, especially for immigrants who were scared of the Canadian methods or had no money. In ten years, some two hundred babies were born at our place. The fee was $75—for pre- and post-natal care and confinement."

Immigrants joined together to set up medical plans, and credit associations. The Canadian-Netherlands Immigration Council came into being, providing a united voice to the bureaucrats and new programs to benefit newcomers (more on that in the next chapter).

In Vancouver, some newcomers set up the Catholic Netherlands Organization in the early 1950s to provide information, help, and fellowship. A big city could be a very lonely place, especially for those who didn't speak the language and found their environment strange. The CNO was given advance notice that a certain family or single person would be arriving at the station. Then they ensured that someone would be on hand to extend a welcome, offer assistance in finding a job and housing, and provide information on further services available through church and government agencies.

"We encouraged the newcomers to settle in their neighborhood parish and not form a Dutch community," says Leo Hoens, one of the organizers of the CNO. "They could still have a lot of contact with the Dutch. There were a number of Dutch priests around the city, including one who was specifically assigned to assist the Dutch immigrants. We made available Roman Catholic literature in the Dutch language, and we organized social evenings."

One day in 1979, two hundred people, smiling and bubbling with pleasantries, gathered at John VanderHeyden's farm, two miles from Picture Butte, Alberta. They all seemed to know each other. It

Community Spirit

There were many examples of immigrants helping immigrants. Someone in need or difficulty often received a lot of kindness. Community spirit was alive and well.

Mr. and Mrs. George Keep of Brampton, Ontario, will never forget the army of volunteer workers from Holland Marsh who marched to their vegetable fields when illness struck the family.

"In the fall of 1958, two years after we started our own ten-acre operation, my husband came down with a bad case of pneumonia," says Mrs. Keep. "Many volunteers helped us to get the crop out of the ground. In 1961, my husband got tuberculosis, and was admitted to a sanatorium, where he stayed for eight months. Again, a big group of people came over to get the potatoes out and to look after things. We sure appreciated that."

Direction in British Columbia

Fieldman A. DeJong (with hat) of the Christian Reformed Church meets immigrant Peter Heida at the train station in Vancouver in 1958.

Enjoying the New Life

One of the young men sponsored by Leonard Mol was William Grin, formerly of Broek op Langendijk, Noord-Holland. He was one of three emigrants aboard the freighter Leerdam which sailed from Antwerp, Belgium, to New York City in May, 1947. This old hangar was his first home in Canada. After working in the tobacco harvest in 1948, he returned to Holland to marry his sweetheart. They settled in Chatham, Ontario, in early 1949. Grin says: "In Holland, I had gotten fed up with bureaucracy and the lack of elbow room. I looked forward to starting a new life with unlimited horizons. I have been delighted with Canada since day one."

looked like a happy reunion—which it was in a way.

These people had come to honor the person who, more than anyone else, had helped them through the difficult early times of their immigration, providing spiritual strength, sound counsel, and a helping hand. Many of them were in Canada because he had advised them to emigrate. They loved him for it.

At the center of all the attention was

Rev. Frans Verhagen, a Roman Catholic priest, who was about to return to The Netherlands. But before his departure, the people wanted to show their profound respect and gratitude for all his work in helping Roman Catholics get settled in Alberta.

"We all loved him," says Vander-Heyden, the host. "He was always the optimist. When the going got rough, he would encourage us to continue on. He

Above: Rev. Frans Verhagen is presented with a cake at the farewell party in 1979. Right: Verhagen poses with a bride and groom after conducting a wedding ceremony in Coaldale, Alberta, in 1955.

could always see a brighter future. And he was right. Yes, he was a real support for the people here."

As a young man in Noord-Brabant, VanderHeyden had heard Father Verhagen advocate emigration to Canada at meetings of the *Noordbrabantse Christelijke Boerenbond* (N.C.B.), a Catholic organization. The priest, adviser for the group in Helmont, could easily see that many of his young charges would never realize their dream of owning their own farm unless they moved away from the congestion and the shortage of land in The Netherlands. His message was simple: seek your future elsewhere, and take your beliefs with you.

Father Verhagen, a farmer's son himself, began to be concerned about the plight of the young farmers shortly after the war. He began to press for the establishment of a *Pater van den Elsen Instituut*, named after the founder of the N.C.B.

"I had discovered that the Nazis had built five dwellings in the Peel area for the retraining of young Dutch farmers who were to be settled in the Ukraine, then occupied by the Germans. My proposal was to use these facilities to train young farmers who wanted to emigrate to Canada and to establish an agricultural trades school under the direction of the brothers from Heythuisen. It was clear that many of the boys could never become farmers. I felt that the psychological distance between farming and a factory job was just too great. That's why I envisaged a program that would turn a farmer into a tradesman, such as a carpenter or a mason." The priest insisted that prospective emigrants be taught the English language and the operation of farm machines, including milking machines, which were in common use in Canada. His proposal, however, ran into stumbling blocks. Some officials in the church, particularly those in the *Katholieke Nederlandse Boeren en Tuindersbond* (K.N.T.B.), an agricultural organization, had their eyes on Brazil and France, which were predominantly Catholic. In fact, in southern France a castle with some surrounding land had been purchased for Dutch farmers to use. This plan never really succeeded because the French authorities didn't co-operate. Brazil was more receptive. Many farmers from Noord-Brabant and Limburg eventually settled in Hollambra, a Dutch colony in Brazil.

Despite the setbacks, Father Verhagen continued to talk about Canada. He held sessions for prospective emigrants once a month at Hotel de Kroon in Gemert. Following mass, discussions took place on all aspects of life in Canada. The Protestant-led *Christelijke Emigratie Centrale* was eager to share its experiences. English lessons were also offered. Before long, language courses were being conducted in communities throughout Noord-Brabant.

In 1947, the year Canada opened its doors, the Catholics finally organized their own emigration society. Its first and only director, Dr. Jos Van Campen, recalled once: "When I began my work in The Hague, there was a stack of information on Brazil on one side of my desk and another stack of information on France on the other side. And between these stacks I kept on talking to farmers who wanted to go to Canada."

A number of priests followed close on the heels of the first immigrants. Their task wasn't easy. Recalls Rev. Alphons VanderVorst of Ottawa: "When I arrived in Canada in 1948, no special care was given to the Dutch, except perhaps by the Capuchin Fathers in Blenheim, Ontario. All one could do in those days was give a helping hand, because there was not yet any organization to fall back on."

Later on, a representative of the Catholic church, Mgr. Hanssen, assistant bishop of Roermond, was sent on a scouting mission to Canada.

Roman Catholic immigrants sit on the grass in Dundas, Ontario for a religious service. Events organized by the Catholic Netherlands Organization included games and a picnic.

Multicultural History Society of Ontario

"As soon as he came back, he came to Gemert, where I was still the curate," says Father Verhagen. "He talked a mile a minute about his trip. He urged me to go to Canada to set up a good Canadian Catholic organization for the reception of young farmers from The Netherlands. I replied that I would love to go, provided there were no objections from my superiors who were afraid that The Netherlands might suffer a shortage of priests."

The *Groote Beer* dropped him off at Halifax where his tour of the vast country began. In Nova Scotia, he met many immigrants who had graduated from his orientation courses. Some had bought farms with the aid of low-cost loans from the Nova Scotia Land Settlement Board and the extension department of the Catholic university at Antigonish. In the following weeks, as he traveled inland and then on to the Pacific coast, he saw other examples of immigrants being helped, in some places by Dutch priests. Where no organized help existed, he urged prewar immigrants and priests of local parishes to arrange for sponsors and to keep in touch with new arrivals.

After completing his exploratory mission, Father Verhagen went to Calgary to work for the Catholic immigration society. He visited the parishes in the diocese, saw the possibilities for the settlement of large families, and evolved a plan whereby two members of each parish, usually a man from the Holy Name Society and a woman from the Catholic Women's League, would look after local immigration matters. In addition, offices were set up in Calgary, Lethbridge, and Medicine Hat. There was even a monthly publication for the settlers, called *Onze Toekomst.*

Father Verhagen worked out of Coaldale, where he had been posted at the end of 1952. He recalls: "It was hard work in those days." But as a result of that hard work, thousands of Dutch Catholic immigrants settled in Alberta.

He was called back to The Netherlands in 1958, and oversaw the building of a church in a new subdivision in Tilburg. However, his heart was still in Canada. At his request, he returned to Alberta to resume his work among the immigrants. Today, after a few visits back and forth, he's back in The Netherlands.

"There's nothing here for old priests," says his brother, William, who settled in Alberta in 1954. "So he went back to Holland, and is living now with one hundred others in a priests' home in Nijmegen. In the past few years, he's had some medical problems, but he's very well looked after. I'm sure, though, that his thoughts are often still in Canada."

And then there were To and Michel Van Gendt, who moved away from the city of Utrecht in 1955, settled in Hamilton, Ontario, and opened their home to hundreds of immigrants who had nowhere else to go.

"Shortly after we arrived in Canada," says Van Gendt, "we saw that something was wrong. The Reformed churches were well organized in looking after their people. But it was a different story for the Catholics. Quite a number of immigrants were not sponsored, and they had nowhere to go. They were just lost."

The couple told the Dutch consulate in Toronto that they wanted to help. As a result, they were regularly given lists showing the names of emigrants and the dates of their arrival. They made sure they were at the station, often waiting until after midnight.

"We always took all the people home and gave them coffee and sandwiches while we figured out what to do with them," says Mrs. Van Gendt. "Sometimes we phoned friends to arrange accommodation. But we often had as many as

Michel VanGendt opened his door to newcomers.

twenty people at our house at night, sleeping on mattresses and cots in the hallways."

Van Gendt charged $1 a day for adults and fifty cents for children to cover the cost of food, lodging, and extra services such as washing clothes. After all, he earned only a laborer's wages.

After eight or nine years of providing shelter, the couple still always made sure that sandwiches were ready and a bath was running for the children, but the overnight stay was in a hotel that charged $6 a night.

"We helped the immigrants find work," says Van Gendt, now of Dundas, Ontario. "We also gave them advice about the new country, especially the do's and don'ts of buying insurance. People borrowed bedding and kitchen utensils until they could get their own. I lent out money—and sometimes didn't get it back."

In 1957, Van Gendt was one of the organizers of the Catholic Netherlands Organization for the Hamilton area. This group provided used furniture, sponsored dances and picnics, and arranged other special events, such as a St. Nicholas evening, all in an effort to make the newcomer feel at home.

Queen Juliana stopped at the Van Gendts' home when she toured the immigrant community in 1967. She stayed for an hour, and even made an unexpected tour of the house, because she wanted to see how an immigrant family lived. Before leaving, she commented to Mrs. Van Gendt: "You have been doing a wonderful job. You've been just like a *soldatenmoeder* (a good mother to soldiers) here. We all are proud of your work."

Jacob Prins is an important name in the annals of the history of the Dutch in Canada. As fieldman of the Christian Reformed Church for northern British Columbia, Prins directed immigrants to the Bulkley Valley, an area hardly touched before the war, but one that he was convinced was full of opportunities. Little wonder that he became known as the Father of the Bulkley Valley.

Prins used glowing terms to describe the valley to audiences in The Netherlands and Canada. In 1951, when addressing immigrants in Ladner, British Columbia, he was asked: "Can you grow potatoes there?" His answer must have been pretty convincing, for approximately twenty immigrants left Ladner for the valley.

He didn't beat around the bush either. He told people that the valley needed settlers who were not complainers, ones who were willing to work through a severe winter climate. Real pioneers were sought.

Prins screened his people. Anyone not

Queen Juliana is welcomed to the VanGendt home in Dundas, Ontario, in 1967.

considered hardy enough for the primitive conditions simply wasn't placed there. He kept a close eye on the ones he did direct to the area, making sure all their problems were looked after. He advised the settlers to start their own churches, and even read a sermon once for a small group gathered at Telkwa.

Many people of the Bulkley Valley remember Prins fondly.

John Boonstra Sr. and his family left Haulerwijk, Friesland, in 1948 and settled in the beetfields of Iron Springs, Alberta. They stayed there for two years. When Boonstra read in *De Wachter*, a Dutch-language publication for immigrants, that Thys Stad of Houston had a farm for sale, he wrote to Prins. The answer: come and have a look. During his visit, Boonstra ventured farther into the valley and bought a farm near Round Lake. On the way back to Houston, he and Prins left the train for a cup of coffee while it made a brief stop at McBride. Boonstra kept a nervous eye on the train, even getting up a couple of times. Prins, perfectly at ease, teased: "Are you afraid that it will leave without you, Boonstra?"

Earlier, Prins had placed the Fritz Buursema family in McBride. In The Netherlands, the Buursemas had learned the acreage of their host farm, and so had assumed that their landlord was quite rich. What a surprise when they were met at the train in March, 1949, by a 76-year-old man with a team of horses hitched to a flat wagon. The Buursemas arrived at a house that had not seen a woman's hand for years. They first thought that the inside walls had been tarred, but it turned out to be soot from a cracked stove and from smoking oil lamps. Some energetic scrubbing followed. The farmer com-

plained when the wash-water leaked through the floor boards and rained on his potatoes in the cellar. One of the neighbors, however, was more complimentary. When he entered the house, he asked: "How did you make this hell into heaven?"

Fritz and his wife, Riek, moved into McBride when their one-year contract with the farmer ran out. During an extremely cold spell that winter, Prins came for a visit to check up on his charges. Riek told him: "I've made your bed upstairs." But Prins replied: "Why don't I stay here by the stove? I can move these two chairs together. In the train, I sleep like that all the time."

Another immigrant who experienced Prins's persuasive ways was Siepie Beerda, now Mrs. Shirley Reitsma of Evelyn, near Smithers. She was traveling across Canada by train to her sister and brother-in-law, Sophie and Hark VanderMeulen in Smithers. In Winnipeg, she ignored advice to transfer to another train. Even in Edmonton, she didn't want to get off. Fortunately Prins was there. He told her: "Yes, I know Hark and Sophie. You can stay with my daughter here, while we make arrangements to get you to Smithers." Then she finally gave in and left the train.

A lot of the work Prins did, like the work of many other fieldmen, went unobserved. Only later did people begin to ask: "What would I have done without him?" Prins, like his colleagues, did make observations about the people he helped. He once told Mrs. Riek Buursema: "The ones who cry right away make good immigrants. It's the ones who start crying later on who don't make it."

Chapter 20

Forging a Visible Identity

Canadian-born Princess Margriet of The Netherlands and her husband, Pieter Van Vollenhoven, ride in a carriage drawn by Frisian horses to take part in a ground-breaking ceremony for the 120-bed Faith Nursing Home at the Holland Christian Homes complex in Brampton, Ontario, in October, 1983. The carriage and horses belong to Jack Botma and his daughter Shirley of Wyoming, Ontario. The princess also officially opened an exhibit of forty works from the royal collection of the Mauritshuis gallery in The Hague at the Art Gallery of Ontario in Toronto.

Forging a Visible Identity

Jan Heersink, who left his mayor's post in The Netherlands to work among the immigrants, becoming one himself, didn't like the fragmented way the interests of the newcomers were being looked after. There was nothing wrong with each church having its own organization to look after the welfare of the Dutch. But a united front, with some clout, was needed to make overtures to government authorities and to plan projects for the common good.

This need was met by the creation in 1953 of the Canadian-Netherlands Immigration Council, consisting of representatives of the Canadian Reformed Churches, the Christian Reformed Church, the Reformed Church, and the Roman Catholic Church. The Holland-America Line, whose ships continued to ferry emigrants, and the KLM, the Dutch airline whose services were becoming increasingly popular, also were represented. A lawyer sat in on the meetings.

"We began to act jointly," says Heersink, the CNIC chairman. "Everyone agreed that this was much better. The sometimes fierce competition between the churches seemed to disappear. For example, we took turns meeting the boats in Halifax. Working together, we put energy into improving things for the immigrants, often with good results."

One of the changes enabled immigrants to qualify for the government's family allowance payments on the day of their arrival, instead of having to wait for a year. Farm wages were improved. Financial support was arranged for immigrants who were involved in difficulties through no fault of their own. The matter of hospital insurance also received close attention.

The council even tried to arrange low-cost loans for immigrants. Talks were held with the two co-operative banks (the *Boerenleenbank* headquartered in Eindhoven and the *Raiffeisenbank* headquartered in Utrecht; the two merged some years ago and the name was changed to *Rabobank*) and the *Nationale Handelsbank* in The Netherlands and the Mercantile Bank of Canada. The total plan, however, was not carried out. Instead, local credit unions were established which would serve the same purpose.

CNIC members knew that many immigrants often longed to return to the Old Country for a visit, to see a loved one or a friend, to tour the familiar spots, or to stay over for Christmas and New Year's. It was also no secret that many people in The Netherlands wanted to visit Canada to see how their relatives were faring and whether all the claims made in letters were true. So an effort was launched to arrange bargain charter flights. This contributed to the establishment of *Wereld Contact*, a Netherlands-based organization which arranges group flights to Canada and other areas of Dutch settlement.

The CNIC, which began in the social aid field, eventually became an agency which sponsored emigrants and found jobs and living quarters for them. The council actively promoted emigration to Canada. Representatives addressed thousands of prospective emigrants and hundreds of students of agricultural, technical, and industrial schools in The Netherlands.

"Another big achievement of CNIC was the youth program," says Heersink. "We arranged to have a number of sons of Dutch farmers spend a year in Canada to get acquainted with the agricultural

A group of young farmers has just arrived in Halifax. Among those on hand to greet them are John VanderVliet (center) and Jan Heersink (right).

methods here, to look over the country, and to report their impressions to a wide circle of people upon their return."

In March, 1958, John VanderVliet, secretary-treasurer of the council, reported to his church's Immigration Committee that seventy-five young farmers—twenty-four Roman Catholic, nineteen Reformed, twenty-six Christian Reformed, two Canadian Reformed, two Old Christian Reformed, and two of no religion—were to arrive with the *Groote*

Beer on May 1. Organizations in The Netherlands were in favor of placing them all in southern Ontario. CNIC wanted them placed in at least five provinces. In the end, Canadian immigration officials decreed that spreading was compulsory.

VanderVliet commented at the time: "This is an experiment which might develop into a larger movement in the coming years, if it is handled properly." No major problems were encountered. Another group of young farmers arrived

Getting a Financial Foothold

This is the modern DUCA Credit Union building in Metropolitan Toronto.

In the early 1950s, when most immigrants had just enough money to make ends meet, it was advantageous to have a minister with some knowledge of monetary matters. Dollars meant getting on the road to stability. The church would also benefit.

Rev. John Van Harmelen of the Christian Reformed Church in Brampton, Ontario, put his own financial good sense to work for others. One of his first acts after his arrival was to see the manager of the local branch of the Royal Bank of Canada and arrange a source of money for immigrants.

"Approximately one hundred families got loans to help them get started," recalls the minister. "One needed a car, another a stove and fridge, another some furniture, and so on. Some wanted to start a business. I co-signed. You know, not one person let me down. Their payments were made on time, and I was able to go back

to the bank time and time again in Brampton, and later in Oshawa and Whitby. Our people were very thankful. Even in later years, some showed their gratitude for this initial help."

Across Canada, this story was repeated. At a time when lending institutions were hesitant to do business with immigrants, many of whom supported large families, established Canadians stood ready to say a few persuasive words, and even to co-sign. But this was not enough. The high cost of borrowing discouraged many people, particularly those who wanted to buy their own farms. Ever cautious, they refused to sink themselves into a seemingly unfathomable debt. As might have been expected, the Dutch immigrants eventually took matters into their own hands and organized self-help financial institutions.

During his work among the early immigrants, Rev. Jan Van Wezel came face to face many times with a common plight: lack of capital and insufficient credit. From conversations with immigration officials, he learned about the credit union movement in Canada. These co-operative societies used the savings of members to help other members acquire a car, appliances, or even a home. The priest immediately saw the possibilities.

On November 14, 1950, a meeting was held in London, Ontario, and fifty persons chartered the Dutch and Flemish Catholic Immigrants Credit Union Ltd. Father Van Wezel took home $16 that night. It was a humble beginning for an organization which would grow to some twelve thousand members, with assets in the tens of millions. Later, St. Willibrord was added to the name, honoring the English missionary who brought Chris-

the following year, paying their own way. The program became so successful that it served as a model to be followed in other countries. It is still going strong, placing young men and women in jobs in the tobacco fields of southern Ontario, in general farming, and in other agricultural areas.

CNIC tried to have influence in a number of other fields, including the granting of loans for university study. But a time came, in the late 1960s, when most

The Royal Bank of Canada was eager for immigrant business. Harry DeJong, who arrived with the Waterman *in 1947, received this letter, inviting him to do his banking at the nearest branch.*

tianity to The Netherlands in the 7th century.

The infant credit union proved to be a convenient place where immigrants could bank their so-called black dollars—money they had smuggled out of The Netherlands to beat the strict exchange controls. It's not hard to understand why some people decided to take their money with them instead of leaving it sitting in a Dutch bank. Some immigrant farmers, conscious of the language problem and afraid of bureaucratic interference, were hesitant to deposit such funds in their Canadian bank account.

Father Van Wezel found that these people were glad to entrust their money to him. He put it in an account at the Royal Bank at Dundas and Quebec Streets in London. It soon became obvious that someone with a talent for accounting was needed to record the growing number of transactions.

Jacobus Bontje, a director of the credit union, came to the rescue. Bontje, who had emigrated with ten of his thirteen children, ran a boarding house for immigrants who slept in his attic, dubbed the *Ridderzaal* (the Hall of Knights in The Hague). He wrote to his nephew in The Hague, Ted Smeenk, who had some accounting experience, expounding the virtues of Canada.

Smeenk took the bait. When he arrived in Canada with his wife and three small children, he became the first part-time manager and secretary-treasurer of the St. Willibrord Credit Union. Father Van Wezel handed him the Royal Bank account book and a small page from a notebook with the names and addresses of contributors and the individual totals of

their deposits.

Other credit unions were established in Ontario for the benefit of the immigrants. The name DUCA is now a household word among Dutch immigrants. This abbreviation was first used by the Dutch-Canadian Community Credit Union, set up in the 1950s with a handful of members and a few hundred dollars. Now, with assets in the millions, various branches offer Dutch-Canadians and others a full range of financial services. Many newcomers owe them a vote of thanks for their present financial stability.

The Dutch government helped DUCA at first. It extended a financial guarantee to a co-operative bank in The Netherlands, which then extended a loan to the credit union. As a result, additional long-term credits were available to members who needed to make a large outlay, such as for the purchase of a farm.

Several credit unions were also established in the West.

The Christian Credit Union Ltd. building in Edmonton, Alberta.

The 1949 class of the Christian school at Holland Marsh.

of the work could be left in the hands of established organizations. Without fanfare, the council disbanded.

In 1908, a group of Dutch Roman Catholics under the leadership of Father Van Aaken settled on Canadian Pacific Railway land near Strathmore, east of Calgary, Alberta. The priest's plans for a church did not materialize right away. But the parents made sure they had one institution—a school at which their children were taught the ABCs and the Christian faith.

Most of the prewar immigrants, whether Catholic or Protestant, believed that the Bible should be in the classroom. That's what they had been used to in The Netherlands, and that's what they wanted for their children. Sometimes Canada seemed to threaten all that they believed. However, most had no choice but to send their youngsters to the nearest secular school. Their numbers were too few and their resources too small to allow them to build their own schools.

It wasn't until after the postwar set-

tlers had become financially stable and built their churches that the construction of Christian schools got under way in earnest. The members of the Christian Reformed Church were particularly active in this field. Today, there are 115 Christian education institutions associated with Christian Schools International—ninety-two elementary schools, twenty secondary schools, two colleges, and one graduate institution. The total number of students is approaching the seventeen thousand mark.

The operation of these schools demands significant sacrifice from parents. In Ontario, for example, the government does not give financial support at the elementary level. Repeated requests, petitions and protests have failed to sway the authorities to approve grant and tax support. In Holland Marsh, where the first school was established in 1943, parents first paid $10 a month for their children's education. The budget for 1982-83 expected a parental contribution of $205 a month, twelve times a year.

Mrs. Reina Feyen of Chatham, Ontario, recalls the launching of a school

Parents pose for a photo before they start working to get the Christian school in Vancouver ready for the new term in 1953. The school started in 1949 with one teacher and eleven pupils.
At left, the flag is raised at the official opening of the William of Orange School in New Westminster, British Columbia, in September, 1955, the first Canadian Reformed school established in Canada.

society and having to pay $3 a week into a building fund. The school was opened in 1957. "I remember that for many years mothers went tomato picking so that they could pay the cost of sending their children to this school. We also started a Mothers Club, later the Home and School Club, to work for the school."

With careful budgeting, the immigrants have been able to keep their schools going. "We had to be careful with our money," say Peter and Tina DeGroot of Lethbridge, Alberta, "but our children got a Christian education, and three are teachers now. This is important for us. We want to be a Christian influence in this community and this country. At first, our church and school were seen as strictly ethnic—and they were. Now they are seen more as part of the community. This is

especially true of the school, where many families from other than the Christian Reformed Church are now involved."

The school societies which Canadian Reformed congregations set up often began their programs with a Friday evening school or a Saturday school. The children were taught by church members who were public school teachers, by those who had followed a teaching course in The Netherlands, and by others who were deemed capable of instructing in Bible study, church history, and sometimes the Dutch language. Ministers were often asked to help.

The first complete elementary school of the Canadian Reformed Churches, the William of Orange School, was opened in New Westminster, British Columbia, on September 7, 1955, with an enrolment of sixty-four pupils. Others followed. There are now nineteen Canadian Reformed schools in Canada.

Other denominations also have established schools.

Already in the 1950s, immigrants of the Reformed faith were thinking of setting

Redeemer Reformed Christian College serves young people from across Ontario and also promotes adult education in the greater Hamilton area.

board chairman of the association, was appointed the college's first president. At a membership meeting in the spring, it was decided that Redeemer College would open its doors in September, 1982, somewhere in the greater Hamilton area. Other staff appointments were made in the ensuing months, and the work of preparing for the opening began.

On September 6, 1982, Redeemer held its first convocation. More than 1,700 friends and supporters of the college crowded into Centenary United Church in Hamilton to thank God for His blessings and to request continued guidance.

Around fifty students were expected for the first academic year, and then, as response increased, the projection was elevated to seventy-five. At the first registration, ninety-seven young men and women signed up as full-time students. An additional thirty-one registered as part-timers.

The one hundred and four names on its membership rolls have become more than five thousand. An incredible start!

Redeemer offers a full range of college-level liberal arts curriculum. The program includes courses in religion and theology, English composition, literature, French, geography, history, mathematics, music, philosophy, physics, biology, chemistry, political science, psychology, art, business, computer science, drama, Dutch, economics, German, and sociology.

An official notes: "As Redeemer College looks to the future, it is committed to offering a four-year degree-granting program with a full range of course options. As we are able to offer more courses, we anticipate that student enrolment will also increase significantly."

In Edmonton, a Christian liberal arts institution called The King's College was

up a Christian college in Ontario. Not much came of those plans, but the idea did not disappear.

1973 brought new initiatives. A feasibility study committee was appointed. Its efforts led to the formation of the Ontario Christian College Association. This group, formally organized on November 13, 1976, initially had one hundred and four members. In December of 1980, the provincial government granted a charter to the association, giving it permission to incorporate Redeemer Reformed Christian College.

Early in 1981, Rev. Henry R. De Bolster, long a staunch promoter of Christian education at all levels, and formerly

established in 1979. It now offers university-level education to nearly one hundred and sixty students.

As early as 1965, men and women from diverse walks of life saw the need for a regional, non-denominational Christian college in Western Canada. In December, 1970, they incorporated the Christian College Association (Alberta) and through a constitution and statement of principles gave written expression to their vision of Scripturally-directed higher education. During the following years, the association adopted a master development plan. Many new members joined, and in January, 1978, the membership voted to proceed with the opening of the college in September, 1979.

On November 16, 1979, the Alberta legislature approved the granting of a charter to The King's College. With three thousand financial supporters and seventy-five students, King's opened its doors, offering first-year courses in biology, economics, English, history, music, interdisciplinary studies, philosophy, psychology, sociology, and theology. The program was expanded the following year, and enrolment increased to one hundred and forty. In addition, extension courses attracted more than four hundred people in six different Western Canadian communities.

In 1981, the college community outgrew its facilities and moved to the

present campus at 10766 - 97 Street. Students can now register in a third year of study, and an expanded curriculum includes courses in chemistry, education, and mathematics.

An official explains: "In the quality of education in student services, in the extension lecture series, in concerts and recitals, in faculty research, and in its organizational structure and functioning, The King's College seeks to promote the kingdom of Jesus Christ by serving the community of His people."

The Canadian Reformed Churches bought a large house in Hamilton, On-

Student life is an important part of a Christian college experience. The young men and women of The King's College in Edmonton, Alberta, are encouraged to be involved in the college community and in the world outside.

tario, and launched a seminary for the training of new ministers. In September, 1969, more than one thousand church members packed into Hamilton's Central Presbyterian Church for the official opening ceremonies. The theological college began with five faculty members and four students.

Rev. W.W.J. VanOene writes in his book, *Inheritance Preserved:* "The burdens which the membership bears to maintain the college are considerable, but the hundreds who come every year anew to attend the convocations prove by their very presence that the college has the love of the membership. As long as that is the case, both college and churches will flourish."

Fourteen ministers who are either serving congregations in Canada or working in mission fields abroad have received their Bachelor of Divinity degree from the college.

Hamilton is also the home of a Canadian Reformed teachers' college which uses the facilities of the local church. It has a faculty of three full-time and four part-time teachers.

The Association for the Advancement of Christian Scholarship and the Institute for

Immigrant Hospitality to Travelers from Other Countries

Rev. John Dresselhuis talks with a seaman in Vancouver.

Seafarers from thousands of ships and dozens of nations call at the port in Montreal and at other places along the St. Lawrence Seaway. There, the Christian Reformed Church established a ministry in 1965, a ministry which reaches out to people from all over the world.

Among his many duties, Rev. Hans Uittenbosch, the chaplain, visits hospitals, conducts chapel services, and distributes literature. But he considers meeting incoming ships the heart of his waterfront ministry.

"The privacy of the cabin affords a climate of personal ministry," he says. "Serious discussions can also be held in a quiet corner in the galley, the hallways, the bar, the recreation room, or on the deck."

When immigrants still come by boat, he meets them. As he wrote in a report: "I welcome immigrants from The Netherlands, regardless of their religious affiliation. They are met personally on board, they are provided with information about Canada, they receive the address of the church and minister in the place where they intend to settle . . ."

In 1969, the First Christian Reformed Church in Vancouver embarked on a similar outreach program; it called a full-time minister to work among the thousands of seamen in the port area.

Rev. J.E.F. Dresselhuis visited the ships—an average of forty-two a month. Most of the seamen on board couldn't speak English, so he had to depend heavily on the printed page and cassette recordings in appropriate languages. He could see results.

Christian Studies date back to 1956, the year in which the Association for Reformed Scientific Studies was founded. There were two influences that shaped the association—a group of Dutch immigrants of Reformed faith, and a college professor, Dr. H. Evan Runner, and his students. From both directions came the insistence that, because Jesus Christ is Lord of all of life, the realm of education is also subject to His renewing power, and that, therefore, Christians are called to promote the development of Scripturally-directed learning.

In 1955, four men—Rev. François Guillaume, Pieter Speelman, Casper

Opening day at the Theological College of the Canadian Reformed Churches.

"Thousands of seamen accept Christian literature," he reported once. "Many invite me to their cabins or their place of work on board."

Rev. Uittenbosch's work is the subject of a forty-eight-minute documentary film, Sea Salt, produced by John R. Hamilton of Del Rey Communications of Chicago, Illinois, and available from CRC-TV. The film crew followed the chaplain aboard dozens of ships over a two-week period.

These harbor ministries are clear examples of changes occuring in immigrant churches. Finally they have become established, and are no longer dependent on their sister congregations in the United States. On their own, they are reaching out beyond the immigrant community. Maybe someday the Canadians will stop referring to them as "Dutch churches."

Soon after the Council of the Christian Reformed Churches in Canada was established in November, 1966, it embarked on two important projects: contact with the government, and mission work among urban Indians. It also worked toward the establishment of a church office in Canada.

The Christian Reformed Church is widely known for its outspoken views on a wide number of issues affecting today's society. The synod is repeatedly being asked by churches to speak from the Scriptures on such matters as warfare, nuclear weapons, and the incompatibility of lodge membership with church membership. The church council in Canada also speaks from a Reformed perspective to those who make decisions in various levels of government.

There are more aspects of this denomination's outreach. More than two hundred congregations of eight other denominations in Canada now use the religious education material of the Christian Reformed Church. And continuing discussions are held with other church bodies, such as the Reformed Church (this denomination has also established a council in Canada), to encourage the development of local inter-church contact.

Rev. Hans Uittenbosch meets with crew members and officers on board a Soviet ship in Montreal in the 1960s.

VandeRiet and Rev. Henry Venema—met in Toronto to begin working for the establishment of a Christian university in Canada. By the spring of 1956, they were able to establish the Association for Reformed Scientific Studies with a membership of around sixty. Its first public meeting, held in November, 1956, attracted a wider audience, including Dr. Runner and some of his students from Calvin College in Grand Rapids.

The association formulated an educational creed and invited professors from The Netherlands—many of them from the Free University in Amsterdam—for lecture tours across North America. It also sponsored student conferences, held during the summer months near Unionville, Ontario. In 1963, it hired a part-time director, Dr. Paul Schrotenboer, who helped to focus attempts to establish a Christian institution for higher learning in Canada. In the spring of 1967, John Olthuis became executive director of the organization, the name of which was changed in the following year to the Association for the Advancement of Christian Scholarship (AACS).

The Institute for Christian Studies, which was to become the major focus of AACS activity, opened its doors for the first time in October, 1967. The research and teaching which took place there during the late 1960s and early 1970s was a powerful and creative attempt to take new approaches to various academic disciplines. Such efforts, together with calls for renewal in church and society, stirred up the Christian Reformed community. The Institute became a centre of controversy for a while, but as it matured, coming to emphasize cooperation rather than confrontation, its controversial nature began to subside. The results of its scholarly work have been widely disseminated, and its academic stature is widely recognized. The Institute, based in Toronto, employs an eight-member teaching faculty. Most of its students come from Canada and the United States.

The AACS, with Dr. Robert VanderVennen as current executive director, continues its support of the Institute, and also sponsors various publications, seminars, lectures, and academic conferences. A major educational service is the Campus Outreach program, which brings students of the Institute to a number of secular campuses in Ontario to teach Christian perspective courses.

There was a time when the Dutch postwar immigrant groups included only a handful of people older than fifty. No one had to think about caring for the elderly.

However, the situation was different ten or fifteen years later. Across Canada, groups were organized to study what could be done for the immigrants who were getting on in years.

In 1965, the Hamilton classis of the Christian Reformed Church mandated the deacons in that area to look into the need for a home for the aged of Dutch background. Many things happened to delay the building of such a home. Then, in 1976, a committee in Grimsby contacted the deacons on the board set up by Classis Hamilton. The two groups went to work in earnest, but they encountered more difficulties.

Since provincial restraint policies were just coming into effect, no money would be available for a home for the aged with full care for the residents. In the spring of 1977, shortly after the Christian Reformed Church in Grimsby had sold part of its property for the proposed home, the Ontario housing ministry put a land freeze on the Niagara Peninsula. No construction could be started on this land, because up to that time it had been planted in peaches. The government minister was petitioned, many church members wrote to their representatives in the legislature, and prayers were offered. In the late sum-

Emmanuel Home for senior citizens in Edmonton, Alberta.

mer of that year, in a rare exception, the minister lifted the freeze on the property.

Then, when building plans were complete, an application for the town to extend its sewer line to the property was rejected. A petition to the ministry of the environment produced favorable results. The local government was instructed to include the home in its sewer expansion plans. All the red tape was out of the way.

A drive was held in late 1977 and early 1978, netting more than $400,000. A large mortgage—$700,000—had to be taken out to finance the construction of a seventy-four bed building and the purchase of equipment.

Says Rita Otten, secretary of the Shalom Manor board: "From time to time, the need for this home has become very clear. It's a place where people

Retirement Homes

Ontario Premier William Davis (seated at right) was on hand for the official opening of the second phase of the housing complex for seniors at Brampton. Trinity Tower and Hope Tower house many people of Dutch origin.

In 1951, the Christian Reformed Church Co-operative Medical and Hospital Society was formed to provide its members with medical insurance, a commodity not available to citizens of Canada at large. This organization, run as a true co-operative with membership not restricted to any one denomination, insured some 1,500 families at its peak. Such insurance took pressure off church deaconal funds, the only other source of help for needy families with medical expenses.

In the '60s, when government health insurance schemes came into being, it became obvious that the society had served its purpose. The membership decided at the annual meeting on April 27, 1962, that steps should be taken to consolidate the capital and to proceed with another project—the organization of a society for the establishment of a home for the aged.

A few years later, on July 8, 1969, Holland Christian Homes was incorporated for the purpose of providing care for the elderly. But much groundwork was yet to be done. Not until 1974 was a ten-acre parcel purchased in Brampton, near Toronto, from the Salem Christian Mental Health Association. Actual construction of the first senior citizens home, Trinity Tower, began in 1977. In 1982, the second home, Hope Tower, was completed, together with a social and recreation area called Ebenezer Center. In December, 1983, construction was to begin on a 160-unit rest home and a 120-bed nursing home.

Holland Christian Homes, with more than 1,500 members at present, serves the region at large, without discrimination based on race, color, and religious or political views. Yet approximately ninety per cent of the present population of three hundred and ten elderly people were born in The Netherlands.

receive care, where there is an atmosphere of Christian love, where the staff understands you if Dutch is the only language you have left. Now we have a waiting list of more than fifty people, which means we should expand in the very near future."

With the first-generation immigrants getting on in years, homes suited to their particular needs were established in several areas. Western Canada led the way. The Ebenezer Home in Abbotsford, British Columbia, celebrated its tenth anniversary in 1982. The next facility built was the Emmanuel Home in Edmonton, Alberta. There are other homes in such cities as Chatham, Ottawa, Sarnia, and St. Thomas, some of them operating on a cooperative basis in which the residents buy a share. More are in the planning stages.

In June of 1983, the 30-unit Ebenezer Villa adjacent to the Cornerstone Reformed Church in Hamilton was officially opened. Planning for a center for the aged had begun in 1956. It is now home for a number of elderly people from the Canadian Reformed and Christian Reformed Churches, who pay $325 a month for a one-bedroom unit and $375 for a two-bedroom one.

One of the residents, Cor Guther, said at the opening: "What is most important is that we all get along so well with each other. After all, we are all brothers and sisters in the faith . . ."

Some immigrants were adamantly opposed to joining unions of any kind and didn't hesitate to let others know about their views. One of them, Willem Vander Molen of Chilliwack, British Columbia, recalls an incident at a construction site where he was foreman and where some fellow Canadian Reformed members were employed as laborers.

"A well-dressed gentleman came to the job site one day. Noticing that I was the foreman, he asked me how many men were working for me. As he had not identified himself, I asked him who he was. He said he was a representative of a certain labor union. I then told him to go to the office. This made him angry. In a heated exchange, I told him that I would not answer his questions. It was a matter of principle. At least seven church members were on the job, and would never join a labor union. As foreman, I did not have to join, but I couldn't betray my church members."

Two days later, the union official returned to the site, accompanied by another man. The same questions were asked. The same answers were given. The two men, obviously angered, told Vander-Molen that he would be without a job in six weeks. Then they stomped away.

Within a few weeks, rumors began to circulate that the firm would be picketed. The boss heard them, too, and promptly called in his foreman and asked that everything be done to avoid trouble. The answer was an unequivocal no.

"A couple of days later, my work was finished. The other church members were laid off too."

But VanderMolen knew that he had stood up for his principles: he didn't want to join a union and he certainly didn't want to be coerced into signing a card and paying dues. However, his road wasn't easy when he got other jobs. One time, a burly Polish laborer, who had fought against the Germans in The Netherlands toward the end of the war, defended him from physical violence when he had refused to sign up.

And VanderMolen remained proud of his principles.

"A breath of fresh air."

That's what R.C. Cornish, then editor of the *Trentonian and Tri-County News* in Trenton, Ontario, said about the Christian Labor Association of Canada back in 1967 when the organization held its fifteenth annual convention.

Cornish explained that his interest in the CLAC had been aroused by its insistence

Ebenezer Villa in Hamilton, Ontario, opened in June of 1983.

Peter Van Duyvenvoorde of the CLAC pickets the picketers. His point: the AFL-CIO should not be allowed to monopolize jobs and workers' opinions. Below: The Guide, the official publication of the Christian Labour Association of Canada.

that workers be free to join the union of their choice and its conviction that "Christianity is to be carried into every sphere of life, and not limited to Sunday." With his observation, the editor had pinpointed quite accurately what lies at the core of CLAC's existence.

Others have focused on those same characteristics. For example, in 1977, Professor Abraham Rotstein of the University of Toronto referred to the CLAC as "a sprinkling of yeast in the Canadian body politic" and a reminder that the "witnesses to His Kingdom are alive and well and living in Canada."

However, such respect hasn't been the only reaction. Often this Christian labor union has met with misunderstanding and intolerance as well. Other unions have looked upon it as a divisive nuisance. Whereas traditional North American unions are organized on the basis of trades or places of employment, the CLAC appeals to workers on the basis of their Christian commitment. This challenges the prevailing idea that unions are religiously neutral groups seeking only to maximize their own bargaining power.

When a few men and women gathered in Vancouver, Edmonton, Sarnia, Aylmer, London, and Hamilton in the fall of 1951 to talk about forming a Christian union, they scarcely knew where to start. But they began anyway. And on February 20, 1952, the CLAC was formally established with a national executive.

Slowly, assisted by those who knew a similar organization in the United States and Christian trade unions in The Netherlands, the movement grew. A serious obstacle arose when the Ontario Labor Relations Board decided in 1954 that the specific Christian basis of the CLAC violated the requirements of the Labor Relations Act and of the Fair Employment Practices Act. This board's refusal to certify the CLAC led to a great deal of soul-searching and, unfortunately, to a split in the ranks of the fledgling organization in 1958—a split that was finally healed in 1979.

In March of 1963, Chief Justice J.C. McRuer of the Ontario Supreme Court ruled that the Ontario Labor Relations Board had erred in refusing to certify the CLAC. He argued that no organization is neutral, and that the union which begins its meeting with prayer and a Scripture reading is just as much entitled to be certified as a union committed to the theories of Karl Marx. This significant breakthrough paved the way for expansion.

By 1982, the membership had risen to around six thousand. Many groups of workers in a variety of trades and professions were represented. Offices with full-time staff members existed in British Columbia, Alberta, and four Ontario locations.

"The CLAC has especially emphasized the need to overcome the adversary principle in collective bargaining," says Harry Antonides, director of research. "Conse-

In 1954, the immigrant farmers in Ontario began to speak with united voice; the Christian Farmers' Federation of Ontario was formed. Its purpose: to promote and apply Christian ideas and principles to the solution of agricultural problems and to advance the social and economic interests of its members.

Elbert VanDonkersgoed, the executive director and the driving force behind the movement, explained once: "Agriculture has problems. Christians need to work together to find solutions to these problems. There *is* a better way." The Federation has a membership of six hundred and fifty. A sister organization in Alberta has three hundred and fifty members.

There's also a charitable organization known as Christian Stewardship Services, operated out of Toronto by its executive director, Harry Houtman. It has one principal goal: helping Canadians with their stewardship responsibilities. To this end, it conducts educational seminars, offers planned giving programs, distributes literature, and provides personal, confidential estate planning and financial counselling.

The organization, sponsored and funded by more than twenty Christian causes, explains: "Effective stewardship blesses our own lives, the lives of our neighbors, and the existence of organizations dedicated to the furtherance of the kingdom of God."

quently, it has been promoting a new form of co-determination in the workplace so that the us-versus-them mentality can make way for one in which both labor and management co-operate in a setting of mutual respect and trust. It is for this reason that we have paid much attention to the way work itself and collective bargaining need to be restructured."

In April of 1963, a dream was realized by 153 Reformed people of Dutch origin. With the incorporation of the CJL Foundation, they established an organization which offered a Christian witness in the field of labor relations. The guiding principle was that workers should be free to support the trade unions of their choice.

The foundation enjoyed some important victories. Among them was the well-known Hoogendoorn case, which established that workers whose principles conflicted with their union's had a right to independent representation before those bodies deciding on their case. Another landmark decision was the so-called charity clause in the Ontario Labor Relations Act, which allowed workers the right to pay the equivalent of union dues to a recognized charity.

During those first years, the seed of another dream began to germinate—the need for a solid Christian political presence in Canada. On CJL's tenth anniversary, at the 1973 annual membership meeting in Toronto, it was decided to add political research and action to the organization's agenda.

That decision marked a turning point. Even as CJL embraced a new task, it opened itself to the support, wisdom, and participation of a wider community of believers. Dr. Bernard Zylstra, then a member of the CJL board of directors, highlighted the turning point, speaking of CJL's deep political roots that extended back to the 19th-century social and political reformer, Abraham Kuyper. But, he said, depending upon only those roots was not enough. "Our background is not large enough for the job ahead."

Since 1973, the research program of CJL—now Citizens for Public Justice—has included examining the role of progress and economic growth as guiding ideals in Canadian politics. Foundational research continues in such areas as criminal justice and social policy. The organization has taken part in the public policy formation process on issues such as energy, justice for native people, and human rights. And work continues on labor and educational equality issues.

Citizens for Public Justice has expanded in many directions since its formation. In contrast to 1963, when the 153 original members shared a common ethnic and denominational background, its current 2,200 supporters represent a hearty mixture of faith traditions and national origins.

Immigrants suffering from mental health problems as a result of immigration, dislocation, marital or personal conflicts have access to expert care throughout Canada. In Ontario, for example, there's Salem, a non-profit, interdenominational Christian organization for people with emotional problems which prevent them from achieving the best possible use of their abilities to think, feel, and perceive. It provides personal, marriage, and family counseling, psychological counseling services at Christian schools in and around Toronto and St. Catharines, marriage enrichment conferences, personal enrichment weekends, and service to the Christian community in the form of lectures and workshops. A similar service is provided in the West by Cascade Christian Counseling. It is based in Surrey, British Columbia.

"A satisfied immigrant is a good immigrant. Our radio will help make the immigrants good Canadians, because it will help put them at ease."

Maja Van Steensel, representative of the international service of the Canadian Broadcasting Corporation, was in The Hague in early 1950 to announce plans for a special service intended to ease a bit of the loneliness and strangeness that gripped immigrant women who were left by themselves for most of the day. While their husbands were at work and their children at school, they would be able to listen to a morning radio program in their own language. There would be music and news from The Netherlands. And there would be educational segments: for example, explanations of the meaning of Valentine's Day and of all the wares that a hardware store had to offer.

The Dutch continue to use the radio to-

day. Many churches have regular programs in the English language, catering to their own members and other interested listeners. *Radio Nederland Wereldomroep* distributes programs in English, French and Dutch to more than 140 stations across Canada. Then there are independent programs in such centers as Vancouver, Edmonton, Winnipeg, Toronto, Montreal, and Truro, Nova Scotia, all featuring classical and light music, news, interviews, and some chit-chat.

On CHIN in Toronto, hosts John and Atie Bosch find that most of the musical numbers requested by listeners are oldies.

"That's logical," John explained once. "The people here remember the numbers that were popular when they left The Netherlands."

Even Oshawa, a city east of Toronto, has its own program. The announcer is

Jack Brouwer of Radio Nederland *in his studio.*

Jack Brouwer, who began his weekly show on CKQT in 1955, two years after leaving Vlaardingen, Zuid-Holland. He had been a reporter for *Het Parool*, one of the national newspapers. He comments proudly: "I guess it's the oldest continuous Dutch radio program in Canada. I haven't missed a week."

Brouwer also has a program on Toronto's CHIN called *Zingend Gelovend*, featuring sacred music. But that's not all. As the representative in Canada for *Radio Nederland*, he produces and distributes such programs as *Holland Calling, Topics from Holland,* and *Dutch Concert Hall,* provides material and suggestions for the shortwave broadcasts from The Netherlands, and looks after the expand-ing transcription service for radio stations across Canada.

"The primary objective of *Radio Nederland* is to make its listeners aware of what's going on in Holland," says Brouwer, who left his job at Philips Electronics Industries Ltd. in Toronto in 1973 to make broadcasting his full-time career. "We try to give a picture of what goes on there. It goes without saying, of course, that the Dutch-Canadians form a big part of our audience."

Many of the listeners are in the Vancouver area, where Jan Van Bruchem, Brouwer's forerunner, has made a name for himself in the broadcasting world. He loves to tell the story of an elderly Dutch couple who wanted to return to The

The Immigrant Press Keeps Track of Dutch-Canadian History

Let's not forget the printed word. The immigrants have known such religious publications as *Contact, The Calvinist, Calvinist Contact, The Banner, De Wachter, The Pioneer, Clarion* (formerly called *Canadian Reformed Magazine*), *The Reformed Perspective, The Messenger,* and others. These carried news of the churches in Canada and the United States, in-depth articles on a variety of topics, and items of general interest to the newcomers, including the occasional piece from overseas. A new venture, *Christian Renewal,* was launched in 1982.

For up-to-date news, the immigrants have a choice. *The Windmill Herald* is published in New Westminster, British Columbia, *De Hollandse Krant* in Langley, British Columbia, *Hollandia News* in Chatham, Ontario, and *De Nederlandse Courant* in Toronto.

Hollandia News and *De Nederlandse Courant* have been in existence since 1954. The *Windmill Herald,* known originally as *Goed Nieuws,* came into be-

Netherlands when their children moved east. They figured they would be just as close to them if they lived in Europe, and there they would be able to enjoy the companionship of relatives and friends in familiar surroundings. In fact, they were even receiving some pension money from The Netherlands. Then something caused a sudden change of mind: the daily Dutch program on CJVB in Vancouver. The familiar music and the up-to-date news from The Netherlands made them feel less homesick and lonely. They decided instead to retire to Vancouver Island and build their final home on a specially-selected spot where the reception of the station's signal would be perfect.

Van Bruchem begins his program with *Goede morgen luisteraars* (Good morning, listeners), and then keeps his faithful audience entertained for a full hour. He's more than an announcer; he's the owner of CJVB, a station that caters to Vancouver's large ethnic community with round-the-clock programming in twenty-three languages. This successful venture is the culmination of dreams he had when he left Limburg in 1952 at the age of twenty-two. He brought with him his experience as a sound technician with Philips and as a broadcaster with the Netherlands Radio Union.

His first Dutch-language program on CKBB in Barrie, Ontario, went out to the farmers in Holland Marsh. It paved the way for his syndicated radio program,

ing a few years later. *De Hollandse Krant* first appeared in 1969.

Albert VanderHeide acquired *Goed Nieuws* in 1969 from the founder, T.P. Blom, who was forced out by increased postal rates and other interests. The publication had been a give-away, with the advertisers paying the cost.

"We developed an editorial policy of sorts, to provide some depth and develop a real newspaper," says VanderHeide. "Since Dutch-Canadians were traveling 'home' in great numbers, and visitors from The Netherlands were also arriving by the thousands, it had become important to keep up with the news from the Old Country. Otherwise, 'culture shock' could spoil a holiday. People did not find home to be what they remembered. Attitudes had changed. The country had gone into rapid social and economic development. Prosperity abounded. Old truths were no longer important, or so it seemed to many immigrants."

In 1975, VanderHeide also acquired the defunct *Hollandia News* to cover the Ontario market, which had been difficult to reach because of poor postal service. This paper had been founded by John and Jean Vellinga. John died in 1974 and his wife became ill in 1975. As a result, *Hollandia News* did not appear for about eight months.

VanderHeide, publisher and editor of both papers, is convinced that there is a continuing need for publications in the

Thea Schryer, editor of De Nederlandse Courant; *the late Dick Farenhorst, for many years editor of* Calvinist Contact; *Albert VanderHeide, editor of the* Windmill Herald *and* Hollandia News.

Dutch language.

"The need will most definitely outlast the economic viability of the papers. Many immigrants, no matter how well-integrated and well-versed in the language of their chosen country, do revert to their mother tongue when the aging process accelerates."

As a side interest, both papers have built up an extensive collection of material on the Dutch immigrants in North America, including books, magazines, pamphlets, photographs, correspondence, and news clippings.

"Occasionally, items from our collection are published," says VanderHeide. "The information is often used for reference purposes too. Some day all of it will have to be organized in a scientific manner."

De Hollandse Krant, published once a month by Gerard Bonekamp, is distributed on all CP and Wardair flights to Amsterdam. *De Nederlandse Courant* is owned and edited by Mrs. Thea Schryer.

John Hultink of Paideia Press.

Publishing Books in Canada

Dutch immigrants certainly don't lack access to good literature. Books in the Dutch language are available in libraries, and stores across Canada, mainly due to the efforts of Pieter Speelman of Speelman's Bookhouse Ltd. in Rexdale, Ontario.

Books which cater to the interests of many immigrants are produced for them in Canada by Paideia Press.

This firm, operating out of a converted barn which overlooks vineyards west of St. Catharines, Ontario, has 165 titles in print, many of them translated from the Dutch language, and another forty titles in various stages of production. Paideia Press, which sells books all over the English-speaking world, also co-published with McGraw-Hill Ryerson Ltd. the popular *A Liberation Album*, and from time to time distributes a Dutch-language book such as *Beatrix in Ballingschap*.

The man behind this enterprise is John Hultink, formerly of Zwolle, Overijssel, who came to Canada as a nine-year-old in 1952 with his parents and four brothers. He grew up in the Wallaceburg, Ontario, area. At sixteen, he quit school—"I hated it"—and got a job in a supermarket. A few years later, when a second store opened, he was offered the manager's job. But by this time he had concluded that he didn't want to stand in a grocery store for the rest of his life and that he should go back to school and possibly enter the ministry. He enrolled in a pre-seminary program at Calvin College in Grand Rapids, Michigan, and majored in philosophy. Instead of the ministry, he entered the field of Christian education. His publishing business, really an extension of that work, grew out of an idea which had first come to him in college. He wanted to give Christians in North America access to "some of those Dutch books that open the Scriptures as only Reformed books can."

He began publishing in February, 1977. S.G. De Graaf's four-volume *Promise and Deliverance*, translated from the Dutch, became an instant success. It's his best seller, with more than 50,000 volumes sold. Other religious, popular, and children's books followed in rapid succession. Works by well-known Dutch authors such as Anne DeVries, Piet Jongeling, Meindert DeJong, and W.G. VandeHulst have reached a wide audience.

"Many people questioned the saleability of translations," says Hultink. "But I proved the enterprise viable. Over the years, we've received many letters and telephone calls from people who have said their lives are enriched because of the books brought out by Paideia Press. That's what makes us continue this challenging work."

Holland Calling. Thousands of Dutch-Canadians who tuned in each week will remember the familiar ending: "Keep in touch with the Dutch." When Van Bruchem heard about ethnic radio stations starting up first in Montreal, and then in Toronto, he knew that he wanted to own and operate such a station.

"Everyone looks forward to that one hour," says one of his faithful listeners, Leo Hoens. "It's a ray of sunshine for people in hospital and those on in years. There's no question that Jan is making it a better world for all of us."

The television medium is also used in a number of Canadian cities. One of the popular producers and hosts is Lisette Van Gessel of Toronto, who once traveled throughout Canada to promote Dutch cheese. A Dutch magazine, *Margriet*, reported in 1982: "Canada is a land of many opportunities, and Lisette Van Gessel, who emigrated ten years ago, has taken good advantage of that. Consider this: like a real Mies Bouwman (a TV personality in The Netherlands), she has her own TV program in Toronto. In the Dutch language even. And her success multiplies: other Canadian cities are following her example and broadcasting programs for the Netherlanders in their area." She has helped to establish programs in Montreal, Ottawa, Winnipeg, and Vancouver. Other cities, including Calgary, may join the list.

Her program, Dutch Magazine, on Channel 47, includes introductory chit-chat, newsreels, films from The Netherlands, commentaries and inter-

Lisette Van Gessel talks with Princess Juliana in Toronto in 1981.

views. Her guests have included Mayor Polak of Amsterdam, in town as part of the Toronto-Amsterdam twinning, a program that promotes cultural exchange; Juliana, who had come to open an exhibit of Van Gogh paintings; Princess Margriet and her husband, Pieter Van Vollenhoven; renowned soccer star Johan Cruyff, who played professionally in North America for a number of seasons . . .

One group directly concerned with the question of Netherlands identity is the Canadian Association for the Advancement of Netherlandic Studies, established in June, 1971. Its members wish to stimulate an awareness of, and interest in, Dutch and Flemish culture, to encourage academic and public libraries

In October, 1979, the Netherlands Luncheon Club celebrated its 25th anniversary in Toronto. Special guests were members of a Dutch economic mission to Canada, including K.H. Beyen, secretary of state of the Dutch ministry of economic affairs. Among those shown in the photo is Jan Heersink (second from left), the founder of the club.

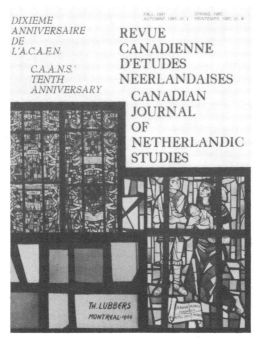

DIXIEME
ANNIVERSAIRE
DE
L'A.C.A.E.N.

C.A.A.N.S.'
TENTH
ANNIVERSARY

FALL 1981   SPRING 1982
AUTOMNE 1981. III. I   PRINTEMPS 1982. III. II

REVUE
CANADIENNE
D'ETUDES
NEERLANDAISES
CANADIAN
JOURNAL
OF
NETHERLANDIC
STUDIES

TH. LUBBERS
MONTREAL·1964

At first CAANS distributed a newsletter which has since been replaced by a journal edited by Adrian VandenHoven of the University of Windsor.

in Canada to give substantial representation to Netherlandic literature and culture, to encourage universities and other educational bodies to include Netherlandic studies in their programs, and to promote the inviting of Netherlandic scholars to Canada.

This organization, consisting mostly of people in the teaching field and other professions, has grown steadily. Local chapters have been formed in Windsor, Toronto, and Waterloo, all university centers in Ontario, and in Montreal. Additional chapters are planned for Ottawa, Edmonton, and Vancouver.

CAANS has organized annual seminars at the Learned Societies conferences held at different universities across Canada. But most of the activity takes place at the local level. For example, the Toronto chapter, formed in 1979, has held its own conferences, and it has organized Dutch language classes. Several schools in Metropolitan Toronto are now teaching Dutch classes on Saturday morning, and the University of Toronto teaches two full credit courses in the Dutch language. In such ways, CAANS fulfills its mandate.

In 1954, Jan Heersink and a number of other business and professional people in the Toronto-Hamilton area decided that they needed regular contact with each other. The result was the formation of the Netherlands Luncheon Club.

"It's been a success," says Heersink, now an honorary member. "We still meet once a month in Toronto to listen to a speaker and to associate with one another. There are some one hundred and twenty members. The contact the club provides can't help but be of benefit."

Vancouver, another hub of the Canadian business world, also had a Dutch businessmen's association. Indeed, there is much for people in business and the professions to talk about. Both Canada and The Netherlands have benefited tremendously from the postwar immigration—economically, socially, and culturally. Dutch scientists, technicians, engineers, medical doctors, educators, theologians, geologists, linguists, and foresters have all found their niche in private and public institutions in Canada. Bankers, insurance executives, and investment personnel have also made places for themselves. Many immigrants have started their own businesses. And well-known firms of Dutch or partly Dutch origin, including Philips, Shell, Unilever, International Fertilizers, and Amstel Brewery, have become part of the Canadian industrial scene.

Dr. A.S. Tuinman, emigration attaché in Ottawa in the early years, wrote in 1956: "The importance of the immigrant in developing trade relations between The Netherlands and Canada should not be overlooked. Two functions may be distinguished, one *commercially active*, and the other *consumptive*. Immigrants who become merchants are the commercially active ones, promoting the sale of Netherlands articles either through importation or wholesale and retail trade. Trade has considerably increased in quantity as well as in variety as a result of the painstaking efforts. Here is market research of a particularly valuable kind. Nearly all the articles which The Netherlands has to offer are tried in the Canadian market and as a result it is proved by practice which articles can be sold. These pioneers deserve the greatest possible interest and cooperation from The Netherlands trade and industry. The consumptive importance of the immigrants lies in the fact that they are often the first consumers in Canada of the products, thus stimulating the efforts of traders. The economic importance of immigration is also evident from the extension of freight and passenger traffic, postage service and financial transactions. In additon to the commercially active and consumptive functions, the immigrants create a general goodwill which is important for the relation between the two countries."

Twenty-five years later, many of the same conditions hold, and many of the dynamics operate.

The singers and instrumentalists of the Ontario Christian Music Assembly have performed before many appreciative audiences since 1961. There was even a concert tour of The Netherlands in 1981 to mark the 20th anniversary. The five organizations that make up the organization are the two mixed choirs Praise the Lord of Bowmanville and Toronto, the music society Euphonia of Toronto, the chamber orchestra Pro Musica of Toronto, and the youth choir The Lord Is My Shepherd of Toronto. The director is Leendert Kooij, an associate of the Royal Conservatory of Toronto. Someone wrote once: "To see him perform is to watch pure energy. His enthusiasm, which is not easily paralleled, inspires both performers and audience."

Chapter 21

After a Decade

After a Decade

When the *Groote Beer* came alongside the dock at Quebec City in April, 1958, Gerald Prins leaned over the railing and peered at the people waiting on shore. He tried to spot the fieldman with whom he had corresponded, even though he had no idea what the man looked like.

"We saw someone on the dock below us, dressed in a brown overcoat, looking intently at the passengers. His eyes focused on us. I said to my wife: 'That's the fieldman.' I raised my hand, and he did the same."

The two men shook hands on board. After passing on some advice, the fieldman promised to notify Rev. Hans Wittenbosch, the minister of the Christian Reformed Church at Renfrew, Ontario, that the family would be arriving by train at around nine o'clock the following morning. Everything seemed to be going according to plan. There was nothing to worry about.

However, when Prins and his family, tired but full of eager anticipation, stepped out of the train at Renfrew, nobody was there to greet them. They just stood next to their suitcases, looking around and wondering what to do. Prins, feeling uncomfortable, clutched in his hand the last letter that had been forwarded to him by Rev. Wittenbosch.

"A couple of men—they looked like railway people—stared at us. They must have known that we were immigrants. The *pofbroek* of my ten-year-old son surely gave us away. Anyway, one of them walked toward us. I showed him the envelope and pointed to the address of the minister. He then motioned that he would make a phone call. When he returned, he pointed to his pocket watch, indicating that the minister would be arriving within minutes."

Rev. Wittenbosch, accompanied by a member of his congregation who had happened to be in his house when the phone rang, pulled up in an auto. They welcomed the newcomers to Canada and apologized for the mixup in communications. In the same breath, the minister explained that he had not received any word from the fieldman; the call from the railway worker had caught him completely by surprise.

Everyone and everything was squeezed

into the car somehow. First they would go to the minister's house, for more introductions and a cup of coffee, and then to the little house that had been cleaned by members of the church and outfitted with beds, chairs, a table, wood for the furnace, and a bag of potatoes for the kitchen.

Toward noon, the minister finally got a call from the fieldman, saying the Prins family was on the train headed for Renfrew.

"You're too late with your news," said the minister. "They're home already."

That happened more than a decade after the *Waterman*'s first arrival in Montreal with more than a thousand newcomers on board. Even after all those years of experience, the responsible authorities slipped up now and then. To err is human. But such experiences weren't quickly forgotten.

Mrs. G.J. Ferwerda of London, Ontario, doesn't smile either when she looks back upon the day when she stepped onto Canadian soil and was placed in the hands

Another family is about to sail for Canada in 1957. Mr. and Mrs. Jaap DeWaard of Amsterdam and their six children wave goodbye to relatives from the Waterman.

Mrs. G.J. Ferwerda, who immigrated as a registered nurse.

Many of the first postwar immigrants were bachelors. After a few years, some of them returned to The Netherlands to visit relatives and friends, hoping, perhaps, to find a bride. Willem Hutten and Menko Postma (at left) join three others on board the Ryndam during a voyage to the Old Country.

Dutch immigrants board the Seven Seas at Quebec City in December, 1957, for a return trip to The Netherlands. Some went for holidays; others went back to stay. At the desk in the foreground is Rimmer Tjalsma, now a regional representative for Wereld Contact, a popular travel organization in The Netherlands.

of a fieldman who obviously didn't know too much about nursing, her vocation. She was single then (surnamed Woelders), a registered nurse with postgraduate study in obstetrics, public health, and pediatrics, who had left Heemstede, Noord-Holland, with intentions of settling in Canada.

Her story:

"The *Waterman* was like a rocking-horse. I was seasick most of the time, and quite lonely. I was glad when we finally arrived at the port, where I was to meet the fieldman. I did not have much money left—only $25. I was sent to a big hall with many beds, even though I told the people at the desk that I would be picked up.

"Dinner was served in a restaurant— stew and dumplings, which cost $1.25! What a taste! No more dumplings for me, thank you. A while later, the fieldman arrived and led me out of the 'prison.' We met a young woman who had immigrated a few months earlier, and she told me that I needed an application form from the nurses' office in the city to apply for registration. The fieldman contradicted her, saying I could start working tomorrow without registering. What did I know?

"We went to the fieldman's house, quite a ways from the city, where I would stay for the night. I went outside to see the surroundings and discovered an outhouse for two. I thought: 'Why don't they tear that old thing down?' A short time later, I found out that it was still in use and that I had to use it too. The next day, the fieldman took me to the local hospital for an interview with the director. She said I could work as a nurse's aide, later as a registered nurse. I had to spell my name verbally, which I did very poorly—as I found out when I got my first paycheque three months later. The fieldman never corrected my spelling. He just grinned.

"We decided that I should wait for my registration, but nothing was done so that I could obtain it. I earned my board by cleaning the house, feeding the chickens, and picking stones off the field. I felt very lonely. Many an afternoon I went into the woods, sat down on a tree stump, and thought of how I could go back without money. The immigrants I met here were so different from the people I was used to associating with. They all seemed to be friends together, and I did not feel at home among them.

"The home missionary for the region came to my rescue. One day, he and his wife took me to the city to pick up an application form. What a relief. Again, the fieldman was far from helpful. He just grinned when I asked him what some question meant. When the form was finally done, it had to be completed by the director of my training hospital.

"The weeks went by ever so slowly. I didn't have too much to wear. I had left most of my clothes in Holland, thinking that I would start working right away. The fieldman's wife made me a dress, which I appreciated. At last, the form came back. It had to be taken to the office in the city. Instead of lending me some money, the fieldman made me hitch-hike the sixty miles to the city. Thank God, I traveled safely. The ladies in the office were very kind and concerned. But when I was going to hand in the form, I couldn't find it. I turned my purse inside out. It was not there. I had been so nervous after all those weeks of waiting that I had left it in the house. I was given a receipt just the same, with the promise that I would mail the form that night. I was so happy that I bounced out of the office and fell down a flight of concrete steps. I hitch-hiked back and went to the hospital, where I was hired right away. That same evening at nine o'clock, the fieldman drove me to the nurses' residence, where I could stay for the time being. Finally I could start working in my own field and live on my own."

In 1957, the Immigration Committee for Canada of the Christian Reformed Church was still immersed in the work for which it had been set up. Canada's door was still open to immigrants. In fact, in that year many more newcomers had arrived compared to the two previous years.

"Interest for immigration is often stimulated by adverse economic conditions, political disturbances, and threats of war," John VanderVliet, the secretary, explained in a report to the church's synod. "The Suez Canal crisis late in 1956 caused an avalanche of inquiries to fall upon my office. About seven hundred letters were received in two months. Some of them were written on the spur of the moment and eventually withdrawn, but others resulted in valuable contacts and subsequent immigrations to Canada. In total, some six thousand letters were dispatched during the year."

His report showed that Canada was the most popular destination for the Dutch emigrants that year. The United States was a few thousand behind, and Australia was in third place. More than half of those who stepped onto Canadian soil ended up in Ontario. British Columbia was next in popularity, followed by Alberta, Quebec, Manitoba, Nova Scotia, Saskatchewan, New Brunswick, and Prince Edward Island. Three went to the Yukon and one landed in Newfoundland.

"At all the arrivals of boats as well as planes," stated VanderVliet, "a representative of the Immigration Committee was present to bid our people a cordial welcome in the name of the Christian Reformed Church and to assist them with baggage difficulties, changes in destination, telegrams, etc. This, to our mind, is a very important task. The fact that the

This firm advertised its emigration services in The Netherlands.

She Came as Miss Verploegh, Now She's Mrs. Sedo

One of the arrivals in 1957 was Mrs. Titie Sedo of Weston, Ontario, then single and thirty years old, and no stranger to emigration fever. Her father, Dr. Henri Verploegh, had once planned to settle down in England to run a clinic for tuberculosis with an English doctor. But when the First World War demolished that plan, he started his own Institute of Rheumatology and Rhoentgentherapy in The Hague. He always tried new ideas, new cures, new methods of helping patients. He used to remark: "I am fifty years ahead of my time . . ."

The doctor died of a heart attack when Titie was only twelve years old. Her mother died in 1956 after a long struggle with cancer. Titie, a secretary, then looked for a completely different kind of life.

"I wanted to strike out, to do new things, so I joined an international correspondence club and wrote in the various languages to many countries. This was very exciting, and I became anxious to travel and actually see those places across the ocean. And so came the moment when I flew to Canada in March of 1957."

She planned to start in Montreal, whose cosmopolitan nature attracted her.

"It was like Europe—all different kinds of people of different nationalities. I loved Canada the minute I stepped onto its soil. I noticed the bright blue sky—it was often so cloudy in Holland—the huge piles of snow, and the enormous billboards alongside the road."

She rented a room at the YWCA. Later, she boarded with a French widow near McGill University.

"From the very beginning, I felt at home. The people were absolutely wonderful. Young or old, Canadians or immigrants, they were always friendly and willing to help. Here I could spread my wings. In Holland, I had always felt limited, wondering, 'What will people think?' or 'I'm not supposed to do this.' Here nobody cared about what I did or didn't do."

One of her first purchases in Canada was a radio, which helped her fight spasms of loneliness. She also joined the YWCA, where she met people while swimming, fencing, learning to cook and being part of a keep-fit class. She took up

Tapping the sap from a maple tree was a new experience for Mrs. Titie Sedo, single at the time. She is with her husband in the lower photo.

ballroom dancing, and got her bronze swimming medal.

Although she had been assured in The Netherlands that she would have no trouble finding a job as a secretary, Titie was given the same response wherever she applied: "You have no Canadian experience." Job hunting became frustrating. Then, at the suggestion of her landlady, she tried Office Overload and was given a job offer on the first day.

After six months in Canada, she met her future husband, a Slovac, who had left Czechoslovakia in 1949. They were married half a year later in Toronto. Their two sons are married to girls of Italian and Greek-Macedonian descent.

"I always will love Holland," says Mrs. Sedo. "Every now and then I go back for a visit to see the old familiar faces and places again, and to speak Dutch once more."

church, their church, is the first one to reach out a friendly hand immediately upon their arrival in this country never fails to impress them profoundly. As a rule, no spiritual work is being done in the reception hall, because everyone is busy with his belongings, his family, and with preparations for the long trip inland. Our fieldmen, however, do hand out leaflets containing information on churches and addresses, church papers, and other Christian literature. Our services at the ports of entry are highly appreciated by our own newcomers and also by the port authorities."

Really, not too much had changed at the ports over the years.

According to VanderVliet, settlement conditions in Canada were from fair to good. However, towards the fall of 1957, fieldmen began to experience a difficult period because of the influx of refugees from the 1956 Hungarian Revolution, government loan restrictions which resulted in layoffs in the building trades, and the increasing number of immigrants from Great Britain.

"Jobs were scarce and housing in the large cities became unobtainable. Yet, the monthly reports at Christmas revealed that only a small number of our people were unemployed, compared with the thousands of other newcomers who were idle at that time. This situation was due largely to the tireless efforts of the fieldmen of our church to keep everyone working, thereby saving the diaconates many thousands of dollars and keeping disappointment and defeat from the lives of many."

VanderVliet underscored the role of the fieldmen for a purpose. He was concerned about a growing feeling within the church that the network of fieldmen was a waste of money now that there were enough congregations across the country to help newcomers with employment and housing. In fact, the synod had decided to reduce its financial support for 1958, and VanderVliet had to cut the work week of four full-time fieldmen to four days and of one to three days.

"The work of the Immigration Committee is more than meeting immigrants at the docks and providing them with a house and a job," he stated. "The work continues: in the after-care, when adverse conditions call for action, in the establishment and maintenance of the reputation and the honor of the Christian Reformed Church, and in the promotion of all such conditions as will help the immigrant in a material, social, and spiritual way. This system has so impressed other denominations that, at a time when our own church tries desperately to break down the apparatus built up with great effort throughout the last eleven years, they are eager to copy our method."

In an article in *Calvinist Contact*, the Christian weekly, he pursued his case.

First Impressions Hadn't Changed

H. John Meyer

The appearance of Halifax hadn't changed much in ten years. The newcomers who disembarked there in 1957 found the harborfront just as dismal as the people had in the earlier years. In fact, H. John Meyer, now of Nepean, Ontario, found his arrival on the *Waterman* on July 20 quite disillusioning.

"We knew that we would arrive at Halifax harbor in the middle of the night, and so we had put the children to bed. Of course, nobody could sleep. When we heard the ship's engines slow down, we dressed the children and took them on deck. And here it was: a dark night, a steady drizzle, and vaguely in the distance a string of lights. It was exactly what we had left behind us—hardly an inspiring experience. The *Waterman* docked in the morning and the debarkation formalities were started. Everybody tried very hard to make us feel welcome, but the five hours between debarkation and boarding the train for Montreal did not give us much time to take advantage of any hospitality. Besides, the weather had not improved one bit, which made us feel somewhat downhearted."

On a later visit to Nova Scotia, Meyer saw it in one of its more pleasant moods.

"It is beautiful country—just like the travel folders say."

"During 1957, an average of twenty-two children were born for every hundred families in Canada. This compares with fifteen in the United States. The difference can be attributed to the fact that immigrants tend to have young families, while those in the United States are more established. Despite the high birth rate in Canadian churches—2,000 in 1957—the original immigration can be credited with being the most important single factor in the growth of the Canadian wing of the Christian Reformed Church."

His statistics on the number of newcomers translated into the establishment of six average-sized congregations each year.

"Is it not advisable to supervise this growth? The addition of six churches a year should be monitored closely by a church that has always expressed interest in orderly growth, not only because the immigrants deserve it but also because we do not want to lose the interest of future immigrants. Some argue that most new immigrants are assisted by relatives already in Canada, implying that they need no special attention from the church. But of the 237 random cases we examined, only eighty-four had relatives in Canada. Even if that estimate is conservative, those who have no relatives here need the assistance provided by the fieldmen. Only through a rational policy, conducted by a church committee, can the present wave of immigration bring such positive results. Let the church continue its interest in the immigration process in Canada. It is the most economical and most effective system."

1957 Immigrant Profiles: A Variety of Experiences

A frank look at how the arrivals of 1957 coped in their new environment was provided by Rev. John Van Harmelen in a broadcast over the NCRV network in Hilversum, the radio center of The Netherlands.

- "Family A——is composed of father, mother, and two school children. Relatives first opened their doors to the family. After that, they rented a house, six kilometers from the city, for $35 a month. The father first found employment in construction and later in the brick factory. During the winter, he was unemployed for a while and drew $30 a week in unemployment insurance. During the off hours, he sells goods."

- "Family B——consists of father, mother, and three school children. They were picked up at the airport by our immigration committee. There was no house for them. Before their arrival, an announcement was made from the pulpit, asking members of the congregation to take these people in until a house could be found. Three members volunteered. Two weeks later, this family rented a basement at $50 a month. The man had been employed at KLM, but he could not find a comparative position here because he first had to be a Canadian citizen, which takes five years of uninterrupted residence in Canada. He went to work in a factory as an unskilled laborer and earned $50 a week. Then they found some friends who agreed to rent a house with them at $115 a month. The friends lived upstairs, the family in question down. In the meantime, we are looking for a better position for the man. At the moment, he is working in a store, earning $55 a week with the potential of making $70. During the evening, he teaches music privately to earn extra income. Although they were not advised to emigrate to Canada, they are doing quite well and do not want to go back, despite the loss of a pleasant job with KLM."

- "Family C——man, woman, and four small children. They were first put up by friends, and were assisted by our immigration committee in finding work and better accommodation. The man was an airplane engine mechanic, knew a bit of English, but couldn't find a comparable position because of the large influx of English mechanics in 1957. He went to work in a garage, earning $55 a week. After three months, he was dismissed because he refused to work on Sundays. Then he began to sell household appliances such as washing machines and refrigerators. That didn't work very well,

Despite such appeals, the special funding continued to dwindle, and the reduction seemed inevitable.

Now Canada was getting a new breed of immigrant from The Netherlands. Many of them were well educated and adept in a variety of skilled and professional fields. One of them, Petrus Meyboom, came over with a master's degree in geology from the University of Utrecht. Geologists were in big demand at that time.

Until 1961, he worked as a ground-water geologist for the Alberta Research Council in Edmonton. He used the results of this work for a doctoral thesis which he defended in Utrecht.

"In 1961," says Dr. Meyboom, "I joined the Geological Survey of Canada in Ot-

Dr. Petrus Meyboom on location in Alberta.

especially because his automobile expenses were much too high relative to his gross income. He remained optimistic, however, and kept an eye on the airplane manufacturer. Because he kept applying and because he had excellent papers, he was finally hired. Now he has it made and earns a generous salary. Though the first year wasn't exactly a success, they are now happy and blessed."

- "**Family D**———a man, woman, and three children. He had been archivist in The Netherlands. He was a handy man, with a lot of incentive, and found a job as a carpenter. To his great surprise, he was paid $1.75 per hour. They were also housed by relatives for awhile, and lived in a gorgeous basement for $45 a month. He was one of those who had been advised by his relatives not to emigrate. They had asked him: what is an archivist going to do in Canada? But he likes Canada very much and apparently has forgotten about his archives."

- "**Family E**———a man, his wife, and two children. The man was in typewriter service and knew English pretty well. The day after arrival in Canada, he went to look for work and found a job in his field. He has been doing that for almost a year now. His first house, for which he paid

$35 a month, left much to be desired. He now lives in a much nicer house, right in the city, and pays $60 a month. If you ask the mother what she likes best about Canada, she will point to the fact that she can give her children whatever they need. That's easy to see, too, since oranges cost only six cents apiece, bananas fifteen cents a pound, eggs four cents apiece, and good quality meat seventy cents a pound. Very few mothers complain about the cost of food in Canada. For $10 to $15, you can get a cart full of groceries in one of these self-serve stores."

- "**Bachelor A**———had no trade, which was too bad. He went to work in a nursery and is still there. The living seemed to be good enough for him to have his girlfriend come over from The Netherlands. They are now married—the law required them to get married within thirty days—and are living in a decent apartment for $60 a month. His young wife helps in the nursery, packaging and shipping flowers. Their combined income is more than $80 a week. They will have no trouble making it."

- "**Bachelor B**———is a farm laborer. He was placed immediately on a farm, with a wage of $100 a month plus room and board. He later went to another farm. But he had enough money left over for a used

tawa and conducted geological research in all the prairie provinces until 1967. In that year, I received Canada's Centennial medal for my work in groundwater geology. The following year, I changed my career to public administration and I occupied progressively more senior positions in the departments of finance, environment, supply and services, and science and technology. At present, I'm deputy secretary for administration policy of the Treasury Board of Canada."

Soon after their arrival in Montreal, H. John Meyer and his wife began to look for a house.

"This was quite an experience for us, coming from Holland with its multitude of housing problems. Imagine going 'shopping' for a house, seeing half a dozen in one evening, and being particular about your choice. No waiting period of so many years, no formalities, no endless red tape, no half a ton of all kinds of forms, requests, certificates, and what have you. Just a simple straight deal between the owner and yourself. It was almost unbelievable."

Many of the earlier immigrants were preoccupied with acquiring new housing too. They didn't like sending their hard-earned dollars to a landlord's bank account. For years, many of them struggled to scrape together enough for a downpayment on a house. Others bought a lot in a carefully chosen location and started saving anew for the materials needed to put a house on it. Some got a Dutch contractor to do the work. Others, experienced or not, tackled the job themselves.

"Many people were building in those days," says S.P. Knuist of London, Ontario. "So you looked around and saw how others did it, you talked, asked questions, got some pointers on how to and how not to. Then you recruited a number of friends. Friends were always eager to help so that they could learn from some of the mistakes that you were going to make."

Knuist got his home-building experience by agreeing to help a friend in Kamloops, British Columbia, where he lived first.

"Even though my friend was a carpenter by trade, it was quite a challenge. Now he had to measure in inches rather than centimeters and abide by an unfamiliar building code. But we made progress. We started in the spring, and by the summer his family could move in. It took a few more months to finish the outside. Since then, the man has established himself as a building contractor and has built many other houses."

An immigrant couple, Henry and Gerda Kuiperij, often dreamed of having a house of their own. They were getting a little tired of their rented frame dwelling. There was no electricity. And the outside pump, the only source of water, produced a mere trickle at the best of times. With small children and lots of clothes to wash, this inconvenience was very annoying.

"During the winter, I couldn't get the clothes dry outside," recalls Mrs. Kuiperij, now of Acton, Ontario. "So I had to take the wash inside and hang it on lines in the living room. All that moisture stayed inside. We could scrape the ice off the ceiling and the baseboards."

Her husband saw a prefabricated

Immigrant Profiles

car, which gave him some freedom of movement."

● "Family F———a large family, composed of father and mother, a couple of older sons and a couple of older daughters. They were assisted by relatives. They rented a house for $75 a month. They all got jobs. They soon made it over the top, for every week a fair portion of their wages was deposited in the bank. The man is already looking for a house to buy. He is employed year round in the workshop of a large construction company. The boys are carpenters, and the girls hire themselves out to Canadian homes as domestic help, earning $1 an hour."

● "Family G———a young family, recently married. The man had no trade, and yet he started with a construction company and earned a good wage. His wife was a hairdresser, thereby earning additional income. In the winter, however, the man was temporarily out of work. Unemployment insurance paid him $30 a week. He found other temporary work at $60 a week, and in the spring went back to the construction company."

Such were the stories Rev. Van Harmelen told: fair stories about good times and bad.

uiperij Built His Own Home

Above: Henry Kuiperij dug the hole for his basement by hand.
Left: The family lived in the basement during the winter.
Below left: The unloading of the prefabricated parts drew some attention.
Below: Kuiperij worked long hours to get his house ready.

house, liked it, and thought: "If someone else can do it, I can too." So they decided to start saving every extra penny. Two years later, the landlady gave notice that they had to get out of the house. After recovering from the shock, the couple decided that this would be a good time to start building. They bought a half-acre parcel of farmland from a relative.

In late April, as soon as the frost was out of the ground, Kuiperij picked up a shovel and began to dig the hole for his basement. It was a backbreaking job, because the ground was hard and full of rocks and boulders. Often, he had to use a pick. There just wasn't the money to hire someone with power equipment.

"My husband finally got the job done.

He then ordered building blocks, cement, sand, etc., and started building the walls from the inside. He hadn't made the hole any bigger than was necessary. We later learned that the walls should be tarred on the outside to stop water from seeping in. Fortunately, it was high ground, and we never experienced a wet basement. We never ordered or bought more than we needed. Paying the bills every month, we were able to keep up."

In the beginning of August, Kuiperij was ready to pour the floor. But an unexpected problem arose—there was no cement available anywhere in the district. Weeks went by before he was able to lay his hands on a quantity.

"We moved into the basement in Oc-

Helping Hands

In the spring of 1951, Ed DeJong bought one acre of land between Aldershot and Waterdown, Ontario, for $500. He went to a construction site to observe the laying of concrete blocks, and then started building his own basement. Jack Dykstra, a cousin, arrived from Edmonton to give him a hand. They lived in the basement while building the rest of the house out of materials from an old house purchased for $200 and from an old sanatorium. Two other young men, Ike Jorritsma and Johnny Post, helped DeJong with the construction in exchange for room and board. A fifth, Frans Klaver, was killed in a tunnel project at Niagara Falls where all of them were working. The house, which took twenty months to complete, was sold in 1953. DeJong, formerly of Sexbierum, Friesland, now lives in Ontario, California, and trucks to forty-eight states.

tober," says Mrs. Kuiperij. "Less than half of the floor was poured. The outside door wasn't even on its hinges yet. We propped it up with a pole from the inside. The inside walls weren't finished. But the partitions, made out of two-by-fours, were. We hung up a few blankets and a bedspread, creating a little room to keep the heat in. This was only for a short time. All the walls were finished before the real cold weather set in."

The next summer, during Kuiperij's vacation, the prefabricated house arrived. All the pieces were numbered, so it wasn't too difficult to put everything in place. It just took a lot of hammering under a blazing sun. The insulation and the inside finish would have to wait for two years. Kuiperij had to put in electrical wiring and plumbing first and he didn't want to borrow more than was actually needed.

There were a few problems. A building permit was needed before the hydro people would connect the house to the supply line. Kuiperij, who had never heard of such a permit, went to the township office, paid $6 for the piece of paper, and got his connection. There were also a few headaches before water was found on the property.

Five years after Kuiperij first started digging, the house was finally finished.

While some people worked, others played.

Here and there, a handful of young immigrants got together and kicked around a ball until darkness forced them to go home. They were indulging in soccer, the world's No. 1 sport, the sport that occupied the free hours of many boys in The Netherlands.

In those years, the sportsminded Canadian was preoccupied with baseball, football, and hockey. Soccer was being played in Canada only by European immigrants. The Dutch showed that they were a force to be reckoned with. Many of the older boys with some experience in organized play in The Netherlands joined existing teams. Others banded together and fielded teams with Old Country names such as *Excelsior*. In a number of centers, the immigrants set up their own sports clubs, with soccer as one of the main activities. *Kaatsen*, a popular sport in Friesland, was also imported. It involves hitting a small ball with the hand. In Ontario, a number of clubs were organized and matches were held. This game, like cricket, will never have universal appeal. But don't mention

that to those enthusiasts who think it's the best game in the world.

Whenever immigrants got together, one of the main subjects of conversation was the war, even in 1957. The five dark years of German occupation had left a lasting mark. People wanted and needed to tell others about their adventures, tragedies, and humorous experiences. Even Canadians loved to listen to their fellow workers talk about those days still fresh in most people's memories.

There were some immigrants who still bore psychological scars and didn't want to talk about their experiences. They winced whenever they heard fellow Dutchmen tell war stories, often in exaggerated

Peter Vriend of Houston, British Columbia, tries to outwit his nephew, Allan Vriend, in chess, a popular game among immigrants.

A 1958 photo of the Neerlandia soccer club of Toronto, founded in 1950.

terms. They simply wanted to forget. But that was difficult, as it was for one woman, Joan, in St. Marys, Ontario.

Colin Campbell, a neighbor from across the street, recalls: "The Royal Canadian Air Force maintained a large base at Centralia, north of St. Marys, and the huge stacks of the St. Marys Cement Company provided a highly visible corner for their triangular training flights. One day, as my wife Bea and I talked with Joan on the sidewalk in front of our home, the roar of a fleet of airplanes suddenly burst on our ears. A look of terror came

Henry J. Martens, a member of the Dutch army in Canada, holds his young daughter in 1941. Most Canadians had no idea of the hardships and suffering experienced by the Dutch during five years of German occupation. They listened with interest to the stories told by immigrants. The photo below, taken shortly after the German capitulation, shows Allied servicemen carrying the coffin of Jannetje Johanna Schaft, one of the many resistance members who paid the ultimate price. Her body was found in a mass grave in the dunes near Haarlem, Noord-Holland.

over her face and her hands flew to her ears as she looked about wildly for a second or two. We were astonished. Joan then explained that it was an instinctive reaction, the result of undergoing many bombing raids when one looked frantically for any available cover. We in Canada have never experienced such horror. It gave us a little insight into what the people of Holland, and millions of others, have endured in modern warfare."

Another one who remembered the war years—although in a much different way—was Henry J. Martens of High River, Alberta. He emigrated to Canada aboard the *Volendam* in September, 1927, at the age of twenty-three, and eventually ended up making $10 a month looking after race horses and helping with crops. Two years later, he was back in The Netherlands, intending to marry his girlfriend and bring her to Canada. But her parents wouldn't let her go. In March, 1930, he returned alone. He married a Canadian girl from High River in 1939, the year the world was plunged into darkness by Hitler's invasion of Poland.

After the Germans overran The Netherlands in May, 1940, he joined the Royal Netherlands Army, which had established a recruiting and training center in Stratford, Ontario. Six weeks later—he had already received some military training in The Netherlands—he was on his way east. He never got a chance to go overseas, however. He developed leg trouble, was admitted to a

military hospital, and was sent home with an honorable discharge in March, 1941.

He returned to High River, went to work with a friend, built a house, and raised a family. By this time, he was deeply rooted in Canadian society. But he retained a soft spot for The Netherlands, always scanning the papers from overseas to keep up with the news.

"In 1949, I took my wife and children to Holland for a visit and we stayed six months. In 1975, we went back again, with our oldest daughter and her husband and son. And we were there again in 1982. After all these years, I haven't forgotten Holland. Why, I was ready to fight for her."

Each of the adults above is either a former resident of Sneek, Friesland, or married to one. And all are now from the greater Vancouver area, attending the annual Sneeker picnic.

John Mud of Brantford, Ontario, playing Kaatsen at the annual Frisian picnic at Paris, Ontario, on July 1, 1983. While the men play, the women knit.

Queen Juliana, accompanied by Dr. A.S. Tuinman, visited immigrants in April of 1952.

Prince Bernhard, consort of Juliana, arrived on the first KLM flight to Dorval Airport near Montreal on May 30, 1949. The flight took 19.5 hours.

Juliana has made a number of visits to Canada. She is shown here in 1967, surrounded by immigrants eager to catch a glimpse of her.

By 1957, Queen Juliana's first visit to the immigrants in Canada was a pleasant memory. She had come in 1952 to see how they were faring in the country that had provided a safe haven for her and her daughters during the war.

Dr. A.S. Tuinman, emigration attaché in Ottawa then, recalls: "Due to the time available, only a few families in Ontario were visited on that occasion. Although the route had not been published, it had leaked out. And all along the road there were immigrants, men, women, and children cheering and waving flags and wearing orange. The queen talked with them at length and was visibly impressed by their perseverance and accomplishments. She was indefatigable, visiting families, admiring the landscape, and walking through the countryside all day, to the despair of the exhausted court dignitaries who tried to keep up with her. For luncheon, the party went to a small restaurant run by a Dutch couple. They served a delicious *huzarensla*. As I remember it, her visit became a feast for all concerned."

Jake Feenstra of Woodstock, Ontario, also has a happy memory of Juliana, although he never met her.

In 1948, as a bachelor farmhand from Bolsward, Friesland, he was on a farm in the Ottawa area only a few days when he got acquainted with a war bride. The news that some newcomers from The Netherlands were in the area had spread fast, and she had come to the farm to welcome him and to extend an invitation.

"She told me that a reception was being planned by the Dutch embassy to mark the accession to the throne of Juliana. And I and a number of others were invited. That was completely unexpected. Here I was, a poor immigrant just off the boat, being asked to mingle with high society. I'll never forget it."

When Prince Bernhard visited the St. Lawrence Seaway project at Cornwall, Ontario, in May of 1958, he was presented a gift by immigrants Edda Harrison, Trynie DeVries, and Henny VanderVeer.

Chapter 22

But Life Goes On

Frans Klaver, newly arrived in Canada, is shown with his sister, Mrs. Harry L. DeJong, and her two children in 1951.

July, 1953, began happily for the Christian Reformed congregation in Wellandport, Ontario. Everyone was looking forward to the opening of the new church building. But three days before the dedication, sad news arrived: one of the members, twenty-one-year-old Frans Klaver, who had emigrated in 1951 from Tzummarum, Friesland, had died as the result of a fall while working at a tunnel project at Niagara Falls. This tragedy put a damper on the events at the church. On July 31, a few days after the dedication, most of the members turned out for the funeral, conducted by Rev. Wiebe Van Dyk, a recent arrival from The Netherlands.

But Life Goes On

Rev. Harri Zegerius of the Reformed Church office in Hamilton, Ontario, received a message from Ottawa on an afternoon in the early '50s: "Arie DeMik is in Victoria Hospital, London, with lung cancer. New immigrants from Gouda, with little English. They don't know what's up. Will you go and talk to them?"

The next morning, on the way to a short speaking tour in Michigan, the minister stopped at the hospital and found Arie, a small man with dark hair and startling blue eyes, sitting on the edge of his bed, panting for breath.

"Dominee," he said, "I don't know what's happening. I've been working in a greenhouse for some months and things have been going well. But for some days now, I've been very short of breath. *Dominee,* I hope I'll be O.K. We don't want much from Canada—not to be rich. Just a little place near some water, a cow, a few ducks, a peaceful life for my wife and son."

Rev. Zegerius clasped the man's hand and said: "Your illness is not that simple. I'm sure that they will do all they can. But there comes a time, Arie, when we have to turn our hearts to God, for God is our final hope. And, Arie, some of our humble dreams can be fulfilled only on the other side of the river. Let me read from the Bible and say a prayer."

The minister's next task was to look for the wife and son. He finally found them in a little house near a stream and some greenhouses. Very carefully, he approached the seriousness of the situation. But finally he had to say it—Arie didn't have much longer to live. The woman collapsed on the floor. Quite some time elapsed before he dared to leave her and the son to their grief. He hoped they would remember his prayer.

Then he traveled on to his speaking engagements. He would try to tell the long-time settlers in Grand Rapids what it's like to be an immigrant, what it's like to die in a strange land. He wondered if they would understand.

On his way home, five days later, he asked the receptionist at the desk in Victoria Hospital: "May I see Arie DeMik?"

There was silence, then the words: "Arie DeMik was buried yesterday."

Rev. Zegerius was deep in thought as he drove on to Hamilton. He hoped that he had said what needed to be said, that he had shown some of Christ's compassion.

Then it was time to deal with other immigrants and other problems—lots of them. The blue-eyed man from Gouda slipped into the background. But he was never quite forgotten.

On the morning of November 17, 1972, thirty-seven-year-old Harry Roefs stepped into his car and headed for his brother-in-law's farm in West Bay, Nova Scotia, where he was helping put up a barn. He looked forward to this work. After all, he and his father had received help, too, when they were putting up their own new barn. Recalls his mother, Anna: "Before leaving, he had told his father: 'Just feed the cows and leave the milking to me. I'll do it tonight when I get home.' My husband was already in his 70s and he found it difficult to lug the heavy milking machines around. So he didn't argue."

The couple spent a quiet day on the farm. At 2:30, there was a knock on the door: their priest. "We were wondering what was up, because he didn't visit us that often. When he had come inside, he said: 'I have some bad news for you.

The burial of a Dutch immigrant, Mrs. Syrt Wolters of the Victoria, British Columbia, area, who died in September of 1959.

Harry Roefs at work harvesting tomatoes.

A Death in the Old Country

After four and a half years in Canada, Mrs. Leo Hovius received some dreaded news in a letter from relatives in The Netherlands: her father was seriously ill and was not expected to recover. Her husband still had some money in The Netherlands and had time on his hands—he was out of work—so they decided to go back for a trip.

Nowadays, an urgent phone call concerning an overseas emergency prompts a quick visit to a travel agent, who arranges an immediate booking on a transatlantic flight. But in the early 1950s, an airplane was still a novelty, a mode of travel only for those with money. Hovius and his wife left their belongings in the care of an acquaintance and set sail for The Netherlands aboard the *Maasdam*.

"My father had died before we arrived," says Mrs. Hovius. "In fact, he had already been buried. Nevertheless, everyone was delighted that we had come."

Leo's father took him to his barn and said: "Look at all the nice cattle. That can be yours if you take over the farm. Mother and I will get a house in the village."

Leo shook his head and said: "It's too late. Canada is now my country."

He and his wife didn't feel quite at home in The Netherlands. There was something about Canada that made them want to go back and tackle the hardships that surely would be awaiting them. They stayed for three months and then headed home aboard the *Rijndam*, accompanied by Mrs. Hovius' brother and his wife, emigrants on the way to British Columbia.

Harry was involved in a car accident this morning. He's not dead. But he's in serious condition in the hospital in Antigonish.' We just stood there, not knowing what to say or do. The news was like a thunderbolt out of a clear sky."

Members of the family and Harry's fianceé were notified. Some went to the hospital. A kind neighbor offered to milk the cows.

"When they returned from the hospital, the word was bad. Harry was critical, with head injuries. He had spent hours on the operating table. But he was still in a coma when they left."

The next day, his father and mother went to the hospital. Their son, who had been so full of life, was dying. They wouldn't be able to run the farm without him. His mother thought: "Is this what we came to Canada for?"

"It was the hardest moment in our lives," she recalls. "Harry was lying there. We could see he was very sick. His eyes were open, but he didn't respond to anything we said or asked. There was no sign of recognition."

The Roefs later learned that their son, bleeding profusely, had lain in the ambulance for more than an hour while rescuers tried to free the other driver from the wreckage.

"A doctor in Halifax told us that if Harry had been brought to the hospital earlier, they might have been able to do something for him. But it was too late. We later wrote here and there to protest, but we ran into stone walls. Was it because we were poor immigrants?"

Harry clung to life. His parents made the 160-mile round trip to the hospital two or three times a week, sometimes traveling through storms so severe that they wondered whether they would return home safely. It was a bleak winter.

Harry never came out of the coma. He died on June 29, 1973.

On December 1, 1977, a terrible auto accident claimed the lives of Mrs. John Kap of Sarnia, Ontario, sixty-three years old, and her daughters, thirty-one and thirty-four. For a long time, Kap, who had been on the *Waterman* in 1947, walked around aimlessly, asking himself: "Why? Why us? Why was a successful marriage of nearly forty years so abruptly ended?" There was no answer.

Kap now says: "It was a terrible blow to our family, although it couldn't be compared to Job, who lost everything. God

Great Expectations Dashed by Illness

John Eisen tries out the scooter and the home-built sidecar.

In the fall of 1956, John Eisen's brother and wife and two children returned to The Netherlands. He had never really felt at home in Canada. His thoughts had wandered constantly to his old home in that little country beside the sea. John, however, was intent on staying.

He had thought for several years about going to Calvin College in Grand Rapids, Michigan. He hoped to study for the ministry or some other helping profession.

"In September, 1957, I was accepted on probation, for I had only one and a half years of H.B.S. schooling in The Netherlands. That school year, I hitch-hiked more than four thousand miles between Grand Rapids and Toronto.

John's mother returned to The Netherlands in the fall of 1957. Her death from a heart attack the following year saddened him deeply. It was because of her courage and faith that he was in the New World, trying hard to get an education and become secure for the rest of his life. But there was joy and brightness too: his marriage in Toronto to Tjits, a girl he had met during a visit to The Netherlands.

"Together we went back to Grand Rapids. For the first five months, Tjits worked in the kitchen of the college, and I became a Watkins salesman. We bought a scooter so that we could get around. And in Sepember, 1959, we bought a rather big house and boarded nine or ten students to make ends meet. That same month, our John was born."

After a shaky start in Canada, everything seemed to be going well for John. He and the other students played Monopoly every Saturday night for three years, a period filled with much fun and fellowship. He and his wife and the baby once took the scooter to Holland Marsh and back. Little John slept in a home-built sidecar. A customs officer at the Port Huron border crossing looked suspiciously at the wooden box and asked: "What have you got in there? Chickens?" Eisen replied: "No, the baby." The officer didn't believe him and took a peek. Then, with a wide grin, he shouted to his colleagues: "Hey guys, look here! A baby!"

In May, 1962, Eisen graduated with a B.A. in sociology. His dream of making something worthwhile out of his life was close to becoming reality. There was something that worried him, however. On many days, he didn't feel well. Something was wrong with his body, but doctors could not diagnose the ailment.

He found a job as a rehabilitation social worker for the Ontario government and settled in Toronto. Later he was transferred to Renfrew, northwest of Ottawa. As the months passed, he felt his condition growing worse. In February, 1964, he went to hospital for observation and received the shocking news that he had multiple sclerosis, a disease of the central nervous system.

Although he couldn't do regular work any more, he didn't give up. He started making quartet games—centered on things like Canadian history, geography and language. And in 1965, he and his wife began selling Dutch products, as we noted in an earlier chapter.

"As we had to face the reality of chronic illness, our Lord was with us," says Eisen. "He has given us the courage to go on. Many members of our congregation also helped. They bought for us a stencilling machine for about $400. The government provides a dependent father's allowance. Furthermore, we've been gladdened and inspired to see how we can survive as a family when we all work together."

stayed close at hand and will continue to do so until the end. He promised us that."

In 1972, tragedy struck the family of another of the early arrivals—Dirk Van Rooyen of the Chatham, Ontario, area. His son, whom he had brought with him to Canada in 1948, was killed at the age of thirty, leaving behind a wife and three children. While operating a bulldozer, he had struck a garage door, causing a steel hoist to crash down, which crushed his spine just below the neck.

Van Rooyen and his wife had been touched by tragedy before. They hadn't been in Canada long when they lost their baby of fourteen months. Psalm 91 had

An Expensive Recovery

Fully recovered after three operations, Jelle Ganzevoort enjoys skating on the lake in 1952.

For years, Jelle Ganzevoort had known that there was something awry with his body. Ever since an operation in The Hague in 1925 to correct a stomach disorder, he had felt discomfort. But when he went to doctors in The Netherlands, and later in Canada—he left Heerenveen, Friesland, in 1948, sailing on the *Kota Inten*—he got the same answer: we can't find anything wrong with you.

He held a succession of jobs in the St. Catharines, Ontario, area, including work as a nurseryman, a laborer in a cement-block factory, and a bulldozer operator, but all the while he knew that something was wrong. He began swallowing forty-two aspirins a day to ease the pain.

In desperation, he went to another doctor, who ordered an immediate operation. It was none too soon. He could have been dead the next morning because of a break in his intestines, which would have poisoned his system. Two more operations followed. After one of them, the doctor commented: "You know, we've put more than a thousand stitches in you. It goes to show that you can't kill a Dutchman."

The doctor's bill for the three operations amounted to $600. Ganzevoort, who had no medical or hospital insurance, dug into his savings and paid the fee promptly. The doctor, in turn, used the money to pay the colleagues who had assisted in the operations, and he probably took a net loss in the process. But no one helped with the hospital bill, which totalled a daunting $3,600. Ganzevoort borrowed the money. Then he resolved to pay off his debt as quickly as possible by getting a second job.

"I knew that the Dutch immigrants liked horse meat. And I also knew someone who slaughtered horses. So I got into business, buying the meat for ten cents a pound and selling it for twenty cents. I once sold nine hundred pounds in one week, meaning I had around $90 extra in my pocket."

His days were long. He worked at his regular job from seven to five, ate a quick lunch at home, and then made his rounds of the Dutch immigrants, often not getting home to his family until 10 p.m. The thought of eating horsemeat was repugnant to Canadians. Once Ganzevoort was even brought before a judge to face some obscure charge related to the horsemeat business. The case was dismissed.

"I sold horse meat for five years and got rid of all my debts. Someone else then took over the business. There was a lot of hard work in those early days. We had no choice but to work hard . . ."

comforted them and now it came to them again: "He that dwelleth in the secret place of the Most High shall abide under the shadow of the Almighty . . ."

After months of waiting on a farm near Mount Forest, Ontario, John and Gerda Hesselink finally received their shipped belongings. There was much excitement as they unpacked the crates and looked for a place for everything. Life had been so different since the packers came to the farm near Winterswijk, Gelderland, in October, 1951, and the family—Hesselink, his wife, sons Bertus and Albert, his widowed mother, and three brothers and one sister, all unmarried—moved to Canada. But the arrival of the crates seemed to put everyone in a good mood.

One day, while Mrs. Hesselink was still busily sorting her belongings, the farmer's wife came running into the house. Mrs. Hesselink couldn't understand much of what the woman was saying, but she guessed from her behavior that something serious had happened. She rushed to the barn where her husband had been working and found him lying in pain on the floor. He had slipped on straw in the hayloft and had plunged eighteen feet, breaking his back.

"He thought he was going to die. He told me to go back to Holland with the children. We prayed together. Then the ambulance came to take him to the hospital."

Hesselink survived, but the lower part of his body was paralyzed. He spent ten months in Toronto hospitals. In the meantime, as the medical bills multiplied, he had to decide on how to make a living. The fall had shattered his dreams of starting his own farm in Canada.

"We decided to start a store, and we chose the village of Drayton as the location," recalls Hesselink. "In 1953, we rented a little house on Wellington Street and turned part of it into a store. We placed our first order with National Grocers for $300. We hardly knew what to order. We knew we needed sugar, coffee, tea, margarine, tobacco, and toilet paper. It was hard to change from farming to a business life, especially in a new land with its language difficulties."

Within a year, the business had outgrown the house and was moved into a store across the street. More lines were added. Hardware, dry goods, paint, and wallpaper complemented the grocery and

John Hesselink, paralyzed as the result of an accident, enjoys the company of his sons. Below, he prices Dutch-made underwear in his living room in 1956. In its earlier days, Hesselink's store had a Dutch baby-buggy in the window.

Dutch imports sections.

Hesselink used crutches to get about, postponing the use of a wheelchair as long as he could. For business trips, he drove a specially equipped car. Later, his injury became complicated by a rare spinal disease which causes increasing paralysis. He was in hospital frequently for treatment, but always returned to his post behind the counter. Then major surgery forced his retirement. He now uses a wheelchair to get around, and contents himself by doing the bookkeeping for the business—the enlarged Hesselink Shopping Center is managed by his son, Albert—and by working for the church.

The Reformed Church helped him and his wife get started in business. When they were faced with the medical bills, a sum of $2,000 was scraped together from Church World Service funds and from churches in the Classis of Muskegon. From month to month, they saved what they could and repaid their obligation.

In 1968, Rev. Harri Zegerius, then pastor of the First Reformed Church of Portage, Michigan, revisited the family in Drayton. He wrote later in *The Church Herald:* "The striking thing about this family is not its helplessness, but its faith. There is no bitterness against an undeserved blow, no hopelessness in the face of a difficult future . . . After dinner, the man asked for his chequebook and then handed me a cheque for $1,000. He said something like this: 'You were here to provide help when we needed it. We want you to handle this gift. Find a place in the Reformed Church where it is needed as we once needed such help. We want the church to know that there is gratitude not only for the Word of God proclaimed, but for the kindly deed done for those in bitter need.' I left that little town confirmed in

Natural Phenomenon Brought Dutch-style Disaster

Arie VanderKooij stands knee-deep in water during the flooding of Holland Marsh in 1954.

In early February of 1953, terrible news came from The Netherlands: a spring tide accompanied by gale-force winds had driven a solid mass of water against the dikes in the southwestern delta area of The Netherlands. As dikes were breached, the water entered some low-lying polders gradually, rising slowly. But elsewhere, it was a different story. The boiling sea rushed over the land, sweeping away all that stood in its path.

On that ill-fated night, as alarm bells pealed a warning and cattle lowed in terror, close to two thousand people lost their lives. Thousands were left homeless. The cattle stock, the pride of the country, was decimated. Many towns and villages and thousands of acres of arable land disappeared below the swirling brine.

Mourning settled over The Netherlands. The news traveled quickly to the immigrant community in Canada, bringing shock and sadness. People felt touched by the disaster, even though they were now in another land. Many went door-to-door to collect money for a relief fund.

In mid-October of the following year, it was Canada's turn to be hit by a vicious storm. Meteorologists called it Hurricane Hazel. First it battered Haiti and part of Cuba before smashing its way into the Carolinas and then inland all the way to Ontario.

Prolonged torrential rains turned normally placid streams into raging torrents. Flooding and high winds caused hundreds of deaths and damage to property costing millions of dollars. A dike broke too—in Holland Marsh, where Dutch farmers watched helplessly as a blanket of water covered their fields and surrounded their houses.

that intangible work of the ministry . . ."

Hesselink says Canada has been good to him and his family, regardless of the accident and the hard times that followed.

"It didn't turn out the way we planned; we didn't become farmers. When I look at the store, I sometimes wonder how it was all possible. It took a lot of work and dedication. You know, Canada needed people, and the Dutch came. Some say they made the move for the children or for a better future. That may have been true, but I'm convinced that the emigration movement was part of God's plan. Knowing that to be true for us, we've never regretted coming to Canada."

The Christian Reformed Church at Woodstock, Ontario, before the tornado struck in 1979. The aftermath is shown below. The school on the site, also destroyed, was replaced by a modern new structure.

Shortly before 7 p.m. on Tuesday, August 7, 1979, the warm, muggy air in Woodstock, Ontario, grew calm. The cloud cover turned an eerie orange-grey. The unnatural air and sky seemed to forebode something terrible.

A stiff breeze set up. The clouds, now black, began to swirl. Before long, the wind grew more intense; gusts swept along the summer dust. Rain began to pelt down. It was obvious that a fierce storm, the kind that can uproot trees and flatten ripening crops, was about to hit. People ran for shelter.

Suddenly, there was a great roar. People who turned to look at the sky saw a monstrous, swirling black cloud which was sucking up shingles, branches, and birds. Several small funnels touched the ground behind it.

The tornado cut a swath of utter destruction. It reduced some homes to rubble, and tore the roofs from others. It pulled trees out of the ground and overturned cars. Farms lay in ruins. There were some deaths and hundreds of injuries.

When it was all over, people picked themselves up or climbed out of their various hiding places to survey the damage. What they saw made them sick.

A shock awaited the Dutch-Canadians who lived in the southeast section of the city, where the twisters had struck. The damage to their own houses was bad enough. But when they heard that the nearby Christian Reformed Church and the Christian school next to it were demolished, they were stunned. Some broke down in tears.

In its early years, the congregation had worshipped in a basement. Later, instead of building the sanctuary on top of that basement, they decided to buy land adja-

cent to Highway 401, the freeway that crosses Ontario, and construct a new church. Many people contributed countless hours of volunteer labor and hard-earned dollars. Now it was all gone: what had taken immigrants years of painstaking effort to build up had been destroyed in a few seconds.

The shock, however, soon changed into determination to rebuild, to start anew, to put up buildings that were even better than the previous ones. And that's what happened.

The homes and farms of many Dutch people were extensively damaged.

Through insurance settlements, a general relief drive, and the helping hand of friends and neighbors, the victims struggled back to their feet. But for one family, the scars remain. Corrie Ryksen, thirty-three years old, was killed when the vicious winds tore into her farmhouse near the village of Harley. Her nine-year-old

daughter, Annita, sustained serious head injuries. The father and the other children were in the barn and escaped the brunt of the storm.

In British Columbia's Bulkley Valley, where the well-known colonizer, Jacob Prins, was active before and after the war, disaster struck the Dutch community one night in November, 1947; the little Christian Reformed church at Houston, built with much sacrifice, was reduced to ashes.

Members of the congregation felt sad and bewildered, but they did not despair; they launched plans for a new building immediately. The town offered a community hall as an interim meeting place, and catechism classes were held in the public school and in an Anglican Mission House.

In December of 1958, nearly a decade had passed since the new church building had been dedicated. And then fire struck again. The damage was considerable. Again, the community came to the aid of the congregation. This time services were held in the public school auditorium and catechism classes were conducted in the village council room. By March 12, 1961, the congregation was once again worshipping in its own building.

The Iron Springs, Alberta, Christian Reformed Church in 1951.

A Terrible Day in Iron Springs

In 1958, fire struck the Christian Reformed Church in Iron Springs, Alberta. The pastor, Rev. Peter Van Egmond, wrote about that terrible day soon after.

"Tragedy struck our congregation on Sunday, March 9, when fire completely destroyed our house of worship. My wife noticed the blaze first, at 5:15 in the morning. However, before we could summon any help, thick smoke had made it impossible for us to enter the building. Nothing could be saved—chairs, Bibles, hymnals, communion set, and books of the young people's societies all have been destroyed. Water is scarce here; what we had was hardly enough to keep the parsonage wet. The house is located about one hundred feet south of the church site. It was snowing, and a sharp, cold wind from the northwest blew sparks and burning debris over the house. The heat inside was almost unbearable. If the wind had shifted just a bit to the north, the parsonage would have been lost too. Within a few hours, our church building was reduced to a sad smoking mass of rubble and ashes. The first postwar immigrant church of Western Canada was gone . . ."

From the other side of the world comes a news item in the Dutch press: "In Woubrugge, a rural community near Leiden, people are showing compassion for A. Schuilenburg, a former resident, who emigrated to Canada. While the family was visiting Holland, their house in Canada burned to the ground. A plumber was at fault. The insurance didn't cover the loss and the plumber didn't have any money. So the local football society in Woubrugge has plans for organizing a huge festive evening to assist this family in the task of reconstructing home and good fortune."

That's life; it has its ups and downs. One can't escape its trials by moving to another country. Tragedy and bad fortune can strike anyone—anywhere. Let's now turn to a happier aspect of the immigration story—to romance and weddings. For life does go on.

Mrs. Anne VanWijngaarden of the Wellandport, Ontario, area tells this story: "Just after the war, in 1947 or so, a young fellow in the south of Holland met a nice girl. This happens every day, you say. Well, this was a bit different. He was nineteen and she was sixteen. They sort of liked each other and met off and on. Then, one day, the young man said that he was going to Canada. Well, she didn't think much of the idea, and the relationship went cold. He left in 1948, found a job which paid thirty-five cents an hour, and counted himself lucky. After the excitement of emigrating and settling had passed, he found that he missed the nice girl back home. She was surprised to see a letter from Canada in the mail, but she responded. That's how a three-year correspondence courtship got started. Finally, in August of 1951, a young lady set off for Canada to meet this young stranger

Community Springs Back after Burnout

Early in the morning on February 24, 1983, fire broke out in several areas of the fifty-year-old frame building which housed the Bulkley Valley Christian High School of Smithers, British Columbia. Within minutes, flames were leaping through the entire structure. By 5 a.m., there was nothing left but a tangle of twisted pipes, charred wood, and ashes.

Other than a few items rescued from the principal's office, everything was lost: teaching material, school records, artwork, trophies, music sheets, gym equipment, lab supplies, a new piano, and personal items belonging to staff and students. There was shock and disbelief, but no one despaired.

While firefighters were still dousing the flames, the teaching staff gathered at the vice-principal's home to pray and to discuss this unexpected development. Further discussions with the school board and members of the school society were held during the next few days. Interim accommodation was arranged. Books and supplies were borrowed from other schools. Within days, classes were under way again.

Immediately after the fire, the students organized a bottle drive and a bake sale and raised more than $1,000. They found the response from the local community overwhelming. In fact, when word of the fire spread, people from across Canada offered help and money.

A few weeks later, another fire of suspicious origin heavily damaged the Christian School at Rocky Mountain House, Alberta. Again, people from near and far responded. Again, there was evidence of the underlying comradeship among the Dutch community, coast to coast.

People watch helplessly as fire destroys the Bulkley Valley Christian High School of Smithers, British Columbia, in late February, 1983.

It's a common story: Peter Van Dyk of Gemert, Noord-Brabant, came to Canada in 1947, followed in May of 1948 by Theodora Selten, the woman he wanted to marry. The ceremony had to take place within a month of her arrival. In this way the Canadian government safeguarded against young women becoming dependent on the state. The reunited couple is shown near Quebec City with Jan VandeElzen, another new arrival from Gemert.

—after all, three years is quite a time. She arrived in Toronto, where they were supposed to meet. But she couldn't spot him. She had to get off the train, but then what? She sank down on a suitcase while a helpful fieldman went to look for the young man. Just before the train was to leave, he found him. The fieldman, after telling the young man where to find the girl, hopped on board. Can you imagine how the young woman must have felt when that train pulled out and there was no boyfriend in sight? Well, he soon appeared, accompanied by some friends. She was escorted to a car, where she and her young man got into the back seat to begin to get acquainted again. She was impressed with the vehicle. Then, after a few hours of driving, they pulled up to a gas station, where she and he changed over to an old jalopy. But that didn't seem to lower her opinion of him; in December of that year they were married."

When Mrs. J. Dening of Edmonton, Alberta, was a single girl in The Netherlands, she couldn't wait for the day to come when she would step on the boat to Canada. Her boyfriend had gone ahead of her, and he had been there thirteen months already—a long time for the two to be parted.

She felt nervous on the day of departure. But when a sister said: "God is the same all over the world," she felt eased in her mind and comforted.

But the nervous fear overwhelmed her again when she and her two girl compa-

nions sat waiting at the train station in Edmonton for their boyfriends to show up. After hours of waiting, one of the girls said: "If we'd known this, we would have stayed in Holland."

But the boys hadn't forgotten them. They were waiting at another station, wondering what had become of their girls. There were no harsh words, of course, when everyone finally was reunited.

The single immigrants—and there were many—kept their eyes open for future wives. They had to look around at the girls attending the young people's society meetings, at the new families arriving in their community. These boys, far away from relatives and friends, were lonely and in need of companionship.

Rev. Henry Numan of the Christian Reformed Church once told this story: "In those days, there were some single men who came to church for other than spiritual reasons. People there could speak Dutch and there were girls. Not enough girls, mind you. But there were girls. And that kept the boys coming. Some only came for a short time, but others experienced a conversion. One fellow I remember was a big farm boy who had never been inside a church before. But he came every Sunday, and he even started to come to catechism, because he cared about a girl. One evening, I asked the first question of the Heidelberg Catechism: 'What is your only comfort in life and death?' I looked at him. He looked back, and said: 'Een kop koffie, dominee' (A cup of coffee, Reverend). Everyone roared, and so did I. I hear that he's an elder in the Christian Reformed Church now."

Anno Slomp of Nobleford, Alberta, who came in 1954 with thirteen other members of his family, but without his fiancée, remembers well the loneliness.

"We wrote letters to each other every week. But that only seemed to make it worse. One time, I made a stupid mistake on the beet farm where I worked. The farmer said: 'What's the matter, Anno? Didn't you get a letter this week?' He had guessed it. Well, she came over after a year and we got married two weeks later."

Romance sometimes upset a family's carefully-laid plans for emigrating as smoothly as possible. The press in The Netherlands recorded more than one instance of an older teen who simply rebelled against the family and stayed behind with a sweetheart when the time came for everyone to leave—even though the fare had been paid.

One headline in February, 1952, read: "*Groote Beer* Leaves Without Girl." The eighteen-year-old daughter of a flax worker from Leerdam, south of Utrecht, had been left behind. She and her boyfriend of three months, a soldier from Wormerveer, north of Amsterdam, had disappeared without a trace. So the rest of the family, disappointed and worried, sailed to Canada without her. Another case, a few years later, involved a nineteen-year-old youth from Leiden, Zuid-Holland, who decided that his girlfriend was worth more than a new life in Canada. He went into hiding, and his family had no choice but to leave on the *Ryndam* as scheduled.

There was nothing fancy about many of the early weddings in Canada. The immigrants were struggling to make something out of nothing and couldn't afford such luxuries as tuxedos, lavish ban-

Wedding in English

Mrs. Ann De Jong of Matsqui, British Columbia, had come to Canada to be a bride, too, at the age of thirty-two.

In 1960, her husband-to-be, Jack, was a lonely immigrant with whom she had corresponded at the suggestion of a friend.

"At the time I didn't mean to become serious," she recalls. "I had a good and satisfying job as a nanny, and was involved in first aid and the Red Cross. I thought it was fun to hear about that faraway country. But one thing led to another and, after three years of writing, he asked me to come to Canada to be his wife."

Her parents were adamantly against her going. They had never met the boy, and British Columbia was half a world away. But she had made up her mind. She took English lessons in 's-Hertogenbosch, Noord-Brabant, and applied for emigration in The Hague. After two months, she was called in for an interview and a medical examination. Then she had to sign that she was willing to marry within a month after arrival or return to The Netherlands. With this regulation, the government safeguarded against young women becoming dependent on the state.

Before long, she was in an airplane winging its way across the ocean, destination Vancouver. Her luggage, including her wedding dress, had been sent on ahead.

"I recognized my friend from the pictures he had sent me. He introduced me to two people who were with him—he called them Grandma and Grandpa Nielsen— and they took me to their home in Surrey. Over the years, those people became as dear to us as our own parents. I stayed with them for the month prior to the wedding. On the third week, I was treated to a bridal shower. I was just overwhelmed by the best wishes and gifts from people who didn't even know me. All I could say was 'Thank you, thank you, thank you.' The week after, a lot of the Dutch ladies living in that area gave me a Dutch shower. That was easier, because I could thank them properly."

Since the wedding ceremony was to be in English, the bride-to-be rehearsed her words carefully. On the big day, she even got some help from the Roman Catholic priest, who proceeded slowly so that she wouldn't miss anything.

Piet and Mary Provoost on their wedding day.

A One-photograph Wedding

"I wasn't married in the white wedding dress most girls dream about," says Mrs. Mary Provoost of Aylmer, Ontario, who tied the knot in 1950. She had met her husband in a greenhouse during tobacco planting time. "My mother insisted on a suit, because it was more practical then. The wedding took place on my parents' farm at six o'clock in the evening. We each had one attendant. People were sitting in rows, facing us and the minister. Later on, we had a *Hollandse broodtafel* (a selection of sandwiches). There were no skits; just a nice get-together with family and friends. After the ceremony, we went to have our picture taken by the photographer. Yes, that's right—one picture."

The following evening, the farm was a beehive of activity once again: this time, the newly-married couple were entertaining the young people of the church, all of whom had been invited for fun and games.

"We were given very few presents, as you can imagine. Just before the wedding, Mom took me upstairs and gave me a few things to start out with—a couple of sheets, pillow cases, and towels, still packed in a wooden suitcase from Holland. I made do with them for a long time."

Return Trip for a Wife

No, this was no honeymoon cabin. Its cramped space was shared by two brothers, Jake and Henry Feenstra, who had settled in the Woodstock, Ontario, area in the late 1940s. They had bought the structure, fixed it up a bit, and then placed it on two acres of land they had purchased.

"It wasn't much," recalls Jake. "It held a bunkbed and an oil stove. We slept and ate breakfast there, but we had to go to town for lunch. We lived in it for a year. It was a small beginning."

Jake met and fell in love with a girl from The Netherlands who was visiting a friend in Woodstock. They decided to get married—in The Netherlands, where all the relatives could be present. The ceremony took place in 1950 in the coastal village of Valkenburg, Zuid-Holland.

"People swarmed all around me," says Jake. "They all wanted to know about Canada. Well, I told them the truth, that a lot of tears were being shed and that a lot of families were living in poor conditions. And yet I felt that most of them didn't believe me."

The newly-wed couple found that it was impossible to get berths on a liner bound for Canada. They finally located two placed on the *Edam*, a freighter, that would leave from Antwerp, Belgium, with some twenty-five other passengers.

"It took that old ship fifteen days to get across. We ran into a heavy storm which we rode out for five days. What a terrible

*Mr. and Mrs. Jake Feenstra after their wedding in The
therlands. The garage made out of the kist *was big enough
to accommodate Feenstra's car.*

ship. The captain came around now and
then to ask us how we were. Well, we certainly weren't enjoying anything. Our
main concern was to get safely to
Canada."

Included in Jake's *kist* was an assortment of cheese-making equipment.

"Somebody in Canada had promised to
pay half the freight if I would take it
along. That was a good deal for me. The
man made cheese and sold it at the church
on Sundays, because that's where he could
find most of the immigrants together."

The *kist*, by the way, was eventually
turned into a garage.

Another Happy Story

The photo above shows Mr. and Mrs.
Peter Meliefste of Coaldale, Alberta, and
their two oldest children, Corny and Inga,
in front of their rented house in 1953.
Twenty years later, Mrs. Meliefste, a
teacher at the Coaldale Christian School,
and the same two children were the
recipients of degrees granted by the
University of Lethbridge. Mother, who
already had her B.Ed., added a B.A.
degree to her credits. Inga received a
B.Ed. and Corny a B.A. Afterward, Inga
taught for a number of years in Cloverdale, British Columbia, and then got married and quit teaching. Corny also became
a teacher and has been principal of the
Dufferin Christian School in Carman,
Manitoba, for the last ten years. In the
1973 photo, the three are standing in front
of the family's own house.

The Van Aert family, parents and sixteen children, before emigrating from Etten-Leur, Noord-Brabant, in 1950. They first lived near Winnipeg and later moved to Vancouver. In February, 1982, the parents celebrated their 50th wedding anniversary by renewing their vows in a Roman Catholic ceremony. There are now more than 130 family members.

The Griffioen family—father and mother, seventeen children, a son-in-law, and a grandchild—arrived in British Columbia in 1952.

quets, expensive gifts, and honeymoons on exotic islands.

Less than three weeks after her arrival in Smithers, British Columbia, in 1950, Aafke Wieling was to become the bride of John Koldijk in a ceremony at the Christian Reformed Church in Houston. They drove into Houston with John's brother, Siebren, the only relative in Canada, and a friend, Roel Groen.

"We went in an old pickup," recalls Mrs. Koldijk. "John was driving and Roel and Siebren were sitting in the back. Roel was playing his mouth organ and eating dust at the same time. There were no paved roads yet. Before we entered Houston, we had to stop by a creek and wash up a little bit."

After the ceremony, members of the congregation threw a nice party in the church basement. Then it was back to the farm. There was work to be done.

The Griffioen family of Tuindorp, a village near Utrecht, made the news when it arrived in Canada in 1952. Mother and father brought along seventeen children, one son-in-law, and one grandchild. While traveling by train from New York City to British Columbia, the family was the darling of the press. This publicity helped create the public perception that the Dutch immigrant families were large.

The photos on these two pages show a few of these families. Since most of the children of immigrants are now married and have families of their own, the number of people in Canada who can claim Dutch descent is staggering. The 1981 census figures show there are 408,240 who claim one ethnic origin. Add to that the ones who have more than one ethnic origin—for example, a Dutch mother and a Scottish father—and the total could exceed 500,000.

This photo was taken in New Westminster, British Columbia, in 1963 at the 40th wedding anniversary of Bernhard and Elizabeth Bohmer, who emigrated from Renkem, Gelderland, with eleven children. At their 60th anniversary, there were sixty grandchildren and twenty great-grandchildren.

Mr. and Mrs. J. Kuik hope to celebrate their 65th wedding anniversary on December 28, 1983.

CARMAN, MANITOBA

WINNIPEG, MANITOBA

Family Album

A Story

Photos of the immigration experience, whether mounted neatly in albums or filed haphazardly in old shoeboxes (an Old Country custom), are popular at family gatherings. Even the children of immigrants love to travel back in time to relive with nostalgia their family's first years in Canada. Photographs call for quiet moments of reflection. They bring back memories.

These photos are from the family album of Mr. and Mrs. Klaas Terpstra of Hamilton, Ontario. They show their two daughters, Tina and Alberta, during the years following their emigration from Leeuwarden, Friesland, in 1951. Tina is now Mrs. Richie of Hamilton, Ontario, and Alberta now lives in Hamilton as well.

On the Volendam.

Feeding the chickens on the farm at Stirling, Ontario, in 1951.

Mr. and Mrs. Jacob Kuik came to Canada in July, 1950, with seven children, one of whom was married. The tree, prepared for the couple's 65th wedding anniversary on December 28, 1983, shows how the family has branched out over the years. When the tree was drawn, there were 127 members, including the parents. The Kuiks live in Carman, Manitoba.

Playmates at a birthday party in 1953.

Growing girls in new summer dresses, 1956.

The sisters go skating in 1954.

Summer of '57: time to cool off.

1955: a trip to Niagara Falls.

1958: backyard fun.

Christmas dinner in Edmonton in 1958.

Tina and Alberta visit a cousin in California in 1963.

Tina with sons Travis and Tom in 1982.

Alberta at the graduation of brother Nick in 1983.

Chapter 23
"Thank You, Canada!"

For the liberation of their homeland in 1945, Dutch-Canadians from coast to coast have said thank you to Canada in various ways, including the planting of tulip bulbs.

"Thank You, Canada!"

On Sunday, August 31, 1947, the thoughts of the newcomers drifted back to The Netherlands. It was the birthday of Queen Wilhelmina, the day to wear orange and to pray for the safety and the continuance of the royal house. The next day would be a national holiday in The Netherlands, with parades, games for the youngsters, fireworks, and revelling until late into the night.

In Holland Marsh, Arie VanderKooij planted the Dutch tri-color he had brought with him from The Netherlands on the bed of his farmer's truck. Fluttering brightly in the wind, it said that even in faraway Canada the queen and her family were not forgotten. (And he still has that flag.)

All across Canada, wherever clusters of immigrants gathered for worship, there was orange. Boys wore orange sashes and girls were decked out in orange dresses and hair-ribbons. There were prayers for Wilhelmina, a symbol of faith and strength. And after the services, everyone sang *Het Wilhelmus*, the Dutch national anthem, with new vigor. The clear voices of the children rang out above those of their parents.

Mrs. F. Huizinga, formerly of Zwaagwesteinde, Friesland, remembers celebrating the special day in 1948, a few months after arriving on a farm near Dobbinton, Ontario.

"My husband asked the farmer if he could get off work early. At four o'clock, the party started. The girls put on white dresses with orange sashes and ribbons, and the boys wore white shorts, white shirts, and orange caps. Two other Dutch families joined us. First we had a parade, Dad leading with the trumpet. We went around the house and the barn to the garden, where everybody sang *Wilhelmus* loud enough to send the birds flying. Then we went in for supper. After supper, our Canadian sponsors came in. Everybody played games, sang songs and told stories. Our Canadian friends agreed that the Dutch people sure knew how to have a good time."

As the years passed, the adults would continue to remember the queen, and her successor, Juliana, although not with such fervor as before. Their children would lose touch with Dutch royalty altogether.

1947: behind the VanderKooijs stands the truck with the Dutch tri-color.

1948: orange hats, sashes and ribbons brighten the party of the Huizinga family.

Rev. Adam Persenaire assisted many immigrants in Ontario on behalf of the Christian Reformed Church. He is shown at left, solemnizing the first wedding in the new church at Jarvis, Ontario.

New Canadian at Heart

Most of the immigrants have adapted themselves to the Canadian holidays and celebrations—Victoria Day, Labor Day, Thanksgiving, Halloween. They've become Canadianized. They still carry on some of the customs from the Old Country. But they do so for sentimental reasons, or for the sake of cultural heritage. Most of the immigrants now call themselves Canadians—and without shame or hesitation.

N.D. De Jong of Toronto, who married a Canadian girl, expresses the thoughts of many with these words: "I don't go to Dutch clubs or events. Nevertheless, I believe there is a little bit of Dutch left in me. After thirty years, I still eat *oliebollen* and *appelflappen* on New Year's Eve. And I love a big plate of kale with a juicy sausage during the cold winter months. My mouth waters when I think of croquettes, Dutch cheese, eel, and salted herring. Still, whenever I'm in Holland for a visit, I don't feel much at home there. Canada is my country now."

In the early '50s, they could begin to look to Elizabeth II of England, who ruled the Commonwealth, including Canada. And they came to feel more at home singing God Save the Queen, O Canada, and The Maple Leaf Forever.

The early postwar immigrants got lots of sound advice about Canada and its people from prewar settlers, ministers, fieldmen and others who knew the ropes. These words, mostly positive, were never forgotten.

Recalls C.M. Hogeterp of Hamilton, Ontario: "Shortly after we arrived in 1947, John VanderVliet told me never to think about going back to Holland. We started here with nothing but courage. We had nothing to go back to; we could only go ahead. And every year we did make gains. There were some who had something to fall back on in case things didn't turn out well, and it took them longer than it took us to get acquainted with the Canadian way of life, to feel at home here. Sure, there were rough times for us too. But I was always convinced that our being in Canada was the Lord's will. We never, for one moment, considered going back to Holland."

Ever since he entered the door of the farmhouse in 1947 and saw a table spread with good food, a welcome for him and his family, he had thought highly of Canadians, his hosts, the ones who opened up their doors and provided opportunities for those who didn't even know their language.

"When I finally realized my dream and bought my own farm, most of my money was gone. But I had to come up with another $500 to pay principal and interest to my lawyer. I had always paid the bills on time, and now I thought I was in trouble. Then a Canadian, a stranger, really, heard about my plight and invited me over. Without asking any questions, he told his wife to write out a cheque for $500. 'There's no interest,' he said. 'And pay it back when you can.' What can you say about people like that?"

Hogeterp also remembers the advice of Rev. Adam Persenaire, the home missionary: "Don't move away from this area. People will respect you if you stay. And when you need help, they'll be there to give it."

Like most other immigrants, Hogeterp and his wife look upon their years in Canada as a success. They now live comfortably in a new retirement village in suburban Hamilton, always looking forward to visits of their grandchildren. All their seven children are married to Dutch spouses, two of them from the same village in Friesland where the Hogeterps once lived. Their only son, Peter, is a minister of the Christian Reformed Church.

"When he was five years old, we used to ask him what he wanted to be," says Mrs. Hogeterp. "He always said the same thing: *dominee*. Well, he did become a *dominee*. We're proud, of course. But we're proud of all the blessings that the Lord has surrounded us with in this wonderful country."

When Mr. and Mrs. H. John Meyer moved from Montreal to Regina, Saskatchewan, where he was to work as an industrial consultant with the provincial Department of Industry and Commerce, they believed they had an important decision to make: Were they going to become Canadians or were they going to remain a Dutch family in Canada?

"In Montreal," he says, "we had joined the Christian Reformed Church. Being part of that community certainly helped us to overcome the initial problems of settling. However, the group tended to be a community unto itself, partly as a matter of survival, I think. Whatever it was, it gave us somewhat of a schizophrenic feeling: not really being Dutch or Canadian. Moving to Regina helped us make the break that we felt we should make. If we were to be Canadians, we wanted to do it completely." (Mr. Meyer wrote these views in 1966 at the request of the Department of Citizenship and Immigration.)

Occasionally the couple had attended services of the Presbyterian Church. Now they concluded that this denomination was basically as Calvinistic as any of the Reformed churches in The Netherlands.

"And so we decided to join the Presbyterian Church in Regina. Just how important this decision was for our assimilation, we came to realize only later. But Canadian society being what it is, particularly in the West, many social activities, relationships, and friendships depend on the church one belongs to . . ."

Meyer believes that his desire to be a good Canadian citizen was held against him at first. He sensed this when he visited his relatives in The Netherlands. And he certainly sensed it whenever he met immigrants who continued to identify with the Dutch community and the Reformed churches.

"Sometimes we felt an implied reproach; apparently we were considered disloyal to our heritage. However, we didn't want to be disloyal. Sure, we couldn't get excited any more about the day-to-day happenings in Holland, and some of the cabinet crises there seemed to us more senseless than when we lived

T. Roy Adams

The Standard, St. Catharines

Bemedalled Mayor

One of the staunchest supporters of the Club the Netherlands of St. Catharines, Ontario, has been a Canadian, T. Roy Adams, that city's mayor, who plays horn in the band. As president of the Lincoln and Welland Regiment Association, a post he has held for more than twenty-five years, he has done much to enhance relations between the Canadians and the Dutch on both sides of the ocean.

In May, 1983, Mayor Adams was honored by the municipal executive of Bergen op Zoom, the Noord-Brabant community which was liberated by the Lincoln and Welland Regiment on October 27, 1944. He was given the municipality's silver medal of honor.

Jan Heersink, the Dutch vice-consul who presented the medal, told Mayor Adams: "I would like to repeat our pledge to you, given on March 21, 1981: 'We, people of Dutch descent, do hereby promise and pledge that as long as you keep on playing your (bilingual) horn in the band *Hollands Glorie*, we will do our share to see that you will be the mayor here . . . as long as you enjoy having us around.' "

The Hryciw family

A Part
of the Canadian Mosaic

Elizabeth Hryciw of Calgary says: "I am proud of my Dutch heritage and of my Dutch green thumb, but I feel that I am a Canadian more than anything else. All of us children have married Canadians and none of us speak Dutch to our children, although we teach them little children's verses and sing Dutch children's songs to them. If I were to maintain their cultural heritage, I would have to teach them Ukrainian, French and German, too, for my father-in-law is Polish and my mother-in-law French Swiss. I have many picture books of Holland and my children enjoy looking through them. Although I can still speak Dutch, I use it only when traveling or when acting as an interpreter for Dutch patients who can't speak English. I have Dutch friends, but I did not seek them out because of their nationality. My parents, who live in Aylmer, retain many Dutch customs. When they have a big party, it's always Dutch-style, and Canadians love the fun as much as the Dutch do. They have no regrets about coming to Canada. They have done much better and have achieved much more than they ever could have in Holland. If it weren't for the relatives there whom they like to visit, I doubt that they would go back at all."

there. But we were—and are—as proud as ever of our heritage and our history."

Meyer, a senior civil servant, is an active member of St. Andrew Presbyterian Church in Ottawa, which Juliana attended during the war.

John Snyders of Brooks, Alberta, says: "We've done well in Canada. I came with a wife, three kids, and five suitcases. Now I have some real estate and a business that employs nineteen men. But the money is not the most important thing. What is important is the satisfaction that work brings. We built a business and helped build this community and our church. And now our young people are taking over from us. That feels good. At first, our relatives in Holland pitied us. For a long time, they thought of us as poor relatives who had made a mistake but wouldn't admit it. We visited them, but they didn't really believe that we were doing well. Of course, we wanted to justify our move. And having come to love this country, too, I think we must have bragged a lot. The other thing that we wouldn't accept at first was that some immigrants couldn't see any good in Canada. We thought of the people who moved back to Holland as traitors. One family who went back told us they were moving to Calgary. But someone saw their *kist* with a Dutch address on it. The poor people didn't dare to tell us the truth because of how critical and unaccepting we were. We needed to prove that *we* had made the right move—at their expense."

Mrs. Fredrika Jentink of Grande Prairie, Alberta, recalls: "I was homesick. I hadn't been anxious to go anyway. When you want to go, you'll take a lot. But if you're kind of dragged, it's a different story. But now I have no regrets. We've had a good life. Our children are doing fine. And we have our own place. We came to Canada because we wanted to own a farm. In southern Alberta, the land was expensive, and so in 1955 we moved to the Peace River country. After working for a farmer for a year, we bought a half section for $6,500. We used the farmer's machinery, and that is how we started. Even though we had hard times at first, we were never as poor in Canada as we had been in Holland in the 1930s. My husband was a *klompenmaker* and he made very little money. We really had to scratch then. In Canada, we always had lots to eat and we always had wood or coal for the stove. And the Lord saved us from any serious sickness."

Teunis Schinkel of Chatham, Ontario, asks: "Was our immigration a success? If we moved to Canada to keep the family together, we didn't succeed in that. One daughter stayed behind in Holland. Another moved back after fifteen years in Canada, something we didn't find pleasant. And a son lives in the Yukon, thousands of kilometers away. Yet . . . at a dinner to mark our 55th wedding anniversary, there were seventy family members present—and that wasn't everyone. I made a little speech, saying: 'We're here with seventy. Jacob came to Egypt with seventy and they became a nation. I'm sure the Schinkels will never grow into a nation. But I hope that all of you will become a blessing for the nation of Canada.' "

Mrs. Huibert Van Drunen of Stratford, Ontario, says: "Yes, our immigration was a success. Maybe not financially—we don't own a big farm or a beautiful mansion to show off. Yet the Lord has blessed us greatly. We and our children and their families belong here."

John Kap of Sarnia, Ontario, says: "A success? I'll leave the answer to God. I can only say, thank you, Lord, that I am in Canada."

Joe and Kitty Vaessen of North York, Ontario, wanted to become Canadian citizens before the birth of their first child. They didn't like the idea of a baby being Canadian and its parents Dutch. Besides, they wanted to tell their children later on: "We were Canadian before you were."

Three weeks before the fifth anniversary sary of their arrival in Canada, the couple went to register for their citizenship. Vaessen, considering the occasion to be an important milestone in his life, had taken the day off work.

"When we arrived at the citizenship administration office, we were told that we were three weeks too early and that we had to come back later. We were disappointed about this reception and told the lady that the chances of our coming back were very remote indeed, because we probably could not get another day off just to register for our citizenship papers. The lady told us to wait for a moment while

Mrs. Louie Ypma receives her Canadian citizenship papers in a ceremony in Port Arthur, Ontario, in 1954. Many immigrants became citizens as soon as the five-year residency requirement had been fulfilled.

she checked with the higher-ups. After a few minutes, she came back and asked whether we knew that a fee had to be paid on the day of registration. We told her that we knew, and that we each had $10. 'Well,' she said, 'come on in.' "

Now, never having regretted that he became a citizen, Vaessen has this advice: "The greatest contribution we can make to this country is to be good, hard-working, ambitious citizens. And I really believe we are doing a fine job at that."

S.P. Knuist of London, Ontario, who also became a citizen, comments: "We wanted to belong here for the rest of our lives and be Canadians. I didn't feel that I was losing a country. No, I was gaining one. Canada is our home."

Yet there are some people who have lived here for more than three decades, who are still Dutch, and who will be until they die.

Why?

"I just never got around to it yet."

The Big Step to Acquiring Canadian Citizenship

New citizens for Canada: Ben and Tina Afman and their children.

Ben and Tina Afman decided to become Canadian citizens—a logical step which most immigrants took—while they were sitting in a restaurant feasting on the food their new country had to offer.

"Why not?" says Mrs. Afman. "We couldn't go back. After five years of hard work, we still didn't have enough money to pay for a trip back if we had wanted to go. In Holland, we would need a house, furniture, a job . . . Canada had been

good to us. We appreciated the baby bonus cheque that came every month from the government. And we were looking forward to having the right to vote, and to crossing the United States border without the need for a passport. Yes, we wanted to become citizens of Canada."

They sent away for information. Three weeks later, the postman brought forms and booklets. They also went to night school to get a better grasp of the English language. Finally a notice came that they and their daughter, Edna, who was over sixteen, were to appear in the courtroom in Barrie, Ontario, on June 18, 1958. The pressure was on.

"Every night we studied about the history of Canada and about the Commonwealth. We also tried to remember every prime minister of the country. This wasn't easy, because we could hardly pronounce the names, let alone remember them. We had more success with the provinces and their capitals."

The Afmans were at the courthouse more than an hour before the citizenship sitting was to begin. No one else seemed to be around. Since the door was open, they walked inside and had a look around. Before long, others began to arrive. Soon there was a babble of voices in many tongues. A bang of the gavel brought immediate silence. All eyes turned toward the judge, who was sitting in his lofty perch. He knocked again and said loudly: "Arise!"

"We didn't know what the word meant. We were sitting in the front row, so we goofed right at the start by not getting up. If he would have said 'Stand up,' we

"There's no need to change. I get all the benefits. And why have the right to vote? They can't get anybody good to run this country anyway."

"Maybe I'll want to go back to Holland some day."

"I never thought of it."

Tulips, tulips and more tulips. Ottawa in May resembles *Keukenhof*, the renowned floral showplace in the bulb-growing area along The Netherlands' North Sea coast. In fact, the profusion of colors in Ottawa is Dutch.

Ottawa's love affair with tulips dates back to the Second World War, when Princess Juliana and her daughters took refuge in the capital. In 1945, to express her gratitude to the city and its people for their hospitality during those dark years, the future queen donated 100,000 tulip bulbs to Ottawa. These were immediately planted on Parliament Hill and along the

would have known what was what. We got the message, however, when one of the policemen at the door simply raised his arms. We all jumped to our feet like a little army in training."

The judge began calling names in alphabetical order. Afman and his wife didn't like that one bit: they were first, and couldn't copy anyone.

"Ben Afman, come forward and take the stand."

He entered the little gate that led to the enclosure beside the judge. Then, following instructions, he placed his hand on the Bible.

"Are you Ben Afman?"

"Yes, sir."

"Where were you born?"

"In Holland, sir."

"What do you think about communism?"

"I don't like it, sir."

"Why did you come to Canada?"

"It's a big and free country. There's more opportunity to spread our wings here."

"Are you sure of what you are doing? Giving up your country is almost the same as giving up your birthright."

"Yes, I'm quite sure. We like it here very much, sir."

It was Tina's turn next. When her name was called, she asked her husband to accompany her. But he shook his head and whispered: "Don't be scared. There's nothing to it." One of the policemen took her by the arm and led her to the front. She sat down, shaking like a leaf, and pronounced firmly: "I do too."

Laughter erupted.

The late Ben Afman and his wife, Tina.

"Not so fast, lady," said the judge. "Put your hand on the Bible and swear to God."

Tina's eyes couldn't leave the photograph of Queen Elizabeth that hung behind the judge. He asked: "Do you like the queen?"

"I like all queens," she replied.

"Do you like flowers?"

"Yes."

"You can go back to your seat now."

Although relieved, the Afmans were a bit disappointed in the questions. They had studied hard to learn more about Canada and the English language. Yet not once had the judge referred to these subjects.

"We shook hands with our new fellow Canadians and went home to celebrate with a cup of tea and a piece of cake and to admire the English Bible that had been presented to us by a representative of the Gideon Bible Society."

CANADA

CERTIFICATE OF
CANADIAN CITIZENSHIP
DEPARTMENT OF CITIZENSHIP AND IMMIGRATION

337069

CERTIFICAT DE
CITOYENNETÉ CANADIENNE
MINISTÈRE DE LA CITOYENNETÉ ET DE L'IMMIGRATION

This is to certify that

ALBERTUS (ALBERT) VAN DER MEY

Ce certificat atteste que

DEPUTY MINISTER
SOUS-MINISTRE

MINISTER
MINISTRE

PRINTED IN CANADA

The new Canadian citizens received certificates and congratulatory letters.

THE SECRETARY OF STATE OF CANADA

Ottawa, April 9, 1947.

Dear Sir,

I wish to take this opportunity of congratulating you personally upon the attainment of Canadian citizenship. By this certificate of citizenship you have been granted the rights and privileges of a citizen of Canada. These rights and privileges entitle you to freedom of speech, religion, thought, and action, the right to vote as you choose, and the right to be secure in your possessions.

Your citizenship carries with it the obligation of defending your adopted country in time of need, of living in peaceful brotherhood with your fellow Canadians, and of doing your part in the preservation of Canadian ideals and institutions.

I extend to you a warm welcome on this solemn occasion and I invite you to share with us the ancient liberties of a free people living together in harmony, under a democratic Government which recognizes the rights of all its citizens.

Secretary of State.

Marinus Cornelis Mol, Esq.,
R.R.No.4,
Chatham, Ont.

Rideau Canal. Juliana was so moved by that gesture that she decided to make further gifts of 10,000 bulbs a year.

Over the years, the National Capital Commission has planted millions of tulips. Many Ottawans have followed suit, and their colorful flowerbeds add to the display. Along the Ottawa River, daffodils mingle with the tulips, and crocuses bloom all over the city, and the sight warms the hearts of Dutch immigrants.

In 1970, twenty-five years after the liberation of their homeland by the Canadian troops under Allied command, Dutch-Canadians from coast to coast took part in fund-raising events and celebrations to show their gratitude. Some seven thousand Canadians had died on Dutch soil in the closing months of the war. Operation Thank You Canada was to be a fitting tribute to this sacrifice.

Immigrants also took advantage of the occasion to say a general thank you to Canada—for letting them come, for giving them the opportunity to start afresh and make something of their lives.

Specially-developed tulip bulbs were donated to municipalities and horticultural societies: orange for the royal family and red to represent the spilled blood of the Canadian troops. Plaques were presented to regiments. Services were held at cenotaphs across the country. People remembered.

The main events were focused on Ottawa during the Victoria Day weekend. Hundreds of immigrants converged on the capital for festivities, a gala dinner and an interdenominational church service. The highlight was the symbolic presentation of a gift from Canada's Dutch community—a $90,000 Dutch-built baroque concert organ which would belong to the National Arts Centre in Ottawa, and thereby to all Canadians. A Golden Memorial Book containing the names of the donors to the organ fund was handed over by Jan Van Bruchem, chairman of the Dutch-Canadian Committee 1945-70.

Earlier he had said: "We, the Dutch and the Dutch-Canadians, will have to live with the knowledge that whatever we do to show our gratitude, it will never measure up to the level and magnitude of what the Canadians did for us."

There are other signs of gratitude in Canada, including the statue that was erected in a small park in Stratford, Ontario, by former soldiers. They had been recruited and trained to serve in the Royal Netherlands Army when the day came to wrest control away from Hitler's military machine. A former furniture factory in Stratford had served as barracks.

In Victoria, the picturesque capital of British Columbia, there's also a visible touch of the Dutch: a carillon tower almost thirty meters high, built by the provincial government. Its bells were donated by the Dutch-Canadian community of the province in commemoration of Canada's centennial in 1967. The first stone was laid by Queen Juliana.

When the Ontario city of Guelph celebrated its 150th birthday in 1977, it was given a windmill by the Holland-Canada Club. This Dutch symbol and the drawbridge are located in Riverside Park.

Guelph Daily Mercury

Province of British Columbia

Province of British Columbia

Provincial carillonneur Herman Bergink gives a recital from the carillon tower in Victoria, British Columbia; the tower is pictured at left.

Thank You

Twenty-five years after the end of the war, Operation Thank You Canada was launched to commemorate the 25th anniversary of the end of the war. Looking over the plans are Lt.-General Guy G. Simonds, honorary chairman of the committee, Jan Van Bruchem, the chairman, and J.W. Stuurman, the Dutch consul-general in Toronto. At top, Dutch-Canadians walk toward the cenotaph in St. Catharines, Ontario, for a memorial service in 1970. At right, immigrants lay tulips at the base of the national war memorial in Ottawa.

"THANK YOU, CANADA."

THE DUTCH-CANADIAN COMMITTEE 1945-70.

TEXT: BARBARA GAASENBEEK.

MUSIC: LORNE BETTS
ARRANGEMENT: WIM DE BRUYN.

'tWas spring in nine-teen for-ty-five in star-ving Ne-ther-lands In suffe-ring and hope-less strife, We prayed God, free our hands, Ca-na-di-ans, they came to save, And for our lives their lives they gave ni-ty.

Canadian graves in Holland lay:	The Dutch in Canada, they feel
This sacrifice will be,	A bond that's strong and true.
A debt we only can repay	Proud of their heritage, they seal
With love and loyalty.	The old into the new:
Together going hand in hand,	Our Canada, so young and free.
We build the future of this land.	God, give us peace and unity.

The official Thank You Canada *song.*

On the quarter hour, the tower's distinctive and cheery tones pervade the area near the parliament buildings. The sixty-two bronze bells, imported from The Netherlands, are activated by a time clock and a 'player piano' roll. At least twice a week, passersby are treated to a recital by provincial carillonneur Herman Bergink, a skilled musician who at the age of thirteen was a church organist in Enschede, Overijssel. He has to climb some eighty-five steps to the playing cabin. Then, using both feet and fists, he lets the music, a touch of The Netherlands, peal out upon appreciative ears below. Bergink, who came to Canada in 1957, is also director of music of Grace Lutheran Church in Victoria.

The Dutch in other communities also said thank you in various ways over the years, sometimes before 1970 and sometimes after.

In Vancouver, the Shaughnessy Hospital was given a rooftop garden accessible by stairs and elevator, enabling war veterans to enjoy the sunshine and fresh air. In Edmonton, a street-organ named *De Cello* was donated. In Calgary, the Dutch raised funds for chimes for the Calgary Tower. And in Guelph, Ontario, a windmill that pumps water was built in a park.

Near the end of the Second World War, a crippled Allied bomber returning from a mission over Germany flew over the home of Nan Mulder at the tip of Noord-Holland.

"It was around midnight when we heard it going over. We looked outside and saw that it was on fire. The pilot seemed to be steering it toward the Waddenzee. A few seconds later, we heard a thud and that was it."

At dawn, Mulder and three others ventured to the north dike of the former Wieringen Island and spotted the wreckage a short distance from shore.

"The tide at that hour was very low, so we decided to have a closer look. As we

Thousands of Canadian soldiers who died during the liberation of The Netherlands are buried at cemeteries in Groesbeek, Holten, and Bergen op Zoom (below). At far left, tulips brighten the grave-sites of four Allied airmen. At bottom left is a photo of one of them, Sam Zareikin (right), with his brother Joe, who also died in the war.

were walking to the plane, a German soldier on the dike a little to the south of us fired some warning shots. We decided not to press our luck, and returned home."

The bodies of the crew members were buried near the dike. Mulder's wife, Gertrude, and several other members of her church's *Zusterkring* looked after the graves. In this way, the Mulders got to know the names of the victims, including Sam Zareikin, a twenty-six-year-old pilot officer with 102 Squadron of the Royal Canadian Air Force.

In 1948, when they knew that Canada would be their new country, the couple wrote a letter to Zareikin's parents. It took more than half a year for the letter to reach them in Los Angeles, California, where they had moved shortly after the war.

"All we have ever heard from the War Department was that our son was missing in action," replied Zareikin Sr. "We have written to several agencies in England and Canada, including the Red Cross, but they could not give us any information. Would you or anyone in your village know the manner in which my son and his crew lost their lives? Were they alive when found? Is he buried in a single grave or in one grave with his crew?"

The Mulders passed on whatever information they had, including the address of a Jewish family which Zareikin had requested. In appreciation, he forwarded a food parcel, saying: "Your consul in Los Angeles advised us what might be helpful, and we were very happy that we could send it to you."

Yes, not only the Dutch were thankful.

In Vancouver, Ray Koot has been saying thank you to Canada for thirty-one years by donating regularly to the Red Cross blood bank.

He comes from Arnhem, a city that suffered much during the Second World War. As a high school boy, he was a member of the underground, writing down broadcasts which came to the resistance forces over the BBC's *Radio Oranje*. "I'd type up twenty copies and deliver them on my bicycle." He later went into hiding in the north of the country to avoid being drafted into forced labor. In the spring of 1945, he got through the army lines around Arnhem through the kindness of Canadian soldiers.

"You've no idea of the relief and exhilaration we felt after the five long years of the occupation," he told an interviewer from the *Vancouver Province*. "It was tremendous. When I came here in 1952, I started wondering: 'How can I repay Canada?' I had a steady job. I decided that giving blood to the Red Cross was the least I could do."

While Red Cross workers tapped him for his 115th pint of A positive, he remarked: "I'll be a donor as long as they let me."

Perhaps the ones who appreciate Canada the most are those who returned to The Netherlands after a number of years in the new land—and then came back to Canada after all.

Rev. Harri Zegerius of the Reformed Church tells this story about a stranger he met in Chatham, Ontario, one day: "I parked on one of the main streets and went to put a coin in the meter. Next to me a man was fidgeting with another meter. I could see that he was a Dutchman—you know, the haircut, the facial features. I told him in Dutch: 'You have to do it this way.' Well, when he knew that I could understand his language, he started cursing Canada. There was nothing right with it. He was going to return to Holland, pronto. Less than a year later, I

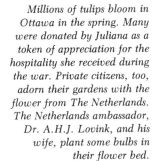

Millions of tulips bloom in Ottawa in the spring. Many were donated by Juliana as a token of appreciation for the hospitality she received during the war. Private citizens, too, adorn their gardens with the flower from The Netherlands. The Netherlands ambassador, Dr. A.H.J. Lovink, and his wife, plant some bulbs in their flower bed.

Malak, Ottawa

was meeting a ship at Halifax. And the first person I saw walking off the plank was this fellow from Chatham. I couldn't believe my eyes. He had tried it again in Holland, but had decided to return to Canada, more convinced than ever that in Holland there was no elbow room."

Twenty years after his emigration, ex-fieldman Rimmer Tjalsma also decided to return to The Netherlands with his wife and young children. They arrived around Christmas, not a good time to start looking for a job. Before long, they were back in Canada.

"We realized we did the wrong thing to go back to Holland," he says. "We just couldn't fit in any more."

The same story could be told by some of the prewar immigrants who returned to The Netherlands when the Depression hit, believing that life would be better in the country they had left behind. After the war, they were among the passengers on the first immigrant boats heading for Canada.

Frank Flach of Brampton, Ontario, who left Maassluis, Zuid-Holland, in 1924, and sailed to Canada on the *Veendam*, says: "I know the names of a number of people who went through this experience. When they first left Holland, they took with them a mental picture of the country, and the picture remained unchanged. So when things turned bad in Canada, they figured that things were still all right in Holland. Well, the Depression was felt there, too, and then came the war. Little wonder that they hurried back to Canada at the first opportunity, now with grownup children."

As their first years of immigration passed, immigrants began to notice and experience various degrees of so-called Canadianization. Naturally, parents felt anxious when, for example, a daughter was going out with a Canadian boy of different faith. But as time progressed, such developments became more acceptable. Most people began to realize that assimilation was not only inevitable, but necessary.

The Christian Reformed community in Kentville, Nova Scotia, followed a fairly typical pattern. At first, English hymns were introduced. A year later, the church held its first English service. By 1958, one service was held in English and the other in Dutch. Gradually the proportion of English was increased until by the early 1970s all Dutch was eliminated.

Not all of the older members agreed with the consistory's decision to go English. A man who had been an elder during that period recalls: "There was quite a fight." However, efforts to please everyone by introducing a third Sunday service, in Dutch, met with little approval. In the end, aging parents preferred to attend church with their children, even if the services were in English.

Nowadays the congregation hardly sounds or seems Dutch, apart from the traditions and heritage which shape its life.

When Gerald Prins returned to Kampen in 1974 for a visit, a former co-worker asked: "If you had known in 1958 what you know now about Canada, would you have emigrated?"

Mr. and Mrs. Gerald Prins in Renfrew, Ontario.

Prins replied: "If I had known then what I know now, I would have gone to Canada twenty-five years earlier."

Immigrants on vacation in The Netherlands are often asked by still-dubious relatives and acquaintances how they can say that life has been good to them in the new land. The Netherlanders point to their own economic boom and the personal prosperity of the '60s and '70s as if to say: "You should have stayed. The ones who didn't go had it good."

Prins abhors such talk. A lot of it is hindsight, he says. Much is also based on the belief that a good job, money and social status make a successful person. Prins, a carpenter, never measured his success or failure in a material way. He looked at the values in life, upheld through Christian beliefs and a lifestyle to match, and the blessings his family received during the years in Canada.

An elderly man told him in Kampen in 1974: "I would never have gone." He then mentioned how his sons had succeeded in their business, how much the business grossed, and how much they each earn

personally. Angry about this boasting, Prins pulled out his own wallet and snapped: "If your biggest value in life is the size of your wallet, then I can understand why you can't find a good word for emigration. You know, there are values in life that can't be compared with money."

The old man, a former church elder, quickly changed the topic.

The same subject arose when a visitor from The Netherlands stopped by in Renfrew. This man, after spending a few weeks in Canada, said he had seen and heard enough to form an opinion against emigration. Nearly everyone, he said, would have been better off if they had stayed in The Netherlands.

Prins made no bones about what he thought: "What right do you have to judge our emigration as an unwise move? The decision was made by us, and thousands of others, in consultation with the Lord. Emigration is a very personal happening. I'm not going to express an opinion about your life. Maybe you had made the wisest decision by staying in Holland. But that was your business . . ."

Mrs. Reina Feyen, who visited The Netherlands after eleven years in Canada, was relieved when she stepped on Canadian soil again.

"I found everything very small in Holland. What I once thought was a big canal looked like a ditch. The street I remembered as wide was now so narrow it frightened me. I also learned that I had grown out of the way of life there. It was all so changed. But then we had changed, too."

Gary Eggink of the Jarvis, Ontario, area came back to Canada after a visit to The Netherlands convinced him that his parents' decision to emigrate had been the right one. He found The Netherlands a nice place to spend a vacation. But he would never think of trying to make a living there.

Why?

"There's more freedom and less government intervention in Canada; there are more chances here for an entrepreneur; there is virtually no chance there to start your own business; in Holland, you need a licence to get out of bed in the morning; the social benefits are so high there that the small businessman can hardly afford to hire help; any assets you have are highly taxed; the country is much too crowded; luxuries we take for granted (eating out, well-heated homes, pleasant-riding cars) are exceptions for the average man; last but not least, the churches leave much to be desired."

Mrs. Trudy Joldersma's life in Canada has not been easy. Debts were a constant worry during thirteen years of farm life. In the end, she and her husband decided to sell.

"All around us, we saw sons leaving the farm to look for industrial jobs. We wanted higher education for our two sons and two daughters, and a small community was not very conducive to this goal. So we moved to Hamilton, Ontario."

Her husband started a small but promising construction business. It seemed as if their financial worries would be a thing of the past. It was not to last, however. After two and a half years of this blessedness, her husband was killed by his own tractor. She still doesn't know how it happened.

"Left with four children, ranging in age from six to fourteen, I upgraded my education in a government adult retraining program. It certainly was no small task entering school at age 44 and with only a Grade 7 education in another language. I did secretarial work for seven years, and then stepped out to do something more relaxing. Now I'm in my seventh year of being a visiting homemaker, working with the sick, elderly and handicapped."

And her children?

"My vision for my children's future was that they should become educated contributors to Canadian society, in whatever academic field they might choose. By the grace of God, I believe I see that goal coming to fruition. Two of them are in Christian education, higher and elementary, one is a lawyer, and one is working on her Ph.D. I also taught them with fervor to love and take pride in their country, while at the same time I instilled in them an interest in their roots. This, too, has paid off. All four of them speak and read Dutch, and three have spent one or more vacations in Holland."

Mrs. Netty Oosterman of the Lambeth, Ontario, area found herself mingling more with Canadians than with people of Dutch origin when she joined a Baptist church after five years in Canada.

"But do we feel a hundred percent Canadian? No. Nor do we feel a hundred percent Dutch. We will always be in-between. That hurts sometimes. But that's the price immigrants pay. Our comfort is in knowing that this world is not our final destination; we are all just traveling through to a Perfect Country."

Now that the first generation of Dutch immigrants is getting on in years, there are many among their ranks who reflect upon the immigration years. They wonder privately and within their family circles whether they made the right move so many years ago. They have doubts.

Feelings of guilt haunt some of them. They're disturbed about how things developed: the children are drifting away from the church, some of them are marrying people of other faiths and nationalities, many are scattered across the country far away from home, contact with relatives in The Netherlands is diminishing . . . They ask: "If we had stayed, would this have happened?"

Often they conclude their pondering by blaming Canada for whatever guilt or disappointment plagues them. In fact, some immigrants never speak kindly of their adopted country.

A good example of this behavior was presented to television viewers in The Netherlands in the spring of 1983. From the NCRV studio in Hilversum, a number of immigrants who had returned to their native land expressed one bad feeling after another about Canada. Their negative feelings were to be expected. But surprising, and perhaps shocking, was the way these views were echoed by a number of handpicked immigrants from southern Ontario who were in a Toronto studio and connected to the others by satellite. The audience was given a highly distorted view of the welfare of Dutch immigrants in Canada.

Immigrants who head back for The Netherlands are either fed up with unemployment or alleged prejudice or are simply overcome by longings for beloved relatives and old surroundings. One study concluded that one out of every three immigrants would eventually return, although many people have found that figure hard to believe. Regardless of the numbers, people do leave Canada.

But then there are the others—many others—who solidly back the sentiments expressed by immigrant Ted Smeenk of London, Ontario, when he learned about the NCRV television program: "It fills us with pity and sympathy for the misguided, unhappy souls who think of themselves as 'homeless' and 'displaced' and as second-class citizens in a country that is made up of immigrants, where Dutchmen are held in the highest esteem, where tolerance of color, creed, and national origin is unequaled and guaranteed in the Charter of Rights, where Dutch immigrants have risen to occupy seats in various levels of government, and where others have become engineers, lawyers, doctors, and business owners."

Chapter 24

Making an Impact

Top: The Grandville Island Hotel in Vancouver is one of the many fine commercial and industrial buildings in Western Canada built by J.C. Kerkhoff and Sons Construction Ltd. This division is one of a number in the Kerkhoff Group, founded in 1970 by Johan C. Kerkhoff. The company's work includes design, engineering, and construction, as well as window, door and specialty millwork manufacturing. Kerkhoff's five sons—C.W. (Casey), Willem, Dirk, Peter, and Maarten—are actively involved in management and operations. The non-union firm is based in Chilliwack.

Bottom Left: Ike Rusticus (right) came to Canada thirty-four years ago with dreams of operating his own slaughterhouse. After milking cows and working as an employee in various slaughter houses in British Columbia, he managed to take over a business in 1955. With hog producer Cors De Lint (left), who came to Canada in 1978, he now operates Britco Export Packers Ltd. in Langley, British Columbia.

Bottom Right: Nicolaas Van Duyvendyk, born in The Netherlands in 1923, is assistant deputy minister, finance, of Transport Canada. He served with the Canadian armed forces in The Netherlands and later with the Royal Netherlands Air Force in the Far East. From 1947 to 1954, he was employed by a major oil company in Indonesia as a senior financial officer. Following his immigration to Canada in 1954, he held positions of chief financial officer, general auditor and controller until 1968 when he joined the public service. He was appointed assistant deputy minister, field operations service, Department of Consumer and Corporate Affairs, in January, 1975; assistant deputy minister, finance, personnel and administration, Department of Veterans Affairs, in February, 1977, followed by his present appointment in April, 1980. He was also chairman of the Ottawa Board of Education in 1977 and 1978.

Making an Impact

Harry (left) and Bill Voortman discuss business at their
modern plant near
Burlington, Ontario.

Some people call them Canada's Dutch-born cookie monsters. But people with a sweet tooth—and that's most of us—know them as brothers Bill and Harry Voortman. Their firm's Dutch-style cookies and other baked delights give thousands of immigrants a taste of home when it's time for tea or coffee. And obviously the Canadians love their cookies too.

The modern W.H. Voortman Ltd. plant near Burlington, Ontario, which employs as many as two hundred during peak production periods, is the pride and joy of Bill and Harry, formerly of Hellendoorn, Overijssel. They didn't get to be cookie monsters by chance. It was in their blood.

Their father, John, was one of seventeen bakers in his village after the war. The competition was too keen for any of them to make an adequate living. Voortman couldn't see any future for himself and his teenaged sons. Little wonder that when he began to advocate emigration, they took him up on it eagerly.

The widowed father and sons left for Canada in 1948, arriving in Picton, Ontario. Of course, Voortman didn't work in a bakery right away. He had been admitted as an agriculturalist, so he labored on

a farm. His sons, however, found work in a bakery, doing the things they knew well. But they weren't satisfied. They longed for the day when they could strike out on their own, as their father had done.

"That's why we had emigrated," says Bill. "Our plan was to bake some cookies in the evenings. But we needed an oven for that. We watched the want ads in the paper. Then one night we read that someone had an oven, a mixer, and some other baking things for sale. We went to him right away."

The next step was to find a place to do their baking. In 1950, they rented the back room of a house for $50 a month. Now they were set to begin their business, to supplement the $28 a week each was making at Hamilton's National System Baking Company. They specialized in *snijkoek* (honeycake) and *roggebrood* (pumpernickel). By the end of the first year, they had sold $6,000 worth of products and grossed $500, a mere $10 a week. Yet this return was enough to convince them to start working full-time.

They found a more spacious location, again for $50 a month. Then the brothers went into debt for $1,250 to purchase other equipment and began working up to

The Voortman brothers started baking in the back room of a house in 1950 (upper left). As the business grew, they kept moving the operation to larger quarters. Their present building near Burlington is shown at lower right. The center photo, from an earlier plant, shows cookies coming off the production line by the thousands. Voortman products are shipped far and near.

twenty hours a day. As with most new businesses, the first five years were difficult. At times, Bill and Harry wondered why they had started. Nobody seemed to have any faith in them, and so investment capital, though they didn't need much, was hard to get. Their attempt to wholesale doughnuts and pies failed due to their lack of experience. But the honeycake and pumpernickel were reaching expanding markets. This gave them enough encouragement to persevere.

The brothers eventually contacted someone who owned a piece of machinery from The Netherlands that could be used to manufacture *speculaas* and *kerstkransjes*, other Old Country delights. The man wanted $800, but the Voortmans didn't have that kind of money. They continued to bake cookies manually. A year later, they returned to the man, found out he still had the equipment, and bought it for $390. Still the $90 for a new motor had to be paid by instalment. Now the Voortmans were ready for expanded production.

"Most of our customers were immigrants," says Harry, now in charge of

Construction
Building Up Canada Became a Family Concern

Rob Dibble

The ten Van Vliet brothers and one of their accomplishments —the Bloedel Floral Conservatory in Queen Elizabeth Park in Vancouver.

sales and promotion. "They kept us afloat. Then we started selling to Canadians too."

They expanded the product line, and obtained more and more retail outlets. As the business grew, larger facilities became a necessity. Adjacent to the Queen Elizabeth Way southwest of Toronto, the latest plant was built for $2.5 million, and produces dozens of different cookies and other products which are shipped across Canada and even into the United States.

Says Harry: "I don't really regret what we did. But I wouldn't advise sixteen and eighteen-year-old boys to go into business with no money at all, and to work eighteen to twenty hours a day, because you miss out on everything else in life."

When William Dam boarded the *Waterman* in 1947 with his wife, Maria, and their four children, he had one goal in mind: to set up his own seed business in Canada. For years he had worked with seeds in Ootmarsum, north of Enschede, but with no chance of starting on his own. So he would try elsewhere. And if he

---

In early summer of 1952, twenty-two-year-old Neil Van Vliet, the eldest of a family of ten sons, arrived with the *Waterman* in Halifax and boarded the train for Edmonton. In Winnipeg, the Canadian immigration authorities suggested he get off the train and go to work on a farm in Manitoba. Flat broke and with no relatives or contacts in Canada, he took their advice. He worked for a farmer at McConnell until he was no longer needed in the fall.

Next, Neil was hired by the CPR in Winnipeg and transferred to the engineering department in Edmonton. With a permanent job, he was able to sponsor two of his brothers, Joe and Fred, who crossed with the *Groote Beer* and arrived in the Alberta capital in May of 1953. They both started working for Canada Packers the next day.

In June, Neil found a new job as a building inspector at the Cold Lake Airport which was just under construction. A year later, he moved back to Edmonton. With his brother Fred and an acquaintance who was a bricklayer, he started to build a house on speculation. Brother Joe kept his steady job to make sure there would be food on the table.

That summer, brother John came with the *Rijndam* to join his brothers in the fledgling business. In 1956, Van Vliet Construction Co. Ltd. was incorporated, and the brothers entered the contracting world.

Their parents came for a visit the following year to attend Fred's wedding, and brought along brothers Pete and Tony. Nick came in 1960 and Paul and

George in 1962, making a total of nine brothers in Canada. Of the nine, only Joe, who was on a farm outside of Edmonton in 1958, was not directly involved in the construction business at that time.

After building public works projects across northern Alberta, the brothers decided in 1965 to venture to Vancouver. The following year, they completed all their operations in Alberta and everyone, including Joe, moved to the Vancouver suburbs. The last of the brothers, Jack, moved to Canada in 1969 and joined the firm.

They have to their credit such outstanding buildings as the Bloedel Floral Conservatory in Queen Elizabeth Park in Vancouver and the new courthouse in the city's downtown. They have also built many highway structures in the lower mainland, residential highrises, commercial buildings such as the tower for the Delta Airport Inn Hotel, and the underground complex below the streets around Pacific Centre and Robson Square.

Now the Van Vliets own two different companies: Double V Construction Ltd., operated by Nick and Paul, and Van Construction Division of Van Vliet Construction Co. Ltd., operated by the other eight brothers, with Neil as general manager, Fred as general superintendent, Tony as purchaser, John, Jack and George as building superintendents, Pete in charge of all concrete operations, and Joe in charge of equipment operations.

All ten married Dutch girls. The combined number of offspring stands at fifty.

Dutch-style Meat Sells

Simon De Groot Sr. sold his butcher shops in The Hague in 1953 and emigrated to Canada with his family, anxious to start the same type of business and cater to the particular palates of immigrants. In February, 1954, he purchased a rundown butcher shop in downtown Toronto, and his business was launched. It did so well that, before long, four sons were helping out.

"In those years," says Kees De Groot, the current president, "many new immigrants came over from Holland and other parts of Europe, bringing along a demand for our Dutch-style meat products. Out of the retail store, we built up a small wholesale business. In 1958, the wholesale and retail were split up, and we rebuilt an old movie theatre for the wholesale division. This part of the business kept growing until we could not accept any new customers."

At that point, the De Groots purchased industrial acreage in Brampton, near Toronto, and contracted Vroom Construction to build a 20,000-square-foot plant. It was officially opened in February, 1975.

"Since then, there has been a big growth in our business. In our first twenty

Above: An interior view of the Simon De Groot meat plant. Below: Simon De Groot Sr. and his wife, Johanna, on their 50th wedding anniversary.

years, we did business mainly with new Canadians. It is very satisfying to notice that when you make quality products, you can sell to everybody. We sell to institutions, supermarkets, caterers, wholesalers, delicatessen stores, etc. Our plant in Brampton is big enough to handle this growth, and we have plenty of room for further expansion."

The firm's only retail store at 481 Church Street, its original location, is doing better than ever. Simon De Groot Jr. is the manager there. Father De Groot died in 1974.

"It's a pity that he never saw the new plant," says Kees. "He would have been very proud of it."

hadn't succeeded within five years, he would promptly return to The Netherlands.

Dam, thirty-four years old and full of vigor, arrived in Sarnia, Ontario. During the next few years, he held a succession of jobs—in sugar and tobacco, in a foundry, as a dock laborer, and in a synthetic rubber factory. He often arrived home dead tired. But it wasn't the end of the day for him. He had started his seed business, catering initially to the Dutch immigrants who longed for some of the vegetables from back home, such as kale, endive, and certain varieties of beans. He often worked until two or three o'clock in the morning, slept a few hours, and then got up early to be at the factory on time.

This was the type of initiative and industriousness that impressed Canadians. Dutch immigrants have worked long and hard, earning their success. Many have made their presence felt in various fields—in the business world, in the intellectual community and in the arts. They have made an impact on Canadian society.

Dam's part-time business grew by leaps and bounds. He acquired land near Dundas, Ontario, a populous area with many Dutch settlers, and began a full-time operation. Today some thirteen thousand customers from coast to coast and across the border order seeds from a colorful William Dam catalogue.

"We have our own trial garden," says Dam. "With that, we can determine which varieties will do very well in this climate. Seed growing is done by experts all over the world, and we import through the Department of Agriculture. We started our business with mainly Dutch customers and later on with all kinds of immigrants from Europe. In the last ten years, we have been selling to everyone, mainly because of our untreated seeds and the boom in home gardening."

A good way to make an impact on what goes on in a democratic community is to join the decision-making process. That's what some immigrants did, beginning on the local level. They became influential members of society as they showed how much they cared about what happened in their adopted land.

Sad to say, there are still many immigrants who shy away from playing a larger role in the community. They feel that their voices are neither as strong nor as important as the voices of native-born Canadians. They still feel like foreigners.

J.A. Grootenboer, a farmer near Murillo, Ontario, became interested in local politics soon after he was appointed weed inspector for Oliver township in 1965. He was active in a number of organizations, including the church, the agricultural society, the milk producers, the co-op, and the soil and crop improvement association. He knew many people and their problems. So he decided to take a logical step: run for a seat on the township council. He was elected in 1966.

"The many hours of hard work on the farm and the many long meetings, sometimes until after midnight, took their toll," he says. "I suffered a mild heart attack and was in the hospital for a month. So I had to slow down a bit. In 1968, after two years on council, I declined nomination. The council then appointed me to the committee of adjustment, which didn't require as much work."

But he wasn't satisfied with being on the outside. He rejoined the council after the next election, and he eventually became reeve, the highest position in the township.

William Dam at work in his office.

Partners in Decision-making

Wim Vander Zalm (above) gained prominence as mayor of Surrey, British Columbia, and as a member of the British Columbia legislature. Peter Elzinga (right) is a member of the House of Commons and president of the national Progressive Conservative party.

Wim Vander Zalm came to Canada in 1947 as a twelve-year-old. He became interested in politics when the municipal council of Surrey, British Columbia, gave permission for a gravel pit to be dug on land that had been earmarked for a park. The land was in his neighborhood, and he led the residents of the area in their protest.

Although the gravel pit was dug anyway, the experience of representing people and their legitimate concerns kindled Vander Zalm's interest in local affairs. Within two years, he was elected alderman, and four years later, in 1969, he became mayor of the largest municipality in the British Commonwealth. But bigger things awaited him. In 1975, he was elected to the British Columbia legislature as a member of the ruling Social Credit Party, and the premier appointed him immediately to the cabinet as minister of human resources.

In private life, Vander Zalm is president of the largest chain of retail garden centers in Western Canada and is also president of Canada's largest greenhouse lettuce growing operation. He has done well for an immigrant boy who first worked in the bulb fields and then, after graduating from high school, took over the family bulb growing business when his father, formerly of Noordwijkerhout, Zuid-Holland, suffered a heart attack.

"I didn't have a lot of education," he told an interviewer from The Netherlands shortly after being named British Columbia's minister of education in August, 1982. "But with sound knowledge, a level-headed approach, and a determination to succeed, one can go a long way in Canada."

A number of other people of Dutch origin have appeared on the Canadian political scene, from the municipal council level to the Canadian senate. One notable one is Peter Elzinga, born in Edmonton, Alberta, in 1944 and the grandson of a pioneering couple from Friesland who settled at Neerlandia. Elzinga, first elected to the Canadian parliament in 1974, has gained national prominence as president of the federal Progressive Conservative party.

Daughter of Immigrants Influences Canadian Literature

Born of Dutch immigrant parents in 1954 in Wetaskiwin, Alberta, Aritha Van Herk grew up on a farm near Edberg, Alberta, and received B.A. and M.A. degrees from the University of Alberta. Her first novel, *Judith*, won the Seal Books First Novel Award in 1978, and several of her short stories have been anthologized. Her most recent novel, *The Tent Peg*, was published in 1981. A critic and lecturer as well as an author, Ms. Van Herk has taught at the University of British Columbia, and is currently assistant professor at the University of Calgary, teaching English literature and creative writing.

Sharing Her Talent

Lini Grol: "The doctor encouraged me to quit nursing and turn my scissor-cutting hobby into a full-time practice."

In 1961, while working as a nurse in Welland, Ontario, Lini Grol was visited at home by a doctor. It wasn't a social call; she was convalescing after an illness.

The doctor noticed black and white scissor-cuts hanging on a wall, found out that Lini had been involved in this art since a patient had shown her how to do it before the war, and offered a comment: "No wonder you're sick. How can you hold down a full-time nursing job and pursue all this in your spare time? You've got more than you can handle."

He was right, and he didn't even know the whole story. Before the war, in Nijmegen, she had written short feature stories and poetry. Then, in 1950, came her first major work: a textbook for psychiatric nurses. Even when she went to South Africa, having been bitten by the travel bug that seems to prey on nurses, she continued to employ her pen and scissors. And she certainly didn't let up after moving to Canada in 1954, lured by the great demand for nurses here at that time.

"The doctor encouraged me to quit nursing and turn my scissor-cutting hobby into a full-time practice," she recalls. "He said Canada had more than enough good nurses, but not enough people in the arts. The doctor died soon after that. I felt that Providence had told me something. So I followed his advice and turned my full attention to the arts, staying on as a part-time nurse until 1979 so that at least I could pay the bills."

She produced books on poetry and folk tales and even one on her favorite pasttime—scissor-cutting. She set up her own publishing house, Trillium Books. She held readings of her work and exhibited her art. And she opened up her own studio in Pelham, a small community in the Niagara Peninsula.

"I may not be a Rembrandt," she says, "but at least I've been able to share what talent I have."

Art

Matth Cupido presents an original print to Governor General Edward Schreyer. The Dutch-born artist has recently settled in Nova Scotia, having lived and worked in British Columbia and Ontario.

Photography

Award-winning photographer, John DeVisser, immigrated to Canada in 1952. Based in Port Hope, Ontario, he has published sixteen books of his own photographs and has contributed widely to other Canadian books and magazines.

Hobbies
Landlocked Skipper

Henk Fietje puts the finishing touches to one of his models.

Many other immigrants brought along their hobbies, skills, and talents. One man who first settled in Woodstock, Ontario, brought with him thousands of butterflies from around the world, mounted in boxes. A geologist in Manitouwadge, Ontario, has become famous among rockhounds, having collected more than two thousand specimens. And then there's Henk 'Skipper' Fietje of Cambridge, On-

tario, an ex-sailor who spends most of his daytime hours doing what he likes best—building model ships.

Born and raised on boats, Fietje spent his first twenty-two years on sail-driven cargo vessels that plied the canals and rivers of The Netherlands and Germany and the coastal waters. His wife, Jantje, also came from a family that worked and lived on the water.

When sailing ships in The Netherlands switched to diesel power in the early 1930s, Fietje began to lose interest in the sailing life. Besides, the Depression had robbed shipping of its profits. So he switched to a landlubber's job.

"But the thought of sailing never left me, even after we moved to Canada. I had some time on my hands, and so I began to build model sailing ships."

His small apartment looks like a miniature shipyard. Models and parts of models cover shelves, tables, and the floor. And if you draw aside a curtain and look into another room, you'll find more of them. Carved memories—that's what they are.

Cinema
Dutch-Canadian Film Producer

For centuries, the Dutch have been known for their contributions to the visual arts. One thinks immediately of Rembrandt, Hals, Vermeer and Van Gogh, to name just a few. It's no surprise that the emigration movement exported such talent. People of Dutch extraction throughout Canada are indeed leaving their mark in painting, sculpture, photography, theatre, and film.

John and Henia Muller of Toronto, a husband-and-wife team of film and television producers, are probably best known for their film *Liberation!*, a one-hour documentary aired on the national CBC-TV network. The popular book, *A Liberation Album*, the story of the liberation of The Netherlands by Canadian troops, evolved from this production.

In 1977, John was invited by the Canada Council's cultural exchange program to work with the late Marshall McLuhan in Toronto. During that year, John and Henia fell in love with Canada and decided to return as landed immigrants. They came to stay in the fall of 1978 with their small children, Gideon and Naomi.

"We could have flown across the Atlantic in seven to eight hours," says John. "Instead, we chose to take a ten-day sea voyage. Our trip on the Polish liner *Stefan Batory* (formerly the *Maasdam*), from Rotterdam to Montreal, made us feel the distance between the two countries. Our son will always remember that long leap he made in the fall of '78."

While based at Huizen, Noord-Holland, the Mullers had produced documentary programs for Dutch networks. In Toronto, they set up M&M Film Productions Ltd. and increased their audience considerably. Their other productions include *Water: Friend or Foe*, a one-hour special on water management in The Netherlands, shown on the CBC's *The Nature of Things*, *Vincent Price's Dracula*, a film about the real and fictional Vlad Dracula, and promotional films for government and industry.

Film producer John Muller and his son, Gideon, enjoy the Canadian outdoors. Below, Henia Muller and her children get a taste of winter.

Some Dutch-Canadian Educators

Steven M. Koning, principal of King Edward Elementary School in Toronto.

Gerry Ensing, executive director of the Federation of Independent School Associations in British Columbia.

Haijo J. Westra

A. Van Vliet, teacher of home economics at Centennial Elementary School in Regina.

John Hofstee, head of the business education department of Listowel District Secondary School in Ontario.

Melle Huizinga, teacher of English as a second language at Alberta Vocational Center in Edmonton.

Reindert J. Klein, coordinator of English at Fine Arts Core Education School in Montreal.

Robert De Haan, assistant head of physics at Sir Allan MacNab Secondary School in Hamilton, Ontario.

Haijo J. Westra, a professor of classics at the University of Calgary, came to Canada alone in May of 1968, at the age of twenty.

After completing one year of study at the University of Amsterdam, he couldn't see himself living in a garret for seven years while he obtained his doctorate, only to spend another one or two years as a draftee in the army. Besides, he wanted to see the world, and establish his independence, including financial independence.

"After an extremely pleasant voyage on the *Maasdam*," he says, "I landed in Quebec City, where I took a 'cours d'initiation'. However, I had made friends on the boat and decided to join my friends in Montreal, where, after a long search, I finally found a job in the library of McGill University. In March of 1969, I moved to Vancouver with an English girl I had met coming over. We lived in Kitsilano, close to the beach. Again after looking for a long time, I found a job, this time with a Japanese automobile company. In 1970, we got married, and I went back to school to finish my education and to find a profession."

At the University of British Columbia, he studied classics and English, and from there he went on to obtain his doctorate at the University of Toronto. By that time his marriage had broken down because of diverging goals and interests. But it wasn't long before he was remarried, this time to a Canadian girl who shared his academic interests and aspirations.

Dr. Westra now says: "Life here hasn't always been easy, but I feel that my decision to emigrate has been beneficial in many ways. In Holland, I would have followed a set, predictable pattern. But by leaving, I broke the mould and gained more control over my life."

Agriculture
Down-to-earth Living

Holland Marsh, the fertile market gardening area north of Toronto named after Samuel Holland, the Dutch-born surveyor of early Eastern Canada, was created by prewar settlers. But the ones who came after the war also brought along expertise in land reclamation. Across Canada, various individuals bought parcels of marshy land and, through ditching, tiling, and diking, made it arable and productive. The project that gained the most attention was the draining of a tract of alluvial land in British Columbia in order to develop an agricultural settlement.

Pitt Polder is on the north side of the Fraser River Valley, about twenty-five miles east of Vancouver. During the spring runoffs from the mountains to the north, a lake used to overflow the polder area. Sometimes the water stood eight feet deep. Little wonder that this land was bypassed during the settlement of the Fraser Valley.

An attempt was made in 1911 to develop the area. A group of Vancouver businessmen used Chinese to construct dikes, cut ditches, and install a pumping station. But the dikes were too low, and the costs of further reclamation were prohibitive. New owners brought a small group of Mennonites to the land in the early 1920s, but these people were flooded out before they were well established. A local gun club took over and set up a private duck hunting preserve. But the flooding and a decline in the duck population eventually led members to decide to sell.

Then the Dutch took over.

In 1949, Dr. Jan Blom arrived in Vancouver in search of investment opportunities in western Canada. He became interested in the possibilities of converting the gun club lands to agricultural use through improved drainage techniques practised in The Netherlands. Tests showed that the silty soil was potentially good farmland.

Dr. Blom took out an option on more than seven thousand acres and returned to The Netherlands to seek backing and technical advice. The land was bought and Pitt Polder Limited came into being, with Dr. Blom as managing director. Engineering work began in 1951. And before long, Dutch immigrants with some

Ministry of Agriculture and Food

experience in reclamation work were employed to bolster existing dikes, build new ones, dig ditches, install two electrical pumps, and lay out a system of roads.

These laborers were given priority in applying for land—each unit was approximately eighty acres—and no rent was asked of them for the first year.

Before being leased, each unit was prepared for occupation by Pitt Polder Limited. The land was cleared of its marsh and brush cover, and field ditches and tiles were installed. Then a cover crop of oats, clover, and grasses was planted.

After the lease was signed, the company built on the unit a house designed for a family with five to seven children, a barn, and certain auxiliary buildings. And the houses were enlarged by the company upon the birth of the eighth child in a farm family.

Top: Harvesting lettuce in Holland Marsh.
Lower: The Pitt Polder Management Building and sheds.

Floriculture
They Still Love Flowers

Dutch immigrants built up the flower-growing business in Canada. They introduced the auction clock system for selling their products efficiently. They made reputations as excellent gardeners. The floral beauty at Niagara Falls was created by a Dutchman.

In many other areas of enterprise, the Dutchman has also excelled, leaving his mark. Perhaps this is because the newcomers brought with them so many ideas. Some were constantly thinking of ways to make money. One man even thought of exporting bullrushes, an item apparently in demand in The Netherlands for its decorative value.

The Dutch auction clock is used in three Canadian cities to expedite the sale of flowers. Tobacco growers in Ontario also use it to sell their crop.

Color abounds in the Niagara Falls area. The person directly responsible for keeping this tourist haven rich in flowers of every kind and color is a Dutch immigrant, Tony Alkemade, manager of the greenhouse operated by the Niagara Parks Commission. This floral clock, the largest timepiece of its kind in the world, showcases Alkemade's work.

The Dutch brought their love of flowers with them to Canada. Many homes blossom with color, indoors and out. Mr. and Mrs. George Keep of Brampton, Ontario, enjoy the flower garden at their former home. Only a color photo begins to do justice to its beauty.

Dundas, Ontario, has been dubbed the cactus capital of North America because of the successful enterprise of an immigrant. At any given time, more than one million cacti are growing in the greenhouses of Ben Veldhuis Ltd., give or take a hundred thousand. No one goes around counting them.

As a boy in Almelo, Overijssel, Veldhuis had kept his own private cactus garden in a corner of his father's greenhouse. The fascination stayed with him when he emigrated to Canada as a thirteen-year-old in 1927. At that time, he was old enough to work in his father's nurseries in nearby Burlington. However, it wasn't until 1952 that the first Ben Veldhuis cactus operation came into being. It consisted of six greenhouses. Veldhuis has never looked back. The complex in Dundas, augmented by facilities near Orlando, Florida, and Leamington, Ontario, has been regarded for years as the biggest cactus growing operation on the continent.

Veldhuis became so well known in the world of international horticulture, both as a nurseryman and a judge, that a letter addressed simply and erroneously to *Cactus, Ontario, USA* found its way to Dundas.

He once regretted that his world-wide business travels left him little time to spend in his favorite spot—the greenhouse. "In the morning, there's something special about being out there among the plants. It makes a man feel good."

A lot of other people seem to think so too. The cacti, the succulents, and the tropical foliage plants attract thousands of visitors each year.

David Hendrik Bakker clutches a loaf of bread as he walks through a devastated neighborhood in the village of Scherpenzeel, Gelderland, in May, 1940. His house was among those destroyed during the fighting that followed the German invasion. The war pushed many people toward emigration. Mr. Bakker's son, John, and six grandchildren moved to Canada. The aerial photo shows part of the vast J.C. Bakker and Sons nursery in St. Catharines, Ontario.

Before Hitler's armies marched through The Netherlands, the nursery business was still suffering the disastrous effects of the Depression. A limited market prevented growers from making much money. They were able to squeeze out a living with raspberries, strawberries, and a few fruit trees.

Then, when the war came, business went from bad to worse. Many nurserymen went bankrupt. Some struggled on, managing to survive by trading goods.

J.C. Bakker of Scherpenzeel, Gelderland, was hit especially hard. His village was in the path of one of The Netherlands' main lines of defence. During the winter of 1939-40, when rumors of an invasion were rife, the Dutch military tested the flooding scheme which they hoped would halt the Germans in their tracks. Unfortunately, that winter was severely harsh, the water froze solid, and Bakker's nursery was destroyed. When the invasion came a few months later, Bakker and the other villagers were evacuated from the line of artillery fire. They returned ten days after the Dutch surrender, only to find much of the village in ruins.

Bakker helped with the cleanup. Live explosives had to be defused. Dead cows and horses had to be removed. Order had to be brought to the rubble. During the ensuing occupation, Bakker grew some tobacco and beans and exchanged much of the crop for bread and other necessities for his family.

"Before my father was married, he'd had dreams of leaving for another part of the world," says his oldest son, Dave. "After the war, things weren't much bet-

Mr. and Mrs. J.C. Bakker and two of their five children share a happy moment after their crates arrive.

ter. Dad grew some fruit trees and roses, but his heart wasn't in it. With all the postwar regulations, he couldn't see a future in The Netherlands for his children. It was very tough for a younger grower to get started; there just wasn't any land available.

So he decided to pack his bags and move to Canada. He could have left with the *Waterman* in June of 1947, but the notice of departure didn't allow enough time for the orderly disposal of the business and other arrangements. In the winter, he received approval for emigration for a second time. The family, seven persons in all, was booked on the *Kota Inten*, scheduled to leave in March, 1948. Now

Horticulture
From the Depths of the Earth to Hot and Sunny Greenhouses

Andy Olsthoorn sits on a lifeboat for a farewell photo in 1951. He's among the young men who headed into the bush and returned with a bear. While working at a hydro-electric project in British Columbia, he literally lived—in the clouds.

Ambition. Many of the young bachelor immigrants had plenty of it. They came here with one aim in mind: to succeed. Some did.

When Andy Olsthoorn, twenty years old and single, boarded the *Volendam* in April of 1951, his goal was to be his own boss eventually. He'd had only four years of schooling, but that didn't daunt him. While working in greenhouses in the Maasdijk-'s-Gravenzande area of Zuid-Holland, he had done some buying and selling. He seemed to have ability in that field, and he was determined to follow it through once he had established himself in Canada.

However, success didn't come quickly. At first, Olsthoorn went from job to job, scraping for a living. He worked for a farmer in the Ottawa area, then headed south for the tobacco harvest. Jobs in Lon-

there was plenty of time for packing the suitcases. The only disappointment was the hefty capital gains tax which Bakker had to pay to the Dutch government.

"We all had visions of going across in style on a luxury liner," recalls Dave, eighteen years old at the time. "What a disappointment when we saw the *Kota Inten*. It looked like a tub. It took eleven days or so for us to get to Halifax. A propeller clutch broke during a storm, and at a given point we could go at only half speed. One farmer on board spread the word that Halifax was the warmest spot in Canada, that even coconuts were growing there. He really meant what he said. What did we know? Well, when we got

close to Halifax, the crew gave the deck its daily wash with seawater, and the water froze. You can imagine how cold it was. The farmer didn't show his face anywhere."

To Dave, his father had decided to emigrate none too soon.

"I was called into the army about the time we left. Even when I was already here, I kept on getting letters by ordinary mail, saying I had to report for duty at such and such a time and bring a sandwich along as the registration etc. might take the whole day. I ignored these, of course. Later I got another notice, temporarily excusing me from going into the service."

don and Woodstock followed. In the spring of 1952, he went north to Sudbury to work in a copper-nickel mine with a number of other young Dutch immigrants. The pay was superb—around $130 a week. There was even time for bear-hunting in the bush. But he hadn't come to Canada to spend the rest of his working life underground. So he moved on.

After a stint with a tunnel project in Niagara Falls, he went off to Kelowna, British Columbia, to help build a four-thousand-foot tunnel at a hydro-electric project. A helicopter brought him to work each day in the remote mountain area.

Eventually he went back east—all the way to The Netherlands. There he met the girl who would later become his wife. Returning to Canada, he worked in the bush in Quebec, and then worked at a General Motors plant. Later he became a truck driver, transporting fruit to Montreal in the summer and fuel in the winter.

"At last I started on my own in Ontario," he says. "I bought a flower business in Kitchener. I sold it again and bought a business at Beamsville. There I finally began doing what I liked best—what the Dutch call *handel*. I went from store to store, peddling vegetables and fruit."

Olsthoorn found success—and satisfaction. Now his export-import business keeps him on the road in Canada, the United States, and Europe for six months of a year, but he doesn't mind. After all,

The men are carted through the dark tunnel they are building.

he had come to Canada with that goal in mind.

Near Beamsville, he grows vegetables, fruit, and flowers under 160,000 square feet of glass and in the open air. The products are shipped to market through Lakeshore Produce, a wholesale firm run with two partners, Tom Hanemeyer and Dick VanderEnden. Vegetables such as yellow and brown peppers, lettuce, and cucumbers are imported from The Netherlands and Spain and distributed across North America. Olsthoorn's other holdings include a forty-acre operation in Florida that specializes in tropical plants for sale in supermarkets.

"You've got to hustle," he says. "That's the only way to get ahead."

When the family arrived in the Niagara Peninsula, the area appealed to them right away because it more closely resembled The Netherlands than anything else they had passed through in Canada. The fruit trees were a surprise. No one in The Netherlands had told them to expect orchards and vineyards. That's how inadequate the information often was.

Bakker Sr. began working at C.H. Prudhomme and Sons Ltd., a nursery at Beamsville, where a number of other new arrivals had found employment.

"In retrospect, those were good days," says Dave. "We didn't have much—I think we could take along $300 in total—and we didn't expect much. There was work, and that was important. We were free from worry."

Right from the start, there were signs that this family would not only make it, but make it big. During the first spring, Dave and a younger brother landed a contract for growing tomatoes, rented some land, and set to work. Unfortunately, they didn't make any money; however, they knew that they were on the right track.

The following year, the family launched its nursery business. Bakker Sr., who had no trouble with English, rented six acres near St. Catharines, ordered seedlings from The Netherlands and grafting stock from British Columbia, and made a beginning. The first years were tough. Until the nursery stock developed, cash crops such as tomatoes and gladioli were necessary to bring in some returns. Says Dave: "You name it and we've grown it."

"There wasn't enough work in the business yet for all of us, so I started working for General Motors," he continues. "I found that very boring. When the nursery picked up, I quit GM and started working again at the job I liked best. In those days, most of the money we made was put into one pot. We got pocket money of $2 a week, cigarettes were supplied, and on birthdays we got a new white shirt. That was the only way the family could get ahead. Most of the money was pumped into the business. I remember my mother splurging for our second Christmas in Canada—she bought herself a coffee pot, because we needed a new one."

Today, as a result of years of hard work and dogged determination, things are much different. The nursery, operated by Dave and brother John, covers one hundred and fifty acres, employs up to fifty people, and can be classed as one of the most modern and efficient operations of its kind in North America.

Bakker Sr. died in the spring of 1983. A week before his death, he told his minister, Rev. Henry Jonker: "I came to Canada to establish myself and my family. But how beautiful it is to look back and to see that the Lord has led me, my wife, and my family to establish His name in this new land."

Says Rev. Jonker: "He marvelled at the way God used his wrong-intentioned immigration to get him involved in His own way in establishing the churches and the Christian schools in this area. Yes, his life covered a distance—from strength and pride to humble dependence."

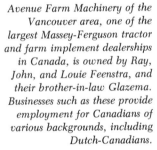

Avenue Farm Machinery of the Vancouver area, one of the largest Massey-Ferguson tractor and farm implement dealerships in Canada, is owned by Ray, John, and Louie Feenstra, and their brother-in-law Glazema. Businesses such as these provide employment for Canadians of various backgrounds, including Dutch-Canadians.

Kees Verburg, a farmer in the Strathroy area of Ontario, had an idea too. He shared it with a friend employed by the *Christelijke Emigratie Centrale* in The Netherlands.

"I suppose that you know that there is a kind of dairy in Holland that makes a kind of milk product that stores well," he wrote. "It isn't an ordinary milk powder. There is demand for it all over Europe. Something like that would have great possibilities in Canada. If one hundred Dutch farmers would import the inventory for one such factory or dairy, and invest six thousand guilders each to buy farms suitable for dairying, we could really start something. In a radius of about fifty miles, I would be able to buy up a hundred farms without attracting too much attention."

Of course, a lot of ideas never became reality. But one venture that did get off the ground, albeit briefly, involved importing farm implements from The Netherlands.

A group of ten Dutch manufacturers were given a grant from their government to set up a modest sales organization in Ontario. The purpose was to sell equipment to Dutch settlers, who could then use the capital that they weren't allowed to take with them to Canada because of the exchange restrictions.

"We started in the early spring of 1952," recalls Felix Leupen of London, Ontario, one of the principals of the importing enterprise known as NVFL. "C. Van Rijn, who lived near Grimsby, was the main sales agent. I lived at that time in Portland, near Brockville, and looked after everything else—administration, assembly, delivery, etc. Among the assortment we had to offer prospective clients were farm wagons on rubber tires, Ford-Ferguson tractors with power takeoff, plows, manure spreaders, hay tethers, fertilizer spreaders, harrows, chain harrows, packers, sorting machines for tomatoes and potatoes, and a variety of spades, shovels and other hand instruments. We also managed to sell a few *greppelploegen*, ditching plows. These huge monsters were drawn by four light tractors. In the Holland Marsh area, they dug trenches which lowered the water level and enabled the farmers to grow longer carrots. It was a sight to behold. People driving along Highway 400 stopped to see what was going on."

Leupen also remembers supplying technical help to the farmers in Holland Marsh after Hurricane Hazel caused

The auger-type pump used in Holland Marsh after the 1954 flood.

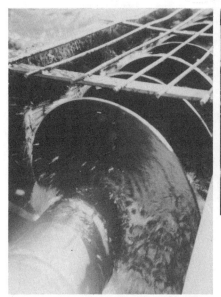

Farm implements from The Netherlands were sold in Canada in the early 1950s.

widespread flooding in 1954.

"We brought in a large pump, just like a huge auger, that removed water at a very high rate and dumped it into the surrounding canal. Everything floating in the water, debris of all kinds, was pumped away too."

Another interesting incident stands out in his memory: "A farmer, F. Smits in Athens, Ontario, ordered all he could. The stuff arrived in a railroad car. But there were no papers with it. Oh boy! I finally managed to get the shipment released by putting up a stiff bond. Finally, the papers arrived. When I took them to the customs people, we discovered strange writing on the envelope. It turned out that the papers had gone all the way to Athens, Greece."

The venture died a slow death.

"Due to the great difference in soil types, especially the hard pan not known in Holland, plows had to be adapted. In general, quite a few adaptations had to be made if the machinery we sold to the Dutch farmer was to appeal to the Canadian farmer. Only in a few cases did we manage to sell into the Canadian market. Fruit-sorting machines did well, and also the cyclone-type fertilizer spreader made by Vicon-Lely. However, the NVFL was a short-term solution to a short-term problem. As time passed, the economy in Europe grew stronger and the normal flow of money between Canada and Holland resumed." The NVFL, known in Canada as Holland Farm Implements, came to an end in 1955.

Here's the story of Alec Popma of Abbotsford, British Columbia: "I was born on a six-cow farm in Friesland, was a paperboy from the age of ten to thirteen, had seven years of grade school, and then worked on farms in Friesland and Drenthe. During the war, I went into hiding for two years on a farm at Zaandam, Noord-Holland, where I met my wife, Jenny. After the war, I started working

"I started with one cow and some heifers. Two of our married sons are working now on the 200-head dairy farm."

for the candy and chocolate factory of Albert Heyn. Then, in April of 1952, we emigrated to Canada with two children. I worked as a farmhand for four years at Deroche and Abbotsford, and then rented a ten-acre farm at Matsqui. I started with one cow and some heifers, and I worked in the peat and on the sawdust truck for a year. After that, we rented a forty-acre farm, which we bought after three years and lived on for fifteen years. By then, the herd had increased to forty-five head. In 1972, we sold the place and bought a 160-acre farm, lock, stock, and barrel, and took our own herd with us. The Lord has blessed us with seven children, and two of our married sons are now working on the 200-head dairy farm. Although my wife and I have moved off the place, we're still involved, but we do take things a little easier."

This story can be repeated hundreds of times across Canada. It's a typical story. It's a story of an immigrant who has made an impact in Canada.

There are so many successful Dutch farmers across Canada, like Berend Flinkert for example, a dairy farmer northwest of Kitchener, Ontario, whose milk quota ranks among the largest in the province. Most of them emigrated with only a few pennies in their pocket. But they had ambition, an essential ingredient for success. John De Graaf is another one of them.

He left Rijsbergen, Noord-Brabant, in October, 1951, in search of more elbow room for himself, his wife, Corrie, and their four children. In Quebec City, they boarded a train that took them to St. John, New Brunswick. There De Graaf began working in the fields at the St. Patrick's Orphanage, operated by the Diocese of St. John, earning $65 a month plus a free house and free vegetables.

"It seems that when people sponsored immigrants, they thought that they were going to hire slaves, dirt-cheap labor. But they got surprises. I couldn't speak the language, but I knew my work. I wasn't a slave; I was a farmer. I outworked the manager and the assistant manager and everybody else. They didn't know what farming was."

De Graaf, somewhat disgruntled, left the orphanage when his one-year contract expired. He moved to St. Andrews, where he became herdsman on the Van Horne estate. He recalls: "This was the best place I ever worked for. All I had to do was look after the cattle. But in 1955, they held a dispersal sale and sold the whole thing, so I had to look for another place."

He bought a small farm at Meagherville, and lived there until 1962. That was the year his wife died.

"I really didn't know what to do. Go back to Holland? My parents told me: 'Come back home.' I had five children then. But soon I had decided not to go back, and to look for another place instead. I put the farm up for sale, and had

Another sign showing the Dutch presence. Below, the modern facilities of the dairy farm of the Ten Brinke brothers at Chilliwack, British Columbia.

Dutch dairymen often have a nice sign at the entrance to their yards. Throughout Canada, Dutch names have appeared on all types of businesses.

a buyer within two weeks. I had heard a lot about Nova Scotia, especially about the Annapolis Valley, so I decided to write to the farm loan board to ask about places for sale. In a short time, I had a catalogue listing a hundred farms. I bought another small, rundown place with a milk quota, some broilers, a pheasant hunting reserve, and a small orchard."

The orchard grew. Today De Graaf and his son Adrian have approximately seventy acres of trees. That's a lot of apples. But there's a second source of income: poultry.

"We started with a flock of four thousand turkey broilers," says De Graaf. "But that operation failed because we knew nothing about handling the birds. Still we stuck to it. Old apple warehouses in the neighborhood came up for sale, and we renovated them and put in turkeys. We ended up with a capacity for 33,000 turkeys and 29,000 chickens."

He has held a number of positions on marketing boards, including nine years as chairman of the Nova Scotia Turkey Marketing Board. This was quite a feat for someone who had seen perhaps a dozen turkeys in his life before coming to Canada. Turkey is not a favorite dish in The Netherlands.

De Graaf, who remarried in 1964, talks proudly of his children—four boys and one girl. Many immigrants do. After all, one of the reasons they had come to Canada was to secure them a stable future. When that has been realized, despite all the woes and setbacks, why shouldn't they show some satisfaction?

"The oldest one, Keith, lives in the neighborhood here and is a tobacco and hog producer. The second one, Hank, is an electrician in New Brunswick. The third one, Toosie, is married to a tobacco and hog producer, one of the Ansems family. The fourth one, Adrian, took over what we call the home place three years ago. And Peter lives in Sussex, New Brunswick, where he is a DeLaval dealer."

De Graaf remembers his first days in Canada very well. Despite his misgivings about the work at the orphanage, he felt at home right away. "We are Roman Catholics, and they were having the service in Latin at the time, and that was just like home." His love for the country grew; now it is unshakeable.

So it still hurts a bit when, after thirty-two years, someone says: "John De Graaf over there—the Dutchman." It bothers him to be singled out as a Dutchman, and not accepted as a fellow Canadian. Still, there is some inner satisfaction when people continue to recognize his ethnic background. He knows that he has made an impact.

When Harry L. DeJong was a five-year-old whippersnapper in Sexbierum, Friesland, he knew that The Netherlands wasn't the place for him. He had already been told how many of his relatives had gone to the New World, some as early as the 1700s. An uncle (he's still alive) went to New Jersey in 1918. Even his father, fed up with working for other people, made frequent noises about moving to the United States.

"As I grew older, Dad kept on advising me to move to the States. He said: 'Don't work for the farmers in Friesland. They'll treat you like a slave.' I agreed that seventy-hour weeks were not for me. I also didn't like the insecurity of the system. In November, you had to tell the farmer whether you wanted to stay for another year; but the farmer could say that he didn't want you anymore too. And yet custom dictated that moving day was on May 12, some six months later. Can you imagine the unpleasant feelings if you had to stay for half a year with a farmer who didn't want you any longer? I didn't want to experience such things."

Unrest in Europe and dark clouds of war descending upon the continent postponed any plans young DeJong entertained for moving away. During the German occupation, he worked at many jobs in the Wieringermeer polder on the other side of the IJsselmeer. Back home, in Sexbierum, he learned to operate a windmill. In the darkness of the evening, he ground grain for members of the underground and for bakers who wanted to circumvent the rationing system. When the Canadian liberators arrived to general jubilation, the local police threw him in jail for two days for some dubious offence: trading grain, a controlled commodity, for cigarettes.

"I wanted to go to the uncle in New Jersey. I wrote him in 1946 that I was going to get married and then join him. He wrote back to say that I should come alone. He would have to sponsor us for some time, and he just couldn't afford to look after two extra people. Well, I had no plans of going by myself."

Then Canadian and Dutch authorities reached an understanding for the admittance of a number of agriculturalists to Canada. DeJong was interested and he applied. A few weeks before the scheduled departure of the *Waterman*, in June, 1947, he received notice of his acceptance. Hectic days followed. A wedding ceremony had to be planned. He arranged for his parents to move into a double house that he and a friend had built on a rented lot.

DeJong and his bride, Edith, had no idea where they would be placed in Canada. In Montreal, they were put in the hands of John Vellinga, fieldman of the Christian Reformed Church, who directed them to a farm near Waterloo, Ontario.

"The conditions didn't suit us. We lived in the farmer's house, in a bedroom upstairs. We told him that we wanted to live in a house by ourselves. He understood that. So I contacted Vellinga, and he found another place near Stratford."

During the four months at the first farm, a cordial relationship had been established. In fact, when DeJong was

Mr. and Mrs. Harry DeJong after the baptism of their first child, Tessie, at the Christian Reformed Church in Kitchener in 1948. The baptismal font had to be borrowed from the congregation in Hamilton. The couple, shown below in 1983, eventually had five children.

about to leave, the farmer, a Mennonite, invited the neighbors over. Even some people from the city, who had fought in The Netherlands, came to say goodbye. DeJong and his wife were given enough food to last them all winter.

At the second farm near Stratford, frictions developed between boss and employee. "The farmer had a severe drinking problem, and it was impossible to work for him. I got in touch with Vellinga again. In March, 1948, we moved to

DeJong milks his Jersey.

a farm near St. George. The pay wasn't too bad—$90 a month. But again, there were problems with the boss."

In the fall, the farmer gave DeJong one month's notice that he wouldn't be needed any more, since there was no work during the winter.

"Well, I told him that if that were the case, I would move out tomorrow. He just laughed. The next day, I milked the cows and fed the pigs and started carrying the furniture outside. You should have seen that farmer. He shouted: 'You can't leave! The apples have to be picked!' But nothing could change my mind."

He and his wife moved into a house in Hamilton owned by a couple they had befriended on the *Waterman*. They rented two rooms for $2 a week. Part of this cost was recovered when DeJong began to earn $1.50 for driving his neighbors to their construction jobs at the site of an addition to the Dofasco steel mill. They got paid eighty-five cents an hour.

"In those days, we were always looking for ways to make some extra money. One day, I spotted an ad in the *Hamilton Spec-*

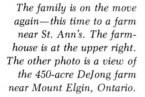

The family is on the move again—this time to a farm near St. Ann's. The farmhouse is at the upper right. The other photo is a view of the 450-acre DeJong farm near Mount Elgin, Ontario.

tator: The Canada Steamship Line needed 150 workers, and all applicants were asked to report at the dock at 6 p.m. I went, and found myself standing among hundreds of men. A big fellow with a cigar in his mouth stood on a platform looking us over. If he saw someone he liked, he would point him out to a skinny man standing beside him with a box full of copper numbers. The number would be thrown to the lucky applicant. The big man would yell: 'We'll try you for an hour. If you're no good, we'll send you home without pay.' That's how things were done before the union came in."

DeJong worked several nights a week for ninety cents an hour, laboring hard until two or three o'clock in the morning. The big fellow with his ever-present cigar handed out the pay on Saturday nights.

When the job at Dofasco was finished, DeJong got himself on the payroll at Natco Tile, a brickmaking firm near Burlington. He worked from 3 to 11 p.m., seven days a week, and got paid $65. He never had a day off except for Christmas.

"We lived in a house owned by the factory. There were four acres of land with it, so I bought a Jersey for $85. The milk came in handy because we had a few mouths to feed—there were three boarders as well as the family. By April, 1951, I was fed up with the job. I was never home. We didn't have any friends anymore. My children didn't even know me."

His next job was at a feed mill near Burlington. The pay was only $42.50 a week, but he had Saturday afternoons and Sundays off. While there, the thought of acquiring a farm of his own kept entering his mind. His aim had been to work in cash crops—sugarbeets and potatoes—because that's what he had done in Friesland. But he was willing to give dairying a try.

"I bought a 75-acre farm at St. Anns, south of Smithville, for $7,500, with a four percent mortgage. I had three cows, including the Jersey. My first monthly milk cheque was $35. That wasn't enough to live on, of course. As quite a few other immigrants did, I worked eight hours a day—and sometimes a double shift—at a tunnel project in Niagara Falls. My brother-in-law, Frans Klaver, died after a fall on the job site. The average wage was $102. All of that wasn't clear, because the income tax system began around that time."

In 1953, in search of bigger things, he bought a farm of 136 acres at Smithville. The price, including thirty-nine head of cattle, two horses, machinery, and a milk quota, was $26,500. His first milk cheque totalled $513.

The year was also made memorable by the visit of his parents, ostensibly for a holiday. One day, his father, Lieuwe, sixty-two years old, announced that he had come to stay. In fact, the house in Sexbierum had been sold before their departure. Harry and Edith were flabbergasted.

"My parents lived on the farm until 1956. Then they went back to Friesland. My mother never felt at home in Canada. And my father couldn't drive, so they were pretty well stuck in one place."

In 1972, DeJong sold the farm for $75,000. In its place, he bought a 450-acre spread near Mount Elgin with four houses and three sets of buildings. The total price was $310,000.

Harry DeJong's milk record for August, 1953.

"I had three boys, so I decided to buy one big farm to keep us all together. That was my goal."

The farm was profitable. Before too long, the mailman brought a milk cheque for $16,500. One day, 4,800 pounds of milk—the equivalent of sixty full cans—were produced. An additional two hundred acres were rented for grain and corn. The future looked prosperous.

However, DeJong found that two of his sons didn't want to spend the rest of their lives on a farm. They wanted to strike out on their own, in other fields. Only Louis loved farming; he was given one-fourth ownership.

In 1977, at the age of fifty-six, DeJong decided to call it quits. He could hardly work anymore because of a back injury sustained in 1966. Tax laws discouraged him from renewing an effort to get his sons interested in taking over the operation. So he sold everything, grossing a bit over $1 million, including $750,000 for the land. His son Louis kept sixty head of cattle, some machinery, and a big milk quota, and bought a smaller farm near Troy.

"I bought a house with five acres near Dundas," says DeJong. "I do a bit of gardening there. Work for the Christian Reformed Church in Ancaster also keeps me busy. I still wish the boys would have taken over the farm. I wanted them to become partners. But it didn't work out that way. Anyway, my story shows that it was possible for immigrants to make something of themselves. My wife and I came to Canada with only $350. We always strived to get a better job, a bigger house. That paid off."

Henk Van Silfhout

There was no pressing need for Henk Van Silfhout and his wife to emigrate to Canada in 1957. He was an economist in his mid-thirties, with a secure job in Tilburg, Noord-Brabant; she was a lawyer.

"But I found my work in the field of management advisory service with a specialty in tax not very exciting," he recalls. "So I thought it was a good time to start looking for another job. I didn't intend to emigrate; I merely wanted some North American experience, and planned to return to The Netherlands after five years or so."

Things did not turn out as expected. He got his experience, but he and his wife came to like the country so well that thoughts of moving back vanished. They were here to stay.

Mrs. VanSilfhout, who had taken her law training in the Napoleonic code practised in The Netherlands, switched to her second love: teaching at the secondary school level. She was proficient in Latin, French, and mathematics. Her husband started as a junior economist in the economics department of the Bank of Nova Scotia in Toronto, and worked his way up. In the mid-60s, he began work at Nesbitt-Thomson, a stock brokerage firm. Later, he joined Greenshields Inc., and from there went to Wisener-MacKellar, where he became vice-president. In 1972 he struck out on his own, offering a specialized management investment service.

"I saw the possibilities of such a private service," he says. "I believe immigrants have a better chance of succeeding if they try to do something differently. There are already many examples of this."

The couple lives on a 400-acre farm at Mallorytown, Ontario, midway between the major financial centers of Toronto and Montreal.

After six years in the Dutch air force, Simon Kouwenhoven of Delft, Zuid-Holland, felt that flying was in his blood. In 1957, he emigrated to Canada with his wife and one child, hoping to take up a career in the air. He was fascinated by the idea of becoming a bush pilot.

To his dismay, he found that no one was looking for a pilot. Anxious for any kind of work, he became a junior in training—"the lowest on the totem pole"—at the Bank of Montreal in New Westminster, British Columbia. The business schooling that he had received in The Netherlands came in handy.

Kouwenhoven found that he loved the banking world. And his bosses admired his abilities. With this combination, he moved up the corporate ladder quickly. He worked in various branches in British Columbia, became manager of a large branch, and then was named a district manager. Other promotions followed. He's now in Calgary, a senior vice-president in charge of the bank's Alberta division, which has 160 branches.

Does he miss flying?

"I've traveled with commercial aircraft and executive jets, and I've found that flying doesn't fascinate me anymore," he says. "I prefer to be on the ground—in a bank."

Chapter 25

They're Still Coming

New immigrants arrive by airplane in 1982. They are Rob, Marjon, Lars, Peter and Robin Wunsche.

They're Still Coming

Koosje Bol, a pretty eighteen-year-old from the city of Utrecht, was having breakfast with her family aboard the *Groote Beer* as it approached Montreal in May, 1954, when the captain suddenly appeared at the table. He had received a radio message from the Royal Netherlands Embassy in Ottawa: Koosje would be the 100,000th Dutch immigrant to be welcomed by Canada since the end of the war. It was a major milestone; a celebrative ceremony awaited her.

After a moment of silence at the table, everyone began to congratulate the girl, described by one reporter as "a demure and lovely representative of a country which has been steadily tightening its bonds with Canada, and which has cheerfully lost many of its best citizens to this country since 1947."

"I'm kind of frightened," Koosje said in broken English. "What does it all mean?"

Flash-bulbs popped when the boat landed. There were handshakes. At a reception, there were speeches and presentations, including a plate inscribed: "To commemorate the arrival in Canada of the 100,000th settler from Holland since its liberation by the Canadians."

It was a proud moment for Dr. A.H.J. Lovink, the Dutch ambassador, who was on hand for the ceremony. (While ambassador to Australia, he welcomed the 100,000th Dutch immigrant to that country in 1958.) Equally proud were the Canadian officials, including Walter Harris, Canada's immigration minister. Warm words made the message clear: Canada loved the industrious people from The Netherlands, and its doors were open to many more.

And before long, another milestone will be reached in Canada: the 200,000th postwar arrival.

"The Hollanders are the best farmers I've ever seen."

The compliment came from Ralph Maybank, parliamentary assistant to the minister of mines and resources, during an interview in 1950. Hundreds of Dutch immigrants were already established on their own farms. Canadian officials, who had

Royal Netherlands Embassy, Ottawa

Koosje waves to the officials and newsmen on hand to greet her.

Royal Netherlands Embassy, Ottawa

Celebrating the arrival of the 100,000th immigrant gave Canadian and Dutch officials a chance to get together. Shown here are Walter Harris (left), the Canadian immigration minister, and Dr. A.S. Tuinman, the Dutch emigration attaché.

It was always a great occasion when parents of immigrants came over for a visit. The grandchildren were delighted; after all, they didn't have many relatives in Canada. Mrs. M. Polderman of Kruiningen, Zeeland, holds her grandson, Peter, during a visit to her family in Vancouver in 1956.

The parents of Henry Kuiperij of Acton, Ontario visited Canada in 1954, and took delight in roadside picnic tables. The elderly couple lived in Hardenberg, Overijssel.

let them into the country to give the agricultural sector a much-needed boost, were pleased.

"At first, the Hollander is somewhat awed about the vastness of this land," said Maybank. "But he adjusts quickly, and within a year he's adapted to the Canadian way of life. Really, we are happy with the Dutch farmers. I've seen farms that are fine examples for Canadian farmers. And the bulbs that are being grown on the West Coast are of such quality that they could be exported to Holland. We haven't got any better immigrants than the Hollanders."

He wasn't alone in his sentiments.

Lester B. Pearson, Canada's minister of external affairs, said at Schiphol airport near Amsterdam in 1951: "We consider ourselves fortunate to have new Canadians from good old Holland in our midst. The more of this type of people that we get, the better it will be for us. They're first-rate tradesmen, and of high moral character."

Pierre Depuy, the Canadian ambassador to The Netherlands, said in the same year: "Canada isn't a paradise. But it's a country that offers excellent opportunities to capable people. The ones with initiative can definitely succeed there. We consider the Dutch very good settlers. They are people who can adapt easily. The Canadians place them at the top of immigrating nationalities."

The industriousness of the Dutch immigrants did not go unnoticed by Colin Campbell, who was an employee at Maxwell Limited in St. Marys, Ontario, before he became a teacher. He particularly admired a new arrival named John, a man of fine physique, who gave full measure on any job he was assigned. In fact, John put so much effort into the production of power lawn-mowers that he made his co-workers a bit envious.

"Under our contract with the union," recalls Campbell, now of Wallaceburg, Ontario, "no piece-work rates were to be changed, once established by time study, unless the operation was changed. Our Canadian workers were accustomed to producing per worker about thirty-six to forty mowers a day. By working steadily and diligently, John was able to assemble at least fifty a day. Our men were furious; they were afraid that the management would have the assembly operation re-timed and the piece-work rates cut. Of course, this didn't happen. John could not understand, nor could I, why our Canadian workmen were content to produce at

about eighty per cent of their readily attainable production. I understand that low productivity is still a formidable problem in North American industry."

Colin's wife, Beatrice, a retired high school teacher, recalls with fondness the hours she spent teaching English to immigrants at an evening class in St. Marys.

"These people were adults, and it was not an easy assignment. Some of them were fairly proficient in understanding and speaking English, while others, mainly ladies who were at home every day, could speak only their native tongue. But it would have been difficult to find anywhere a more pleasant, responsive and appreciative group. We formed some delightful friendships with these good people—friendships which have endured over the years. I look back on that experience as a time of real inspiration and blessing to me."

When she moved to Wallaceburg in the mid-1950s, Beatrice Campbell was asked to teach a similar night school class.

"Again I found it to be a most rewarding experience. The adults were so eager to become proficient in English and so appreciative of instruction. There were

times when the vagaries of the English language were quite frustrating, and we laughed sometimes at the confusion of sounds and meanings. Occasionally now, we meet some of these friends and they certainly no longer have any language problem."

The speed with which many of the newcomers succeeded left some of the Canadians a bit bewildered. Willem Buitenwerf of St. Catharines, who came here in 1952, recalls: "I couldn't read the thoughts of the Canadians, but I got the impression that many of them thought at first: 'What are those people doing here?' Later, you could notice that some of them were jealous, because the Dutch were getting their own farms and making it in business."

But such feelings belonged to the minority. Most people were appreciative of the contributions the Dutch were making to improving life in their new land. Some Canadian officials even went to The Netherlands—to Nieuwe Pekela, Groningen—to present a plaque honoring the early Dutch settlers of Holland Marsh. Many of the settlers had come from that part of The Netherlands.

They come to Canada by the thousands each year. They struggle with bulging suitcases in crowded terminals and stations, searching for a familiar face in the crowd. They are of all ages, they are dressed in modern clothes, and they arrive with expensive camera equipment slung over their shoulders. They are tourists—from The Netherlands.

Relatives of immigrants, curious to find out how their kin were faring in the new land, have been coming to Canada ever since the early 1950s. At first, they were mainly parents, eager to visit their children and to have a first look at their Canadian-born grandchildren. These people, mostly retired, would stay for months. And, finances permitting, they would come back more than once, often exclaiming to friends in The Netherlands that Canada was a wonderful country and that they would prefer to stay here permanently if only they were younger.

"But times have changed," says Rimmer Tjalsma of Mississauga, Ontario, a former fieldman, and now regional representative of *Wereld Contact*, the organization which sends thousands to Canada, Australia, and the other areas of the world where the Dutch are concentrated. "A generation of brothers, sisters, nephews, and nieces has discovered that in this age of jet travel, Canada isn't so far away. These people come to visit their relatives. But more than that, they come as tourists, to see the sights that they read about in letters. Many of them spend only a few days with their family and then go traveling on their own. A trip to Canada is taking on more and more the character of an ordinary vacation."

Grandpa and Grandma from The Netherlands have come for a visit. This photo, dated 1959, was supplied by William Van Oosten of Chatham, Ontario.

Rimmer Tjalsma: "In this age of jet travel, Canada isn't so far away."

In the early days, many problems had to be solved before an ideal travel system came into being.

Gerrit J. Ter Brugge of Weston, Ontario, formerly an engineer with the department of land and water use of the Dutch ministry of agriculture, knows all about the difficulties. As head of the provincial office in Gelderland, he was adviser of the *Gelderse Mij Van Landbouw*, an agricultural group that organized a charter flight for members who wanted to visit their children in Canada. This venture ran afoul of the stringent rules of the International Air Traffic Association, and the plane was grounded in Toronto. Through the intervention of Jan Heersink, Dutch vice-consul, the worried passengers

Wereld Contact produces a quality magazine for its members.

were able to return to The Netherlands.

This incident motivated a number of people to set up a general, non-profit travel organization with the name *Wereld Contact* and with an annual membership fee of six guilders a family. Ter Brugge was a member of the board.

"That was in 1959," he says. "Most of our first members came from the provinces of Friesland, Groningen, Drenthe, Overijssel, and Gelderland. They were older people, many of them unable to speak a word of English and some with no travel experience beyond their provincial borders. They put total trust in the board."

The first group flight to Toronto was announced in 1961. The price, including compulsory insurance, was 875 guilders,

much lower than the regular fares. Seventy-four members signed up. The inaugural flight would take place with a propeller-driven DC-4 of Intercontinental U.S. Inc.

Then the woes started. Permission to land in Toronto was denied. This meant that the passengers had to fly to Buffalo, New York, and take a bus to Toronto. On the day of departure, the board members and the participants were on time at the Zestienhoven airport in Rotterdam; however, the aircraft was undergoing mechanical repairs in Gander, Newfoundland. Frantic efforts to get a replacement aircraft were in vain.

After two days of waiting at the new Savoy Hotel in Rotterdam, the passengers, ten of them older than seventy (G.B. Wisselink of Varsseveld, Gelderland, was eighty-six), received word that they could fly by jet from Geneva, Switzerland, to New York City. Their travel schedule now was as follows: by plane to Geneva, then to New York, then to Buffalo, and by bus to Toronto.

Says Ter Brugge: "That first trip was something else. One old farmer, confused by the many times he had to transfer from hotels to buses to airfields, woke up midway across the Atlantic and impatiently asked the tour leader: 'Jan, when are we leaving?'"

Wereld Contact has shown phenomenal growth since it was established with 150 members. Today the membership stands at an astounding 50,000, far ahead of the two sister organizations: *Ouders van Emigranten*, with about 25,000 members, and the smaller *Wij Komen.*

"At first, we were able to organize cheap flights," says Piet Madderom of Zuid-Scharwoude, Noord-Holland, one of the many volunteers without whom the organization would not exist. "But those days are in the past. Now the people travel on regular flights. Still, they have the services of a flight leader and they are welcomed at the point of arrival by a representative—in Toronto, it's Mr. Tjalsma—who looks after any problem that may arise while they are away from home."

Wereld Contact does more than arrange flights for its members. Over the years, its cultural committee has developed a varied program to benefit people on both sides of the Atlantic. It has sent a choir to Canada, is working on a book on the history of The Netherlands, intended for the second-generation Dutch in other lands; it has arranged for an ex-

change of students, and for the setting up of an English course taught by Madderom.

"This course has been very popular," he says. "Some 10,000 members have been enrolled in it. It's taught during the winter at forty places in The Netherlands.

Members of *Wereld Contact* want to know a few things about the English language before they travel to Canada. Most of their grandchildren there can't express themselves in Dutch. Even their own children have a habit of unknowingly inserting English words and phrases into Dutch conversations. Besides, an older person can be proud of going back to school and learning something new.

On October 1, 1967, following a "white paper" and parliamentary study, Canada introduced new immigration regulations. For the first time, the principles governing the selection of immigrants were spelled out in detail. These provided for an assessment system requiring immigration officers to apply the same standards in the same way to potential immigrants from all areas of the world. The new regulations were intended to link the selection standards more closely to the economic and manpower requirements of Canada.

The assessment system was based on the following factors: education and training, personal assessment, occupational demand, occupational skill, age, arranged employment, knowledge of English and/or French, relatives in Canada, and employment opportunities in the area of destination. This became known as the points system.

Three categories of immigrants were introduced: sponsored dependents, admissible subject only to the usual requirements

of good health and good character; nominated immigrants, involving certain categories of non-dependent relatives; and independent applicants—those applying abroad on their own initiative.

More changes were made in later years. In the 1970s, following a detailed study, the government issued a "green paper." After exhaustive public and parliamentary review, a new Immigration Act and its associated regulations came into effect. One of the key elements to be preserved was this: "When it is a question of selecting immigrants who will enter the labor force, immigration policy shall operate in close harmony with all the major areas of economic and social policy, and in particular with manpower policy."

Basically, the points system remained the same. But there were some other changes. The category of sponsored dependents became the family class and was extended to include parents and grandparents. Nominated relatives became known as assisted relatives. And regulations were drafted to include specific provision for the admission of the

A big banner reading Welcome to Canada *greeted six young students from Arnhem when they arrived at the Toronto airport in 1979 to start a fourteen-day exchange visit with students at the Hamilton and District Christian High School (above). The visit was arranged by* Wereld Contact *as part of its cultural development program.*

entrepreneur, the retired, and those demonstrably capable of self-employment.

In 1979, the regulations were amended once again. Now the visa officer had no choice but to say no to assisted relatives and independent applicants who received a zero rating under the point system's occupational demand factor.

People were still knocking on Canada's door in the early 1980s. It was not being opened as often, however, because jobs were scarce in an economy suffering recession. On the other hand, prospective employers, and other independent people, who seemed unlikely to become a burden on the state, were welcomed with open arms.

"Things have changed quite a bit since the 1950s," says Geert Belgraver, counsellor for agricultural, social, and immigration affairs at the Royal Netherlands Embassy on Slater Street in Ottawa. "In recent years, immigration has become more restrictive. At first the authorities looked at whether there was a need for the

A Dairy Farm "Second to None"

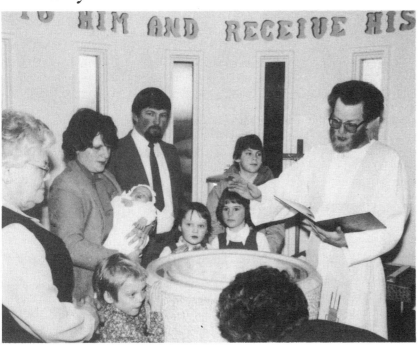

Gina, the Canadian-born daughter of Herman and Maria Schuts, is christened by Rev. Mike Hughes at St. Bernhard's Roman Catholic Church in Waterford, Ontario, in March, 1982. At left is Mrs. Schuts' mother, Mrs. Martina Peters, a visitor from The Netherlands.

In 1971, Herman Schuts and his wife, Maria, began farming near the village of Schayk, Noord-Brabant. They possessed nothing much but love for cows and the desire to succeed. Within a few years, through hard work and sacrifice, they had established a sizeable dairy herd and a pig operation.

But the couple wasn't happy. Their plans for expansion were thwarted by the high price of land in short supply. Thoughts of spacious Canada, where one of their relatives already lived, kept entering their minds.

They toured Ontario for three weeks in 1979. After viewing many farms that were for sale, they returned to Schayk with an option to purchase a 300-acre dairy farm,

complete with 200 Holsteins, a large number of heifers, and a milk quota near Boston, south of Brantford, Ontario. A few months later, the family—mother, father, and two children—was back in Canada to stay.

Schuts was determined to carry on what he had started in The Netherlands, where farming is highly mechanized and specialized. His plan was to establish an ultra-modern operation, with many labor-saving devices. Within a few months, his farm had become the talk of the neighborhood.

The 20,000-square-foot, all-steel barn is home for 185 Holsteins and 140 heifers, a computerized feeding system, divided into six sections, runs the length of the structure. Each cow is fed a computer-controlled diet based on the animal's weight and nutritional requirements, and the production needs. Manure is stored in a large tank beneath the barn before being pumped to the field as fertilizer.

A crowding gate powered by air pressure is used to push the cows from the free-stall barn to the 5,000-square-foot milking parlor, which can handle twenty at a time. The milking system includes an automatic shutoff. In fact, it's so automated that the whole milking operation can be carried out by two persons.

The farm also has a confinement area complete with intercom and closed-circuit television systems so that from the house a close watch can be kept on calving.

More than four thousand people attended an open house of the farm. School classes regularly tour the facility.

"Many people have had the wrong im-

applicant's trade. They simply wanted to avoid the risk of a failure and having to pay out social benefits. Then the screening became even tougher. Workers could be admitted only after clearance had been given by the employment office. In other words, if an unemployed Canadian could be placed in the job eyed by a prospective immigrant, the door would stay closed."

Little wonder that only one out of ten applicants is being accepted. The fact that Canadians appreciate the industriousness of the Dutch doesn't matter. The law, strictly non-discriminatory, cannot be bent. Still, newcomers are being admitted.

Why do so many people still want to leave The Netherland? What compels them to move away from their familiar environment? Surely, The Netherlands is progressive, relatively prosperous, a far cry from the days when it was struggling to recover from the ravages of war.

Belgraver believes the economic factor is small. There are other reasons.

"Many people think they can find a freer lifestyle in Canada. They see fewer regulations, fewer responsibilities, and

Geert Belgraver

Below: An aerial view of the Schuts farm near Boston, Ontario. The modern steel barn has a computerized feeding system.

pression," says Mrs. Schuts. "They thought we came here with a bundle of money. We came here with some know-how and a desire to move ahead. We still had to go to the bank and borrow at twenty-four per cent. But we are working hard as a team. We don't know what vacation is. Because of that, we are moving ahead."

Says Herman: "I'm a person who likes to do things right. I hire consultants. I leave nothing to chance. My aim is to build up a dairy herd second to none."

lots of room in which to manoeuvre. There are those who want to go back to nature—they are dreaming of a small farm, or a little house out in the country. Worries about pollution and fear of another world conflict also cause people to pull up their stakes. Then there are those who are deeply concerned about the decline in moral values and the deterioration in spiritual life in Holland."

Many fly to Canada to have a look first before deciding to apply for admittance. Money seems to be no problem.

"In the late '40s and in the '50s," says Belgraver, "the emigrants thought they were leaving for good. They went to start a new life in a new country. Nowadays, it's different. This is the age of jet travel and instant communications. Emigration is no longer a leap into the unknown."

Mr. and Mrs. Gerrit J. Ter Brugge were lonely in The Netherlands. Their oldest son, an economist, had emigrated to Canada in 1966. Their second son, a medical doctor, had followed in 1970. They missed their children and grandchildren. Their family life felt empty.

There was only one way to bridge the gap: move to Canada too.

"I made up my mind to go," recalls Ter Brugge, an engineer in government service until his retirement at age sixty-five. "My wife, however, was hesitant to take such a big step. In the end, the advice of our younger son was decisive. He told us: 'Don't expect us young people to go to Holland so often. We have to build our own future, and it's too expensive to take an entire family to Holland every year."

The couple sold their house in Zeist, just east of Utrecht, obtained medical clearance, flew to Canada in early 1982, and moved into an apartment in Weston, Ontario. He was sixty-seven; she sixty-six.

"Our emigration was nothing like

—1981———————————————

We Left The Netherlands of Today but Still Long for the Old Hollan

Major and Mrs. Eugene Roosegaarde Bisschop

When the Germans invaded The Netherlands in the spring of 1940, Eugène Roosegaarde Bisschop was an ensign-platoon commander of the Fourth Auto Battallion with the Fourth Army Corps, manning a forward position at the *Grebbelinie*, one of the main lines of defence. The Dutch forces were pushed back by the powerful German army. With thousands of others, he was taken prisoner after the capitulation of General H.G. Winkelman, the supreme commander. A few weeks later, Hitler ordered the release of the Dutch soldiers, calling this a "magnanimous gesture."

Roosegaarde Bisschop decided to continue the fight—underground. In The Hague, he worked for the C.C.D. (*Crisiscontroledienst*), a government organization set up to control the transport of food. During the war years, that job gave him many opportunities to help subvert German operations. Later, he joined the *Binnenlandse Strijdkrachten*, the internal security forces under the command of Prince Bernhard which were responsible for keeping law and order in the liberated areas and rounding up collaborators.

emigrating in the fifties," says Ter Brugge. "It was more just a move. We didn't have to worry about how to make a living. Our school English wasn't a hundred percent, but we could help ourselves reasonably."

Acquaintances in The Netherlands had told them: "One should never transplant old trees" and, "At your age, you won't be able to make new friends so easily." But their experience has so far confirmed their decision. They have formed new friendships in an animated church and church-society life. Their long-time association with *Wereld Contact*, the popular travel organization—he's an honorary board member—had already made them familiar to many people in Canada before their emigration.

"I was a little afraid that living in an apartment in a big city would be disappointing," he says. "But there are advantages: no snowshovelling, no cutting the

A surprise cake from her children marked Mrs. Ter Brugge's first year in Canada.

"We arrested a number of National Socialists—N.S.B.ers—and turned them over to the police. But within a few days, they were walking on the streets again, smiling and talking boisterously. They had been freed through some technicality. I just couldn't understand it. I was deeply disillusioned."

Roosegaarde Bisschop, who became a career officer after the war and rose to the rank of major, has been disillusioned with The Netherlands in many respects. Events of the last decade have been especially disheartening: the vociferous and influential voices of the leftists, the harassment of those who publicly oppose "this devilish propaganda," widespread disrespect for authority, and other signs of decay in all facets of Dutch society.

"People are protesting against the missiles that have yet to be placed in Europe for their protection. Yet they don't protest all the missiles the Soviet Union is already aiming at them. There are so many other things that make us sick. For instance, the over-socialized society, the churches advocating one-sided leftist political views, the total lack of discipline, the change in rules allowing a soldier to wear earrings . . . What's all this leading to?"

Major and Mrs. Roosegaarde Bisschop

didn't want to stay in The Netherlands to find out. In 1981, they left their home in Arnhem and moved to Canada, the land of their liberators, and bought a house in Brantford, Ontario. Their two daughters are also in North America. Now they spend much time telling others of the dangers they see in encroaching communism and advocating the platform of the *OSL-Stichtingen*, an organization composed of the *Oud-Strijders Legioen* (the Legion) for active and ex-servicemen, the *Stichting Politieke Bewustwording* for civilians, and *Constructief Jong Nederland*, the youth department. The organization has realistic views on defence, freedom, and security, in relation to the unremitting Soviet buildup of both conventional and nuclear weapons.

The retired major, a qualified professional musician (Royal Conservatory, The Hague), also has time for instruction of army cadets and for giving private lessons in piano, theory, and ensemble playing.

"People ask me now and then if I ever get homesick, or if I want to go back to Holland," he says. "I tell them that I became homesick when things really started to go sour there. I'm homesick for the good old Holland that I once knew."

Gerrit J. Ter Brugge enjoys the Canadian sunshine.

grass, a secure feeling when you shut the door behind you. Besides, we found a nest of a red-tailed hawk less than a hundred meters away."

Their greatest satisfaction so far has been their chance to better understand how their children have adapted themselves to their new culture. Misunderstandings caused by distance and time had contributed to their loneliness.

"We experienced the emigration as a refreshing reunion with our children and grandchildren," says Ter Brugge. "For the first time, we're together for birthday parties, Mother's Day, Father's Day, and so on. And without depending on them too much, we do feel as if we have gotten our children back."

Mrs. Wilma Roberts of Calgary, Alberta, who is married to a Canadian, still finds that she has quite a bit of Dutch left in

—1982—

"Why import? I'll raise them right here."

Jim Pot's sheep farm at Mount Stewart, Prince Edward Island.

her—it just won't go away. Sometimes she considers this a nuisance. Yet, deep down, there is pride about her heritage.

"I believe Canadians can learn a lot from the Dutch, especially about caring for other people. One day, two years ago, I was helping an organization for the mentally retarded by phoning for canvassers. Long lists were given to me. Whenever I hit a Dutch name, I felt hopeful: they nearly always said yes. In the cancer canvass, too, I noticed that several Dutch people were involved. They do what they can, while Canadians often use 'I am too busy' as an excuse. My minister has often told me: 'There should be more people like you around. I always notice that where there are Dutch people, there's hope—hope for doing it, not just saying it, no matter the task. Their commitments in life are different, deep-rooted, and valuable to everyone.' "

Harry Cunliffe of Ottawa, who was in charge of Canadian immigration matters in The Hague for a number of recent years, says: "The contrast between the simple, unlettered folk who came in the early years and those of the present day is the outstanding impression of my posting in The Hague. The majority of our recent interviews have been done in English without benefit of an office interpreter. Most applicants have been well qualified, and with sufficient capital or Canadian connections to ensure their own quick establishment. The applicant who had not visited Canada was an exception. The motivations for emigration tended to be as various as the people. I like to think that the immigration movement has been the principal factor in establishing the Dutch-Canadian sense of kinship. As one early immigrant said to me: 'Canada is good for the Dutchman—but the Dutchman is good for Canada too.' "

James Pot is also one of the new immigrants. He was a teacher in The Netherlands. In 1982, he bided time near St. Catharines, Ontario, waiting for the chance to move to the Maritimes, preferably Prince Edward Island, and start a sheep farming operation.

"I came to Canada to be able to spend the rest of my life a bit differently than I spent the first half. I doubt if you can call that making a new start, but it has the makings of it. I come from a long line of farmers and craftsmen, and it's not easy to get away from what's in the blood. All my life I've been making things, designing things—from setting up new curricula and new ways of teaching to doing land-scaping and carpentry in my spare time. In the process, I found out that I liked working outside much better than working inside, and walking around much better than sitting around."

So he brought his family to spacious Canada.

"For the last two years or so, we've been busy acquainting ourselves with farming in general and with the possibilities of farming in Canada. To make a long story short, we've decided to try our luck with sheep. When we learned that New Zealand ships some twenty-two million pounds of lamb to Canada on an annual basis, we didn't need much more convincing. It's been all sheep talk wherever we've gone since. We've read all that we could lay our hands on. We'll probably settle down somewhere in the Maritimes, maybe Prince Edward Island, depending somewhat on the financial involvement of the provincial government in agriculture."

A lot has happened since we first talked with Pot in 1982. He did indeed buy a farm in Prince Edward Island, with government assistance, and launched a sheep operation.

"The 254 ewes and eight rams are not really enough to run a viable sheep enterprise," he says, "but we hope to expand a bit next year. We should have four hundred eventually, hopefully in two years' time. Luckily the ewes are not too expensive—around $100. But the last two rams I bought were about $300."

He has no regrets so far about moving to the island.

"There's tremendous potential here. Thousands of acres are going wild; nobody is using them. So what we need are more farmers. And even though we've had quite a few immigrants in recent times, there's still plenty of room for more."

Friendly sheep on the Pot farm.

Chapter 26

Reclaiming the Heritage

Aart Oosterman of the Lambeth, Ontario, area has built a model windmill which lets passersby know that he is Dutch.

Reclaiming the Heritage

It's good to keep a bit of Dutch around the house.

Some farmers still wear wooden shoes because they are warm and comfortable.

Some people would rather suck a King peppermint than a butterscotch Lifesaver.

And doesn't that slice of Gouda taste a lot better than grocery store cheese?

Some women prefer the Dutch way of hanging curtains. Some men love to puff on a Hofnar cigar.

And who really turns his nose up at the *oliebollen* that stink up the house on New Year's Eve?

There's nothing wrong with a little bit of Dutch. But at first, a lot of people thought there was. They went to a Dutch church, were friendly with Dutch people, bought some of their groceries at the Dutch store, and acted every bit as Dutch as their neighbor left behind in, let's say, Sexbierum. They even went to Dutch social evenings, arranged by clubs or church groups, for skits, songs and other familiar entertainment. But, strangely, they didn't want to be known outside of their Dutch circle as an immigrant from The Netherlands.

It wasn't that they were ashamed of their heritage. Rather, they were intent on getting ahead, on proving to themselves and their relatives that immigration had been worthwhile. And so, outside of their circle, they tried to stop being Dutch. So lay the road to success. The authorities had always emphasized how well the Dutch could assimilate. Better, in fact, than most other ethnic groups in Canada. The barrage of such compliments was well-meant. Most Dutch-Canadians felt proud to be singled out for this honor—they were being regarded as true Canadians.

At first the Dutch didn't build social halls. Their entertainment was private, often held in homes or rented halls. In any case, it was the churches, as we have seen, which were the main centers for social activities. From the outside, it seemed as if the Dutch couldn't care less about preserving their culture and their heritage. And there might have been some truth in that. But it was never so entirely—and it certainly isn't so now.

Bob Gosschalk, the former insurance agent who opened up a can of worms in

1950 with allegations of ill treatment and poor conditions for Dutch immigrants, has observed a marked change in recent years in the attitude of Dutch-Canadians toward the open display of their heritage.

"At first, the newcomers were anxious to integrate into Canadian society because that was the thing to do. There was really no ethnic identity except in the churches and in some rural communities. But now things are changing. The second generation seems to be interested in rediscovering their heritage. And the people over fifty, once so anxious to assimilate in order to get ahead, are now saying: 'Hey, we're still Dutch!' "

Gosschalk is a member of the Toronto-based Canadian Netherlands Business and Professional Association, one of whose principal aims is to rekindle interest in Dutch culture. In the summer of 1980, the association organized an exhibition at the Harbourfront Gallery of paintings, drawings and sculptures by prominent contemporary artists of Dutch descent. The show did very well.

Hendrik Reinders, whose father led some ten families to their new land in

Mrs. Dini Hendriksen's mother, her sister Alie, and her daughter Gerri make oliebollen *in southern British Columbia on New Year's Eve, 1952. The custom is still carried on in many Dutch households.*

It's tulip festival time in Drayton, Ontario. The dancers are from the Christian school in the village.

The Dutch are also known for their organ music. The talent has been exported to Canada. Clockwise are organists Chris Teeuwsen, Andre Knevel, and Dr. J.J.K. Kloppers, a few of the many who play at concerts and church services throughout the country.

1952, has never agreed with the notion that immigrants should assimilate, become part of a melting pot society, and thus risk losing whatever culture and identity they possess.

"I'm sure the success of the Dutch people here in the Drayton area is to a great degree due to what I call the *Hollandse gemeenschap* (Dutch community). We came to a strange country. But by staying close together, by helping each other, by worshipping together, we gave each other the strength to carry on. The Canadians know what we have achieved. Maybe their own desire for our assimilation has abated a bit."

Many of the early immigrants found it difficult to adapt to the Canadian social environment. They didn't feel totally at home among the Canadians, who always did things a little differently from what they had been used to. Inevitably, the Dutch met separately. At these clubs, in rented halls, people could have fun among familiar faces, speak their mother-tongue with no embarrassment, and celebrate events that meant something to them.

They were quite happy to retain a bit of Dutch.

One of the better known clubs in southern Ontario serves the large concentration of Dutch-Canadians in the Niagara Peninsula. Called the Club the Netherlands of St. Catharines, it has a number of stated aims, such as providing its members with social and festive evenings, continuing the traditions and cultural habits of the Old Country, and encouraging its members to be or become good Canadian citizens.

There's a band, *Hollands Glorie*, that entertains in the community. So does a

Harbourfront Gallery 1980

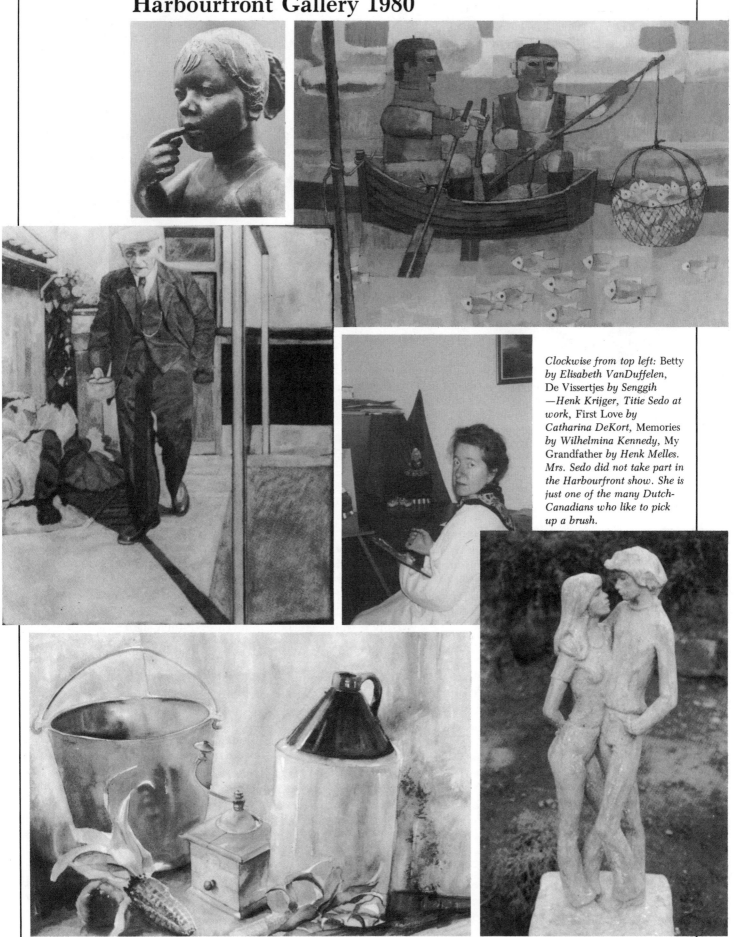

Clockwise from top left: Betty *by Elisabeth VanDuffelen,* De Vissertjes *by Senggih —Henk Krijger, Titie Sedo at work,* First Love *by Catharina DeKort,* Memories *by Wilhelmina Kennedy,* My Grandfather *by Henk Melles. Mrs. Sedo did not take part in the Harbourfront show. She is just one of the many Dutch-Canadians who like to pick up a brush.*

Members of the Hollands Glorie
band of St. Catharines, Ontario,
don wooden shoes and go out
into the community to entertain.

folk dance group, *De Klompendansers.*
Bowlers and card players have their weekly outings. Dutch language classes are
held. There are also dance evenings, concerts, and special events such as the annual St. Nicholas party for children and
the *Achterhoekse Avond,* an evening of
food and fellowship traditional for people
from a certain region of Gelderland.

Says Frank Niesink, the club's
secretary: "We feel that by means of these
many events and happenings, the aims of
the club are being fulfilled, and that the
existence of a club like this helps uphold
the Dutch heritage and culture."

In 1960 a small group of Dutch immigrants in London, Ontario, most of
them from the southern provinces of
Noord-Brabant and Limburg, met to form
a club which would become the Dutch-
Canadian Society of London. They felt
the need to relax and socialize together
now that the most difficult years of immigration were history. Surely many
others of their background would have
much to share with each other.

Dance evenings were held in the Polish
war veteran clubhouse. Executive

members of the club had their hands full
selling tickets, decorating the hall, keeping an eye on things, pouring drinks,
washing glasses, cleaning up. But they
didn't mind; they loved the camaraderie.
The response from the immigrant community was so encouraging that the executive launched plans for a new
building. Five years later, nine immigrants put their signatures on a $38,000
undertaking, and construction was begun.
Volunteers dug in mud, hammered in rain
and hail, and struggled to connect pipes
long after the sun had called it a day.

Since its opening in 1965, the
clubhouse, with its orange and black interior panels, has been a true social centre. Dances are held regularly. There are
film nights, picnics, a tulip festival, programs for children, and special events to
celebrate St. Nicholas Day, Christmas,
and New Year's Eve. The building is also
used for meetings, wedding receptions,
card clubs, billiard games, and other activities. But above all, it's the home of the
Dykehoppers, the carnival society
established in 1966 by Dutch-Canadians
who like to whoop it up in the traditional
style of south Holland during the winter
months. During carnival time, members

entertain across Ontario. They have even traveled to The Netherlands to join the festivities there.

One December, during the annual St. Nicholas party, with the usual magician, film, fruit, cookies, and presents, there was something unusual: the Dutch Santa Claus arrived with no fewer than fourteen 'younger' cohorts dressed in red skirts, sporting white beards, and riding tricycles and an assortment of other vehicles. The Canadian Santa then made a sudden appearance, complaining vociforously that the saint from Holland—or rather, Spain—was intruding on his territory. An amusing verbal battle ensued. Of course, the good old saint won. He promptly celebrated by dancing with every damsel in sight.

Ethnic Club with a Visible Presence

May 16, 1981, was a great day for the Dutch community in Calgary. The Dutch ambassador, Naboth Van Dyl, was on hand for the official opening of Port of Holland, a splendid clubhouse for the Dutch-Canadian Club of the Albertan city. On a hill which overlooks the magnificent Bow Valley, it is a proud symbol of what the immigrants are attempting to do nowadays to preserve their culture in their new land.

Says N.C. DeWit, now the past-president: "The club is a non-profit organization hoping to promote our Dutch heritage and traditions among all Canadians and at the same time provide goodwill and fellowship for people of Dutch origin."

Financing the project wasn't easy. A building fund was set up and debentures were sold to members. Provincial government departments also helped out.

"We have had two tough years," says DeWit, "but with the help of many loyal members, we have made it this far. We can now see daylight at the end of the tunnel."

In the meantime, Port of Holland is a beehive of activity.

"Every week, subgroups such as the choir, carnival society, billiards club, drama club and card club use the facilities. The Ladies Auxiliary is always thinking of ways to make the place cozier and better. Volunteers arrive every Wednesday to help out with the bingo, and the social committee arranges monthly dances. Dutch language lessons are offered, and a new library was opened last fall. Now the club is busy forming a travel agency . . ."

Mr. and Mrs. N.C. DeWit stand in front of Port of Holland, the beautiful clubhouse in Calgary.

Canadian veterans of the Second World War receive tulips from Dutch-Canadians while parading in London, Ontario, in 1981.

The wooden shoe dancers of London entertain at a community social function.

Dutch clubs have come and gone. One of them, the *Nederlandse Vereniging* in Toronto, established in 1952, was popular for a time. Then it fell by the wayside, the result of a dispute about membership and, no doubt, undercut by mutterings from official quarters that the Dutch should assimilate.

This club once organized an amateur theatre group to entertain its members at special gatherings. They would make their debut during a program to commemorate the tenth anniversary of the end of the war.

More than one thousand people gathered in the Palace Pier on Lakeshore Road in Toronto to enjoy the variety entertainment. Someone recited a moving poem. There was a dog act. A church choir rendered a few numbers. Before long, it was time for the theatre group.

"The play was about a Russian spy who

had to hunt and kill," recalls Mrs. Elly Werfhorst of Scarborough, Ontario, whose husband was in the cast. "The story had absolutely nothing to do with the war or the liberation, but was being staged because it was the first project this small group had tackled so far. My husband was the detective who had to speak English—after all, the story was set in London—with a Russian accent. He sounded like a Dutchman speaking Italian. That was hard to listen to with a straight face."

The curtain went up. The actors performed beautifully—however, nobody in the audience could hear what they were saying. A few people urged audibly: "Louder!" But not until one fellow bellowed from the balcony, "Hey, the sound is off!" did the people on stage take notice.

"For a few moments, the performers tried to help out by turning to us and shouting their lines," says Mrs. Werfhorst, "but that wasn't much fun and didn't really help one bit. So Menno De Groot and his wonderful singers filled the gap while electricians and would-be electricians tried to get the sound system working again."

But the problem could not be solved, and so the play was cancelled. There were a few sad faces. But they soon disappeared in the sea of smiles that bobbed and swirled on the dance floor.

Feeling sorry for the cast, the Dutch consul-general in Toronto organized an evening for them to perform for their families and friends.

"Did we laugh! Tears streamed down our faces while we watched this comedy that really was supposed to be high drama. My husband had forgotten to bring his detective cap, so he borrowed a boy's red baseball cap. No one who had to play opposite him could keep a straight face."

When Adriaan Dekker of Willowdale, Ontario, retired a number of years ago, a thought suddenly struck him: many of his fellow immigrants of the early 1950s were also recent retirees now, and probably feeling bored and lonely in the big city of Toronto.

"Those people had worked long and hard ever since they came to Canada and in their work had much contact with other people. But when that work ended, usually at someone's 65th birthday, you could see that many of them were losing

This band member is having as much fun as his audience.

That Dutch delicacy, the salted herring, is a must for guests at social functions. The men on the right are Bob Johnston and Bob Welch, then both members of the Ontario legislature.

At a food festival in Ottawa in 1962, Netherlands ambassador A.H.J. Lovink and his wife sample Dutch cheese. Dutch food and wares are on display at most ethnic festivals in the country.

The top photo records the fifth anniversary of Gezelligheid Kent Geen Tijd, *a Dutch over-fifties group in North York, Ontario. Below it is a 1963 photo of the members of the* Ons Genoegen *club of the First Christian Reformed Church, Rocky Mountain House, Alberta.*

their social contacts. They started to complain that they weren't happy any more."

Dekker, a former bank employee, realized that something could be done. He pioneered an effort which eventually led to the establishment in 1977 of the Dutch-Canadian Seniors Club, an organization that incorporated programs of two existing groups and added some new ones as well. The need was evident. A few days after sending an invitation to some 1,800 Hollanders of fifty-five years and older in the Toronto area, Dekker counted 84 members. Now the membership is close to the 300 mark.

"You can see people come alive again," he says. "Here they find friendships with people their own age and thereby make contact with many other people. It often happens that after a while they visit each other at home. You know, that's our aim. I'm convinced that many people are happier in their senior years as a result of the fellowship that we provide for them."

Many of the members get together each Thursday in the community center of North York, a Toronto suburb, to play billiards, shuffleboard, cards, bingo, chess and checkers. There's a library of books in the Dutch language. Creative activities such as ceramics, woodworking and handicrafts are also organized. Furthermore, general interest courses and excursions are arranged. And once a year there's a *Nederlandse Koffietafel,* a

This Dutch folklore group was formed to perform a klompendans *for Prince Bernhard, Juliana's consort, when he visited British Columbia in 1958 for a semi-official function.*

Top: A sea of children at a St. Nicholas party in Ontario.
Above left: St. Nicholas joins a Santa Claus parade in
Brantford, Ontario.
Above right: Dutch couples whoop it up on St. Nicholas
Eve.
Right: Ted Smeenk plays St. Nicholas for children at St.
Patrick's School in London, Ontario, in 1953, continuing a
custom he started in Voorburg, near The Hague.

gathering of members, friends and interested persons.

"There's no membership fee," explains Dekker. "All we ask for is an admittance of fifty cents on Thursdays. People are asked to bring their lunch, but coffee and cookies are gratis."

The churches also play a large part in keeping seniors occupied. In Lethbridge, Alberta, for example, the Golden Age Club caters to those over sixty-five with games, socializing, coffee and singing.

"The main recreation for the men is the hotly contested shuffleboard competition," says an observer. "The women play a variety of games such as boggle, scrabble and cards. Everybody speaks Dutch, of course."

The more than thirty Dutch-Canadian organizations in the Metropolitan Toronto area are under an umbrella group called the Dutch-Canadian Association of Greater Toronto. Headed by the energetic Mrs. Gé Spaans, this voluntary charitable group aims at stimulating and promoting cultural activities which put the Dutch and their heritage in the limelight. It also serves as an information center for new immigrants, schools, and students doing projects on The Netherlands or the Dutch-Canadian community. Furthermore, it strives to cooperate with Canadian organizations and other ethnic groups.

One of Mrs. Spaans' pet projects is the Netherlands Bazaar, run by a non-denominational committee of volunteers. The proceeds of this event, held once every two years, provide assistance to needy families of Dutch background. Hundreds of food parcels are distributed before Christmas and financial aid is extended. Also, in the last two years, twenty-two children of needy families were given the opportunity to attend summer camp for two weeks.

"We have also held many St. Nicholas programs in schools and libraries," reports Mrs. Spaans.

St. Nicholas? The Dutch Santa Claus? What's he doing in Canada when, according to the authorities, the Dutch are supposed to be assimilated? What does that corpulent fellow from the North Pole think about this encroachment?

At first it was difficult for the early immigrants to get used to Santa Claus and

Wim Van Duyn

the exchanging of presents on Christmas Day. They were sad and angry to see how commercialism seemed to shove the real reason for the holiday into the background. They preferred the familiar *Sinterklaas*, who appeared every year in early December to give presents to those who had been good (the bad ones got some too). Christmas Day was strictly reserved for going to church and enjoying a family get-together at home. Even nowadays, some families follow the old way or distribute gifts on Christmas Eve, not Christmas Day.

On December 5, the eve of St. Nicholas Day, the early immigrants could let go and have fun for a while. *Sinterklaas* and his Moorish aide, *Zwarte Piet*, often showed up at church bazaars. House parties were common.

"In the '50s, we took every opportunity to get together with a few other couples—birthdays, births, new jobs, card games—but *Sinterklaasavond* was always special," says S.P. Knuist, then of Kamloops, British Columbia. "We knew each other well. We all had come to

The Dutch coat of arms, one of the many items for sale at a bazaar in Toronto.

Canada at about the same time. We rejoiced with each other, helped each other, and respected each other's privacy. For *Sinterklaas*, we drew names and gave presents. And we made sure there was plenty of good food and drink. We had lots of fun, which took away the homesickness that always surfaced at that time of year. We sang the familiar songs—*Sinterklaas is Jarig, Hoor de Wind Waait Door de Bomen*—and the harmony improved as the evening progressed. We also did skits and dressed up in funny clothes. Yes, we really enjoyed those evenings."

Later, St. Nicholas almost disappeared from the Canadian scene. Many immigrants, absorbed in Canadian society, felt that it was ridiculous to cling to the old ways. After all, what did *Sinterklaas* mean to the children?

Well, things have changed. Many ethnic groups, including the Dutch, are bringing their culture out into the open. Much rediscovering is going on. People are no longer ashamed to tell others that they are Canadians—but with the Dutch still in them.

British Columbia, so far away from Spain, seems to be a favorite haunt of *Sinterklaas*, the Spanish saint.

Through the efforts of the Vancouver Island Netherlands Association, the saint arrived at the Victoria harbor in style in 1982—on a boat supplied by Seaspan International. The provincial carillonneur, Herman Bergink, added an appropriate touch to the festive atmosphere by ringing out seasonal tunes which anyone from The Netherlands would remember from his or her childhood.

Across the Strait of Georgia, in Vancouver, the Dutch-Canadian organization Je Maintiendrai did its best to ensure that the tradition would live on. *Sinterklaas*, speaking fluent Dutch, entered the hall in regal splendor. His aide, *Zwarte Piet*, handed out gifts left and right, to the delight of young and old.

The seniors weren't forgotten. At the Ebenezer home in Abbotsford, the white-bearded saint dropped in to spread good cheer. His helper distributed something else: *pepernoten*, morsels the size of marbles, which the residents' young visitors accepted eagerly.

At the home of Piet and Dina Vanden Brink in Vancouver, a number of Canadians were introduced to the saint and his helper. They had been invited to an old-fashioned St. Nicholas party, held annually by the VandenBrinks to thank their friends for all the help they had received during a difficult period. (VandenBrink had become an invalid after an accidental injury sustained while helping a neighbor.)

The saint made his grand entrance with his black cohort at his side. He called everyone over to receive a present. Then the tension rose; as always, he would pick out someone who, according to the notations in his book, had misbehaved during the year. This unfortunate person would be trussed up in a sack, and transported back to Spain. VandenBrink's former boss was the culprit this year.

Pepernoten had been properly dropped in a dish, not thrown across the floor, as custom would have it. *Zwarte Piet*, a Canadian, must have known that Canadians wouldn't think of picking up food from the floor and eating it.

Dutch Connections

Well-known artists and groups from The Netherlands—organist Feike Asma, the Concertgebouw Orchestra of Amsterdam, Paul Van Vliet, Toon Hermans, Henk Elsink, Max Teilleur, and a multitude of choirs, including Mastreechter Staar, have come to Canada to entertain the immigrants. The halls are always packed. Why? It's that Dutch, of course, a heritage worth claiming.

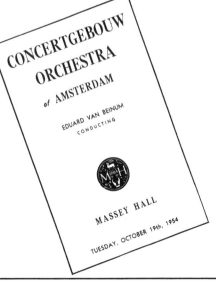

Chapter 27

Dutch Immigrant Ships

Groote Beer

A. Duncan

The Groote Beer, *the* Waterman, *and the*
Zuiderkruis *are three of the more well known
Dutch immigrant ships. Built during the war on
America's west coast (Portland, Oregon) all three
belonged to the Victory class. These ships were
built with a multi-purpose design in mind, for use
after as well as during the war.*

*The three ships were created for the purpose of
transporting troops (capacity 1,500-1,600 men). At
the end of 1946 all three ships were bought by the
Dutch government and in the summer of 1947
made their first voyages to Indonesia. The* Groote
Beer *then came under the management of "De
Stoomvaart Maatschappij, Nederland."*

In 1951 the Groote Beer *was remodelled. She
became an immigrant ship able to accommodate
approximately 850 passengers. Management again
transferred, this time to the Holland-America Line.
In 1960 ownership was transferred to Scheepvaart
Maatschappij Trans Oceaan. The* Waterman *and*
Zuiderkruis *also became this company's responsibility.*

*In the late fifties, the great influx of immigrants
over, a new purpose was found for these ships. In
1964 the Greek shipowner, John S. Latvis, became
the proprietor of the* Groote Beer. *He re-christened
the ship the* Marianne IV *and she was put to work
as a cruise ship in the Mediterranean. From June
1965 to March 1967 she again sailed under the
name of the* Groote Beer *for the Holland-America
Line. On October 2, 1968 she was finally thrown
on the scrap heap.*

*From previous page:
Three in a row at Rotterdam:* Statendam, Nieuw
Amsterdam *and* Ryndam *belonging to the Holland-
America Line.*

A. Duncan

Historisch Scheepvaart Museum

Waterman

Originally a freighter, the Waterman was converted to a passenger ship. In 1947 it was sold by the War Shipping Administration to the Dutch government as a troop carrier. In 1951 it was rebuilt as an immigrant ship.

A. Duncan

Historisch Scheepvaart Museum

Zuiderkruis

Built in 1944 as a freighter it was later converted to a passenger ship. Bought by the Dutch government in 1947 and renamed Zuiderkruis. In 1951 it was rebuilt as an immigrant ship. It made its maiden voyage from Rotterdam to Quebec City in July, 1951.

Ryndam

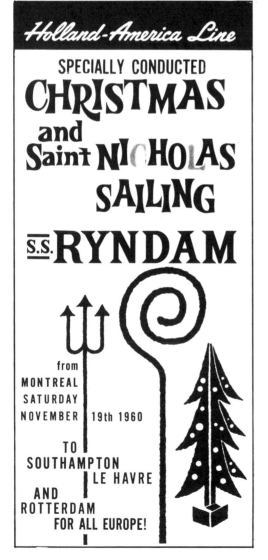

Holland-America Line

SPECIALLY CONDUCTED

CHRISTMAS
and
Saint NICHOLAS
SAILING

s.s. RYNDAM

from
MONTREAL
SATURDAY
NOVEMBER 19th 1960

TO
SOUTHAMPTON
LE HAVRE
AND
ROTTERDAM
FOR ALL EUROPE!

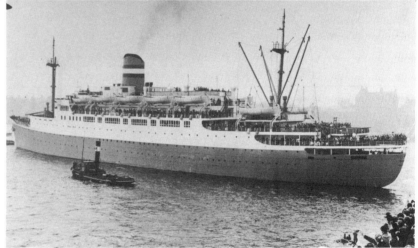

Ryndam

The Ryndam made its maiden voyage from Rotterdam to New York on July 16, 1951. During May of 1960 it began a regular service for the Holland-America Line between Rotterdam and Montreal.

Maasdam

A sister ship to the Ryndam, both ships were the first two-class liners with heavy tourist-class dominance. The Maasdam made her voyage from Rotterdam—Montreal—New York on August 11, 1952. She was heavily damaged after striking two wrecks in Bremerhaven harbour in 1963. Sold and refitted in 1968 as Stefan Batory.

Gemeentelijke Archiefdienst Rotterdam

This is how the Maasdam *dining room looked on her maiden voyage. In November, 1958, in Halifax, St. Nicholas and Black Peter were greeted on board by Captain Hogervorst, social directress, Mrs. Byvoet, and host, Rimmer Tjalsma. At left is the* Maasdam *as the Polish Ocean Lines'* Stefan Batory.

Volendam

Launched on July 6, 1922 and made her maiden voyage from Rotterdam to New York on November 4, 1922. In May of 1940 the Volendam *temporarily housed the exiled Dutch government while at* Falmouth, England. In 1946 it was used for shipping Dutch troops to Indonesia and sailing immigrants from Rotterdam to Australia. In 1947 it commenced summer sailings between Rotterdam and New York.

Veendam

Made her maiden voyage from Rotterdam to New York on April 18, 1923. Caught at Rotterdam during the Nazi invasion in 1940. Commenced postwar sailing from Rotterdam to New York in January of 1947.

The Kota Inten *served as a troop carrier to the former Dutch East Indies and made several trips to North America.*

The Tabinta, *a converted freighter which carried such products as fertilizer before the war years, transported thousands of Dutch immigrants to Canada during the late forties.*

Nieuw Amsterdam

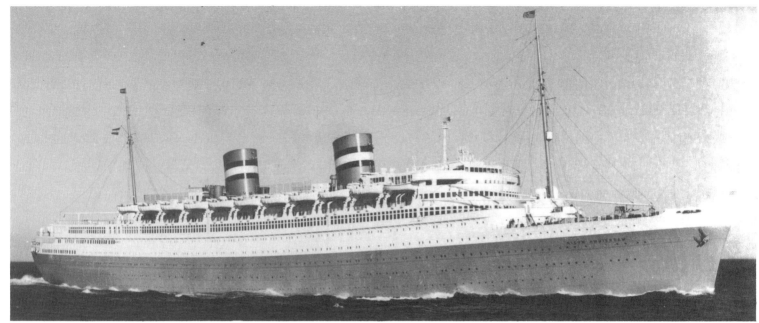

Rotterdam

Statendam

Gemeentelijke Archiefdienst Rotterdam

Bill Miller Collection

Nieuw Amsterdam

Holland's flagship and largest liner from 1938-59. One of the most popular and beloved of Atlantic liners. She arrived in New York on October 29, 1947 on her first postwar voyage from Rotterdam.

Rotterdam

Holland's largest liner and flagship. Made her maiden voyage from Rotterdam to New York on September 3, 1959.

Statendam

Named by Her Royal Highness Beatrix. Departed from Rotterdam on February 6, 1957 on her maiden voyage to New York.

Westerdam

Floated on July 27, 1940 and sunk in August, 1940 in an Allied air raid in Rotterdam. Later refloated and deliberately sunk by the Dutch underground to avoid use by the Nazi occupation forces. After being refloated and refitted the Westerdam made her maiden voyage from Rotterdam to New York on June, 1946.

Noordam

Sailed her maiden voyage from Rotterdam to New York on September 28, 1938. Transferred to New York—Dutch East Indies service during the war. Resumed her Rotterdam-New York sailings July, 1946.

Bloemfontein

The Bloemfontein *was built at Amsterdam and completed on October 18, 1934 for the Holland-Africa Line. During the war years the ship was taken over by the United States War Shipping Administration. She was broken up in 1959 in Hong Kong.*

Bill Miller Collection

Boissevain

The Boissevain *was built by Blohm & Voss at Hamburg, Germany. She plied the seas for the Koninklijke Parketvaart Mij. From 1940 to 1946 she served as a troop transport ship. Later she served the Java-Chine Line of Amsterdam. She was broken up in 1968.*

A. Duncan

Oranje II

The name Oranje *was chosen as a tribute to the Dutch Royal family. Launched in September 1938, the Oranje was given praise for her role in the war effort. She was transferred to a new around-the-world service in February, 1950 that included the Dutch Indies as well as Australia.*

Roger Sherlock

Sibajak

Of the immigrant ships, the Sibajak *may well have had the most varied service of all. The ship had distant ties with the Dutch East Indies before their declaration of independence; she served the Allies as troop transport ship under the management of P. & O. She cruised the Atlantic as immigrant ship with docking points at Rotterdam, Quebec and New York and ended her service in Indonesia before she ended up on the scrap heap in Hong Kong.*

Johan Van Oldenbarnevelt

Launched on August 3, 1929 she was the largest ship ever built in Holland. Transported Dutch government troops to Indonesia in 1946 and began immigrant sailings to Australia. Made an Atlantic crossing in June, 1954 with students travelling from Rotterdam to Quebec City.

Willem Ruys

Built in 1939 the Willem Ruys *was given the 'royal' prefix by Her Majesty Queen Wilhelmina becoming the* Willem Ruys *in 1947. The ship collided with the* Oranje *in 1953. In 1958 she made her first sailing to New York and charter sailings to Montreal.*

L.M. Correia

Anna Salen

The Anna Salen *took Dutch immigrants on a stand-by basis for other Dutch carriers.*

Bill Miller Collection

Aquitania

The Aquitania *served as a Canadian immigrant ship in 1948-1949 sailing from Southampton to Halifax.*

Bill Miller Collection

Arosa Sky

The Arosa Sky *made her maiden voyage for the Arosa Line on May 10, 1957 sailing from Bremerhaven to Halifax and New York.*

Bill Miller Collection

Arosa Sun

Launched in 1929 the Arosa Sun *left Marseilles on her maiden voyage to the Far East via the Suez. In August of 1955 she began sailings from Bremerhaven to Canada.*

A. Duncan

Beaverbrae

Canadian Pacific Steamships

Launched in 1938 for the Hamburg-America Line the Beaverbrae *was bought by the Canadian Pacific in 1947 and rebuilt as an immigrant ship at Sorel, Quebec.*

Berlin

Roger Sherlock

From 1924 to 1954 the Berlin *sailed as the* Gripsholm *for the Swedish America Line. She began service between Bremerhaven and New York in 1955.*

Bremen

The Bremen *was launched as the* Pasteur *for Compagnie Sud-Atlantique flying the French flag. Departed on July 9, 1959 from Bremerhaven on her maiden voyage to New York.*

Castel Bianco

Bill Miller Collection

The Castel Bianco *was a turbine steamer built in Baltimore, Maryland as a victory ship for the United States Maritime Commission. Originally named* Vassar Victory. *She was broken up in 1974.*

Columbia

Completed in 1913 as Katoomba *for McIlwraith & McEachern Proprietary Limited, the* Columbia *was refloated in 1949 and commenced sailings between Bremerhaven and Montreal on June 10, 1950.*

A. Duncan

Edam

The Edam *and* Leerdam *were built in 1921 for the purpose of transporting Polish immigrants to the United States but by the time the ships were completed the United States had cut the flow of immigrants to a trickle. After the war they were used to carry Dutch immigrants, especially to New York. Both ships were broken up in 1953.*

A. Duncan

Fairsea

Performed service between Bremerhaven and Quebec City and Bremerhaven and New York from 1953 to 1957. Also served as an Australian immigrant ship.

A. Duncan

Franconia

The Franconia *was launched on December 14, 1954 and sailed her maiden voyage from Greenock to Quebec City and Montreal on July 1, 1955.*

M. Lennon

Homeric

The Homeric *was launched as* Mariposa *under the American Flag. She made her maiden voyage to New York on January 24, 1955.*

Italia

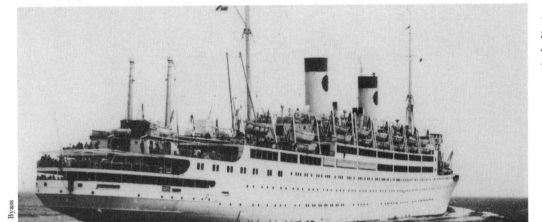

The Italia *traveled from Southampton to Quebec City and Montreal between 1949 and 1951.*

Leerdam

The Leerdam *and* Edam *were built in 1921 for the purpose of transporting Polish immigrants to the United States but by the time the ships were completed the United States had cut the flow of immigrants to a trickle. After the war they were used to carry Dutch immigrants, especially to New York. Both ships were broken up in 1953.*

Mauretania

The Mauretania *commenced her maiden voyage from Liverpool to New York on June 17, 1939. Converted to a government troop ship from 1940-1946 and commenced regular duties from Southampton to New York on June 10, 1947.*

Neptunia

The Neptunia *sailed from Bremerhaven to Southampton to New York beginning on April 8, 1951. She was transferred to the Neptunia Shipping Company in 1954.*

L.M. Correia

Queen Elizabeth

The Queen Elizabeth *was the largest passenger liner ever built. She sailed regularly from Southampton to New York. Some immigrants were fortunate enough to make their trans-Atlantic journey in style.*

L.M. Correia

Queen Mary

The Queen Mary *was the world's fastest liner from 1938 until 1957. Most of her sailings took place between Southampton and Quebec City. During the winter she sailed to Halifax.*

L.M. Correia

II Samaria

The Samaria *was placed on the Southampton-Quebec City run on July 12, 1951. The Samaria ran aground just below Quebec City in 1952, but was refloated without difficulty. She commenced her last voyage, Quebec City-Southampton, on November 23, 1955. She was a sister ship to the* Scythia.

Bill Miller Collection

Scythia

Most of her sailings from 1950-1957 were between Southampton and Quebec City, occasionally sailing to New York via Halifax.

Seven Seas

From 1949-1955 she sailed immigrants from Europe to Australia. On April 30, 1955 she made her maiden voyage from Bremerhaven to Quebec City and Montreal.

Skaubryn

A former cargo ship, it was rebuilt in March 1951 as an immigrant ship. Commenced sailings from Bremerhaven to Quebec City on June 18, 1957.

Washington

Performed postwar austerity service between Bremerhaven, Southampton and New York.

Bill Miller Collection

Roger Sherlock

M. Cassar

Bill Miller Collection

They Manned
the Boats

Drizzle fell as the *Volendam* approached the pier in Halifax in 1950. A bone-chilling dampness hung in the air. It was a miserable day, hardly appropriate for welcoming a boatful of emigrants to their new homeland.

Cornelis Van Herk, a second mate on the aged ex-troop carrier, was overcome with sadness as he watched family after family, many people weak from seasickness, walk silently down the gangplank and disappear into the darkness of the reception building.

"They had to wait for hours," he recalls at his home in Voorburg, near The Hague. "It was so cold . . . fathers walking around . . . mothers with children in their arms. The checking of the papers took so long. And then they had to wait for the trains. I felt very sorry for them. I wondered why they had come to such a land of mist and gloominess instead of sticking it out in Holland. I couldn't understand it then. Only later did the reasons slowly dawn upon me: the poverty after the war, large areas in ruin, the shortage of houses, the fear of more warfare . . ."

During the nine-day voyage, the Holland-America Line employee—he became a captain in 1959—gained a deep respect for his passengers. He knew that just getting ready to board the ship had been a difficult time. And then the trip on the old boat, with the barest of conveniences, would tax whatever emotional reserves they had left. But the people didn't complain. Van Herk concluded: "They didn't mind the discomforts as long as they were being taken to the promised land."

The company's regulations discouraged the crew from conversing with the passengers. But it would have been impolite not to answer a question. While strolling along the deck in uniform, Van Herk could not escape attention from people who wanted to know about this or that. One of them asked: "Lieutenant, what time is the bar open? I'm dying for a beer."

"For the most part," says Van Herk, "the passengers were subdued and stayed in their own little circle. They seemed rather shy. They were simple people, farmers from the eastern and northern areas of the country, who seemed to take everything in stride. They weren't used to

Captain Cornelis Van Herk: "They didn't mind the discomforts as long as they were being taken to the promised land."

luxuries, and didn't expect any."

The storms that often rage across the North Atlantic did not leave the *Volendam* untouched. The old ship, with considerable woodwork, creaked and groaned as it rolled with the waves.

"I'm sure the noise must have been scary. Some people must have thought that the ship was about to break up and head for the bottom. And all that tossing around certainly didn't help those with weak stomachs. On some days, it seemed as if most passengers were staying in their beds. Sure, there were pills for seasickness. But I believe the pills just put you to sleep—when you sleep, you don't feel sick. But the sickness is still there when you wake up."

Was much food wasted when hardly anyone showed up in the dining hall?

"I wondered about that myself. So I asked the cook. He knew that in bad weather only a few people would be well enough to eat, and so he cooked accordingly. Of course, there were always leftovers. Most of it went overboard."

Van Herk, who traveled the North Atlantic routes many times, found most of the trips somewhat monotonous. There was usually nothing to see except water, the occasional whale or dolphin, and more water.

"If you were lucky, you could spot fishing boats from Canada or Portugal near Newfoundland. But by then the trip would be nearly over. In the summer, fog banks could close in for days. We'd have to sound the fog-horn every two minutes. No, such trips weren't much to write home about."

In the spring, the captain had to be wary of icebergs.

"We followed special routes based on reports from the Coast Guard. The ocean was littered with ice in May and June, and we marked the reported sightings on a map. You can't fool around with those things."

Van Herk knows of a few instances when woozy emigrants leaned over the railing to vomit and lost their dentures in the process. There were some anxious moments during severe storms, when the decks were roped off and passengers were advised to stay in their quarters. And a buzz of excitement made the rounds during that trip with the *Volendam* in 1950 after a baby was born on board. But most of the trips were uneventful.

Van Herk realized, of course, that the crossing wasn't routine for his passengers.

"When we were approaching Halifax in 1950, I saw them line up at the railing,

Captain H. Hogervorst of the Maasdam *talks with some passengers during a crossing to Canada in 1956. In the other photo, crew members from the Dutch East Indies pose with young emigrants on the deck of the* Tabinta *in 1949.*

Not every immigrant arrived in Canada by boat; the airplane gained increasing popularity in the '50s. The photos show the arrival in 1952 of the first KLM Super Constellation at Montreal, a typical pose in 1954 of an immigrant family, and stewardesses talking to members of the Royal Canadian Mounted Police after the arrival in Montreal in 1949 of the first KLM flight from Amsterdam.

looking at the new land, and I wondered what they were thinking. One man asked the person next to him: 'Well, what do you think of it?' The answer: 'It looks pretty good.' Really, the Halifax waterfront couldn't have impressed anyone much. It was pretty drab. But these people were so happy that the voyage was over, and that they were finally about to set foot in Canada . . .''

The captain, forced into early retirement because of illness, retains a deep admiration for the immigrants.

"Many of them were farm folk, and they knew how to work hard. Such people could tackle a hard new life in Canada. Within a few years, many of them had their own farms. I have great respect for them, as I'm sure most people in Holland do."